W9-CNF-633

Plays of Our Time

Plays

OF

Our Time

E D I T E D   B Y

Bennett Cerf .

Random House · *New York*

• Published 1967 in New York by RANDOM HOUSE, INC.

MANUFACTURED IN THE UNITED STATES OF AMERICA

Contents

The Iceman
Cometh

BY

Eugene O'Neill

Characters

HARRY HOPE, proprietor of a saloon and rooming house*

ED MOSHER, Hope's brother-in-law, one-time circus man*

PAT MCGLOIN, one-time Police Lieutenant*

WILLIE OBAN, a Harvard Law School alumnus*

JOE MOTT, one-time proprietor of a Negro gambling house

PIET WETJOEN ("THE GENERAL"), one-time leader of a Boer commando*

CECIL LEWIS ("THE CAPTAIN"), one-time Captain of British infantry*

JAMES CAMERON ("JIMMY TOMORROW"), one-time Boer War correspondent*

HUGO KALAMAR, one-time editor of Anarchist periodicals

LARRY SLADE, one-time Syndicalist-Anarchist*

ROCKY PIOGGI, night bartender*

DON PARRITT*

PEARL*

MARGIE* } street walkers

CORA

CHUCK MORELLO, day bartender*

THEODORE HICKMAN (HICKEY), a hardware salesman

MORAN

LIEB

* Roomers at Harry Hope's.

Synopsis of Scenes

ACT ONE

Scene—Back room and a section of the bar at Harry Hope's—early morning in summer, 1912.

ACT TWO

Scene—Back room, around midnight of the same day.

ACT THREE

Scene—Bar and a section of the back room—morning of the following day.

ACT FOUR

Scene—Same as Act One. Back room and a section of the bar—around 1:30 A.M. of the next day.

Harry Hope's is a Raines-Law hotel of the period, a cheap ginmill of the five-cent whiskey, last-resort variety situated on the downtown West Side of New York. The building, owned by Hope, is a narrow five-story structure of the tenement type, the second floor a flat occupied by the proprietor. The renting of rooms on the upper floors, under the Raines-Law loopholes, makes the establishment legally a hotel and gives it the privilege of serving liquor in the back room of the bar after closing hours and on Sundays, provided a meal is served with the booze, thus making a back room legally a hotel restaurant. This food provision was generally circumvented by putting a property sandwich in the middle of each table, an old desiccated ruin of dust-laden bread and mummified ham or cheese which only the drunkest yokel from the sticks ever regarded as anything but a noisome table decoration. But at Harry Hope's, Hope being a former minor Tammanyite and still possessing friends, this food technicality is ignored as irrelevant, except during the fleeting alarms of reform agitation. Even Hope's back room is not a separate room, but simply the rear of the barroom divided from the bar by drawing a dirty black curtain across the room.

ACT ONE

SCENE: *The back room and a section of the bar of* HARRY HOPE'S *saloon on an early morning in summer, 1912. The right wall of the back room is a dirty black curtain which separates it from the bar. At rear, this curtain is drawn back from the wall so the bartender can get in and out. The back room is crammed with round tables and chairs placed so close together that it is a difficult squeeze to pass between them. In the middle of the rear wall is a door opening on a hallway. In the left corner, built out into the room, is the toilet with a sign "This is it" on the door. Against the middle of the left wall is a nickel-in-the-slot phonograph. Two windows, so glazed with grime one cannot see through them, are in the left wall, looking out on a backyard. The walls and ceiling once were white, but it was a long time ago, and they are now so splotched, peeled, stained and dusty that their color can best be described as dirty. The floor, with iron spittoons placed here and there, is covered with sawdust. Lighting comes from single wall brackets, two at left and two at rear.*

There are three rows of tables, from front to back. Three are in the front line. The one at left-front has four chairs; the one at center-front, four; the one at right-front, five. At rear of, and half between, front tables one and two is a table of the second row with five chairs. A table, similarly placed at rear of front tables two and three, also has five chairs. The third row of tables, four chairs to one and six to the other, is against the rear wall on either side of the door.

At right of this dividing curtain is a section of the barroom, with the end of the bar seen at rear, a door to the hall at left of it. At front is a table with four chairs. Light comes from the street windows off right, the gray subdued light of early morning in a narrow street. In the back room, LARRY SLADE *and* HUGO KALMAR *are at the table at left-front,* HUGO *in a chair facing right,* LARRY *at rear of table facing front, with an empty chair between them. A fourth chair is at right of table, facing left.* HUGO *is a small man in his late fifties. He has a head much too big for his body, a high forehead, crinkly long black hair streaked with gray, a square face with a pug nose, a walrus mustache, black eyes which peer near-sightedly from behind thick-lensed spectacles, tiny hands and feet. He is dressed in thread-bare black clothes and his white shirt is frayed at collar and cuffs, but everything about him is fastidiously clean. Even his flowing Windsor tie is neatly tied. There is a foreign atmosphere about him, the stamp of an alien radical, a strong resemblance to the type Anarchist as portrayed, bomb in hand, in newspaper cartoons. He is asleep now, bent forward in his chair, his arms folded on the table, his head resting sideways on his arms.*

LARRY SLADE *is sixty. He is tall, raw-boned, with coarse straight white hair, worn long and raggedly cut. He has a gaunt Irish face with a big nose, high cheekbones, a lantern jaw with a week's stub-ble of beard, a mystic's meditative pale-blue eyes with a gleam of sharp sardonic humor in them. As slovenly as* HUGO *is neat, his clothes are dirty and much slept in. His gray flannel shirt, open at the neck, has the appearance of having never been washed. From the way he methodically scratches himself with his long-fingered, hairy hands, he is lousy and reconciled to being so. He is the only occupant of the room who is not asleep. He stares in front of him, an expression of tired tolerance giving his face the quality of a pity-ing but weary old priest's.*

All four chairs at the middle table, front, are occupied. JOE MOTT *sits at left-front of the table, facing front. Behind him, facing right-front, is* PIET WETJOEN ("The General"). *At center of the table, rear,* JAMES CAMERON ("Jimmy Tomorrow") *sits facing front. At right of table, opposite* JOE, *is* CECIL LEWIS ("The Captain").

JOE MOTT *is a Negro, about fifty years old, brown-skinned, stocky, wearing a light suit that had once been flashily sporty but is now about to fall apart. His pointed tan buttoned shoes, faded pink shirt and bright tie belong to the same vintage. Still, he manages to pre-serve an atmosphere of nattiness and there is nothing dirty about his appearance. His face is only mildly negroid in type. The nose is thin and his lips are not noticeably thick. His hair is crinkly and he is beginning to get bald. A scar from a knife slash runs from his left cheekbone to jaw. His face would be hard and tough if it were not for its good nature and lazy humor. He is asleep, his nodding head supported by his left hand.*

PIET WETJOEN, *the Boer, is in his fifties, a huge man with a bald head and a long grizzled beard. He is slovenly dressed in a dirty shapeless patched suit, spotted by food. A Dutch farmer type, his once great muscular strength has been debauched into flaccid tallow. But despite his blubbery mouth and sodden bloodshot blue eyes, there is still a suggestion of old authority lurking in him like a memory of the drowned. He is hunched forward, both elbows on the table, his hand on each side of his head for support.*

JAMES CAMERON *("Jimmy Tomorrow") is about the same size and age as* HUGO, *a small man. Like* HUGO, *he wears threadbare black, and everything about him is clean. But the resemblance ceases there.* JIMMY *has a face like an old well-bred, gentle bloodhound's, with folds of flesh hanging from each side of his mouth, and big brown friendly guileless eyes, more bloodshot than any bloodhound's ever were. He has mouse-colored thinning hair, a little bulbous nose, buck teeth in a small rabbit mouth. But his forehead is fine, his eyes are intelligent and there once was a competent ability in him. His speech is educated, with the ghost of a Scotch rhythm in it. His manners are those of a gentleman. There is a quality about him of a prim, Victorian old maid, and at the same time of a likable, affectionate boy who has never grown up. He sleeps, chin on chest, hands folded in his lap.*

CECIL LEWIS *("The Captain") is as obviously English as Yorkshire pudding and just as obviously the former army officer. He is going on sixty. His hair and military mustache are white, his eyes bright blue, his complexion that of a turkey. His lean figure is still erect and square-shouldered. He is stripped to the waist, his coat, shirt, undershirt, collar and tie crushed up into a pillow on the table in front of him, his head sideways on this pillow, facing front, his arms dangling toward the floor. On his lower left shoulder is the big ragged scar of an old wound.*

At the table at right, front, HARRY HOPE, *the proprietor, sits in the middle, facing front, with* PAT MCGLOIN *on his right and* ED MOSHER *on his left, the other two chairs being unoccupied.*

Both MCGLOIN *and* MOSHER *are big paunchy men.* MCGLOIN *has his old occupation of policeman stamped all over him. He is in his fifties, sandy-haired, bullet-headed, jowly, with protruding ears and little round eyes. His face must once have been brutal and greedy, but time and whiskey have melted it down into a good-humored, parasite's characterlessness. He wears old clothes and is slovenly. He is slumped sideways on his chair, his head drooping jerkily toward one shoulder.*

ED MOSHER *is going on sixty. He has a round kewpie's face—a kewpie who is an unshaven habitual drunkard. He looks like an enlarged, elderly, bald edition of the village fat boy—a sly fat boy, congenitally indolent, a practical joker, a born grafter and con merchant. But amusing and essentially harmless, even in his most enterprising days, because always too lazy to carry crookedness beyond petty swindling. The influence of his old circus career is apparent in his get-up. His worn clothes are flashy; he wears phony rings and a heavy brass watch-chain (not connected to a watch). Like* MCGLOIN, *he is slovenly. His head is thrown back, his big mouth open.*

HARRY HOPE *is sixty, white-haired, so thin the description "bag of bones" was made for him. He has the face of an old family horse, prone to tantrums, with balkiness always smoldering in its wall eyes, waiting for any excuse to shy and pretend to take the bit in its teeth.* HOPE *is one of those men whom everyone likes on sight, a softhearted slob, without malice, feeling superior to no one, a sinner among sinners, a born easy mark for every appeal. He attempts to hide his defenselessness behind a testy truculent manner, but this has never fooled anyone. He is a little deaf, but not half as deaf as he sometimes pretends. His sight is failing but is not as bad as he complains it is. He wears five-and-ten-cent-store spectacles which are so out of alignment that one eye at times peers half over one glass while the other eye looks half under the other. He has badly fitting store teeth, which click like castanets when he begins to fume. He is dressed in an old coat from one suit and pants from another.*

In a chair facing right at the table in the second line, between the first two tables, front, sits WILLIE OBAN, *his head on his left arm outstretched along the table edge. He is in his late thirties, of average height, thin. His haggard, dissipated face has a small nose, a pointed chin, blue eyes with colorless lashes and brows. His blond hair, badly in need of a cut, clings in a limp part to his skull. His eyelids flutter continually as if any light were too strong for his eyes. The clothes he wears belong on a scarecrow. They seem constructed of an inferior grade of dirty blotting paper. His shoes are even more disreputable, wrecks of imitation leather, one laced with twine, the other with a bit of wire. He has no socks, and his bare feet show through holes in the soles, with his big toes sticking out of the uppers. He keeps muttering and twitching in his sleep.*

As the curtain rises, ROCKY, *the night bartender, comes from the*

*bar through the curtain and stands looking over the back room. He
is a Neapolitan-American in his late twenties, squat and muscular,
with a flat, swarthy face and beady eyes. The sleeves of his collarless
shirt are rolled up on his thick, powerful arms and he wears a soiled
apron. A tough guy but sentimental, in his way, and good-natured.
He signals to* LARRY *with a cautious "Sstt" and motions him to see
if* HOPE *is asleep.* LARRY *rises from his chair to look at* HOPE *and nods
to* ROCKY. ROCKY *goes back to the bar but immediately returns with
a bottle of bar whiskey and a glass. He squeezes between the tables
to* LARRY.

ROCKY (*In a low voice out of the side of his mouth*) Make it fast.
(LARRY *pours a drink and gulps it down.* ROCKY *takes the bottle
and puts it on the table where* WILLIE OBAN *is*) Don't want de
Boss to get wise when he's got one of his tightwad buns on. (*He
chuckles with an amused glance at* HOPE) Jees, ain't de old
bastard a riot when he starts dat bull about turnin' over a new
leaf? "Not a damned drink on de house," he tells me, "and all
dese bums got to pay up deir room rent. Beginnin' tomorrow," he
says. Jees, yuh'd tink he meant it!
(*He sits down in the chair at* LARRY's *left*)
LARRY (*Grinning*) I'll be glad to pay up—tomorrow. And I know
my fellow inmates will promise the same. They've all a touching
credulity concerning tomorrows. (*A half-drunken mockery in his
eyes*) It'll be a great day for them, tomorrow—the Feast of All
Fools, with brass bands playing! Their ships will come in, loaded
to the gunwales with cancelled regrets and promises fulfilled and
clean slates and new leases!
ROCKY (*Cynically*) Yeah, and a ton of hop!
LARRY (*Leans toward him, a comical intensity in his low voice*)
Don't mock the faith! Have you no respect for religion, you un-
regenerate Wop? What's it matter if the truth is that their favor-
ing breeze has the stink of nickel whiskey on its breath, and their
sea is a growler of lager and ale, and their ships are long since
looted and scuttled and sunk on the bottom? To hell with the
truth! As the history of the world proves, the truth has no bearing on anything. It's irrelevant and immaterial, as the lawyers
say. The lie of a pipe dream is what gives life to the whole mis-
begotten mad lot of us, drunk or sober. And that's enough
philosophic wisdom to give you for one drink of rot-gut.

ROCKY (*Grins kiddingly*) De old Foolosopher, like Hickey calls yuh, ain't yuh? I s'pose you don't fall for no pipe dream?

LARRY (*A bit stiffly*) I don't, no. Mine are all dead and buried behind me. What's before me is the comforting fact that death is a fine long sleep, and I'm damned tired, and it can't come too soon for me.

ROCKY Yeah, just hangin' around hopin' you'll croak, ain't yuh? Well, I'm bettin' you'll have a good long wait. Jees, somebody'll have to take an axe to croak you!

LARRY (*Grins*) Yes, it's my bad luck to be cursed with an iron constitution that even Harry's booze can't corrode.

ROCKY De old anarchist wise guy dat knows all de answers! Dat's you, huh?

LARRY (*Frowns*) Forget the anarchist part of it. I'm through with the Movement long since. I saw men didn't want to be saved from themselves, for that would mean they'd have to give up greed, and they'll never pay that price for liberty. So I said to the world, God bless all here, and may the best man win and die of gluttony! And I took a seat in the grandstand of philosophical detachment to fall asleep observing the cannibals do their death dance. (*He chuckles at his own fancy—reaches over and shakes Hugo's shoulder*) Ain't I telling him the truth, Comrade Hugo?

ROCKY Aw, fer Chris' sake, don't get dat bughouse bum started!

HUGO (*Raises his head and peers at* ROCKY *blearily through his thick spectacles—in a guttural declamatory tone*) Capitalist swine! Bourgeois stool pigeons! Have the slaves no right to sleep even? (*Then he grins at* ROCKY *and his manner changes to a giggling, wheedling playfulness, as though he were talking to a child*) Hello, leedle Rocky! Leedle monkey-face! Vere is your leedle slave girls? (*With an abrupt change to a bullying tone*) Don't be a fool! Loan me a dollar! Damned bourgeois Wop! The great Malatesta is my good friend! Buy me a trink!
(*He seems to run down, and is overcome by drowsiness. His head sinks to the table again and he is at once fast asleep*)

ROCKY He's out again. (*More exasperated than angry*) He's lucky no one don't take his cracks serious or he'd wake up every mornin' in a hospital.

LARRY (*Regarding* HUGO *with pity*) No. No one takes him seriously. That's his epitaph. Not even the comrades any more. If I've been through with the Movement long since, it's been through with him, and, thanks to whiskey, he's the only one doesn't know it.

ROCKY　I've let him get by wid too much. He's goin' to pull dat slave-girl stuff on me once too often. (*His manner changes to defensive argument*) Hell, yuh'd tink I wuz a pimp or somethin'. Everybody knows me knows I ain't. A pimp don't hold no job. I'm a bartender. Dem tarts, Margie and Poil, dey're just a side line to pick up some extra dough. Strictly business, like dey was fighters and I was deir manager, see? I fix the cops fer dem so's dey can hustle widout gettin' pinched. Hell, dey'd be on de Island most of de time if it wasn't fer me. And I don't beat dem up like a pimp would. I treat dem fine. Dey like me. We're pals, see? What if I do take deir dough? Dey'd on'y trow it away. Tarts can't hang on to dough. But I'm a bartender and I work hard for my livin' in dis dump. You know dat, Larry.

LARRY　(*With inner sardonic amusement—flatteringly*) A shrewd business man, who doesn't miss any opportunity to get on in the world. That's what I'd call you.

ROCKY　(*Pleased*) Sure ting. Dat's me. Grab another ball, Larry. (LARRY *pours a drink from the bottle on* WILLIE's *table and gulps it down.* ROCKY *glances around the room*) Yuh'd never tink all dese bums had a good bed upstairs to go to. Scared if dey hit the hay dey wouldn't be here when Hickey showed up, and dey'd miss a coupla drinks. Dat's what kept you up too, ain't it?

LARRY　It is. But not so much the hope of booze, if you can believe that. I've got the blues and Hickey's a great one to make a joke of everything and cheer you up.

ROCKY　Yeah, some kidder! Remember how he woiks up dat gag about his wife, when he's cockeyed, cryin' over her picture and den springin' it on yuh all of a sudden dat he left her in de hay wid de iceman? (*He laughs*) I wonder what's happened to him. Yuh could set your watch by his periodicals before dis. Always got here a coupla days before Harry's birthday party, and now he's on'y got till tonight to make it. I hope he shows soon. Dis dump is like de morgue wid all dese bums passed out.

(WILLIE OBAN *jerks and twitches in his sleep and begins to mumble. They watch him*)

WILLIE　(*Blurts from his dream*) It's a lie! (*Miserably*) Papa! Papa!

LARRY　Poor devil. (*Then angry with himself*) But to hell with pity! It does no good. I'm through with it!

ROCKY　Dreamin' about his old man. From what de old-timers say, de old gent sure made a pile of dough in de bucket-shop game before de cops got him. (*He considers* WILLIE *frowningly*) Jees, I've seen him bad before but never dis bad. Look at dat get-up. Been playin' de old reliever game. Sold his suit and shoes at Solly's two days ago. Solly give him two bucks and a bum outfit. Yesterday he sells de bum one back to Solly for four bits and gets dese rags to put on. Now he's through. Dat's Solly's final edition he wouldn't take back for nuttin'. Willie sure is on de bottom. I ain't never seen no one so bad, except Hickey on de end of a coupla his bats.

LARRY (*Sardonically*)　It's a great game, the pursuit of happiness.

ROCKY　Harry don't know what to do about him. He called up his old lady's lawyer like he always does when Willie gets licked. Yuh remember dey used to send down a private dick to give him the rush to a cure, but de lawyer tells Harry nix, de old lady's off of Willie for keeps dis time and he can go to hell.

LARRY (*Watches* WILLIE, *who is shaking in his sleep like an old dog*)　There's the consolation that he hasn't far to go! (*As if replying to this,* WILLIE *comes to a crisis of jerks and moans.* LARRY *adds in a comically intense, crazy whisper*) Be God, he's knocking on the door right now!

WILLIE (*Suddenly yells in his nightmare*)　It's a God-damned lie! (*He begins to sob*) Oh, Papa! Jesus! (*All the occupants of the room stir on their chairs but none of them wakes up except* HOPE)

ROCKY (*Grabs his shoulder and shakes him*)　Hey, you! Nix! Cut out de noise! (WILLIE *opens his eyes to stare around him with a bewildered horror*)

HOPE (*Opens one eye to peer over his spectacles—drowsily*) Who's that yelling?

ROCKY　Willie, Boss. De Brooklyn boys is after him.

HOPE (*Querulously*)　Well, why don't you give the poor feller a drink and keep him quiet? Bejees, can't I get a wink of sleep in my own back room?

ROCKY (*Indignantly to* LARRY)　Listen to that blind-eyed, deef old bastard, will yuh? He give me strict orders not to let Willie hang up no more drinks, no matter—

HOPE (*Mechanically puts a hand to his ear in the gesture of deafness*)　What's that? I can't hear you. (*Then drowsily irascible*) You're a cockeyed liar. Never refused a drink to anyone needed it bad in my life! Told you to use your judgment. Ought to know better. You're too busy thinking up ways to cheat me. Oh, I ain't as blind as you think. I can still see a cash register, bejees!

ROCKY (*Grins at him affectionately now—flatteringly*) Sure, Boss. Swell chance of foolin' you!

HOPE I'm wise to you and your sidekick, Chuck. Bejees, you're burglars, not barkeeps! Blind-eyed, deef old bastard, am I? Oh, I heard you! Heard you often when you didn't think. You and Chuck laughing behind my back, telling people you throw the money up in the air and whatever sticks to the ceiling is my share! A fine couple of crooks! You'd steal the pennies off your dead mother's eyes!

ROCKY (*Winks at* LARRY) Aw, Harry, me and Chuck was on'y kiddin'.

HOPE (*More drowsily*) I'll fire both of you. Bejees, if you think you can play me for an easy mark, you've come to the wrong house. No one ever played Harry Hope for a sucker!

ROCKY (*To* LARRY) No one but everybody.

HOPE (*His eyes shut again—mutters*) Least you could do—keep things quiet—

(*He falls asleep*)

WILLIE (*Pleadingly*) Give me a drink, Rocky. Harry said it was all right. God, I need a drink.

ROCKY Den grab it. It's right under your nose.

WILLIE (*Avidly*) Thanks.

(*He takes the bottle with both twitching hands and tilts it to his lips and gulps down the whiskey in big swallows*)

ROCKY (*Sharply*) When! When! (*He grabs the bottle*) I didn't say, take a bath! (*Showing the bottle to* LARRY—*indignantly*) Jees, look! He's killed a half pint or more!

(*He turns on* WILLIE *angrily, but* WILLIE *has closed his eyes and is sitting quietly, shuddering, waiting for the effect*)

LARRY (*With a pitying glance*) Leave him be, the poor devil. A half pint of that dynamite in one swig will fix him for a while—if it doesn't kill him.

ROCKY (*Shrugs his shoulders and sits down again*) Aw right by me. It ain't my booze.

(*Behind him, in the chair at left of the middle table,* JOE MOTT, *the Negro, has been waking up*)

JOE (*His eyes blinking sleepily*) Whose booze? Gimme some. I don't care whose. Where's Hickey? Ain't he come yet? What time's it, Rocky?

ROCKY Gettin' near time to open up. Time you begun to sweep up in de bar.

JOE (*Lazily*) Never mind de time. If Hickey ain't come, it's time Joe goes to sleep again. I was dreamin' Hickey come in de door, crackin' one of dem drummer's jokes, wavin' a big bankroll and we was all goin' be drunk for two weeks. Wake up and no luck. (*Suddenly his eyes open wide*) Wait a minute, dough. I got idea. Say, Larry, how 'bout dat young guy, Parritt, come to look you up last night and rented a room? Where's he at?

LARRY Up in his room, asleep. No hope in him, anyway, Joe. He's broke.

JOE Dat what he told you? Me and Rocky knows different. Had a roll when he paid you his room rent, didn't he, Rocky? I seen it.

ROCKY Yeah. He flashed it like he forgot and den tried to hide it quick.

LARRY (*Surprised and resentful*) He did, did he?

ROCKY Yeah, I figgered he don't belong, but he said he was a friend of yours.

LARRY He's a liar. I wouldn't know him if he hadn't told me who he was. His mother and I were friends years ago on the Coast. (*He hesitates—then lowering his voice*) You've read in the papers about that bombing on the Coast when several people got killed? Well, the one woman they pinched, Rosa Parritt, is his mother. They'll be coming up for trial soon, and there's no chance for them. She'll get life, I think. I'm telling you this so you'll know why if Don acts a bit queer, and not jump on him. He must be hard hit. He's her only kid.

ROCKY (*Nods—then thoughtfully*) Why ain't he out dere stickin' by her?

LARRY (*Frowns*) Don't ask questions. Maybe there's a good reason.

ROCKY (*Stares at him—understandingly*) Sure. I get it. (*Then wonderingly*) But den what kind of a sap is he to hang on to his right name?

LARRY (*Irritably*) I'm telling you I don't know anything and I don't want to know. To hell with the Movement and all connected with it! I'm out of it, and everything else, and damned glad to be.

ROCKY (*Shrugs his shoulders—indifferently*) Well, don't tink I'm interested in dis Parritt guy. He's nuttin' to me.

JOE Me neider. If dere's one ting more'n anudder I cares nuttin' about, it's de sucker game you and Hugo call de Movement. (*He chuckles—reminiscently*) Reminds me of damn fool argument me and Mose Porter has de udder night. He's drunk and I'm drunker. He says, "Socialist and Anarchist, we ought to shoot dem dead. Dey's all no-good sons of bitches." I says, "Hold on, you talk 's if Anarchists and Socialists was de same." "Dey is," he says. "Dey's both no-good bastards." "No, dey ain't," I says. "I'll explain the difference. De Anarchist he never works. He drinks but he never buys, and if he do ever get a nickel, he blows it in on bombs, and he wouldn't give you nothin'. So go ahead and shoot him. But de Socialist, sometimes, he's got a job, and if he gets ten bucks, he's bound by his religion to split fifty-fifty wid you. You say— how about my cut, Comrade? And you gets de five. So you don't shoot no Socialists while I'm around. Dat is, not if dey got any-thing. Of course, if dey's broke, den dey's no-good bastards, too." (*He laughs, immensely tickled*)

LARRY (*Grins with sardonic appreciation*) Be God, Joe, you've got all the beauty of human nature and the practical wisdom of the world in that little parable.

ROCKY (*Winks at* JOE) Sure, Larry ain't de on'y wise guy in dis dump, hey, Joe? (*At a sound from the hall he turns as* DON PAR-RITT *appears in the doorway.* ROCKY *speaks to* LARRY *out of the side of his mouth*) Here's your guy.

(PARRITT *comes forward. He is eighteen, tall and broad-shouldered but thin, gangling and awkward. His face is good-looking, with blond curly hair and large regular features, but his personality is unpleasant. There is a shifting defiance and in-gratiation in his light-blue eyes and an irritating aggressiveness in his manner. His clothes and shoes are new, comparatively ex-pensive, sporty in style. He looks as though he belonged in a pool room patronized by would-be sports. He glances around defen-sively, sees* LARRY *and comes forward*)

PARRITT Hello, Larry. (*He nods to* ROCKY *and* JOE) Hello.

(*They nod and size him up with expressionless eyes*)

LARRY (*Without cordiality*) What's up? I thought you'd be asleep.

PARRITT Couldn't make it. I got sick of lying awake. Thought I might as well see if you were around.

LARRY (*Indicates the chair on the right of table*) Sit down and join the bums then. (PARRITT *sits down.* LARRY *adds meaning-fully*) The rules of the house are that drinks may be served at all hours.

PARRITT (*Forcing a smile*) I get you. But, hell, I'm just about broke. (*He catches* ROCKY's *and* JOE's *contemptuous glances— quickly*) Oh, I know you guys saw— You think I've got a roll. Well, you're all wrong. I'll show you. (*He takes a small wad of dollar bills from his pocket*) It's all ones. And I've got to live on it till I get a job. (*Then with defensive truculence*) You think I fixed up a phony, don't you? Why the hell would I? Where would I get a real roll? You don't get rich doing what I've been doing. Ask Larry. You're lucky in the Movement if you have enough to eat.

(LARRY *regards him puzzledly*)

ROCKY (*Coldly*) What's de song and dance about? We ain't said nuttin'.

PARRITT (*Lamely—placating them now*) Why, I was just putting you right. But I don't want you to think I'm a tightwad. I'll buy a drink if you want one.

JOE (*Cheering up*) If? Man, when I don't want a drink, you call de morgue, tell dem come take Joe's body away, 'cause he's sure enuf dead. Gimme de bottle quick, Rocky, before he changes his mind!

(ROCKY *passes him the bottle and glass. He pours a brimful drink and tosses it down his throat, and hands the bottle and glass to* LARRY)

ROCKY I'll take a cigar when I go in de bar. What're you havin'?

PARRITT Nothing. I'm on the wagon. What's the damage?

(*He holds out a dollar bill*)

ROCKY Fifteen cents.

(*He makes change from his pocket*)

PARRITT Must be some booze!

LARRY It's cyanide cut with carbolic acid to give it a mellow flavor. Here's luck!

(*He drinks*)

ROCKY Guess I'll get back in de bar and catch a coupla winks before opening-up time.

(*He squeezes through the tables and disappears, right-rear, behind the curtain. In the section of bar at right, he comes forward and sits at the table and slumps back, closing his eyes and yawning*)

JOE (*Stares calculatingly at* PARRITT *and then looks away—aloud to himself, philosophically*) One-drink guy. Dat well done run dry. No hope till Harry's birthday party. 'Less Hickey shows up. (*He turns to* LARRY) If Hickey comes, Larry, you wake me up if you has to bat me wid a chair.

(*He settles himself and immediately falls asleep*)

PARRITT Who's Hickey?

LARRY A hardware drummer. An old friend of Harry Hope's and all the gang. He's a grand guy. He comes here twice a year regularly on a periodical drunk and blows in all his money.

PARRITT (*With a disparaging glance around*) Must be hard up for a place to hang out.

LARRY It has its points for him. He never runs into anyone he knows in his business here.

PARRITT (*Lowering his voice*) Yes, that's what I want, too. I've got to stay under cover, Larry, like I told you last night.

LARRY You did a lot of hinting. You didn't tell me anything.

PARRITT You can guess, can't you? (*He changes the subject abruptly*) I've been in some dumps on the Coast, but this is the limit. What kind of joint is it, anyway?

LARRY (*With a sardonic grin*) What is it? It's the No Chance Saloon. It's Bedrock Bar, The End of the Line Café, The Bottom of the Sea Rathskeller! Don't you notice the beautiful calm in the atmosphere? That's because it's the last harbor. No one here has to worry about where they're going next, because there is no farther they can go. It's a great comfort to them. Although even here they keep up the appearances of life with a few harmless pipe dreams about their yesterdays and tomorrows, as you'll see for yourself if you're here long.

PARRITT (*Stares at him curiously*) What's your pipe dream, Larry?

LARRY (*Hiding resentment*) Oh, I'm the exception. I haven't any left, thank God. (*Shortly*) Don't complain about this place. You couldn't find a better for lying low.

PARRITT I'm glad of that, Larry. I don't feel any too damned good. I was knocked off my base by that business on the Coast, and since then it's been no fun dodging around the country, thinking every guy you see might be a dick.

LARRY (*Sympathetically now*) No, it wouldn't be. But you're safe here. The cops ignore this dump. They think it's as harmless as a graveyard. (*He grins sardonically*) And, be God, they're right.

PARRITT It's been lonely as hell. (*Impulsively*) Christ, Larry, I was glad to find you. I kept saying to myself, "If I can only find Larry. He's the one guy in the world who can understand—"

(*He hesitates, staring at* LARRY *with a strange appeal*)

LARRY (*Watching him puzzledly*) Understand what?

PARRITT (*Hastily*) Why, all I've been through. (*Looking away*) Oh, I know you're thinking, This guy has a hell of a nerve. I haven't seen him since he was a kid. I'd forgotten he was alive. But I've never forgotten you, Larry. You were the only friend of Mother's who ever paid attention to me, or knew I was alive. All the others were too busy with the Movement. Even Mother. And I had no Old Man. You used to take me on your knee and tell me stories and crack jokes and make me laugh. You'd ask me questions and take what I said seriously. I guess I got to feel in the years you lived with us that you'd taken the place of my Old Man. (*Embarrassedly*) But, hell, that sounds like a lot of mush. I suppose you don't remember a damned thing about it.

LARRY (*Moved in spite of himself*) I remember well. You were a serious lonely little shaver. (*Then resenting being moved, changes the subject*) How is it they didn't pick you up when they got your mother and the rest?

PARRITT (*In a lowered voice but eagerly, as if he wanted this chance to tell about it*) I wasn't around, and as soon as I heard the news I went under cover. You've noticed my glad rags. I was staked to them—as a disguise, sort of. I hung around pool rooms and gambling joints and hooker shops, where they'd never look for a Wobblie, pretending I was a sport. Anyway, they'd grabbed everyone important, so I suppose they didn't think of me until afterward.

LARRY The papers say the cops got them all dead to rights, that the Burns dicks knew every move before it was made, and someone inside the Movement must have sold out and tipped them off.

PARRITT (*Turns to look* LARRY *in the eyes—slowly*) Yes, I guess that must be true, Larry. It hasn't come out who it was. It may never come out. I suppose whoever it was made a bargain with the Burns men to keep him out of it. They won't need his evidence.

LARRY (*Tensely*) By God, I hate to believe it of any of the crowd, if I am through long since with any connection with them. I know they're damned fools, most of them, as stupidly greedy for power as the worst capitalist they attack, but I'd swear there couldn't be a yellow stool pigeon among them.

PARRITT Sure. I'd have sworn that, too, Larry.

LARRY I hope his soul rots in hell, whoever it is!

PARRITT   Yes, so do I.

LARRY   (*After a pause—shortly*)   How did you locate me? I hoped I'd found a place of retirement here where no one in the Movement would ever come to disturb my peace.

PARRITT   I found out through Mother.

LARRY   I asked her not to tell anyone.

PARRITT   She didn't tell me, but she'd kept all your letters and I found where she'd hidden them in the flat. I sneaked up there one night after she was arrested.

LARRY   I'd never have thought she was a woman who'd keep letters.

PARRITT   No, I wouldn't, either. There's nothing soft or sentimental about Mother.

LARRY   I never answered her last letters. I haven't written her in a couple of years—or anyone else. I've gotten beyond the desire to communicate with the world—or, what's more to the point, to let it bother me any more with its greedy madness.

PARRITT   It's funny Mother kept in touch with you so long. When she's finished with anyone, she's finished. She's always been proud of that. And you know how she feels about the Movement. Like a revivalist preacher about religion. Anyone who loses faith in it is more than dead to her; he's a Judas who ought to be boiled in oil. Yet she seemed to forgive you.

LARRY   (*Sardonically*)   She didn't, don't worry. She wrote to denounce me and try to bring the sinner to repentance and a belief in the One True Faith again.

PARRITT   What made you leave the Movement, Larry? Was it on account of Mother?

LARRY   (*Starts*)   Don't be a damned fool! What the hell put that in your head?

PARRITT   Why, nothing—except I remember what a fight you had with her before you left.

LARRY   (*Resentfully*)   Well, if you do, I don't. That was eleven years ago. You were only seven. If we did quarrel, it was because I told her I'd become convinced the Movement was only a beautiful pipe dream.

PARRITT   (*With a strange smile*)   I don't remember it that way.

LARRY   Then you can blame your imagination—and forget it. (*He changes the subject abruptly*)   You asked me why I quit the Movement. I had a lot of good reasons. One was myself, and another was my comrades, and the last was the breed of swine called men in general. For myself, I was forced to admit, at the end of thirty years' devotion to the Cause, that I was never made for it. I was born condemned to be one of those who has to see all sides of a question. When you're damned like that, the questions multiply for you until in the end it's all question and no answer. As history proves, to be a worldly success at anything, especially revolution, you have to wear blinders like a horse and see only straight in front of you. You have to see, too, that this is all black, and that is all white. As for my comrades in the Great Cause, I felt as Horace Walpole did about England, that he could love it if it weren't for the people in it. The material the ideal free society must be constructed from is men themselves and you can't build a marble temple out of a mixture of mud and manure. When man's soul isn't a sow's ear, it will be time enough to dream of silk purses. (*He chuckles sardonically—then irritably as if suddenly provoked at himself for talking so much*) Well, that's why I quit the Movement, if it leaves you any wiser. At any rate, you see it had nothing to do with your mother.

PARRITT (*Smiles almost mockingly*) Oh, sure, I see. But I'll bet Mother has always thought it was on her account. You know her, Larry. To hear her go on sometimes, you'd think she was the Movement.

LARRY (*Stares at him, puzzled and repelled—sharply*) That's a hell of a way for you to talk, after what happened to her!

PARRITT (*At once confused and guilty*) Don't get me wrong. I wasn't sneering, Larry. Only kidding. I've said the same thing to her lots of times to kid her. But you're right. I know I shouldn't now. I keep forgetting she's in jail. It doesn't seem real. I can't believe it about her. She's always been so free. I— But I don't want to think of it. (LARRY *is moved to a puzzled pity in spite of himself.* PARRITT *changes the subject*) What have you been doing all the years since you left—the Coast, Larry?

LARRY (*Sardonically*) Nothing I could help doing. If I don't believe in the Movement, I don't believe in anything else either, especially not the State. I've refused to become a useful member of its society. I've been a philosophical drunken bum, and proud of it. (*Abruptly his tone sharpens with resentful warning*) Listen to me. I hope you've deduced that I've my own reason for answering the impertinent questions of a stranger, for that's all you are to me. I have a strong hunch you've come here expecting something of me. I'm warning you, at the start, so there'll be no misunderstanding, that I've nothing left to give, and I want to be left alone, and I'll thank you to keep your life to yourself. I feel you're looking for some answer to something. I have no answer to give anyone, not even myself. Unless you can call what Heine wrote in his poem to morphine an answer.

(*He quotes a translation of the closing couplet sardonically*)

"Lo, sleep is good; better is death; in sooth,
  The best of all were never to be born."

PARRITT (*Shrinks a bit frightenedly*) That's the hell of an answer. (*Then with a forced grin of bravado*) Still, you never know when it might come in handy.

(*He looks away.* LARRY *stares at him puzzledly, interested in spite of himself and at the same time vaguely uneasy*)

LARRY (*Forcing a casual tone*) I don't suppose you've had much chance to hear news of your mother since she's been in jail?

PARRITT No. No chance. (*He hesitates—then blurts out*) Anyway, I don't think she wants to hear from me. We had a fight just before that business happened. She bawled me out because I was going around with tarts. That got my goat, coming from her. I told her, "You've always acted the free woman, you've never let anything stop you from—" (*He checks himself—goes on hurriedly*) That made her sore. She said she wouldn't give a damn what I did except she'd begun to suspect I was too interested in outside things and losing interest in the Movement.

LARRY (*Stares at him*) And were you?

PARRITT (*Hesitates—then with intensity*) Sure I was! I'm no damned fool! I couldn't go on believing forever that gang was going to change the world by shooting off their loud traps on soapboxes and sneaking around blowing up a lousy building or a bridge! I got wise it was all a crazy pipe dream! (*Appealingly*) The same as you did, Larry. That's why I came to you. I knew you'd understand. What finished me was this last business of someone selling out. How can you believe anything after a thing like that happens? It knocks you cold! You don't know what the hell is what! You're through! (*Appealingly*) You know how I feel, don't you, Larry?

(LARRY *stares at him, moved by sympathy and pity in spite of himself, disturbed, and resentful at being disturbed, and puzzled by something he feels about* PARRITT *that isn't right. But before he can reply,* HUGO *suddenly raises his head from his arms in a half-awake alcoholic daze and speaks)*

HUGO (*Quotes aloud to himself in a guttural declamatory style*) "The days grow hot, O Babylon! 'Tis cool beneath thy villow trees!" (PARRITT *turns startledly as* HUGO *peers muzzily without recognition at him.* HUGO *exclaims automatically in his tone of denunciation)* Gottammed stool pigeon!

PARRITT (*Shrinks away—stammers*) What? Who do you mean? (*Then furiously*) You lousy bum, you can't call me that! (*He draws back his fist*)

HUGO (*Ignores this—recognizing him now, bursts into his childish teasing giggle*) Hello, leedle Don! Leedle monkey-face. I did not recognize you. You have grown big boy. How is your mother? Where you come from? (*He breaks into his wheedling, bullying tone*) Don't be a fool! Loan me a dollar! Buy me a trink! (*As if this exhausted him, he abruptly forgets it and plumps his head down on his arms again and is asleep*)

PARRITT (*With eager relief*) Sure, I'll buy you a drink, Hugo. I'm broke, but I can afford one for you. I'm sorry I got sore. I ought to have remembered when you're soused you call everyone a stool pigeon. But it's no damned joke right at this time. (*He turns to* LARRY, *who is regarding him now fixedly with an uneasy expression as if he suddenly were afraid of his own thoughts—forcing a smile*) Gee, he's passed out again. (*He stiffens defensively*) What are you giving me the hard look for? Oh, I know. You thought I was going to hit him? What do you think I am? I've always had a lot of respect for Hugo. I've always stood up for him when people in the Movement panned him for an old drunken has-been. He had the guts to serve ten years in the can in his own country and get his eyes ruined in solitary. I'd like to see some of them here stick that. Well, they'll get a chance now to show— (*Hastily*) I don't mean— But let's forget that. Tell me some more about this dump. Who are all these tanks? Who's that guy trying to catch pneumonia? (*He indicates* LEWIS)

LARRY (*Stares at him almost frightenedly—then looks away and grasps eagerly this chance to change the subject. He begins to describe the sleepers with sardonic relish but at the same time showing his affection for them*) That's Captain Lewis, a one-time hero of the British Army. He strips to display that scar on his back he got from a native spear whenever he's completely plastered. The bewhiskered bloke opposite him is General Wetjoen, who led a commando in the War. The two of them met when they came here to work in the Boer War spectacle at the St. Louis Fair and they've been bosom pals ever since. They dream the hours away in happy dispute over the brave days in South Africa when they tried to murder each other. The little guy between them was in it, too, as correspondent for some English paper. His nickname here is Jimmy Tomorrow. He's the leader of our Tomorrow Movement.

PARRITT What do they do for a living?

LARRY As little as possible. Once in a while one of them makes a successful touch somewhere, and some of them get a few dollars a month from connections at home who pay it on condition they never come back. For the rest, they live on free lunch and their old friend, Harry Hope, who doesn't give a damn what anyone does or doesn't do, as long as he likes you.

PARRITT It must be a tough life.

LARRY It's not. Don't waste your pity. They wouldn't thank you for it. They manage to get drunk, by hook or crook, and keep their pipe dreams, and that's all they ask of life. I've never known more contented men. It isn't often that men attain the true goal of their heart's desire. The same applies to Harry himself and his two cronies at the far table. He's so satisfied with life he's never set foot out of this place since his wife died twenty years ago. He has no need of the outside world at all. This place has a fine trade from the Market people across the street and the waterfront workers, so in spite of Harry's thirst and his generous heart, he comes out even. He never worries in hard times because there's always old friends from the days when he was a jitney Tammany politician, and a friendly brewery to tide him over. Don't ask me what his two pals work at because they don't. Except at being his lifetime guests. The one facing this way is his brother-in-law, Ed Mosher, who once worked for a circus in the ticket wagon. Pat McGloin, the other one, was a police lieutenant back in the flush times of graft when everything went. But he got too greedy and when the usual reform investigation came he was caught red-handed and thrown off the Force. (*He nods at* JOE) Joe here has a yesterday in the same flush period. He ran a colored gambling house then and was a hell of a sport, so they say. Well, that's our whole family circle of inmates, except the two barkeeps and their girls, three ladies of the pavement that room on the third floor.

PARRITT (*Bitterly*)   To hell with them! I never want to see a whore again! (*As* LARRY *flashes him a puzzled glance, he adds confusedly*) I mean, they always get you in dutch.

(*While he is speaking* WILLIE OBAN *has opened his eyes. He leans toward them, drunk now from the effect of the huge drink he took, and speaks with a mocking suavity*)

WILLIE   Why omit me from your Who's Who in Dypsomania, Larry? An unpardonable slight, especially as I am the only inmate of royal blood. (*To* PARRITT—*ramblingly*) Educated at Harvard, too. You must have noticed the atmosphere of culture here. My humble contribution. Yes, Generous Stranger—I trust you're generous—I was born in the purple, the son, but unfortunately not the heir, of the late world-famous Bill Oban, King of the Bucket Shops. A revolution deposed him, conducted by the District Attorney. He was sent into exile. In fact, not to mince matters, they locked him in the can and threw away the key. Alas, his was an adventurous spirit that pined in confinement. And so he died. Forgive these reminiscences. Undoubtedly all this is well known to you. Everyone in the world knows.

PARRITT (*Uncomfortably*)   Tough luck. No, I never heard of him.

WILLIE (*Blinks at him incredulously*)   Never heard? I thought everyone in the world— Why, even at Harvard I discovered my father was well known by reputation, although that was some time before the District Attorney gave him so much unwelcome publicity. Yes, even as a freshman I was notorious. I was accepted socially with all the warm cordiality that Henry Wadsworth Longfellow would have shown a drunken Negress dancing the cancan at high noon on Brattle Street. Harvard was my father's idea. He was an ambitious man. Dictatorial, too. Always knowing what was best for me. But I did make myself a brilliant student. A dirty trick on my classmates, inspired by revenge, I fear. (*He quotes*) "Dear college days, with pleasure rife! The grandest gladdest days of life!" But, of course, that is a Yale hymn, and they're given to rah-rah exaggeration at New Haven. I was a brilliant student at Law School, too. My father wanted a lawyer in the family. He was a calculating man. A thorough knowledge of the law close at hand in the house to help him find fresh ways to evade it. But I discovered the loophole of whiskey and escaped his jurisdiction. (*Abruptly to* PARRITT) Speaking of whiskey, sir, reminds me—and, I hope, reminds you—that when meeting a Prince the customary salutation is "What'll you have?"

PARRITT (*With defensive resentment*) Nix! All you guys seem to think I'm made of dough. Where would I get the coin to blow everyone?

WILLIE (*Sceptically*) Broke? You haven't the thirsty look of the impecunious. I'd judge you to be a plutocrat, your pockets stuffed with ill-gotten gains. Two or three dollars, at least. And don't think we will question how you got it. As Vespasian remarked, the smell of all whiskey is sweet.

PARRITT What do you mean, how I got it? (*To* LARRY, *forcing a laugh*) It's a laugh, calling me a plutocrat, isn't it, Larry, when I've been in the Movement all my life.

(LARRY *gives him an uneasy suspicious glance, then looks away, as if avoiding something he does not wish to see*)

WILLIE (*Disgustedly*) Ah, one of those, eh? I believe you now, all right! Go away and blow yourself up, that's a good lad. Hugo is the only licensed preacher of that gospel here. A dangerous terrorist, Hugo! He would as soon blow the collar off a schooner of beer as look at you! (*To* LARRY) Let us ignore this useless youth, Larry. Let us join in prayer that Hickey, the Great Salesman, will soon arrive bringing the blessed bourgeois long green! Would that Hickey or Death would come! Meanwhile, I will sing a song. A beautiful old New England folk ballad which I picked up at Harvard amid the debris of education.

(*He sings in a boisterous baritone, rapping on the table with his knuckles at the indicated spots in the song:*)

"Jack, oh, Jack, was a sailor lad
 And he came to a tavern for gin.
 He rapped and he rapped with a (*Rap, rap, rap*)
 But never a soul seemed in."

(*The drunks at the tables stir.* ROCKY *gets up from his chair in the bar and starts back for the entrance to the back room.* HOPE *cocks one irritable eye over his specs.* JOE MOTT *opens both of his and grins.* WILLIE *interposes some drunken whimsical exposition to* LARRY) The origin of this beautiful ditty is veiled in mystery, Larry. There was a legend bruited about in Cambridge lavatories that Waldo Emerson composed it during his uninformative period as a minister, while he was trying to write a sermon. But my own opinion is, it goes back much further, and Jonathan Edwards was the author of both words and music.

(*He sings:*)

"He rapped and rapped, and tapped and tapped
  Enough to wake the dead
  Till he heard a damsel (*Rap, rap, rap*)
  On a window right over his head."

(*The drunks are blinking their eyes now, grumbling and cursing.* ROCKY *appears from the bar at rear, right, yawning*)

HOPE (*With fuming irritation*) Rocky! Bejees, can't you keep that crazy bastard quiet?

(ROCKY *starts for* WILLIE)

WILLIE And now the influence of a good woman enters our mariner's life. Well, perhaps "good" isn't the word. But very, very kind.

(*He sings:*)

"Oh, come up," she cried, "my sailor lad,
  And you and I'll agree,
  And I'll show you the prettiest (*Rap, rap, rap*)
  That ever you did see."

(*He speaks*) You see, Larry? The lewd Puritan touch, obviously, and it grows more marked as we go on.

(*He sings:*)

"Oh, he put his arm around her waist,
  He gazed in her bright blue eyes
  And then he—"

(*But here* ROCKY *shakes him roughly by the shoulder*)

ROCKY Piano! What d'yuh tink dis dump is, a dump?

HOPE Give him the bum's rush upstairs! Lock him in his room!

ROCKY (*Yanks* WILLIE *by the arm*) Come on, Bum.

WILLIE (*Dissolves into pitiable terror*) No! Please, Rocky! I'll go crazy up in that room alone! It's haunted! I— (*He calls to* HOPE) Please, Harry! Let me stay here! I'll be quiet!

HOPE (*Immediately relents—indignantly*) What the hell you doing to him, Rocky? I didn't tell you to beat up the poor guy. Leave him alone, long as he's quiet.

(ROCKY *lets go of* WILLIE *disgustedly and goes back to his chair in the bar*)

WILLIE (*Huskily*) Thanks, Harry. You're a good scout.
(*He closes his eyes and sinks back in his chair exhaustedly, twitching and quivering again*)

HOPE (*Addressing* MCGLOIN *and* MOSHER, *who are sleepily awake— accusingly*) Always the way. Can't trust nobody. Leave it to that Dago to keep order and it's like bedlam in a cathouse, singing and everything. And you two big barflies are a hell of a help to me, ain't you? Eat and sleep and get drunk! All you're good for, bejees! Well, you can take that "I'll-have-the-same" look off your maps! There ain't going to be no more drinks on the house till hell freezes over! (*Neither of the two is impressed either by his insults or his threats. They grin hangover grins of tolerant affection at him and wink at each other.* HARRY *fumes*) Yeah, grin! Wink, bejees! Fine pair of sons of bitches to have glued on me for life!

(*But he can't get a rise out of them and he subsides into a fuming mumble. Meanwhile, at the middle table,* CAPTAIN LEWIS *and* GENERAL WETJOEN *are as wide awake as heavy hangovers permit.* JIMMY TOMORROW *nods, his eyes blinking.* LEWIS *is gazing across the table at* JOE MOTT, *who is still chuckling to himself over* WILLIE'S *song. The expression on* LEWIS's *face is that of one who can't believe his eyes*)

LEWIS (*Aloud to himself, with a muzzy wonder*) Good God! Have I been drinking at the same table with a bloody Kaffir?

JOE (*Grinning*) Hello, Captain. You comin' up for air? Kaffir? Who's he?

WETJOEN (*Blurrily*) Kaffir, dot's a nigger, Joe. (JOE *stiffens and his eyes narrow.* WETJOEN *goes on with heavy jocosity*) Dot's joke on him, Joe. He don't know you. He's still plind drunk, the ploody Limey chentleman! A great mistake I missed him at the pattle of Modder River. Vit mine rifle I shoot damn fool Limey officers py the dozen, but him I miss. De pity of it! (*He chuckles and slaps* LEWIS *on his bare shoulder*) Hey, wake up, Cecil, you ploody fool! Don't you know your old friend, Joe? He's no damned Kaffir! He's white, Joe is!

LEWIS (*Light dawning—contritely*) My profound apologies, Joseph, old chum. Eyesight a trifle blurry, I'm afraid. Whitest colored man I ever knew. Proud to call you my friend. No hard feelings, what?
(*He holds out his hand*)

JOE (*At once grins good-naturedly and shakes his hand*) No, Captain, I know it's mistake. Youse regular, if you is a Limey. (*Then his face hardening*) But I don't stand for "nigger" from nobody. Never did. In de old days, people calls me "nigger" wakes up in de hospital. I was de leader ob de Dirty Half-Dozen Gang. All six of us colored boys, we was tough and I was de toughest.

WETJOEN (*Inspired to boastful reminiscence*) Me, in old days in Transvaal, I vas so tough and strong I grab axle of ox wagon mit full load and lift like feather.

LEWIS (*Smiling amiably*) As for you, my balmy Boer that walks like a man, I say again it was a grave error in our foreign policy ever to set you free, once we nabbed you and your commando with Cronje. We should have taken you to the London zoo and incarcerated you in the baboons' cage. With a sign: "Spectators may distinguish the true baboon by his blue behind."

WETJOEN (*Grins*) Gott! To dink, ten better Limey officers, at least, I shoot clean in the mittle of forehead at Spion Kopje, and you I miss! I neffer forgive myself!

(JIMMY TOMORROW *blinks benignantly from one to the other with a gentle drunken smile*)

JIMMY (*Sentimentally*) Now, come, Cecil, Piet! We must forget the War. Boer and Briton, each fought fairly and played the game till the better man won and then we shook hands. We are all brothers within the Empire united beneath the flag on which the sun never sets. (*Tears come to his eyes. He quotes with great sentiment, if with slight application*) "Ship me somewhere east of Suez—"

LARRY (*Breaks in sardonically*) Be God, you're there already, Jimmy. Worst is best here, and East is West, and tomorrow is yesterday. What more do you want?

JIMMY (*With bleary benevolence, shaking his head in mild rebuke*) No, Larry, old friend, you can't deceive me. You pretend a bitter, cynic philosophy, but in your heart you are the kindest man among us.

LARRY (*Disconcerted—irritably*) The hell you say!

PARRITT (*Leans toward him—confidentially*) What a bunch of cuckoos!

JIMMY (*As if reminded of something—with a pathetic attempt at a brisk, no-more-nonsense air*) Tomorrow, yes. It's high time I straightened out and got down to business again. (*He brushes his sleeve fastidiously*) I must have this suit cleaned and pressed. I can't look like a tramp when I—

JOE (*Who has been brooding—interrupts*) Yes, suh, white folks always said I was white. In de days when I was flush, Joe Mott's de only colored man dey allows in de white gamblin' houses. "You're all right, Joe, you're white," dey says. (*He chuckles*) Wouldn't let me play craps, dough. Dey know I could make dem dice behave. "Any odder game and any limit you like, Joe," dey says. Man, de money I lost! (*He chuckles—then with an underlying defensiveness*) Look at de Big Chief in dem days. He knew I was white. I'd saved my dough so I could start my own gamblin' house. Folks in de know tells me, see de man at de top, den you never has trouble. You git Harry Hope give you a letter to de Chief. And Harry does. Don't you, Harry?

HOPE (*Preoccupied with his own thoughts*) Eh? Sure. Big Bill was a good friend of mine. I had plenty of friends high up in those days. Still could have if I wanted to go out and see them. Sure, I gave you a letter. I said you was white. What the hell of it?

JOE (*To* CAPTAIN LEWIS *who has relapsed into a sleepy daze and is listening to him with an absurd strained attention without comprehending a word*) Dere. You see, Captain. I went to see de Chief, shakin' in my boots, and dere he is sittin' behind a big desk, lookin' as big as a freight train. He don't look up. He keeps me waitin' and waitin', and after 'bout an hour, seems like to me, he says slow and quiet like dere wasn't no harm in him, "You want to open a gamblin' joint, does you, Joe?" But he don't give me no time to answer. He jumps up, lookin' as big as two freight trains, and he pounds his fist like a ham on de desk, and he shouts, "You black son of a bitch, Harry says you're white and you better be white or dere's a little iron room up de river waitin' for you!" Den he sits down and says quiet again, "All right. You can open. Git de hell outa here!" So I opens, and he finds out I'se white, sure 'nuff, 'cause I run wide open for years and pays my sugar on de dot, and de cops and I is friends. (*He chuckles with pride*) Dem old days! Many's de night I come in here. Dis was a first-class hangout for sports in dem days. Good whiskey, fifteen cents, two for two bits. I t'rows down a fifty-dollar bill like it was trash paper and says, "Drink it up, boys, I don't want no change." Ain't dat right, Harry?

HOPE (*Caustically*) Yes, and bejees, if I ever seen you throw fifty cents on the bar now, I'd know I had delirium tremens! You've told that story ten million times and if I have to hear it again, that'll give me D.T.s anyway!

JOE (*Chuckling*) Gittin' drunk every day for twenty years ain't give you de Brooklyn boys. You needn't be scared of me!

LEWIS (*Suddenly turns and beams on* HOPE) Thank you, Harry, old chum. I will have a drink, now you mention it, seeing it's so near your birthday.

(*The others laugh*)

HOPE (*Puts his hand to his ear—angrily*) What's that? I can't hear you.

LEWIS (*Sadly*) No, I fancied you wouldn't.

HOPE I don't have to hear, bejees! Booze is the only thing you ever talk about!

LEWIS (*Sadly*) True. Yet there was a time when my conversation was more comprehensive. But as I became burdened with years, it seemed rather pointless to discuss my other subject.

HOPE You can't joke with me! How much room rent do you owe me, tell me that?

LEWIS Sorry. Adding has always baffled me. Subtraction is my forte.

HOPE (*Snarling*) Arrh! Think you're funny! Captain, bejees! Showing off your wounds! Put on your clothes, for Christ's sake! This ain't no Turkish bath! Lousy Limey army! Took 'em years to lick a gang of Dutch hayseeds!

WETJOEN Dot's right, Harry. Gif him hell!

HOPE No lip out of you, neither, you Dutch spinach! General, hell! Salvation Army, that's what you'd ought t'been General in! Bragging what a shot you were, and, bejees, you missed him! And he missed you, that's just as bad! And now the two of you bum on me! (*Threateningly*) But you've broke the camel's back this time, bejees! You pay up tomorrow or out you go!

LEWIS (*Earnestly*) My dear fellow, I give you my word of honor as an officer and a gentleman, you shall be paid tomorrow.

WETJOEN Ve swear it, Harry! Tomorrow vidout fail!

MCGLOIN (*A twinkle in his eye*) There you are, Harry. Sure, what could be fairer?

MOSHER (*With a wink at* MCGLOIN) Yes, you can't ask more than that, Harry. A promise is a promise—as I've often discovered.

HOPE (*Turns on them*) I mean the both of you, too! An old grafting flatfoot and a circus bunco steerer! Fine company for me, bejees! Couple of con men living in my flat since Christ knows when! Getting fat as hogs, too! And you ain't even got the decency to get me upstairs where I got a good bed! Let me sleep on a chair like a bum! Kept me down here waitin' for Hickey to show up, hoping I'd blow you to more drinks!

MCGLOIN Ed and I did our damnedest to get you up, didn't we, Ed?

MOSHER We did. But you said you couldn't bear the flat because it was one of those nights when memory brought poor old Bessie back to you.

HOPE (*His face instantly becoming long and sad and sentimental—mournfully*) Yes, that's right, boys. I remember now. I could almost see her in every room just as she used to be—and it's twenty years since she—

(*His throat and eyes fill up. A suitable sentimental hush falls on the room*)

LARRY (*In a sardonic whisper to* PARRITT) Isn't a pipe dream of yesterday a touching thing? By all accounts, Bessie nagged the hell out of him.

JIMMY (*Who has been dreaming, a look of prim resolution on his face, speaks aloud to himself*) No more of this sitting around and loafing. Time I took hold of myself. I must have my shoes soled and heeled and shined first thing tomorrow morning. A general spruce-up. I want to have a well-groomed appearance when I—

(*His voice fades out as he stares in front of him. No one pays any attention to him except* LARRY *and* PARRITT)

LARRY (*As before, in a sardonic aside to* PARRITT) The tomorrow movement is a sad and beautiful thing, too!

MCGLOIN (*With a huge sentimental sigh—and a calculating look at* HOPE) Poor old Bessie! You don't find her like in these days. A sweeter woman never drew breath.

MOSHER (*In a similar calculating mood*) Good old Bess. A man couldn't want a better sister than she was to me.

HOPE (*Mournfully*) Twenty years, and I've never set foot out of this house since the day I buried her. Didn't have the heart. Once she'd gone, I didn't give a damn for anything. I lost all my ambition. Without her, nothing seemed worth the trouble. You remember, Ed, you, too, Mac—the boys was going to nominate me for Alderman. It was all fixed. Bessie wanted it and she was so proud. But when she was taken, I told them, "No, boys, I can't do it. I simply haven't the heart. I'm through." I would have won the election easy, too. (*He says this a bit defiantly*) Oh, I know there was jealous wise guys said the boys was giving me the nomination because they knew they couldn't win that year in this ward. But that's a damned lie! I knew every man, woman and child in the ward, almost. Bessie made me make friends with everyone, helped me remember all their names. I'd have been elected easy.

MCGLOIN You would, Harry. It was a sure thing.

MOSHER A dead cinch, Harry. Everyone knows that.

HOPE Sure they do. But after Bessie died, I didn't have the heart. Still, I know while she'd appreciate my grief, she wouldn't want it to keep me cooped up in here all my life. So I've made up my mind I'll go out soon. Take a walk around the ward, see all the friends I used to know, get together with the boys and maybe tell 'em I'll let 'em deal me a hand in their game again. Yes, bejees, I'll do it. My birthday, tomorrow, that'd be the right time to turn over a new leaf. Sixty. That ain't too old.

MCGLOIN (*Flatteringly*) It's the prime of life, Harry.

MOSHER Wonderful thing about you, Harry, you keep young as you ever was.

JIMMY (*Dreaming aloud again*) Get my things from the laundry. They must still have them. Clean collar and shirt. If I wash the ones I've got on any more, they'll fall apart. Socks, too. I want to make a good appearance. I met Dick Trumbull on the street a year or two ago. He said, "Jimmy, the publicity department's never been the same since you got—resigned. It's dead as hell." I said, "I know. I've heard rumors the management were at their wits' end and would be only too glad to have me run it for them again. I think all I'd have to do would be go and see them and they'd offer me the position. Don't you think so, Dick?" He said, "Sure, they would, Jimmy. Only take my advice and wait a while until business conditions are better. Then you can strike them for a bigger salary than you got before, do you see?" I said, "Yes, I do see, Dick, and many thanks for the tip." Well, conditions must be better by this time. All I have to do is get fixed up with a decent front tomorrow, and it's as good as done.

HOPE (*Glances at* JIMMY *with a condescending affectionate pity—in a hushed voice*) Poor Jimmy's off on his pipe dream again. Bejees, he takes the cake!

(*This is too much for* LARRY. *He cannot restrain a sardonic guffaw. But no one pays any attention to him*)

LEWIS (*Opens his eyes, which are drowsing again—dreamily to* WETJOEN) I'm sorry we had to postpone our trip again this April,

Piet. I hoped the blasted old estate would be settled up by then. The damned lawyers can't hold up the settlement much longer. We'll make it next year, even if we have to work and earn our passage money, eh? You'll stay with me at the old place as long as you like, then you can take the *Union Castle* from Southampton to Cape Town. (*Sentimentally, with real yearning*) England in April. I want you to see that, Piet. The old veldt has its points, I'll admit, but it isn't home—especially home in April.

WETJOEN (*Blinks drowsily at him—dreamily*) Ja, Cecil, I know how beautiful it must be, from all you tell me many times. I vill enjoy it. But I shall enjoy more ven I am home, too. The veldt, ja! You could put England on it, and it would look like a farmer's small garden. Py Gott, there is space to be free, the air like vine is, you don't need booze to be drunk! My relations vill so surprised be. They vill not know me, it is so many years. Dey vill be so glad I haf come home at last.

JOE (*Dreamily*) I'll make my stake and get my new gamblin' house open before you boys leave. You got to come to de openin'. I'll treat you white. If you're broke, I'll stake you to buck any game you chooses. If you wins, dat's velvet for you. If you loses, it don't count. Can't treat you no whiter dan dat, can I?

HOPE (*Again with condescending pity*) Bejees, Jimmy's started them off smoking the same hop.

(*But the three are finished, their eyes closed again in sleep or a drowse*)

LARRY (*Aloud to himself—in his comically tense, crazy whisper*) Be God, this bughouse will drive me stark, raving loony yet!

HOPE (*Turns on him with fuming suspicion*) What? What d'you say?

LARRY (*Placatingly*) Nothing, Harry. I had a crazy thought in my head.

HOPE (*Irascibly*) Crazy is right! Yah! The old wise guy! Wise, hell! A damned old fool Anarchist I-Won't-Worker! I'm sick of you and Hugo, too. Bejees, you'll pay up tomorrow, or I'll start a Harry Hope Revolution! I'll tie a dispossess bomb to your tails that'll blow you out in the street! Bejees, I'll make your Movement move!

(*The witticism delights him and he bursts into a shrill cackle. At once* MCGLOIN *and* MOSHER *guffaw enthusiastically*)

MOSHER (*Flatteringly*) Harry, you sure say the funniest things! (*He reaches on the table as if he expected a glass to be there—*

then starts with well-acted surprise) Hell, where's my drink? That Rocky is too damned fast cleaning tables. Why, I'd only taken one sip of it.

HOPE (*His smiling face congealing*) No, you don't! (*Acidly*) Any time you only take one sip of a drink, you'll have lockjaw and paralysis! Think you can kid me with those old circus con games? —me, that's known you since you was knee-high, and, bejees, you was a crook even then!

MCGLOIN (*Grinning*) It's not like you to be so hard-hearted, Harry. Sure, it's hot, parching work laughing at your jokes so early in the morning on an empty stomach!

HOPE Yah! You, Mac! Another crook! Who asked you to laugh? We was talking about poor old Bessie, and you and her no-good brother start to laugh! A hell of a thing! Talking mush about her, too! "Good old Bess." Bejees, she'd never forgive me if she knew I had you two bums living in her flat, throwing ashes and cigar butts on her carpet. You know her opinion of you, Mac. "That Pat McGloin is the biggest drunken grafter that ever disgraced the police force," she used to say to me. "I hope they send him to Sing Sing for life."

MCGLOIN (*Unperturbed*) She didn't mean it. She was angry at me because you used to get me drunk. But Bess had a heart of gold underneath her sharpness. She knew I was innocent of all the charges.

WILLIE (*Jumps to his feet drunkenly and points a finger at* MCGLOIN *—imitating the manner of a cross-examiner—coldly*) One moment, please. Lieutenant McGloin! Are you aware you are under oath? Do you realize what the penalty for perjury is? (*Purringly*) Come now, Lieutenant, isn't it a fact that you're as guilty as hell? No, don't say, "How about your old man?" I am asking the questions. The fact that he was a crooked old bucket-shop bastard has no bearing on your case. (*With a change to maudlin joviality*) Gentlemen of the Jury, court will now recess while the D.A. sings out a little ditty he learned at Harvard. It was composed in a wanton moment by the Dean of the Divinity School on a moonlight night in July, 1776, while sobering up in a Turkish bath. (*He sings:*)

"Oh, come up," she cried, "my sailor lad,
   And you and I'll agree.
   And I'll show you the prettiest (*Rap, rap, rap on table*)
   That ever you did see."

(*Suddenly he catches* HOPE's *eyes fixed on him condemningly, and sees* ROCKY *appearing from the bar. He collapses back on his chair, pleading miserably*) Please, Harry! I'll be quiet! Don't make Rocky bounce me upstairs! I'll go crazy alone! (*To* MCGLOIN) I apologize, Mac. Don't get sore. I was only kidding you.

(ROCKY, *at a relenting glance from* HOPE, *returns to the bar*)

MCGLOIN (*Good-naturedly*) Sure, kid all you like, Willie. I'm hardened to it. (*He pauses—seriously*) But I'm telling you some day before long I'm going to make them reopen my case. Everyone knows there was no real evidence against me, and I took the fall for the ones higher up. I'll be found innocent this time and reinstated. (*Wistfully*) I'd like to have my old job on the Force back. The boys tell me there's fine pickings these days, and I'm not getting rich here, sitting with a parched throat waiting for Harry Hope to buy a drink.

(*He glances reproachfully at* HOPE)

WILLIE Of course, you'll be reinstated, Mac. All you need is a brilliant young attorney to handle your case. I'll be straightened out and on the wagon in a day or two. I've never practiced but I was one of the most brilliant students in Law School, and your case is just the opportunity I need to start. (*Darkly*) Don't worry about my not forcing the D.A. to reopen your case. I went through my father's papers before the cops destroyed them, and I remember a lot of people, even if I can't prove— (*Coaxingly*) You will let me take your case, won't you, Mac?

MCGLOIN (*Soothingly*) Sure I will and it'll make your reputation, Willie.

(MOSHER *winks at* HOPE, *shaking his head, and* HOPE *answers with identical pantomime, as though to say, "Poor dopes, they're off again!"*)

LARRY (*Aloud to himself more than to* PARRITT—*with irritable wonder*) Ah, be damned! Haven't I heard their visions a thousand times? Why should they get under my skin now? I've got the blues, I guess. I wish to hell Hickey'd turn up.

MOSHER (*Calculatingly solicitous—whispering to* HOPE) Poor Willie needs a drink bad, Harry—and I think if we all joined him it'd make him feel he was among friends and cheer him up.

HOPE More circus con tricks! (*Scathingly*) You talking of your dear sister! Bessie had you sized up. She used to tell me, "I don't know what you can see in that worthless, drunken, petty-larceny brother of mine. If I had my way," she'd say, "he'd get booted out in the gutter on his fat behind." Sometimes she didn't say behind, either.

MOSHER (*Grins genially*) Yes, dear old Bess had a quick temper, but there was no real harm in her. (*He chuckles reminiscently*) Remember the time she sent me down to the bar to change a ten-dollar bill for her?

HOPE (*Has to grin himself*) Bejees, do I! She coulda bit a piece out of a stove lid, after she found it out.
(*He cackles appreciatively*)

MOSHER I was sure surprised when she gave me the ten spot. Bess usually had better sense, but she was in a hurry to go to church. I didn't really mean to do it, but you know how habit gets you. Besides, I still worked then, and the circus season was going to begin soon, and I needed a little practice to keep my hand in. Or, you never can tell, the first rube that came to my wagon for a ticket might have left with the right change and I'd be disgraced. (*He chuckles*) I said, "I'm sorry, Bess, but I had to take it all in dimes. Here, hold out your hands and I'll count it out for you, so you won't kick afterwards I short-changed you." (*He begins a count which grows more rapid as he goes on*) Ten, twenty, thirty, forty, fifty, sixty, seventy, eighty, ninety, a dollar. Ten, twenty, thirty, forty, fifty, sixty— You're counting with me, Bess, aren't you?—eighty, ninety, two dollars. Ten, twenty— Those are pretty shoes you got on, Bess—forty, fifty, seventy, eighty, ninety, three dollars. Ten, twenty, thirty— What's on at the church tonight, Bess?—fifty, sixty, seventy, ninety, four dollars. Ten, twenty, thirty, fifty, seventy, eighty, ninety— That's a swell new hat, Bess, looks very becoming—six dollars. (*He chuckles*) And so on. I'm bum at it now for lack of practice, but in those days I could have short-changed the Keeper of the Mint.

HOPE (*Grinning*) Stung her for two dollars and a half, wasn't it, Ed?

MOSHER Yes. A fine percentage, if I do say so, when you're dealing to someone who's sober and can count. I'm sorry to say she discovered my mistakes in arithmetic just after I beat it around the corner. She counted it over herself. Bess somehow never had the confidence in me a sister should. (*He sighs tenderly*) Dear old Bess.

HOPE (*Indignant now*) You're a fine guy bragging how you short-changed your own sister! Bejees, if there was a war and you was in it, they'd have to padlock the pockets of the dead!

MOSHER (*A bit hurt at this*) That's going pretty strong, Harry. I always gave a sucker some chance. There wouldn't be no fun robbing the dead. (*He becomes reminiscently melancholy*) Gosh, thinking of the old ticket wagon brings those days back. The greatest life on earth with the greatest show on earth! The grandest crowd of regular guys ever gathered under one tent! I'd sure like to shake their hands again!

HOPE (*Acidly*) They'd have guns in theirs. They'd shoot you on sight. You've touched every damned one of them. Bejees, you've even borrowed fish from the trained seals and peanuts from every elephant that remembered you!

(*This fancy tickles him and he gives a cackling laugh*)

MOSHER (*Overlooking this—dreamily*) You know, Harry, I've made up my mind I'll see the boss in a couple of days and ask for my old job. I can get back my magic touch with change easy, and I can throw him a line of bull that'll kid him I won't be so unreasonable about sharing the profits next time. (*With insinuating complaint*) There's no percentage in hanging around this dive, taking care of you and shooing away your snakes, when I don't even get an eye-opener for my trouble.

HOPE (*Implacably*) No! (MOSHER *sighs and gives up and closes his eyes. The others, except* LARRY *and* PARRITT, *are all dozing again now.* HOPE *goes on grumbling*) Go to hell or the circus, for all I care. Good riddance, bejees! I'm sick of you! (*Then worriedly*) Say, Ed, what the hell you think's happened to Hickey? I hope he'll turn up. Always got a million funny stories. You and the other bums have begun to give me the graveyard fantods. I'd like a good laugh with old Hickey. (*He chuckles at a memory*) Remember that gag he always pulls about his wife and the iceman? He'd make a cat laugh!

(ROCKY *appears from the bar. He comes front, behind* MOSHER'S *chair, and begins pushing the black curtain along the rod to the rear wall*)

ROCKY Openin' time, Boss. (*He presses a button at rear which switches off the lights. The back room becomes drabber and dingier than ever in the gray daylight that comes from the street windows, off right, and what light can penetrate the grime of the two backyard windows at left.* ROCKY *turns back to* HOPE—*grumpily*) Why don't you go up to bed, Boss? Hickey'd never turn up dis time of de mornin'!

HOPE (*Starts and listens*) Someone's coming now.

ROCKY (*Listens*) Aw, dat's on'y my two pigs. It's about time dey showed.

(*He goes back toward the door at left of the bar*)

HOPE (*Sourly disappointed*) You keep them dumb broads quiet. I don't want to go to bed. I'm going to catch a couple more winks here and I don't want no damn-fool laughing and screeching. (*He settles himself in his chair, grumbling*) Never thought I'd see the day when Harry Hope's would have tarts rooming in it. What'd Bessie think? But I don't let 'em use my rooms for business. And they're good kids. Good as anyone else. They got to make a living. Pay their rent, too, which is more than I can say for— (*He cocks an eye over his specs at* MOSHER *and grins with satisfaction*) Bejees, Ed, I'll bet Bessie is doing somersaults in her grave!

(*He chuckles. But* MOSHER's *eyes are closed, his head nodding, and he doesn't reply, so* HOPE *closes his eyes.* ROCKY *has opened the barroom door at rear and is standing in the hall beyond it, facing right. A girl's laugh is heard*)

ROCKY (*Warningly*) Nix! Piano!

(*He comes in, beckoning them to follow. He goes behind the bar and gets a whiskey bottle and glasses and chairs.* MARGIE *and* PEARL *follow him, casting a glance around. Everyone except* LARRY *and* PARRITT *is asleep or dozing. Even* PARRITT *has his eyes closed. The two girls, neither much over twenty, are typical dollar street walkers, dressed in the usual tawdry get-up.* PEARL *is obviously Italian with black hair and eyes.* MARGIE *has brown hair and hazel eyes, a slum New Yorker of mixed blood. Both are plump and have a certain prettiness that shows even through their blobby make-up. Each retains a vestige of youthful freshness, although the game is beginning to get them and give them hard, worn expressions. Both are sentimental, feather-brained, giggly, lazy, good-natured and reasonably contented with life. Their attitude toward* ROCKY *is much that of two maternal, affectionate sisters toward a bullying brother whom they like to tease and spoil. His attitude toward them is that of the owner of two performing pets he has trained to do a profitable act under his management. He feels a proud proprietor's affection for them, and is tolerantly lax in his discipline*)

MARGIE (*Glancing around*) Jees, Poil, it's de Morgue wid all de stiffs on deck. (*She catches* LARRY's *eye and smiles affectionately*) Hello, Old Wise Guy, ain't you died yet?

LARRY (*Grinning*) Not yet, Margie. But I'm waiting impatiently for the end.

(PARRITT *opens his eyes to look at the two girls, but as soon as they glance at him he closes them again and turns his head away*)

MARGIE (*As she and* PEARL *come to the table at right, front, followed by* ROCKY) Who's de new guy? Friend of yours, Larry? (*Automatically she smiles seductively at* PARRITT *and addresses him in a professional chant*) Wanta have a good time, kid?

PEARL Aw, he's passed out. Hell wid him!

HOPE (*Cocks an eye over his specs at them—with drowsy irritation*) You dumb broads cut the loud talk.

(*He shuts his eye again*)

ROCKY (*Admonishing them good-naturedly*) Sit down before I knock yuh down. (MARGIE *and* PEARL *sit at left, and rear, of table,* ROCKY *at right of it. The girls pour drinks.* ROCKY *begins in a brisk, business-like manner but in a lowered voice with an eye on* HOPE) Well, how'd you tramps do?

MARGIE Pretty good. Didn't we, Poil?

PEARL Sure. We nailed a coupla all-night guys.

MARGIE On Sixth Avenoo. Boobs from de sticks.

PEARL Stinko, de bot' of 'em.

MARGIE We thought we was in luck. We steered dem to a real hotel. We figgered dey was too stinko to bother us much and we could cop a good sleep in beds that ain't got cobble stones in de mattress like de ones in dis dump.

PEARL But we was outa luck. Dey didn't bother us much dat way, but dey wouldn't go to sleep either, see? Jees, I never hoid such gabby guys.

MARGIE Dey got onta politics, drinkin' outa de bottle. Dey forgot we was around. "De Bull Moosers is de on'y reg'lar guys," one guy says. And de other guy says, "You're a God-damned liar! And I'm a Republican!" Den dey'd laugh.

PEARL Den dey'd get mad and make a bluff dey was goin' to scrap, and den dey'd make up and cry and sing "School Days." Jees, imagine tryin' to sleep wid dat on de phonograph!

MARGIE Maybe you tink we wasn't glad when de house dick come up and told us all to git dressed and take de air!

PEARL We told de guys we'd wait for dem 'round de corner.

MARGIE So here we are.

ROCKY (*Sententiously*)   Yeah. I see you. But I don't see no dough yet.

PEARL (*With a wink at* MARGIE—*teasingly*)   Right on de job, ain't he, Margie?

MARGIE   Yeah, our little business man! Dat's him!

ROCKY   Come on! Dig!

(*They both pull up their skirts to get the money from their stockings.* ROCKY *watches this move carefully*)

PEARL (*Amused*)   Pipe him keepin' cases, Margie.

MARGIE (*Amused*)   Scared we're holdin' out on him.

PEARL   Way he grabs, yuh'd tink it was him done de woik. (*She holds out a little roll of bills to* ROCKY) Here y'are, Grafter!

MARGIE (*Holding hers out*)   We hope it chokes yuh.

(ROCKY *counts the money quickly and shoves it in his pocket*)

ROCKY (*Genially*)   You dumb baby dolls gimme a pain. What would you do wid money if I wasn't around? Give it all to some pimp.

PEARL (*Teasingly*)   Jees, what's the difference—? (*Hastily*) Aw, I don't mean dat, Rocky.

ROCKY (*His eyes growing hard—slowly*)   A lotta difference, get me?

PEARL   Don't get sore. Jees, can't yuh take a little kiddin'?

MARGIE   Sure, Rocky, Poil was on'y kiddin'. (*Soothingly*) We know yuh got a reg'lar job. Dat's why we like yuh, see? Yuh don't live offa us. Yuh're a bartender.

ROCKY (*Genially again*)   Sure, I'm a bartender. Everyone knows me knows dat. And I treat you goils right, don't I? Jees, I'm wise yuh hold out on me, but I know it ain't much, so what the hell, I let yuh get away wid it. I tink yuh're a coupla good kids. Yuh're aces wid me, see?

PEARL   You're aces wid us, too. Ain't he, Margie?

MARGIE   Sure, he's aces. (ROCKY *beams complacently and takes the glasses back to the bar.* MARGIE *whispers*) Yuh sap, don't yuh know enough not to kid him on dat? Serve yuh right if he beat yuh up!

PEARL (*Admiringly*)   Jees, I'll bet he'd give yuh an awful beatin', too, once he started. Ginnies got awful tempers.

MARGIE   Anyway, we wouldn't keep no pimp, like we was reg'lar old whores. We ain't dat bad.

PEARL   No. We're tarts, but dat's all.

ROCKY (*Rinsing glasses behind the bar*)   Cora got back around three o'clock. She woke up Chuck and dragged him outa de hay

to go to a chop suey joint. (*Disgustedly*) Imagine him standin'
for dat stuff!

MARGIE (*Disgustedly*)   I'll bet dey been sittin' around kiddin' demselves wid dat old pipe dream about gettin' married and settlin'
down on a farm. Jees, when Chuck's on de wagon, dey never lay
off dat dope! Dey give yuh an earful every time yuh talk to 'em!

PEARL   Yeah. Chuck wid a silly grin on his ugly map, de big boob,
and Cora gigglin' like she was in grammar school and some tough
guy'd just told her babies wasn't brung down de chimney by a
boid!

MARGIE   And her on de turf long before me and you was! And bot'
of 'em arguin' all de time, Cora sayin' she's scared to marry him
because he'll go on drunks again. Just as dough any drunk could
scare Cora!

PEARL   And him swearin', de big liar, he'll never go on no more
periodicals! An' den her pretendin'— But it gives me a pain to
talk about it. We ought to phone de booby hatch to send round
de wagon for 'em.

ROCKY (*Comes back to the table—disgustedly*)   Yeah, of all de
pipe dreams in dis dump, dey got de nuttiest! And nuttin' stops
dem. Dey been dreamin' it for years, every time Chuck goes on
de wagon. I never could figger it. What would gettin' married
get dem? But de farm stuff is de sappiest part. When bot' of 'em
was dragged up in dis ward and ain't never been nearer a farm
dan Coney Island! Jees, dey'd tink dey'd gone deef if dey didn't
hear de El rattle! Dey'd get D.T.s if dey ever hoid a cricket choip!
I hoid crickets once on my cousin's place in Joisey. I couldn't sleep
a wink. Dey give me de heebie-jeebies. (*With deeper disgust*)
Jees, can yuh picture a good barkeep like Chuck diggin' spuds?
And imagine a whore hustlin' de cows home! For Christ sake!
Ain't dat a sweet picture!

MARGIE (*Rebukingly*)   Yuh oughtn't to call Cora dat, Rocky. She's
a good kid. She may be a tart, but—

ROCKY (*Considerately*)   Sure, dat's all I meant, a tart.

PEARL (*Giggling*)   But he's right about de damned cows, Margie.
Jees, I bet Cora don't know which end of de cow has de horns!
I'm goin' to ask her.

(*There is the noise of a door opening in the hall and the sound of
a man's and woman's arguing voices*)

ROCKY   Here's your chance. Dat's dem two nuts now.

(CORA *and* CHUCK *look in from the hallway and then come in.* CORA *is a thin peroxide blonde, a few years older than* PEARL *and* MARGIE, *dressed in similar style, her round face showing more of the wear and tear of her trade than theirs, but still with traces of a doll-like prettiness.* CHUCK *is a tough, thick-necked, barrel-chested Italian-American, with a fat, amiable, swarthy face. He has on a straw hat with a vivid band, a loud suit, tie and shirt, and yellow shoes. His eyes are clear and he looks healthy and strong as an ox)*

CORA (*Gaily*)   Hello, bums. (*She looks around*) Jees, de Morgue on a rainy Sunday night! (*She waves to* LARRY—*affectionately*) Hello, Old Wise Guy! Ain't you croaked yet?

LARRY (*Grins*)   Not yet, Cora. It's damned tiring, this waiting for the end.

CORA   Aw, gwan, you'll never die! Yuh'll have to hire someone to croak yuh wid an axe.

HOPE (*Cocks one sleepy eye at her—irritably*)   You dumb hookers, cut the loud noise! This ain't a cathouse!

CORA (*Teasingly*)   My, Harry! Such language!

HOPE (*Closes his eyes—to himself with a gratified chuckle*)   Bejees, I'll bet Bessie's turning over in her grave!

(CORA *sits down between* MARGIE *and* PEARL. CHUCK *takes an empty chair from* HOPE's *table and puts it by hers and sits down. At* LARRY's *table,* PARRITT *is glaring resentfully toward the girls*)

PARRITT   If I'd known this dump was a hooker hangout, I'd never have come here.

LARRY (*Watching him*)   You seem down on the ladies.

PARRITT (*Vindictively*)   I hate every bitch that ever lived! They're all alike! (*Catching himself guiltily*) You can understand how I feel, can't you, when it was getting mixed up with a tart that made me have that fight with Mother? (*Then with a resentful sneer*) But what the hell does it matter to you? You're in the grandstand. You're through with life.

LARRY (*Sharply*)   I'm glad you remember it. I don't want to know a damned thing about your business.

(*He closes his eyes and settles on his chair as if preparing for sleep.* PARRITT *stares at him sneeringly. Then he looks away and his expression becomes furtive and frightened*)

CORA   Who's de guy wid Larry?

ROCKY   A tightwad. To hell wid him.

PEARL   Say, Cora, wise me up. Which end of a cow is de horns on?

CORA (*Embarrassed*) Aw, don't bring dat up. I'm sick of hearin' about dat farm.

ROCKY You got nuttin' on us!

CORA (*Ignoring this*) Me and dis overgrown tramp has been scrappin' about it. He says Joisey's de best place, and I says Long Island because we'll be near Coney. And I tells him, "How do I know yuh're off of periodicals for life? I don't give a damn how drunk yuh get, the way we are, but I don't wanta be married to no soak."

CHUCK And I tells her I'm off de stuff for life. Den she beefs we won't be married a month before I'll trow it in her face she was a tart. "Jees, Baby," I tells her. "Why should I? What de hell yuh tink I tink I'm marryin', a voigin? Why should I kick as long as yuh lay off it and don't do no cheatin' wid de iceman or nobody?" (*He gives her a rough hug*) Dat's on de level, Baby. (*He kisses her*)

CORA (*Kissing him*) Aw, yuh big tramp!

ROCKY (*Shakes his head with profound disgust*) Can yuh tie it? I'll buy a drink. I'll do anything. (*He gets up*)

CORA No, dis round's on me. I run into luck. Dat's why I dragged Chuck outa bed to celebrate. It was a sailor. I rolled him. (*She giggles*) Listen, it was a scream. I've run into some nutty souses, but dis guy was de nuttiest. De booze dey dish out around de Brooklyn Navy Yard must be as turrible bug-juice as Harry's. My dogs was givin' out when I seen dis guy holdin' up a lamppost, so I hurried to get him before a cop did. I says, "Hello, Handsome, wanta have a good time?" Jees, he was paralyzed! One of dem polite jags. He tries to bow to me, imagine, and I had to prop him up or he'd fell on his nose. And what d'yuh tink he said? "Lady," he says, "can yuh kindly tell me de nearest way to de Museum of Natural History?" (*They all laugh*) Can yuh imagine! At two A.M. As if I'd know where de dump was anyway. But I says, "Sure ting, Honey Boy, I'll be only too glad." So I steered him into a side street where it was dark and propped him against a wall and give him a frisk. (*She giggles*) And what d'yuh tink he does? Jees, I ain't lyin', he begins to laugh, de big sap! He says, "Quit ticklin' me." While I was friskin' him for his roll! I near died! Den I toined him 'round and give him a push to start him. "Just keep goin'," I told him. "It's a big white building on your right. You can't miss it." He must be swimmin' in de North River yet! (*They all laugh*)

CHUCK   Ain't Uncle Sam de sap to trust guys like dat wid dough!

CORA   (*With a business-like air*)   I picked twelve bucks offa him. Come on, Rocky. Set 'em up. (ROCKY *goes back to the bar.* CORA *looks around the room*) Say, Chuck's kiddin' about de iceman a minute ago reminds me. Where de hell's Hickey?

ROCKY   Dat's what we're all wonderin'.

CORA   He oughta be here. Me and Chuck seen him.

ROCKY   (*Excited, comes back from the bar, forgetting the drinks*) You seen Hickey? (*He nudges* HOPE) Hey, Boss, come to! Cora's seen Hickey.

(HOPE *is instantly wide awake and everyone in the place, except* HUGO *and* PARRITT, *begins to rouse up hopefully, as if a mysterious wireless message had gone round*)

HOPE   Where'd you see him, Cora?

CORA   Right on de next corner. He was standin' dere. We said, "Welcome to our city. De gang is expectin' yuh wid deir tongues hangin' out a yard long." And I kidded him, "How's de iceman, Hickey? How's he doin' at your house?" He laughs and says, "Fine." And he says, "Tell de gang I'll be along in a minute. I'm just finishin' figurin' out de best way to save dem and bring dem peace."

HOPE   (*Chuckles*)   Bejees, he's thought up a new gag! It's a wonder he didn't borry a Salvation Army uniform and show up in that! Go out and get him, Rocky. Tell him we're waitin' to be saved! (ROCKY *goes out, grinning*)

CORA   Yeah, Harry, he was only kiddin'. But he was funny, too, somehow. He was different, or somethin'.

CHUCK   Sure, he was sober, Baby. Dat's what made him different. We ain't never seen him when he wasn't on a drunk, or had de willies gettin' over it.

CORA   Sure! Gee, ain't I dumb?

HOPE   (*With conviction*)   The dumbest broad I ever seen! (*Then puzzledly*) Sober? That's funny. He's always lapped up a good starter on his way here. Well, bejees, he won't be sober long! He'll be good and ripe for my birthday party tonight at twelve. (*He chuckles with excited anticipation—addressing all of them*) Listen! He's fixed some new gag to pull on us. We'll pretend to let him kid us, see? And we'll kid the pants off him.

(*They all say laughingly, "Sure, Harry," "Righto," "That's the stuff," "We'll fix him," etc., etc., their faces excited with the same eager anticipation.* ROCKY *appears in the doorway at the end of the bar with* HICKEY, *his arm around* HICKEY's *shoulders*)

ROCKY (*With an affectionate grin*) Here's the old son of a bitch! (*They all stand up and greet him with affectionate acclaim, "Hello, Hickey!" etc. Even* HUGO *comes out of his coma to raise his head and blink through his thick spectacles with a welcoming giggle*)

HICKEY (*Jovially*) Hello, Gang! (*He stands a moment, beaming around at all of them affectionately. He is about fifty, a little under medium height, with a stout, roly-poly figure. His face is round and smooth and big-boyish with bright blue eyes, a button nose, a small, pursed mouth. His head is bald except for a fringe of hair around his temples and the back of his head. His expression is fixed in a salesman's winning smile of self-confident affability and hearty good fellowship. His eyes have the twinkle of a humor which delights in kidding others but can also enjoy equally a joke on himself. He exudes a friendly, generous personality that makes everyone like him on sight. You get the impression, too, that he must have real ability in his line. There is an efficient, business-like approach in his manner, and his eyes can take you in shrewdly at a glance. He has the salesman's mannerisms of speech, an easy flow of glib, persuasive convincingness. His clothes are those of a successful drummer whose territory consists of minor cities and small towns—not flashy but conspicuously spic and span. He immediately puts on an entrance act, places a hand affectedly on his chest, throws back his head, and sings in a fal-setto tenor*) "It's always fair weather, when good fellows get together!" (*Changing to a comic bass and another tune*) "And an-other little drink won't do us any harm!" (*They all roar with laughter at this burlesque which his personality makes really funny. He waves his hand in a lordly manner to* ROCKY) Do your duty, Brother Rocky. Bring on the rat poison! (ROCKY *grins and goes behind the bar to get drinks amid an approving cheer from the crowd.* HICKEY *comes forward to shake hands with* HOPE—*with affectionate heartiness*) How goes it, Governor?

HOPE (*Enthusiastically*) Bejees, Hickey, you old bastard, it's good to see you! (HICKEY *shakes hands with* MOSHER *and* MCGLOIN; *leans right to shake hands with* MARGIE *and* PEARL; *moves to the middle table to shake hands with* LEWIS, JOE MOTT, WETJOEN *and* JIMMY; *waves to* WILLIE, LARRY *and* HUGO. *He greets each by name with the same affectionate heartiness and there is an inter-*

change of "How's the kid?" "How's the old scout?" "How's the boy?" "How's everything?" etc., etc. ROCKY *begins setting out drinks, whiskey glasses with chasers, and a bottle for each table, starting with* LARRY's *table.* HOPE *says:*) Sit down, Hickey. Sit down. (HICKEY *takes the chair, facing front, at the front of the table in the second row which is half between* HOPE's *table and the one where* JIMMY TOMORROW *is.* HOPE *goes on with excited pleasure*) Bejees, Hickey, it seems natural to see your ugly, grinning map. (*With a scornful nod to* CORA) This dumb broad was tryin' to tell us you'd changed, but you ain't a damned bit. Tell us about yourself. How've you been doin'? Bejees, you look like a million dollars.

ROCKY (*Coming to* HICKEY's *table, puts a bottle of whiskey, a glass and a chaser on it—then hands* HICKEY *a key*) Here's your key, Hickey. Same old room.

HICKEY (*Shoves the key in his pocket*) Thanks, Rocky. I'm going up in a little while and grab a snooze. Haven't been able to sleep lately and I'm tired as hell. A couple of hours good kip will fix me.

HOPE (*As* ROCKY *puts drinks on his table*) First time I ever heard you worry about sleep. Bejees, you never would go to bed. (*He raises his glass, and all the others except* PARRITT *do likewise*) Get a few slugs under your belt and you'll forget sleeping. Here's mud in your eye, Hickey.

(*They all join in with the usual humorous toasts*)

HICKEY (*Heartily*) Drink hearty, boys and girls!

(*They all drink, but* HICKEY *drinks only his chaser*)

HOPE Bejees, is that a new stunt, drinking your chaser first?

HICKEY No, I forgot to tell Rocky— You'll have to excuse me, boys and girls, but I'm off the stuff. For keeps.

(*They stare at him in amazed incredulity*)

HOPE What the hell— (*Then with a wink at the others, kiddingly*) Sure! Joined the Salvation Army, ain't you? Been elected President of the W.C.T.U.? Take that bottle away from him, Rocky. We don't want to tempt him into sin.

(*He chuckles and the others laugh*)

HICKEY (*Earnestly*) No, honest, Harry. I know it's hard to believe but— (*He pauses—then adds simply*) Cora was right, Harry. I have changed. I mean, about booze. I don't need it any more.

(*They all stare, hoping it's a gag, but impressed and disappointed and made vaguely uneasy by the change they now sense in him*)

HOPE (*His kidding a bit forced*) Yeah, go ahead, kid the pants off

us! Bejees, Cora said you was coming to save us! Well, go on.
Get this joke off your chest! Start the service! Sing a God-damned
hymn if you like. We'll all join in the chorus. "No drunkard can
enter this beautiful home." That's a good one.

(*He forces a cackle*)

HICKEY (*Grinning*) Oh, hell, Governor! You don't think I'd come
around here peddling some brand of temperance bunk, do you?
You know me better than that! Just because I'm through with the
stuff don't mean I'm going Prohibition. Hell, I'm not that ungrateful! It's given me too many good times. I feel exactly the same as
I always did. If anyone wants to get drunk, if that's the only way
they can be happy, and feel at peace with themselves, why the
hell shouldn't they? They have my full and entire sympathy. I
know all about that game from soup to nuts. I'm the guy that
wrote the book. The only reason I've quit is— Well, I finally had
the guts to face myself and throw overboard the damned lying
pipe dream that'd been making me miserable, and do what I had
to do for the happiness of all concerned—and then all at once I
found I was at peace with myself and I didn't need booze any
more. That's all there was to it. (*He pauses. They are staring at
him, uneasy and beginning to feel defensive.* HICKEY *looks round
and grins affectionately—apologetically*) But what the hell! Don't
let me be a wet blanket, making fool speeches about myself. Set
'em up again, Rocky. Here. (*He pulls a big roll from his pocket
and peels off a ten-dollar bill. The faces of all brighten*) Keep the
balls coming until this is killed. Then ask for more.

ROCKY Jees, a roll dat'd choke a hippopotamus! Fill up, youse guys.
(*They all pour out drinks*)

HOPE That sounds more like you, Hickey. That water-wagon bull—
Cut out the act and have a drink, for Christ's sake.

HICKEY It's no act, Governor. But don't get me wrong. That don't
mean I'm a teetotal grouch and can't be in the party. Hell, why
d'you suppose I'm here except to have a party, same as I've always
done, and help celebrate your birthday tonight? You've all been
good pals to me, the best friends I've ever had. I've been thinking
about you ever since I left the house—all the time I was walking
over here—

HOPE Walking? Bejees, do you mean to say you walked?

HICKEY I sure did. All the way from the wilds of darkest Astoria.
Didn't mind it a bit, either. I seemed to get here before I knew it.

I'm a bit tired and sleepy but otherwise I feel great. (*Kiddingly*)
That ought to encourage you, Governor—show you a little walk
around the ward is nothing to be so scared about. (*He winks at
the others.* HOPE *stiffens resentfully for a second.* HICKEY *goes on*)
I didn't make such bad time either for a fat guy, considering it's a
hell of a ways, and I sat in the park a while thinking. It was going
on twelve when I went in the bedroom to tell Evelyn I was leaving. Six hours, say. No, less than that. I'd been standing on the
corner some time before Cora and Chuck came along, thinking
about all of you. Of course, I was only kidding Cora with that stuff
about saving you. (*Then seriously*) No, I wasn't either. But I
didn't mean booze. I meant save you from pipe dreams. I know
now, from my experience, they're the things that really poison and
ruin a guy's life and keep him from finding any peace. If you knew
how free and contented I feel now. I'm like a new man. And the
cure for them is so damned simple, once you have the nerve. Just
the old dope of honesty is the best policy—honesty with yourself,
I mean. Just stop lying about yourself and kidding yourself about
tomorrows. (*He is staring ahead of him now as if he were talking
aloud to himself as much as to them. Their eyes are fixed on him
with uneasy resentment. His manner becomes apologetic again*)
Hell, this begins to sound like a damned sermon on the way to
lead the good life. Forget that part of it. It's in my blood, I guess.
My old man used to whale salvation into my heinie with a birch
rod. He was a preacher in the sticks of Indiana, like I've told you.
I got my knack of sales gab from him, too. He was the boy who
could sell those Hoosier hayseeds building lots along the Golden
Street! (*Taking on a salesman's persuasiveness*) Now listen, boys
and girls, don't look at me as if I was trying to sell you a goldbrick. Nothing up my sleeve, honest. Let's take an example. Any
one of you. Take you, Governor. That walk around the ward you
never take—

HOPE (*Defensively sharp*) What about it?

HICKEY (*Grinning affectionately*) Why, you know as well as I do,
Harry. Everything about it.

HOPE (*Defiantly*) Bejees, I'm going to take it!

HICKEY Sure, you're going to—this time. Because I'm going to help
you. I know it's the thing you've got to do before you'll ever know
what real peace means. (*He looks at* JIMMY TOMORROW) Same
thing with you, Jimmy. You've got to try and get your old job
back. And no tomorrow about it! (*As* JIMMY *stiffens with a pa-*

thetic attempt at dignity—placatingly) No, don't tell me, Jimmy. I know all about tomorrow. I'm the guy that wrote the book.

JIMMY I don't understand you. I admit I've foolishly delayed, but as it happens, I'd just made up my mind that as soon as I could get straightened out—

HICKEY Fine! That's the spirit! And I'm going to help you. You've been damned kind to me, Jimmy, and I want to prove how grateful I am. When it's all over and you don't have to nag at yourself any more, you'll be grateful to me, too! (*He looks around at the others*) And all the rest of you, ladies included, are in the same boat, one way or another.

LARRY (*Who has been listening with sardonic appreciation—in his comically intense, crazy whisper*) Be God, you've hit the nail on the head, Hickey! This dump is the Palace of Pipe Dreams!

HICKEY (*Grins at him with affectionate kidding*) Well, well! The Old Grandstand Foolosopher speaks! You think you're the big exception, eh? Life doesn't mean a damn to you any more, does it? You're retired from the circus. You're just waiting impatiently for the end—the good old Long Sleep! (*He chuckles*) Well, I think a lot of you, Larry, you old bastard. I'll try and make an honest man of you, too!

LARRY (*Stung*) What the devil are you hinting at, anyway?

HICKEY You don't have to ask me, do you, a wise old guy like you? Just ask yourself. I'll bet you know.

PARRITT (*Is watching LARRY's face with a curious sneering satisfaction*) He's got your number all right, Larry! (*He turns to HICKEY*) That's the stuff, Hickey. Show the old faker up! He's got no right to sneak out of everything.

HICKEY (*Regards him with surprise at first, then with a puzzled interest*) Hello. A stranger in our midst. I didn't notice you before, Brother.

PARRITT (*Embarrassed, his eyes shifting away*) My name's Parritt. I'm an old friend of Larry's. (*His eyes come back to HICKEY to find him still sizing him up—defensively*) Well? What are you staring at?

HICKEY (*Continuing to stare—puzzledly*) No offense, Brother. I was trying to figure— Haven't we met before some place?

PARRITT (*Reassured*) No. First time I've ever been East.

HICKEY No, you're right. I know that's not it. In my game, to be a shark at it, you teach yourself never to forget a name or a face. But still I know damned well I recognized something about you. We're members of the same lodge—in some way.

PARRITT (*Uneasy again*)   What are you talking about? You're nuts.

HICKEY (*Dryly*)   Don't try to kid me, Little Boy. I'm a good sales-man—so damned good the firm was glad to take me back after every drunk—and what made me good was I could size up any-one. (*Frowningly puzzled again*) But I don't see— (*Suddenly breezily good-natured*) Never mind. I can tell you're having trou-ble with yourself and I'll be glad to do anything I can to help a friend of Larry's.

LARRY   Mind your own business, Hickey. He's nothing to you—or to me, either. (HICKEY *gives him a keen inquisitive glance.* LARRY *looks away and goes on sarcastically*) You're keeping us all in suspense. Tell us more about how you're going to save us.

HICKEY (*Good-naturedly but seeming a little hurt*)   Hell, don't get sore, Larry. Not at me. We've always been good pals, haven't we? I know I've always liked you a lot.

LARRY (*A bit shamefaced*)   Well, so have I liked you. Forget it, Hickey.

HICKEY (*Beaming*)   Fine! That's the spirit! (*Looking around at the others, who have forgotten their drinks*) What's the matter, every-body? What is this, a funeral? Come on and drink up! A little action! (*They all drink*) Have another. Hell, this is a celebration! Forget it, if anything I've said sounds too serious. I don't want to be a pain in the neck. Any time you think I'm talking out of turn, just tell me to go chase myself! (*He yawns with growing drowsiness and his voice grows a bit muffled*) No, boys and girls, I'm not trying to put anything over on you. It's just that I know now from experience what a lying pipe dream can do to you—and how damned relieved and contented with yourself you feel when you're rid of it. (*He yawns again*) God, I'm sleepy all of a sud-den. That long walk is beginning to get me. I better go upstairs. Hell of a trick to go dead on you like this. (*He starts to get up but relaxes again. His eyes blink as he tries to keep them open*) No, boys and girls, I've never known what real peace was until now. It's a grand feeling, like when you're sick and suffering like hell and the Doc gives you a shot in the arm, and the pain goes, and you drift off. (*His eyes close*) You can let go of yourself at last. Let yourself sink down to the bottom of the sea. Rest in peace. There's no farther you have to go. Not a single damned hope or dream left to nag you. You'll all know what I mean after you— (*He pauses—mumbles*) Excuse—all in—got to grab forty winks— Drink up, everybody—on me—

(*The sleep of complete exhaustion overpowers him. His chin sags to his chest. They stare at him with puzzled uneasy fascination*)

HOPE (*Forcing a tone of irritation*) Bejees, that's a fine stunt, to go to sleep on us! (*Then fumingly to the crowd*) Well, what the hell's the matter with you bums? Why don't you drink up? You're always crying for booze, and now you've got it under your nose, you sit like dummies! (*They start and gulp down their whiskies and pour another.* HOPE *stares at* HICKEY) Bejees, I can't figure Hickey. I still say he's kidding us. Kid his own grandmother, Hickey would. What d'you think, Jimmy?

JIMMY (*Unconvincingly*) It must be another of his jokes, Harry, although— Well, he does appear changed. But he'll probably be his natural self again tomorrow— (*Hastily*) I mean, when he wakes up.

LARRY (*Staring at* HICKEY *frowningly—more aloud to himself than to them*) You'll make a mistake if you think he's only kidding.

PARRITT (*In a low confidential voice*) I don't like that guy, Larry. He's too damned nosy. I'm going to steer clear of him.

(LARRY *gives him a suspicious glance, then looks hastily away*)

JIMMY (*With an attempt at open-minded reasonableness*) Still, Harry, I have to admit there was some sense in his nonsense. It is time I got my job back—although I hardly need him to remind me.

HOPE (*With an air of frankness*) Yes, and I ought to take a walk around the ward. But I don't need no Hickey to tell me, seeing I got it all set for my birthday tomorrow.

LARRY (*Sardonically*) Ha! (*Then in his comically intense, crazy whisper*) Be God, it looks like he's going to make two sales of his peace at least! But you'd better make sure first it's the real McCoy and not poison.

HOPE (*Disturbed—angrily*) You bughouse I-Won't-Work harp, who asked you to shove in an oar? What the hell d'you mean, poison? Just because he has your number— (*He immediately feels ashamed of this taunt and adds apologetically*) Bejees, Larry, you're always croaking about something to do with death. It gets my nanny. Come on, fellers, let's drink up. (*They drink.* HOPE's *eyes are fixed on* HICKEY *again*) Stone cold sober and dead to the world! Spilling that business about pipe dreams! Bejees, I don't get it. (*He bursts out again in angry complaint*) He ain't like the old Hickey! He'll be a fine wet blanket to have around at my birthday party! I wish to hell he'd never turned up!

MOSHER (*Who has been the least impressed by* HICKEY's *talk and is the first to recover and feel the effect of the drinks on top of his hangover—genially*) Give him time, Harry, and he'll come out of it. I've watched many cases of almost fatal teetotalism, but they all came out of it completely cured and as drunk as ever. My opinion is the poor sap is temporarily bughouse from over-work. (*Musingly*) You can't be too careful about work. It's the deadliest habit known to science, a great physician once told me. He practiced on street corners under a torchlight. He was posi-tively the only doctor in the world who claimed that rattlesnake oil, rubbed on the prat, would cure heart failure in three days. I remember well his saying to me, "You are naturally delicate, Ed, but if you drink a pint of bad whiskey before breakfast every evening, and never work if you can help it, you may live to a ripe old age. It's staying sober and working that cuts men off in their prime."

(*While he is talking, they turn to him with eager grins. They are longing to laugh, and as he finishes they roar. Even* PARRITT *laughs.* HICKEY *sleeps on like a dead man, but* HUGO, *who had passed into his customary coma again, head on table, looks up through his thick spectacles and giggles foolishly*)

HUGO (*Blinking around at them. As the laughter dies he speaks in his giggling, wheedling manner, as if he were playfully teasing children*) Laugh, leedle bourgeois monkey-faces! Laugh like fools, leedle stupid peoples! (*His tone suddenly changes to one of guttural soapbox denunciation and he pounds on the table with a small fist*) I vill laugh, too! But I vill laugh last! I vill laugh at you! (*He declaims his favorite quotation*) "The days grow hot, O Babylon! 'Tis cool beneath thy villow trees!"

(*They all hoot him down in a chorus of amused jeering.* HUGO *is not offended. This is evidently their customary reaction. He giggles good-naturedly.* HICKEY *sleeps on. They have all forgotten their uneasiness about him now and ignore him*)

LEWIS (*Tipsily*) Well, now that our little Robespierre has got the daily bit of guillotining off his chest, tell me more about your doctor friend, Ed. He strikes me as the only bloody sensible medico I ever heard of. I think we should appoint him house physician here without a moment's delay.

(*They all laughingly assent*)

MOSHER (*Warming to his subject, shakes his head sadly*) Too late! The old Doc has passed on to his Maker. A victim of overwork, too. He didn't follow his own advice. Kept his nose to the grindstone and sold one bottle of snake oil too many. Only eighty years old when he was taken. The saddest part was that he knew he was doomed. The last time we got paralyzed together he told me: "This game will get me yet, Ed. You see before you a broken man, a martyr to medical science. If I had any nerves I'd have a nervous breakdown. You won't believe me, but this last year there was actually one night I had so many patients, I didn't even have time to get drunk. The shock to my system brought on a stroke which, as a doctor, I recognized was the beginning of the end." Poor old Doc! When he said this he started crying. "I hate to go before my task is completed, Ed," he sobbed. "I'd hoped I'd live to see the day when, thanks to my miraculous cure, there wouldn't be a single vacant cemetery lot left in this glorious country." (*There is a roar of laughter. He waits for it to die and then goes on sadly*) I miss Doc. He was a gentleman of the old school. I'll bet he's standing on a street corner in hell right now, making suckers of the damned, telling them there's nothing like snake oil for a bad burn.

(*There is another roar of laughter. This time it penetrates* HICKEY's *exhausted slumber. He stirs on his chair, trying to wake up, managing to raise his head a little and force his eyes half open. He speaks with a drowsy, affectionately encouraging smile. At once the laughter stops abruptly and they turn to him startledly*)

HICKEY That's the spirit—don't let me be a wet blanket—all I want is to see you happy—

(*He slips back into heavy sleep again. They all stare at him, their faces again puzzled, resentful and uneasy*)

Curtain

ACT TWO

SCENE: *The back room only. The black curtain dividing it from the bar is the right wall of the scene. It is getting on toward midnight of the same day.*

The back room has been prepared for a festivity. At center, front, four of the circular tables are pushed together to form one long table with an uneven line of chairs behind it, and chairs at each end. This improvised banquet table is covered with old table cloths, borrowed from a neighboring beanery, and is laid with glasses, plates and cutlery before each of the seventeen chairs. Bottles of bar whiskey are placed at intervals within reach of any sitter. An old upright piano and stool have been moved in and stand against the wall at left, front. At right, front, is a table without chairs. The other tables and chairs that had been in the room have been moved out, leaving a clear floor space at rear for dancing. The floor has been swept clean of sawdust and scrubbed. Even the walls show evidence of having been washed, although the result is only to heighten their splotchy leprous look. The electric light brackets are adorned with festoons of red ribbon. In the middle of the separate table at right, front, is a birthday cake with six candles. Several packages, tied with ribbon, are also on the table. There are two necktie boxes, two cigar boxes, a fifth containing a half dozen handkerchiefs, the sixth is a square jeweler's watch box.

As the curtain rises, CORA, CHUCK, HUGO, LARRY, MARGIE, PEARL *and* ROCKY *are discovered.* CHUCK, ROCKY *and the three girls have dressed up for the occasion.* CORA *is arranging a bouquet of flowers in a vase, the vase being a big schooner glass from the bar, on top of the piano.* CHUCK *sits in a chair at the foot (left) of the banquet table. He has turned it so he can watch her. Near the middle of the row of chairs behind the table,* LARRY *sits, facing front, a drink of whiskey before him. He is staring before him in frowning, disturbed meditation. Next to him, on his left,* HUGO *is in his habitual position, passed out, arms on table, head on arms, a full whiskey glass by his head. By the separate table at right, front,* MARGIE *and* PEARL *are arranging the cake and presents, and* ROCKY *stands by them. All of them, with the exception of* CHUCK *and* ROCKY, *have had plenty to drink and show it, but no one, except* HUGO, *seems to be drunk. They are trying to act up in the spirit of the occasion but there is something forced about their manner, an undercurrent of nervous irritation and preoccupation.*

CORA (*Standing back from the piano to regard the flower effect*) How's dat, Kid?

CHUCK (*Grumpily*) What de hell do I know about flowers?

CORA Yuh can see dey're pretty, can't yuh, yuh big dummy?

CHUCK (*Mollifyingly*) Yeah, Baby, sure. If yuh like 'em, dey're aw right wid me.

(CORA *goes back to give the schooner of flowers a few more touches*)

MARGIE (*Admiring the cake*) Some cake, huh, Poil? Lookit! Six candles. Each for ten years.

PEARL When do we light de candles, Rocky?

ROCKY (*Grumpily*) Ask dat bughouse Hickey. He's elected himself boss of dis boithday racket. Just before Harry comes down, he says. Den Harry blows dem out wid one breath, for luck. Hickey was goin' to have sixty candles, but I says, Jees, if de old guy took dat big a breath, he'd croak himself.

MARGIE (*Challengingly*) Well, anyways, it's some cake, ain't it?

ROCKY (*Without enthusiasm*) Sure, it's aw right by me. But what de hell is Harry goin' to do wid a cake? If he ever et a hunk, it'd croak him.

PEARL Jees, yuh're a dope! Ain't he, Margie?

MARGIE A dope is right!

ROCKY (*Stung*) You broads better watch your step or—

PEARL (*Defiantly*) Or what?

MARGIE Yeah! Or what?

(*They glare at him truculently*)

ROCKY Say, what de hell's got into youse? It'll be twelve o'clock and Harry's boithday before long. I ain't lookin' for no trouble.

PEARL (*Ashamed*) Aw, we ain't neider, Rocky.

(*For the moment this argument subsides*)

CORA (*Over her shoulder to* CHUCK—*acidly*) A guy what can't see flowers is pretty must be some dumbbell.

CHUCK Yeah? Well, if I was as dumb as you— (*Then mollifyingly*) Jees, yuh got your scrappin' pants on, ain't yuh? (*Grins good-naturedly*) Hell, Baby, what's eatin' yuh? All I'm tinkin' is, flowers is dat louse Hickey's stunt. We never had no flowers for Harry's boithday before. What de hell can Harry do wid flowers? He don't know a cauliflower from a geranium.

ROCKY Yeah, Chuck, it's like I'm tellin' dese broads about de cake. Dat's Hickey's wrinkle, too. (*Bitterly*) Jees, ever since he woke up, yuh can't hold him. He's taken on de party like it was his boithday.

MARGIE Well, he's payin' for everything, ain't he?

ROCKY Aw, I don't mind de boithday stuff so much. What gets my goat is de way he's tryin' to run de whole dump and everyone in it. He's buttin' in all over de place, tellin' everybody where dey get off. On'y he don't really tell yuh. He just keeps hintin' around.

PEARL Yeah. He was hintin' to me and Margie.

MARGIE Yeah, de lousy drummer.

ROCKY He just gives yuh an earful of dat line of bull about yuh got to be honest wid yourself and not kid yourself, and have de guts to be what yuh are. I got sore. I told him dat's aw right for de bums in dis dump. I hope he makes dem wake up. I'm sick of listenin' to dem hop demselves up. But it don't go wid me, see? I don't kid myself wid no pipe dream. (PEARL *and* MARGIE *exchange a derisive look. He catches it and his eyes narrow*) What are yuh grinnin' at?

PEARL (*Her face hard—scornfully*) Nuttin'.

MARGIE Nuttin'.

ROCKY It better be nuttin'! Don't let Hickey put no ideas in your nuts if you wanta stay healthy! (*Then angrily*) I wish de louse never showed up! I hope he don't come back from de delicatessen. He's gettin' everyone nuts. He's ridin' someone every minute. He's got Harry and Jimmy Tomorrow run ragged, and de rest is hidin' in deir rooms so dey won't have to listen to him. Dey're all actin' cagey wid de booze, too, like dey was scared if dey get too drunk, dey might spill deir guts, or somethin'. And everybody's gettin' a prize grouch on.

CORA Yeah, he's been hintin' round to me and Chuck, too. Yuh'd tink he suspected me and Chuck hadn't no real intention of gettin' married. Yuh'd tink he suspected Chuck wasn't goin' to lay off periodicals—or maybe even didn't want to.

CHUCK He didn't say it right out or I'da socked him one. I told him, "I'm on de wagon for keeps and Cora knows it."

CORA I told him, "Sure, I know it. And Chuck ain't never goin' to trow it in my face dat I was a tart, neider. And if yuh tink we're just kiddin' ourselves, we'll show yuh!"

CHUCK We're goin' to show him!

CORA We got it all fixed. We've decided Joisey is where we want de farm, and we'll get married dere, too, because yuh don't need no license. We're goin' to get married tomorrow. Ain't we, Honey?

CHUCK You bet, Baby.

ROCKY (*Disgusted*) Christ, Chuck, are yuh lettin' dat bughouse louse Hickey kid yuh into—

CORA (*Turns on him angrily*) Nobody's kiddin' him into it, nor me neider! And Hickey's right. If dis big tramp's goin' to marry me, he ought to do it, and not just shoot off his old bazoo about it.

ROCKY (*Ignoring her*) Yuh can't be dat dumb, Chuck.

CORA You keep outa dis! And don't start beefin' about crickets on de farm drivin' us nuts. You and your crickets! Yuh'd tink dey was elephants!

MARGIE (*Coming to* ROCKY'S *defense—sneeringly*) Don't notice dat broad, Rocky. Yuh heard her say "tomorrow," didn't yuh? It's de same old crap.

CORA (*Glares at her*) Is dat so?

PEARL (*Lines up with* MARGIE—*sneeringly*) Imagine Cora a bride! Dat's a hot one! Jees, Cora, if all de guys you've stayed wid was side by side, yuh could walk on 'em from here to Texas!

CORA (*Starts moving toward her threateningly*) Yuh can't talk like dat to me, yuh fat Dago hooker! I may be a tart, but I ain't a cheap old whore like you!

PEARL (*Furiously*) I'll show yuh who's a whore!

(*They start to fly at each other, but* CHUCK *and* ROCKY *grab them from behind*)

CHUCK (*Forcing* CORA *onto a chair*) Sit down and cool off, Baby.

ROCKY (*Doing the same to* PEARL) Nix on de rough stuff, Poil.

MARGIE (*Glaring at* CORA) Why don't you leave Poil alone, Rocky? She'll fix dat blonde's clock! Or if she don't, I will!

ROCKY Shut up, you! (*Disgustedly*) Jees, what dames! D'yuh wanta gum Harry's party?

PEARL (*A bit shamefaced—sulkily*) Who wants to? But nobody can't call me a —.

ROCKY (*Exasperatedly*) Aw, bury it! What are you, a voigin?
(PEARL *stares at him, her face growing hard and bitter. So does* MARGIE)

PEARL Yuh mean you tink I'm a whore, too, huh?

MARGIE Yeah, and me?

ROCKY Now don't start nuttin'!

PEARL I suppose it'd tickle you if me and Margie did what dat louse, Hickey, was hintin' and come right out and admitted we was whores.

ROCKY Aw right! What of it? It's de truth, ain't it?

CORA (*Lining up with* PEARL *and* MARGIE—*indignantly*) Jees, Rocky, dat's a fine hell of a ting to say to two goils dat's been as good to yuh as Poil and Margie! (*To* PEARL) I didn't mean to call yuh dat, Poil. I was on'y mad.

PEARL (*Accepts the apology gratefully*) Sure, I was mad, too, Cora. No hard feelin's.

ROCKY (*Relieved*) Dere. Dat fixes everyting, don't it?

PEARL (*Turns on him—hard and bitter*) Aw right, Rocky. We're whores. You know what dat makes you, don't you?

ROCKY (*Angrily*) Look out, now!

MARGIE A lousy little pimp, dat's what!

ROCKY I'll loin yuh!
(*He gives her a slap on the side of the face*)

PEARL A dirty little Ginny pimp, dat's what!

ROCKY (*Gives her a slap, too*) And dat'll loin you!
(*But they only stare at him with hard sneering eyes*)

MARGIE He's provin' it to us, Poil.

PEARL Yeah! Hickey's convoited him. He's give up his pipe dream!

ROCKY (*Furious and at the same time bewildered by their defiance*) Lay off me or I'll beat de hell—

CHUCK (*Growls*) Aw, lay off dem. Harry's party ain't no time to beat up your stable.

ROCKY (*Turns to him*) Whose stable? Who d'yuh tink yuh're talkin' to? I ain't never beat dem up! What d'yuh tink I am? I just give dem a slap, like any guy would his wife, if she got too gabby. Why don't yuh tell dem to lay off me? I don't want no trouble on Harry's boithday party.

MARGIE (*A victorious gleam in her eye—tauntingly*) Aw right, den, yuh poor little Ginny. I'll lay off yuh till de party's over if Poil will.

PEARL (*Tauntingly*) Sure, I will. For Harry's sake, not yours, yuh little Wop!

ROCKY (*Stung*) Say, listen, youse! Don't get no wrong idea— (*But an interruption comes from* LARRY *who bursts into a sardonic laugh. They all jump startledly and look at him with unanimous hostility.* ROCKY *transfers his anger to him*) Who de hell yuh laughin' at, yuh half-dead old stew bum?

CORA (*Sneeringly*) At himself, he ought to be! Jees, Hickey's sure got his number!

LARRY (*Ignoring them, turns to* HUGO *and shakes him by the shoulder—in his comically intense, crazy whisper*) Wake up, Comrade! Here's the Revolution starting on all sides of you and you're sleeping through it! Be God, it's not to Bakunin's ghost you ought to pray in your dreams, but to the great Nihilist, Hickey! He's started a movement that'll blow up the world!

HUGO (*Blinks at him through his thick spectacles—with guttural denunciation*) You, Larry! Renegade! Traitor! I vill have you shot! (*He giggles*) Don't be a fool! Buy me a trink! (*He sees the drink in front of him, and gulps it down. He begins to sing the Carmagnole in a guttural basso, pounding on the table with his glass*) "Dansons la Carmagnole! Vive le son! Vive le son! Dansons la Carmagnole! Vive le son des canons!"

ROCKY Can dat noise!

HUGO (*Ignores this—to* LARRY, *in a low tone of hatred*) That bourgeois svine, Hickey! He laughs like good fellow, he makes jokes, he dares make hints to me so I see what he dares to think. He thinks I am finish, it is too late, and so I do not vish the Day come because it vill not be my Day. Oh, I see what he thinks! He thinks lies even vorse, dat I— (*He stops abruptly with a guilty look, as if afraid he was letting something slip—then revengefully*) I vill have him hanged the first one of all on de first lamppost! (*He changes his mood abruptly and peers around at* ROCKY *and the others—giggling again*) Vhy you so serious, leedle monkey-faces? It's all great joke, no? So ve get drunk, and ve laugh like hell, and den ve die, and de pipe dream vanish! (*A bitter mocking contempt creeps into his tone*) But be of good cheer, leedle stupid peoples! "The days grow hot, O Babylon!" Soon, leedle proletarians, ve vill have free picnic in the cool shade, ve vill eat hot dogs and trink free beer beneath the villow trees! Like hogs, yes! Like beautiful leedle hogs! (*He stops startledly, as if confused and amazed at what he has heard himself say. He mutters with hatred*) Dot Gottamned liar, Hickey. It is he who makes me sneer. I want to sleep.

(*He lets his head fall forward on his folded arms again and closes his eyes.* LARRY *gives him a pitying look, then quickly drinks his drink*)

CORA (*Uneasily*) Hickey ain't overlookin' no bets, is he? He's even give Hugo de woiks.

LARRY I warned you this morning he wasn't kidding.

MARGIE (*Sneering*) De old wise guy!

PEARL Yeah, still pretendin' he's de one exception, like Hickey told him. He don't do no pipe dreamin'! Oh, no!

LARRY (*Sharply resentful*) I—! (*Then abruptly he is drunkenly good-natured, and you feel this drunken manner is an evasive exaggeration*) All right, take it out on me, if it makes you more content. Sure, I love every hair of your heads, my great big beautiful baby dolls, and there's nothing I wouldn't do for you!

PEARL (*Stiffly*) De old Irish bunk, huh? We ain't big. And we ain't your baby dolls! (*Suddenly she is mollified and smiles*) But we admit we're beautiful. Huh, Margie?

MARGIE (*Smiling*) Sure ting! But what would he do wid beautiful dolls, even if he had de price, de old goat? (*She laughs teasingly —then pats* LARRY *on the shoulder affectionately*) Aw, yuh're aw right at dat, Larry, if yuh are full of bull!

PEARL Sure. Yuh're aces wid us. We're noivous, dat's all. Dat lousy drummer—why can't he be like he's always been? I never seen a guy change so. You pretend to be such a fox, Larry. What d'yuh tink's happened to him?

LARRY I don't know. With all his gab I notice he's kept that to himself so far. Maybe he's saving the great revelation for Harry's party. (*Then irritably*) To hell with him! I don't want to know. Let him mind his own business and I'll mind mine.

CHUCK Yeah, dat's what I say.

CORA Say, Larry, where's dat young friend of yours disappeared to?

LARRY I don't care where he is, except I wish it was a thousand miles away! (*Then, as he sees they are surprised at his vehemence, he adds hastily*) He's a pest.

ROCKY (*Breaks in with his own preoccupation*) I don't give a damn what happened to Hickey, but I know what's gonna happen if he don't watch his step. I told him, "I'll take a lot from you, Hickey, like everyone else in dis dump, because yuh've always been a grand guy. But dere's tings I don't take from you nor nobody, see? Remember dat, or you'll wake up in a hospital—or maybe worse, wid your wife and de iceman walkin' slow behind yuh."

CORA Aw, yuh shouldn't make dat iceman crack, Rocky. It's aw right for him to kid about it but—I notice Hickey ain't pulled dat old iceman gag dis time. (*Excitedly*) D'yuh suppose dat he did catch his wife cheatin'? I don't mean wid no iceman, but wid some guy.

ROCKY Aw, dat's de bunk. He ain't pulled dat gag or showed her photo around because he ain't drunk. And if he'd caught her cheatin' he'd be drunk, wouldn't he? He'd have beat her up and den gone on de woist drunk he'd ever staged. Like any other guy'd do.

(*The girls nod, convinced by this reasoning*)

CHUCK Sure! Rocky's got de right dope, Baby. He'd be paralyzed. (*While he is speaking, the Negro,* JOE, *comes in from the hallway. There is a noticeable change in him. He walks with a tough, truculent swagger and his good-natured face is set in sullen suspicion*)

JOE (*To* ROCKY—*defiantly*) I's stood tellin' people dis dump is closed for de night all I's goin' to. Let Harry hire a doorman, pay him wages, if he wants one.

ROCKY (*Scowling*) Yeah? Harry's pretty damned good to you.

JOE (*Shamefaced*) Sure he is. I don't mean dat. Anyways, it's all right. I told Schwartz, de cop, we's closed for de party. He'll keep folks away. (*Aggressively again*) I want a big drink, dat's what!

CHUCK Who's stoppin' yuh? Yuh can have all yuh want on Hickey.

JOE (*Has taken a glass from the table and has his hand on a bottle when* HICKEY's *name is mentioned. He draws his hand back as if he were going to refuse—then grabs it defiantly and pours a big drink*) All right, I's earned all de drinks on him I could drink in a year for listenin' to his crazy bull. And here's hopin' he gets de lockjaw! (*He drinks and pours out another*) I drinks on him but I don't drink wid him. No, suh, never no more!

ROCKY Aw, bull! Hickey's aw right. What's he done to you?

JOE (*Sullenly*) Dat's my business. I ain't buttin' in yours, is I? (*Bitterly*) Sure, you think he's all right. He's a white man, ain't he? (*His tone becomes aggressive*) Listen to me, you white boys! Don't you get it in your heads I's pretendin' to be what I ain't, or dat I ain't proud to be what I is, get me? Or you and me's goin' to have trouble!

(*He picks up his drink and walks left as far away from them as he can get and slumps down on the piano stool*)

MARGIE (*In a low angry tone*) What a noive! Just because we act nice to him, he gets a swelled nut! If dat ain't a coon all over!

CHUCK Talkin' fight talk, huh? I'll moider de nigger!

(*He takes a threatening step toward* JOE, *who is staring before him guiltily now*)

JOE (*Speaks up shamefacedly*) Listen, boys, I's sorry. I didn't mean dat. You been good friends to me. I's nuts, I guess. Dat Hickey, he gets my head all mixed up wit' craziness.

(*Their faces at once clear of resentment against him*)

CORA Aw, dat's aw right, Joe. De boys wasn't takin' yuh serious. (*Then to the others, forcing a laugh*) Jees, what'd I say, Hickey ain't overlookin' no bets. Even Joe. (*She pauses—then adds puzzledly*) De funny ting is, yuh can't stay sore at de bum when he's around. When he forgets de bughouse preachin', and quits tellin' yuh where yuh get off, he's de same old Hickey. Yuh can't help likin' de louse. And yuh got to admit he's got de right dope— (*She adds hastily*) I mean, on some of de bums here.

MARGIE (*With a sneering look at* ROCKY) Yeah, he's coitinly got one guy I know sized up right! Huh, Poil?

PEARL He coitinly has!

ROCKY Cut it out, I told yuh!

LARRY (*Is staring before him broodingly. He speaks more aloud to himself than to them*) It's nothing to me what happened to him. But I have a feeling he's dying to tell us, inside him, and yet he's afraid. He's like that damned kid. It's strange the queer way he seemed to recognize him. If he's afraid, it explains why he's off booze. Like that damned kid again. Afraid if he got drunk, he'd tell—

(*While he is speaking,* HICKEY *comes in the doorway at rear. He looks the same as in the previous act, except that now his face beams with the excited expectation of a boy going to a party. His arms are piled with packages*)

HICKEY (*Booms in imitation of a familiar Polo Grounds bleacherite cry—with rising volume*) Well! Well!! Well!!! (*They all jump startledly. He comes forward, grinning*) Here I am in the nick of time. Give me a hand with these bundles, somebody.

(MARGIE *and* PEARL *start taking them from his arms and putting them on the table. Now that he is present, all their attitudes show the reaction* CORA *has expressed. They can't help liking him and forgiving him*)

MARGIE   Jees, Hickey, yuh scared me outa a year's growth, sneakin' in like dat.

HICKEY   Sneaking? Why, me and the taxi man made enough noise getting my big surprise in the hall to wake the dead. You were all so busy drinking in words of wisdom from the Old Wise Guy here, you couldn't hear anything else. (*He grins at* LARRY) From what I heard, Larry, you're not so good when you start playing Sherlock Holmes. You've got me all wrong. I'm not afraid of anything now—not even myself. You better stick to the part of Old Cemetery, the Barker for the Big Sleep—that is, if you can still let yourself get away with it!

(*He chuckles and gives* LARRY *a friendly slap on the back.* LARRY *gives him a bitter angry look*)

CORA   (*Giggles*)   Old Cemetery! That's him, Hickey. We'll have to call him dat.

HICKEY   (*Watching* LARRY *quizzically*)   Beginning to do a lot of puzzling about me, aren't you, Larry? But that won't help you. You've got to think of yourself. I couldn't give you my peace. You've got to find your own. All I can do is help you, and the rest of the gang, by showing you the way to find it.

(*He has said this with a simple persuasive earnestness. He pauses, and for a second they stare at him with fascinated resentful uneasiness*)

ROCKY (*Breaks the spell*)   Aw, hire a church!

HICKEY (*Placatingly*)   All right! All right! Don't get sore, boys and girls. I guess that did sound too much like a lousy preacher. Let's forget it and get busy on the party.

(*They look relieved*)

CHUCK   Is dose bundles grub, Hickey? You bought enough already to feed an army.

HICKEY (*With boyish excitement again*)   Can't be too much! I want this to be the biggest birthday Harry's ever had. You and Rocky go in the hall and get the big surprise. My arms are busted lugging it.

(*They catch his excitement.* CHUCK *and* ROCKY *go out, grinning expectantly. The three girls gather around* HICKEY, *full of thrilled curiosity*)

PEARL   Jees, yuh got us all het up! What is it, Hickey?

HICKEY   Wait and see. I got it as a treat for the three of you more than anyone. I thought to myself, I'll bet this is what will please those whores more than anything. (*They wince as if he had slapped them, but before they have a chance to be angry, he goes on affectionately*) I said to myself, I don't care how much it costs, they're worth it. They're the best little scouts in the world, and they've been damned kind to me when I was down and out! Nothing is too good for them. (*Earnestly*) I mean every word of that, too—and then some! (*Then, as if he noticed the expression on their faces for the first time*) What's the matter? You look sore. What—? (*Then he chuckles*) Oh, I see. But you know how I feel about that. You know I didn't say it to offend you. So don't be silly now.

MARGIE (*Lets out a tense breath*) Aw right, Hickey. Let it slide.

HICKEY (*Jubilantly, as* CHUCK *and* ROCKY *enter carrying a big wicker basket*) Look! There it comes! Unveil it, boys.

(*They pull off a covering burlap bag. The basket is piled with quarts of champagne*)

PEARL (*With childish excitement*) It's champagne! Jees, Hickey, if you ain't a sport!

(*She gives him a hug, forgetting all animosity, as do the other girls*)

MARGIE I never been soused on champagne. Let's get stinko, Poil.

PEARL You betcha my life! De bot' of us!

(*A holiday spirit of gay festivity has seized them all. Even* JOE MOTT *is standing up to look at the wine with an admiring grin, and* HUGO *raises his head to blink at it*)

JOE You sure is hittin' de high spots, Hickey. (*Boastfully*) Man, when I runs my gamblin' house, I drinks dat old bubbly water in steins! (*He stops guiltily and gives* HICKEY *a look of defiance*) I's goin' to drink it dat way again, too, soon's I make my stake! And dat ain't no pipe dream, neider!

(*He sits down where he was, his back turned to them*)

ROCKY What'll we drink it outa, Hickey? Dere ain't no wine glasses.

HICKEY (*Enthusiastically*) Joe has the right idea! Schooners! That's the spirit for Harry's birthday!

(ROCKY *and* CHUCK *carry the basket of wine into the bar. The three girls go back and stand around the entrance to the bar, chatting excitedly among themselves and to* CHUCK *and* ROCKY *in the bar*)

HUGO (*With his silly giggle*) Ve vill trink vine beneath the villow trees!

HICKEY (*Grins at him*) That's the spirit, Brother—and let the lousy slaves drink vinegar!

(HUGO *blinks at him startledly, then looks away*)

HUGO (*Mutters*) Gottamned liar!

(*He puts his head back on his arms and closes his eyes, but this time his habitual pass-out has a quality of hiding*)

LARRY (*Gives* HUGO *a pitying glance—in a low tone of anger*) Leave Hugo be! He rotted ten years in prison for his faith! He's earned his dream! Have you no decency or pity?

HICKEY (*Quizzically*) Hello, what's this? I thought you were in the grandstand. (*Then with a simple earnestness, taking a chair by* LARRY, *and putting a hand on his shoulder*) Listen, Larry, you're getting me all wrong. Hell, you ought to know me better. I've always been the best-natured slob in the world. Of course, I have pity. But now I've seen the light, it isn't my old kind of pity—the kind yours is. It isn't the kind that lets itself off easy by encouraging some poor guy to go on kidding himself with a lie—the kind that leaves the poor slob worse off because it makes him feel guiltier than ever—the kind that makes his lying hopes nag at him and reproach him until he's a rotten skunk in his own eyes. I know all about that kind of pity. I've had a bellyful of it in my time, and it's all wrong! (*With a salesman's persuasiveness*) No, sir. The kind of pity I feel now is after final results that will really save the poor guy, and make him contented with what he is, and quit battling himself, and find peace for the rest of his life. Oh, I know how you resent the way I have to show you up to yourself. I don't blame you. I know from my own experience it's bitter medicine, facing yourself in the mirror with the old false whiskers off. But you forget that, once you're cured. You'll be grateful to me when all at once you find you're able to admit, without feeling ashamed, that all the grandstand foolosopher bunk and the waiting for the Big Sleep stuff is a pipe dream. You'll say to yourself, I'm just an old man who is scared of life, but even more scared of dying. So I'm keeping drunk and hanging on to life at any price, and what of it? Then you'll know what real peace means, Larry, because you won't be scared of either life or death any more. You simply won't give a damn! Any more than I do!

LARRY (*Has been staring into his eyes with a fascinated wondering dread*) Be God, if I'm not beginning to think you've gone mad! (*With a rush of anger*) You're a liar!

HICKEY (*Injuredly*) Now, listen, that's no way to talk to an old pal who's trying to help you. Hell, if you really wanted to die, you'd just take a hop off your fire escape, wouldn't you? And if you really were in the grandstand, you wouldn't be pitying everyone. Oh, I know the truth is tough at first. It was for me. All I ask is for you to suspend judgment and give it a chance. I'll absolutely guarantee— Hell, Larry, I'm no fool. Do you suppose I'd deliberately set out to get under everyone's skin and put myself in dutch with all my old pals, if I wasn't certain, from my own experience, that it means contentment in the end for all of you? (LARRY *again is staring at him fascinatedly.* HICKEY *grins*) As for my being bughouse, you can't crawl out of it that way. Hell, I'm too damned sane. I can size up guys, and turn 'em inside out, better than I ever could. Even where they're strangers like that Parritt kid. He's licked, Larry. I think there is only one possible way out you can help him to take. That is, if you have the right kind of pity for him.

LARRY (*Uneasily*) What do you mean? (*Attempting indifference*) I'm not advising him, except to leave me out of his troubles. He's nothing to me.

HICKEY (*Shakes his head*) You'll find he won't agree to that. He'll keep after you until he makes you help him. Because he has to be punished, so he can forgive himself. He's lost all his guts. He can't manage it alone, and you're the only one he can turn to.

LARRY For the love of God, mind your own business! (*With forced scorn*) A lot you know about him! He's hardly spoken to you!

HICKEY No, that's right. But I do know a lot about him just the same. I've had hell inside me. I can spot it in others. (*Frowning*) Maybe that's what gives me the feeling there's something familiar about him, something between us. (*He shakes his head*) No, it's more than that. I can't figure it. Tell me about him. For instance, I don't imagine he's married, is he?

LARRY No.

HICKEY Hasn't he been mixed up with some woman? I don't mean trollops. I mean the old real love stuff that crucifies you.

LARRY (*With a calculating relieved look at him—encouraging him along this line*) Maybe you're right. I wouldn't be surprised.

HICKEY (*Grins at him quizzically*) I see. You think I'm on the wrong track and you're glad I am. Because then I won't suspect whatever he did about the Great Cause. That's another lie you tell yourself, Larry, that the good old Cause means nothing to you any more. (LARRY *is about to burst out in denial but* HICKEY *goes on*) But you're all wrong about Parritt. That isn't what's got him stopped. It's what's behind that. And it's a woman. I recognize the symptoms.

LARRY (*Sneeringly*) And you're the boy who's never wrong! Don't be a damned fool. His trouble is he was brought up a devout believer in the Movement and now he's lost his faith. It's a shock, but he's young and he'll soon find another dream just as good. (*He adds sardonically*) Or as bad.

HICKEY All right. I'll let it go at that, Larry. He's nothing to me except I'm glad he's here because he'll help me make you wake up to yourself. I don't even like the guy, or the feeling there's anything between us. But you'll find I'm right just the same, when you get to the final showdown with him.

LARRY There'll be no showdown! I don't give a tinker's damn—

HICKEY Sticking to the old grandstand, eh? Well, I knew you'd be the toughest to convince of all the gang, Larry. And, along with Harry and Jimmy Tomorrow, you're the one I want most to help. (*He puts an arm around* LARRY's *shoulder and gives him an affectionate hug*) I've always liked you a lot, you old bastard! (*He gets up and his manner changes to his bustling party excitement—glancing at his watch*) Well, well, not much time before twelve. Let's get busy, boys and girls. (*He looks over the table where the cake is*) Cake all set. Good. And my presents, and yours, girls, and Chuck's, and Rocky's. Fine. Harry'll certainly be touched by your thought of him. (*He goes back to the girls*) You go in the bar, Pearl and Margie, and get the grub ready so it can be brought right in. There'll be some drinking and toasts first, of course. My idea is to use the wine for that, so get it all set. I'll go upstairs now and root everyone out. Harry the last. I'll come back with him. Somebody light the candles on the cake when you hear us coming, and you start playing Harry's favorite tune, Cora. Hustle now, everybody. We want this to come off in style.

(*He bustles into the hall.* MARGIE *and* PEARL *disappear in the bar.* CORA *goes to the piano.* JOE *gets off the stool sullenly to let her sit down*)

CORA I got to practice. I ain't laid my mits on a box in Gawd knows when. (*With the soft pedal down, she begins gropingly to pick out "The Sunshine of Paradise Alley"*) Is dat right, Joe? I've forgotten dat has-been tune. (*She picks out a few more notes*) Come on, Joe, hum de tune so I can follow.

(JOE *begins to hum and sing in a low voice and correct her. He forgets his sullenness and becomes his old self again*)

LARRY (*Suddenly gives a laugh—in his comically intense, crazy tone*) Be God, it's a second feast of Belshazzar, with Hickey to do the writing on the wall!

CORA Aw, shut up, Old Cemetery! Always beefin'! (WILLIE *comes in from the hall. He is in a pitiable state, his face pasty, haggard with sleeplessness and nerves, his eyes sick and haunted. He is sober.* CORA *greets him over her shoulder kiddingly*) If it ain't Prince Willie! (*Then kindly*) Gee, kid, yuh look sick. Git a coupla shots in yuh.

WILLIE (*Tensely*) No, thanks. Not now. I'm tapering off.

(*He sits down weakly on* LARRY'S *right*)

CORA (*Astonished*) What d'yuh know? He means it!

WILLIE (*Leaning toward* LARRY *confidentially—in a low shaken voice*) It's been hell up in that damned room, Larry! The things I've imagined! (*He shudders*) I thought I'd go crazy. (*With pathetic boastful pride*) But I've got it beat now. By tomorrow morning I'll be on the wagon. I'll get back my clothes the first thing. Hickey's loaning me the money. I'm going to do what I've always said—go to the D.A.'s office. He was a good friend of my Old Man's. He was only assistant, then. He was in on the graft, but my Old Man never squealed on him. So he certainly owes it to me to give me a chance. And he knows that I really was a brilliant law student. (*Self-reassuringly*) Oh, I know I can make good, now I'm getting off the booze forever. (*Moved*) I owe a lot to Hickey. He's made me wake up to myself—see what a fool— It wasn't nice to face but— (*With bitter resentment*) It isn't what he says. It's what you feel behind—what he hints— Christ, you'd think all I really wanted to do with my life was sit here and stay drunk. (*With hatred*) I'll show him!

LARRY (*Masking pity behind a sardonic tone*) If you want my advice, you'll put the nearest bottle to your mouth until you don't give a damn for Hickey!

WILLIE (*Stares at a bottle greedily, tempted for a moment—then bitterly*) That's fine advice! I thought you were my friend!

(*He gets up with a hurt glance at* LARRY, *and moves away to take a chair in back of the left end of the table, where he sits in dejected, shaking misery, his chin on his chest*)

JOE (*To* CORA) No, like dis. (*He beats time with his finger and sings in a low voice)* "She is the sunshine of Paradise Alley." (*She plays*) Dat's more like it. Try it again.

(*She begins to play through the chorus again.* DON PARRITT *enters from the hall. There is a frightened look on his face. He slinks in furtively, as if he were escaping from someone. He looks relieved when he sees* LARRY *and comes and slips into the chair on his right.* LARRY *pretends not to notice his coming, but he instinctively shrinks with repulsion.* PARRITT *leans toward him and speaks ingratiatingly in a low secretive tone)*

PARRITT   Gee, I'm glad you're here, Larry. That damned fool, Hickey, knocked on my door. I opened up because I thought it must be you, and he came busting in and made me come downstairs. I don't know what for. I don't belong in this birthday celebration. I don't know this gang and I don't want to be mixed up with them. All I came here for was to find you.

LARRY   (*Tensely*)   I've warned you—

PARRITT   (*Goes on as if he hadn't heard*)   Can't you make Hickey mind his own business? I don't like that guy, Larry. The way he acts, you'd think he had something on me. Why, just now he pats me on the shoulder, like he was sympathizing with me, and says, "I know how it is, Son, but you can't hide from yourself, not even here on the bottom of the sea. You've got to face the truth and then do what must be done for your own peace and the happiness of all concerned." What did he mean by that, Larry?

LARRY   How the hell would I know?

PARRITT   Then he grins and says, "Never mind, Larry's getting wise to himself. I think you can rely on his help in the end. He'll have to choose between living and dying, and he'll never choose to die while there is a breath left in the old bastard!" And then he laughs like it was a joke on you. (*He pauses.* LARRY *is rigid on his chair, staring before him.* PARRITT *asks him with a sudden taunt in his voice*) Well, what do you say to that, Larry?

LARRY   I've nothing to say. Except you're a bigger fool than he is to listen to him.

PARRITT   (*With a sneer*)   Is that so? He's no fool where you're concerned. He's got your number, all right! (LARRY's *face tightens but he keeps silent.* PARRITT *changes to a contrite, appealing air*) I don't mean that. But you keep acting as if you were sore at me, and that gets my goat. You know what I want most is to be friends with you, Larry. I haven't a single friend left in the world. I hoped you— (*Bitterly*) And you could be, too, without it hurting

you. You ought to, for Mother's sake. She really loved you. You
loved her, too, didn't you?

LARRY (*Tensely*) Leave what's dead in its grave.

PARRITT I suppose, because I was only a kid, you didn't think I was
wise about you and her. Well, I was. I've been wise, ever since I
can remember, to all the guys she's had, although she'd tried to
kid me along it wasn't so. That was a silly stunt for a free Anarchist woman, wasn't it, being ashamed of being free?

LARRY Shut your damned trap!

PARRITT (*Guiltily but with a strange undertone of satisfaction*)
Yes, I know I shouldn't say that now. I keep forgetting she isn't
free any more. (*He pauses*) Do you know, Larry, you're the one
of them all she cared most about? Anyone else who left the Movement would have been dead to her, but she couldn't forget you.
She'd always make excuses for you. I used to try and get her goat
about you. I'd say, "Larry's got brains and yet he thinks the Movement is just a crazy pipe dream." She'd blame it on booze getting
you. She'd kid herself that you'd give up booze and come back to
the Movement—tomorrow! She'd say, "Larry can't kill in himself
a faith he's given his life to, not without killing himself." (*He grins
sneeringly*) How about it, Larry? Was she right? (LARRY *remains
silent. He goes on insistently*) I suppose what she really meant
was, come back to her. She was always getting the Movement
mixed up with herself. But I'm sure she really must have loved
you, Larry. As much as she could love anyone besides herself.
But she wasn't faithful to you, even at that, was she? That's why
you finally walked out on her, isn't it? I remember that last fight
you had with her. I was listening. I was on your side, even if she
was my mother, because I liked you so much; you'd been so good
to me—like a father. I remember her putting on her high-and-
mighty free-woman stuff, saying you were still a slave to bourgeois
morality and jealousy and you thought a woman you loved was a
piece of private property you owned. I remember that you got
mad and you told her, "I don't like living with a whore, if that's
what you mean!"

LARRY (*Bursts out*) You lie! I never called her that!

PARRITT (*Goes on as if* LARRY *hadn't spoken*) I think that's why
she still respects you, because it was you who left her. You were
the only one to beat her to it. She got sick of the others before
they did of her. I don't think she ever cared much about them,
anyway. She just had to keep on having lovers to prove to herself

how free she was (*He pauses—then with a bitter repulsion*) It made home a lousy place. I felt like you did about it. I'd get feeling it was like living in a whorehouse—only worse, because she didn't have to make her living—

LARRY   You bastard! She's your mother! Have you no shame?

PARRITT (*Bitterly*)   No! She brought me up to believe that family-respect stuff is all bourgeois, property-owning crap. Why should I be ashamed?

LARRY (*Making a move to get up*)   I've had enough!

PARRITT (*Catches his arm—pleadingly*)   No! Don't leave me! Please! I promise I won't mention her again! (LARRY *sinks back in his chair*) I only did it to make you understand better. I know this isn't the place to— Why didn't you come up to my room, like I asked you? I kept waiting. We could talk everything over there.

LARRY   There's nothing to talk over!

PARRITT   But I've got to talk to you. Or I'll talk to Hickey. He won't let me alone! I feel he knows, anyway! And I know he'd understand, all right—in his way. But I hate his guts! I don't want anything to do with him! I'm scared of him, honest. There's something not human behind his damned grinning and kidding.

LARRY (*Starts*)   Ah! You feel that, too?

PARRITT (*Pleadingly*)   But I can't go on like this. I've got to decide what I've got to do. I've got to tell you, Larry!

LARRY (*Again starts up*)   I won't listen!

PARRITT (*Again holds him by the arm*)   All right! I won't. Don't go! (LARRY *lets himself be pulled down on his chair.* PARRITT *examines his face and becomes insultingly scornful*) Who do you think you're kidding? I know damned well you've guessed—

LARRY   I've guessed nothing!

PARRITT   But I want you to guess now! I'm glad you have! I know now, since Hickey's been after me, that I meant you to guess right from the start. That's why I came to you. (*Hurrying on with an attempt at a plausible frank air that makes what he says seem doubly false*) I want you to understand the reason. You see, I began studying American history. I got admiring Washington and Jefferson and Jackson and Lincoln. I began to feel patriotic and love this country. I saw it was the best government in the world, where everybody was equal and had a chance. I saw that all the ideas behind the Movement came from a lot of Russians like Bakunin and Kropotkin and were meant for Europe, but we didn't need them here in a democracy where we were free already. I didn't want this country to be destroyed for a damned foreign pipe dream. After all, I'm from old American pioneer stock. I began to feel I was a traitor for helping a lot of cranks and bums and free women plot to overthrow our government. And then I saw it was my duty to my country—

LARRY (*Nauseated—turns on him*) You stinking rotten liar! Do you think you can fool me with such hypocrite's cant! (*Then turning away*) I don't give a damn what you did! It's on your head— whatever it was! I don't want to know—and I won't know!

PARRITT (*As if* LARRY *had never spoken—falteringly*) But I never thought Mother would be caught. Please believe that, Larry. You know I never would have—

LARRY (*His face haggard, drawing a deep breath and closing his eyes—as if he were trying to hammer something into his own brain*) All I know is I'm sick of life! I'm through! I've forgotten myself! I'm drowned and contented on the bottom of a bottle. Honor or dishonor, faith or treachery are nothing to me but the opposites of the same stupidity which is ruler and king of life, and in the end they rot into dust in the same grave. All things are the same meaningless joke to me, for they grin at me from the one skull of death. So go away. You're wasting breath. I've forgotten your mother.

PARRITT (*Jeers angrily*) The old foolosopher, eh? (*He spits out contemptuously*) You lousy old faker!

LARRY (*So distracted he pleads weakly*) For the love of God, leave me in peace the little time that's left to me!

PARRITT Aw, don't pull that pitiful old-man junk on me! You old bastard, you'll never die as long as there's a free drink of whiskey left!

LARRY (*Stung—furiously*) Look out how you try to taunt me back into life, I warn you! I might remember the thing they call justice there, and the punishment for— (*He checks himself with an effort—then with a real indifference that comes from exhaustion*) I'm old and tired. To hell with you! You're as mad as Hickey, and as big a liar. I'd never let myself believe a word you told me.

PARRITT (*Threateningly*) The hell you won't! Wait till Hickey gets through with you!

(PEARL *and* MARGIE *come in from the bar. At the sight of them,* PARRITT *instantly subsides and becomes self-conscious and defensive, scowling at them and then quickly looking away*)

MARGIE (*Eyes him jeeringly*) Why, hello, Tightwad Kid. Come to join de party? Gee, don't he act bashful, Poil?

PEARL Yeah. Especially wid his dough. (PARRITT *slinks to a chair at the left end of the table, pretending he hasn't heard them. Suddenly there is a noise of angry, cursing voices and a scuffle from the hall.* PEARL *yells*) Hey, Rocky! Fight in de hall!

(ROCKY *and* CHUCK *run from behind the bar curtain and rush into the hall.* ROCKY's *voice is heard in irritated astonishment,* "What de hell?" *and then the scuffle stops and* ROCKY *appears holding* CAPTAIN LEWIS *by the arm, followed by* CHUCK *with a similar hold on* GENERAL WETJOEN. *Although these two have been drinking they are both sober, for them. Their faces are sullenly angry, their clothes disarranged from the tussle*)

ROCKY (*Leading* LEWIS *forward—astonished, amused and irritated*) Can yuh beat it? I've heard youse two call each odder every name yuh could think of but I never seen you— (*Indignantly*) A swell time to stage your first bout, on Harry's boithday party! What started de scrap?

LEWIS (*Forcing a casual tone*) Nothing, old chap. Our business, you know. That bloody ass, Hickey, made some insinuation about me, and the boorish Boer had the impertinence to agree with him.

WETJOEN Dot's a lie! Hickey made joke about me, and this Limey said yes, it was true!

ROCKY Well, sit down, de bot' of yuh, and cut out de rough stuff. (*He and* CHUCK *dump them down in adjoining chairs toward the left end of the table, where, like two sulky boys, they turn their backs on each other as far as possible in chairs which both face front*)

MARGIE (*Laughs*) Jees, lookit de two bums! Like a coupla kids! Kiss and make up, for Gawd's sakes!

ROCKY Yeah. Harry's party begins in a minute and we don't want no soreheads around.

LEWIS (*Stiffly*) Very well. In deference to the occasion, I apologize, General Wetjoen—provided that you do also.

WETJOEN (*Sulkily*) I apologize, Captain Lewis—because Harry is my goot friend.

ROCKY Aw, hell! If yuh can't do better'n dat—!

(MOSHER *and* MCGLOIN *enter together from the hall. Both have been drinking but are not drunk*)

PEARL Here's de star boarders.

(*They advance, their heads together, so interested in a discussion they are oblivious to everyone*)

MCGLOIN   I'm telling you, Ed, it's serious this time. That bastard, Hickey, has got Harry on the hip. (*As he talks,* MARGIE, PEARL, ROCKY *and* CHUCK *prick up their ears and gather round.* CORA, *at the piano, keeps running through the tune, with soft pedal, and singing the chorus half under her breath, with* JOE *still correcting her mistakes. At the table,* LARRY, PARRITT, WILLIE, WETJOEN *and* LEWIS *sit motionless, staring in front of them.* HUGO *seems asleep in his habitual position*) And you know it isn't going to do us no good if he gets him to take that walk tomorrow.

MOSHER   You're damned right. Harry'll mosey around the ward, dropping in on everyone who knew him when. (*Indignantly*) And they'll all give him a phony glad hand and a ton of good advice about what a sucker he is to stand for us.

MCGLOIN   He's sure to call on Bessie's relations to do a little cryin' over dear Bessie. And you know what that bitch and all her family thought of me.

MOSHER (*With a flash of his usual humor—rebukingly*)   Remember, Lieutenant, you are speaking of my sister! Dear Bessie wasn't a bitch. She was a God-damned bitch! But if you think my loving relatives will have time to discuss you, you don't know them. They'll be too busy telling Harry what a drunken crook I am and saying he ought to have me put in Sing Sing!

MCGLOIN (*Dejectedly*)   Yes, once Bessie's relations get their hooks in him, it'll be as tough for us as if she wasn't gone.

MOSHER (*Dejectedly*)   Yes, Harry has always been weak and easily influenced, and now he's getting old he'll be an easy mark for those grafters. (*Then with forced reassurance*) Oh, hell, Mac, we're saps to worry. We've heard Harry pull that bluff about taking a walk every birthday he's had for twenty years.

MCGLOIN (*Doubtfully*)   But Hickey wasn't sicking him on those times. Just the opposite. He was asking Harry what he wanted to go out for when there was plenty of whiskey here.

MOSHER (*With a change to forced carelessness*)   Well, after all, I don't care whether he goes out or not. I'm clearing out tomorrow morning anyway. I'm just sorry for you, Mac.

MCGLOIN (*Resentfully*)   You needn't be, then. Ain't I going myself? I was only feeling sorry for you.

MOSHER   Yes, my mind is made up. Hickey may be a lousy, interfering pest, now he's gone teetotal on us, but there's a lot of truth in some of his bull. Hanging around here getting plastered with you, Mac, is pleasant, I won't deny, but the old booze gets you in the end, if you keep lapping it up. It's time I quit for a while. (*With forced enthusiasm*) Besides, I feel the call of the old care-free circus life in my blood again. I'll see the boss tomorrow. It's late in the season but he'll be glad to take me on. And won't all the old gang be tickled to death when I show up on the lot!

MCGLOIN   Maybe—if they've got a rope handy!

MOSHER (*Turns on him—angrily*)   Listen! I'm damned sick of that kidding!

MCGLOIN   You are, are you? Well, I'm sicker of your kidding me about getting reinstated on the Force. And whatever you'd like, I can't spend my life sitting here with you, ruining my stomach with rotgut. I'm tapering off, and in the morning I'll be fresh as a daisy. I'll go and have a private chin with the Commissioner. (*With forced enthusiasm*) Man alive, from what the boys tell me, there's sugar galore these days, and I'll soon be ridin' around in a big red automobile—

MOSHER (*Derisively—beckoning an imaginary Chinese*)   Here, One Lung Hop! Put fresh peanut oil in the lamp and cook the Lieutenant another dozen pills! It's his gowed-up night!

MCGLOIN (*Stung—pulls back a fist threateningly*)   One more crack like that and I'll—!

MOSHER (*Putting up his fists*)   Yes? Just start—!

(CHUCK *and* ROCKY *jump between them*)

ROCKY   Hey! Are you guys nuts? Jees, it's Harry's boithday party! (*They both look guilty*) Sit down and behave.

MOSHER (*Grumpily*)   All right. Only tell him to lay off me.

(*He lets* ROCKY *push him in a chair, at the right end of the table, rear*)

MCGLOIN (*Grumpily*)   Tell him to lay off me.

(*He lets* CHUCK *push him into the chair on* MOSHER's *left. At this moment* HICKEY *bursts in from the hall, bustling and excited*)

HICKEY   Everything all set? Fine! (*He glances at his watch*) Half a minute to go. Harry's starting down with Jimmy. I had a hard time getting them to move! They'd rather stay hiding up there, kidding each other along. (*He chuckles*) Harry don't even want to remember it's his birthday now! (*He hears a noise from the stairs*) Here they come! (*Urgently*) Light the candles! Get ready to play, Cora! Stand up, everybody! Get that wine ready, Chuck and Rocky! (MARGIE *and* PEARL *light the candles on the cake.*

CORA *gets her hands set over the piano keys, watching over her shoulder.* ROCKY *and* CHUCK *go in the bar. Everybody at the table stands up mechanically.* HUGO *is the last, suddenly coming to and scrambling to his feet.* HARRY HOPE *and* JIMMY TOMORROW *appear in the hall outside the door.* HICKEY *looks up from his watch*) On the dot! It's twelve! (*Like a cheer leader*) Come on now, everybody, with a Happy Birthday, Harry!

(*With his voice leading they all shout "Happy Birthday, Harry!" in a spiritless chorus.* HICKEY *signals to* CORA, *who starts playing and singing in a whiskey soprano "She's the Sunshine of Paradise Alley."* HOPE *and* JIMMY *stand in the doorway. Both have been drinking heavily. In* HOPE *the effect is apparent only in a bristling, touchy, pugnacious attitude. It is entirely different from the usual irascible beefing he delights in and which no one takes seriously. Now he really has a chip on his shoulder.* JIMMY, *on the other hand, is plainly drunk, but it has not had the desired effect, for beneath a pathetic assumption of gentlemanly poise, he is obviously frightened and shrinking back within himself.* HICKEY *grabs* HOPE's *hand and pumps it up and down. For a moment* HOPE *appears unconscious of this handshake. Then he jerks his hand away angrily*)

HOPE   Cut out the glad hand, Hickey. D'you think I'm a sucker? I know you, bejees, you sneaking, lying drummer! (*With rising anger, to the others*) And all you bums! What the hell you trying to do, yelling and raising the roof? Want the cops to close the joint and get my license taken away? (*He yells at* CORA *who has stopped singing but continues to play mechanically with many mistakes*) Hey, you dumb tart, quit banging that box! Bejees, the least you could do is learn the tune!

CORA   (*Stops—deeply hurt*)   Aw, Harry! Jees, ain't I—
        (*Her eyes begin to fill*)

HOPE   (*Glaring at the other girls*)   And you two hookers, screaming at the top of your lungs! What d'you think this is, a dollar cathouse? Bejees, that's where you belong!

PEARL   (*Miserably*)   Aw, Harry—
        (*She begins to cry*)

MARGIE   Jees, Harry, I never thought you'd say that—like yuh meant it. (*She puts her arm around* PEARL—*on the verge of tears herself*) Aw, don't bawl, Poil. He don't mean it.

HICKEY   (*Reproachfully*)   Now, Harry! Don't take it out on the gang because you're upset about yourself. Anyway, I've promised you

you'll come through all right, haven't I? So quit worrying. (*He slaps* HOPE *on the back encouragingly.* HOPE *flashes him a glance of hate*) Be yourself, Governor. You don't want to bawl out the old gang just when they're congratulating you on your birthday, do you? Hell, that's no way!

HOPE (*Looking guilty and shamefaced now—forcing an unconvincing attempt at his natural tone*) Bejees, they ain't as dumb as you. They know I was only kidding them. They know I appreciate their congratulations. Don't you, fellers? (*There is a listless chorus of "Sure, Harry," "Yes," "Of course we do," etc. He comes forward to the two girls, with* JIMMY *and* HICKEY *following him, and pats them clumsily*) Bejees, I like you broads. You know I was only kidding.

(*Instantly they forgive him and smile affectionately*)

MARGIE Sure we know, Harry.

PEARL Sure.

HICKEY (*Grinning*) Sure. Harry's the greatest kidder in this dump and that's saying something! Look how he's kidded himself for twenty years! (*As* HOPE *gives him a bitter, angry glance, he digs him in the ribs with his elbow playfully*) Unless I'm wrong, Governor, and I'm betting I'm not. We'll soon know, eh? Tomorrow morning. No, by God, it's *this* morning now!

JIMMY (*With a dazed dread*) This morning?

HICKEY Yes, it's today at last, Jimmy. (*He pats him on the back*) Don't be so scared! I've promised I'll help you.

JIMMY (*Trying to hide his dread behind an offended, drunken dignity*) I don't understand you. Kindly remember I'm fully capable of settling my own affairs!

HICKEY (*Earnestly*) Well, isn't that exactly what I want you to do, settle with yourself once and for all? (*He speaks in his ear in confidential warning*) Only watch out on the booze, Jimmy. You know, not too much from now on. You've had a lot already, and you don't want to let yourself duck out of it by being too drunk to move—not this time!

(JIMMY *gives him a guilty, stricken look and turns away and slumps into the chair on* MOSHER'S *right*)

HOPE (*To* MARGIE—*still guiltily*) Bejees, Margie, you know I didn't mean it. It's that lousy drummer riding me that's got my goat.

MARGIE I know. (*She puts a protecting arm around* HOPE *and turns him to face the table with the cake and presents*) Come on. You ain't noticed your cake yet. Ain't it grand?

HOPE (*Trying to brighten up*) Say, that's pretty. Ain't ever had a cake since Bessie— Six candles. Each for ten years, eh? Bejees, that's thoughtful of you.

PEARL It was Hickey got it.

HOPE (*His tone forced*) Well, it was thoughtful of him. He means well, I guess. (*His eyes, fixed on the cake, harden angrily*) To hell with his cake.

(*He starts to turn away.* PEARL *grabs his arm*)

PEARL Wait, Harry. Yuh ain't seen de presents from Margie and me and Cora and Chuck and Rocky. And dere's a watch all engraved wid your name and de date from Hickey.

HOPE To hell with it! Bejees, he can keep it!

(*This time he does turn away*)

PEARL Jees, he ain't even goin' to look at our presents.

MARGIE (*Bitterly*) Dis is all wrong. We gotta put some life in dis party or I'll go nuts! Hey, Cora, what's de matter wid dat box? Can't yuh play for Harry? Yuh don't have to stop just because he kidded yuh!

HOPE (*Rouses himself—with forced heartiness*) Yes, come on, Cora. You was playing it fine. (CORA *begins to play half-heartedly.* HOPE *suddenly becomes almost tearfully sentimental*) It was Bessie's favorite tune. She was always singing it. It brings her back. I wish—

(*He chokes up*)

HICKEY (*Grins at him—amusedly*) Yes, we've all heard you tell us you thought the world of her, Governor.

HOPE (*Looks at him with frightened suspicion*) Well, so I did, bejees! Everyone knows I did! (*Threateningly*) Bejees, if you say I didn't—

HICKEY (*Soothingly*) Now, Governor. I didn't say anything. You're the only one knows the truth about that.

(HOPE *stares at him confusedly.* CORA *continues to play. For a moment there is a pause, broken by* JIMMY TOMORROW *who speaks with muzzy, self-pitying melancholy out of a sentimental dream*)

JIMMY Marjorie's favorite song was "Loch Lomond." She was beautiful and she played the piano beautifully and she had a beautiful voice. (*With gentle sorrow*) You were lucky, Harry. Bessie died. But there are more bitter sorrows than losing the woman one loves by the hand of death—

HICKEY (*With an amused wink at* HOPE) Now, listen, Jimmy, you needn't go on. We've all heard that story about how you came back to Cape Town and found her in the hay with a staff officer. We know you like to believe that was what started you on the booze and ruined your life.

JIMMY (*Stammers*) I—I'm talking to Harry. Will you kindly keep out of— (*With a pitiful defiance*) My life is not ruined!

HICKEY (*Ignoring this—with a kidding grin*) But I'll bet when you admit the truth to yourself, you'll confess you were pretty sick of her hating you for getting drunk. I'll bet you were really damned relieved when she gave you such a good excuse. (JIMMY *stares at him strickenly.* HICKEY *pats him on the back again—with sincere sympathy*) I know how it is, Jimmy. I—

(*He stops abruptly and for a second he seems to lose his self-assurance and become confused*)

LARRY (*Seizing on this with vindictive relish*) Ha! So that's what happened to you, is it? Your iceman joke finally came home to roost, did it? (*He grins tauntingly*) You should have remembered there's truth in the old superstition that you'd better look out what you call because in the end it comes to you!

HICKEY (*Himself again—grins to* LARRY *kiddingly*) Is that a fact, Larry? Well, well! Then you'd better watch out how you keep calling for that old Big Sleep! (LARRY *starts and for a second looks superstitiously frightened. Abruptly* HICKEY *changes to his jovial, bustling, master-of-ceremonies manner*) But what are we waiting for, boys and girls? Let's start the party rolling! (*He shouts to the bar*) Hey, Chuck and Rocky! Bring on the big surprise! Governor, you sit at the head of the table here. (*He makes* HARRY *sit down on the chair at the end of the table, right. To* MARGIE *and* PEARL) Come on, girls, sit down. (*They sit side by side on* JIMMY's *right.* HICKEY *bustles down to the left end of table*) I'll sit here at the foot.

(*He sits, with* CORA *on his left and* JOE *on her left.* ROCKY *and* CHUCK *appear from the bar, each bearing a big tray laden with schooners of champagne which they start shoving in front of each member of the party*)

ROCKY (*With forced cheeriness*) Real champagne, bums! Cheer up! What is dis, a funeral? Jees, mixin' champagne wid Harry's redeye will knock yuh paralyzed! Ain't yuh never satisfied?

(*He and* CHUCK *finish serving out the schooners, grab the last two themselves and sit down in the two vacant chairs remaining near the middle of the table. As they do so,* HICKEY *rises, a schooner in his hand*)

HICKEY (*Rapping on the table for order when there is nothing but a dead silence*) Order! Order, Ladies and Gents! (*He catches* LARRY's *eyes on the glass in his hand*) Yes, Larry, I'm going to drink with you this time. To prove I'm not teetotal because I'm afraid booze would make me spill my secrets, as you think. (LARRY *looks sheepish.* HICKEY *chuckles and goes on*) No, I gave you the simple truth about that. I don't need booze or anything else any more. But I want to be sociable and propose a toast in honor of our old friend, Harry, and drink it with you. (*His eyes fix on* HUGO, *who is out again, his head on his plate— To* CHUCK, *who is on* HUGO's *left*) Wake up our demon bomb-tosser, Chuck. We don't want corpses at this feast.

CHUCK (*Gives* HUGO *a shake*) Hey, Hugo, come up for air! Don't yuh see de champagne?

(HUGO *blinks around and giggles foolishly*)

HUGO Ve vill eat birthday cake and trink champagne beneath the villow tree! (*He grabs his schooner and takes a greedy gulp—then sets it back on the table with a grimace of distaste—in a strange, arrogantly disdainful tone, as if he were rebuking a butler*) Dis vine is unfit to trink. It has not properly been iced.

HICKEY (*Amusedly*) Always a high-toned swell at heart, eh, Hugo? God help us poor bums if you'd ever get to telling us where to get off! You'd have been drinking our blood beneath those willow trees! (*He chuckles.* HUGO *shrinks back in his chair, blinking at him, but* HICKEY *is now looking up the table at* HOPE. *He starts his toast, and as he goes on he becomes more moved and obviously sincere*) Here's the toast, Ladies and Gents! Here's to Harry Hope, who's been a friend in need to every one of us! Here's to the old Governor, the best sport and the kindest, biggest-hearted guy in the world! Here's wishing you all the luck there is, Harry, and long life and happiness! Come on, everybody! To Harry! Bottoms up!

(*They have all caught his sincerity with eager relief. They raise their schooners with an enthusiastic chorus of "Here's how, Harry!" "Here's luck, Harry!" etc., and gulp half the wine down,* HICKEY *leading them in this*)

HOPE (*Deeply moved—his voice husky*) Bejees, thanks, all of you. Bejees, Hickey, you old son of a bitch, that's white of you! Bejees, I know you meant it, too.

HICKEY (*Moved*) Of course I meant it, Harry, old friend! And I mean it when I say I hope today will be the biggest day in your life, and in the lives of everyone here, the beginning of a new life of peace and contentment where no pipe dreams can ever nag at you again. Here's to that, Harry!

(*He drains the remainder of his drink, but this time he drinks alone. In an instant the attitude of everyone has reverted to uneasy, suspicious defensiveness*)

ROCKY (*Growls*)   Aw, forget dat bughouse line of bull for a minute, can't yuh?

HICKEY (*Sitting down—good-naturedly*)   You're right, Rocky, I'm talking too much. It's Harry we want to hear from. Come on, Harry! (*He pounds his schooner on the table*) Speech! Speech! (*They try to recapture their momentary enthusiasm, rap their schooners on the table, call "Speech," but there is a hollow ring in it.* HOPE *gets to his feet reluctantly, with a forced smile, a smoldering resentment beginning to show in his manner*)

HOPE (*Lamely*)   Bejees, I'm no good at speeches. All I can say is thanks to everybody again for remembering me on my birthday. (*Bitterness coming out*) Only don't think because I'm sixty I'll be a bigger damned fool easy mark than ever! No, bejees! Like Hickey says, it's going to be a new day! This dump has got to be run like other dumps, so I can make some money and not just split even. People has got to pay what they owe me! I'm not running a damned orphan asylum for bums and crooks! Nor a God-damned hooker shanty, either! Nor an Old Men's Home for lousy Anarchist tramps that ought to be in jail! I'm sick of being played for a sucker! (*They stare at him with stunned, bewildered hurt. He goes on in a sort of furious desperation, as if he hated himself for every word he said, and yet couldn't stop*) And don't think you're kidding me right now, either! I know damned well you're giving me the laugh behind my back, thinking to yourselves, The old, lying, pipe-dreaming faker, we've heard his bull about taking a walk around the ward for years, he'll never make it! He's yellow, he ain't got the guts, he's scared he'll find out— (*He glares around at them almost with hatred*) But I'll show you, bejees! (*He glares at* HICKEY) I'll show you, too, you son of a bitch of a frying-pan-peddling bastard!

HICKEY (*Heartily encouraging*)   That's the stuff, Harry! Of course you'll try to show me! That's what I want you to do!

(HARRY *glances at him with helpless dread—then drops his eyes and looks furtively around the table. All at once he becomes miserably contrite*)

HOPE (*His voice catching*) Listen, all of you! Bejees, forgive me. I lost my temper! I ain't feeling well! I got a hell of a grouch on! Bejees, you know you're all as welcome here as the flowers in May!

(*They look at him with eager forgiveness.* ROCKY *is the first one who can voice it*)

ROCKY Aw, sure, Boss, you're always aces wid us, see?

HICKEY (*Rises to his feet again. He addresses them now with the simple, convincing sincerity of one making a confession of which he is genuinely ashamed*) Listen, everybody! I know you are sick of my gabbing, but I think this is the spot where I owe it to you to do a little explaining and apologize for some of the rough stuff I've had to pull on you. I know how it must look to you. As if I was a damned busybody who was not only interfering in your private business, but even sicking some of you on to nag at each other. Well, I have to admit that's true, and I'm damned sorry about it. But it simply had to be done! You must believe that! You know old Hickey. I was never one to start trouble. But this time I had to—for your own good! I had to make you help me with each other. I saw I couldn't do what I was after alone. Not in the time at my disposal. I knew when I came here I wouldn't be able to stay with you long. I'm slated to leave on a trip. I saw I'd have to hustle and use every means I could. (*With a joking boastfulness*) Why, if I had enough time, I'd get a lot of sport out of selling my line of salvation to each of you all by my lonesome. Like it was fun in the old days, when I traveled house to house, to convince some dame, who was sicking the dog on me, her house wouldn't be properly furnished unless she bought another wash boiler. And I could do it with you, all right. I know every one of you, inside and out, by heart. I may have been drunk when I've been here before, but old Hickey could never be so drunk he didn't have to see through people. I mean, everyone except himself. And, finally, he had to see through himself, too. (*He pauses. They stare at him, bitter, uneasy and fascinated. His manner changes to deep earnestness*) But here's the point to get. I swear I'd never act like I have if I wasn't absolutely sure it will be worth it to you in the end, after you're rid of the damned guilt that makes you lie to yourselves you're something you're not, and the remorse that nags at you and makes you hide behind lousy pipe dreams about tomorrow. You'll be in a today where there is no yesterday or tomorrow to worry you. You won't give a damn what you are any more. I wouldn't say this unless I knew, Brothers and Sisters. This peace is real! It's a fact! I know! Because I've got it! Here! Now! Right in front of you! You see the difference in me! You remember how I used to be! Even when I had two quarts of rotgut under my belt and joked and sang "Sweet Adeline," I still felt like a guilty skunk. But you can all see that I don't give a damn about anything now. And I promise you, by the time this day is over, I'll have every one of you feeling the same way! (*He pauses. They stare at him fascinatedly. He adds with a grin*) I guess that'll be about all from me, boys and girls—for the present. So let's get on with the party.

(*He starts to sit down*)

LARRY (*Sharply*) Wait! (*Insistently—with a sneer*) I think it would help us poor pipe-dreaming sinners along the sawdust trail to salvation if you told us now what it was happened to you that converted you to this great peace you've found. (*More and more with a deliberate, provocative taunting*) I notice you didn't deny it when I asked you about the iceman. Did this great revelation of the evil habit of dreaming about tomorrow come to you after you found your wife was sick of you?

(*While he is speaking the faces of the gang have lighted up vindictively, as if all at once they saw a chance to revenge themselves. As he finishes, a chorus of sneering taunts begins, punctuated by nasty, jeering laughter*)

HOPE Bejees, you've hit it, Larry! I've noticed he hasn't shown her picture around this time!

MOSHER He hasn't got it! The iceman took it away from him!

MARGIE Jees, look at him! Who could blame her?

PEARL She must be hard up to fall for an iceman!

CORA Imagine a sap like him advisin' me and Chuck to git married!

CHUCK Yeah! He done so good wid it!

JIMMY At least I can say Marjorie chose an officer and a gentleman.

LEWIS Come to look at you, Hickey, old chap, you've sprouted horns like a bloody antelope!

WETJOEN Pigger, py Gott! Like a water buffalo's!

WILLIE (*Sings to his Sailor Lad tune*)

"Come up," she cried, "my iceman lad,
    And you and I'll agree—"

(*They all join in a jeering chorus, rapping with knuckles or glasses
on the table at the indicated spot in the lyric*)

"And I'll show you the prettiest (*Rap, rap, rap*)
    That ever you did see!"

(*A roar of derisive, dirty laughter. But* HICKEY *has remained unmoved by all this taunting. He grins good-naturedly, as if he
enjoyed the joke at his expense, and joins in the laughter*)

HICKEY   Well, boys and girls, I'm glad to see you getting in good
spirits for Harry's party, even if the joke is on me. I admit I asked
for it by always pulling that iceman gag in the old days. So laugh
all you like. (*He pauses. They do not laugh now. They are again
staring at him with baffled uneasiness. He goes on thoughtfully*)
Well, this forces my hand, I guess, your bringing up the subject
of Evelyn. I didn't want to tell you yet. It's hardly an appropriate
time. I meant to wait until the party was over. But you're getting
the wrong idea about poor Evelyn, and I've got to stop that.
(*He pauses again. There is a tense stillness in the room. He bows
his head a little and says quietly*) I'm sorry to tell you my dearly
beloved wife is dead.

(*A gasp comes from the stunned company. They look away from
him, shocked and miserably ashamed of themselves, except* LARRY
who continues to stare at him)

LARRY   (*Aloud to himself with a superstitious shrinking*)   Be God,
I felt he'd brought the touch of death on him! (*Then suddenly
he is even more ashamed of himself than the others and stam-
mers*) Forgive me, Hickey! I'd like to cut my dirty tongue out!
(*This releases a chorus of shamefaced mumbles from the crowd.
"Sorry, Hickey." "I'm sorry, Hickey." "We're sorry, Hickey."*)

HICKEY   (*Looking around at them—in a kindly, reassuring tone*)
Now look here, everybody. You mustn't let this be a wet blanket
on Harry's party. You're still getting me all wrong. There's no
reason— You see, I don't feel any grief. (*They gaze at him
startledly. He goes on with convincing sincerity*) I've got to feel
glad, for her sake. Because she's at peace. She's rid of me at last.
Hell, I don't have to tell you—you all know what I was like. You
can imagine what she went through, married to a no-good
cheater and drunk like I was. And there was no way out of it

for her. Because she loved me. But now she is at peace like she always longed to be. So why should I feel sad? She wouldn't want me to feel sad. Why, all that Evelyn ever wanted out of life was to make me happy.

(*He stops, looking around at them with a simple, gentle frankness. They stare at him in bewildered, incredulous confusion*)

Curtain

ACT THREE

SCENE: *Barroom of* HARRY HOPE'S, *including a part of what had been the back room in Acts One and Two. In the right wall are two big windows, with the swinging doors to the street between them. The bar itself is at rear. Behind it is a mirror, covered with white mosquito netting to keep off the flies, and a shelf on which are barrels of cheap whiskey with spiggots and a small show case of bottled goods. At left of the bar is the doorway to the hall. There is a table at left, front, of barroom proper, with four chairs. At right, front, is a small free-lunch counter, facing left, with a space between it and the window for the dealer to stand when he dishes out soup at the noon hour. Over the mirror behind the bar are framed photographs of Richard Croker and Big Tim Sullivan, flanked by framed lithographs of John L. Sullivan and Gentleman Jim Corbett in ring costume.*

At left, in what had been the back room, with the dividing curtain drawn, the banquet table of Act Two has been broken up, and the tables are again in the crowded arrangement of Act One. Of these, we see one in the front row with five chairs at left of the barroom table, another with five chairs at left-rear of it, a third back by the rear wall with five chairs, and finally, at extreme left-front, one with four chairs, partly on and partly off stage, left.

It is around the middle of the morning of HOPE'S *birthday, a hot summer day. There is sunlight in the street outside, but it does not hit the windows and the light in the back-room section is dim.*

JOE MOTT *is moving around, a box of sawdust under his arm, strewing it over the floor. His manner is sullen, his face set in gloom. He ignores everyone. As the scene progresses, he finishes his sawdusting job, goes behind the lunch counter and cuts loaves of bread.* ROCKY *is behind the bar, wiping it, washing glasses, etc. He wears his working clothes, sleeves rolled up. He looks sleepy, irritable and worried. At the barroom table, front,* LARRY *sits in a chair, facing*

*right-front. He has no drink in front of him. He stares ahead, deep
in harried thought. On his right, in a chair facing right, HUGO sits
sprawled forward, arms and head on the table as usual, a whiskey
glass beside his limp hand. At rear of the front table at left of them,
in a chair facing left, PARRITT is sitting. He is staring in front of him
in a tense, strained immobility.*

*As the curtain rises, ROCKY finishes his work behind the bar. He
comes forward and drops wearily in the chair at right of LARRY's
table, facing left.*

ROCKY   Nuttin' now till de noon rush from de Market. I'm goin' to
rest my fanny. (*Irritably*) If I ain't a sap to let Chuck kid me into
workin' his time so's he can take de mornin' off. But I got sick of
arguin' wid 'im. I says, "Aw right, git married! What's it to me?"
Hickey's got de bot' of dem bugs. (*Bitterly*) Some party last
night, huh? Jees, what a funeral! It was jinxed from de start, but
his tellin' about his wife croakin' put de K.O. on it.

LARRY   Yes, it turned out it wasn't a birthday feast but a wake!

ROCKY   Him promisin' he'd cut out de bughouse bull about peace—
and den he went on talkin' and talkin' like he couldn't stop! And
all de gang sneakin' upstairs, leavin' free booze and eats like dey
was poison! It didn't do dem no good if dey thought dey'd shake
him. He's been hoppin' from room to room all night. Yuh can't
stop him. He's got his Reform Wave goin' strong dis mornin'!
Did yuh notice him drag Jimmy out de foist ting to get his laundry and his clothes pressed so he wouldn't have no excuse? And
he give Willie de dough to buy his stuff back from Solly's. And
all de rest been brushin' and shavin' demselves wid de shakes—

LARRY   (*Defiantly*)   He didn't come to my room! He's afraid I might
ask him a few questions.

ROCKY   (*Scornfully*)   Yeah? It don't look to me he's scared of yuh.
I'd say you was scared of him.

LARRY   (*Stung*)   You'd lie, then!

PARRITT   (*Jerks round to look at LARRY—sneeringly*)   Don't let him
kid you, Rocky. He had his door locked. I couldn't get in, either.

ROCKY   Yeah, who d'yuh tink yuh're kiddin', Larry? He's showed
you up, aw right. Like he says, if yuh was so anxious to croak, why
wouldn't yuh hop off your fire escape long ago?

LARRY   (*Defiantly*)   Because it'd be a coward's quitting, that's why!

PARRITT   He's all quitter, Rocky. He's a yellow old faker!

LARRY (*Turns on him*) You lying punk! Remember what I warned you—!

ROCKY (*Scowls at* PARRITT) Yeah, keep outta dis, you! Where d'yuh get a license to butt in? Shall I give him de bum's rush, Larry? If you don't want him around, nobody else don't.

LARRY (*Forcing an indifferent tone*) No. Let him stay. I don't mind him. He's nothing to me.

(ROCKY *shrugs his shoulders and yawns sleepily*)

PARRITT You're right, I have nowhere to go now. You're the only one in the world I can turn to.

ROCKY (*Drowsily*) Yuh're a soft old sap, Larry. He's a no-good louse like Hickey. He don't belong. (*He yawns*) I'm all in. Not a wink of sleep. Can't keep my peepers open.

(*His eyes close and his head nods.* PARRITT *gives him a glance and then gets up and slinks over to slide into the chair on* LARRY'S *left, between him and* ROCKY. LARRY *shrinks away, but determinedly ignores him*)

PARRITT (*Bending toward him—in a low, ingratiating, apologetic voice*) I'm sorry for riding you, Larry. But you get my goat when you act as if you didn't care a damn what happened to me, and keep your door locked so I can't talk to you. (*Then hopefully*) But that was to keep Hickey out, wasn't it? I don't blame you. I'm getting to hate him. I'm getting more and more scared of him. Especially since he told us his wife was dead. It's that queer feeling he gives me that I'm mixed up with him some way. I don't know why, but it started me thinking about Mother—as if she was dead. (*With a strange undercurrent of something like satisfaction in his pitying tone*) I suppose she might as well be. Inside herself, I mean. It must kill her when she thinks of me—I know she doesn't want to, but she can't help it. After all, I'm her only kid. She used to spoil me and made a pet of me. Once in a great while, I mean. When she remembered me. As if she wanted to make up for something. As if she felt guilty. So she must have loved me a little, even if she never let it interfere with her freedom. (*With a strange pathetic wistfulness*) Do you know, Larry, I once had a sneaking suspicion that maybe, if the truth was known, you were my father.

LARRY (*Violently*) You damned fool! Who put that insane idea in your head? You know it's a lie! Anyone in the Coast crowd could tell you I never laid eyes on your mother till after you were born.

PARRITT Well, I'd hardly ask them, would I? I know you're right, though, because I asked her. She brought me up to be frank and ask her anything, and she'd always tell me the truth. (*Abruptly*) But I was talking about how she must feel now about me. My getting through with the Movement. She'll never forgive that. The Movement is her life. And it must be the final knockout for her if she knows I was the one who sold—

LARRY Shut up, damn you!

PARRITT It'll kill her. And I'm sure she knows it must have been me. (*Suddenly with desperate urgency*) But I never thought the cops would get her! You've got to believe that! You've got to see what my only reason was! I'll admit what I told you last night was a lie—that bunk about getting patriotic and my duty to my country. But here's the true reason, Larry—the only reason! It was just for money! I got stuck on a whore and wanted dough to blow in on her and have a good time! That's all I did it for! Just money! Honest!

(*He has the terrible grotesque air, in confessing his sordid baseness, of one who gives an excuse which exonerates him from any real guilt*)

LARRY (*Grabs him by the shoulder and shakes him*) God damn you, shut up! What the hell is it to me?

(ROCKY *starts awake*)

ROCKY What's comin' off here?

LARRY (*Controlling himself*) Nothing. This gabby young punk was talking my ear off, that's all. He's a worse pest than Hickey.

ROCKY (*Drowsily*) Yeah, Hickey— Say, listen, what d'yuh mean about him bein' scared you'd ask him questions? What questions?

LARRY Well, I feel he's hiding something. You notice he didn't say what his wife died of.

ROCKY (*Rebukingly*) Aw, lay off dat. De poor guy— What are yuh gettin' at, anyway? Yuh don't tink it's just a gag of his?

LARRY I don't. I'm damned sure he's brought death here with him. I feel the cold touch of it on him.

ROCKY Aw, bunk! You got croakin' on de brain, Old Cemetery. (*Suddenly* ROCKY's *eyes widen*) Say! D'yuh mean yuh tink she committed suicide, 'count of his cheatin' or someting?

LARRY (*Grimly*) It wouldn't surprise me. I'd be the last to blame her.

ROCKY (*Scornfully*) But dat's crazy! Jees, if she'd done dat, he wouldn't tell us he was glad about it, would he? He ain't dat big a bastard.

PARRITT (*Speaks up from his own preoccupation—strangely*) You
know better than that, Larry. You know she'd never commit suicide. She's like you. She'll hang on to life even when there's nothing left but—

LARRY (*Stung—turns on him viciously*) And how about you? Be
God, if you had any guts or decency—!
(*He stops guiltily*)

PARRITT (*Sneeringly*) I'd take that hop off your fire escape you're
too yellow to take, I suppose?

LARRY (*As if to himself*) No! Who am I to judge? I'm done with
judging.

PARRITT (*Tauntingly*) Yes I suppose you'd like that, wouldn't you?

ROCKY (*Irritably mystified*) What de hell's all dis about? (*To
PARRITT*) What d'you know about Hickey's wife? How d'yuh know
she didn't—?

LARRY (*With forced belittling casualness*) He doesn't. Hickey's
addled the little brains he's got. Shove him back to his own table,
Rocky. I'm sick of him.

ROCKY (*To PARRITT, threateningly*) Yuh heard Larry? I'd like an
excuse to give yuh a good punch in de snoot. So move quick!

PARRITT (*Gets up—to LARRY*) If you think moving to another table
will get rid of me! (*He moves away—then adds with bitter reproach*) Gee, Larry, that's a hell of a way to treat me, when I've
trusted you, and I need your help.
(*He sits down in his old place and sinks into a wounded, self-
pitying brooding*)

ROCKY (*Going back to his train of thought*) Jees, if she committed
suicide, yuh got to feel sorry for Hickey, huh? Yuh can understand how he'd go bughouse and not be responsible for all de
crazy stunts he's stagin' here. (*Then puzzledly*) But how can yuh
be sorry for him when he says he's glad she croaked, and yuh can
tell he means it? (*With weary exasperation*) Aw, nuts! I don't
get nowhere tryin' to figger his game. (*His face hardening*) But
I know dis. He better lay off me and my stable! (*He pauses—then
sighs*) Jees, Larry, what a night dem two pigs give me! When
de party went dead, dey pinched a coupla bottles and brung dem
up deir room and got stinko. I don't get a wink of sleep, see? Just
as I'd drop off on a chair here, dey'd come down lookin' for
trouble. Or else dey'd raise hell upstairs, laughin' and singin', so
I'd get scared dey'd get de joint pinched and go up to tell dem
to can de noise. And every time dey'd crawl my frame wid de
same old argument. Dey'd say, "So yuh agreed wid Hickey, do

yuh, yuh dirty little Ginny? We're whores, are we? Well, we agree wid Hickey about you, see! Yuh're nuttin' but a lousy pimp!" Den I'd slap dem. Not beat 'em up, like a pimp would. Just slap dem. But it don't do no good. Dey'd keep at it over and over. Jees, I get de earache just thinkin' of it! "Listen," dey'd say, "if we're whores we gotta right to have a reg'lar pimp and not stand for no punk imitation! We're sick of wearin' out our dogs poundin' sidewalks for a double-crossin' bartender, when all de thanks we get is he looks down on us. We'll find a guy who really needs us to take care of him and ain't ashamed of it. Don't expect us to work tonight, 'cause we won't, see? Not if de streets was blocked wid sailors! We're goin' on strike and yuh can like it or lump it!" (*He shakes his head*) Whores goin' on strike! Can yuh tie dat? (*Going on with his story*) Dey says, "We're takin' a holiday. We're goin' to beat it down to Coney Island and shoot the chutes and maybe we'll come back and maybe we won't. And you can go to hell!" So dey put on deir lids and beat it, de bot' of dem stinko.

(*He sighs dejectedly. He seems grotesquely like a harried family man, henpecked and browbeaten by a nagging wife.* LARRY *is deep in his own bitter preoccupation and hasn't listened to him.* CHUCK *enters from the hall at rear. He has his straw hat with the gaudy band in his hand and wears a Sunday-best blue suit with a high stiff collar. He looks sleepy, hot, uncomfortable and grouchy*)

CHUCK (*Glumly*) Hey, Rocky. Cora wants a sherry flip. For her noives.

ROCKY (*Turns indignantly*) Sherry flip! Christ, she don't need nuttin' for her noive! What's she tink dis is, de Waldorf?

CHUCK Yeah, I told her, what would we use for sherry, and dere wasn't no egg unless she laid one. She says, "Is dere a law yuh can't go out and buy de makings, yuh big tramp?" (*Resentfully puts his straw hat on his head at a defiant tilt*) To hell wid her! She'll drink booze or nuttin'!

(*He goes behind the bar to draw a glass of whiskey from a barrel*)

ROCKY (*Sarcastically*) Jees, a guy oughta give his bride anything she wants on de weddin' day, I should tink! (*As* CHUCK *comes from behind the bar,* ROCKY *surveys him derisively*) Pipe de bridegroom, Larry! All dolled up for de killin'!

(LARRY *pays no attention*)

CHUCK Aw, shut up!

ROCKY   One week on dat farm in Joisey, dat's what I give yuh! Yuh'll come runnin' in here some night yellin' for a shot of booze 'cause de crickets is after yuh! (*Disgustedly*) Jees, Chuck, dat louse Hickey's coitinly made a prize coupla suckers outa youse.

CHUCK   (*Unguardedly*) Yeah. I'd like to give him one sock in de puss—just one! (*Then angrily*) Aw, can dat! What's he got to do wid it? Ain't we always said we was goin' to? So we're goin' to, see? And don't give me no argument! (*He stares at* ROCKY *truculently. But* ROCKY *only shrugs his shoulders with weary disgust and* CHUCK *subsides into complaining gloom*) If on'y Cora'd cut out de beefin'. She don't gimme a minute's rest all night. De same old stuff over and over! Do I really want to marry her? I says, "Sure, Baby, why not?" She says, "Yeah, but after a week yuh'll be tinkin' what a sap you was. Yuh'll make dat an excuse to go off on a periodical, and den I'll be tied for life to a no-good soak, and de foist ting I know yuh'll have me out hustlin' again, your own wife!" Den she'd bust out cryin', and I'd get sore. "Yuh're a liar," I'd say. "I ain't never taken your dough 'cept when I was drunk and not workin'!" "Yeah," she'd say, "and how long will yuh stay sober now? Don't tink yuh can kid me wid dat water-wagon bull! I've heard it too often." Dat'd make me sore and I'd say, "Don't call me a liar. But I wish I was drunk right now, because if I was, yuh wouldn't be keepin' me awake all night beefin'. If yuh opened your yap, I'd knock de stuffin' outa yuh!" Den she'd yell, "Dat's a sweet way to talk to de goil yuh're goin' to marry." (*He sighs explosively*) Jees, she's got me hangin' on de ropes! (*He glances with vengeful yearning at the drink of whiskey in his hand*) Jees, would I like to get a quart of dis redeye under my belt!

ROCKY   Well, why de hell don't yuh?

CHUCK   (*Instantly suspicious and angry*) Sure! You'd like dat, wouldn't yuh? I'm wise to you! Yuh don't wanta see me get married and settle down like a reg'lar guy! Yuh'd like me to stay paralyzed all de time, so's I'd be like you, a lousy pimp!

ROCKY   (*Springs to his feet, his face hardened viciously*) Listen! I don't take dat even from you, see!

CHUCK   (*Puts his drink on the bar and clenches his fists*) Yeah? Wanta make sometin' of it? (*Jeeringly*) Don't make me laugh! I can lick ten of youse wid one mit!

ROCKY   (*Reaching for his hip pocket*) Not wid lead in your belly, yuh won't!

JOE (*Has stopped cutting when the quarrel started—expostulating*) Hey, you, Rocky and Chuck! Cut it out! You's ole friends! Don't let dat Hickey make you crazy!

CHUCK (*Turns on him*) Keep outa our business, yuh black bastard!

ROCKY (*Like* CHUCK, *turns on* JOE, *as if their own quarrel was forgotten and they became natural allies against an alien*) Stay where yuh belong, yuh doity nigger!

JOE (*Snarling with rage, springs from behind the lunch counter with the bread knife in his hand*) You white sons of bitches! I'll rip your guts out!

(CHUCK *snatches a whiskey bottle from the bar and raises it above his head to hurl at* JOE. ROCKY *jerks a short-barreled, nickel-plated revolver from his hip pocket. At this moment* LARRY *pounds on the table with his fist and bursts into a sardonic laugh*)

LARRY That's it! Murder each other, you damned loons, with Hickey's blessing! Didn't I tell you he'd brought death with him? (*His interruption startles them. They pause to stare at him, their fighting fury suddenly dies out and they appear deflated and sheepish*)

ROCKY (*To* JOE) Aw right, you. Leggo dat shiv and I'll put dis gat away.

(JOE *sullenly goes back behind the counter and slaps the knife on top of it.* ROCKY *slips the revolver back in his pocket.* CHUCK *lowers the bottle to the bar.* HUGO, *who has awakened and raised his head when* LARRY *pounded on the table, now giggles foolishly*)

HUGO Hello, leedle peoples! Neffer mind! Soon you vill eat hot dogs beneath the villow trees and trink free vine— (*Abruptly in a haughty fastidious tone*) The champagne vas not properly iced. (*With guttural anger*) Gottamned liar, Hickey! Does that prove I vant to be aristocrat? I love only the proletariat! I vill lead them! I vill be like a Gott to them! They vill be my slaves! (*He stops in bewildered self-amazement—to* LARRY *appealingly*) I am very trunk, no, Larry? I talk foolishness. I am so trunk, Larry, old friend, am I not, I don't know vhat I say?

LARRY (*Pityingly*) You're raving drunk, Hugo. I've never seen you so paralyzed. Lay your head down now and sleep it off.

HUGO (*Gratefully*) Yes. I should sleep. I am too crazy trunk. (*He puts his head on his arms and closes his eyes*)

JOE (*Behind the lunch counter—brooding superstitiously*) You's right, Larry. Bad luck come in de door when Hickey come. I's an ole gamblin' man and I knows bad luck when I feels it! (*Then defiantly*) But it's white man's bad luck. He can't jinx me! (*He comes from behind the counter and goes to the bar—addressing* ROCKY *stiffly*) De bread's cut and I's finished my job. Do I get de drink I's earned? (ROCKY *gives him a hostile look but shoves a bottle and glass at him.* JOE *pours a brimful drink—sullenly*) I's finished wid dis dump for keeps. (*He takes a key from his pocket and slaps it on the bar*) Here's de key to my room. I ain't comin' back. I's goin' to my own folks where I belong. I don't stay where I's not wanted. I's sick and tired of messin' round wid white men. (*He gulps down his drink—then looking around defiantly he deliberately throws his whiskey glass on the floor and smashes it*)

ROCKY Hey! What de hell—!

JOE (*With a sneering dignity*) I's on'y savin' you de trouble, White Boy. Now you don't have to break it, soon's my back's turned, so's no white man kick about drinkin' from de same glass. (*He walks stiffly to the street door—then turns for a parting shot— boastfully*) I's tired of loafin' 'round wid a lot of bums. I's a gamblin' man. I's gonna get in a big crap game and win me a big bankroll. Den I'll get de okay to open up my old gamblin' house for colored men. Den maybe I comes back here sometime to see de bums. Maybe I throw a twenty-dollar bill on de bar and say, "Drink it up," and listen when dey all pat me on de back and say, "Joe, you sure is white." But I'll say, "No, I'm black and my dough is black man's dough, and you's proud to drink wid me or you don't get no drink!" Or maybe I just says, "You can all go to hell. I don't lower myself drinkin' wid no white trash!" (*He opens the door to go out—then turns again*) And dat ain't no pipe dream! I'll git de money for my stake today, somehow, somewheres! If I has to borrow a gun and stick up some white man, I gets it! You wait and see!

(*He swaggers out through the swinging doors*)

CHUCK (*Angrily*) Can yuh beat de noive of dat dinge! Jees, if I wasn't dressed up, I'd go out and mop up de street wid him!

ROCKY Aw, let him go, de poor old dope! Him and his gamblin' house! He'll be back tonight askin' Harry for his room and bummin' me for a ball. (*Vengefully*) Den I'll be de one to smash de glass. I'll loin him his place!

(*The swinging doors are pushed open and* WILLIE OBAN *enters from the street. He is shaved and wears an expensive, well-cut suit, good shoes and clean linen. He is absolutely sober, but his face is sick, and his nerves in a shocking state of shakes*)

CHUCK Another guy all dolled up! Got your clothes from Solly's, huh, Willie? (*Derisively*) Now yuh can sell dem back to him again tomorrow.

WILLIE (*Stiffly*) No, I—I'm through with that stuff. Never again. (*He comes to the bar*)

ROCKY (*Sympathetically*) Yuh look sick, Willie. Take a ball to pick yuh up.

(*He pushes a bottle toward him*)

WILLIE (*Eyes the bottle yearningly but shakes his head—determinedly*) No, thanks. The only way to stop is to stop. I'd have no chance if I went to the D.A.'s office smelling of booze.

CHUCK Yuh're really goin' dere?

WILLIE (*Stiffly*) I said I was, didn't I? I just came back here to rest a few minutes, not because I needed any booze. I'll show that cheap drummer I don't have to have any Dutch courage— (*Guiltily*) But he's been very kind and generous staking me. He can't help his insulting manner, I suppose. (*He turns away from the bar*) My legs are a bit shaky yet. I better sit down a while. (*He goes back and sits at the left of the second table, facing* PARRITT, *who gives him a scowling, suspicious glance and then ignores him.* ROCKY *looks at* CHUCK *and taps his head disgustedly.* CAPTAIN LEWIS *appears in the doorway from the hall*)

CHUCK (*Mutters*) Here's anudder one.

(LEWIS *looks spruce and clean-shaven. His ancient tweed suit has been brushed and his frayed linen is clean. His manner is full of a forced, jaunty self-assurance. But he is sick and beset by katzen-jammer*)

LEWIS Good morning, gentlemen all. (*He passes along the front of bar to look out in the street*) A jolly fine morning, too. (*He turns back to the bar*) An eye-opener? I think not. Not required, Rocky, old chum. Feel extremely fit, as a matter of fact. Though can't say I slept much, thanks to that interfering ass, Hickey, and that stupid bounder of a Boer. (*His face hardens*) I've had about all I can take from that fellow. It's my own fault, of course, for allowing a brute of a Dutch farmer to become familiar. Well, it's come to a parting of the ways now, and good riddance. Which reminds me, here's my key. (*He puts it on the bar*) I shan't be coming back. Sorry to be leaving good old Harry and the rest of you, of course, but I can't continue to live under the same roof with that fellow.

(*He stops, stiffening into hostility as* WETJOEN *enters from the hall, and pointedly turns his back on him.* WETJOEN *glares at him sneeringly. He, too, has made an effort to spruce up his appearance, and his bearing has a forced swagger of conscious physical strength. Behind this, he is sick and feebly holding his booze-sodden body together*)

ROCKY (*To* LEWIS—*disgustedly putting the key on the shelf in back of the bar*) So Hickey's kidded the pants offa you, too? Yuh tink yuh're leavin' here, huh?

WETJOEN (*Jeeringly*) Ja! Dot's vhat he kids himself.

LEWIS (*Ignores him—airily*) Yes, I'm leaving, Rocky. But that ass, Hickey, has nothing to do with it. Been thinking things over. Time I turned over a new leaf, and all that.

WETJOEN He's going to get a job! Dot's what he says!

ROCKY What at, for Chris' sake?

LEWIS (*Keeping his airy manner*) Oh, anything. I mean, not manual labor, naturally, but anything that calls for a bit of brains and education. However humble. Beggars can't be choosers. I'll see a pal of mine at the Consulate. He promised any time I felt an energetic fit he'd get me a post with the Cunard—clark in the office or something of the kind.

WETJOEN Ja! At Limey Consulate they promise anything to get rid of him vhen he comes there tronk! They're scared to call the police and have him pinched because it vould scandal in the papers make about a Limey officer and chentleman!

LEWIS As a matter of fact, Rocky, I only wish a post temporarily. Means to an end, you know. Save up enough for a first-class passage home, that's the bright idea.

WETJOEN He's sailing back to home, sveet home! Dot's biggest pipe dream of all. What leetle brain the poor Limey has left, dot isn't in whiskey pickled, Hickey has made crazy!

(LEWIS's *fists clench, but he manages to ignore this*)

CHUCK (*Feels sorry for* LEWIS *and turns on* WETJOEN—*sarcastically*) Hickey ain't made no sucker outa you, huh? You're too foxy, huh? But I'll bet you tink yuh're goin' out and land a job, too.

WETJOEN (*Bristles*) I am, ja. For me, it is easy. Because I put on no airs of chentleman. I am not ashamed to vork with my hands. I vas a farmer before the war ven ploody Limey thieves steal my country. (*Boastfully*) Anyone I ask for job can see vith one look I have the great strength to do work of ten ordinary mens.

LEWIS (*Sneeringly*) Yes, Chuck, you remember he gave a demonstration of his extraordinary muscles last night when he helped to move the piano.

CHUCK Yuh couldn't even hold up your corner. It was your fault de damned box almost fell down de stairs.

WETJOEN My hands vas sweaty! Could I help dot my hands slip? I could de whole veight of it lift! In old days in Transvaal, I lift loaded oxcart by the axle! So vhy shouldn't I get job? Dot longshoreman boss, Dan, he tell me any time I like, he take me on. And Benny from de Market he promise me same.

LEWIS You remember, Rocky, it was one of those rare occasions when the Boer that walks like a man—spelled with a double o, by the way—was buying drinks and Dan and Benny were stony. They'd bloody well have promised him the moon.

ROCKY Yeah, yuh big boob, dem boids was on'y kiddin' yuh.

WETJOEN (*Angrily*) Dot's lie! You vill see dis morning I get job! I'll show dot bloody Limey chentleman, and dot liar, Hickey! And I need vork only leetle vhile to save money for my passage home. I need not much money because I am not ashamed to travel steerage. I don't put on first-cabin airs! (*Tauntingly*) Und *I can* go home to my country! Vhen I get there, they vill let *me* come in!

LEWIS (*Grows rigid—his voice trembling with repressed anger*) There was a rumor in South Africa, Rocky, that a certain Boer officer—if you call the leaders of a rabble of farmers officers—kept advising Cronje to retreat and not stand and fight—

WETJOEN And I vas right! I vas right! He got surrounded at Poardeberg! He had to surrender!

LEWIS (*Ignoring him*) Good strategy, no doubt, but a suspicion grew afterwards into a conviction among the Boers that the officer's caution was prompted by a desire to make his personal escape. His countrymen felt extremely savage about it, and his family disowned him. So I imagine there would be no welcoming committee waiting on the dock, nor delighted relatives making the veldt ring with their happy cries—

WETJOEN (*With guilty rage*) All lies! You Gottamned Limey—
(*Trying to control himself and copy* LEWIS's *manner*) I also haf heard rumors of a Limey officer who, after the war, lost all his

money gambling vhen he vas tronk. But they found out it vas regiment money, too, he lost—

LEWIS (*Loses his control and starts for him*) You bloody Dutch scum!

ROCKY (*Leans over the bar and stops* LEWIS *with a straight-arm swipe on the chest*) Cut it out!

(*At the same moment* CHUCK *grabs* WETJOEN *and yanks him back*)

WETJOEN (*Struggling*) Let him come! I saw them come before— at Modder River, Magersfontein, Spion Kopje—waving their silly swords, so afraid they couldn't show off how brave they vas!—and I kill them vith my rifle so easy! (*Vindictively*) Listen to me, you Cecil! Often vhen I am tronk and kidding you I say I am sorry I missed you, but now, py Gott, I am sober, and I don't joke, and I say it!

LARRY (*Gives a sardonic guffaw—with his comically crazy, intense whisper*) Be God, you can't say Hickey hasn't the miraculous touch to raise the dead, when he can start the Boer War raging again!

(*This interruption acts like a cold douche on* LEWIS *and* WETJOEN. *They subside, and* ROCKY *and* CHUCK *let go of them.* LEWIS *turns his back on the Boer*)

LEWIS (*Attempting a return of his jaunty manner, as if nothing had happened*) Well, time I was on my merry way to see my chap at the Consulate. The early bird catches the job, what? Good-bye and good luck, Rocky, and everyone.

(*He starts for the street door*)

WETJOEN Py Gott, if dot Limey can go, I can go!

(*He hurries after* LEWIS. *But* LEWIS, *his hand about to push the swinging doors open, hesitates, as though struck by a sudden paralysis of the will, and* WETJOEN *has to jerk back to avoid bumping into him. For a second they stand there, one behind the other, staring over the swinging doors into the street*)

ROCKY Well, why don't yuh beat it?

LEWIS (*Guiltily casual*) Eh? Oh, just happened to think. Hardly the decent thing to pop off without saying good-bye to old Harry. One of the best, Harry. And good old Jimmy, too. They ought to be down any moment. (*He pretends to notice* WETJOEN *for the first time and steps away from the door—apologizing as to a stranger*) Sorry. I seem to be blocking your way out.

WETJOEN (*Stiffly*) No. I vait to say good-bye to Harry and Jimmy, too.

(*He goes to right of door behind the lunch counter and looks through the window, his back to the room.* LEWIS *takes up a similar stand at the window on the left of door*)

CHUCK Jees, can yuh beat dem simps! (*He picks up* CORA's *drink at the end of the bar*) Hell, I'd forgot Cora. She'll be trowin' a fit. (*He goes into the hall with the drink*)

ROCKY (*Looks after him disgustedly*) Dat's right, wait on her and spoil her, yuh poor sap!

(*He shakes his head and begins to wipe the bar mechanically*)

WILLIE (*Is regarding* PARRITT *across the table from him with an eager, calculating eye. He leans over and speaks in a low confidential tone*) Look here, Parritt. I'd like to have a talk with you.

PARRITT (*Starts—scowling defensively*) What about?

WILLIE (*His manner becoming his idea of a crafty criminal lawyer's*) About the trouble you're in. Oh, I know. You don't admit it. You're quite right. That's my advice. Deny everything. Keep your mouth shut. Make no statements whatever without first consulting your attorney.

PARRITT Say! What the hell—?

WILLIE But you can trust me. I'm a lawyer, and it's just occurred to me you and I ought to co-operate. Of course I'm going to see the D.A. this morning about a job on his staff. But that may take time. There may not be an immediate opening. Meanwhile it would be a good idea for me to take a case or two, on my own, and prove my brilliant record in law school was no flash in the pan. So why not retain me as your attorney?

PARRITT You're crazy! What do I want with a lawyer?

WILLIE That's right. Don't admit anything. But you can trust me, so let's not beat about the bush. You got in trouble out on the Coast, eh? And now you're hiding out. Any fool can spot that. (*Lowering his voice still more*) You feel safe here, and maybe you are, for a while. But remember, they get you in the end. I know from my father's experience. No one could have felt safer than he did. When anyone mentioned the law to him, he nearly died laughing. But—

PARRITT You crazy mutt! (*Turning to* LARRY *with a strained laugh*) Did you get that, Larry? This damned fool thinks the cops are after me!

LARRY (*Bursts out with his true reaction before he thinks to ignore him*) I wish to God they were! And so should you, if you had the honor of a louse!

(PARRITT *stares into his eyes guiltily for a second. Then he smiles sneeringly*)

PARRITT And you're the guy who kids himself he's through with the Movement! You old lying faker, you're still in love with it!

(LARRY *ignores him again now*)

WILLIE (*Disappointedly*) Then you're not in trouble, Parritt? I was hoping— But never mind. No offense meant. Forget it.

PARRITT (*Condescendingly—his eyes on* LARRY) Sure. That's all right, Willie. I'm not sore at you. It's that damned old faker that gets my goat. (*He slips out of his chair and goes quietly over to sit in the chair beside* LARRY *he had occupied before—in a low, insinuating, intimate tone*) I think I understand, Larry. It's really Mother you still love—isn't it?—in spite of the dirty deal she gave you. But hell, what did you expect? She was never true to anyone but herself and the Movement. But I understand how you can't help still feeling—because I still love her, too. (*Pleading in a strained, desperate tone*) You know I do, don't you? You must! So you see I couldn't have expected they'd catch her! You've got to believe me that I sold them out just to get a few lousy dollars to blow in on a whore. No other reason, honest! There couldn't possibly be any other reason!

(*Again he has a strange air of exonerating himself from guilt by this shameless confession*)

LARRY (*Trying not to listen, has listened with increasing tension*) For the love of Christ will you leave me in peace! I've told you you can't make me judge you! But if you don't keep still, you'll be saying something soon that will make you vomit your own soul like a drink of nickel rotgut that won't stay down! (*He pushes back his chair and springs to his feet*) To hell with you! (*He goes to the bar*)

PARRITT (*Jumps up and starts to follow him—desperately*) Don't go, Larry! You've got to help me!

(*But* LARRY *is at the bar, back turned, and* ROCKY *is scowling at him. He stops, shrinking back into himself helplessly, and turns away. He goes to the table where he had been before, and this time he takes the chair at rear facing directly front. He puts his elbows on the table, holding his head in his hands as if he had a splitting headache*)

LARRY Set 'em up, Rocky. I swore I'd have no more drinks on

Hickey, if I died of drought, but I've changed my mind! Be God, he owes it to me, and I'd get blind to the world now if it was the Iceman of Death himself treating! (*He stops, startledly, a superstitious awe coming into his face*) What made me say that, I wonder. (*With a sardonic laugh*) Well, be God, it fits, for Death was the Iceman Hickey called to his home!

ROCKY   Aw, forget dat iceman gag! De poor dame is dead. (*Pushing a bottle and glass at* LARRY) Gwan and get paralyzed! I'll be glad to see one bum in dis dump act natural.

(LARRY *downs a drink and pours another.* ED MOSHER *appears in the doorway from the hall. The same change which is apparent in the manner and appearance of the others shows in him. He is sick, his nerves are shattered, his eyes are apprehensive, but he, too, puts on an exaggeratedly self-confident bearing. He saunters to the bar between* LARRY *and the street entrance*)

MOSHER   Morning, Rocky. Hello, Larry. Glad to see Brother Hickey hasn't corrupted you to temperance. I wouldn't mind a shot myself. (*As* ROCKY *shoves a bottle toward him he shakes his head*) But I remember the only breath-killer in this dump is coffee beans. The boss would never fall for that. No man can run a circus successfully who believes guys chew coffee beans because they like them. (*He pushes the bottle away*) No, much as I need one after the hell of a night I've had— (*He scowls*) That drummer son of a drummer! I had to lock him out. But I could hear him through the wall doing his spiel to someone all night long. Still at it with Jimmy and Harry when I came down just now. But the hardest to take was that flannel-mouth, flatfoot Mick trying to tell me where I got off! I had to lock him out, too.

(*As he says this,* MCGLOIN *comes in the doorway from the hall. The change in his appearance and manner is identical with that of* MOSHER *and the others*)

MCGLOIN   He's a liar, Rocky! It was me locked him out!

(MOSHER *starts to flare up—then ignores him. They turn their backs on each other.* MCGLOIN *starts into the back-room section*)

WILLIE   Come and sit here, Mac. You're just the man I want to see. If I'm to take your case, we ought to have a talk before we leave.

MCGLOIN   (*Contemptuously*)   We'll have no talk. You damned fool, do you think I'd have your father's son for my lawyer? They'd take one look at you and bounce us both out on our necks! (WILLIE *winces and shrinks down in his chair.* MCGLOIN *goes to the first table beyond him and sits with his back to the bar*) I don't need a lawyer, anyway. To hell with the law! All I've got to do is see the right ones and get them to pass the word. They will, too. They know I was framed. And once they've passed the word, it's as good as done, law or no law.

MOSHER God, I'm glad I'm leaving this madhouse! (*He pulls his key from his pocket and slaps it on the bar*) Here's my key, Rocky.

MCGLOIN (*Pulls his from his pocket*) And here's mine. (*He tosses it to* ROCKY) I'd rather sleep in the gutter than pass another night under the same roof with that loon, Hickey, and a lying circus grifter! (*He adds darkly*) And if that hat fits anyone here, let him put it on!

(MOSHER *turns toward him furiously but* ROCKY *leans over the bar and grabs his arm*)

ROCKY Nix! Take it easy! (MOSHER *subsides.* ROCKY *tosses the keys on the shelf—disgustedly*) You boids gimme a pain. It'd soive you right if I wouldn't give de keys back to yuh tonight.

(*They both turn on him resentfully, but there is an interruption as* CORA *appears in the doorway from the hall with* CHUCK *behind her. She is drunk, dressed in her gaudy best, her face plastered with rouge and mascara, her hair a bit disheveled, her hat on anyhow*)

CORA (*Comes a few steps inside the bar—with a strained bright giggle*) Hello, everybody! Here we go! Hickey just told us, ain't it time we beat it, if we're really goin'. So we're showin' de bastard, ain't we, Honey? He's comin' right down wid Harry and Jimmy. Jees, dem two look like dey was goin' to de electric chair! (*With frightened anger*) If I had to listen to any more of Hickey's bunk, I'd brain him. (*She puts her hand on* CHUCK's *arm*) Come on, Honey. Let's get started before he comes down.

CHUCK (*Sullenly*) Sure, anyting yuh say, Baby.

CORA (*Turns on him truculently*) Yeah? Well, I say we stop at de foist reg'lar dump and yuh gotta blow me to a sherry flip—or four or five, if I want 'em!—or all bets is off!

CHUCK Aw, yuh got a fine bun on now!

CORA Cheap skate! I know what's eatin' you, Tightwad! Well, use my dough, den, if yuh're so stingy. Yuh'll grab it all, anyway, right after de ceremony. I know you! (*She hikes her skirt up and reaches inside the top of her stocking*) Here, yuh big tramp!

CHUCK (*Knocks her hand away—angrily*) Keep your lousy dough! And don't show off your legs to dese bums when yuh're goin' to be married, if yuh don't want a sock in de puss!

CORA (*Pleased—meekly*) Aw right, Honey. (*Looking around with a foolish laugh*) Say, why don't all you barflies come to de weddin'? (*But they are all sunk in their own apprehensions and ignore her. She hesitates, miserably uncertain*) Well, we're goin', guys. (*There is no comment. Her eyes fasten on* ROCKY—*desperately*) Say, Rocky, yuh gone deef? I said me and Chuck was goin' now.

ROCKY (*Wiping the bar—with elaborate indifference*) Well, goodbye. Give my love to Joisey.

CORA (*Tearfully indignant*) Ain't yuh goin' to wish us happiness, yuh doity little Ginny?

ROCKY Sure. Here's hopin' yuh don't moider each odder before next week.

CHUCK (*Angrily*) Aw, Baby, what d'we care for dat pimp? (ROCKY *turns on him threateningly, but* CHUCK *hears someone upstairs in the hall and grabs* CORA'S *arm*) Here's Hickey comin'! Let's get outa here!

(*They hurry into the hall. The street door is heard slamming behind them*)

ROCKY (*Gloomily pronounces an obituary*) One regular guy and one all-right tart gone to hell. (*Fiercely*) Dat louse Hickey oughta be croaked!

(*There is a muttered growl of assent from most of the gathering. Then* HARRY HOPE *enters from the hall, followed by* JIMMY TOMORROW, *with* HICKEY *on his heels.* HOPE *and* JIMMY *are both putting up a front of self-assurance, but* CORA'S *description of them was apt. There is a desperate bluff in their manner as they walk in, which suggests the last march of the condemned.* HOPE *is dressed in an old black Sunday suit, black tie, shoes, socks, which give him the appearance of being in mourning.* JIMMY'S *clothes are pressed, his shoes shined, his white linen immaculate. He has a hangover and his gently appealing dog's eyes have a boiled look.* HICKEY'S *face is a bit drawn from lack of sleep and his voice is hoarse from continual talking, but his bustling energy appears nervously intensified, and his beaming expression is one of triumphant accomplishment*)

HICKEY Well, here we are! We've got this far, at least! (*He pats* JIMMY *on the back*) Good work, Jimmy. I told you you weren't half as sick as you pretended. No excuse whatever for postponing—

JIMMY I'll thank you to keep your hands off me! I merely mentioned I would feel more fit tomorrow. But it might as well be today, I suppose.

HICKEY   Finish it now, so it'll be dead forever, and you can be free! (*He passes him to clap* HOPE *encouragingly on the shoulder*) Cheer up, Harry. You found your rheumatism didn't bother you coming downstairs, didn't you? I told you it wouldn't. (*He winks around at the others. With the exception of* HUGO *and* PARRITT, *all their eyes are fixed on him with bitter animosity. He gives* HOPE *a playful nudge in the ribs*) You're the damnedest one for alibis, Governor! As bad as Jimmy!

HOPE   (*Putting on his deaf manner*) Eh? I can't hear— (*Defiantly*) You're a liar! I've had rheumatism on and off for twenty years. Ever since Bessie died. Everybody knows that.

HICKEY   Yes, we know it's the kind of rheumatism you turn on and off! We're on to you, you old faker!

(*He claps him on the shoulder again, chuckling*)

HOPE   (*Looks humiliated and guilty—by way of escape he glares around at the others*) Bejees, what are all you bums hanging round staring at me for? Think you was watching a circus! Why don't you get the hell out of here and 'tend to your own business, like Hickey's told you?

(*They look at him reproachfully, their eyes hurt. They fidget as if trying to move*)

HICKEY   Yes, Harry, I certainly thought they'd have had the guts to be gone by this time. (*He grins*) Or maybe I did have my doubts. (*Abruptly he becomes sincerely sympathetic and earnest*) Because I know exactly what you're up against, boys. I know how damned yellow a man can be when it comes to making himself face the truth. I've been through the mill, and I had to face a worse bastard in myself than any of you will have to in yourselves. I know you become such a coward you'll grab at any lousy excuse to get out of killing your pipe dreams. And yet, as I've told you over and over, it's exactly those damned tomorrow dreams which keep you from making peace with yourself. So you've got to kill them like I did mine. (*He pauses. They glare at him with fear and hatred. They seem about to curse him, to spring at him. But they remain silent and motionless. His manner changes and he becomes kindly bullying*) Come on, boys! Get moving! Who'll start the ball rolling? You, Captain, and you, General. You're nearest the door. And besides, you're old war heroes! You ought to lead the forlorn hope! Come on, now, show us a

little of that good old battle of Modder River spirit we've heard
so much about! You can't hang around all day looking as if you
were scared the street outside would bite you!

LEWIS (*Turns with humiliated rage—with an attempt at jaunty
casualness*) Right you are, Mister Bloody Nosey Parker! Time
I pushed off. Was only waiting to say good-bye to you, Harry,
old chum.

HOPE (*Dejectedly*) Good-bye, Captain. Hope you have luck.

LEWIS Oh, I'm bound to, Old Chap, and the same to you.
(*He pushes the swinging doors open and makes a brave exit,
turning to his right and marching off outside the window at right
of door*)

WETJOEN Py Gott, if dot Limey can, I can!
(*He pushes the door open and lumbers through it like a bull
charging an obstacle. He turns left and disappears off rear, outside the farthest window*)

HICKEY (*Exhortingly*) Next? Come on, Ed. It's a fine summer's
day and the call of the old circus lot must be in your blood!
(MOSHER *glares at him, then goes to the door.* MCGLOIN *jumps up
from his chair and starts moving toward the door.* HICKEY *claps
him on the back as he passes*) That's the stuff, Mac.

MOSHER Good-bye, Harry.
(*He goes out, turning right outside*)

MCGLOIN (*Glowering after him*) If that crooked grifter has the
guts—
(*He goes out, turning left outside.* HICKEY *glances at* WILLIE *who,
before he can speak, jumps from his chair*)

WILLIE Good-bye, Harry, and thanks for all your kindness.

HICKEY (*Claps him on the back*) That's the way, Willie! The D.A.'s
a busy man. He can't wait all day for you, you know.
(WILLIE *hurries to the door*)

HOPE (*Dully*) Good luck, Willie.
(WILLIE *goes out and turns right outside. While he is doing so,*
JIMMY, *in a sick panic, sneaks to the bar and furtively reaches for*
LARRY's *glass of whiskey*)

HICKEY And now it's your turn, Jimmy, old pal. (*He sees what*
JIMMY *is at and grabs his arm just as he is about to down the
drink*) Now, now, Jimmy! You can't do that to yourself. One drink
on top of your hangover and an empty stomach and you'll be
oreyeyed. Then you'll tell yourself you wouldn't stand a chance
if you went up soused to get your old job back.

JIMMY (*Pleads abjectly*) Tomorrow! I will tomorrow! I'll be in good shape tomorrow! (*Abruptly getting control of himself—with shaken firmness*) All right. I'm going. Take your hands off me.

HICKEY That's the ticket! You'll thank me when it's all over.

JIMMY (*In a burst of futile fury*) You dirty swine!

(*He tries to throw the drink in* HICKEY's *face, but his aim is poor and it lands on* HICKEY's *coat.* JIMMY *turns and dashes through the door, disappearing outside the window at right of door*)

HICKEY (*Brushing the whiskey off his coat—humorously*) All set for an alcohol rub! But no hard feelings. I know how he feels. I wrote the book. I've seen the day when if anyone forced me to face the truth about my pipe dreams, I'd have shot them dead. (*He turns to* HOPE—*encouragingly*) Well, Governor, Jimmy made the grade. It's up to you. If he's got the guts to go through with the test, then certainly you—

LARRY (*Bursts out*) Leave Harry alone, damn you!

HICKEY (*Grins at him*) I'd make up my mind about myself if I was you, Larry, and not bother over Harry. He'll come through all right. I've promised him that. He doesn't need anyone's bum pity. Do you, Governor?

HOPE (*With a pathetic attempt at his old fuming assertiveness*) No, bejees! Keep your nose out of this, Larry. What's Hickey got to do with it? I've always been going to take this walk, ain't I? Bejees, you bums want to keep me locked up in here 's if I was in jail! I've stood it long enough! I'm free, white and twenty-one, and I'll do as I damned please, bejees! You keep your nose out, too, Hickey! You'd think you was boss of this dump, not me. Sure, I'm all right! Why shouldn't I be? What the hell's to be scared of, just taking a stroll around my own ward? (*As he talks he has been moving toward the door. Now he reaches it*) What's the weather like outside, Rocky?

ROCKY Fine day, Boss.

HOPE What's that? Can't hear you. Don't look fine to me. Looks 's if it'd pour down cats and dogs any minute. My rheumatism— (*He catches himself*) No, must be my eyes. Half blind, bejees. Makes things look black. I see now it's a fine day. Too damned hot for a walk, though, if you ask me. Well, do me good to sweat the booze out of me. But I'll have to watch out for the damned automobiles. Wasn't none of them around the last time, twenty years ago. From what I've seen of 'em through the window, they'd run over you as soon as look at you. Not that I'm scared of 'em.

I can take care of myself. (*He puts a reluctant hand on the swinging door*) Well, so long— (*He stops and looks back—with frightened irascibility*) Bejees, where are you, Hickey? It's time we got started.

HICKEY (*Grins and shakes his head*) No, Harry. Can't be done. You've got to keep a date with yourself alone.

HOPE (*With forced fuming*) Hell of a guy, you are! Thought you'd be willing to help me across the street, knowing I'm half blind. Half deaf, too. Can't bear those damned automobiles. Hell with you! Bejees, I've never needed no one's help and I don't now! (*Egging himself on*) I'll take a good long walk now I've started. See all my old friends. Bejees, they must have given me up for dead. Twenty years is a long time. But they know it was grief over Bessie's death that made me— (*He puts his hand on the door*) Well, the sooner I get started— (*Then he drops his hand—with sentimental melancholy*) You know, Hickey, that's what gets me. Can't help thinking the last time I went out was to Bessie's funeral. After she'd gone, I didn't feel life was worth living. Swore I'd never go out again. (*Pathetically*) Somehow, I can't feel it's right for me to go, Hickey, even now. It's like I was doing wrong to her memory.

HICKEY Now, Governor, you can't let yourself get away with that one any more!

HOPE (*Cupping his hand to his ear*) What's that? Can't hear you. (*Sentimentally again but with desperation*) I remember now clear as day the last time before she— It was a fine Sunday morning. We went out to church together.

(*His voice breaks on a sob*)

HICKEY (*Amused*) It's a great act, Governor. But I know better, and so do you. You never did want to go to church or any place else with her. She was always on your neck, making you have ambition and go out and do things, when all you wanted was to get drunk in peace.

HOPE (*Falteringly*) Can't hear a word you're saying. You're a God-damned liar, anyway! (*Then in a sudden fury, his voice trembling with hatred*) Bejees, you son of a bitch, if there was a mad dog outside I'd go and shake hands with it rather than stay here with you!

(*The momentum of his fit of rage does it. He pushes the door open and strides blindly out into the street and as blindly past the window behind the free-lunch counter*)

ROCKY (*In amazement*) Jees, he made it! I'd a give yuh fifty to one he'd never— (*He goes to the end of the bar to look through the window—disgustedly*) Aw, he's stopped. I'll bet yuh he's comin' back.

HICKEY Of course, he's coming back. So are all the others. By tonight they'll all be here again. You dumbbell, that's the whole point.

ROCKY (*Excitedly*) No, he ain't neider! He's gone to de coib. He's lookin' up and down. Scared stiff of automobiles. Jees, dey ain't more'n two an hour comes down dis street, de old boob! (*He watches excitedly, as if it were a race he had a bet on, oblivious to what happens in the bar*)

LARRY (*Turns on* HICKEY *with bitter defiance*) And now it's my turn, I suppose? What is it I'm to do to achieve this blessed peace of yours?

HICKEY (*Grins at him*) Why, we've discussed all that, Larry. Just stop lying to yourself—

LARRY You think when I say I'm finished with life, and tired of watching the stupid greed of the human circus, and I'll welcome closing my eyes in the long sleep of death—you think that's a coward's lie?

HICKEY (*Chuckling*) Well, what do you think, Larry?

LARRY (*With increasing bitter intensity, more as if he were fighting with himself than with* HICKEY) I'm afraid to live, am I?—and even more afraid to die! So I sit here, with my pride drowned on the bottom of a bottle, keeping drunk so I won't see myself shaking in my britches with fright, or hear myself whining and praying: Beloved Christ, let me live a little longer at any price! If it's only for a few days more, or a few hours even, have mercy, Almighty God, and let me still clutch greedily to my yellow heart this sweet treasure, this jewel beyond price, the dirty, stinking bit of withered old flesh which is my beautiful little life! (*He laughs with a sneering, vindictive self-loathing, staring inward at himself with contempt and hatred. Then abruptly he makes* HICKEY *again the antagonist*) You think you'll make me admit that to myself?

HICKEY (*Chuckling*) But you just did admit it, didn't you?

PARRITT (*Lifts his head from his hands to glare at* LARRY—*jeeringly*) That's the stuff, Hickey! Show the old yellow faker up! He can't play dead on me like this! He's got to help me!

HICKEY Yes, Larry, you've got to settle with him. I'm leaving you entirely in his hands. He'll do as good a job as I could at making you give up that old grandstand bluff.

LARRY (*Angrily*) I'll see the two of you in hell first!

ROCKY (*Calls excitedly from the end of the bar*) Jees, Harry's startin' across de street! He's goin' to fool yuh, Hickey, yuh bastard! (*He pauses, watching—then worriedly*) What de hell's he stoppin' for? Right in de middle of de street! Yuh'd tink he was paralyzed or somethin'! (*Disgustedly*) Aw, he's quittin'! He's turned back! Jees, look at de old bastard travel! Here he comes! (*Hope passes the window outside the free-lunch counter in a shambling, panic-stricken run. He comes lurching blindly through the swinging doors and stumbles to the bar at* LARRY's *right*)

HOPE Bejees, give me a drink quick! Scared me out of a year's growth! Bejees, that guy ought to be pinched! Bejees, it ain't safe to walk in the streets! Bejees, that ends me! Never again! Give me that bottle! (*He slops a glass full and drains it and pours another— To* ROCKY, *who is regarding him with scorn—appealingly*) You seen it, didn't you, Rocky?

ROCKY Seen what?

HOPE That automobile, you dumb Wop! Feller driving it must be drunk or crazy. He'd run right over me if I hadn't jumped. (*Ingratiatingly*) Come on, Larry, have a drink. Everybody have a drink. Have a cigar, Rocky. I know you hardly ever touch it.

ROCKY (*Resentfully*) Well, dis is de time I do touch it! (*Pouring a drink*) I'm goin' to get stinko, see! And if yuh don't like it, yuh know what yuh can do! I gotta good mind to chuck my job, anyways. (*Disgustedly*) Jees, Harry, I thought yuh had some guts! I was bettin' yuh'd make it and show dat four-flusher up. (*He nods at* HICKEY—*then snorts*) Automobile, hell! Who d'yuh tink yuh're kiddin'? Dey wasn' no automobile! Yuh just quit cold!

HOPE (*Feebly*) Guess I ought to know! Bejees, it almost killed me!

HICKEY (*Comes to the bar between him and* LARRY, *and puts a hand on his shoulder—kindly*) Now, now, Governor. Don't be foolish. You've faced the test and come through. You're rid of all that nagging dream stuff now. You know you can't believe it any more.

HOPE (*Appeals pleadingly to* LARRY) Larry, you saw it, didn't you? Drink up! Have another! Have all you want! Bejees, we'll go on a grand old souse together! You saw that automobile, didn't you?

LARRY (*Compassionately, avoiding his eyes*) Sure, I saw it, Harry. You had a narrow escape. Be God, I thought you were a goner!

HICKEY (*Turns on him with a flash of sincere indignation*) What

the hell's the matter with you, Larry? You know what I told you
about the wrong kind of pity. Leave Harry alone! You'd think
I was trying to harm him, the fool way you act! My oldest friend!
What kind of a louse do you think I am? There isn't anything I
wouldn't do for Harry, and he knows it! All I've wanted to do is
fix it so he'll be finally at peace with himself for the rest of his
days! And if you'll only wait until the final returns are in, you'll
find that's exactly what I've accomplished! (*He turns to* HOPE *and
pats his shoulder—coaxingly*) Come now, Governor. What's the
use of being stubborn, now when it's all over and dead? Give
up that ghost automobile.

HOPE (*Beginning to collapse within himself—dully*) Yes, what's the
use—now? All a lie! No automobile. But, bejees, something ran
over me! Must have been myself, I guess. (*He forces a feeble
smile—then wearily*) Guess I'll sit down. Feel all in. Like a corpse,
bejees. (*He picks a bottle and glass from the bar and walks to the
first table and slumps down in the chair, facing left-front. His
shaking hand misjudges the distance and he sets the bottle on the
table with a jar that rouses* HUGO, *who lifts his head from his arms
and blinks at him through his thick spectacles.* HOPE *speaks to
him in a flat, dead voice*) Hello, Hugo. Coming up for air? Stay
passed out, that's the right dope. There ain't any cool willow trees
—except you grow your own in a bottle.

(*He pours a drink and gulps it down*)

HUGO (*With his silly giggle*) Hello, Harry, stupid proletarian
monkey-face! I vill trink champagne beneath the villow— (*With
a change to aristocratic fastidiousness*) But the slaves must ice it
properly! (*With guttural rage*) Gottamned Hickey! Peddler pimp
for nouveau-riche capitalism! Vhen I lead the jackass mob to the
sack of Babylon, I vill make them hang him to a lamppost the
first one!

HOPE (*Spiritlessly*) Good work. I'll help pull on the rope. Have a
drink, Hugo.

HUGO (*Frightenedly*) No, thank you. I am too trunk now. I hear
myself say crazy things. Do not listen, please. Larry vill tell you
I haf never been so crazy trunk. I must sleep it off. (*He starts to
put his head on his arms but stops and stares at* HOPE *with growing
uneasiness*) Vhat's matter, Harry? You look funny. You look dead.
Vhat's happened? I don't know you. Listen, I feel I am dying, too.
Because I am so crazy trunk! It is very necessary I sleep. But I
can't sleep here vith you. You look dead.

(*He scrambles to his feet in a confused panic, turns his back on* HOPE *and settles into the chair at the next table which faces left. He thrusts his head down on his arms like an ostrich hiding its head in the sand. He does not notice* PARRITT, *nor* PARRITT *him*)

LARRY (*To* HICKEY *with bitter condemnation*) Another one who's begun to enjoy your peace!

HICKEY Oh, I know it's tough on him right now, the same as it is on Harry. But that's only the first shock. I promise you they'll both come through all right.

LARRY And you believe that! I see you do! You mad fool!

HICKEY Of course, I believe it! I tell you I know from my own experience!

HOPE (*Spiritlessly*) Close that big clam of yours, Hickey. Bejees, you're a worse gabber than that nagging bitch, Bessie, was. (*He drinks his drink mechanically and pours another*)

ROCKY (*In amazement*) Jees, did yuh hear dat?

HOPE (*Dully*) What's wrong with this booze? There's no kick in it.

ROCKY (*Worriedly*) Jees, Larry, Hugo had it right. He does look like he'd croaked.

HICKEY (*Annoyed*) Don't be a damned fool! Give him time. He's coming along all right. (*He calls to* HOPE *with a first trace of underlying uneasiness*) You're all right, aren't you, Harry?

HOPE (*Dully*) I want to pass out like Hugo.

LARRY (*Turns to* HICKEY—*with bitter anger*) It's the peace of death you've brought him.

HICKEY (*For the first time loses his temper*) That's a lie! (*But he controls this instantly and grins*) Well, well, you did manage to get a rise out of me that time. I think such a hell of a lot of Harry— (*Impatiently*) You know that's damned foolishness. Look at me. I've been through it. Do I look dead? Just leave Harry alone and wait until the shock wears off and you'll see. He'll be a new man. Like I am. (*He calls to* HOPE *coaxingly*) How's it coming, Governor? Beginning to feel free, aren't you? Relieved and not guilty any more?

HOPE (*Grumbles spiritlessly*) Bejees, you must have been monkeying with the booze, too, you interfering bastard! There's no life in it now. I want to get drunk and pass out. Let's all pass out. Who the hell cares?

HICKEY (*Lowering his voice—worriedly to* LARRY) I admit I didn't think he'd be hit so hard. He's always been a happy-go-lucky slob. Like I was. Of course, it hit me hard, too. But only for a minute.

Then I felt as if a ton of guilt had been lifted off my mind. I saw what had happened was the only possible way for the peace of all concerned.

LARRY (*Sharply*) What was it happened? Tell us that! And don't try to get out of it! I want a straight answer! (*Vindictively*) I think it was something you drove someone else to do!

HICKEY (*Puzzled*) Someone else?

LARRY (*Accusingly*) What did your wife die of? You've kept that a deep secret, I notice—for some reason!

HICKEY (*Reproachfully*) You're not very considerate, Larry. But, if you insist on knowing now, there's no reason you shouldn't. It was a bullet through the head that killed Evelyn.

(*There is a second's tense silence*)

HOPE (*Dully*) Who the hell cares? To hell with her and that nagging old hag, Bessie.

ROCKY Christ. You had de right dope, Larry.

LARRY (*Revengefully*) You drove your poor wife to suicide? I knew it! Be God, I don't blame her! I'd almost do as much myself to be rid of you! It's what you'd like to drive us all to— (*Abruptly he is ashamed of himself and pitying*) I'm sorry, Hickey. I'm a rotten louse to throw that in your face.

HICKEY (*Quietly*) Oh, that's all right, Larry. But don't jump at conclusions. I didn't say poor Evelyn committed suicide. It's the last thing she'd ever have done, as long as I was alive for her to take care of and forgive. If you'd known her at all, you'd never get such a crazy suspicion. (*He pauses—then slowly*) No, I'm sorry to have to tell you my poor wife was killed.

(LARRY *stares at him with growing horror and shrinks back along the bar away from him.* PARRITT *jerks his head up from his hands and looks around frightenedly, not at* HICKEY, *but at* LARRY. ROCKY's *round eyes are popping.* HOPE *stares dully at the table top.* HUGO, *his head hidden in his arms, gives no sign of life*)

LARRY (*Shakenly*) Then she—was murdered.

PARRITT (*Springs to his feet—stammers defensively*) You're a liar, Larry! You must be crazy to say that to me! You know she's still alive!

(*But no one pays any attention to him*)

ROCKY (*Blurts out*) Moidered? Who done it?

LARRY (*His eyes fixed with fascinated horror on* HICKEY—*frightenedly*) Don't ask questions, you dumb Wop! It's none of our damned business! Leave Hickey alone!

HICKEY (*Smiles at him with affectionate amusement*) Still the old grandstand bluff, Larry? Or is it some more bum pity? (*He turns to* ROCKY—*matter-of-factly*) The police don't know who killed her yet, Rocky. But I expect they will before very long. (*As if that finished the subject, he comes forward to* HOPE *and sits beside him, with an arm around his shoulder—affectionately coaxing*) Coming along fine now, aren't you, Governor? Getting over the first shock? Beginning to feel free from guilt and lying hopes and at peace with yourself?

HOPE (*With a dull callousness*) Somebody croaked your Evelyn, eh? Bejees, my bets are on the iceman! But who the hell cares? Let's get drunk and pass out. (*He tosses down his drink with a lifeless, automatic movement—complainingly*) Bejees, what did you do to the booze, Hickey? There's no damned life left in it.

PARRITT (*Stammers, his eyes on* LARRY, *whose eyes in turn remain fixed on* HICKEY) Don't look like that, Larry! You've got to believe what I told you! It had nothing to do with her! It was just to get a few lousy dollars!

HUGO (*Suddenly raises his head from his arms and, looking straight in front of him, pounds on the table frightenedly with his small fists*) Don't be a fool! Buy me a trink! But no more vine! It is not properly iced! (*With guttural rage*) Gottamned stupid proletarian slaves! Buy me a trink or I vill have you shot! (*He collapses into abject begging*) Please, for Gott's sake! I am not trunk enough! I cannot sleep! Life is a crazy monkey-face! Always there is blood beneath the villow trees! I hate it and I am afraid! (*He hides his face on his arms, sobbing muffledly*) Please, I am crazy trunk! I say crazy things! For Gott's sake, do not listen to me!

(*But no one pays any attention to him.* LARRY *stands shrunk back against the bar.* ROCKY *is leaning over it. They stare at* HICKEY. PARRITT *stands looking pleadingly at* LARRY)

HICKEY (*Gazes with worried kindliness at* HOPE) You're beginning to worry me, Governor. Something's holding you up somewhere. I don't see why— You've faced the truth about yourself. You've done what you had to do to kill your nagging pipe dreams. Oh, I know it knocks you cold. But only for a minute. Then you see it was the only possible way to peace. And you feel happy. Like I did. That's what worries me about you, Governor. It's time you began to feel happy—

Curtain

ACT FOUR

SCENE: *Same as Act One—the back room with the curtain separating it from the section of the barroom with its single table at right of curtain, front. It is around half past one in the morning of the following day.*

The tables in the back room have a new arrangement. The one at left, front, before the window to the yard, is in the same position. So is the one at the right, rear, of it in the second row. But this table now has only one chair. This chair is at right of it, facing directly front. The two tables on either side of the door at rear are unchanged. But the table which was at center, front, has been pushed toward right so that it and the table at right, rear, of it in the second row, and the last table at right in the front row, are now jammed so closely together that they form one group.

LARRY, HUGO and PARRITT are at the table at left, front. LARRY is at left of it, beside the window, facing front. HUGO sits at rear, facing front, his head on his arms in his habitual position, but he is not asleep. On HUGO's left is PARRITT, his chair facing left, front. At right of table, an empty chair, facing left. LARRY's chin is on his chest, his eyes fixed on the floor. He will not look at PARRITT, who keeps staring at him with a sneering, pleading challenge.

Two bottles of whiskey are on each table, whiskey and chaser glasses, a pitcher of water.

The one chair by the table at right, rear, of them is vacant.

At the first table at right of center, CORA sits at left, front, of it, facing front. Around the rear of this table are four empty chairs. Opposite CORA, in a sixth chair, is CAPTAIN LEWIS, also facing front. On his left, MCGLOIN is facing front in a chair before the middle table of his group. At right, rear, of him, also at this table, GENERAL WETJOEN sits facing front. In back of this table are three empty chairs.

At right, rear, of WETJOEN, but beside the last table of the group, sits WILLIE. *On* WILLIE'S *left, at rear of table, is* HOPE. *On* HOPE'S *left, at right, rear, of table, is* MOSHER. *Finally, at right of table is* JIMMY TOMORROW. *All of the four sit facing front.*

There is an atmosphere of oppressive stagnation in the room, and a quality of insensibility about all the people in this group at right. They are like wax figures, set stiffly on their chairs, carrying out mechanically the motions of getting drunk but sunk in a numb stupor which is impervious to stimulation.

In the bar section, JOE *is sprawled in the chair at right of table, facing left. His head rolls forward in a sodden slumber.* ROCKY *is standing behind his chair, regarding him with dull hostility.* ROCKY'S *face is set in an expression of tired, callous toughness. He looks now like a minor Wop gangster.*

ROCKY (*Shakes* JOE *by the shoulder*) Come on, yuh damned nigger! Beat it in de back room! It's after hours. (*But* JOE *remains inert.* ROCKY *gives up*) Aw, to hell wid it. Let de dump get pinched. I'm through wid dis lousy job, anyway! (*He hears someone at rear and calls*) Who's dat? (CHUCK *appears from rear. He has been drinking heavily, but there is no lift to his jag; his manner is grouchy and sullen. He has evidently been brawling. His knuckles are raw and there is a mouse under one eye. He has lost his straw hat, his tie is awry, and his blue suit is dirty.* ROCKY *eyes him indifferently*) Been scrappin', huh? Started off on your periodical, ain't yuh?

(*For a second there is a gleam of satisfaction in his eyes*)

CHUCK Yeah, ain't yuh glad? (*Truculently*) What's it to yuh?

ROCKY Not a damn ting. But dis is someting to me. I'm out on my feet holdin' down your job. Yuh said if I'd take your day, yuh'd relieve me at six, and here it's half past one A.M. Well, yuh're takin' over now, get me, no matter how plastered yuh are!

CHUCK Plastered, hell! I wisht I was. I've lapped up a gallon, but it don't hit me right. And to hell wid de job. I'm goin' to tell Harry I'm quittin'.

ROCKY Yeah? Well, I'm quittin', too.

CHUCK I've played sucker for dat crummy blonde long enough, lettin' her kid me into woikin'. From now on I take it easy.

ROCKY I'm glad yuh're gettin' some sense.

CHUCK And I hope yuh're gettin' some. What a prize sap you been, tendin' bar when yuh got two good hustlers in your stable!

ROCKY Yeah, but I ain't no sap now. I'll loin dem, when dey get back from Coney. (*Sneeringly*) Jees, dat Cora sure played you for a dope, feedin' yuh dat marriage-on-de-farm hop!

CHUCK (*Dully*) Yeah. Hickey got it right. A lousy pipe dream. It was her pulling sherry flips on me woke me up. All de way walkin' to de ferry, every ginmill we come to she'd drag me in to blow her. I got tinkin', Christ, what won't she want when she gets de ring on her finger and I'm hooked? So I tells her at de ferry, "Kiddo, yuh can go to Joisey, or to hell, but count me out."

ROCKY She says it was her told you to go to hell, because yuh'd started hittin' de booze.

CHUCK (*Ignoring this*) I got tinkin', too, Jees, won't I look sweet wid a wife dat if yuh put all de guys she's stayed wid side by side, dey'd reach to Chicago. (*He sighs gloomily*) Dat kind of dame, yuh can't trust 'em. De minute your back is toined, dey're cheatin' wid de iceman or someone. Hickey done me a favor, makin' me wake up. (*He pauses—then adds pathetically*) On'y it was fun, kinda, me and Cora kiddin' ourselves— (*Suddenly his face hardens with hatred*) Where is dat son of a bitch, Hickey? I want one good sock at dat guy—just one!—and de next buttin' in he'll do will be in de morgue! I'll take a chance on goin' to de Chair—!

ROCKY (*Starts—in a low warning voice*) Piano! Keep away from him, Chuck! He ain't here now, anyway. He went out to phone, he said. He wouldn't call from here. I got a hunch he's beat it. But if he does come back, yuh don't know him, if anyone asks yuh, get me? (*As* CHUCK *looks at him with dull surprise he lowers his voice to a whisper*) De Chair, maybe dat's where he's goin'. I don't know nuttin', see, but it looks like he croaked his wife.

CHUCK (*With a flash of interest*) Yuh mean she really was cheatin' on him? Den I don't blame de guy—

ROCKY Who's blamin' him? When a dame asks for it— But I don't know nuttin' about it, see?

CHUCK Is any of de gang wise?

ROCKY Larry is. And de boss ought to be. I tried to wise de rest of dem up to stay clear of him, but dey're all so licked, I don't know if dey got it. (*He pauses—vindictively*) I don't give a damn what he done to his wife, but if he gets de Hot Seat I won't go into no mournin'!

CHUCK Me, neider!

ROCKY Not after his trowin' it in my face I'm a pimp. What if I am? Why de hell not? And what he's done to Harry. Jees, de poor old slob is so licked he can't even get drunk. And all de gang. Dey're all licked. I couldn't help feelin' sorry for de poor bums when dey showed up tonight, one by one, lookin' like pooches wid deir tails between deir legs, dat everyone'd been kickin' till dey was too punch-drunk to feel it no more. Jimmy Tomorrow was de last. Schwartz, de copper, brung him in. Seen him sittin' on de dock on West Street, lookin' at de water and cryin'! Schwartz thought he was drunk and I let him tink it. But he was cold sober. He was tryin' to jump in and didn't have de noive, I figgered it. Noive! Jees, dere ain't enough guts left in de whole gang to battle a mosquito!

CHUCK Aw, to hell wid 'em! Who cares? Gimme a drink. (ROCKY *pushes the bottle toward him apathetically*) I see you been hittin' de redeye, too.

ROCKY Yeah. But it don't do no good. I can't get drunk right. (CHUCK *drinks.* JOE *mumbles in his sleep.* CHUCK *regards him resentfully*) Dis doity dinge was able to get his snootful and pass out. Jees, even Hickey can't faze a nigger! Yuh'd tink he was fazed if yuh'd seen him come in. Stinko, and he pulled a gat and said he'd plug Hickey for insultin' him. Den he dropped it and begun to cry and said he wasn't a gamblin' man or a tough guy no more; he was yellow. He'd borrowed de gat to stick up someone, and den didn't have de guts. He got drunk panhandlin' drinks in nigger joints, I s'pose. I guess dey felt sorry for him.

CHUCK He ain't got no business in de bar after hours. Why don't yuh chuck him out?

ROCKY (*Apathetically*) Aw, to hell wid it. Who cares?

CHUCK (*Lapsing into the same mood*) Yeah. I don't.

JOE (*Suddenly lunges to his feet dazedly—mumbles in humbled apology*) Scuse me, White Boys. Scuse me for livin'. I don't want to be where I's not wanted.

(*He makes his way swayingly to the opening in the curtain at rear and tacks down to the middle table of the three at right, front. He feels his way around it to the table at its left and gets to the chair in back of* CAPTAIN LEWIS)

CHUCK (*Gets up—in a callous, brutal tone*) My pig's in de back room, ain't she? I wanna collect de dough I wouldn't take dis mornin', like a sucker, before she blows it.

(*He goes rear*)

ROCKY (*Getting up*) I'm comin', too. I'm trough woikin'. I ain't no lousy bartender.

(CHUCK *comes through the curtain and looks for* CORA *as* JOE *flops down in the chair in back of* CAPTAIN LEWIS)

JOE (*Taps* LEWIS *on the shoulder—servilely apologetic*) If you objects to my sittin' here, Captain, just tell me and I pulls my freight.

LEWIS No apology required, old chap. Anybody could tell you I should feel honored a bloody Kaffir would lower himself to sit beside me.

(JOE *stares at him with sodden perplexity—then closes his eyes.* CHUCK *comes forward to take the chair behind* CORA'S, *as* ROCKY *enters the back room and starts over toward* LARRY'S *table*)

CHUCK (*His voice hard*) I'm waitin', Baby. Dig!

CORA (*With apathetic obedience*) Sure. I been expectin' yuh. I got it all ready. Here. (*She passes a small roll of bills she has in her hand over her shoulder, without looking at him. He takes it, glances at it suspiciously, then shoves it in his pocket without a word of acknowledgment.* CORA *speaks with a tired wonder at herself rather than resentment toward him*) Jees, imagine me kiddin' myself I wanted to marry a drunken pimp.

CHUCK Dat's nuttin', Baby. Imagine de sap I'da been, when I can get your dough just as easy widout it!

ROCKY (*Takes the chair on* PARRITT'S *left, facing* LARRY—*dully*) Hello, Old Cemetery. (LARRY *doesn't seem to hear. To* PARRITT) Hello, Tightwad. You still around?

PARRITT (*Keeps his eyes on* LARRY—*in a jeeringly challenging tone*) Ask Larry! He knows I'm here, all right, although he's pretending not to! He'd like to forget I'm alive! He's trying to kid himself with that grandstand philosopher stuff! But he knows he can't get away with it now! He kept himself locked in his room until a while ago, alone with a bottle of booze, but he couldn't make it work! He couldn't even get drunk! He had to come out! There must have been something there he was even more scared to face than he is Hickey and me! I guess he got looking at the fire escape and thinking how handy it was, if he was really sick of life and only had the nerve to die! (*He pauses sneeringly.* LARRY'S *face has tautened, but he pretends he doesn't hear.* ROCKY *pays no attention. His head has sunk forward, and he stares at the table top, sunk in the same stupor as the other occupants of the room.* PARRITT *goes on, his tone becoming more insistent*) He's been thinking of me, too, Rocky. Trying to figure a way to get out of helping me! He doesn't want to be bothered understanding. But he does understand all right! He used to love her, too. So he thinks I ought to take a hop off the fire escape! (*He pauses.* LARRY's *hands on the table have clinched into fists, as his nails dig into his palms, but he remains silent.* PARRITT *breaks and starts pleading*) For God's sake, Larry, can't you say something? Hickey's got me all balled up. Thinking of what he must have done has got me so I don't know any more what I did or why. I can't go on like this! I've got to know what I ought to do—

LARRY (*In a stifled tone*) God damn you! Are you trying to make me your executioner?

PARRITT (*Starts frightenedly*) Execution? Then you do think—?

LARRY I don't think anything!

PARRITT (*With forced jeering*) I suppose you think I ought to die because I sold out a lot of loud-mouthed fakers, who were cheating suckers with a phony pipe dream, and put them where they ought to be, in jail? (*He forces a laugh*) Don't make me laugh! I ought to get a medal! What a damned old sap you are! You must still believe in the Movement! (*He nudges* ROCKY *with his elbow*) Hickey's right about him, isn't he, Rocky? An old no-good drunken tramp, as dumb as he is, ought to take a hop off the fire escape!

ROCKY (*Dully*) Sure. Why don't he? Or you? Or me? What de hell's de difference? Who cares? (*There is a faint stir from all the crowd, as if this sentiment struck a responsive chord in their numbed minds. They mumble almost in chorus as one voice, like sleepers talking out of a dully irritating dream,* "The hell with it!" "Who cares?" *Then the sodden silence descends again on the room.* ROCKY *looks from* PARRITT *to* LARRY *puzzledly. He mutters*) What am I doin' here wid youse two? I remember I had someting on my mind to tell yuh. What—? Oh, I got it now. (*He looks from one to the other of their oblivious faces with a strange, sly, calculating look—ingratiatingly*) I was tinking how you was bot' reg'lar guys. I tinks, ain't two guys like dem saps to be hangin' round like a coupla stew bums and wastin' demselves. Not dat I blame yuh for not woikin'. On'y suckers woik. But dere's no percentage in bein' broke when yuh can grab good jack for yourself and make someone else woik for yuh, is dere? I mean, like I do. So I tinks, Dey're my pals and I ought to wise up two good guys like dem to play my system, and not be lousy barflies, no good to demselves or nobody else. (*He addresses* PARRITT *now—persuasively*) What yuh tink, Parritt? Ain't I right? Sure, I am. So don't be a sucker, see? Yuh ain't a bad-lookin' guy. Yuh could easy make some gal who's a good hustler, an' start a stable. I'd help yuh and wise yuh up to de inside dope on de game. (*He pauses inquiringly.* PARRITT *gives no sign of having heard him.* ROCKY *asks impatiently*) Well, what about it? What if dey do call yuh a pimp? What de hell do you care—any more'n I do.

PARRITT (*Without looking at him—vindictively*) I'm through with whores. I wish they were all in jail—or dead!

ROCKY (*Ignores this—disappointedly*) So yuh won't touch it, huh? Aw right, stay a bum! (*He turns to* LARRY) Jees, Larry, he's sure one dumb boob, ain't he? Dead from de neck up! He don't know a good ting when he sees it. (*Oily, even persuasive again*) But how about you, Larry? You ain't dumb. So why not, huh? Sure, yuh're old, but dat don't matter. All de hustlers tink yuh're aces. Dey fall for yuh like yuh was deir uncle or old man or someting. Dey'd like takin' care of yuh. And de cops 'round here, dey like yuh, too. It'd be a pipe for yuh, 'specially wid me to help yuh and wise yuh up. Yuh wouldn't have to worry where de next drink's comin' from, or wear doity clothes. (*Hopefully*) Well, don't it look good to yuh?

LARRY (*Glances at him—for a moment he is stirred to sardonic pity*) No, it doesn't look good, Rocky. I mean, the peace Hickey's brought you. It isn't contented enough, if you have to make everyone else a pimp, too.

ROCKY (*Stares at him stupidly—then pushes his chair back and gets up, grumbling*) I'm a sap to waste time on yuh. A stew bum is a stew bum and yuh can't change him. (*He turns away—then turns back for an afterthought*) Like I was sayin' to Chuck, yuh better keep away from Hickey. If anyone asks yuh, yuh don't know nuttin', get me? Yuh never even hoid he had a wife. (*His face hardens*) Jees, we all ought to git drunk and stage a celebration when dat bastard goes to de Chair.

LARRY (*Vindictively*) Be God, I'll celebrate with you and drink long life to him in hell! (*Then guiltily and pityingly*) No! The poor mad devil— (*Then with angry self-contempt*) Ah, pity again! The wrong kind! He'll welcome the Chair!

PARRITT (*Contemptuously*) Yes, what are you so damned scared of death for? I don't want your lousy pity.

ROCKY Christ, I hope he don't come back, Larry. We don't know nuttin' now. We're on'y guessin', see? But if de bastard keeps on talkin'—

LARRY (*Grimly*) He'll come back. He'll keep on talking. He's got to. He's lost his confidence that the peace he's sold us is the real McCoy, and it's made him uneasy about his own. He'll have to prove to us—

(*As he is speaking* HICKEY *appears silently in the doorway at rear. He has lost his beaming salesman's grin. His manner is no longer self-assured. His expression is uneasy, baffled and resentful. It has the stubborn set of an obsessed determination. His eyes are on* LARRY *as he comes in. As he speaks, there is a start from all the crowd, a shrinking away from him*)

HICKEY (*Angrily*) That's a damned lie, Larry! I haven't lost confidence a damned bit! Why should I? (*Boastfully*) By God, whenever I made up my mind to sell someone something I knew they ought to want, I've sold 'em! (*He suddenly looks confused—haltingly*) I mean— It isn't kind of you, Larry, to make that kind of crack when I've been doing my best to help—

ROCKY (*Moving away from him toward right—sharply*) Keep away from me! I don't know nuttin' about yuh, see?

(*His tone is threatening but his manner as he turns his back and ducks quickly across to the bar entrance is that of one in flight. In the bar he comes forward and slumps in a chair at the table, facing front*)

HICKEY (*Comes to the table at right, rear, of* LARRY's *table and sits in the one chair there, facing front. He looks over the crowd at right, hopefully and then disappointedly. He speaks with a strained attempt at his old affectionate jollying manner*) Well, well! How are you coming along, everybody? Sorry I had to leave you for a while, but there was something I had to get finally settled. It's all fixed now.

HOPE (*In the voice of one reiterating mechanically a hopeless complaint*) When are you going to do something about this booze, Hickey? Bejees, we all know you did something to take the life out of it. It's like drinking dishwater! We can't pass out! And you promised us peace.

(*His group all join in in a dull, complaining chorus, "We can't pass out! You promised us peace!"*)

HICKEY (*Bursts into resentful exasperation*) For God's sake, Harry, are you still harping on that damned nonsense! You've kept it up all afternoon and night! And you've got everybody else singing the same crazy tune! I've had about all I can stand— That's why I phoned— (*He controls himself*) Excuse me, boys and girls. I don't mean that. I'm just worried about you, when you play dead

on me like this. I was hoping by the time I got back you'd be like
you ought to be! I thought you were deliberately holding back,
while I was around, because you didn't want to give me the satisfaction of showing me I'd had the right dope. And I did have! I
know from my own experience. (*Exasperatedly*) But I've explained that a million times! And you've all done what you
needed to do! By rights you should be contented now, without a
single damned hope or lying dream left to torment you! But here
you are, acting like a lot of stiffs cheating the undertaker! (*He
looks around accusingly*) I can't figure it—unless it's just your
damned pigheaded stubbornness! (*He breaks—miserably*) Hell,
you oughtn't to act this way with me! You're my old pals, the only
friends I've got. You know the one thing I want is to see you all
happy before I go— (*Rousing himself to his old brisk, master-of-
ceremonies manner*) And there's damned little time left now. I've
made a date for two o'clock. We've got to get busy right away and
find out what's wrong. (*There is a sodden silence. He goes on
exasperatedly*) Can't you appreciate what you've got, for God's
sake? Don't you know you're free now to be yourselves, without
having to feel remorse or guilt, or lie to yourselves about reform-
ing tomorrow? Can't you see there is no tomorrow now? You're
rid of it forever! You've killed it! You don't have to care a damn
about anything any more! You've finally got the game of life
licked, don't you see that? (*Angrily exhorting*) Then why the hell
don't you get pie-eyed and celebrate? Why don't you laugh and
sing "Sweet Adeline"? (*With bitterly hurt accusation*) The only
reason I can think of is, you're putting on this rotten half-dead act
just to get back at me! Because you hate my guts! (*He breaks
again*) God, don't do that, gang! It makes me feel like hell to
think you hate me. It makes me feel you suspect I must have
hated you. But that's a lie! Oh, I know I used to hate everyone
in the world who wasn't as rotten a bastard as I was! But that was
when I was still living in hell—before I faced the truth and saw
the one possible way to free poor Evelyn and give her the peace
she'd always dreamed about.

(*He pauses. Everyone in the group stirs with awakening dread
and they all begin to grow tense on their chairs*)

CHUCK (*Without looking at* HICKEY—*with dull, resentful viciousness*)
Aw, put a bag over it! To hell wid Evelyn! What if she was
cheatin'? And who cares what yuh did to her? Dat's your funeral.
We don't give a damn, see? (*There is a dull, resentful chorus of*

assent, "We don't give a damn." CHUCK *adds dully*) All we want outa you is keep de hell away from us and give us a rest.

(*A muttered chorus of assent*)

HICKEY (*As if he hadn't heard this—an obsessed look on his face*) The one possible way to make up to her for all I'd made her go through, and get her rid of me so I couldn't make her suffer any more, and she wouldn't have to forgive me again! I saw I couldn't do it by killing myself, like I wanted to for a long time. That would have been the last straw for her. She'd have died of a broken heart to think I could do that to her. She'd have blamed herself for it, too. Or I couldn't just run away from her. She'd have died of grief and humiliation if I'd done that to her. She'd have thought I'd stopped loving her. (*He adds with a strange impressive simplicity*) You see, Evelyn loved me. And I loved her. That was the trouble. It would have been easy to find a way out if she hadn't loved me so much. Or if I hadn't loved her. But as it was, there was only one possible way. (*He pauses—then adds simply*) I had to kill her.

(*There is a second's dead silence as he finishes—then a tense indrawn breath like a gasp from the crowd, and a general shrinking movement*)

LARRY (*Bursts out*) You mad fool, can't you keep your mouth shut! We may hate you for what you've done here this time, but we remember the old times, too, when you brought kindness and laughter with you instead of death! We don't want to know things that will make us help send you to the Chair!

PARRITT (*With angry scorn*) Ah, shut up, you yellow faker! Can't you face anything? Wouldn't I deserve the Chair, too, if I'd— It's worse if you kill someone and they have to go on living. I'd be glad of the Chair! It'd wipe it out! It'd square me with myself!

HICKEY (*Disturbed—with a movement of repulsion*) I wish you'd get rid of that bastard, Larry. I can't have him pretending there's something in common between him and me. It's what's in your heart that counts. There was love in my heart, not hate.

PARRITT (*Glares at him in angry terror*) You're a liar! I don't hate her! I couldn't! And it had nothing to do with her, anyway! You ask Larry!

LARRY (*Grabs his shoulder and shakes him furiously*) God damn you, stop shoving your rotten soul in my lap!

(PARRITT *subsides, hiding his face in his hands and shuddering*)

HICKEY (*Goes on quietly now*) Don't worry about the Chair, Larry.

I know it's still hard for you not to be terrified by death, but when
you've made peace with yourself, like I have, you won't give a
damn. (*He addresses the group at right again—earnestly*) Listen,
everybody. I've made up my mind the only way I can clear things
up for you, so you'll realize how contented and carefree you ought
to feel, now I've made you get rid of your pipe dreams, is to show
you what a pipe dream did to me and Evelyn. I'm certain if I tell
you about it from the beginning, you'll appreciate what I've done
for you and why I did it, and how damned grateful you ought to
be—instead of hating me. (*He begins eagerly in a strange running
narrative manner*) You see, even when we were kids, Evelyn and
me—

HOPE (*Bursts out, pounding with his glass on the table*) No! Who
the hell cares? We don't want to hear it. All we want is to pass
out and get drunk and a little peace!

(*They are all, except* LARRY *and* PARRITT, *seized by the same fit
and pound with their glasses, even* HUGO, *and* ROCKY *in the bar,
and shout in chorus, "Who the hell cares? We want to pass out!"*)

HICKEY (*With an expression of wounded hurt*) All right, if that's
the way you feel. I don't want to cram it down your throats. I
don't need to tell anyone. I don't feel guilty. I'm only worried
about you.

HOPE   What did you do to this booze? That's what we'd like to hear.
Bejees, you done something. There's no life or kick in it now. (*He
appeals mechanically to* JIMMY TOMORROW) Ain't that right,
Jimmy?

JIMMY (*More than any of them, his face has a wax-figure blankness
that makes it look embalmed. He answers in a precise, completely
lifeless voice, but his reply is not to* HARRY's *question, and he does
not look at him or anyone else*) Yes. Quite right. It was all a
stupid lie—my nonsense about tomorrow. Naturally, they would
never give me my position back. I would never dream of asking
them. It would be hopeless. I didn't resign. I was fired for drunkenness. And that was years ago. I'm much worse now. And it
was absurd of me to excuse my drunkenness by pretending it was
my wife's adultery that ruined my life. As Hickey guessed, I was
a drunkard before that. Long before. I discovered early in life
that living frightened me when I was sober. I have forgotten
why I married Marjorie. I can't even remember now if she was
pretty. She was a blonde, I think, but I couldn't swear to it. I had
some idea of wanting a home, perhaps. But, of course, I much

preferred the nearest pub. Why Marjorie married me, God knows. It's impossible to believe she loved me. She soon found I much preferred drinking all night with my pals to being in bed with her. So, naturally, she was unfaithful. I didn't blame her. I really didn't care. I was glad to be free—even grateful to her, I think, for giving me such a good tragic excuse to drink as much as I damned well pleased.

(*He stops like a mechanical doll that has run down. No one gives any sign of having heard him. There is a heavy silence. Then* ROCKY, *at the table in the bar, turns grouchily as he hears a noise behind him. Two men come quietly forward. One,* MORAN, *is middle-aged. The other,* LIEB, *is in his twenties. They look ordinary in every way, without anything distinctive to indicate what they do for a living*)

ROCKY (*Grumpily*) In de back room if yuh wanta drink.

(MORAN *makes a peremptory sign to be quiet. All of a sudden* ROCKY *senses they are detectives and springs up to face them, his expression freezing into a wary blankness.* MORAN *pulls back his coat to show his badge*)

MORAN (*In a low voice*) Guy named Hickman in the back room?

ROCKY Tink I know de names of all de guys—?

MORAN Listen, you! This is murder. And don't be a sap. It was Hickman himself phoned in and said we'd find him here around two.

ROCKY (*Dully*) So dat's who he phoned to. (*He shrugs his shoulders*) Aw right, if he asked for it. He's de fat guy sittin' alone. (*He slumps down in his chair again*) And if yuh want a confession all yuh got to do is listen. He'll be tellin' all about it soon. Yuh can't stop de bastard talkin'.

(MORAN *gives him a curious look, then whispers to* LIEB, *who disappears rear and a moment later appears in the hall doorway of the back room. He spots* HICKEY *and slides into a chair at the left of the doorway, cutting off escape by the hall.* MORAN *goes back and stands in the opening in the curtain leading to the back room. He sees* HICKEY *and stands watching him and listening*)

HICKEY (*Suddenly bursts out*) I've got to tell you! Your being the way you are now gets my goat! It's all wrong! It puts things in my mind—about myself. It makes me think, if I got balled up about you, how do I know I wasn't balled up about myself? And that's plain damned foolishness. When you know the story of me and Evelyn, you'll see there wasn't any other possible way out of

it, for her sake. Only I've got to start way back at the beginning
or you won't understand. (*He starts his story, his tone again
becoming musingly reminiscent*) You see, even as a kid I was always restless. I had to keep on the go. You've heard the old saying, "Ministers' sons are sons of guns." Well, that was me, and then
some. Home was like a jail. I didn't fall for the religious bunk.
Listening to my old man whooping up hell fire and scaring those
Hoosier suckers into shelling out their dough only handed me a
laugh, although I had to hand it to him, the way he sold them
nothing for something. I guess I take after him, and that's what
made me a good salesman. Well, anyway, as I said, home was
like jail, and so was school, and so was that damned hick town.
The only place I liked was the pool rooms, where I could smoke
Sweet Caporals, and mop up a couple of beers, thinking I was a
hell-on-wheels sport. We had one hooker shop in town, and, of
course, I liked that, too. Not that I hardly ever had entrance
money. My old man was a tight old bastard. But I liked to sit
around in the parlor and joke with the girls, and they liked me
because I could kid 'em along and make 'em laugh. Well, you
know what a small town is. Everyone got wise to me. They all
said I was a no-good tramp. I didn't give a damn what they said.
I hated everybody in the place. That is, except Evelyn. I loved
Evelyn. Even as a kid. And Evelyn loved me.
(*He pauses. No one moves or gives any sign except by the dread
in their eyes that they have heard him. Except* PARRITT, *who takes
his hands from his face to look at* LARRY *pleadingly*)
PARRITT   I loved Mother, Larry! No matter what she did! I still do!
Even though I know she wishes now I was dead! You believe
that, don't you? Christ, why can't you say something?
HICKEY (*Too absorbed in his story now to notice this—goes on in a
tone of fond, sentimental reminiscence*) Yes, sir, as far back as
I can remember, Evelyn and I loved each other. She always stuck
up for me. She wouldn't believe the gossip—or she'd pretend she
didn't. No one could convince her I was no good. Evelyn was
stubborn as all hell once she'd made up her mind. Even when I'd
admit things and ask her forgiveness, she'd make excuses for me
and defend me against myself. She'd kiss me and say she knew I
didn't mean it and I wouldn't do it again. So I'd promise I
wouldn't. I'd have to promise, she was so sweet and good, though
I knew darned well— (*A touch of strange bitterness comes into
his voice for a moment*) No, sir, you couldn't stop Evelyn. Noth-

ing on earth could shake her faith in me. Even I couldn't. She was
a sucker for a pipe dream. (*Then quickly*) Well, naturally, her
family forbid her seeing me. They were one of the town's best,
rich for that hick burg, owned the trolley line and lumber company. Strict Methodists, too. They hated my guts. But they
couldn't stop Evelyn. She'd sneak notes to me and meet me on
the sly. I was getting more restless. The town was getting more
like a jail. I made up my mind to beat it. I knew exactly what I
wanted to be by that time. I'd met a lot of drummers around the
hotel and liked 'em. They were always telling jokes. They were
sports. They kept moving. I liked their life. And I knew I could
kid people and sell things. The hitch was how to get the railroad
fare to the Big Town. I told Mollie Arlington my trouble. She
was the madame of the cathouse. She liked me. She laughed and
said, "Hell, I'll stake you, Kid! I'll bet on you. With that grin of
yours and that line of bull, you ought to be able to sell skunks for
good ratters!" (*He chuckles*) Mollie was all right. She gave me
confidence in myself. I paid her back, the first money I earned.
Wrote her a kidding letter, I remember, saying I was peddling
baby carriages and she and the girls had better take advantage
of our bargain offer. (*He chuckles*) But that's ahead of my story.
The night before I left town, I had a date with Evelyn. I got all
worked up, she was so pretty and sweet and good. I told her
straight, "You better forget me, Evelyn, for your own sake. I'm no
good and never will be. I'm not worthy to wipe your shoes." I
broke down and cried. She just said, looking white and scared,
"Why, Teddy? Don't you still love me?" I said, "Love you? God,
Evelyn, I love you more than anything in the world. And I always
will!" She said, "Then nothing else matters, Teddy, because nothing but death could stop my loving you. So I'll wait, and when
you're ready you send for me and we'll be married. I know I can
make you happy, Teddy, and once you're happy you won't want
to do any of the bad things you've done any more." And I said,
"Of course, I won't, Evelyn!" I meant it, too. I believed it. I loved
her so much she could make me believe anything.

(*He sighs. There is a suspended, waiting silence. Even the two
detectives are drawn into it. Then* HOPE *breaks into dully exasperated, brutally callous protest*)

HOPE   Get it over, you long-winded bastard! You married her, and
you caught her cheating with the iceman, and you croaked her,
and who the hell cares? What's she to us? All we want is to pass

out in peace, bejees! (*A chorus of dull, resentful protest from all the group. They mumble, like sleepers who curse a person who keeps awakening them,* "What's it to us? We want to pass out in peace!" HOPE *drinks and they mechanically follow his example. He pours another and they do the same. He complains with a stupid, nagging insistence*) No life in the booze! No kick! Dishwater. Bejees, I'll never pass out!

HICKEY (*Goes on as if there had been no interruption*) So I beat it to the Big Town. I got a job easy, and it was a cinch for me to make good. I had the knack. It was like a game, sizing people up quick, spotting what their pet pipe dreams were, and then kidding 'em along that line, pretending you believed what they wanted to believe about themselves. Then they liked you, they trusted you, they wanted to buy something to show their gratitude. It was fun. But still, all the while I felt guilty, as if I had no right to be having such a good time away from Evelyn. In each letter I'd tell her how I missed her, but I'd keep warning her, too. I'd tell her all my faults, how I liked my booze every once in a while, and so on. But there was no shaking Evelyn's belief in me, or her dreams about the future. After each letter of hers, I'd be as full of faith as she was. So as soon as I got enough saved to start us off, I sent for her and we got married. Christ, wasn't I happy for a while! And wasn't she happy! I don't care what anyone says, I'll bet there never was two people who loved each other more than me and Evelyn. Not only then but always after, in spite of everything I did— (*He pauses—then sadly*) Well, it's all there, at the start, everything that happened afterwards. I never could learn to handle temptation. I'd want to reform and mean it. I'd promise Evelyn, and I'd promise myself, and I'd believe it. I'd tell her, it's the last time. And she'd say, "I know it's the last time, Teddy. You'll never do it again." That's what made it so hard. That's what made me feel such a rotten skunk—her always forgiving me. My playing around with women, for instance. It was only a harmless good time to me. Didn't mean anything. But I'd know what it meant to Evelyn. So I'd say to myself, never again. But you know how it is, traveling around. The damned hotel rooms. I'd get seeing things in the wall paper. I'd get bored as hell. Lonely and homesick. But at the same time sick of home. I'd feel free and I'd want to celebrate a little. I never drank on the job, so it had to be dames. Any tart. What I'd want was some tramp I could be myself with without being ashamed—someone I could tell a dirty joke to and she'd laugh.

CORA (*With a dull, weary bitterness*) Jees, all de lousy jokes I've had to listen to and pretend was funny!

HICKEY (*Goes on obliviously*) Sometimes I'd try some joke I thought was a corker on Evelyn. She'd always make herself laugh. But I could tell she thought it was dirty, not funny. And Evelyn always knew about the tarts I'd been with when I came home from a trip. She'd kiss me and look in my eyes, and she'd know. I'd see in her eyes how she was trying not to know, and then telling herself even if it was true, he couldn't help it, they tempt him, and he's lonely, he hasn't got me, it's only his body, anyway, he doesn't love them, I'm the only one he loves. She was right, too. I never loved anyone else. Couldn't if I wanted to. (*He pauses*) She forgave me even when it all had to come out in the open. You know how it is when you keep taking chances. You may be lucky for a long time, but you get nicked in the end. I picked up a nail from some tart in Altoona.

CORA (*Dully, without resentment*) Yeah. And she picked it up from some guy. It's all in de game. What de hell of it?

HICKEY I had to do a lot of lying and stalling when I got home. It didn't do any good. The quack I went to got all my dough and then told me I was cured and I took his word. But I wasn't, and poor Evelyn— But she did her best to make me believe she fell for my lie about how traveling men get things from drinking cups on trains. Anyway, she forgave me. The same way she forgave me every time I'd turn up after a periodical drunk. You all know what I'd be like at the end of one. You've seen me. Like something lying in the gutter that no alley cat would lower itself to drag in—something they threw out of the D.T. ward in Bellevue along with the garbage, something that ought to be dead and isn't! (*His face is convulsed with self-loathing*) Evelyn wouldn't have heard from me in a month or more. She'd have been waiting there alone, with the neighbors shaking their heads and feeling sorry for her out loud. That was before she got me to move to the outskirts, where there weren't any next-door neighbors. And then the door would open and in I'd stumble—looking like what I've said—into her home, where she kept everything so spotless and clean. And I'd sworn it would never happen again, and now I'd have to start swearing again this was the last time. I could see disgust having a battle in her eyes with love. Love always won. She'd make herself kiss me, as if nothing had happened, as if I'd just come home from a business trip. She'd never complain or bawl me out. (*He bursts out in a tone of anguish that has anger and hatred beneath it*) Christ, can you imagine what a guilty skunk she made me feel! If she'd only admitted once she didn't believe any more in her pipe dream that some day I'd behave! But she never would. Evelyn was stubborn as hell. Once she'd set her heart on anything, you couldn't shake her faith that it had to come true—tomorrow! It was the same old story, over and over, for years and years. It kept piling up, inside her and inside me. God, can you picture all I made her suffer, and all the guilt she made me feel, and how I hated myself! If she only hadn't been so damned good—if she'd been the same kind of wife I was a husband. God, I used to pray sometimes she'd—I'd even say to her, "Go on, why don't you, Evelyn? It'd serve me right. I wouldn't mind. I'd forgive you." Of course, I'd pretend I was kidding—the same way I used to joke here about her being in the hay with the iceman. She'd have been so hurt if I'd said it seriously. She'd have thought I'd stopped loving her. (*He pauses—then looking around at them*) I suppose you think I'm a liar, that no woman could have stood all she stood and still loved me so much—that it isn't human for any woman to be so pitying and forgiving. Well, I'm not lying, and if you'd ever seen her, you'd realize I wasn't. It was written all over her face, sweetness and love and pity and forgiveness. (*He reaches mechanically for the inside pocket of his coat*) Wait! I'll show you. I always carry her picture. (*Suddenly he looks startled. He stares before him, his hand falling back—quietly*) No, I'm forgetting I tore it up—afterwards. I didn't need it any more.

(*He pauses. The silence is like that in the room of a dying man where people hold their breath, waiting for him to die*)

CORA (*With a muffled sob*)   Jees, Hickey! Jees!

(*She shivers and puts her hands over her face*)

PARRITT (*To* LARRY *in a low insistent tone*)   I burnt up Mother's picture, Larry. Her eyes followed me all the time. They seemed to be wishing I was dead!

HICKEY   It kept piling up, like I've said. I got so I thought of it all the time. I hated myself more and more, thinking of all the wrong I'd done to the sweetest woman in the world who loved me so much. I got so I'd curse myself for a lousy bastard every time I saw myself in the mirror. I felt such pity for her it drove me crazy. You wouldn't believe a guy like me, that's knocked around so much, could feel such pity. It got so every night I'd wind up hiding my face in her lap, bawling and begging her forgiveness. And, of course, she'd always comfort me and say, "Never mind, Teddy, I know you won't ever again." Christ, I loved her so, but I began to hate that pipe dream! I began to be afraid I was going bughouse, because sometimes I couldn't forgive her for forgiving me. I even caught myself hating her for making me hate myself so much. There's a limit to the guilt you can feel and the forgiveness and the pity you can take! You have to begin blaming someone else, too. I got so sometimes when she'd kiss me it was like she did it on purpose to humiliate me, as if she'd spit in my face! But all the time I saw how crazy and rotten of me that was, and it made me hate myself all the more. You'd never believe I could hate so much, a good-natured, happy-go-lucky slob like me. And as the time got nearer to when I was due to come here for my drunk around Harry's birthday, I got nearly crazy. I kept swearing to her every night that this time I really wouldn't, until I'd made it a real final test to myself—and to her. And she kept encouraging me and saying, "I can see you really mean it now, Teddy. I know you'll conquer it this time, and we'll be so happy, dear." When she'd say that and kiss me, I'd believe it, too. Then she'd go to bed, and I'd stay up alone because I couldn't sleep and I didn't want to disturb her, tossing and rolling around. I'd get so damned lonely. I'd get thinking how peaceful it was here, sitting around with the old gang, getting drunk and forgetting love, joking and laughing and singing and swapping lies. And finally I knew I'd have to come. And I knew if I came this time, it was the finish. I'd never have the guts to go back and be forgiven again, and that would break Evelyn's heart because to her it would mean I didn't love her any more. (*He pauses*) That last night I'd driven myself crazy trying to figure some way out for her. I went in the bedroom. I was going to tell her it was the end. But I couldn't do that to her. She was sound asleep. I thought, God, if she'd only never wake up, she'd never know! And then it came to me—the only possible way out, for her sake. I remembered I'd given her a gun for protection while I was away and it was in the bureau drawer. She'd never feel any pain, never wake up from her dream. So I—

HOPE (*Tries to ward this off by pounding with his glass on the table —with brutal, callous exasperation*) Give us a rest, for the love of Christ! Who the hell cares? We want to pass out in peace!

(*They all, except* PARRITT *and* LARRY, *pound with their glasses and grumble in chorus:* "Who the hell cares? We want to pass out in peace!" MORAN, *the detective, moves quietly from the entrance in the curtain across the back of the room to the table where his companion,* LIEB, *is sitting.* ROCKY *notices his leaving and gets up from the table in the rear and goes back to stand and watch in the entrance.* MORAN *exchanges a glance with* LIEB, *motioning him to get up. The latter does so. No one notices them. The clamor of banging glasses dies out as abruptly as it started.* HICKEY *hasn't appeared to hear it*)

HICKEY (*Simply*) So I killed her.

(*There is a moment of dead silence. Even the detectives are caught in it and stand motionless*)

PARRITT (*Suddenly gives up and relaxes limply in his chair—in a low voice in which there is a strange exhausted relief*) I may as well confess, Larry. There's no use lying any more. You know, anyway. I didn't give a damn about the money. It was because I hated her.

HICKEY (*Obliviously*) And then I saw I'd always known that was the only possible way to give her peace and free her from the misery of loving me. I saw it meant peace for me, too, knowing she was at peace. I felt as though a ton of guilt was lifted off my mind. I remember I stood by the bed and suddenly I had to laugh. I couldn't help it, and I knew Evelyn would forgive me. I remember I heard myself speaking to her, as if it was something I'd always wanted to say: "Well, you know what you can do with your pipe dream now, you damned bitch!" (*He stops with a horrified start, as if shocked out of a nightmare, as if he couldn't believe he heard what he had just said. He stammers*) No I never—!

PARRITT (*To* LARRY—*sneeringly*) Yes, that's it! Her and the damned old Movement pipe dream! Eh, Larry?

HICKEY (*Bursts into frantic denial*) No! That's a lie! I never said—! Good God, I couldn't have said that! If I did, I'd gone insane! Why, I loved Evelyn better than anything in life! (*He appeals brokenly to the crowd*) Boys, you're all my old pals! You've known old Hickey for years! You know I'd never— (*His eyes fix on* HOPE) You've known me longer than anyone, Harry. You know I must have been insane, don't you, Governor?

HOPE (*At first with the same defensive callousness—without looking at him*) Who the hell cares? (*Then suddenly he looks at* HICKEY *and there is an extraordinary change in his expression. His face lights up, as if he were grasping at some dawning hope in his mind. He speaks with a groping eagerness*) Insane? You mean—you went really insane?

(*At the tone of his voice, all the group at the tables by him start and stare at him as if they caught his thought. Then they all look at* HICKEY *eagerly, too*)

HICKEY   Yes! Or I couldn't have laughed! I couldn't have said that to her!

(MORAN *walks up behind him on one side, while the second detective,* LIEB, *closes in on him from the other*)

MORAN   (*Taps* HICKEY *on the shoulder*) That's enough, Hickman. You know who we are. You're under arrest. (*He nods to* LIEB, *who slips a pair of handcuffs on* HICKEY's *wrists.* HICKEY *stares at them with stupid incomprehension.* MORAN *takes his arm*) Come along and spill your guts where we can get it on paper.

HICKEY   No, wait, Officer! You owe me a break! I phoned and made it easy for you, didn't I? Just a few minutes! (*To* HOPE—*pleadingly*) You know I couldn't say that to Evelyn, don't you, Harry—unless—

HOPE   (*Eagerly*) And you've been crazy ever since? Everything you've said and done here—

HICKEY   (*For a moment forgets his own obsession and his face takes on its familiar expression of affectionate amusement and he chuckles*) Now, Governor! Up to your old tricks, eh? I see what you're driving at, but I can't let you get away with— (*Then, as* HOPE's *expression turns to resentful callousness again and he looks away, he adds hastily with pleading desperation*) Yes, Harry, of course, I've been out of my mind ever since! All the time I've been here! You saw I was insane, didn't you?

MORAN   (*With cynical disgust*) Can it! I've had enough of your act. Save it for the jury. (*Addressing the crowd, sharply*) Listen, you guys. Don't fall for his lies. He's starting to get foxy now and thinks he'll plead insanity. But he can't get away with it.

(*The crowd at the grouped tables are grasping at* HOPE *now. They glare at him resentfully*)

HOPE   (*Begins to bristle in his old-time manner*) Bejees, you dumb dick, you've got a crust trying to tell us about Hickey! We've known him for years, and every one of us noticed he was nutty the minute he showed up here! Bejees, if you'd heard all the crazy bull he was pulling about bringing us peace—like a bughouse preacher escaped from an asylum! If you'd seen all the damned-fool things he made us do! We only did them because— (*He hesitates—then defiantly*) Because we hoped he'd come out of it if we kidded him along and humored him. (*He looks around at the others*) Ain't that right, fellers?

(*They burst into a chorus of eager assent: "Yes, Harry!" "That's it, Harry!" "That's why!" "We knew he was crazy!" "Just to humor him!"*)

MORAN   A fine bunch of rats! Covering up for a dirty, cold-blooded murderer.

HOPE (*Stung into recovering all his old fuming truculence*)   Is that so? Bejees, you know the old story, when Saint Patrick drove the snakes out of Ireland they swam to New York and joined the police force! Ha! (*He cackles insultingly*) Bejees, we can believe it now when we look at you, can't we, fellers? (*They all growl assent, glowering defiantly at* MORAN. MORAN *glares at them, looking as if he'd like to forget his prisoner and start cleaning out the place.* HOPE *goes on pugnaciously*) You stand up for your rights, bejees, Hickey! Don't let this smart-aleck dick get funny with you. If he pulls any rubber-hose tricks, you let me know! I've still got friends at the Hall! Bejees, I'll have him back in uniform pounding a beat where the only graft he'll get will be stealing tin cans from the goats!

MORAN (*Furiously*)   Listen, you cockeyed old bum, for a plugged nickel I'd— (*Controlling himself, turns to* HICKEY, *who is oblivious to all this, and yanks his arm*) Come on, you!

HICKEY (*With a strange mad earnestness*)   Oh, I want to go, Officer. I can hardly wait now. I should have phoned you from the house right afterwards. It was a waste of time coming here. I've got to explain to Evelyn. But I know she's forgiven me. She knows I was insane. You've got me all wrong, Officer. I want to go to the Chair.

MORAN   Crap!

HICKEY (*Exasperatedly*)   God, you're a dumb dick! Do you suppose I give a damn about life now? Why, you bonehead, I haven't got a single damned lying hope or pipe dream left!

MORAN (*Jerks him around to face the door to the hall*)   Get a move on!

HICKEY (*As they start walking toward rear—insistently*)   All I want you to see is I was out of my mind afterwards, when I laughed at her! I was a raving rotten lunatic or I couldn't have said— Why,

Evelyn was the only thing on God's earth I ever loved! I'd have killed myself before I'd ever have hurt her!

(*They disappear in the hall.* HICKEY's *voice keeps on protesting*)

HOPE (*Calls after him*) Don't worry, Hickey! They can't give you the Chair! We'll testify you was crazy! Won't we, fellers? (*They all assent. Two or three echo* HOPE's *"Don't worry, Hickey." Then from the hall comes the slam of the street door.* HOPE's *face falls— with genuine sorrow*) He's gone. Poor crazy son of a bitch! (*All the group around him are sad and sympathetic, too.* HOPE *reaches for his drink*) Bejees, I need a drink. (*They grab their glasses.* HOPE *says hopefully*) Bejees, maybe it'll have the old kick, now he's gone.

(*He drinks and they follow suit*)

ROCKY (*Comes forward from where he has stood in the bar entrance —hopefully*) Yeah, Boss, maybe we can get drunk now.

(*He sits in the chair by* CHUCK *and pours a drink and tosses it down. Then they all sit still, waiting for the effect, as if this drink were a crucial test, so absorbed in hopeful expectancy that they remain oblivious to what happens at* LARRY's *table*)

LARRY (*His eyes full of pain and pity—in a whisper, aloud to himself*) May the Chair bring him peace at last, the poor tortured bastard!

PARRITT (*Leans toward him—in a strange low insistent voice*) Yes, but he isn't the only one who needs peace, Larry. I can't feel sorry for him. He's lucky. He's through, now. It's all decided for him. I wish it was decided for me. I've never been any good at deciding things. Even about selling out, it was the tart the detective agency got after me who put it in my mind. You remember what Mother's like, Larry. She makes all the decisions. She's always decided what I must do. She doesn't like anyone to be free but herself. (*He pauses, as if waiting for comment, but* LARRY *ignores him*) I suppose you think I ought to have made those dicks take me away with Hickey. But how could I prove it, Larry? They'd think I was nutty. Because she's still alive. You're the only one who can understand how guilty I am. Because you know her and what I've done to her. You know I'm really much guiltier than he is. You know what I did is a much worse murder. Because she is dead and yet she has to live. For a while. But she can't live long in jail. She loves freedom too much. And I can't kid myself like Hickey, that she's at peace. As long as she lives, she'll never be able to forget what I've done to her even in her sleep. She'll never have a second's peace. (*He pauses—then bursts out*) Jesus, Larry, can't you say something? (LARRY *is at the breaking point.* PARRITT *goes on*) And I'm not putting up any bluff, either, that I was crazy afterwards when I laughed to myself and thought, "You know what you can do with your freedom pipe dream now, don't you, you damned old bitch!"

LARRY (*Snaps and turns on him, his face convulsed with detestation. His quivering voice has a condemning command in it*) Go! Get the hell out of life, God damn you, before I choke it out of you! Go up—!

PARRITT (*His manner is at once transformed. He seems suddenly at peace with himself. He speaks simply and gratefully*) Thanks, Larry. I just wanted to be sure. I can see now it's the only possible way I can ever get free from her. I guess I've really known that all my life. (*He pauses—then with a derisive smile*) It ought to comfort Mother a little, too. It'll give her the chance to play the great incorruptible Mother of the Revolution, whose only child is the Proletariat. She'll be able to say: "Justice is done! So may all traitors die!" She'll be able to say: "I am glad he's dead! Long live the Revolution!" (*He adds with a final implacable jeer*) You know her, Larry! Always a ham!

LARRY (*Pleads distractedly*) Go, for the love of Christ, you mad tortured bastard, for your own sake!

(HUGO *is roused by this. He lifts his head and peers uncomprehendingly at* LARRY. *Neither* LARRY *nor* PARRITT *notices him*)

PARRITT (*Stares at* LARRY. *His face begins to crumble as if he were going to break down and sob. He turns his head away, but reaches out fumblingly and pats* LARRY's *arm and stammers*) Jesus, Larry, thanks. That's kind. I knew you were the only one who could understand my side of it.

(*He gets to his feet and turns toward the door*)

HUGO (*Looks at* PARRITT *and bursts into his silly giggle*) Hello, leedle Don, leedle monkey-face! Don't be a fool! Buy me a trink!

PARRITT (*Puts on an act of dramatic bravado—forcing a grin*) Sure, I will, Hugo! Tomorrow! Beneath the willow trees!

(*He walks to the door with a careless swagger and disappears in the hall. From now on,* LARRY *waits, listening for the sound he knows is coming from the backyard outside the window, but trying not to listen, in an agony of horror and cracking nerve*)

HUGO (*Stares after* PARRITT *stupidly*) Stupid fool! Hickey make you crazy, too. (*He turns to the oblivious* LARRY—*with a timid eagerness*) I'm glad, Larry, they take that crazy Hickey avay to asylum. He makes me have bad dreams. He makes me tell lies about myself. He makes me want to spit on all I have ever dreamed. Yes, I am glad they take him to asylum. I don't feel I am dying now. He vas selling death to me, that crazy salesman. I think I have a trink now, Larry.

(*He pours a drink and gulps it down*)

HOPE (*Jubilantly*) Bejees, fellers, I'm feeling the old kick, or I'm a liar! It's putting life back in me! Bejees, if all I've lapped up begins to hit me, I'll be paralyzed before I know it! It was Hickey kept it from— Bejees, I know that sounds crazy, but he was crazy, and he'd got all of us as bughouse as he was. Bejees, it does queer things to you, having to listen day and night to a lunatic's pipe dreams—pretending you believe them, to kid him along and doing any crazy thing he wants to humor him. It's dangerous, too. Look at me pretending to start for a walk just to keep him quiet. I knew damned well it wasn't the right day for it. The sun was broiling and the streets full of automobiles. Bejees, I could feel myself getting sunstroke, and an automobile damn near ran over me. (*He appeals to* ROCKY, *afraid of the result, but daring it*) Ask Rocky. He was watching. Didn't it, Rocky?

ROCKY (*A bit tipsily*) What's dat, Boss? Jees, all de booze I've mopped up is beginning to get to me. (*Earnestly*) De automobile, Boss? Sure, I seen it! Just missed yuh! I thought yuh was a goner. (*He pauses—then looks around at the others, and assumes the old kidding tone of the inmates, but hesitantly, as if still a little afraid*) On de woid of a honest bartender!

(*He tries a wink at the others. They all respond with smiles that are still a little forced and uneasy*)

HOPE (*Flashes him a suspicious glance. Then he understands—with his natural testy manner*) You're a bartender, all right. No one can say different. (ROCKY *looks grateful*) But, bejees, don't pull that honest junk! You and Chuck ought to have cards in the Burglars' Union! (*This time there is an eager laugh from the group.* HOPE *is delighted*) Bejees, it's good to hear someone laugh again! All the time that bas— poor old Hickey was here, I didn't have the heart— Bejees, I'm getting drunk and glad of it! (*He cackles and reaches for the bottle*) Come on, fellers. It's on the house. (*They pour drinks. They begin rapidly to get drunk now.* HOPE *becomes sentimental*) Poor old Hickey! We mustn't hold him responsible for anything he's done. We'll forget that and only

remember him the way we've always known him before—the
kindest, biggest-hearted guy ever wore shoe leather. (*They all
chorus hearty sentimental assent: "That's right, Harry!" "That's
all!" "Finest fellow!" "Best scout!" etc.* HOPE *goes on*) Good luck to
him in Matteawan! Come on, bottoms up!
(*They all drink. At the table by the window* LARRY's *hands grip
the edge of the table. Unconsciously his head is inclined toward
the window as he listens*)

LARRY (*Cannot hold back an anguished exclamation*)   Christ! Why
don't he—!

HUGO (*Beginning to be drunk again—peers at him*)   Vhy don't he
what? Don't be a fool! Hickey's gone. He vas crazy. Have a trink.
(*Then as he receives no reply—with vague uneasiness*) What's
matter vith you, Larry? You look funny. What you listen to out in
backyard, Larry?
(CORA *begins to talk in the group at right*)

CORA (*Tipsily*)   Well, I thank Gawd now me and Chuck did all
we could to humor de poor nut. Jees, imagine us goin' off like we
really meant to git married, when we ain't even picked out a
farm yet!

CHUCK (*Eagerly*)   Sure ting, Baby. We kidded him we was serious.

JIMMY (*Confidently—with a gentle, drunken unction*)   I may as
well say I detected his condition almost at once. All that talk of
his about tomorrow, for example. He had the fixed idea of the
insane. It only makes them worse to cross them.

WILLIE (*Eagerly*)   Same with me, Jimmy. Only I spent the day in
the park. I wasn't such a damned fool as to—

LEWIS (*Getting jauntily drunk*)   Picture my predicament if I *had*
gone to the Consulate. The pal of mine there is a humorous
blighter. He would have got me a job out of pure spite. So I
strolled about and finally came to roost in the park. (*He grins
with affectionate kidding at* WETJOEN) And lo and behold, who
was on the neighboring bench but my old battlefield companion,
the Boer that walks like a man—who, if the British Government
had taken my advice, would have been removed from his fetid
kraal on the veldt straight to the baboon's cage at the London
Zoo, and little children would now be asking their nurses: "Tell
me, Nana, is that the Boer General, the one with the blue behind?"
(*They all laugh uproariously.* LEWIS *leans over and slaps* WET-
JOEN *affectionately on the knee*) No offense meant, Piet, old chap.

WETJOEN (*Beaming at him*)   No offense taken, you tamned Limey!

(WETJOEN *goes on—grinningly*) About a job, I felt the same as you, Cecil.

(*At the table by the window* HUGO *speaks to* LARRY *again*)

HUGO (*With uneasy insistence*) What's matter, Larry? You look scared. What you listen for out there?

(*But* LARRY *doesn't hear, and* JOE *begins talking in the group at right*)

JOE (*With drunken self-assurance*)   No, suh, I wasn't fool enough to git in no crap game. Not while Hickey's around. Crazy people puts a jinx on you.

(MCGLOIN *is now heard. He is leaning across in front of* WETJOEN *to talk to* ED MOSHER *on* HOPE's *left*)

MCGLOIN (*With drunken earnestness*)   I know you saw how it was, Ed. There was no good trying to explain to a crazy guy, but it ain't the right time. You know how getting reinstated is.

MOSHER (*Decidedly*)   Sure, Mac. The same way with the circus. The boys tell me the rubes are wasting all their money buying food and times never was so hard. And I never was one to cheat for chicken feed.

HOPE (*Looks around him in an ecstasy of bleary sentimental content*)   Bejees, I'm cockeyed! Bejees, you're all cockeyed! Bejees, we're all all right! Let's have another!

(*They pour out drinks. At the table by the window* LARRY *has unconsciously shut his eyes as he listens.* HUGO *is peering at him frightenedly now*)

HUGO (*Reiterates stupidly*)   What's matter, Larry? Why you keep eyes shut? You look dead. What you listen for in backyard? (*Then, as* LARRY *doesn't open his eyes or answer, he gets up hastily and moves away from the table, mumbling with frightened anger*) Crazy fool! You vas crazy like Hickey! You give me bad dreams, too.

(*He shrinks quickly past the table where* HICKEY *had sat to the rear of the group at right*)

ROCKY (*Greets him with boisterous affection*)   Hello, dere, Hugo! Welcome to de party!

HOPE   Yes, bejees, Hugo! Sit down! Have a drink! Have ten drinks, bejees!

HUGO (*Forgetting* LARRY *and bad dreams, gives his familiar giggle*) Hello, leedle Harry! Hello, nice, leedle, funny monkey-faces! (*Warming up, changes abruptly to his usual declamatory denunciation*) Gottamned stupid bourgeois! Soon comes the Day of

Judgment! (*They make derisive noises and tell him to sit down. He changes again, giggling good-naturedly, and sits at rear of the middle table*) Give me ten trinks, Harry. Don't be a fool.

(*They laugh.* ROCKY *shoves a glass and bottle at him. The sound of* MARGIE's *and* PEARL's *voices is heard from the hall, drunkenly shrill. All of the group turn toward the door as the two appear. They are drunk and look blowsy and disheveled. Their manner as they enter hardens into a brazen defensive truculence*)

MARGIE (*Stridently*)   Gangway for two good whores!

PEARL   Yeah! And we want a drink quick!

MARGIE (*Glaring at* ROCKY)   Shake de lead outa your pants, Pimp! A little soivice!

ROCKY (*His black bullet eyes sentimental, his round Wop face grinning welcome*)   Well, look who's here! (*He goes to them unsteadily, opening his arms*) Hello, dere, Sweethearts! Jees, I was beginnin' to worry about yuh, honest!

(*He tries to embrace them. They push his arms away, regarding him with amazed suspicion*)

PEARL   What kind of a gag is dis?

HOPE (*Calls to them effusively*)   Come on and join the party, you broads! Bejees, I'm glad to see you!

(*The girls exchange a bewildered glance, taking in the party and the changed atmosphere*)

MARGIE   Jees, what's come off here?

PEARL   Where's dat louse, Hickey?

ROCKY   De cops got him. He'd gone crazy and croaked his wife. (*The girls exclaim, "Jees!" But there is more relief than horror in it.* ROCKY *goes on*) He'll get Matteawan. He ain't responsible. What he's pulled don't mean nuttin'. So forget dat whore stuff. I'll knock de block off anyone calls you whores! I'll fill de bastard full of lead! Yuh're tarts, and what de hell of it? Yuh're as good as anyone! So forget it, see?

(*They let him get his arms around them now. He gives them a hug. All the truculence leaves their faces. They smile and exchange maternally amused glances*)

MARGIE (*With a wink*)   Our little bartender, ain't he, Poil?

PEARL   Yeah, and a cute little Ginny at dat!

(*They laugh*)

MARGIE   And is he stinko!

PEARL   Stinko is right. But he ain't got nuttin' on us. Jees, Rocky, did we have a big time at Coney!

HOPE Bejees, sit down, you dumb broads! Welcome home! Have a drink! Have ten drinks, bejees! (*They take the empty chairs on* CHUCK's *left, warmly welcomed by all.* ROCKY *stands in back of them, a hand on each of their shoulders, grinning with proud proprietorship.* HOPE *beams over and under his crooked spectacles with the air of a host whose party is a huge success, and rambles on happily*) Bejees, this is all right! We'll make this my birthday party, and forget the other. We'll get paralyzed! But who's missing? Where's the Old Wise Guy? Where's Larry?

ROCKY Over by de window, Boss. Jees, he's got his eyes shut. De old bastard's asleep (*They turn to look.* ROCKY *dismisses him*) Aw, to hell wid him. Let's have a drink.

(*They turn away and forget him*)

LARRY (*Torturedly arguing to himself in a shaken whisper*) It's the only way out for him! For the peace of all concerned, as Hickey said! (*Snapping*) God damn his yellow soul, if he doesn't soon, I'll go up and throw him off!—like a dog with its guts ripped out you'd put out of misery!

(*He half rises from his chair just as from outside the window comes the sound of something hurtling down, followed by a muffled, crunching thud.* LARRY *gasps and drops back on his chair, shuddering, hiding his face in his hands. The group at right hear it but are too preoccupied with drinks to pay much attention*)

HOPE (*Wonderingly*) What the hell was that?

ROCKY Aw, nuttin'. Someting fell off de fire escape. A mattress, I'll bet. Some of dese bums been sleepin' on de fire escapes.

HOPE (*His interest diverted by this excuse to beef—testily*) They've got to cut it out! Bejees, this ain't a fresh-air cure. Mattresses cost money.

MOSHER Now don't start crabbing at the party, Harry. Let's drink up.

(HOPE *forgets it and grabs his glass, and they all drink*)

LARRY (*In a whisper of horrified pity*) Poor devil! (*A long-forgotten faith returns to him for a moment and he mumbles*) God rest his soul in peace. (*He opens his eyes—with a bitter self-derision*) Ah, the damned pity—the wrong kind, as Hickey said! Be God, there's no hope! I'll never be a success in the grandstand —or anywhere else! Life is too much for me! I'll be a weak fool looking with pity at the two sides of everything till the day I die! (*With an intense bitter sincerity*) May that day come soon! (*He pauses startledly, surprised at himself—then with a sardonic grin*)

Be God, I'm the only real convert to death Hickey made here.
From the bottom of my coward's heart I mean that now!

HOPE (*Calls effusively*) Hey there, Larry! Come over and get paralyzed! What the hell you doing, sitting there? (*Then as* LARRY
*doesn't reply he immediately forgets him and turns to the party.
They are all very drunk now, just a few drinks ahead of the
passing-out stage, and hilariously happy about it*) Bejees, let's
sing! Let's celebrate! It's my birthday party! Bejees, I'm oreyeyed!
I want to sing!

(*He starts the chorus of "She's the Sunshine of Paradise Alley,"
and instantly they all burst into song. But not the same song. Each
starts the chorus of his or her choice.* JIMMY TOMORROW's *is "A
Wee Dock and Doris";* ED MOSHER's, *"Break the News to Mother";*
WILLIE OBAN's, *the Sailor Lad ditty he sang in Act One;* GENERAL
WETJOEN's, *"Waiting at the Church";* MCGLOIN's, *"Tammany";* CAP-
TAIN LEWIS's, *"The Old Kent Road";* JOE's, *All I Got Was Sympathy";* PEARL's *and* MARGIE's, *"Everybody's Doing It";* ROCKY's,
"You Great Big Beautiful Doll"; CHUCK's, *"The Curse of an Aching
Heart";* CORA's, *"The Oceana Roll"; while* HUGO *jumps to his feet
and, pounding on the table with his fist, bellows in his guttural
basso the French Revolutionary "Carmagnole." A weird cacoph-
ony results from this mixture and they stop singing to roar with
laughter. All but* HUGO, *who keeps on with drunken fervor*)

HUGO

Dansons la Carmagnole!
Vive le son! Vive le son!
Dansons la Carmagnole!
Vive le son des canons!

(*They all turn on him and howl him down with amused derision.
He stops singing to denounce them in his most fiery style*) Capitalist svine! Stupid bourgeois monkeys! (*He declaims*) "The days
grow hot, O Babylon!" (*They all take it up and shout in enthusiastic jeering chorus*) "'Tis cool beneath thy willow trees!"

(*They pound their glasses on the table, roaring with laughter,
and* HUGO *giggles with them. In his chair by the window,* LARRY
stares in front of him, oblivious to their racket)

Curtain

A Streetcar Named Desire

BY

Tennessee Williams

A STREETCAR NAMED DESIRE *was presented at the Barrymore Theatre in New York on December 3, 1947, by Irene Selznick. It was directed by Elia Kazan, with the following cast:*

NEGRO WOMAN	*Gee Gee James*
EUNICE HUBBELL	*Peg Hillias*
STANLEY KOWALSKI	*Marlon Brando*
STELLA KOWALSKI	*Kim Hunter*
STEVE HUBBELL	*Rudy Bond*
HAROLD MITCHELL (MITCH)	*Karl Malden*
MEXICAN WOMAN	*Edna Thomas*
BLANCHE DUBOIS	*Jessica Tandy*
PABLO GONZALES	*Nick Dennis*
A YOUNG COLLECTOR	*Vito Christi*
NURSE	*Ann Dere*
DOCTOR	*Richard Garrick*

Scenery and lighting by Jo Meilziner, costumes by Lucinda Ballard. The action of the play takes place in the spring, summer, and early fall in New Orleans. It was performed with intermissions after Scene Four and Scene Six.

Assistant to the Producer, Irving Schneider
Musical Advisor, Lehman Engel

———————

And so it was I entered the broken world
To trace the visionary company of love, its voice
An instant in the wind (I know not whither hurled)
But not for long to hold each desperate choice.

"The Broken Tower" *by* HART CRANE

SCENE ONE

The exterior of a two-story corner building on a street in New Orleans which is named Elysian Fields and runs between the L & N tracks and the river. The section is poor but, unlike corresponding sections in other American cities, it has a raffish charm. The houses are mostly white frame, weathered grey, with rickety outside stairs and galleries and quaintly ornamented gables. This building contains two flats, upstairs and down. Faded white stairs ascend to the entrances of both.

It is first dark of an evening early in May. The sky that shows around the dim white building is a peculiarly tender blue, almost a turquoise, which invests the scene with a kind of lyricism and gracefully attenuates the atmosphere of decay. You can almost feel the warm breath of the brown river beyond the river warehouses with their faint redolences of bananas and coffee. A corresponding air is evoked by the music of Negro entertainers at a barroom around the corner. In this part of New Orleans you are practically always just around the corner, or a few doors down the street, from a tinny piano being played with the infatuated fluency of brown fingers. This "Blue Piano" expresses the spirit of the life which goes on here.

Two women, one white and one colored, are taking the air on the steps of the building. The white woman is EUNICE, *who occupies the upstairs flat; the colored woman a neighbor, for New Orleans is a cosmopolitan city where there is a relatively warm and easy intermingling of races in the old part of town.*

Above the music of the "Blue Piano" the voices of people on the street can be heard overlapping.

(Two men come around the corner, STANLEY KOWALSKI *and* MITCH. *They are about twenty-eight or thirty years old, roughly dressed in blue denim work clothes.* STANLEY *carries his bowling jacket and a red-stained package from a butcher's. They stop at the foot of the steps)*

STANLEY (*Bellowing*)   Hey, there! Stella, Baby!

(STELLA *comes out on the first floor landing, a gentle young woman, about twenty-five, and of a background obviously quite different from her husband's*)

STELLA (*Mildly*)   Don't holler at me like that. Hi, Mitch.

STANLEY   Catch!

STELLA   What?

STANLEY   Meat!

(*He heaves the package at her. She cries out in protest but manages to catch it: then she laughs breathlessly. Her husband and his companion have already started back around the corner*)

STELLA (*Calling after him*)   Stanley! Where are you going?

STANLEY   Bowling!

STELLA   Can I come watch?

STANLEY   Come on.

(*He goes out*)

STELLA   Be over soon. (*To the white woman*) Hello, Eunice. How are you?

EUNICE   I'm all right. Tell Steve to get him a poor boy's sandwich 'cause nothing's left here.

(*They all laugh; the colored woman does not stop.* STELLA *goes out*)

COLORED WOMAN   What was that package he th'ew at 'er?

(*She rises from steps, laughing louder*)

EUNICE   You hush, now!

NEGRO WOMAN   Catch *what!*

(*She continues to laugh.* BLANCHE *comes around the corner, carrying a valise. She looks at a slip of paper, then at the building, then again at the slip and again at the building. Her expression is one of shocked disbelief. Her appearance is incongruous to this setting. She is daintily dressed in a white suit with a fluffy bodice, necklace and earrings of pearl, white gloves and hat, looking as if she were arriving at a summer tea or cocktail party in the garden district. She is about five years older than Stella. Her delicate beauty must avoid a strong light. There is something about her uncertain manner, as well as her white clothes, that suggests a moth*)

EUNICE (*Finally*)   What's the matter, honey? Are you lost?

BLANCHE (*With faintly hysterical humor*)   They told me to take a street-car named Desire, and then transfer to one called Cemeteries and ride six blocks and get off at—Elysian Fields!

EUNICE That's where you are now.

BLANCHE At Elysian Fields?

EUNICE This here is Elysian Fields.

BLANCHE They mustn't have—understood—what number I wanted . . .

EUNICE What number you lookin' for?

(BLANCHE *wearily refers to the slip of paper*)

BLANCHE Six thirty-two.

EUNICE You don't have to look no further.

BLANCHE (*Uncomprehendingly*) I'm looking for my sister, Stella DuBois. I mean—Mrs. Stanley Kowalski.

EUNICE That's the party.—You just did miss her, though.

BLANCHE This—can this be—her home?

EUNICE She's got the downstairs here and I got the up.

BLANCHE Oh. She's—out?

EUNICE You noticed that bowling alley around the corner?

BLANCHE I'm—not sure I did.

EUNICE Well, that's where she's at, watchin' her husband bowl. (*There is a pause*) You want to leave your suitcase here an' go find her?

BLANCHE No.

NEGRO WOMAN I'll go tell her you come.

BLANCHE Thanks.

NEGRO WOMAN You welcome.

(*She goes out*)

EUNICE She wasn't expecting you?

BLANCHE No. No, not tonight.

EUNICE Well, why don't you just go in and make yourself at home till they get back.

BLANCHE How could I—do that?

EUNICE We own this place so I can let you in.

(*She gets up and opens the downstairs door. A light goes on behind the blind, turning it light blue.* BLANCHE *slowly follows her into the downstairs flat. The surrounding areas dim out as the interior is lighted. Two rooms can be seen, not too clearly defined. The one first entered is primarily a kitchen but contains a folding bed to be used by* BLANCHE. *The room beyond this is a bedroom. Off this room is a narrow door to a bathroom*)

EUNICE (*Defensively, noticing* BLANCHE'S *look*) It's sort of messed up right now but when it's clean it's real sweet.

BLANCHE Is it?

EUNICE   Uh-huh, I think so. So you're Stella's sister?

BLANCHE   Yes. (*Wanting to get rid of her*) Thanks for letting me in.

EUNICE   *Por nada*, as the Mexicans say, *por nada!* Stella spoke of you.

BLANCHE   Yes?

EUNICE   I think she said you taught school.

BLANCHE   Yes.

EUNICE   And you're from Mississippi, huh?

BLANCHE   Yes.

EUNICE   She showed me a picture of your home-place, the plantation.

BLANCHE   Belle Reve?

EUNICE   A great big place with white columns.

BLANCHE   Yes . . .

EUNICE   A place like that must be awful hard to keep up.

BLANCHE   If you will excuse me, I'm just about to drop.

EUNICE   Sure, honey. Why don't you set down?

BLANCHE   What I meant was I'd like to be left alone.

EUNICE   (*Offended*)   Aw. I'll make myself scarce, in that case.

BLANCHE   I didn't mean to be rude, but—

EUNICE   I'll drop by the bowling alley an' hustle her up.

(*She goes out the door.* BLANCHE *sits in a chair very stiffly with her shoulders slightly hunched and her legs pressed close together and her hands tightly clutching her purse as if she were quite cold. After a while the blind look goes out of her eyes and she begins to look slowly around. A cat screeches. She catches her breath with a startled gesture. Suddenly she notices something in a half opened closet. She springs up and crosses to it, and removes a whiskey bottle. She pours a half tumbler of whiskey and tosses it down. She carefully replaces the bottle and washes out the tumbler at the sink. Then she resumes her seat in front of the table*)

BLANCHE   (*Faintly to herself*)   I've got to keep hold of myself!

(STELLA *comes quickly around the corner of the building and runs to the door of the downstairs flat*)

STELLA   (*Calling out joyfully*)   Blanche!

(*For a moment they stare at each other. Then* BLANCHE *springs up and runs to her with a wild cry*)

BLANCHE   Stella, oh, Stella, Stella! Stella for Star!

(*She begins to speak with feverish vivacity as if she feared for either of them to stop and think. They catch each other in a spasmodic embrace*)

BLANCHE   Now, then, let me look at you. But don't you look at me, Stella, no, no, no, not till later, not till I've bathed and rested! And turn that over-light off! Turn that off! I won't be looked at in this merciless glare! (STELLA *laughs and complies*) Come back here now! Oh, my baby! Stella! Stella for Star! (*She embraces her again*) I thought you would never come back to this horrible place! What am I saying? I didn't meant to say that. I meant to be nice about it and say—Oh, what a convenient location and such—Ha-a-ha! Precious lamb! You haven't said a *word* to me.

STELLA   You haven't given me a chance to, honey!

(*She laughs, but her glance at* BLANCHE *is a little anxious*)

BLANCHE   Well, now you talk. Open your pretty mouth and talk while I look around for some liquor! I know you must have some liquor on the place! Where could it be, I wonder? Oh, I spy, I spy! (*She rushes to the closet and removes the bottle; she is shaking all over and panting for breath as she tries to laugh. The bottle nearly slips from her grasp*)

STELLA   (*Noticing*)   Blanche, you sit down and let me pour the drinks. I don't know what we've got to mix with. Maybe a coke's in the icebox. Look'n see, honey, while I'm—

BLANCHE   No coke, honey, not with my nerves tonight! Where—where—where is—?

STELLA   Stanley? Bowling! He loves it. They're having a—found some soda!—tournament . . .

BLANCHE   Just water, baby, to chase it! Now don't get worried, your sister hasn't turned into a drunkard, she's just all shaken up and hot and tired and dirty! You sit down, now, and explain this place to me! What are you doing in a place like this?

STELLA   Now, Blanche—

BLANCHE   Oh, I'm not going to be hypocritical, I'm going to be honestly critical about it! Never, never, never in my worst dreams could I picture— Only Poe! Only Mr. Edgar Allan Poe!—could do it justice! Out there I suppose is the ghoul-haunted woodland of Weir!

(*She laughs*)

STELLA   No, honey, those are the L & N tracks.

BLANCHE   No, now seriously, putting joking aside. Why didn't you tell me, why didn't you write me, honey, why didn't you let me know?

STELLA (*Carefully, pouring herself a drink*) Tell you what, Blanche?

BLANCHE Why, that you had to live in these conditions!

STELLA Aren't you being a little intense about it? It's not that bad at all! New Orleans isn't like other cities.

BLANCHE This has got nothing to do with New Orleans. You might as well say—forgive me, blessed baby! (*She suddenly stops short*) The subject is closed!

STELLA (*A little drily*) Thanks.

(*During the pause,* BLANCHE *stares at her. She smiles at* BLANCHE)

BLANCHE (*Looking down at her glass, which shakes in her hand*) You're all I've got in the world, and you're not glad to see me!

STELLA (*Sincerely*) Why, Blanche, you know that's not true.

BLANCHE No?—I'd forgotten how quiet you were.

STELLA You never did give me a chance to say much, Blanche. So I just got in the habit of being quiet around you.

BLANCHE (*Vaguely*) A good habit to get into . . . (*Then, abruptly*) You haven't asked me how I happened to get away from the school before the spring term ended.

STELLA Well, I thought you'd volunteer that information—if you wanted to tell me.

BLANCHE You thought I'd been fired?

STELLA No, I—thought you might have—resigned . . .

BLANCHE I was so exhausted by all I'd been through my—nerves broke. (*Nervously tamping cigarette*) I was on the verge of—lunacy, almost! So Mr. Graves—Mr. Graves is the high school superintendent—he suggested I take a leave of absence. I couldn't put all of those details into the wire . . . (*She drinks quickly*) Oh, this buzzes right through me and feels so *good!*

STELLA Won't you have another?

BLANCHE No, one's my limit.

STELLA Sure?

BLANCHE You haven't said a word about my appearance.

STELLA You look just fine.

BLANCHE God love you for a liar! Daylight never exposed so total a ruin! But you—you've put on some weight, yes, you're just as plump as a little partridge! And it's so becoming to you!

STELLA Now, Blanche—

BLANCHE Yes, it is, it is or I wouldn't say it! You just have to watch around the hips a little. Stand up.

STELLA Not now.

BLANCHE You hear me? I said stand up! (STELLA *complies reluc-*

tantly) You messy child, you, you've spilt something on that pretty white lace collar! About your hair—you ought to have it cut in a feather bob with your dainty features. Stella, you have a maid, don't you?

STELLA   No. With only two rooms it's—

BLANCHE   What? *Two* rooms, did you say?

STELLA   This one and—
(*She is embarrassed*)

BLANCHE   The other one?
(*She laughs sharply. There is an embarrassed silence*)

BLANCHE   I am going to take just one little tiny nip more, sort of to put the stopper on, so to speak. . . . Then put the bottle away so I won't be tempted. (*She rises*) I want you to look at *my* figure! (*She turns around*) You know I haven't put on one ounce in ten years, Stella? I weigh what I weighed the summer you left Belle Reve. The summer Dad died and you left us . . .

STELLA   (*A little wearily*) It's just incredible, Blanche, how well you're looking.

BLANCHE   (*They both laugh uncomfortably*) But, Stella, there's only two rooms, I don't see where you're going to put me!

STELLA   We're going to put you in here.

BLANCHE   What kind of bed's this—one of those collapsible things? (*She sits on it*)

STELLA   Does it feel all right?

BLANCHE   (*Dubiously*) Wonderful, honey. I don't like a bed that gives much. But there's no door between the two rooms, and Stanley—will it be decent?

STELLA   Stanley is Polish, you know.

BLANCHE   Oh, yes. They're something like Irish, aren't they?

STELLA   Well—

BLANCHE   Only not so—highbrow? (*They both laugh again in the same way*) I brought some nice clothes to meet all your lovely friends in.

STELLA   I'm afraid you won't think they are lovely.

BLANCHE   What are they like?

STELLA   They're Stanley's friends.

BLANCHE   Polacks?

STELLA   They're a mixed lot, Blanche.

BLANCHE   Heterogeneous—types?

STELLA   Oh, yes. Yes, types is right!

BLANCHE   Well—anyhow—I brought nice clothes and I'll wear them. I guess you're hoping I'll say I'll put up at a hotel, but I'm not going to put up at a hotel. I want to be *near* you, got to be *with* somebody, I *can't* be *alone!* Because—as you must have noticed—I'm—*not* very *well* . . .

(*Her voice drops and her look is frightened*)

STELLA   You seem a little bit nervous or overwrought or something.

BLANCHE   Will Stanley like me, or will I be just a visiting in-law, Stella? I couldn't stand that.

STELLA   You'll get along fine together, if you'll just try not to—well—compare him with men that we went out with at home.

BLANCHE   Is he so—different?

STELLA   Yes. A different species.

BLANCHE   In what way; what's he like?

STELLA   Oh, you can't describe someone you're in love with! Here's a picture of him!

(*She hands a photograph to* BLANCHE)

BLANCHE   An officer?

STELLA   A Master Sergeant in the Engineers' Corps. Those are decorations!

BLANCHE   He had those on when you met him?

STELLA   I assure you I wasn't just blinded by all the brass.

BLANCHE   That's not what I—

STELLA   But of course there were things to adjust myself to later on.

BLANCHE   Such as his civilian background! (STELLA *laughs uncertainly*) How did he take it when you said I was coming?

STELLA   Oh, Stanley doesn't know yet.

BLANCHE (*Frightened*)   You—haven't told him?

STELLA   He's on the road a good deal.

BLANCHE   Oh. Travels?

STELLA   Yes.

BLANCHE   Good. I mean—isn't it?

STELLA (*Half to herself*)   I can hardly stand it when he is away for a night . . .

BLANCHE   Why, Stella!

STELLA   When he's away for a week I nearly go wild!

BLANCHE   Gracious!

STELLA   And when he comes back I cry on his lap like a baby . . .

(*She smiles to herself*)

BLANCHE   I guess that is what is meant by being in love . . .

(STELLA *looks up with a radiant smile*) Stella—

STELLA   What?

BLANCHE (*In an uneasy rush*)   I haven't asked you the things you probably thought I was going to ask. And so I'll expect you to be understanding about what *I* have to tell *you*.

STELLA What, Blanche?

(*Her face turns anxious*)

BLANCHE Well, Stella—you're going to reproach me, I know that you're bound to reproach me—but before you do—take into consideration—you left! I stayed and struggled! You came to New Orleans and looked out for yourself! *I* stayed at *Belle Reve* and tried to hold it together! I'm not meaning this in any reproachful way, but *all* the burden descended on *my* shoulders.

STELLA The best I could do was make my own living, Blanche.

(BLANCHE *begins to shake again with intensity*)

BLANCHE I know, I know. But you are the one that abandoned Belle Reve, not I! I stayed and fought for it, bled for it, almost died for it!

STELLA Stop this hysterical outburst and tell me what's happened? What do you mean fought and bled? What kind of—

BLANCHE I knew you would, Stella. I knew you would take this attitude about it!

STELLA About—what?—please!

BLANCHE (*Slowly*) The loss—the loss . . .

STELLA Belle Reve? Lost, is it? No!

BLANCHE Yes, Stella.

(*They stare at each other across the yellow-checked linoleum of the table.* BLANCHE *slowly nods her head and* STELLA *looks slowly down at her hands folded on the table. The music of the "blue piano" grows louder.* BLANCHE *touches her handkerchief to her forehead*)

STELLA But how did it go? What happened?

BLANCHE (*Springing up*) You're a fine one to ask me how it went!

STELLA Blanche!

BLANCHE You're a fine one to sit there *accusing me* of it!

STELLA *Blanche!*

BLANCHE I, I, *I* took the blows in my face and my body! All of those deaths! The long parade to the graveyard! Father, mother! Margaret, that dreadful way! So big with it, it couldn't be put in a coffin! But had to be burned like rubbish! You just came home in time for the funerals, Stella. And funerals are pretty compared to deaths. Funerals are quiet, but deaths—not always. Sometimes their breathing is hoarse, and sometimes it rattles, and sometimes they even cry out to you, "Don't let me go!" Even the old, some-

times, say, "Don't let me go." As if you were able to stop them!
But funerals are quiet, with pretty flowers. And, oh, what
gorgeous boxes they pack them away in! Unless you were there
at the bed when they cried out, "Hold me!" you'd never suspect
there was the struggle for breath and bleeding. You didn't dream,
but I saw! *Saw! Saw!* And now you sit there telling me with your
eyes that I let the place go! How in hell do you think all that
sickness and dying was paid for? Death is expensive, Miss Stella!
And old Cousin Jessie's right after Margaret's, hers! Why, the
Grim Reaper had put up his tent on our doorstep! . . . Stella.
Belle Reve was his headquarters! Honey—that's how it slipped
through my fingers! Which of them left us a fortune? Which of
them left a cent of insurance even? Only poor Jessie—one hundred to pay for her coffin. That was all, Stella! And I with my
pitiful salary at the school. Yes, accuse me! Sit there and stare
at me, thinking I let the place go! *I* let the place go? Where were
you! In bed with your—Polack!

STELLA (*Springing*)   Blanche! You be still! That's enough!
   (*She starts out*)
BLANCHE   Where are you going?
STELLA   I'm going into the bathroom to wash my face.
BLANCHE   Oh, Stella, Stella, you're crying!
STELLA   Does that surprise you?
BLANCHE   Forgive me—I didn't mean to—
   (*The sound of men's voices is heard.* STELLA *goes into the bath-
   room, closing the door behind her. When the men appear, and*
   BLANCHE *realizes it must be* STANLEY *returning, she moves un-
   certainly from the bathroom door to the dressing table, looking
   apprehensively toward the front door.* STANLEY *enters, followed
   by* STEVE *and* MITCH. STANLEY *pauses near his door,* STEVE *by the
   foot of the spiral stair, and* MITCH *is slightly above and to the
   right of them, about to go out. As the men enter, we hear some
   of the following dialogue*)
STANLEY   Is that how he got it?
STEVE   Sure that's how he got it. He hit the old weather-bird for
   300 bucks on a six-number-ticket.
MITCH   Don't tell him those things; he'll believe it.
   (MITCH *starts out*)
STANLEY (*Restraining* MITCH)   Hey, Mitch—come back here.
   (BLANCHE, *at the sound of voices, retires to the bedroom. She
   picks up* STANLEY's *photo from dressing table, looks at it, puts it*

down. When STANLEY *enters the apartment, she darts and hides behind the screen at the head of bed*)

STEVE (*To* STANLEY *and* MITCH) Hey, are we playin' poker to-morrow?

STANLEY Sure—at Mitch's.

MITCH (*Hearing this, returns quickly to the stair rail*) No—not at my place. My mother's still sick!

STANLEY Okay, at my place . . . (MITCH *starts out again*) But you bring the beer! (MITCH *pretends not to hear,—calls out "Goodnight all," and goes out, singing.* EUNICE's *voice is heard, above*)
Break it up down there! I made the spaghetti dish and ate it myself.

STEVE (*Going upstairs*) I told you and phoned you we was playing. (*To the men*) Jax beer!

EUNICE You never phoned me once.

STEVE I told you at breakfast—and phoned you at lunch . . .

EUNICE Well, never mind about that. You just get yourself home here once in a while.

STEVE You want it in the papers?

(*More laughter and shouts of parting come from the men.* STAN-LEY *throws the screen door of the kitchen open and comes in. He is of medium height, about five feet eight or nine, and strongly, compactly built. Animal joy in his being is implicit in all his move-ments and attitudes. Since earliest manhood the center of his life has been pleasure with women, the giving and taking of it, not with weak indulgence, dependently, but with the power and pride of a richly feathered male bird among hens. Branching out from this complete and satisfying center are all the auxiliary chan-nels of his life, such as his heartiness with men, his appreciation of rough humor, his love of good drink and food and games, his car, his radio, everything that is his, that bears his emblem of the gaudy seed-bearer. He sizes women up at a glance, with sexual classifications, crude images flashing into his mind and determin-ing the way he smiles at them*)

BLANCHE (*Drawing involuntarily back from his stare*) You must be Stanley. I'm Blanche.

STANLEY Stella's sister?

BLANCHE Yes.

STANLEY H'lo. Where's the little woman?

BLANCHE In the bathroom.

STANLEY Oh. Didn't know you were coming in town.

BLANCHE I—uh—

STANLEY Where you from, Blanche?

BLANCHE Why, I—live in Laurel.

(*He has crossed to the closet and removed the whiskey bottle*)

STANLEY In Laurel, huh? Oh, yeah. Yeah, in Laurel, that's right. Not in my territory. Liquor goes fast in hot weather. (*He holds the bottle to the light to observe its depletion*) Have a shot?

BLANCHE No, I—rarely touch it.

STANLEY Some people rarely touch it, but it touches them often.

BLANCHE (*Faintly*) Ha-ha.

STANLEY My clothes're stickin' to me. Do you mind if I make myself comfortable?

(*He starts to remove his shirt*)

BLANCHE Please, please do.

STANLEY Be comfortable is my motto.

BLANCHE It's mine, too. It's hard to stay looking fresh. I haven't washed or even powdered my face and—here you are!

STANLEY You know you can catch cold sitting around in damp things, especially when you been exercising hard like bowling is. You're a teacher, aren't you?

BLANCHE Yes.

STANLEY What do you teach, Blanche?

BLANCHE English.

STANLEY I never was a very good English student. How long you here for, Blanche?

BLANCHE I—don't know yet.

STANLEY You going to shack up here?

BLANCHE I thought I would if it's not inconvenient for you all.

STANLEY Good.

BLANCHE Traveling wears me out.

STANLEY Well, take it easy.

(*A cat screeches near the window.* BLANCHE *springs up*)

BLANCHE What's that?

STANLEY Cats . . . Hey, Stella!

STELLA (*Faintly, from the bathroom*) Yes, Stanley.

STANLEY Haven't fallen in, have you? (*He grins at* BLANCHE. *She tries unsuccessfully to smile back. There is a silence*) I'm afraid I'll strike you as being the unrefined type. Stella's spoke of you a good deal. You were married once, weren't you?

(*The music of the polka rises up, faint in the distance*)

BLANCHE Yes. When I was quite young.

STANLEY What happened?

BLANCHE The boy—the boy died. (*She sinks back down*) I'm afraid I'm—going to be sick!

(*Her head falls on her arms*)

SCENE TWO

It is six o'clock the following evening. BLANCHE *is bathing.* STELLA *is completing her toilette.* BLANCHE's *dress, a flowered print, is laid out on* STELLA's *bed.*

STANLEY *enters the kitchen from outside, leaving the door open on the perpetual "blue piano" around the corner.*

STANLEY What's all this monkey doings?

STELLA Oh, Stan! (*She jumps up and kisses him which he accepts with lordly composure*) I'm taking Blanche to Galatoire's for supper and then to a show, because it's your poker night.

STANLEY How about my supper, huh? I'm not going to no Galatoire's for supper!

STELLA I put you a cold plate on ice.

STANLEY Well, isn't that just dandy!

STELLA I'm going to try to keep Blanche out till the party breaks up because I don't know how she would take it. So we'll go to one of the little places in the Quarter afterwards and you'd better give me some money.

STANLEY Where is she?

STELLA She's soaking in a hot tub to quiet her nerves. She's terribly upset.

STANLEY Over what?

STELLA She's been through such an ordeal.

STANLEY Yeah?

STELLA Stan, we've—lost Belle Reve!

STANLEY The place in the country?

STELLA Yes.

STANLEY How?

STELLA (*Vaguely*) Oh, it had to be—sacrificed or something. (*There is a pause while* STANLEY *considers.* STELLA *is changing into her dress*) When she comes in be sure to say something nice about her appearance. And, oh! Don't mention the baby. I haven't said anything yet, I'm waiting until she gets in a quieter condition.

STANLEY (*Ominously*) So?

STELLA And try to understand her and be nice to her, Stan.

BLANCHE (*Singing in the bathroom:*)

"From the land of the sky blue water,
They brought a captive maid!"

STELLA She wasn't expecting to find us in such a small place. You see I'd tried to gloss things over a little in my letters.

STANLEY So?

STELLA And admire her dress and tell her she's looking wonderful. That's important with Blanche. Her little weakness!

STANLEY Yeah. I get the idea. Now let's skip back a little to where you said the country place was disposed of.

STELLA Oh!—yes . . .

STANLEY How about that? Let's have a few more details on that subjeck.

STELLA It's best not to talk much about it until she's calmed down.

STANLEY So that's the deal, huh? Sister Blanche cannot be annoyed with business details right now!

STELLA You saw how she was last night.

STANLEY Uh-hum, I saw how she was. Now let's have a gander at the bill of sale.

STELLA I haven't seen any.

STANLEY She didn't show you no papers, no deed of sale or nothing like that, huh?

STELLA It seems like it wasn't sold.

STANLEY Well, what in hell was it then, give away? To charity?

STELLA Shhh! She'll hear you.

STANLEY I don't care if she hears me. Let's see the papers!

STELLA There weren't any papers, she didn't show any papers, I don't care about papers.

STANLEY Have you ever heard of the Napoleonic code?

STELLA No, Stanley, I haven't heard of the Napoleonic code and if I have, I don't see what it—

STANLEY Let me enlighten you on a point or two, baby.

STELLA Yes?

STANLEY In the state of Louisiana we have the Napoleonic code according to which what belongs to the wife belongs to the husband and vice versa. For instance if I had a piece of property, or you had a piece of property—

STELLA   My head is swimming!

STANLEY   All right. I'll wait till she gets through soaking in a hot tub and then I'll inquire if *she* is acquainted with the Napoleonic code. It looks to me like you have been swindled, baby, and when you're swindled under the Napoleonic code I'm swindled *too*. And I don't like to be *swindled*.

STELLA   There's plenty of time to ask her questions later but if you do now she'll go to pieces again. I don't understand what happened to Belle Reve but you don't know how ridiculous you are being when you suggest that my sister or I or anyone of our family could have perpetrated a swindle on anyone else.

STANLEY   Then where's the money if the place was sold?

STELLA   Not sold—*lost, lost!* (*He stalks into bedroom, and she follows him*) Stanley!

(*He pulls open the wardrobe trunk standing in middle of room and jerks out an armful of dresses*)

STANLEY   Open your eyes to this stuff! You think she got them out of a teacher's pay?

STELLA   Hush!

STANLEY   Look at these feathers and furs that she come here to preen herself in! What's this here? A solid-gold dress, I believe! And this one! What is these here? Fox-pieces! (*He blows on them*) Genuine fox fur-pieces, a half a mile long! Where are your fox-pieces, Stella? Bushy snow-white ones, no less! Where are your white fox-pieces?

STELLA   Those are inexpensive summer furs that Blanche has had a long time.

STANLEY   I got an acquaintance who deals in this sort of merchandise. I'll have him in here to appraise it. I'm willing to bet you there's thousands of dollars invested in this stuff here!

STELLA   Don't be such an idiot, Stanley!

(*He hurls the furs to the daybed. Then he jerks open small drawer in the trunk and pulls up a fistful of costume jewelry*)

STANLEY   And what have we here? The treasure chest of a pirate!

STELLA   Oh, Stanley!

STANLEY   Pearls! Ropes of them! What is this sister of yours, a deep-sea diver? Bracelets of solid gold, too! Where are your pearls and gold bracelets?

STELLA   Shhh! Be still, Stanley!

STANLEY   And diamonds! A crown for an empress!

STELLA   A rhinestone tiara she wore to a costume ball.

STANLEY   What's rhinestone?

STELLA   Next door to glass.

STANLEY   Are you kidding? I have an acquaintance that works in a jewelry store. I'll have him in here to make an appraisal of this. Here's your plantation, or what was left of it, here!

STELLA   You have no idea how stupid and horrid you're being! Now close that trunk before she comes out of the bathroom!

(*He kicks the trunk partly closed and sits on the kitchen table*)

STANLEY   The Kowalskis and the DuBois have different notions.

STELLA   (*Angrily*)   Indeed they have, thank heavens!—*I'm* going outside. (*She snatches up her white hat and gloves and crosses to the outside door*) You come out with me while Blanche is getting dressed.

STANLEY   Since when do you give me orders?

STELLA   Are you going to stay here and insult her?

STANLEY   You're damn tootin' I'm going to stay here.

(STELLA *goes out to the porch.* BLANCHE *comes out of the bathroom in a red satin robe*)

BLANCHE   (*Airily*)   Hello, Stanley! Here I am, all freshly bathed and scented, and feeling like a brand new human being!

(*He lights a cigarette*)

STANLEY   That's good.

BLANCHE   (*Drawing the curtains at the windows*)   Excuse me while I slip on my pretty new dress!

STANLEY   Go right ahead, Blanche.

(*She closes the drapes between the rooms*)

BLANCHE   I understand there's to be a little card party to which we ladies are cordially *not* invited!

STANLEY   (*Ominously*)   Yeah?

(BLANCHE *throws off her robe and slips into a flowered print dress*)

BLANCHE   Where's Stella?

STANLEY   Out on the porch.

BLANCHE   I'm going to ask a favor of you in a moment.

STANLEY   What could that be, I wonder?

BLANCHE   Some buttons in back! You may enter! (*He crosses through drapes with a smoldering look*) How do I look?

STANLEY   You look all right.

BLANCHE   Many thanks! Now the buttons!

STANLEY   I can't do nothing with them.

BLANCHE   You men with your big clumsy fingers. May I have a drag on your cig?

STANLEY   Have one for yourself.

BLANCHE   Why, thanks! . . . It looks like my trunk has exploded.

STANLEY   Me an' Stella were helping you unpack.

BLANCHE   Well, you certainly did a fast and thorough job of it!

STANLEY   It looks like you raided some stylish shops in Paris.

BLANCHE   Ha-ha! Yes—clothes are my passion!

STANLEY   What does it cost for a string of fur-pieces like that?

BLANCHE   Why, those were a tribute from an admirer of mine!

STANLEY   He must have had a lot of—admiration!

BLANCHE   Oh, in my youth I excited some admiration. But look at me now! (*She smiles at him radiantly*) Would you think it possible that I was once considered to be—attractive?

STANLEY   Your looks are okay.

BLANCHE   I was fishing for a compliment, Stanley.

STANLEY   I don't go in for that stuff.

BLANCHE   What—stuff?

STANLEY   Compliments to women about their looks. I never met a woman that didn't know if she was good-looking or not without being told, and some of them give themselves credit for more than they've got. I once went out with a doll who said to me, "I am the glamorous type, I am the glamorous type!" I said, "So what?"

BLANCHE   And what did she say then?

STANLEY   She didn't say nothing. That shut her up like a clam.

BLANCHE   Did it end the romance?

STANLEY   It ended the conversation—that was all. Some men are took in by this Hollywood glamor stuff and some men are not.

BLANCHE   I'm sure you belong in the second category.

STANLEY   That's right.

BLANCHE   I cannot imagine any witch of a woman casting a spell over you.

STANLEY   That's—right.

BLANCHE   You're simple, straightforward and honest, a little bit on the primitive side I should think. To interest you a woman would have to—
    (*She pauses with an indefinite gesture*)

STANLEY (*Slowly*)   Lay . . . her cards on the table.

BLANCHE (*Smiling*)   Well, I never cared for wishy-washy people. That was why, when you walked in here last night, I said to my-

self—"My sister has married a man!"—Of course that was all that
I could tell about you.

STANLEY (*Booming*) Now let's cut the re-bop!

BLANCHE (*Pressing hands to her ears*) Ouuuuu!

STELLA (*Calling from the steps*) Stanley! You come out here and
let Blanche finish dressing!

BLANCHE I'm through dressing, honey.

STELLA Well, you come out, then.

STANLEY Your sister and I are having a little talk.

BLANCHE (*Lightly*) Honey, do me a favor. Run to the drug-store
and get me a lemon-coke with plenty of chipped ice in it!—Will
you do that for me, Sweetie?

STELLA (*Uncertainly*) Yes.

(*She goes around the corner of the building*)

BLANCHE The poor little thing was out there listening to us, and I
have an idea she doesn't understand you as well as I do. . . . All
right; now, Mr. Kowalski, let us proceed without any more double-
talk. I'm ready to answer all questions. I've nothing to hide. What
is it?

STANLEY There is such a thing in this State of Louisiana as the
Napoleonic code, according to which whatever belongs to my wife
is also mine—and vice versa.

BLANCHE My, but you have an impressive judicial air!

(*She sprays herself with her atomizer; then playfully sprays him
with it. He seizes the atomizer and slams it down on the dresser.
She throws back her head and laughs*)

STANLEY If I didn't know that you was my wife's sister I'd get ideas
about you!

BLANCHE Such as what!

STANLEY Don't play so dumb. You know what!

BLANCHE (*She puts the atomizer on the table*) All right. Cards on
the table. That suits me. (*She turns to* STANLEY) I know I fib a
good deal. After all, a woman's charm is fifty per cent illusion, but
when a thing is important I tell the truth, and this is the truth: I
haven't cheated my sister or you or anyone else as long as I have
lived.

STANLEY Where's the papers? In the trunk?

BLANCHE Everything that I own is in that trunk.

(STANLEY *crosses to the trunk, shoves it roughly open and begins
to open compartments*)

BLANCHE What in the name of heaven are you thinking of! What's

in the back of that little boy's mind of yours? That I am absconding with something, attempting some kind of treachery on my sister?—Let me do that! It will be faster and simpler . . . (*She crosses to the trunk and takes out a box*) I keep my papers mostly in this tin box.
(*She opens it*)

STANLEY   What's them underneath?
(*He indicates another sheaf of paper*)

BLANCHE   These are love-letters, yellowing with antiquity, all from one boy. (*He snatches them up. She speaks fiercely*) Give those back to me!

STANLEY   I'll have a look at them first!

BLANCHE   The touch of your hands insults them!

STANLEY   Don't pull that stuff!
(*He rips off the ribbon and starts to examine them.* BLANCHE *snatches them from him, and they cascade to the floor*)

BLANCHE   Now that you've touched them I'll burn them!

STANLEY (*Staring, baffled*)   What in hell are they?

BLANCHE (*On the floor gathering them up*)   Poems a dead boy wrote. I hurt him the way that you would like to hurt me, but you can't! I'm not young and vulnerable any more. But my young husband was and I—never mind about that! Just give them back to me!

STANLEY   What do you mean by saying you'll have to burn them?

BLANCHE   I'm sorry, I must have lost my head for a moment. Everyone has something he won't let others touch because of their—intimate nature . . . (*She now seems faint with exhaustion and she sits down with the strong box and puts on a pair of glasses and goes methodically through a large stack of papers*) Ambler & Ambler. Hmmmmm. . . . Crabtree. . . . More Ambler & Ambler.

STANLEY   What is Ambler & Ambler?

BLANCHE   A firm that made loans on the place.

STANLEY   Then it *was* lost on a mortgage?

BLANCHE (*Touching her forehead*)   That must've been what happened.

STANLEY   I don't want no ifs, ands or buts! What's all the rest of them papers?
(*She hands him the entire box. He carries it to the table and starts to examine the papers*)

BLANCHE (*Picking up a large envelope containing more papers*)

There are thousands of papers, stretching back over hundreds of years, affecting Belle Reve as, piece by piece, our improvident grandfathers and father and uncles and brothers exchanged the land for their epic fornications—to put it plainly! (*She removes her glasses with an exhausted laugh*) The four-letter word deprived us of our plantation, till finally all that was left—and Stella can verify that!—was the house itself and about twenty acres of ground, including a graveyard, to which now all but Stella and I have retreated. (*She pours the contents of the envelope on the table*) Here all of them are, all papers! I hereby endow you with them! Take them, peruse them—commit them to memory, even! I think it's wonderfully fitting that Belle Reve should finally be this bunch of old papers in your big, capable hands! . . . I wonder if Stella's come back with my lemon-coke . . .

(*She leans back and closes her eyes*)

STANLEY   I have a lawyer acquaintance who will study these out.

BLANCHE   Present them to him with a box of aspirin tablets.

STANLEY (*Becoming somewhat sheepish*)   You see, under the Napoleonic code—a man has to take an interest in his wife's affairs—especially now that she's going to have a baby.

(BLANCHE *opens her eyes. The "blue piano" sounds louder*)

BLANCHE   Stella? Stella going to have a baby? (*Dreamily*) I didn't know she was going to have a baby!

(*She gets up and crosses to the outside door.* STELLA *appears around the corner with a carton from the drug-store.* STANLEY *goes into the bedroom with the envelope and the box. The inner rooms fade to darkness and the outside wall of the house is visible.* BLANCHE *meets* STELLA *at the foot of the steps to the sidewalk*)

BLANCHE   Stella, Stella for Star! How lovely to have a baby! It's all right. Everything's all right.

STELLA   I'm sorry he did that to you.

BLANCHE   Oh, I guess he's just not the type that goes for jasmine perfume, but maybe he's what we need to mix with our blood now that we've lost Belle Reve. We thrashed it out. I feel a bit shaky, but I think I handled it nicely, I laughed and treated it all as a joke. (STEVE *and* PABLO *appear, carrying a case of beer*) I called him a little boy and laughed and flirted. Yes, I was flirting with your husband! (*As the men approach*) The guests are gathering for the poker party. (*The two men pass between them, and enter the house*) Which way do we go now, Stella—this way?

STELLA No, this way.

(*She leads* BLANCHE *away*)

BLANCHE (*Laughing*) The blind are leading the blind!

(*A tamale vendor is heard calling*)

VENDOR'S VOICE Red-hot!

SCENE THREE

THE POKER NIGHT

There is a picture of Van Gogh's of a billiard-parlor at night. The kitchen now suggests that sort of lurid nocturnal brilliance, the raw colors of childhood's spectrum. Over the yellow linoleum of the kitchen table hangs an electric bulb with a vivid green glass shade. The poker players—STANLEY, STEVE, MITCH and PABLO—wear colored shirts, solid blues, a purple, a red-and-white check, a light green, and they are men at the peak of their physical manhood, as coarse and direct and powerful as the primary colors. There are vivid slices of watermelon on the table, whiskey bottles and glasses. The bedroom is relatively dim with only the light that spills between the portieres and through the wide window on the street.

For a moment, there is absorbed silence as a hand is dealt.

STEVE   Anything wild this deal?

PABLO   One-eyed jacks are wild.

STEVE   Give me two cards.

PABLO   You, Mitch?

MITCH   I'm out.

PABLO   One.

MITCH   Anyone want a shot?

STANLEY   Yeah. Me.

PABLO   Why don't somebody go to the Chinaman's and bring back a load of chop suey?

STANLEY   When I'm losing you want to eat! Ante up! Openers? Openers! Get y'r ass off the table, Mitch. Nothing belongs on a poker table but cards, chips and whiskey.

(He lurches up and tosses some watermelon rinds to the floor)

MITCH   Kind of on your high horse, ain't you?

STANLEY   How many?

STEVE   Give me three.

STANLEY   One.

MITCH   I'm out again. I oughta go home pretty soon.

STANLEY   Shut up.

MITCH   I gotta sick mother. She don't go to sleep until I come in at night.

STANLEY   Then why don't you stay home with her?

MITCH   She says to go out, so I go, but I don't enjoy it. All the while I keep wondering how she is.

STANLEY   Aw, for the sake of Jesus, go home, then!

PABLO   What've you got?

STEVE   Spade flush.

MITCH   You all are married. But I'll be alone when she goes.—I'm going to the bathroom.

STANLEY   Hurry back and we'll fix you a sugar-tit.

MITCH   Aw, go rut.

(*He crosses through the bedroom into the bathroom*)

STEVE   (*Dealing a hand*)   Seven card stud. (*Telling his joke as he deals*)   This ole farmer is out in back of his house sittin' down th'owing corn to the chickens when all at once he hears a loud cackle and this young hen comes lickety split around the side of the house with the rooster right behind her and gaining on her fast.

STANLEY   (*Impatient with the story*)   Deal!

STEVE   But when the rooster catches sight of the farmer th'owing the corn he puts on the brakes and lets the hen get away and starts pecking corn. And the old farmer says, "Lord God, I hopes I never gits *that* hongry!"

(STEVE *and* PABLO *laugh. The sisters appear around the corner of the building*)

STELLA   The game is still going on.

BLANCHE   How do I look?

STELLA   Lovely, Blanche.

BLANCHE   I feel so hot and frazzled. Wait till I powder before you open the door. Do I look done in?

STELLA   Why no. You are as fresh as a daisy.

BLANCHE   One that's been picked a few days.

(STELLA *opens the door and they enter*)

STELLA   Well, well, well. I see you boys are still at it!

STANLEY   Where you been?

STELLA   Blanche and I took in a show. Blanche, this is Mr. Gonzales and Mr. Hubbell.

BLANCHE   Please don't get up.

STANLEY   Nobody's going to get up, so don't be worried.

STELLA   How much longer is this game going to continue?

STANLEY   Till we get ready to quit.

BLANCHE   Poker is so fascinating. Could I kibitz?

STANLEY   You could not. Why don't you women go up and sit with Eunice?

STELLA   Because it is nearly two-thirty. (BLANCHE *crosses into the bedroom and partially closes the portieres*) Couldn't you call it quits after one more hand?

(*A chair scrapes.* STANLEY *gives a loud whack of his hand on her thigh*)

STELLA (*Sharply*)   That's not fun, Stanley.

(*The men laugh.* STELLA *goes into the bedroom*)

STELLA   It makes me so mad when he does that in front of people.

BLANCHE   I think I will bathe.

STELLA   Again?

BLANCHE   My nerves are in knots. Is the bathroom occupied?

STELLA   I don't know.

(BLANCHE *knocks.* MITCH *opens the door and comes out, still wiping his hands on a towel*)

BLANCHE   Oh!—good evening.

MITCH   Hello.

(*He stares at her*)

STELLA   Blanche, this is Harold Mitchell. My sister, Blanche Du-Bois.

MITCH (*With awkward courtesy*)   How do you do, Miss DuBois.

STELLA   How is your mother now, Mitch?

MITCH   About the same, thanks. She appreciated your sending over that custard.—Excuse me, please.

(*He crosses slowly back into the kitchen, glancing back at* BLANCHE *and coughing a little shyly. He realizes he still has the towel in his hands and with an embarrassed laugh hands it to* STELLA. BLANCHE *looks after him with a certain interest*)

BLANCHE   That one seems—superior to the others.

STELLA   Yes, he is.

BLANCHE   I thought he had a sort of sensitive look.

STELLA   His mother is sick.

BLANCHE   Is he married?

STELLA   No.

BLANCHE   Is he a wolf?

STELLA   Why, Blanche! (BLANCHE *laughs*) I don't think he would be.

BLANCHE   What does—what does he do?
(*She is unbuttoning her dress*)

STELLA   He's on the precision bench in the spare parts department. At the plant Stanley travels for.

BLANCHE   Is that something much?

STELLA   No. Stanley's the only one of his crowd that's likely to get anywhere.

BLANCHE   What makes you think Stanley will?

STELLA   Look at him.

BLANCHE   I've looked at him.

STELLA   Then you should know.

BLANCHE   I'm sorry, but I haven't noticed the stamp of genius even on Stanley's forehead.
(*She takes off the dress and stands in her pink silk brassiere and petticoat in the light through the portieres. The game has continued in undertones*)

STELLA   It isn't on his forehead and it isn't genius.

BLANCHE   Oh. Well, what is it, and where? I would like to know.

STELLA   It's a drive that he has. You're standing in the light, Blanche!

BLANCHE   Oh, am I!
(*She moves out of the yellow streak of light. STELLA has removed her dress and put on a light blue satin kimona*)

STELLA   (*With girlish laughter*)   You ought to see their wives.

BLANCHE   (*Laughingly*)   I can imagine. Big, beefy things, I suppose.

STELLA   You know that one upstairs? (*More laughter*) One time (*laughing*) the plaster—(*laughing*) cracked—

STANLEY   You hens cut out that conversation in there!

STELLA   You can't hear us.

STANLEY   Well, you can hear me and I said to hush up!

STELLA   This is my house and I'll talk as much as I want to!

BLANCHE   Stella, don't start a row.

STELLA   He's half drunk!—I'll be out in a minute.
(*She goes into the bathroom.* BLANCHE *rises and crosses leisurely to a small white radio and turns it on*)

STANLEY   Awright, Mitch, you in?

MITCH   What? Oh!—No, I'm out!
(*BLANCHE moves back into the streak of light. She raises her arms*

and stretches, as she moves indolently back to the chair. Rhumba
music comes over the radio. MITCH rises at the table)

STANLEY   Who turned that on in there?

BLANCHE   I did. Do you mind?

STANLEY   Turn it off!

STEVE   Aw, let the girls have their music.

PABLO   Sure, that's good, leave it on!

STEVE   Sounds like Xavier Cugat!

(STANLEY *jumps up and, crossing to the radio, turns it off. He
stops short at the sight of* BLANCHE *in the chair. She returns his
look without flinching. Then he sits again at the poker table. Two
of the men have started arguing hotly*)

STEVE   I didn't hear you name it.

PABLO   Didn't I name it, Mitch?

MITCH   I wasn't listenin'.

PABLO   What were you doing, then?

STANLEY   He was looking through them drapes. (*He jumps up and
jerks roughly at curtains to close them*) Now deal the hand over
again and let's play cards or quit. Some people get ants when they
win.

(MITCH *rises as* STANLEY *returns to his seat*)

STANLEY   (*Yelling*)   Sit down!

MITCH   I'm going to the "head." Deal me out.

PABLO   Sure he's got ants now. Seven five-dollar bills in his pants
pocket folded up tight as spitballs.

STEVE   Tomorrow you'll see him at the cashier's window getting
them changed into quarters.

STANLEY   And when he goes home he'll deposit them one by one in
a piggy bank his mother give him for Christmas. (*Dealing*) This
game is Spit in the Ocean.

(MITCH *laughs uncomfortably and continues through the portieres.
He stops just inside*)

BLANCHE   (*Softly*)   Hello! The Little Boys' Room is busy right now.

MITCH   We've—been drinking beer.

BLANCHE   I hate beer.

MITCH   It's—a hot weather drink.

BLANCHE   Oh, I don't think so; it always makes me warmer. Have
you got any cigs?

(*She has slipped on the dark red satin wrapper*)

MITCH   Sure.

BLANCHE   What kind are they?

MITCH   Luckies.

BLANCHE   Oh, good. What a pretty case. Silver?

MITCH   Yes. Yes; read the inscription.

BLANCHE   Oh, is there an inscription? I can't make it out. (*He strikes a match and moves closer*) Oh!

(*Reading with feigned difficulty:*)

"And if God choose,
    I shall but love thee better—after—death!"

Why, that's from my favorite sonnet by Mrs. Browning!

MITCH   You know it?

BLANCHE   Certainly I do!

MITCH   There's a story connected with that inscription.

BLANCHE   It sounds like a romance.

MITCH   A pretty sad one.

BLANCHE   Oh?

MITCH   The girl's dead now.

BLANCHE (*In a tone of deep sympathy*)   Oh!

MITCH   She knew she was dying when she give me this. A very strange girl, very sweet—very!

BLANCHE   She must have been fond of you. Sick people have such deep, sincere attachments.

MITCH   That's right, they certainly do.

BLANCHE   Sorrow makes for sincerity, I think.

MITCH   It sure brings it out in people.

BLANCHE   The little there is belongs to people who have experienced some sorrow.

MITCH   I believe you are right about that.

BLANCHE   I'm positive that I am. Show me a person who hasn't known any sorrow and I'll show you a shuperficial— Listen to me! My tongue is a little—thick! You boys are responsible for it. The show let out at eleven and we couldn't come home on account of the poker game so we had to go somewhere and drink. I'm not accustomed to having more than one drink. Two is the limit—and *three!* (*She laughs*) Tonight I had three.

STANLEY   Mitch!

MITCH   Deal me out. I'm talking to Miss—

BLANCHE   DuBois.

MITCH   Miss DuBois?

BLANCHE   It's a French name. It means woods and Blanche means white, so the two together mean white woods. Like an orchard in spring! You can remember it by that.

MITCH You're French?

BLANCHE We are French by extraction. Our first American ancestors were French Huguenots.

MITCH You are Stella's sister, are you not?

BLANCHE Yes, Stella is my precious little sister. I call her little in spite of the fact she's somewhat older than I. Just slightly. Less than a year. Will you do something for me?

MITCH Sure. What?

BLANCHE I bought this adorable little colored paper lantern at a Chinese shop on Bourbon. Put it over the light bulb! Will you, please?

MITCH Be glad to.

BLANCHE I can't stand a naked light bulb, any more than I can a rude remark or a vulgar action.

MITCH (*Adjusting the lantern*) I guess we strike you as being a pretty rough bunch.

BLANCHE I'm very adaptable—to circumstances.

MITCH Well, that's a good thing to be. You are visiting Stanley and Stella?

BLANCHE Stella hasn't been so well lately, and I came down to help her for a while. She's very run down.

MITCH You're not—?

BLANCHE Married? No, no. I'm an old maid schoolteacher!

MITCH You may teach school but you're certainly not an old maid.

BLANCHE Thank you, sir! I appreciate your gallantry!

MITCH So you are in the teaching profession?

BLANCHE Yes. Ah, yes . . .

MITCH Grade school or high school or—

STANLEY (*Bellowing*) *Mitch!*

MITCH *Coming!*

BLANCHE Gracious, what lung-power! . . . I teach high school. In Laurel.

MITCH What do you teach? What subject?

BLANCHE Guess!

MITCH I bet you teach art or music? (BLANCHE *laughs delicately*) Of course I could be wrong. You might teach arithmetic.

BLANCHE Never arithmetic, sir; never arithmetic! (*With a laugh*) I don't even know my multiplication tables! No, I have the misfortune of being an English instructor. I attempt to instill a bunch of bobby-soxers and drug-store Romeos with reverence for Hawthorne and Whitman and Poe!

MITCH I guess that some of them are more interested in other things.

BLANCHE How very right you are! Their literary heritage is not what most of them treasure above all else! But they're sweet things! And in the spring, it's touching to notice them making their first discovery of love! As if nobody had ever known it before! (*The bathroom door opens and* STELLA *comes out.* BLANCHE *continues talking to* MITCH) Oh! Have you finished? Wait—I'll turn on the radio.

(*She turns the knobs on the radio and it begins to play "Wien, Wien, nur du allein."* BLANCHE *waltzes to the music with romantic gestures.* MITCH *is delighted and moves in awkward imitation like a dancing bear.* STANLEY *stalks fiercely through the portieres into the bedroom. He crosses to the small white radio and snatches it off the table. With a shouted oath, he tosses the instrument out the window*)

STELLA *Drunk—drunk—animal thing, you!* (*She rushes through to the poker table*) All of you—please go home! If any of you have one spark of decency in you—

BLANCHE (*Wildly*) Stella, watch out, he's—

(STANLEY *charges after* STELLA)

MEN (*Feebly*) Take it easy, Stanley. Easy, fellow.—Let's all—

STELLA You lay your hands on me and I'll—

(*She backs out of sight. He advances and disappears. There is the sound of a blow.* STELLA *cries out.* BLANCHE *screams and runs into the kitchen. The men rush forward and there is grappling and cursing. Something is overturned with a crash*)

BLANCHE (*Shrilly*) My sister is going to have a baby!

MITCH This is terrible.

BLANCHE Lunacy, absolute lunacy!

MITCH Get him in here, men.

(STANLEY *is forced, pinioned by the two men, into the bedroom. He nearly throws them off. Then all at once he subsides and is limp in their grasp. They speak quietly and lovingly to him and he leans his face on one of their shoulders*)

STELLA (*In a high, unnatural voice, out of sight*) I want to go away, I want to go away!

MITCH Poker shouldn't be played in a house with women.

(BLANCHE *rushes into the bedroom*)

BLANCHE   I want my sister's clothes! We'll go to that woman's upstairs!

MITCH   Where is the clothes?

BLANCHE   (*Opening the closet*)   I've got them! (*She rushes through to* STELLA) Stella, Stella, precious! Dear, dear little sister, don't be afraid!

(*With her arms around* STELLA, BLANCHE *guides her to the outside door and upstairs*)

STANLEY   (*Dully*)   What's the matter; what's happened?

MITCH   You just blew your top, Stan.

PABLO   He's okay, now.

STEVE   Sure, my boy's okay!

MITCH   Put him on the bed and get a wet towel.

PABLO   I think coffee would do him a world of good, now.

STANLEY   (*Thickly*)   I want water.

MITCH   Put him under the shower!

(*The men talk quietly as they lead him to the bathroom*)

STANLEY   Let the rut go of me, you sons of bitches!

(*Sounds of blows are heard. The water goes on full tilt*)

STEVE   Let's get quick out of here!

(*They rush to the poker table and sweep up their winnings on their way out*)

MITCH   (*Sadly but firmly*)   Poker should not be played in a house with women.

(*The door closes on them and the place is still. The* NEGRO *entertainers in the bar around the corner play "Paper Doll" slow and blue. After a moment* STANLEY *comes out of the bathroom dripping water and still in his clinging wet polka dot drawers*)

STANLEY   Stella! (*There is a pause*) My baby doll's left me! (*He breaks into sobs. Then he goes to the phone and dials, still shuddering with sobs*) Eunice? I want my baby! (*He waits a moment; then he hangs up and dials again*) Eunice! I'll keep on ringin' until I talk with my baby!

(*An undistinguishable shrill voice is heard. He hurls phone to floor. Dissonant brass and piano sounds as the rooms dim out to darkness and the outer walls appear in the night light. The "blue piano" plays for a brief interval. Finally,* STANLEY *stumbles half-dressed out to the porch and down the wooden steps to the pavement before the building. There he throws back his head like a baying hound and bellows his wife's name:* "STELLA! STELLA, *sweetheart!* STELLA!")

STANLEY   Stell-*lahhhhh!*

EUNICE   (*Calling down from the door of her upper apartment*)   Quit that howling out there an' go back to bed!

STANLEY   I want my baby down here. Stella, Stella!

EUNICE   She ain't comin' down so you quit! Or you'll git th' law on you!

STANLEY   Stella!

EUNICE   You can't beat on a woman an' then call 'er back! She won't come! And her goin' t' have a baby! . . . You stinker! You whelp of a Polack, you! I hope they do haul you in and turn the fire hose on you, same as the last time!

STANLEY   (*Humbly*)   Eunice, I want my girl to come down with me!

EUNICE   Hah!

(*She slams her door*)

STANLEY   (*With heaven-splitting violence*)   *STELL-LAHHHHH!*
(*The low-tone clarinet moans. The door upstairs opens again.* STELLA *slips down the rickety stairs in her robe. Her eyes are glistening with tears and her hair loose about her throat and shoulders. They stare at each other. Then they come together with low, animal moans. He falls to his knees on the steps and presses his face to her belly, curving a little with maternity. Her eyes go blind with tenderness as she catches his head and raises him level with her. He snatches the screen door open and lifts her off her feet and bears her into the dark flat.* BLANCHE *comes out on the upper landing in her robe and slips fearfully down the steps*)

BLANCHE   Where is my little sister? Stella? Stella?
(*She stops before the dark entrance of her sister's flat. Then catches her breath as if struck. She rushes down to the walk before the house. She looks right and left as if for a sanctuary. The music fades away.* MITCH *appears from around the corner*)

MITCH   Miss DuBois?

BLANCHE   Oh!

MITCH   All quiet on the Potomac now?

BLANCHE   She ran downstairs and went back in there with him.

MITCH   Sure she did.

BLANCHE   I'm terrified!

MITCH   Ho-ho! There's nothing to be scared of. They're crazy about each other.

BLANCHE   I'm not used to such—

MITCH Naw, it's a shame this had to happen when you just got here. But don't take it serious.

BLANCHE Violence! Is so—

MITCH Set down on the steps and have a cigarette with me.

BLANCHE I'm not properly dressed.

MITCH That don't make no difference in the Quarter.

BLANCHE Such a pretty silver case.

MITCH I showed you the inscription, didn't I?

BLANCHE Yes. (*During the pause, she looks up at the sky*) There's so much—so much confusion in the world . . . (*He coughs diffidently*) Thank you for being so kind! I need kindness now.

SCENE FOUR

It is early the following morning. There is a confusion of street cries like a choral chant.

STELLA *is lying down in the bedroom. Her face is serene in the early morning sunlight. One hand rests on her belly, rounding slightly with new maternity. From the other dangles a book of colored comics. Her eyes and lips have that almost narcotized tranquility that is in the faces of Eastern idols.*

The table is sloppy with remains of breakfast and the debris of the preceding night, and STANLEY'S *gaudy pyjamas lie across the threshold of the bathroom. The outside door is slightly ajar on a sky of summer brilliance.*

BLANCHE *appears at this door. She has spent a sleepless night and her appearance entirely contrasts with* STELLA'S. *She presses her knuckles nervously to her lips as she looks through the door, before entering.*

BLANCHE Stella?

STELLA (*Stirring lazily*) Hmmh?

(BLANCHE *utters a moaning cry and runs into the bedroom, throwing herself down beside* STELLA *in a rush of hysterical tenderness*)

BLANCHE Baby, my baby sister!

STELLA (*Drawing away from her*) Blanche, what is the matter with you?

(BLANCHE *straightens up slowly and stands beside the bed looking down at her sister with knuckles pressed to her lips*)

BLANCHE He's left?

STELLA Stan? Yes.

BLANCHE Will he be back?

STELLA He's gone to get the car greased. Why?

BLANCHE Why! I've been half crazy, Stella! When I found out

you'd been insane enough to come back in here after what happened—I started to rush in after you!

STELLA I'm glad you didn't.

BLANCHE What were you thinking of? (STELLA *makes an indefinite
gesture*) Answer me! What? What?

STELLA Please, Blanche! Sit down and stop yelling.

BLANCHE All right, Stella. I will repeat the question quietly now.
How could you come back in this place last night? Why, you
must have slept with him!

(STELLA *gets up in a calm and leisurely way*)

STELLA Blanche, I'd forgotten how excitable you are. You're making much too much fuss about this.

BLANCHE Am I?

STELLA Yes, you are, Blanche. I know how it must have seemed
to you and I'm awful sorry it had to happen, but it wasn't anything
as serious as you seem to take it. In the first place, when men
are drinking and playing poker anything can happen. It's always
a powder-keg. He didn't know what he was doing. . . . He was as
good as a lamb when I came back and he's really very, very
ashamed of himself.

BLANCHE And that—that makes it all right?

STELLA No, it isn't all right for anybody to make such a terrible
row, but—people do sometimes. Stanley's always smashed things.
Why, on our wedding night—soon as we came in here—he
snatched off one of my slippers and rushed about the place smash-
ing the light-bulbs with it.

BLANCHE He did—*what?*

STELLA He smashed all the light-bulbs with the heel of my slipper!
(*She laughs*)

BLANCHE And you—you *let* him? Didn't *run*, didn't *scream?*

STELLA I was—sort of—thrilled by it. (*She waits for a moment*)
Eunice and you had breakfast?

BLANCHE Do you suppose I wanted any breakfast?

STELLA There's some coffee left on the stove.

BLANCHE You're so—matter of fact about it, Stella.

STELLA What other can I be? He's taken the radio to get it fixed.
It didn't land on the pavement so only one tube was smashed.

BLANCHE And you are standing there smiling!

STELLA What do you want me to do?

BLANCHE Pull yourself together and face the facts.

STELLA   What are they, in your opinion?

BLANCHE   In my opinion? You're married to a madman!

STELLA   No!

BLANCHE   Yes, you are, your fix is worse than mine is! Only you're
not being sensible about it. I'm going to *do* something. Get hold
of myself and make myself a new life!

STELLA   Yes?

BLANCHE   But you've given in. And that isn't right, you're not old!
You can get out.

STELLA   (*Slowly and emphatically*)   I'm not in anything I want to
get out of.

BLANCHE   (*Incredulously*)   What—Stella?

STELLA   I said I am not in anything that I have a desire to get out
of. Look at the mess in this room! And those empty bottles! They
went through two cases last night! He promised this morning that
he was going to quit having these poker parties, but you know
how long such a promise is going to keep. Oh, well, it's his pleasure, like mine is movies and bridge. People have got to tolerate
each other's habits, I guess.

BLANCHE   I don't understand you. (STELLA *turns toward her*) I don't
understand your indifference. Is this a Chinese philosophy you've
—cultivated?

STELLA   Is what—what?

BLANCHE   This—shuffling about and mumbling—"One tube smashed
—beer-bottles—mess in the kitchen!"—as if nothing out of the ordinary has happened!

(STELLA *laughs uncertainly and picking up the broom, twirls it in
her hands*)

BLANCHE   Are you deliberately shaking that thing in my face?

STELLA   No.

BLANCHE   Stop it. Let go of that broom. I won't have you cleaning
up for him!

STELLA   Then who's going to do it? Are you?

BLANCHE   I? I!

STELLA   No, I didn't think so.

BLANCHE   Oh, let me think, if only my mind would function! We've
got to get hold of some money, that's the way out!

STELLA   I guess that money is always nice to get hold of.

BLANCHE   Listen to me. I have an idea of some kind. (*Shakily she
twists a cigarette into her holder*) Do you remember Shep Huntleigh? (STELLA *shakes her head*) Of course you remember Shep

Huntleigh. I went out with him at college and wore his pin for a while. Well—

STELLA Well?

BLANCHE I ran into him last winter. You know I went to Miami during the Christmas holidays?

STELLA No.

BLANCHE Well, I did. I took the trip as an investment, thinking I'd meet someone with a million dollars.

STELLA Did you?

BLANCHE Yes. I ran into Shep Huntleigh—I ran into him on Biscayne Boulevard, on Christmas Eve, about dusk . . . getting into his car—Cadillac convertible; must have been a block long!

STELLA I should think it would have been—inconvenient in traffic!

BLANCHE You've heard of oil-wells?

STELLA Yes—remotely.

BLANCHE He has them, all over Texas. Texas is literally spouting gold in his pockets.

STELLA My, my.

BLANCHE Y'know how indifferent I am to money. I think of money in terms of what it does for you. But he could do it, he could certainly do it!

STELLA Do what, Blanche?

BLANCHE Why—set us up in a—shop!

STELLA What kind of a shop?

BLANCHE Oh, a—shop of some kind! He could do it with half what his wife throws away at the races.

STELLA He's married?

BLANCHE Honey, would I be here if the man weren't married? (STELLA *laughs a little.* BLANCHE *suddenly springs up and crosses to phone. She speaks shrilly*) How do I get Western Union?— Operator! Western Union!

STELLA That's a dial phone, honey.

BLANCHE I can't dial, I'm too—

STELLA Just dial O.

BLANCHE O?

STELLA Yes, "O" for Operator!
(BLANCHE *considers a moment; then she puts the phone down*)

BLANCHE Give me a pencil. Where is a slip of paper? I've got to write it down first—the message, I mean . . . (*She goes to the dressing table, and grabs up a sheet of Kleenex and an eyebrow pencil for writing equipment*) Let me see now . . . (*She bites the pencil*) "Darling Shep. Sister and I in desperate situation."

BLANCHE   Oh, no. No, Stella.

STELLA   I beg your pardon!

BLANCHE   "Sister and I in desperate situation. Will explain details later. Would you be interested in—?" (*She bites the pencil again*) "Would you be—interested—in . . ." (*She smashes the pencil on the table and springs up*) You never get anywhere with direct appeals!

STELLA (*With a laugh*)   Don't be so ridiculous, darling!

BLANCHE   But I'll think of something, I've *got* to think of—*some*thing! Don't, don't laugh at me, Stella! Please, please don't—I—I want you to look at the contents of my purse! Here's what's in it! (*She snatches her purse open*) Sixty-five measly cents in coin of the realm!

STELLA (*Crossing to bureau*)   Stanley doesn't give me a regular allowance, he likes to pay bills himself, but—this morning he gave me ten dollars to smooth things over. You take five of it, Blanche, and I'll keep the rest.

STELLA (*Insisting*)   I know how it helps your morale just having a little pocket-money on you.

BLANCHE   No, thank you—I'll take to the streets!

STELLA   Talk sense! How did you happen to get so low on funds?

BLANCHE   Money just goes—it goes places. (*She rubs her forehead*) Sometime today I've got to get hold of a bromo!

STELLA   I'll fix you one now.

BLANCHE   Not yet—I've got to keep thinking!

STELLA   I wish you'd just let things go, at least for a—while . . .

BLANCHE   Stella, I can't live with him! You can, he's your husband. But how could I stay here with him, after last night, with just those curtains between us?

STELLA   Blanche, you saw him at his worst last night.

BLANCHE   On the contrary, I saw him at his best! What such a man has to offer is animal force and he gave a wonderful exhibition of that! But the only way to live with such a man is to—go to bed with him! And that's your job—not mine!

STELLA   After you've rested a little, you'll see it's going to work out. You don't have to worry about anything while you're here. I mean —expenses . . .

BLANCHE   I have to plan for us both, to get us both—out!

STELLA   You take it for granted that I am in something that I want to get out of.

BLANCHE   I take it for granted that you still have sufficient memory of Belle Reve to find this place and these poker players impossible to live with.

STELLA   Well, you're taking entirely too much for granted.

BLANCHE   I can't believe you're in earnest.

STELLA   No?

BLANCHE   I understand how it happened—a little. You saw him in uniform, an officer, not here but—

STELLA   I'm not sure it would have made any difference where I saw him.

BLANCHE   Now don't say it was one of those mysterious electric things between people! If you do I'll laugh in your face.

STELLA   I am not going to say anything more at all about it!

BLANCHE   All right, then, don't!

STELLA   But there are things that happen between a man and a woman in the dark—that sort of make everything else seem—unimportant.

(*Pause*)

BLANCHE   What you are talking about is brutal desire—just—Desire! —the name of that rattle-trap street-car that bangs through the Quarter, up one old narrow street and down another . . .

STELLA   Haven't you ever ridden on that street-car?

BLANCHE   It brought me here.—Where I'm not wanted and where I'm ashamed to be . . .

STELLA   Then don't you think your superior attitude is a bit out of place?

BLANCHE   I am not being or feeling at all superior, Stella. Believe me I'm not! It's just this. This is how I look at it. A man like that is someone to go out with—once—twice—three times when the devil is in you. But live with? Have a child by?

STELLA   I have told you I love him.

BLANCHE   Then I *tremble* for you! I just—*tremble* for you. . . .

STELLA   I can't help your trembling if you insist on trembling!

(*There is a pause*)

BLANCHE   May I—speak—*plainly*?

STELLA   Yes, do. Go ahead. As plainly as you want to.

(*Outside, a train approaches. They are silent till the noise subsides. They are both in the bedroom. Under cover of the train's noise* STANLEY *enters from outside. He stands unseen by the women, holding some packages in his arms, and overhears their following conversation. He wears an undershirt and grease-stained seersucker pants)*

BLANCHE   Well—if you'll forgive me—he's *common!*

STELLA   Why, yes, I suppose he is.

BLANCHE   Suppose! You can't have forgotten that much of our bringing up, Stella, that you just *suppose* that any part of a gentleman's in his nature! *Not one particle, no!* Oh, if he was just—*ordinary!* Just *plain*—but good and wholesome, but—*no.* There's something downright—*bestial*—about him! You're hating me saying this, aren't you?

STELLA   (*Coldly*)   Go on and say it all, Blanche.

BLANCHE   He acts like an animal, has an animal's habits! Eats like one, moves like one, talks like one! There's even something—sub-human—something not quite to the stage of humanity yet! Yes, something—ape-like about him, like one of those pictures I've seen in—anthropological studies! Thousands and thousands of years have passed him right by, and there he is—Stanley Kowalski—survivor of the stone age! Bearing the raw meat home from the kill in the jungle! And you—*you* here—*waiting* for him! Maybe he'll strike you or maybe grunt and kiss you! That is, if kisses have been discovered yet! Night falls and the other apes gather! There in the front of the cave, all grunting like him, and swilling and gnawing and hulking! His poker night!—you call it—this party of apes! Somebody growls—some creature snatches at something—the fight is on! *God!* Maybe we are a long way from being made in God's image, but Stella—my sister—there has been *some* progress since then! Such things as art—as poetry and music—such kinds of new light have come into the world since then! In some kinds of people some tenderer feelings have had some little beginning! That we have got to make *grow!* And *cling* to, and hold as our flag! In this dark march toward whatever it is we're approaching. . . . *Don't—don't hang back with the brutes!*

(*Another train passes outside.* STANLEY *hesitates, licking his lips. Then suddenly he turns stealthily about and withdraws through front door. The women are still unaware of his presence. When the train has passed he calls through the closed front door)*

STANLEY   Hey! Hey, Stella!

STELLA   (*Who has listened gravely to* BLANCHE)   Stanley!

BLANCHE   Stell, I—

(*But* STELLA *has gone to the front door.* STANLEY *enters casually with his packages*)

STANLEY   Hiyuh, Stella. Blanche back?

STELLA   Yes, she's back.

STANLEY   Hiyuh, Blanche.

(*He grins at her*)

STELLA   You must've got under the car.

STANLEY   Them darn mechanics at Fritz's don't know their ass fr'm— Hey!

(STELLA *has embraced him with both arms, fiercely, and full in the view of* BLANCHE. *He laughs and clasps her head to him. Over her head he grins through the curtains at* BLANCHE. *As the lights fade away, with a lingering brightness on their embrace, the music of the "blue piano" and trumpet and drums is heard*)

SCENE FIVE

BLANCHE *is seated in the bedroom fanning herself with a palm leaf as she reads over a just completed letter. Suddenly she bursts into a peal of laughter.* STELLA *is dressing in the bedroom.*

STELLA   What are you laughing at, honey?

BLANCHE   Myself, myself, for being such a liar! I'm writing a letter to Shep. (*She picks up the letter*) "Darling Shep. I am spending the summer on the wing, making flying visits here and there. And who knows, perhaps I shall take a sudden notion to *swoop* down on *Dallas!* How would you feel about that? Ha-ha! (*She laughs nervously and brightly, touching her throat as if actually talking to Shep*) Forewarned is forearmed, as they say!"—How does that sound?

STELLA   Uh-huh . . .

BLANCHE   (*Going on nervously*)   "Most of my sister's friends go north in the summer but some have homes on the Gulf and there has been a continued round of entertainments, teas, cocktails, and luncheons—"

   (*A disturbance is heard upstairs at the* HUBBELLS' *apartment*)

STELLA   Eunice seems to be having some trouble with Steve.

   (EUNICE'S *voice shouts in terrible wrath*)

EUNICE   I heard about you and that blonde!

STEVE   That's a damn lie!

EUNICE   You ain't pulling the wool over my eyes! I wouldn't mind if you'd stay down at the Four Deuces, but you always going up.

STEVE   Who ever seen me up?

EUNICE   I seen you chasing her 'round the balcony—I'm gonna call the vice squad!

STEVE   Don't you throw that at me!

EUNICE   (*Shrieking*)   You hit me! I'm gonna call the police!

   (*A clatter of aluminum striking a wall is heard, followed by a*

man's angry roar, shouts and overturned furniture. There is a
crash; then a relative hush)

BLANCHE (*Brightly*)   Did he *kill* her?

(EUNICE *appears on the steps in daemonic disorder*)

STELLA   No! She's coming downstairs.

EUNICE   Call the police, I'm going to call the police!

(*She rushes around the corner. They laugh lightly.* STANLEY *comes around the corner in his green and scarlet silk bowling shirt. He trots up the steps and bangs into the kitchen.* BLANCHE *registers his entrance with nervous gestures*)

STANLEY   What's a matter with Eun-uss?

STELLA   She and Steve had a row. Has she got the police?

STANLEY   Naw. She's gettin' a drink.

STELLA   That's much more practical!

(STEVE *comes down nursing a bruise on his forehead and looks in the door*)

STEVE   *She here?*

STANLEY   Naw, naw. At the Four Deuces.

STEVE   That rutting hunk!

(*He looks around the corner a bit timidly, then turns with affected boldness and runs after her*)

BLANCHE   I must jot that down in my notebook. Ha-ha! I'm compiling a notebook of quaint little words and phrases I've picked up here.

STANLEY   You won't pick up nothing here you ain't heard before.

BLANCHE   Can I count on that?

STANLEY   You can count on it up to five hundred.

BLANCHE   That's a mighty high number. (*He jerks open the bureau drawer, slams it shut and throws shoes in a corner. At each noise* BLANCHE *winces slightly. Finally she speaks*) What sign were you born under?

STANLEY (*While he is dressing*)   Sign?

BLANCHE   Astrological sign. I bet you were born under Aries. Aries people are forceful and dynamic. They dote on noise! They love to bang things around! You must have had lots of banging around in the army and now that you're out, you make up for it by treating inanimate objects with such a fury!

(STELLA *has been going in and out of closet during this scene. Now she pops her head out of the closet*)

STELLA   Stanley was born just five minutes after Christmas.

BLANCHE   Capricorn—the Goat!

STANLEY What sign were *you* born under?

BLANCHE Oh, my birthday's next month, the fifteenth of September; that's under Virgo.

STANLEY What's Virgo?

BLANCHE Virgo is the Virgin.

STANLEY (*Contemptuously*) Hah! (*He advances a little as he knots his tie*) Say, do you happen to know somebody named Shaw?

(*Her face expresses a faint shock. She reaches for the cologne bottle and dampens her handkerchief as she answers carefully*)

BLANCHE Why, everybody knows somebody named Shaw!

STANLEY Well, this somebody named Shaw is under the impression he met you in Laurel, but I figure he must have got you mixed up with some other party because this other party is someone he met at a hotel called the Flamingo.

(BLANCHE *laughs breathlessly as she touches the cologne-dampened handkerchief to her temples*)

BLANCHE I'm afraid he does have me mixed up with this "other party." The Hotel Flamingo is not the sort of establishment I would dare to be seen in!

STANLEY You know of it?

BLANCHE Yes, I've seen it and smelled it.

STANLEY You must've got pretty close if you could smell it.

BLANCHE The odor of cheap perfume is penetrating.

STANLEY That stuff you use is expensive?

BLANCHE Twenty-five dollars an ounce! I'm nearly out. That's just a hint if you want to remember my birthday!

(*She speaks lightly but her voice has a note of fear*)

STANLEY Shaw must've got you mixed up. He goes in and out of Laurel all the time so he can check on it and clear up any mistake.

(*He turns away and crosses to the portieres.* BLANCHE *closes her eyes as if faint. Her hand trembles as she lifts the handkerchief again to her forehead.* STEVE *and* EUNICE *come around corner.* STEVE'S *arm is around* EUNICE'S *shoulder and she is sobbing luxuriously and he is cooing love-words. There is a murmur of thunder as they go slowly upstairs in a tight embrace*)

STANLEY (*To* STELLA) I'll wait for you at the Four Deuces!

STELLA Hey! Don't I rate one kiss?

STANLEY Not in front of your sister.

(*He goes out.* BLANCHE *rises from her chair. She seems faint; looks about her with an expression of almost panic*)

BLANCHE   Stella! What have you heard about me?

STELLA   Huh?

BLANCHE   What have people been telling you about me?

STELLA   Telling?

BLANCHE   You haven't heard any—unkind—gossip about me?

STELLA   Why, no, Blanche, of course not!

BLANCHE   Honey, there was—a good deal of talk in Laurel.

STELLA   About *you*, Blanche?

BLANCHE   I wasn't so good the last two years or so, after Belle Reve had started to slip through my fingers.

STELLA   All of us do things we—

BLANCHE   I never was hard or self-sufficient enough. When people are soft—soft people have got to shimmer and glow—they've got to put on soft colors, the colors of butterfly wings, and put a— paper lantern over the light. . . . It isn't enough to be soft. You've got to be soft *and attractive*. And I—I'm fading now! I don't know how much longer I can turn the trick.

(*The afternoon has faded to dusk.* STELLA *goes into the bedroom and turns on the light under the paper lantern. She holds a bottled soft drink in her hand*)

BLANCHE   Have you been listening to me?

STELLA   I don't listen to you when you are being morbid!

(*She advances with the bottled coke*)

BLANCHE   (*With abrupt change to gaiety*)   Is that coke for me?

STELLA   Not for anyone else!

BLANCHE   Why, you precious thing, you! Is it just coke?

STELLA   (*Turning*)   You mean you want a shot in it!

BLANCHE   Well, honey, a shot never does a coke any harm! Let me! You mustn't wait on me!

STELLA   I like to wait on you, Blanche. It makes it seem more like home.

(*She goes into the kitchen, finds a glass and pours a shot of whiskey into it*)

BLANCHE   I have to admit I love to be waited on . . . (*She rushes into the bedroom.* STELLA *goes to her with the glass.* BLANCHE *suddenly clutches* STELLA's *free hand with a moaning sound and presses the hand to her lips.* STELLA *is embarrassed by her show of emotion.* BLANCHE *speaks in a choked voice*) You're—you're—so *good* to me! And I—

STELLA   Blanche.

BLANCHE   I know, I won't! You hate me to talk sentimental! But honey, *believe* I feel things more than I *tell* you! I *won't* stay long! I won't, I *promise* I—

STELLA   Blanche!

BLANCHE   (*Hysterically*)   I won't, I promise, *I'll* go! Go *soon!* I will *really!* I *won't* hang around until he—throws me out . . .

STELLA   Now will you stop talking foolish?

BLANCHE   Yes, honey. Watch how you pour—that fizzy stuff foams over!

(BLANCHE *laughs shrilly and grabs the glass, but her hand shakes so it almost slips from her grasp.* STELLA *pours the coke into the glass. It foams over and spills.* BLANCHE *gives a piercing cry*)

STELLA   (*Shocked by the cry*)   Heavens!

BLANCHE   Right on my pretty white skirt!

STELLA   Oh . . . Use my hanky. Blot gently.

BLANCHE   (*Slowly recovering*)   I know—gently—gently . . .

STELLA   Did it stain?

BLANCHE   Not a bit. Ha-ha! Isn't that lucky?

(*She sits down shakily, taking a grateful drink. She holds the glass in both hands and continues to laugh a little*)

STELLA   Why did you scream like that?

BLANCHE   I don't know why I screamed! (*Continuing nervously*) Mitch—Mitch is coming at seven. I guess I am just feeling nervous about our relations. (*She begins to talk rapidly and breathlessly*) He hasn't gotten a thing but a goodnight kiss, that's all I have given him, Stella. I want his respect. And men don't want anything they get too easy. But on the other hand men lose interest quickly. Especially when the girl is over—thirty. They think a girl over thirty ought to—the vulgar term is—"put out." . . . And I— I'm not "putting out." Of course he—he doesn't know—I mean I haven't informed him—of my real age!

STELLA   Why are you sensitive about your age?

BLANCHE   Because of hard knocks my vanity's been given. What I mean is—he thinks I'm sort of—prim and proper, you know! (*She laughs out sharply*) I want to *deceive* him enough to make him— want me . . .

STELLA   Blanche, do you want *him?*

BLANCHE   I want to *rest!* I want to breathe quietly again! Yes—I *want* Mitch . . . *very badly!* Just think! If it happens! I can leave here and not be anyone's problem . . .

(STANLEY *comes around the corner with a drink under his belt*)

STANLEY (*Bawling*)   Hey, Steve! Hey, Eunice! Hey, Stella!

(*There are joyous calls from above. Trumpet and drums are heard from around the corner*)

STELLA (*Kissing* BLANCHE *impulsively*)   It *will* happen!

BLANCHE (*Doubtfully*)   It will?

STELLA   It *will!* (*She goes across into the kitchen, looking back at* BLANCHE) It will, honey, *it will.* . . . But don't take another drink!

(*Her voice catches as she goes out the door to meet her husband.* BLANCHE *sinks faintly back in her chair with her drink.* EUNICE *shrieks with laughter and runs down the steps.* STEVE *bounds after her with goat-like screeches and chases her around corner.* STANLEY *and* STELLA *twine arms as they follow, laughing. Dusk settles deeper. The music from the Four Deuces is slow and blue*)

BLANCHE   Ah, me, ah, me, ah, me . . .

(*Her eyes fall shut and the palm leaf fan drops from her fingers. She slaps her hand on the chair arm a couple of times. There is a little glimmer of lightning about the building. A* YOUNG MAN *comes along the street and rings the bell*)

BLANCHE   Come in.

(*The* YOUNG MAN *appears through the portieres. She regards him with interest*)

BLANCHE   Well, well! What can I do for *you?*

YOUNG MAN   I'm collecting for *The Evening Star.*

BLANCHE   I didn't know that stars took up collections.

YOUNG MAN   It's the paper.

BLANCHE   I know, I was joking—feebly! Will you—have a drink?

YOUNG MAN   No, ma'am. No, thank you. I can't drink on the job.

BLANCHE   Oh, well, now, let's see. . . . No, I don't have a dime! I'm not the lady of the house. I'm her sister from Mississippi. I'm one of those poor relations you've heard about.

YOUNG MAN   That's all right. I'll drop by later.

(*He starts to go out. She approaches a little*)

BLANCHE   Hey! (*He turns back shyly. She puts a cigarette in a long holder*) Could you give me a light?

(*She crosses toward him. They meet at the door between the two rooms*)

YOUNG MAN   Sure. (*He takes out a lighter*) This doesn't always work.

BLANCHE   It's temperamental? (*It flares*) Ah!—thank you. (*He*

starts away again) Hey! (*He turns again, still more uncertainly.
She goes close to him*) Uh—what time is it?

YOUNG MAN   Fifteen of seven, ma'am.

BLANCHE   So late? Don't you just love these long rainy afternoons
in New Orleans when an hour isn't just an hour—but a little piece
of eternity dropped into your hands—and who knows what to do
with it? (*She touches his shoulders*) You—uh—didn't get wet in
the rain?

YOUNG MAN   No, ma'am. I stepped inside.

BLANCHE   In a drug-store? And had a soda?

YOUNG MAN   Uh-huh.

BLANCHE   Chocolate?

YOUNG MAN   No, ma'am. Cherry.

BLANCHE (*Laughing*)   Cherry!

YOUNG MAN   A cherry soda.

BLANCHE   You make my mouth water.
  (*She touches his cheek lightly, and smiles. Then she goes to the
  trunk*)

YOUNG MAN   Well, I'd better be going—

BLANCHE (*Stopping him*)   Young man! (*He turns. She takes a
large, gossamer scarf from the trunk and drapes it about her shoulders. In the ensuing pause, the "blue piano" is heard. It continues
through the rest of this scene and the opening of the next. The
YOUNG MAN clears his throat and looks yearningly at the door*)
Young man! Young, young, young man! Has anyone ever told you
that you look like a young Prince out of the Arabian Nights?
(*The YOUNG MAN laughs uncomfortably and stands like a bashful
kid. BLANCHE speaks softly to him*) Well, you do, honey lamb!
Come here. I want to kiss you, just once, softly and sweetly on
your mouth! (*Without waiting for him to accept, she crosses
quickly to him and presses her lips to his*) Now run along, now,
quickly! It would be nice to keep you, but I've got to be good—
and keep my hands off children.
  (*He stares at her a moment. She opens the door for him and
  blows a kiss at him as he goes down the steps with a dazed look.
  She stands there a little dreamily after he has disappeared. Then
  MITCH appears around the corner with a bunch of roses*)

BLANCHE (*Gaily*)   Look who's coming! My Rosenkavalier! Bow to
me first . . . now present them! *Ahhhh—Merciiii!*
  (*She looks at him over them, coquettishly pressing them to her
  lips. He beams at her self-consciously*)

SCENE SIX

It is about two A.M. on the same evening. The outer wall of the building is visible. BLANCHE *and* MITCH *come in. The utter exhaustion which only a neurasthenic personality can know is evident in* BLANCHE'S *voice and manner.* MITCH *is stolid but depressed. They have probably been out to the amusement park on Lake Pontchartrain, for* MITCH *is bearing, upside down, a plaster statuette of Mae West, the sort of prize won at shooting-galleries and carnival games of chance.*

BLANCHE (*Stopping lifelessly at the steps*) Well— (MITCH *laughs uneasily*) Well . . .

MITCH I guess it must be pretty late—and you're tired.

BLANCHE Even the hot tamale man has deserted the street, and he hangs on till the end. (MITCH *laughs uneasily again*) How will you get home?

MITCH I'll walk over to Bourbon and catch an owl-car.

BLANCHE (*Laughing grimly*) Is that street-car named Desire still grinding along the tracks at this hour?

MITCH (*Heavily*) I'm afraid you haven't gotten much fun out of this evening, Blanche.

BLANCHE I spoiled it for *you.*

MITCH No, you didn't, but I felt all the time that I wasn't giving you much—entertainment.

BLANCHE I simply couldn't rise to the occasion. That was all. I don't think I've ever tried so hard to be gay and made such a dismal mess of it. I get ten points for trying!—I *did* try.

MITCH Why did you try if you didn't feel like it, Blanche?

BLANCHE I was just obeying the law of nature.

MITCH Which law is that?

BLANCHE The one that says the lady must entertain the gentleman —or no dice! See if you can locate my door-key in this purse. When I'm so tired my fingers are all thumbs!

MITCH (*Rooting in her purse*)   This it?

BLANCHE No, honey, that's the key to my trunk which I must soon be packing.

MITCH You mean you are leaving here soon?

BLANCHE I've overstayed my welcome.

MITCH This it?

(*The music fades away*)

BLANCHE Eureka! Honey, you open the door while I take a last look at the sky. (*She leans on the porch rail. He opens the door and stands awkwardly behind her*) I'm looking for the Pleiades, the Seven Sisters, but these girls are not out tonight. Oh, yes, they are, there they are! God bless them! All in a bunch going home from their little bridge party. . . . Y' get the door open? Good boy! I guess you—want to go now . . .

(*He shuffles and coughs a little*)

MITCH Can I—uh—kiss you—goodnight?

BLANCHE Why do you always ask me if you may?

MITCH I don't know whether you want me to or not.

BLANCHE Why should you be so doubtful?

MITCH That night when we parked by the lake and I kissed you, you—

BLANCHE Honey, it wasn't the kiss I objected to. I liked the kiss very much. It was the other little—familiarity—that I—felt obliged to—discourage. . . . I didn't resent it! Not a bit in the world! In fact, I was somewhat flattered that you—desired me! But, honey, you know as well as I do that a single girl, a girl alone in the world, has got to keep a firm hold on her emotions or she'll be lost!

MITCH (*Solemnly*)   Lost?

BLANCHE I guess you are used to girls that like to be lost. The kind that get lost immediately, on the first date!

MITCH I like you to be exactly the way that you are, because in all my—experience—I have never known anyone like you.

(BLANCHE *looks at him gravely; then she bursts into laughter and then claps a hand to her mouth*)

MITCH Are you laughing at me?

BLANCHE No, honey. The lord and lady of the house have not yet returned, so come in. We'll have a night-cap. Let's leave the lights off. Shall we?

MITCH You just—do what you want to.

(BLANCHE *precedes him into the kitchen. The outer wall of the*

*building disappears and the interiors of the two rooms can be
dimly seen*)

BLANCHE (*Remaining in the first room*) The other room's more
comfortable—go on in. This crashing around in the dark is my
search for some liquor.

MITCH You want a drink?

BLANCHE I want *you* to have a drink! You have been so anxious
and solemn all evening, and so have I; we have both been anxious
and solemn and now for these few last remaining moments of
our lives together—I want to create—*joie de vivre!* I'm lighting a
candle.

MITCH That's good.

BLANCHE We are going to be very Bohemian. We are going to pretend that we are sitting in a little artists' cafe on the Left Bank
in Paris! (*She lights a candle stub and puts it in a bottle*) *Je suis
la Dame aux Camellias! Vous êtes—Armand!* Understand French?

MITCH (*Heavily*) Naw. Naw, I—

BLANCHE *Voulez-vous couchez avec moi ce soir? Vous ne com-
prenez pas? Ah, quelle dommage!*—I mean it's a damned good
thing. . . . I've found some liquor! Just enough for two shots without any dividends, honey . . .

MITCH (*Heavily*) That's—good.

(*She enters the bedroom with the drinks and the candle*)

BLANCHE Sit down! Why don't you take off your coat and loosen
your collar?

MITCH I better leave it on.

BLANCHE No. I want you to be comfortable.

MITCH I am ashamed of the way I perspire. My shirt is sticking to
me.

BLANCHE Perspiration is healthy. If people didn't perspire they
would die in five minutes. (*She takes his coat from him*) This is
a nice coat. What kind of material is it?

MITCH They call that stuff alpaca.

BLANCHE Oh. Alpaca.

MITCH It's very light weight alpaca.

BLANCHE Oh. Light weight alpaca.

MITCH I don't like to wear a wash-coat even in summer because I
sweat through it.

BLANCHE Oh.

MITCH And it don't look neat on me. A man with a heavy build has got to be careful of what he puts on him so he don't look too clumsy.

BLANCHE   You are not too heavy.

MITCH   You don't think I am?

BLANCHE   You are not the delicate type. You have a massive bone-structure and a very imposing physique.

MITCH   Thank you. Last Christmas I was given a membership to the New Orleans Athletic Club.

BLANCHE   Oh, good.

MITCH   It was the finest present I ever was given. I work out there with the weights and I swim and I keep myself fit. When I started there, I was getting soft in the belly but now my belly is hard. It is so hard now that a man can punch me in the belly and it don't hurt me. Punch me! Go on! See?

(*She pokes lightly at him*)

BLANCHE   Gracious. (*Her hand touches her chest*)

MITCH   Guess how much I weigh, Blanche?

BLANCHE   Oh, I'd say in the vicinity of—one hundred and eighty?

MITCH   Guess again.

BLANCHE   Not that much?

MITCH   No. More.

BLANCHE   Well, you're a tall man and you can carry a good deal of weight without looking awkward.

MITCH   I weigh two hundred and seven pounds and I'm six feet one and one half inches tall in my bare feet—without shoes on. And that is what I weigh stripped.

BLANCHE   Oh, my goodness, me! It's awe-inspiring.

MITCH   (*Embarrassed*)   My weight is not a very interesting subject to talk about. (*He hesitates for a moment*) What's yours?

BLANCHE   My weight?

MITCH   Yes.

BLANCHE   Guess!

MITCH   Let me lift you.

BLANCHE   Samson! Go on, lift me. (*He comes behind her and puts his hands on her waist and raises her lightly off the ground*) Well?

MITCH   You are light as a feather.

BLANCHE   Ha-ha! (*He lowers her but keeps his hands on her waist.* BLANCHE *speaks with an affectation of demureness*) You may release me now.

MITCH   Huh?

BLANCHE   (*Gaily*)   I said unhand me, sir. (*He fumblingly embraces her. Her voice sounds gently reproving*) Now, Mitch. Just because Stanley and Stella aren't at home is no reason why you shouldn't behave like a gentleman.

MITCH   Just give me a slap whenever I step out of bounds.

BLANCHE   That won't be necessary. You're a natural gentleman, one of the very few that are left in the world. I don't want you to think that I am severe and old maid schoolteacherish or anything like that. It's just—well—

MITCH   Huh?

BLANCHE   I guess it is just that I have—old-fashioned ideals! (*She rolls her eyes, knowing he cannot see her face.* MITCH *goes to the front door. There is a considerable silence between them.* BLANCHE *sighs and* MITCH *coughs self-consciously*)

MITCH (*Finally*)   Where's Stanley and Stella tonight?

BLANCHE   They have gone out. With Mr. and Mrs. Hubbell upstairs.

MITCH   Where did they go?

BLANCHE   I think they were planning to go to a midnight prevue at Loew's State.

MITCH   We should all go out together some night.

BLANCHE   No. That wouldn't be a good plan.

MITCH   Why not?

BLANCHE   You are an old friend of Stanley's?

MITCH   We was together in the Two-forty-first.

BLANCHE   I guess he talks to you frankly?

MITCH   Sure.

BLANCHE   Has he talked to you about me?

MITCH   Oh—not very much.

BLANCHE   The way you say that, I suspect that he has.

MITCH   No, he hasn't said much.

BLANCHE   But what he *has* said. What would you say his attitude toward me was?

MITCH   Why do you want to ask that?

BLANCHE   Well—

MITCH   Don't you get along with him?

BLANCHE   What do you think?

MITCH   I don't think he understands you.

BLANCHE   That is putting it mildly. If it weren't for Stella about to have a baby, I wouldn't be able to endure things here.

MITCH   He isn't—nice to you?

BLANCHE   He is insufferably rude. Goes out of his way to offend me.

MITCH In what way, Blanche?

BLANCHE Why, in every conceivable way.

MITCH I'm surprised to hear that.

BLANCHE Are you?

MITCH Well, I—don't see how anybody could be rude to you.

BLANCHE It's really a pretty frightful situation. You see, there's no privacy here. There's just these portieres between the two rooms at night. He stalks through the rooms in his underwear at night. And I have to ask him to close the bathroom door. That sort of commonness isn't necessary. You probably wonder why I don't move out. Well, I'll tell you frankly. A teacher's salary is barely sufficient for her living-expenses. I didn't save a penny last year and so I had to come here for the summer. That's why I have to put up with my sister's husband. And he has to put up with me, apparently so much against his wishes. . . . Surely he must have told you how much he hates me!

MITCH I don't think he hates you.

BLANCHE He hates me. Or why would he insult me? The first time I laid eyes on him I thought to myself, that man is my executioner! That man will destroy me, unless——

MITCH Blanche—

BLANCHE Yes, honey?

MITCH Can I ask you a question?

BLANCHE Yes. What?

MITCH How old are you?

(*She makes a nervous gesture*)

BLANCHE Why do you want to know?

MITCH I talked to my mother about you and she said, "How old is Blanche?" And I wasn't able to tell her.

(*There is another pause*)

BLANCHE You talked to your mother about me?

MITCH Yes.

BLANCHE Why?

MITCH I told my mother how nice you were, and I liked you.

BLANCHE Were you sincere about that?

MITCH You know I was.

BLANCHE Why did your mother want to know my age?

MITCH Mother is sick.

BLANCHE I'm sorry to hear it. Badly?

MITCH She won't live long. Maybe just a few months.

BLANCHE Oh.

MITCH   She worries because I'm not settled.

BLANCHE   Oh.

MITCH   She wants me to be settled down before she—
(*His voice is hoarse and he clears his throat twice, shuffling nervously around with his hands in and out of his pockets*)

BLANCHE   You love her very much, don't you?

MITCH   Yes.

BLANCHE   I think you have a great capacity for devotion. You will be lonely when she passes on, won't you? (MITCH *clears his throat and nods*) I understand what that is.

MITCH   To be lonely?

BLANCHE   I loved someone, too, and the person I loved I lost.

MITCH   Dead? (*She crosses to the window and sits on the sill, looking out. She pours herself another drink*) A man?

BLANCHE   He was a boy, just a boy, when I was a very young girl. When I was sixteen, I made the discovery—love. All at once and much, much too completely. It was like you suddenly turned a blinding light on something that had always been half in shadow, that's how it struck the world for me. But I was unlucky. Deluded. There was something different about the boy, a nervousness, a softness and tenderness which wasn't like a man's, although he wasn't the least bit effeminate looking—still—that thing was there. . . . He came to me for help. I didn't know that. I didn't find out anything till after our marriage when we'd run away and come back and all I knew was I'd failed him in some mysterious way and wasn't able to give the help he needed but couldn't speak of! He was in the quicksands and clutching at me —but I wasn't holding him out, I was slipping in with him! I didn't know that. I didn't know anything except I loved him unendurably but without being able to help him or help myself. Then I found out. In the worst of all possible ways. By coming suddenly into a room that I thought was empty—which wasn't empty, but had two people in it . . . the boy I had married and an older man who had been his friend for years . . . (*A locomotive is heard approaching outside. She claps her hands to her ears and crouches over. The headlight of the locomotive glares into the room as it thunders past. As the noise recedes she straightens slowly and continues speaking*) Afterwards we pretended that nothing had been discovered. Yes, the three of us drove out to Moon Lake Casino, very drunk and laughing all the way. (*Polka music sounds, in a minor key faint with distance*) We danced the Varsouviana! Suddenly in the middle of the dance the boy I had married broke away from me and ran out of the casino. A few moments later—a shot! (*The Polka stops abruptly.* BLANCHE *rises stiffly. Then, the Polka resumes in a major key*) I ran out—all did!—all ran and gathered about the terrible thing at the edge of the lake! I couldn't get near for the crowding. Then somebody caught my arm. "Don't go any closer! Come back! You don't want to see!" See? See what! Then I heard voices say—Allan! Allan! The Grey boy! He'd stuck the revolver into his mouth, and fired —so that the back of his head had been—blown away! (*She sways and covers her face*) It was because—on the dance-floor—unable to stop myself—I'd suddenly said—"I saw! I know! You disgust me . . ." And then the searchlight which had been turned on the world was turned off again and never for one moment since has there been any light that's stronger than this—kitchen—candle . . . (MITCH *gets up awkwardly and moves toward her a little. The Polka music increases.* MITCH *stands beside her*)

MITCH (*Drawing her slowly into his arms*) You need somebody. And I need somebody, too. Could it be—you and me, Blanche? (*She stares at him vacantly for a moment. Then with a soft cry huddles in his embrace. She makes a sobbing effort to speak but the words won't come. He kisses her forehead and her eyes and finally her lips. The Polka tune fades out. Her breath is drawn and released in long, grateful sobs*)

BLANCHE   Sometimes—there's God—so quickly!

SCENE SEVEN

It is late afternoon in mid-September.
  The portieres are open and a table is set for a birthday supper, with cake and flowers.
  STELLA *is completing the decorations as* STANLEY *comes in.*

STANLEY   What's all this stuff for?

STELLA   Honey, it's Blanche's birthday.

STANLEY   She here?

STELLA   In the bathroom.

STANLEY *(Mimicking)*   "Washing out some things"?

STELLA   I reckon so.

STANLEY   How long she been in there?

STELLA   All afternoon.

STANLEY *(Mimicking)*   "Soaking in a hot tub"?

STELLA   Yes.

STANLEY   Temperature 100 on the nose, and she soaks herself in a hot tub.

STELLA   She says it cools her off for the evening.

STANLEY   And you run out an' get her cokes, I suppose? And serve 'em to Her Majesty in the tub? *(STELLA shrugs)* Set down here a minute.

STELLA   Stanley, I've got things to do.

STANLEY   Set down! I've got th' dope on your big sister, Stella.

STELLA   Stanley, stop picking on Blanche.

STANLEY   That girl calls *me* common!

STELLA   Lately you been doing all you can think of to rub her the wrong way, Stanley, and Blanche is sensitive and you've got to realize that Blanche and I grew up under very different circumstances than you did.

STANLEY   So I been told. And told and told and told! You know she's been feeding us a pack of lies here?

STELLA   No, I don't, and—

STANLEY   Well, she has, however. But now the cat's out of the bag! I found out some things!

STELLA   What—things?

STANLEY   Things I already suspected. But now I got proof from the most reliable sources—which I have checked on!

(BLANCHE *is singing in the bathroom a saccharine popular ballad which is used contrapuntally with* STANLEY's *speech*)

STELLA   (*To* STANLEY)   Lower your voice!

STANLEY   Some canary-bird, huh!

STELLA   Now please tell me quietly what you think you've found out about my sister.

STANLEY   Lie Number One: All this squeamishness she puts on! You should just know the line she's been feeding to Mitch. He thought she had never been more than kissed by a fellow! But Sister Blanche is no lily! Ha-ha! Some lily she is!

STELLA   What have you heard and who from?

STANLEY   Our supply-man down at the plant has been going through Laurel for years and he knows all about her and everybody else in the town of Laurel knows all about her. She is as famous in Laurel as if she was the President of the United States, only she is not respected by any party! This supply-man stops at a hotel called the Flamingo.

BLANCHE

(*Singing blithely*)

"Say, it's only a paper moon, Sailing over a cardboard sea— But it wouldn't be make-believe, If you believed in me!"

STELLA   What about the—Flamingo?

STANLEY   She stayed there, too.

STELLA   My sister lived at Belle Reve.

STANLEY   This is after the home-place had slipped through her lily-white fingers! She moved to the Flamingo! A second-class hotel which has the advantage of not interfering in the private social life of the personalities there! The Flamingo is used to all kinds of goings-on. But even the management of the Flamingo was impressed by Dame Blanche! In fact they was so impressed by Dame Blanche that they requested her to turn in her room-key—for permanently! This happened a couple of weeks before she showed here.

BLANCHE

(*Singing*)

"It's a Barnum and Bailey world, Just as phony as it can be—
But it wouldn't be make-believe, If you believed in me!"

STELLA   What—contemptible—lies!

STANLEY   Sure, I can see how you would be upset by this. She
pulled the wool over your eyes as much as Mitch's!

STELLA   It's pure invention! There's not a word of truth in it and
if I were a man and this creature had dared to invent such things
in my presence—

BLANCHE

(*Singing*)

"Without your love,
It's a honky-tonk parade!
Without your love,
It's a melody played, In a penny arcade . . ."

STANLEY   Honey, I told you I thoroughly checked on these stories!
Now wait till I finished. The trouble with Dame Blanche was that
she couldn't put on her act any more in Laurel! They got wised
up after two or three dates with her and then they quit, and she
goes on to another, the same old line, same old act, same old
hooey! But the town was too small for this to go on forever! And
as time went by she became a town character. Regarded as not
just different but downright loco—nuts. (STELLA *draws back*) And
for the last year or two she has been washed up like poison. That's
why she's here this summer, visiting royalty, putting on all this
act—because she's practically told by the mayor to get out of
town! Yes, did you know there was an army camp near Laurel
and your sister's was one of the places called "Out-of-Bounds"?

BLANCHE

"It's only a paper moon, Just as phony as it can be—
But it wouldn't be make-believe, If you believed in me!"

STANLEY   Well, so much for her being such a refined and particular
type of girl. Which brings us to Lie Number Two.

STELLA   I don't want to hear any more!

STANLEY   She's not going back to teach school! In fact I am willing
to bet you that she never had no idea of returning to Laurel! She
didn't resign temporarily from the high school because of her

nerves! No, siree, Bob! She didn't. They kicked her out of that high school before the spring term ended—and I hate to tell you the reason that step was taken! A seventeen-year-old boy—she'd gotten mixed up with!

BLANCHE

"It's a Barnum and Bailey world, Just as phony as it can be—"

(*In the bathroom the water goes on loud; little breathless cries and peals of laughter are heard as if a child were frolicking in the tub*)

STELLA This is making me—sick!

STANLEY The boy's dad learned about it and got in touch with the high school superintendent. Boy, oh, boy, I'd like to have been in that office when Dame Blanche was called on the carpet! I'd like to have seen her trying to squirm out of that one! But they had her on the hook good and proper that time and she knew that the jig was all up! They told her she better move on to some fresh territory. Yep, it was practickly a town ordinance passed against her!

(*The bathroom door is opened and* BLANCHE *thrusts her head out, holding a towel about her hair*)

BLANCHE Stella!

STELLA (*Faintly*) Yes, Blanche?

BLANCHE Give me another bath-towel to dry my hair with. I've just washed it.

STELLA Yes, Blanche.

(*She crosses in a dazed way from the kitchen to the bathroom door with a towel*)

BLANCHE What's the matter, honey?

STELLA Matter? Why?

BLANCHE You have such a strange expression on your face!

STELLA Oh— (*She tries to laugh*) I guess I'm a little tired!

BLANCHE Why don't you bathe, too, soon as I get out?

STANLEY (*Calling from the kitchen*) How soon is that going to be?

BLANCHE Not so terribly long! Possess your soul in patience!

STANLEY It's not my soul, it's my kidneys I'm worried about!

(BLANCHE *slams the door.* STANLEY *laughs harshly.* STELLA *comes slowly back into the kitchen*)

STANLEY Well, what do you think of it?

STELLA I don't believe all of those stories and I think your supply-man was mean and rotten to tell them. It's possible that some of the things he said are partly true. There are things about my sister I don't approve of—things that caused sorrow at home. She was always—flighty!

STANLEY Flighty!

STELLA But when she was young, very young, she married a boy who wrote poetry. . . . He was extremely good-looking. I think Blanche didn't just love him but worshipped the ground he walked on! Adored him and thought him almost too fine to be human! But then she found out—

STANLEY What?

STELLA This beautiful and talented young man was a degenerate. Didn't your supply-man give you that information?

STANLEY All we discussed was recent history. That must have been a pretty long time ago.

STELLA Yes, it was—a pretty long time ago . . .

(STANLEY *comes up and takes her by the shoulders rather gently. She gently withdraws from him. Automatically she starts sticking little pink candles in the birthday cake*)

STANLEY How many candles you putting in that cake?

STELLA I'll stop at twenty-five.

STANLEY Is company expected?

STELLA We asked Mitch to come over for cake and ice-cream.

(STANLEY *looks a little uncomfortable. He lights a cigarette from the one he has just finished*)

STANLEY I wouldn't be expecting Mitch over tonight.

(STELLA *pauses in her occupation with candles and looks slowly around at* STANLEY)

STELLA *Why?*

STANLEY Mitch is a buddy of mine. We were in the same outfit together—Two-forty-first Engineers. We work in the same plant and now on the same bowling team. You think I could face him if—

STELLA Stanley Kowalski, did you—did you repeat what that—?

STANLEY You're goddam right I told him! I'd have that on my conscience the rest of my life if I knew all that stuff and let my best friend get caught!

STELLA Is Mitch through with her?

STANLEY Wouldn't you be if—?

STELLA I said, *Is Mitch through with her?*

(BLANCHE'S *voice is lifted again, serenely as a bell. She sings "But it wouldn't be make believe if you believed in me"*)

STANLEY   No, I don't think he's necessarily through with her—just wised up!

STELLA   Stanley, she thought Mitch was—going to—going to marry her. I was hoping so, too.

STANLEY   Well, he's not going to marry her. Maybe he *was,* but he's not going to jump in a tank with a school of sharks—now! (*He rises*) Blanche! Oh, Blanche! Can I please get in my bathroom? (*There is a pause*)

BLANCHE   Yes, indeed, sir! Can you wait one second while I dry?

STANLEY   Having waited one hour I guess one second ought to pass in a hurry.

STELLA   And she hasn't got her job? Well, what will she do!

STANLEY   She's not stayin' here after Tuesday. You know that, don't you? Just to make sure I bought her ticket myself. A bus-ticket!

STELLA   In the first place, Blanche wouldn't go on a bus.

STANLEY   She'll go on a bus and like it.

STELLA   No, she won't, no, she won't, Stanley!

STANLEY   *She'll go!* Period. P.S. She'll go *Tuesday!*

STELLA (*Slowly*)   What'll—she—do? What on earth will she—do!

STANLEY   Her future is mapped out for her.

STELLA   What do you mean?

(*BLANCHE sings*)

STANLEY   Hey, canary bird! Toots! Get *OUT* of the *BATHROOM!* (*The bathroom door flies open and* BLANCHE *emerges with a gay peal of laughter, but as* STANLEY *crosses past her, a frightened look appears in her face, almost a look of panic. He doesn't look at her but slams the bathroom door shut as he goes in*)

BLANCHE (*Snatching up a hair-brush*)   Oh, I feel so good after my long, hot bath, I feel so good and cool and—rested!

STELLA (*Sadly and doubtfully from the kitchen*)   Do you, Blanche?

BLANCHE (*Brushing her hair vigorously*)   Yes, I do, so refreshed! (*She tinkles her highball glass*) A hot bath and a long, cold drink always give me a brand new outlook on life! (*She looks through the portieres at* STELLA, *standing between them, and slowly stops brushing*) Something has happened!—What is it?

STELLA (*Turning away quickly*)   Why, nothing has happened, Blanche.

BLANCHE   You're lying! Something has!

(*She stares fearfully at* STELLA, *who pretends to be busy at the table. The distant piano goes into a hectic breakdown*)

SCENE EIGHT

Three-quarters of an hour later.

The view through the big windows is fading gradually into a still-golden dusk. A torch of sunlight blazes on the side of a big water-tank or oil-drum across the empty lot toward the business district which is now pierced by pinpoints of lighted windows or windows reflecting the sunset.

The three people are completing a dismal birthday supper. STANLEY *looks sullen.* STELLA *is embarrassed and sad.*

BLANCHE *has a tight, artificial smile on her drawn face. There is a fourth place at the table which is left vacant.*

BLANCHE (*Suddenly*) Stanley, tell us a joke, tell us a funny story to make us all laugh. I don't know what's the matter, we're all so solemn. Is it because I've been stood up by my beau? (STELLA *laughs feebly*) It's the first time in my entire experience with men, and I've had a good deal of all sorts, that I've actually been stood up by anybody! Ha-ha! I don't know how to take it. . . . Tell us a funny little story, Stanley! Something to help us out.

STANLEY I didn't think you liked my stories, Blanche.

BLANCHE I like them when they're amusing but not indecent.

STANLEY I don't know any refined enough for your taste.

BLANCHE Then let me tell one.

STELLA Yes, you tell one, Blanche. You used to know lots of good stories.

(*The music fades*)

BLANCHE Let me see, now. . . . I must run through my repertoire! Oh, yes—I love parrot stories! Do you all like parrot stories? Well, this one's about the old maid and the parrot. This old maid, she had a parrot that cursed a blue streak and knew more vulgar expressions than Mr. Kowalski!

STANLEY Huh.

BLANCHE   And the only way to hush the parrot up was to put the cover back on its cage so it would think it was night and go back to sleep. Well, one morning the old maid had just uncovered the parrot for the day—when who should she see coming up the front walk but the preacher! Well, she rushed back to the parrot and slipped the cover back on the cage and then she let in the preacher. And the parrot was perfectly still, just as quiet as a mouse, but just as she was asking the preacher how much sugar he wanted in his coffee—the parrot broke the silence with a loud— (*She whistles*)—and said—"God *damn*, but that was a short day!"
   (*She throws back her head and laughs.* STELLA *also makes an ineffectual effort to seem amused.* STANLEY *pays no attention to the story but reaches way over the table to spear his fork into the remaining chop which he eats with his fingers*)

BLANCHE   Apparently Mr. Kowalski was not amused.

STELLA   Mr. Kowalski is too busy making a pig of himself to think of anything else!

STANLEY   That's right, baby.

STELLA   Your face and your fingers are disgustingly greasy. Go and wash up and then help me clear the table.
   (*He hurls a plate to the floor*)

STANLEY   That's how I'll clear the table! (*He seizes her arm*) Don't ever talk that way to me! "Pig—Polack—disgusting—vulgar—greasy!"—them kind of words have been on your tongue and your sister's too much around here! What do you two think you are? A pair of queens? Remember what Huey Long said—"Every Man is a King!" And I am the king around here, so don't forget it! (*He hurls a cup and saucer to the floor*) My place is cleared! You want me to clear your places?
   (STELLA *begins to cry weakly.* STANLEY *stalks out on the porch and lights a cigarette. The Negro entertainers around the corner are heard*)

BLANCHE   What happened while I was bathing? What did he tell you, Stella?

STELLA   Nothing, nothing, nothing!

BLANCHE   I think he told you something about Mitch and me! You know why Mitch didn't come but you won't tell me! (STELLA *shakes her head helplessly*) I'm going to call him!

STELLA   I wouldn't call him, Blanche.

BLANCHE   I am, I'm going to call him on the phone.

STELLA (*Miserably*)   I wish you wouldn't.

BLANCHE I intend to be given some explanation from someone!

(*She rushes to the phone in the bedroom.* STELLA *goes out on the porch and stares reproachfully at her husband. He grunts and turns away from her*)

STELLA I hope you're pleased with your doings. I never had so much trouble swallowing food in my life, looking at that girl's face and the empty chair!

(*She cries quietly*)

BLANCHE (*At the phone*) Hello. Mr. Mitchell, please. . . . Oh. . . . I would like to leave a number if I may. Magnolia 9047. And say it's important to call. . . . Yes, very important. . . . Thank you.

(*She remains by the phone with a lost, frightened look.* STANLEY *turns slowly back toward his wife and takes her clumsily in his arms*)

STANLEY Stell, it's gonna be all right after she goes and after you've had the baby. It's gonna be all right again between you and me the way that it was. You remember that way that it was? Them nights we had together? God, honey, it's gonna be sweet when we can make noise in the night the way that we used to and get the colored lights going with nobody's sister behind the curtains to hear us! (*Their upstairs neighbors are heard in bellowing laughter at something.* STANLEY *chuckles*) Steve an' Eunice . . .

STELLA Come on back in. (*She returns to the kitchen and starts lighting the candles on the white cake*) Blanche?

BLANCHE Yes. (*She returns from the bedroom to the table in the kitchen*) Oh, those pretty, pretty little candles! Oh, don't burn them, Stella.

STELLA I certainly will.

(STANLEY *comes back in*)

BLANCHE You ought to save them for baby's birthdays. Oh, I hope candles are going to glow in his life and I hope that his eyes are going to be like candles, like two blue candles lighted in a white cake!

STANLEY (*Sitting down*) What poetry!

BLANCHE (*She pauses reflectively for a moment*) I shouldn't have called him.

STELLA There's lots of things could have happened.

BLANCHE There's no excuse for it, Stella. I don't have to put up with insults. I won't be taken for granted.

STANLEY   Goddamn, it's hot in here with the steam from the bathroom.

BLANCHE   I've said I was sorry three times. (*The piano fades out*)
I take hot baths for my nerves. Hydro-therapy, they call it. You
healthy Polack, without a nerve in your body, of course you
don't know what anxiety feels like!

STANLEY   I am not a Polack. People from Poland are Poles, not
Polacks. But what I am is a one hundred percent American, born
and raised in the greatest country on earth and proud as hell of
it, so don't ever call me a Polack.

(*The phone rings.* BLANCHE *rises expectantly*)

BLANCHE   Oh, that's for me, I'm sure.

STANLEY   I'm not sure. Keep your seat. (*He crosses leisurely to
phone*) H'lo. Aw, yeh, hello, Mac.

(*He leans against wall, staring insultingly in at* BLANCHE. *She
sinks back in her chair with a frightened look.* STELLA *leans over
and touches her shoulder*)

BLANCHE   Oh, keep your hands off me, Stella. What is the matter
with you? Why do you look at me with that pitying look?

STANLEY   (*Bawling*) QUIET IN THERE!—We've got a noisy
woman on the place.—Go on, Mac. At Riley's? No, I don't wanta
bowl at Riley's. I had a little trouble with Riley last week. I'm the
team-captain, ain't I? All right, then, we're not gonna bowl at
Riley's, we're gonna bowl at the West Side or the Gala! All right,
Mac. See you! (*He hangs up and returns to the table.* BLANCHE
*fiercely controls herself, drinking quickly from her tumbler of
water. He doesn't look at her but reaches in a pocket. Then he
speaks slowly and with false amiability*) Sister Blanche, I've got a
little birthday remembrance for you.

BLANCHE   Oh, have you, Stanley? I wasn't expecting any, I—I don't
know why Stella wants to observe my birthday! I'd much rather
forget it—when you—reach twenty-seven! Well—age is a subject
that you'd prefer to—ignore!

STANLEY   Twenty-seven?

BLANCHE (*Quickly*)   What is it? Is it for *me?*

(*He is holding a little envelope toward her*)

STANLEY   Yes, I hope you like it!

BLANCHE   Why, why— Why, it's a—

STANLEY   Ticket! Back to Laurel! On the Greyhound! Tuesday!
(*The Varsouviana music steals in softly and continues playing.*
STELLA *rises abruptly and turns her back.* BLANCHE *tries to smile.*

Then she tries to laugh. Then she gives both up and springs from the table and runs into the next room. She clutches her throat and then runs into the bathroom. Coughing, gagging sounds are heard) Well!

STELLA   You didn't need to do that.

STANLEY   Don't forget all that I took off her.

STELLA   You needn't have been so cruel to someone alone as she is.

STANLEY   Delicate piece she is.

STELLA   She is. She was. You didn't know Blanche as a girl. Nobody was tender and trusting as she was. But people like you abused her, and forced her to change. (*He crosses into the bedroom, ripping off his shirt, and changes into a brilliant silk bowling shirt. She follows him*) Do you think you're going bowling now?

STANLEY   Sure.

STELLA   You're not going bowling. (*She catches hold of his shirt*) Why did you do this to her?

STANLEY   I done nothing to no one. Let go of my shirt. You've torn it.

STELLA   I want to know why. Tell me why.

STANLEY   When we first met, me and you, you thought I was common. How right you was, baby. I was common as dirt. You showed me the snapshot of the place with the columns. I pulled you down off them columns and how you loved it, having them colored lights going! And wasn't we happy together, wasn't it all okay till she showed here? (STELLA *makes a slight movement. Her look goes suddenly inward as if some interior voice had called her name. She begins a slow, shuffling progress from the bedroom to the kitchen, leaning and resting on the back of the chair and then on the edge of a table with a blind look and listening expression.* STANLEY, *finishing with his shirt, is unaware of her reaction*) And wasn't we happy together? Wasn't it all okay? Till she showed here. Hoity-toity, describing me as an ape. (*He suddenly notices the change in* STELLA) Hey, what is it, Stell?

(*He crosses to her*)

STELLA (*Quietly*)   Take me to the hospital.

(*He is with her now, supporting her with his arm, murmuring indistinguishably as they go outside*)

SCENE NINE

A while later that evening. BLANCHE *is seated in a tense hunched position in a bedroom chair that she has recovered with diagonal green and white stripes. She has on her scarlet satin robe. On the table beside chair is a bottle of liquor and a glass. The rapid, feverish polka tune, the "Varsouviana," is heard. The music is in her mind; she is drinking to escape it and the sense of disaster closing in on her, and she seems to whisper the words of the song. An electric fan is turning back and forth across her.*

MITCH *comes around the corner in work clothes: blue denim shirt and pants. He is unshaven. He climbs the steps to the door and rings.* BLANCHE *is startled.*

BLANCHE   Who is it, please?
MITCH (*Hoarsely*)   Me. Mitch.
   (*The polka tune stops*)
BLANCHE   Mitch!—Just a minute. (*She rushes about frantically, hiding the bottle in a closet, crouching at the mirror and dabbing her face with cologne and powder. She is so excited that her breath is audible as she dashes about. At last she rushes to the door in the kitchen and lets him in*) Mitch!—Y'know, I really shouldn't let you in after the treatment I have received from you this evening! So utterly uncavalier! But hello, beautiful! (*She offers him her lips. He ignores it and pushes past her into the flat. She looks fearfully after him as he stalks into the bedroom*) My, my, what a cold shoulder! And such uncouth apparel! Why, you haven't even shaved! The unforgivable insult to a lady! But I forgive you. I forgive you because it's such a relief to see you. You've stopped that polka tune that I had caught in my head. Have you ever had anything caught in your head? No, of course you haven't, you dumb angel-puss, you'd never get anything awful caught in your head!

(*He stares at her while she follows him while she talks. It is obvious that he has had a few drinks on the way over*)

MITCH Do we have to have that fan on?

BLANCHE No!

MITCH I don't like fans.

BLANCHE Then let's turn it off, honey. I'm not partial to them! (*She presses the switch and the fan nods slowly off. She clears her throat uneasily as* MITCH *plumps himself down on the bed in the bedroom and lights a cigarette*) I don't know what there is to drink. I—haven't investigated.

MITCH I don't want Stan's liquor.

BLANCHE It isn't Stan's. Everything here isn't Stan's. Some things on the premises are actually mine! How is your mother? Isn't your mother well?

MITCH Why?

BLANCHE Something's the matter tonight, but never mind. I won't cross-examine the witness. I'll just— (*She touches her forehead vaguely. The polka tune starts up again*)—pretend I don't notice anything different about you! That—music again . . .

MITCH What music?

BLANCHE The "Varsouviana"! The polka tune they were playing when Allan— Wait! (*A distant revolver shot is heard.* BLANCHE *seems relieved*) There now, the shot! It always stops after that. (*The polka music dies out again*) Yes, now it's stopped.

MITCH Are you boxed out of your mind?

BLANCHE I'll go and see what I can find in the way of— (*She crosses into the closet, pretending to search for the bottle*) Oh, by the way, excuse me for not being dressed. But I'd practically given you up! Had you forgotten your invitation to supper?

MITCH I wasn't going to see you any more.

BLANCHE Wait a minute. I can't hear what you're saying and you talk so little that when you do say something, I don't want to miss a single syllable of it. . . . What am I looking around here for? Oh, yes—liquor! We've had so much excitement around here this evening that I *am* boxed out of my mind! (*She pretends suddenly to find the bottle. He draws his foot up on the bed and stares at her contemptuously*) Here's something. Southern Comfort! What is that, I wonder?

MITCH If you don't know, it must belong to Stan.

BLANCHE Take your foot off the bed. It has a light cover on it. Of

course you boys don't notice things like that. I've done so much
with this place since I've been here.

MITCH   I bet you have.

BLANCHE   You saw it before I came. Well, look at it now! This room
is almost—dainty! I want to keep it that way. I wonder if this stuff
ought to be mixed with something? Ummm, it's sweet, so sweet!
It's terribly, terribly sweet! Why, it's a *liqueur*, I believe! Yes,
that's what it *is,* a liqueur! (MITCH *grunts*) I'm afraid you won't
like it, but try it, and maybe you will.

MITCH   I told you already I don't want none of his liquor and I
mean it. You ought to lay off his liquor. He says you been lapping
it up all summer like a wild-cat!

BLANCHE   What a fantastic statement! Fantastic of him to say it,
fantastic of you to repeat it! I won't descend to the level of such
cheap accusations to answer them, even!

MITCH   Huh.

BLANCHE   What's in your mind? I see something in your eyes!

MITCH (*Getting up*)   It's dark in here.

BLANCHE   I like it dark. The dark is comforting to me.

MITCH   I don't think I ever seen you in the light. (BLANCHE *laughs
breathlessly*) That's a fact!

BLANCHE   Is it?

MITCH   I've never seen you in the afternoon.

BLANCHE   Whose fault is that?

MITCH   You never want to go out in the afternoon.

BLANCHE   Why, Mitch, you're at the plant in the afternoon!

MITCH   Not Sunday afternoon. I've asked you to go out with me
sometimes on Sundays but you always make an excuse. You
never want to go out till after six and then it's always some place
that's not lighted much.

BLANCHE   There is some obscure meaning in this but I fail to
catch it.

MITCH   What it means is I've never had a real good look at you,
Blanche. Let's turn the light on here.

BLANCHE (*Fearfully*)   Light? Which light? What for?

MITCH   This one with the paper thing on it.
    (*He tears the paper lantern off the light bulb. She utters a fright-
    ened gasp*)

BLANCHE   What did you do that for?

MITCH   So I can take a look at you good and plain!

BLANCHE   Of course you don't really mean to be insulting!

MITCH No, just realistic.

BLANCHE I don't want realism. I want magic! (MITCH *laughs*) Yes, yes, magic! I try to give that to people. I misrepresent things to them. I don't tell truth, I tell what *ought* to be truth. And if that is sinful, then let me be damned for it!—*Don't turn the light on!* (MITCH *crosses to the switch. He turns the light on and stares at her. She cries out and covers her face. He turns the light off again*)

MITCH (*Slowly and bitterly*) I don't mind you being older than what I thought. But all the rest of it—Christ! That pitch about your ideals being so old-fashioned and all the malarkey that you've dished out all summer. Oh, I knew you weren't sixteen any more. But I was a fool enough to believe you was straight.

BLANCHE Who told you I wasn't—"straight"? My loving brother-in-law. And you believed him.

MITCH I called him a liar at first. And then I checked on the story. First I asked our supply-man who travels through Laurel. And then I talked directly over long-distance to this merchant.

BLANCHE Who is this merchant?

MITCH Kiefaber.

BLANCHE The merchant Kiefaber of Laurel! I know the man. He whistled at me. I put him in his place. So now for revenge he makes up stories about me.

MITCH Three people, Kiefaber, Stanley and Shaw, swore to them!

BLANCHE Rub-a-dub-dub, three men in a tub! And such a filthy tub!

MITCH Didn't you stay at a hotel called The Flamingo?

BLANCHE Flamingo? No! Tartantula was the name of it! I stayed at a hotel called The Tarantula Arms!

MITCH (*Stupidly*) Tarantula?

BLANCHE Yes, a big spider! That's where I brought my victims. (*She pours herself another drink*) Yes, I had many intimacies with strangers. After the death of Allan—intimacies with strangers was all I seemed able to fill my empty heart with. . . . I think it was panic, just panic, that drove me from one to another, hunting for some protection—here and there, in the most—unlikely places —even, at last, in a seventeen-year-old boy but—somebody wrote the superintendent about it—"This woman is morally unfit for her position!" (*She throws back her head with convulsive, sobbing laughter. Then she repeats the statement, gasps, and drinks*) True? Yes, I suppose—unfit somehow—anyway. . . . So I came here. There was nowhere else I could go. I was played out. You know what played out is? My youth was suddenly gone up the water-spout, and—I met you. You said you needed somebody. Well, I needed somebody, too. I thanked God for you, because you seemed to be gentle—a cleft in the rock of the world that I could hide in! But I guess I was asking, hoping—too much! Kiefaber, Stanley and Shaw have tied an old tin can to the tail of the kite.

(*There is a pause.* MITCH *stares at her dumbly*)

MITCH You lied to me, Blanche.

BLANCHE Don't say I lied to you.

MITCH Lies, lies, inside and out, all lies.

BLANCHE Never inside, I didn't lie in my heart . . .

(*A* VENDOR *comes around the corner. She is a blind Mexican woman in a dark shawl, carrying bunches of those gaudy tin flowers that lower class Mexicans display at funerals and other festive occasions. She is calling barely audibly. Her figure is only faintly visible outside the building*)

MEXICAN WOMAN Flores. Flores. Flores para los muertos. Flores. Flores.

BLANCHE What? Oh! Somebody outside . . .

(*She goes to the door, opens it and stares at the* MEXICAN WOMAN)

MEXICAN WOMAN (*She is at the door and offers* BLANCHE *some of her flowers*) Flores? Flores para los muertos?

BLANCHE (*Frightened*) No, no! Not now! Not now!

(*She darts back into the apartment, slamming the door*)

MEXICAN WOMAN (*She turns away and starts to move down the street*) Flores para los muertos.

(*The polka tune fades in*)

BLANCHE (*As if to herself*) Crumble and fade and—regrets—recriminations . . . "If you'd done this, it wouldn't've cost me that!"

MEXICAN WOMAN Corones para los muertos. Corones . . .

BLANCHE Legacies! Huh. . . . And other things such as bloodstained pillow-slips—"Her linen needs changing"—"Yes Mother. But couldn't we get a colored girl to do it?" No, we couldn't of course. Everything gone but the—

MEXICAN WOMAN Flores.

BLANCHE Death—I used to sit here and she used to sit over there and death was as close as you are. . . . We didn't dare even admit we had ever heard of it!

MEXICAN WOMAN Flores para los muertos, flores—flores . . .

BLANCHE The opposite is desire. So do you wonder? How could you possibly wonder! Not far from Belle Reve, before we had lost Belle Reve, was a camp where they trained young soldiers. On Saturday night they would go in town to get drunk—

MEXICAN WOMAN (*Softly*) Corones . . .

BLANCHE —and on the way back they would stagger onto my lawn and call—"Blanche! Blanche!"—The deaf old lady remaining suspected nothing. But sometimes I slipped outside to answer their calls. . . . Later the paddy-wagon would gather them up like daisies . . . the long way home . . .

(*The* MEXICAN WOMAN *turns slowly and drifts back off with her soft mournful cries.* BLANCHE *goes to the dresser and leans forward on it. After a moment,* MITCH *rises and follows her purposefully. The polka music fades away. He places his hands on her waist and tries to turn her about*)

BLANCHE What do you want?

MITCH (*Fumbling to embrace her*) What I been missing all summer.

BLANCHE Then marry me, Mitch!

MITCH I don't think I want to marry you any more.

BLANCHE No?

MITCH (*Dropping his hands from her waist*) You're not clean enough to bring in the house with my mother.

BLANCHE Go away, then. (*He stares at her*) Get out of here quick before I start screaming fire! (*Her throat is tightening with hysteria*) Get out of here quick before I start screaming fire. (*He still remains staring. She suddenly rushes to the big window with its pale blue square of the soft summer light and cries wildly*) Fire! Fire! Fire!

(*With a startled gasp,* MITCH *turns and goes out the outer door, clatters awkwardly down the steps and around the corner of the building.* BLANCHE *staggers back from the window and falls to her knees. The distant piano is slow and blue*)

SCENE TEN

It is a few hours later that night.

BLANCHE has been drinking fairly steadily since MITCH left. She has dragged her wardrobe trunk into the center of the bedroom. It hangs open with flowery dresses thrown across it. As the drinking and packing went on, a mood of hysterical exhilaration came into her and she has decked herself out in a somewhat soiled and crumpled white satin evening gown and a pair of scuffed silver slippers with brilliants set in their heels.

Now she is placing the rhinestone tiara on her head before the mirror of the dressing-table and murmuring excitedly as if to a group of special admirers.

BLANCHE How about taking a swim, a moonlight swim at the old rock-quarry? If anyone's sober enough to drive a car! Ha-ha! Best way in the world to stop your head buzzing! Only you've got to be careful to dive where the deep pool is—if you hit a rock you don't come up till tomorrow . . .

(Tremblingly she lifts the hand mirror for a closer inspection. She catches her breath and slams the mirror face down with such violence that the glass cracks. She moans a little and attempts to rise. STANLEY appears around the corner of the building. He still has on the vivid green silk bowling shirt. As he rounds the corner the honky-tonk music is heard. It continues softly throughout the scene. He enters the kitchen, slamming the door. As he peers in at BLANCHE, he gives a low whistle. He has had a few drinks on the way and has brought some quart beer bottles home with him)

BLANCHE How is my sister?

STANLEY She is doing okay.

BLANCHE And how is the baby?

STANLEY *(Grinning amiably)* The baby won't come before morning so they told me to go home and get a little shut-eye.

BLANCHE   Does that mean we are to be alone in here?

STANLEY   Yep. Just me and you, Blanche. Unless you got somebody hid under the bed. What've you got on those fine feathers
for?

BLANCHE   Oh, that's right. You left before my wire came.

STANLEY   You got a wire?

BLANCHE   I received a telegram from an old admirer of mine.

STANLEY   Anything good?

BLANCHE   I think so. An invitation.

STANLEY   What to? A fireman's ball?

BLANCHE   (*Throwing back her head*)   A cruise of the Caribbean on
a yacht!

STANLEY   Well, well. What do you know?

BLANCHE   I have never been so surprised in my life.

STANLEY   I guess not.

BLANCHE   It came like a bolt from the blue!

STANLEY   Who did you say it was from?

BLANCHE   An old beau of mine.

STANLEY   The one that give you the white fox-pieces?

BLANCHE   Mr. Shep Huntleigh. I wore his ATO pin my last year
at college. I hadn't seen him again until last Christmas. I ran in
to him on Biscayne Boulevard. Then—just now—this wire—inviting
me on a cruise of the Caribbean! The problem is clothes. I tore
into my trunk to see what I have that's suitable for the tropics!

STANLEY   And come up with that—gorgeous—diamond—tiara?

BLANCHE   This old relic? Ha-ha! It's only rhinestones.

STANLEY   Gosh. I thought it was Tiffany diamonds.
(*He unbuttons his shirt*)

BLANCHE   Well, anyhow, I shall be entertained in style.

STANLEY   Uh-huh. It goes to show, you never know what is coming.

BLANCHE   Just when I thought my luck had begun to fail me—

STANLEY   Into the picture pops this Miami millionaire.

BLANCHE   This man is not from Miami. This man is from Dallas.

STANLEY   This man is from Dallas?

BLANCHE   Yes, this man is from Dallas where gold spouts out of
the ground!

STANLEY   Well, just so he's from somewhere!
(*He starts removing his shirt*)

BLANCHE   Close the curtains before you undress any further.

STANLEY   (*Amiably*)   This is all I'm going to undress right now. (*He
rips the sack off a quart beer bottle*) Seen a bottle-opener? (*She

moves slowly toward the dresser, where she stands with her hands knotted together) I used to have a cousin who could open a beer bottle with his teeth. (*Pounding the bottle cap on the corner of table*) That was his only accomplishment, all he could do—he was just a human bottle-opener. And then one time, at a wedding party, he broke his front teeth off! After that he was so ashamed of himself he used t' sneak out of the house when company came . . . (*The bottle cap pops off and a geyser of foam shoots up.* STANLEY *laughs happily, holding up the bottle over his head*) Ha-ha! Rain from heaven! (*He extends the bottle toward her*) Shall we bury the hatchet and make it a loving-cup? Huh?

BLANCHE No, thank you.

STANLEY Well, it's a red letter night for us both. You having an oil-millionaire and me having a baby.

(*He goes to the bureau in the bedroom and crouches to remove something from the bottom drawer*)

BLANCHE (*Drawing back*) What are you doing in here?

STANLEY Here's something I always break out on special occasions like this. The silk pyjamas I wore on my wedding night!

BLANCHE Oh.

STANLEY When the telephone rings and they say, "You've got a son!" I'll tear this off and wave it like a flag! (*He shakes out a brilliant pyjama coat*) I guess we are both entitled to put on the dog.

(*He goes back to the kitchen with the coat over his arm*)

BLANCHE When I think of how divine it is going to be to have such a thing as privacy once more—I could weep with joy!

STANLEY This millionaire from Dallas is not going to interfere with your privacy any?

BLANCHE It won't be the sort of thing you have in mind. This man is a gentleman and he respects me. (*Improvising feverishly*) What he wants is my companionship. Having great wealth some-times makes people lonely! A cultivated woman, a woman of intelligence and breeding, can enrich a man's life—immeasurably! I have those things to offer, and this doesn't take them away. Physical beauty is passing. A transitory possession. But beauty of the mind and richness of the spirit and tenderness of the heart— and I have all of those things—aren't taken away, but grow! In-crease with the years! How strange that I should be called a desti-tute woman! When I have all of these treasures locked in my heart. (*A choked sob comes from her*) I think of myself as a very,

very rich woman! But I have been foolish—casting my pearls before swine!

STANLEY Swine, huh?

BLANCHE Yes, swine! Swine! And I'm thinking not only of you but of your friend, Mr. Mitchell. He came to see me tonight. He dared to come here in his work-clothes! And to repeat slander to me, vicious stories that he had gotten from you! I gave him his walking papers . . .

STANLEY You did, huh?

BLANCHE But then he came back. He returned with a box of roses to beg my forgiveness! He implored my forgiveness. But some things are not forgivable. Deliberate cruelty is not forgivable. It is the one unforgivable thing in my opinion and it is the one thing of which I have never, never been guilty. And so I told him, I said to him, "Thank you," but it was foolish of me to think that we could ever adapt ourselves to each other. Our ways of life are too different. Our attitudes and our backgrounds are incompatible. We have to be realistic about such things. So farewell, my friend! And let there be no hard feelings . . .

STANLEY Was this before or after the telegram came from the Texas oil millionaire?

BLANCHE What telegram? No! No, after! As a matter of fact, the wire came just as—

STANLEY As a matter of fact there wasn't no wire at all!

BLANCHE Oh, oh!

STANLEY There isn't no millionaire! And Mitch didn't come back with roses 'cause I know where he is—

BLANCHE Oh!

STANLEY There isn't a goddam thing but imagination!

BLANCHE Oh!

STANLEY And lies and conceit and tricks!

BLANCHE Oh!

STANLEY And look at yourself! Take a look at yourself in that worn-out Mardi Gras outfit, rented for fifty cents from some rag-picker! And with the crazy crown on! What queen do you think you are?

BLANCHE Oh—God . . .

STANLEY I've been on to you from the start! Not once did you pull any wool over this boy's eyes! You come in here and sprinkle the place with powder and spray perfume and cover the light bulb with a paper lantern, and lo and behold the place has turned into Egypt and you are the Queen of the Nile! Sitting on your throne and swilling down my liquor! I say—*Ha!—Ha!* Do you hear me? *Ha—ha—ha!*

(*He walks into the bedroom*)

BLANCHE Don't come in here! (*Lurid reflections appear on the walls around* BLANCHE. *The shadows are of a grotesque and menacing form. She catches her breath, crosses to the phone and jiggles the hook.* STANLEY *goes into the bathroom and closes the door*) Operator, operator! Give me long-distance, please. . . . I want to get in touch with Mr. Shep Huntleigh of Dallas. He's so well-known he doesn't require any address. Just ask anybody who —Wait!!—No, I couldn't find it right now. . . . Please understand, I—No! No, wait! . . . One moment! Someone is—Nothing! Hold on, please!

(*She sets the phone down and crosses warily into the kitchen. The night is filled with inhuman voices like cries in a jungle. The shadows and lurid reflections move sinuously as flames along the wall spaces. Through the back wall of the rooms, which have become transparent, can be seen the sidewalk. A prostitute has rolled a drunkard. He pursues her along the walk, overtakes her and there is a struggle. A policeman's whistle breaks it up. The figures disappear. Some moments later the* NEGRO WOMAN *appears around the corner with a sequined bag which the prostitute had dropped on the walk. She is rooting excitedly through it.* BLANCHE *presses her knuckles to her lips and returns slowly to the phone. She speaks in a hoarse whisper*)

BLANCHE Operator! Operator! Never mind long-distance. Get Western Union. There isn't time to be—Western—Western Union! (*She waits anxiously*) Western Union? Yes! I—want to—Take down this message! "In desperate, desperate circumstances! Help me! Caught in a trap. Caught in—" *Oh!*

(*The bathroom door is thrown open and* STANLEY *comes out in the brilliant silk pyjamas. He grins at her as he knots the tasseled sash about his waist. She gasps and backs away from the phone. He stares at her for a count of ten. Then a clicking becomes audible from the telephone, steady and rasping*)

STANLEY You left th' phone off th' hook.

(*He crosses to it deliberately and sets it back on the hook. After he has replaced it, he stares at her again, his mouth slowly curving into a grin, as he weaves between* BLANCHE *and the outer door. The barely audible "blue piano" begins to drum up louder.*

The sound of it turns into the roar of an approaching locomotive. BLANCHE *crouches, pressing her fists to her ears until it has gone by*)

BLANCHE (*Finally straightening*) Let me—let me get by you!

STANLEY Get by me? Sure. Go ahead.

(*He moves back a pace in the doorway*)

BLANCHE You—you stand over there!

(*She indicates a further position*)

STANLEY (*Grinning*) You got plenty of room to walk by me now.

BLANCHE Not with you there! But I've got to get out somehow!

STANLEY You think I'll interfere with you? Ha-ha!

(*The "blue piano" goes softly. She turns confusedly and makes a faint gesture. The inhuman jungle voices rise up. He takes a step toward her, biting his tongue which protrudes between his lips*)

STANLEY (*Softly*) Come to think of it—maybe you wouldn't be bad to—interfere with . . .

(BLANCHE *moves backward through the door into the bedroom*)

BLANCHE Stay back! Don't you come toward me another step or I'll—

STANLEY What?

BLANCHE Some awful thing will happen! It will!

STANLEY What are you putting on now?

(*They are now both inside the bedroom*)

BLANCHE I warn you, don't, I'm in danger!

(*He takes another step. She smashes a bottle on the table and faces him, clutching the broken top*)

STANLEY What did you do that for?

BLANCHE So I could twist the broken end in your face!

STANLEY I bet you would do that!

BLANCHE I would! I will if you—

STANLEY Oh! So you want some rough-house! All right, let's have some rough-house! (*He springs toward her, overturning the table. She cries out and strikes at him with the bottle top but he catches her wrist*) Tiger—tiger! Drop the bottle top! Drop it! We've had this date with each other from the beginning!

(*She moans. The bottle top falls. She sinks to her knees. He picks up her inert figure and carries her to the bed. The hot trumpet and drums from the Four Deuces sound loudly*)

SCENE ELEVEN

It is some weeks later. STELLA *is packing* BLANCHE'S *things. Sound of water can be heard running in the bathroom.*

*The portieres are partly open on the poker players—*STANLEY, STEVE, MITCH *and* PABLO*—who sit around the table in the kitchen. The atmosphere of the kitchen is now the same raw, lurid one of the disastrous poker night.*

The building is framed by the sky of turquoise. STELLA *has been crying as she arranges the flowery dresses in the open trunk.*

EUNICE *comes down the steps from her flat above and enters the kitchen. There is an outburst from the poker table.*

STANLEY Drew to an inside straight and made it, by God.

PABLO *Maldita sea tu suerto!*

STANLEY Put it in English, greaseball.

PABLO I am cursing your rutting luck.

STANLEY (*Prodigiously elated*) You know what luck is? Luck is believing you're lucky. Take at Salerno. I believed I was lucky. I figured that 4 out of 5 would not come through but I would . . . and I did. I put that down as a rule. To hold front position in this rat-race you've got to believe you are lucky.

MITCH You . . . you . . . you. . . . Brag . . . brag . . . bull . . . bull.

(STELLA *goes into the bedroom and starts folding a dress*)

STANLEY What's the matter with him?

EUNICE (*Walking past the table*) I always did say that men are callous things with no feelings, but this does beat anything. Making pigs of yourselves.

(*She comes through the portieres into the bedroom*)

STANLEY What's the matter with her?

STELLA How is my baby?

EUNICE Sleeping like a little angel. Brought you some grapes. (*She puts them on a stool and lowers her voice*) Blanche?

STELLA   Bathing.

EUNICE   How is she?

STELLA   She wouldn't eat anything but asked for a drink.

EUNICE   What did you tell her?

STELLA   I—just told her that—we'd made arrangements for her to rest in the country. She's got it mixed in her mind with Shep Huntleigh.

(BLANCHE *opens the bathroom door slightly*)

BLANCHE   Stella.

STELLA   Yes, Blanche?

BLANCHE   If anyone calls while I'm bathing take the number and tell them I'll call right back.

STELLA   Yes.

BLANCHE   That cool yellow silk—the bouclé. See if it's crushed. If it's not too crushed I'll wear it and on the lapel that silver and turquoise pin in the shape of a seahorse. You will find them in the heart-shaped box I keep my accessories in. And Stella . . . Try and locate a bunch of artificial violets in that box, too, to pin with the seahorse on the lapel of the jacket.

(*She closes the door.* STELLA *turns to* EUNICE)

STELLA   I don't know if I did the right thing.

EUNICE   What else could you do?

STELLA   I couldn't believe her story and go on living with Stanley.

EUNICE   Don't ever believe it. Life has got to go on. No matter what happens, you've got to keep on going.

(*The bathroom door opens a little*)

BLANCHE   (*Looking out*)   Is the coast clear?

STELLA   Yes, Blanche. (*To* EUNICE) Tell her how well she's looking.

BLANCHE   Please close the curtains before I come out.

STELLA   They're closed.

STANLEY   —How many for you?

PABLO   —Two.

STEVE   —Three.

(BLANCHE *appears in the amber light of the door. She has a tragic radiance in her red satin robe following the sculptural lines of her body. The "Varsouviana" rises audibly as* BLANCHE *enters the bedroom*)

BLANCHE   (*With faintly hysterical vivacity*)   I have just washed my hair.

STELLA   Did you?

BLANCHE   I'm not sure I got the soap out.

EUNICE   Such fine hair!

BLANCHE   (*Accepting the compliment*)   It's a problem. Didn't I get a call?

STELLA   Who from, Blanche?

BLANCHE   Shep Huntleigh . . .

STELLA   Why, not yet, honey!

BLANCHE   How strange! I—

(*At the sound of* BLANCHE's *voice* MITCH's *arm supporting his cards has sagged and his gaze is dissolved into space.* STANLEY *slaps him on the shoulder*)

STANLEY   Hey, Mitch, come to!

(*The sound of this new voice shocks* BLANCHE. *She makes a shocked gesture, forming his name with her lips.* STELLA *nods and looks quickly away.* BLANCHE *stands quite still for some moments —the silverbacked mirror in her hand and a look of sorrowful perplexity as though all human experience shows on her face.* BLANCHE *finally speaks but with sudden hysteria*)

BLANCHE   What's going on here?

(*She turns from* STELLA *to* EUNICE *and back to* STELLA. *Her rising voice penetrates the concentration of the game.* MITCH *ducks his head lower but* STANLEY *shoves back his chair as if about to rise.* STEVE *places a restraining hand on his arm*)

BLANCHE   (*Continuing*)   What's happened here? I want an explanation of what's happened here.

STELLA   (*Agonizingly*)   Hush! Hush!

EUNICE   Hush! Hush! Honey.

STELLA   Please, Blanche.

BLANCHE   Why are you looking at me like that? Is something wrong with me?

EUNICE   You look wonderful, Blanche. Don't she look wonderful?

STELLA   Yes.

EUNICE   I understand you are going on a trip.

STELLA   Yes, Blanche *is*. She's going on a vacation.

EUNICE   I'm green with envy.

BLANCHE   Help me, help me get dressed!

STELLA   (*Handing her dress*)   Is this what you—

BLANCHE   Yes, it will do! I'm anxious to get out of here—this place is a trap!

EUNICE   What a pretty blue jacket.

STELLA   It's lilac colored.

BLANCHE You're both mistaken. It's Della Robbia blue. The blue of the robe in the old Madonna pictures. Are these grapes washed?

(*She fingers the bunch of grapes which* EUNICE *had brought in*)

EUNICE Huh?

BLANCHE Washed, I said. Are they washed?

EUNICE They're from the French Market.

BLANCHE That doesn't mean they've been washed. (*The cathedral bells chime*) Those cathedral bells—they're the only clean thing in the Quarter. Well, I'm going now. I'm ready to go.

EUNICE (*Whispering*) She's going to walk out before they get here.

STELLA Wait, Blanche.

BLANCHE I don't want to pass in front of those men.

EUNICE Then wait'll the game breaks up.

STELLA Sit down and . . .

(BLANCHE *turns weakly, hesitantly about. She lets them push her into a chair*)

BLANCHE I can smell the sea air. The rest of my time I'm going to spend on the sea. And when I die, I'm going to die on the sea. You know what I shall die of? (*She plucks a grape*) I shall die of eating an unwashed grape one day out on the ocean. I will die—with my hand in the hand of some nice-looking ship's doctor, a very young one with a small blond mustache and a big silver watch. "Poor lady," they'll say, "the quinine did her no good. That unwashed grape has transported her soul to heaven." (*The cathedral chimes are heard*) And I'll be buried at sea sewn up in a clean white sack and dropped overboard—at noon—in the blaze of summer—and into an ocean as blue as (*Chimes again*) my first lover's eyes!

(*A* DOCTOR *and a* MATRON *have appeared around the corner of the building and climbed the steps to the porch. The gravity of their profession is exaggerated—the unmistakable aura of the state institution with its cynical detachment. The* DOCTOR *rings the doorbell. The murmur of the game is interrupted*)

EUNICE (*Whispering to* STELLA) That must be them.

(STELLA *presses her fists to her lips*)

BLANCHE (*Rising slowly*) What is it?

EUNICE (*Affectedly casual*) Excuse me while I see who's at the door.

STELLA Yes.

(EUNICE *goes into the kitchen*)

BLANCHE (*Tensely*)   I wonder if it's for me.
   (*A whispered colloquy takes place at the door*)
EUNICE (*Returning, brightly*)   Someone is calling for Blanche.
BLANCHE   It *is* for me, then! (*She looks fearfully from one to the other and then to the portieres. The "Varsouviana" faintly plays*) Is it the gentleman I was expecting from Dallas?
EUNICE   I think it is, Blanche.
BLANCHE   I'm not quite ready.
STELLA   Ask him to wait outside.
BLANCHE   I . . .
   (*EUNICE goes back to the portieres. Drums sound very softly*)
STELLA   Everything packed?
BLANCHE   My silver toilet articles are still out.
STELLA   Ah!
EUNICE (*Returning*)   They're waiting in front of the house.
BLANCHE   They! Who's "they"?
EUNICE   There's a lady with him.
BLANCHE   I cannot imagine who this "lady" could be! How is she dressed?
EUNICE   Just—just a sort of a—plain-tailored outfit.
BLANCHE   Possibly she's—
   (*Her voice dies out nervously*)
STELLA   Shall we go, Blanche?
BLANCHE   Must we go through that room?
STELLA   I will go with you.
BLANCHE   How do I look?
STELLA   Lovely.
EUNICE (*Echoing*)   Lovely.
   (*BLANCHE moves fearfully to the portieres. EUNICE draws them open for her. BLANCHE goes into the kitchen*)
BLANCHE (*To the men*)   Please don't get up. I'm only passing through.
   (*She crosses quickly to outside door. STELLA and EUNICE follow. The poker players stand awkwardly at the table—all except MITCH, who remains seated, looking down at the table. BLANCHE steps out on a small porch at the side of the door. She stops short and catches her breath*)
DOCTOR   How do you do?
BLANCHE   You are not the gentleman I was expecting. (*She suddenly gasps and starts back up the steps. She stops by STELLA,*

who stands just outside the door, and speaks in a frightening whisper) That man isn't Shep Huntleigh.

(*The "Varsouviana" is playing distantly.* STELLA *stares back at* BLANCHE. EUNICE *is holding* STELLA's *arm. There is a moment of silence—no sound but that of* STANLEY *steadily shuffling the cards.* BLANCHE *catches her breath again and slips back into the flat. She enters the flat with a peculiar smile, her eyes wide and brilliant. As soon as her sister goes past her,* STELLA *closes her eyes and clenches her hands.* EUNICE *throws her arms comfortingly about her.* BLANCHE *stops just inside the door.* MITCH *keeps staring down at his hands on the table, but the other men look at her curiously. At last she starts around the table toward the bedroom. As she does,* STANLEY *suddenly pushes back his chair and rises as if to block her way. The* MATRON *follows her into the flat*)

STANLEY   Did you forget something?

BLANCHE (*Shrilly*)   Yes! Yes, I forgot something!

(*She rushes past him into the bedroom. Lurid reflections appear on the walls in odd, sinuous shapes. The "Varsouviana" is filtered into a weird distortion, accompanied by the cries and noises of the jungle.* BLANCHE *seizes the back of a chair as if to defend herself*)

STANLEY (*Sotto voce*)   Doc, you better go in.

DOCTOR (*Sotto voce, motioning to the* MATRON)   Nurse, bring her out.

(*The* MATRON *advances on one side,* STANLEY *on the other. Divested of all the softer properties of womanhood, the* MATRON *is a peculiarly sinister figure in her severe dress. Her voice is bold and toneless as a firebell*)

MATRON   Hello, Blanche.

(*The greeting is echoed and re-echoed by other mysterious voices behind the walls, as if reverberated through a canyon of rock*)

STANLEY   She says that she forgot something.

(*The echo sounds in threatening whispers*)

MATRON   That's all right.

STANLEY   What did you forget, Blanche?

BLANCHE   I— I—

MATRON   It don't matter. We can pick it up later.

STANLEY   Sure. We can send it along with the trunk.

BLANCHE (*Retreating in panic*)   I don't know you—I don't know you. I want to be—left alone—please!

MATRON   Now, Blanche!

ECHOES (*Rising and falling*) Now, Blanche—now, Blanche—now, Blanche!

STANLEY You left nothing here but spilt talcum and old empty perfume bottles—unless it's the paper lantern you want to take with you. You want the lantern?

(*He crosses to dressing table and seizes the paper lantern, tearing it off the light bulb, and extends it toward her. She cries out as if the lantern was herself. The* MATRON *steps boldly toward her. She screams and tries to break past the* MATRON. *All the men spring to their feet.* STELLA *runs out to the porch, with* EUNICE *following to comfort her, simultaneously with the confused voices of the men in the kitchen.* STELLA *rushes into* EUNICE'S *embrace on the porch*)

STELLA Oh, my God, Eunice help me! Don't let them do that to her, don't let them hurt her! Oh, God, oh, please God, don't hurt her! What are they doing to her? What are they doing?

(*She tries to break from* EUNICE'S *arms*)

EUNICE No, honey, no, no, honey. Stay here. Don't go back in there. Stay with me and don't look.

STELLA What have I done to my sister? Oh, God, what have I done to my sister?

EUNICE You done the right thing, the only thing you could do. She couldn't stay here; there wasn't no other place for her to go.

(*While* STELLA *and* EUNICE *are speaking on the porch the voices of the men in the kitchen overlap them.* MITCH *has started toward the bedroom.* STANLEY *crosses to block him.* STANLEY *pushes him aside.* MITCH *lunges and strikes at* STANLEY. STANLEY *pushes* MITCH *back.* MITCH *collapses at the table, sobbing. During the preceding scenes, the* MATRON *catches hold of* BLANCHE'S *arm and prevents her flight.* BLANCHE *turns wildly and scratches at the* MATRON. *The heavy woman pinions her arms.* BLANCHE *cries out hoarsely and slips to her knees*)

MATRON These fingernails have to be trimmed. (*The* DOCTOR *comes into the room and she looks at him*) Jacket, Doctor?

DOCTOR Not unless necessary.

(*He takes off his hat and now he becomes personalized. The unhuman quality goes. His voice is gentle and reassuring as he crosses to* BLANCHE *and crouches in front of her. As he speaks her name, her terror subsides a little. The lurid reflections fade from the walls, the inhuman cries and noises die out and her own hoarse crying is calmed*)

DOCTOR   Miss DuBois. (*She turns her face to him and stares at him with desperate pleading. He smiles; then he speaks to the* MATRON) It won't be necessary.

BLANCHE (*Faintly*)   Ask her to let go of me.

DOCTOR (*To the* MATRON)   Let go.

(*The* MATRON *releases her.* BLANCHE *extends her hands toward the* DOCTOR. *He draws her up gently and supports her with his arm and leads her through the portieres*)

BLANCHE (*Holding tight to his arm*)   Whoever you are—I have always depended on the kindness of strangers.

(*The poker players stand back as* BLANCHE *and the* DOCTOR *cross the kitchen to the front door. She allows him to lead her as if she were blind. As they go out on the porch,* STELLA *cries out her sister's name from where she is crouched a few steps up on the stairs*)

STELLA   Blanche! Blanche, Blanche!

(BLANCHE *walks on without turning, followed by the* DOCTOR *and the* MATRON. *They go around the corner of the building.* EUNICE *descends to* STELLA *and places the child in her arms. It is wrapped in a pale blue blanket.* STELLA *accepts the child, sobbingly.* EUNICE *continues downstairs and enters the kitchen where the men, except for* STANLEY, *are returning silently to their places about the table.* STANLEY *has gone out on the porch and stands at the foot of the steps looking at* STELLA)

STANLEY (*A bit uncertainly*)   Stella?

(*She sobs with inhuman abandon. There is something luxurious in her complete surrender to crying now that her sister is gone*)

STANLEY (*Voluptuously, soothingly*)   Now, honey. Now, love. Now, now, love. (*He kneels beside her and his fingers find the opening of her blouse*) Now, now, love. Now, love. . . .

(*The luxurious sobbing, the sensual murmur fade away under the swelling music of the "blue piano" and the muted trumpet*)

STEVE   This game is seven-card stud.

Curtain

Death of
a Salesman

*Certain private conversations
in two acts and a requiem*

BY

Arthur Miller

Copyright, 1949, by Arthur Miller. Reprinted by permission of The Viking Press, Inc. All rights reserved. No part of this book may be reproduced in any form without permission in writing from the publisher, with the exception of anyone wishing to quote brief passages in connection with a review written for inclusion in a magazine or newspaper.

DEATH OF A SALESMAN *was first presented by Kermit Bloomgarden and Walter Fried at the Morosco Theatre in New York on February 10, 1949, with the following cast:*

(In order of appearance)

WILLY LOMAN	*Lee J. Cobb*
LINDA	*Mildred Dunnock*
BIFF	*Arthur Kennedy*
HAPPY	*Cameron Mitchell*
BERNARD	*Don Keefer*
THE WOMAN	*Winifred Cushing*
CHARLEY	*Howard Smith*
UNCLE BEN	*Thomas Chalmers*
HOWARD WAGNER	*Alan Hewitt*
JENNY	*Ann Driscoll*
STANLEY	*Tom Pedi*
MISS FORSYTHE	*Constance Ford*
LETTA	*Hope Cameron*

Staged by Elia Kazan
Setting and lighting by Jo Mielziner
Incidental music composed by Alex North
Costumes designed by Julia Sze

Synopsis of Scenes

The action takes place in Willy Loman's house and yard and in various places he visits in the New York and Boston of today.
Throughout the play, in the stage directions, left and right mean stage left and stage right.

ACT ONE

A melody is heard, played upon a flute. It is small and fine, telling of grass and trees and the horizon. The curtain rises.

Before us is the Salesman's house. We are aware of towering, angular shapes behind it, surrounding it on all sides. Only the blue light of the sky falls upon the house and forestage; the surrounding area shows an angry glow of orange. As more light appears, we see a solid vault of apartment houses around the small, fragile-seeming home. An air of the dream clings to the place, a dream rising out of reality. The kitchen at center seems actual enough, for there is a kitchen table with three chairs, and a refrigerator. But no other fixtures are seen. At the back of the kitchen there is a draped entrance, which leads to the living-room. To the right of the kitchen, on a level raised two feet, is a bedroom furnished only with a brass bedstead and a straight chair. On a shelf over the bed a silver athletic trophy stands. A window opens onto the apartment house at the side.

Behind the kitchen, on a level raised six and a half feet, is the boys' bedroom, at present barely visible. Two beds are dimly seen, and at the back of the room a dormer window. (This bedroom is above the unseen living-room.) At the left a stairway curves up to it from the kitchen.

The entire setting is wholly or, in some places, partially transparent. The roof-line of the house is one-dimensional; under and over it we see the apartment buildings. Before the house lies an apron, curving beyond the forestage into the orchestra. This forward area serves as the back yard as well as the locale of all WILLY'S *imaginings and of his city scenes. Whenever the action is in the present the actors observe the imaginary wall-lines, entering the house only through its door at the left. But in the scenes of the past these boundaries are broken, and characters enter or leave a room by stepping "through" a wall onto the forestage.*

From the right, WILLY LOMAN, *the Salesman, enters, carrying two large sample cases. The flute plays on. He hears but is not aware of it. He is past sixty years of age, dressed quietly. Even as he crosses the stage to the doorway of the house, his exhaustion is apparent. He unlocks the door, comes into the kitchen, and thankfully lets his burden down, feeling the soreness of his palms. A word-sigh escapes his lips—it might be "Oh, boy, oh, boy." He closes the door, then carries his cases out into the living-room, through the draped kitchen doorway.*

LINDA, *his wife, has stirred in her bed at the right. She gets out and puts on a robe, listening. Most often jovial, she has developed an iron repression of her exceptions to* WILLY'S *behavior—she more than loves him, she admires him, as though his mercurial nature, his temper, his massive dreams and little cruelties, served her only as sharp reminders of the turbulent longings within him, longings which she shares but lacks the temperament to utter and follow to their end.*

LINDA (*Hearing* WILLY *outside the bedroom, calls with some trepidation*)   Willy!

WILLY   It's all right. I came back.

LINDA   Why? What happened? (*Slight pause*) Did something happen, Willy?

WILLY   No, nothing happened.

LINDA   You didn't smash the car, did you?

WILLY (*With casual irritation*)   I said nothing happened. Didn't you hear me?

LINDA   Don't you feel well?

WILLY   I'm tired to the death. (*The flute has faded away. He sits on the bed beside her, a little numb*) I couldn't make it. I just couldn't make it, Linda.

LINDA (*Very carefully, delicately*)   Where were you all day? You look terrible.

WILLY   I got as far as a little above Yonkers. I stopped for a cup of coffee. Maybe it was the coffee.

LINDA   What?

WILLY (*After a pause*)   I suddenly couldn't drive any more. The car kept going off onto the shoulder, y'know?

LINDA (*Helpfully*)   Oh. Maybe it was the steering again. I don't think Angelo knows the Studebaker.

WILLY   No, it's me, it's me. Suddenly I realize I'm goin' sixty miles an hour and I don't remember the last five minutes. I'm—I can't seem to—keep my mind to it.

LINDA   Maybe it's your glasses. You never went for your new glasses.

WILLY   No, I see everything. I came back ten miles an hour. It took me nearly four hours from Yonkers.

LINDA   (*Resigned*) Well, you'll just have to take a rest, Willy, you can't continue this way.

WILLY   I just got back from Florida.

LINDA   But you didn't rest your mind. Your mind is overactive, and the mind is what counts, dear.

WILLY   I'll start out in the morning. Maybe I'll feel better in the morning. (*She is taking off his shoes*) These goddam arch supports are killing me.

LINDA   Take an aspirin. Should I get you an aspirin? It'll soothe you.

WILLY   (*With wonder*) I was driving along, you understand? And I was fine. I was even observing the scenery. You can imagine, me looking at scenery, on the road every week of my life. But it's so beautiful up there, Linda, the trees are so thick, and the sun is warm. I opened the windshield and just let the warm air bathe over me. And then all of a sudden I'm goin' off the road! I'm tellin' ya, I absolutely forgot I was driving. If I'd've gone the other way over the white line I might've killed somebody. So I went on again—and five minutes later I'm dreamin' again, and I nearly— (*He presses two fingers against his eyes*) I have such thoughts, I have such strange thoughts.

LINDA   Willy, dear. Talk to them again. There's no reason why you can't work in New York.

WILLY   They don't need me in New York. I'm the New England man. I'm vital in New England.

LINDA   But you're sixty years old. They can't expect you to keep traveling every week.

WILLY   I'll have to send a wire to Portland. I'm supposed to see Brown and Morrison tomorrow morning at ten o'clock to show the line. Goddammit, I could sell them!

(*He starts putting on his jacket*)

LINDA   (*Taking the jacket from him*) Why don't you go down to the place tomorrow and tell Howard you've simply got to work in New York? You're too accommodating, dear.

WILLY   If old man Wagner was alive I'd a been in charge of New York now! That man was a prince, he was a masterful man. But that boy of his, that Howard, he don't appreciate. When I went north the first time, the Wagner Company didn't know where New England was!

LINDA   Why don't you tell those things to Howard, dear?

WILLY   (*Encouraged*)   I will, I definitely will. Is there any cheese?

LINDA   I'll make you a sandwich.

WILLY   No, go to sleep. I'll take some milk. I'll be up right away. The boys in?

LINDA   They're sleeping. Happy took Biff on a date tonight.

WILLY   (*Interested*)   That so?

LINDA   It was so nice to see them shaving together, one behind the other, in the bathroom. And going out together. You notice? The whole house smells of shaving lotion.

WILLY   Figure it out. Work a lifetime to pay off a house. You finally own it, and there's nobody to live in it.

LINDA   Well, dear, life is a casting off. It's always that way.

WILLY   No, no, some people—some people accomplish something. Did Biff say anything after I went this morning?

LINDA   You shouldn't have criticized him, Willy, especially after he just got off the train. You mustn't lose your temper with him.

WILLY   When the hell did I lose my temper? I simply asked him if he was making any money. Is that a criticism?

LINDA   But, dear, how could he make any money?

WILLY   (*Worried and angered*)   There's such an undercurrent in him. He became a moody man. Did he apologize when I left this morning?

LINDA   He was crestfallen, Willy. You know how he admires you. I think if he finds himself, then you'll both be happier and not fight any more.

WILLY   How can he find himself on a farm? Is that a life? A farm-hand? In the beginning, when he was young, I thought, well, a young man, it's good for him to tramp around, take a lot of different jobs. But it's more than ten years now and he has yet to make thirty-five dollars a week!

LINDA   He's finding himself, Willy.

WILLY   Not finding yourself at the age of thirty-four is a disgrace!

LINDA   Shh!

WILLY   The trouble is he's lazy, goddammit!

LINDA   Willy, please!

WILLY   Biff is a lazy bum!

LINDA   They're sleeping. Get something to eat. Go on down.

WILLY   Why did he come home? I would like to know what brought him home.

LINDA   I don't know. I think he's still lost, Willy. I think he's very lost.

WILLY   Biff Loman is lost. In the greatest country in the world a young man with such—personal attractiveness, gets lost. And such a hard worker. There's one thing about Biff—he's not lazy.

LINDA   Never.

WILLY   (*With pity and resolve*)   I'll see him in the morning; I'll have a nice talk with him. I'll get him a job selling. He could be big in no time. My God! Remember how they used to follow him around in high school? When he smiled at one of them their faces lit up. When he walked down the street . . .
(*He loses himself in reminiscences*)

LINDA   (*Trying to bring him out of it*)   Willy, dear, I got a new kind of American-type cheese today. It's whipped.

WILLY   Why do you get American when I like Swiss?

LINDA   I just thought you'd like a change—

WILLY   I don't want a change! I want Swiss cheese. Why am I always being contradicted?

LINDA   (*With a covering laugh*)   I thought it would be a surprise.

WILLY   Why don't you open a window in here, for God's sake?

LINDA   (*With infinite patience*)   They're all open, dear.

WILLY   The way they boxed us in here. Bricks and windows windows and bricks.

LINDA   We should've bought the land next door.

WILLY   The street is lined with cars. There's not a breath of fresh air in the neighborhood. The grass don't grow any more, you can't raise a carrot in the back yard. They should've had a law against apartment houses. Remember those two beautiful elm trees out there? When I and Biff hung the swing between them?

LINDA   Yeah, like being a million miles from the city.

WILLY   They should've arrested the builder for cutting those down. They massacred the neighborhood. (*Lost*) More and more I think of those days, Linda. This time of year it was lilac and wisteria. And then the peonies would come out, and the daffodils. What fragrance in this room!

LINDA   Well, after all, people had to move somewhere.

WILLY   No, there's more people now.

LINDA   I don't think there's more people. I think—

WILLY   There's more people! That's what's ruining this country!

Population is getting out of control. The competition is maddening! Smell the stink from that apartment house! And another one on the other side . . . How can they whip cheese?

(*On* WILLY'S *last line,* BIFF *and* HAPPY *raise themselves up in their beds, listening*)

LINDA Go down, try it. And be quiet.

WILLY (*Turning to* LINDA, *guiltily*) You're not worried about me, are you, sweetheart?

BIFF What's the matter?

HAPPY Listen!

LINDA You've got too much on the ball to worry about.

WILLY You're my foundation and my support, Linda.

LINDA Just try to relax, dear. You make mountains out of molehills.

WILLY I won't fight with him any more. If he wants to go back to Texas, let him go.

LINDA He'll find his way.

WILLY Sure. Certain men just don't get started till later in life. Like Thomas Edison, I think. Or B. F. Goodrich. One of them was deaf. (*He starts for the bedroom doorway*) I'll put my money on Biff.

LINDA And Willy—if it's warm Sunday, we'll drive in the country. And we'll open the windshield, and take lunch.

WILLY No, the windshields don't open on the new cars.

LINDA But you opened it today.

WILLY Me? I didn't. (*He stops*) Now isn't that peculiar! Isn't that a remarkable—

(*He breaks off in amazement and fright as the flute is heard distantly*)

LINDA What, darling?

WILLY That is the most remarkable thing.

LINDA What, dear?

WILLY I was thinking of the Chevvy. (*Slight pause*) Nineteen twenty-eight . . . when I had that red Chevvy—(*Breaks off*) That funny? I coulda sworn I was driving that Chevvy today.

LINDA Well, that's nothing. Something must've reminded you.

WILLY Remarkable. Ts. Remember those days? The way Biff used to simonize that car? The dealer refused to believe there was eighty thousand miles on it. (*He shakes his head*) Heh! (*To* LINDA) Close your eyes, I'll be right up.

(*He walks out of the bedroom*)

HAPPY (*To* BIFF) Jesus, maybe he smashed up the car again!

LINDA (*Calling after* WILLY) Be careful on the stairs, dear! The cheese is on the middle shelf!

(*She turns, goes over to the bed, takes his jacket, and goes out of the bedroom. Light has risen on the boys' room. Unseen,* WILLY *is heard talking to himself,* "Eighty thousand miles," *and a little laugh.* BIFF *gets out of bed, comes downstage a bit, and stands attentively.* BIFF *is two years older than his brother* HAPPY, *well built, but in these days bears a worn air and seems less self-assured. He has succeeded less, and his dreams are stronger and less acceptable than* HAPPY'S. HAPPY *is tall, powerfully made. Sexuality is like a visible color on him, or a scent that many women have discovered. He, like his brother, is lost, but in a different way, for he has never allowed himself to turn his face toward defeat and is thus more confused and hard-skinned, although seemingly more content*)

HAPPY (*Getting out of bed*) He's going to get his license taken away if he keeps that up. I'm getting nervous about him, y'know, Biff?

BIFF His eyes are going.

HAPPY No, I've driven with him. He sees all right. He just doesn't keep his mind on it. I drove into the city with him last week. He stops at a green light and then it turns red and he goes. (*He laughs*)

BIFF Maybe he's color-blind.

HAPPY Pop? Why he's got the finest eye for color in the business. You know that.

BIFF (*Sitting down on his bed*) I'm going to sleep.

HAPPY You're not still sour on Dad, are you, Biff?

BIFF He's all right, I guess.

WILLY (*Underneath them, in the living-room*) Yes, sir, eighty thousand miles—eighty-two thousand!

BIFF You smoking?

HAPPY (*Holding out a pack of cigarettes*) Want one?

BIFF (*Taking a cigarette*) I can never sleep when I smell it.

WILLY What a simonizing job, heh!

HAPPY (*With deep sentiment*) Funny, Biff, y'know? Us sleeping in here again? The old beds. (*He pats his bed affectionately*) All the talk that went across those two beds, huh? Our whole lives.

BIFF Yeah. Lotta dreams and plans.

HAPPY (*With a deep and masculine laugh*) About five hundred women would like to know what was said in this room.

(*They share a soft laugh*)

BIFF   Remember that big Betsy something—what the hell was her name—over on Bushwick Avenue?

HAPPY (*Combing his hair*)   With the collie dog!

BIFF   That's the one. I got you in there, remember?

HAPPY   Yeah, that was my first time—I think. Boy, there was a pig! (*They laugh, almost crudely*) You taught me everything I know about women. Don't forget that.

BIFF   I bet you forgot how bashful you used to be. Especially with girls.

HAPPY   Oh, I still am, Biff.

BIFF   Oh, go on.

HAPPY   I just control it, that's all. I think I got less bashful and you got more so. What happened, Biff? Where's the old humor, the old confidence? (*He shakes* BIFF's *knee*. BIFF *gets up and moves restlessly about the room*) What's the matter?

BIFF   Why does Dad mock me all the time?

HAPPY   He's not mocking you, he—

BIFF   Everything I say there's a twist of mockery on his face. I can't get near him.

HAPPY   He just wants you to make good, that's all. I wanted to talk to you about Dad for a long time, Biff. Something's—happening to him. He—talks to himself.

BIFF   I noticed that this morning. But he always mumbled.

HAPPY   But not so noticeable. It got so embarrassing I sent him to Florida. And you know something? Most of the time he's talking to you.

BIFF   What's he say about me?

HAPPY   I can't make it out.

BIFF   What's he say about me?

HAPPY   I think the fact that you're not settled, that you're still kind of up in the air . . .

BIFF   There's one or two other things depressing him, Happy.

HAPPY   What do you mean?

BIFF   Never mind. Just don't lay it all to me.

HAPPY   But I think if you just got started—I mean—is there any future for you out there?

BIFF   I tell ya, Hap, I don't know what the future is. I don't know —what I'm supposed to want.

HAPPY   What do you mean?

BIFF   Well, I spent six or seven years after high school trying to work myself up. Shipping clerk, salesman, business of one kind or another. And it's a measly manner of existence. To get on that subway on the hot mornings in summer. To devote your whole life to keeping stock, or making phone calls, or selling or buying. To suffer fifty weeks of the year for the sake of a two-week vacation, when all you really desire is to be outdoors, with your shirt off. And always to have to get ahead of the next fella. And still— that's how you build a future.

HAPPY Well, you really enjoy it on a farm? Are you content out there?

BIFF (*With rising agitation*) Hap, I've had twenty or thirty different kinds of jobs since I left home before the war, and it always turns out the same. I just realized it lately. In Nebraska when I herded cattle, and the Dakotas, and Arizona, and now in Texas. It's why I came home now, I guess, because I realized it. This farm I work on, it's spring there now, see? And they've got about fifteen new colts. There's nothing more inspiring or—beautiful than the sight of a mare and a new colt. And it's cool there now, see? Texas is cool now, and it's spring. And whenever spring comes to where I am, I suddenly get the feeling, my God, I'm not gettin' anywhere! What the hell am I doing, playing around with horses, twenty-eight dollars a week! I'm thirty-four years old, I oughta be makin' my future. That's when I come running home. And now, I get here, and I don't know what to do with myself. (*After a pause*) I've always made a point of not wasting my life, and every time I come back here I know that all I've done is to waste my life.

HAPPY You're a poet, you know that, Biff? You're a—you're an idealist!

BIFF No, I'm mixed up very bad. Maybe I oughta get married. Maybe I oughta get stuck into something. Maybe that's my trouble. I'm like a boy. I'm not married, I'm not in business, I just— I'm like a boy. Are you content, Hap? You're a success, aren't you? Are you content?

HAPPY Hell, no!

BIFF Why? You're making money, aren't you?

HAPPY (*Moving about with energy, expressiveness*) All I can do now is wait for the merchandise manager to die. And suppose I get to be merchandise manager? He's a good friend of mine, and he just built a terrific estate on Long Island. And he lived there about two months and sold it, and now he's building another one.

He can't enjoy it once it's finished. And I know that's just what I would do. I don't know what the hell I'm workin' for. Sometimes I sit in my apartment—all alone. And I think of the rent I'm paying. And it's crazy. But then, it's what I always wanted. My own apartment, a car, and plenty of women. And still, goddammit, I'm lonely.

BIFF (*With enthusiasm*) Listen, why don't you come out West with me?

HAPPY You and I, heh?

BIFF Sure, maybe we could buy a ranch. Raise cattle, use our muscles. Men built like we are should be working out in the open.

HAPPY (*Avidly*) The Loman Brothers, heh?

BIFF (*With vast affection*) Sure, we'd be known all over the counties!

HAPPY (*Enthralled*) That's what I dream about, Biff. Sometimes I want to just rip my clothes off in the middle of the store and outbox that goddam merchandise manager. I mean I can outbox, outrun, and outlift anybody in that store, and I have to take orders from those common, petty sons-of-bitches till I can't stand it any more.

BIFF I'm tellin' you, kid, if you were with me I'd be happy out there.

HAPPY (*Enthused*) See, Biff, everybody around me is so false that I'm constantly lowering my ideals . . .

BIFF Baby, together we'd stand up for one another, we'd have someone to trust.

HAPPY If I were around you—

BIFF Hap, the trouble is we weren't brought up to grub for money. I don't know how to do it.

HAPPY Neither can I!

BIFF Then let's go!

HAPPY The only thing is—what can you make out there?

BIFF But look at your friend. Builds an estate and then hasn't the peace of mind to live in it.

HAPPY Yeah, but when he walks into the store the waves part in front of him. That's fifty-two thousand dollars a year coming through the revolving door, and I got more in my pinky finger than he's got in his head.

BIFF Yeah, but you just said—

HAPPY I gotta show some of those pompous, self-important executives over there that Hap Loman can make the grade. I want to

walk into the store the way he walks in. Then I'll go with you,
Biff. We'll be together yet, I swear. But take those two we had
tonight. Now weren't they gorgeous creatures?

BIFF Yeah, yeah, most gorgeous I've had in years.

HAPPY I get that any time I want, Biff. Whenever I feel disgusted.
The only trouble is, it gets like bowling or something. I just keep
knockin' them over and it doesn't mean anything. You still run
around a lot?

BIFF Naa. I'd like to find a girl—steady, somebody with substance.

HAPPY That's what I long for.

BIFF Go on! You'd never come home.

HAPPY I would! Somebody with character, with resistance! Like
Mom, y'know? You're gonna call me a bastard when I tell you
this. That girl Charlotte I was with tonight is engaged to be married in five weeks.

(He tries on his new hat)

BIFF No kiddin'!

HAPPY Sure, the guy's in line for the vice-presidency of the store.
I don't know what gets into me, maybe I just have an overde-
veloped sense of competition or something, but I went and ruined
her, and furthermore I can't get rid of her. And he's the third
executive I've done that to. Isn't that a crummy characteristic?
And to top it all, I go to their weddings! (Indignantly, but laughing) Like I'm not supposed to take bribes. Manufacturers offer
me a hundred-dollar bill now and then to throw an order their
way. You know how honest I am, but it's like this girl, see. I hate
myself for it. Because I don't want the girl, and, still, I take it and
—I love it!

BIFF Let's go to sleep.

HAPPY I guess we didn't settle anything, heh?

BIFF I just got one idea that I think I'm going to try.

HAPPY What's that?

BIFF Remember Bill Oliver?

HAPPY Sure, Oliver is very big now. You want to work for him
again?

BIFF No, but when I quit he said something to me. He put his arm
on my shoulder, and he said, "Biff, if you ever need anything,
come to me."

HAPPY I remember that. That sounds good.

BIFF I think I'll go to see him. If I could get ten thousand or even
seven or eight thousand dollars I could buy a beautiful ranch.

HAPPY   I bet he'd back you. 'Cause he thought highly of you, Biff. I mean, they all do. You're well liked, Biff. That's why I say to come back here, and we both have the apartment. And I'm tellin' you, Biff, any babe you want . . .

BIFF   No, with a ranch I could do the work I like and still be something. I just wonder though. I wonder if Oliver still thinks I stole that carton of basketballs.

HAPPY   Oh, he probably forgot that long ago. It's almost ten years. You're too sensitive. Anyway, he didn't really fire you.

BIFF   Well, I think he was going to. I think that's why I quit. I was never sure whether he knew or not. I know he thought the world of me, though. I was the only one he'd let lock up the place.

WILLY   (*Below*)   You gonna wash the engine, Biff?

HAPPY   Shh!

     (BIFF *looks at* HAPPY, *who is gazing down, listening.* WILLY *is mumbling in the parlor*)

HAPPY   You hear that?

     (*They listen.* WILLY *laughs warmly*)

BIFF   (*Growing angry*)   Doesn't he know Mom can hear that?

WILLY   Don't get your sweater dirty, Biff!

     (*A look of pain crosses* BIFF's *face*)

HAPPY   Isn't that terrible? Don't leave again, will you? You'll find a job here. You gotta stick around. I don't know what to do about him, it's getting embarrassing.

WILLY   What a simonizing job!

BIFF   Mom's hearing that!

WILLY   No kiddin', Biff, you got a date? Wonderful!

HAPPY   Go on to sleep. But talk to him in the morning, will you?

BIFF   (*Reluctantly getting into bed*)   With her in the house. Brother!

HAPPY   (*Getting into bed*)   I wish you'd have a good talk with him.

     (*The light on their room begins to fade*)

BIFF   (*To himself in bed*)   That selfish, stupid . . .

HAPPY   Sh . . . Sleep, Biff.

     (*Their light is out. Well before they have finished speaking,* WILLY's *form is dimly seen below in the darkened kitchen. He opens the refrigerator, searches in there, and takes out a bottle of milk. The apartment houses are fading out, and the entire house and surroundings become covered with leaves. Music insinuates itself as the leaves appear*)

WILLY   Just wanna be careful with those girls, Biff, that's all. Don't make any promises. No promises of any kind. Because a girl, y'know, they always believe what you tell 'em, and you're very young, Biff, you're too young to be talking seriously to girls.

(*Light rises on the kitchen.* WILLY, *talking, shuts the refrigerator door and comes downstage to the kitchen table. He pours milk into a glass. He is totally immersed in himself, smiling faintly*)

WILLY Too young entirely, Biff. You want to watch your schooling first. Then when you're all set, there'll be plenty of girls for a boy like you. (*He smiles broadly at a kitchen chair*) That so? The girls pay for you? (*He laughs*) Boy, you must really be makin' a hit.

(WILLY *is gradually addressing—physically—a point offstage, speaking through the wall of the kitchen, and his voice has been rising in volume to that of a normal conversation*)

WILLY I been wondering why you polish the car so careful. Ha! Don't leave the hubcaps, boys. Get the chamois to the hubcaps. Happy, use newspaper on the windows, it's the easiest thing. Show him how to do it, Biff! You see, Happy? Pad it up, use it like a pad. That's it, that's it, good work. You're doin' all right, Hap. (*He pauses, then nods in approbation for a few seconds, then looks upward*) Biff, first thing we gotta do when we get time is clip that big branch over the house. Afraid it's gonna fall in a storm and hit the roof. Tell you what. We get a rope and sling her around, and then we climb up there with a couple of saws and take her down. Soon as you finish the car, boys, I wanna see ya. I got a surprise for you, boys.

BIFF (*Offstage*) Whatta ya got, Dad?

WILLY No, you finish first. Never leave a job till you're finished— remember that. (*Looking toward the "big trees"*) Biff, up in Albany I saw a beautiful hammock. I think I'll buy it next trip, and we'll hang it right between those two elms. Wouldn't that be something? Just swingin' there under those branches. Boy, that would be . . .

(YOUNG BIFF *and* YOUNG HAPPY *appear from the direction* WILLY *was addressing.* HAPPY *carries rags and a pail of water.* BIFF, *wearing a sweater with a block "S," carries a football*)

BIFF (*Pointing in the direction of the car offstage*) How's that, Pop, professional?

WILLY Terrific. Terrific job, boys. Good work, Biff.

HAPPY Where's the surprise, Pop?

WILLY In the back seat of the car.

HAPPY   Boy!

   (*He runs off*)

BIFF   What is it, Dad? Tell me, what'd you buy?

WILLY   (*Laughing, cuffs him*)   Never mind, something I want you to have.

BIFF   (*Turns and starts off*)   What is it, Hap?

HAPPY   (*Offstage*)   It's a punching bag!

BIFF   Oh, Pop!

WILLY   It's got Gene Tunney's signature on it!

   (HAPPY *runs onstage with a punching bag*)

BIFF   Gee, how'd you know we wanted a punching bag?

WILLY   Well, it's the finest thing for the timing.

HAPPY   (*Lies down on his back and pedals with his feet*)   I'm losing weight, you notice, Pop?

WILLY   (*To* HAPPY)   Jumping rope is good too.

BIFF   Did you see the new football I got?

WILLY   (*Examining the ball*)   Where'd you get a new ball?

BIFF   The coach told me to practice my passing.

WILLY   That so? And he gave you the ball, heh?

BIFF   Well, I borrowed it from the locker room.

   (*He laughs confidentially*)

WILLY   (*Laughing with him at the theft*)   I want you to return that.

HAPPY   I told you he wouldn't like it!

BIFF   (*Angrily*)   Well, I'm bringing it back!

WILLY   (*Stopping the incipient argument, to* HAPPY)   Sure, he's gotta practice with a regulation ball, doesn't he? (*To* BIFF) Coach'll probably congratulate you on your initiative!

BIFF   Oh, he keeps congratulating my initiative all the time, Pop.

WILLY   That's because he likes you. If somebody else took that ball there'd be an uproar. So what's the report, boys, what's the report?

BIFF   Where'd you go this time, Dad? Gee we were lonesome for you.

WILLY   (*Pleased, puts an arm around each boy and they come down to the apron*)   Lonesome, heh?

BIFF   Missed you every minute.

WILLY   Don't say? Tell you a secret, boys. Don't breathe it to a soul. Someday I'll have my own business, and I'll never have to leave home any more.

HAPPY   Like Uncle Charley, heh?

WILLY   Bigger than Uncle Charley! Because Charley is not—liked. He's liked, but he's not—well liked.

Death of a Salesman

BIFF Where'd you go this time, Dad?

WILLY Well, I got on the road, and I went north to Providence. Met the Mayor.

BIFF The Mayor of Providence!

WILLY He was sitting in the hotel lobby.

BIFF What'd he say?

WILLY He said, "Morning!" And I said, "You got a fine city here, Mayor." And then he had coffee with me. And then I went to Waterbury. Waterbury is a fine city. Big clock city, the famous Waterbury clock. Sold a nice bill there. And then Boston—Boston is the cradle of the Revolution. A fine city. And a couple of other towns in Mass., and on to Portland and Bangor and straight home!

BIFF Gee, I'd love to go with you sometime, Dad.

WILLY Soon as summer comes.

HAPPY Promise?

WILLY You and Hap and I, and I'll show you all the towns. America is full of beautiful towns and fine, upstanding people. And they know me, boys, they know me up and down New England. The finest people. And when I bring you fellas up, there'll be open sesame for all of us, 'cause one thing, boys: I have friends. I can park my car in any street in New England, and the cops protect it like their own. This summer, heh?

BIFF *and* HAPPY, *together:* Yeah! You bet!

WILLY We'll take our bathing suits.

HAPPY We'll carry your bags, Pop!

WILLY Oh, won't that be something! Me comin' into the Boston stores with you boys carryin' my bags. What a sensation!

(BIFF *is prancing around, practicing passing the ball*)

WILLY You nervous, Biff, about the game?

BIFF Not if you're gonna be there.

WILLY What do they say about you in school, now that they made you captain?

HAPPY There's a crowd of girls behind him every time the classes change.

BIFF (*Taking* WILLY's *hand*) This Saturday, Pop, this Saturday—just for you, I'm going to break through for a touchdown.

HAPPY You're supposed to pass.

BIFF I'm takin' one play for Pop. You watch me, Pop, and when I take off my helmet, that means I'm breakin' out. Then you watch me crash through that line!

WILLY (*Kisses* BIFF) Oh, wait'll I tell this in Boston!

(BERNARD *enters in knickers. He is younger than* BIFF, *earnest and loyal, a worried boy*)

BERNARD   Biff, where are you? You're supposed to study with me today.

WILLY   Hey, looka Bernard. What're you lookin' so anemic about, Bernard?

BERNARD   He's gotta study, Uncle Willy. He's got Regents next week.

HAPPY   (*Tauntingly, spinning* BERNARD *around*)   Let's box, Bernard!

BERNARD   Biff! (*He gets away from* HAPPY) Listen, Biff, I heard Mr. Birnbaum say that if you don't start studyin' math he's gonna flunk you, and you won't graduate. I heard him!

WILLY   You better study with him, Biff. Go ahead now.

BERNARD   I heard him!

BIFF   Oh, Pop, you didn't see my sneakers!

(*He holds up a foot for* WILLY *to look at*)

WILLY   Hey, that's a beautiful job of printing!

BERNARD   (*Wiping his glasses*)   Just because he printed University of Virginia on his sneakers doesn't mean they've got to graduate him, Uncle Willy!

WILLY   (*Angrily*)   What're you talking about? With scholarships to three universities they're gonna flunk him?

BERNARD   But I heard Mr. Birnbaum say—

WILLY   Don't be a pest, Bernard! (*To his boys*) What an anemic!

BERNARD   Okay, I'm waiting for you in my house, Biff.

(BERNARD *goes off. The Lomans laugh*)

WILLY   Bernard is not well liked, is he?

BIFF   He's liked, but he's not well liked.

HAPPY   That's right, Pop.

WILLY   That's just what I mean. Bernard can get the best marks in school, y'understand, but when he gets out in the business world, y'understand, you are going to be five times ahead of him. That's why I thank Almighty God you're both built like Adonises. Because the man who makes an appearance in the business world, the man who creates personal interest, is the man who gets ahead. Be liked and you will never want. You take me, for instance. I never have to wait in line to see a buyer. "Willy Loman is here!" That's all they have to know, and I go right through.

BIFF   Did you knock them dead, Pop?

WILLY   Knocked 'em cold in Providence, slaughtered 'em in Boston.

HAPPY (*On his back, pedaling again*) I'm losing weight, you notice, Pop?

(LINDA *enters, as of old, a ribbon in her hair, carrying a basket of washing*)

LINDA (*With youthful energy*) Hello, dear!

WILLY Sweetheart!

LINDA How'd the Chevvy run?

WILLY Chevrolet, Linda, is the greatest car ever built. (*To the boys*) Since when do you let your mother carry wash up the stairs?

BIFF Grab hold there, boy!

HAPPY Where to, Mom?

LINDA Hang them up on the line. And you better go down to your friends, Biff. The cellar is full of boys. They don't know what to do with themselves.

BIFF Ah, when Pop comes home they can wait!

WILLY (*Laughs appreciatively*) You better go down and tell them what to do, Biff.

BIFF I think I'll have them sweep out the furnace room.

WILLY Good work, Biff.

BIFF (*Goes through wall-line of kitchen to doorway at back and calls down*) Fellas! Everybody sweep out the furnace room! I'll be right down!

VOICES All right! Okay, Biff.

BIFF George and Sam and Frank, come out back! We're hangin' up the wash! Come on, Hap, on the double!

(*He and* HAPPY *carry out the basket*)

LINDA The way they obey him!

WILLY Well, that's training, the training. I'm tellin' you, I was sellin' thousands and thousands, but I had to come home.

LINDA Oh, the whole block'll be at that game. Did you sell anything?

WILLY I did five hundred gross in Providence and seven hundred gross in Boston,

LINDA No! Wait a minute, I've got a pencil. (*She pulls pencil and paper out of her apron pocket*) That makes your commission . . . Two hundred—my God! Two hundred and twelve dollars!

WILLY Well, I didn't figure it yet, but . . .

LINDA How much did you do?

WILLY Well, I—I did—about a hundred and eighty gross in Providence. Well, no—it came to—roughly two hundred gross on the whole trip.

LINDA (*Without hesitation*) Two hundred gross. That's . . . (*She figures*)

WILLY The trouble was that three of the stores were half closed for inventory in Boston. Otherwise I woulda broke records.

LINDA Well, it makes seventy dollars and some pennies. That's very good.

WILLY What do we owe?

LINDA Well, on the first there's sixteen dollars on the refrigerator—

WILLY Why sixteen?

LINDA Well, the fan belt broke, so it was a dollar eighty.

WILLY But it's brand new.

LINDA Well, the man said that's the way it is. Till they work themselves in, y'know.

(*They move through the wall-line into the kitchen*)

WILLY I hope we didn't get stuck on that machine.

LINDA They got the biggest ads of any of them!

WILLY I know, it's a fine machine. What else?

LINDA Well, there's nine-sixty for the washing machine. And for the vacuum cleaner there's three and a half due on the fifteenth. Then the roof, you got twenty-one dollars remaining.

WILLY It don't leak, does it?

LINDA No, they did a wonderful job. Then you owe Frank for the carburetor.

WILLY I'm not going to pay that man! That goddam Chevrolet, they ought to prohibit the manufacture of that car!

LINDA Well, you owe him three and a half. And odds and ends, comes to around a hundred and twenty dollars by the fifteenth.

WILLY A hundred and twenty dollars! My God, if business don't pick up I don't know what I'm gonna do!

LINDA Well, next week you'll do better.

WILLY Oh, I'll knock 'em dead next week. I'll go to Hartford. I'm very well liked in Hartford. You know, the trouble is, Linda, people don't seem to take to me.

(*They move onto the forestage*)

LINDA Oh, don't be foolish.

WILLY I know it when I walk in. They seem to laugh at me.

LINDA Why? Why would they laugh at you? Don't talk that way, Willy.

(WILLY *moves to the edge of the stage.* LINDA *goes into the kitchen and starts to darn stockings*)

WILLY   I don't know the reason for it, but they just pass me by. I'm not noticed.

LINDA   But you're doing wonderful, dear. You're making seventy to a hundred dollars a week.

WILLY   But I gotta be at it ten, twelve hours a day. Other men— I don't know—they do it easier. I don't know why—I can't stop myself—I talk too much. A man oughta come in with a few words. One thing about Charley. He's a man of few words, and they respect him.

LINDA   You don't talk too much, you're just lively.

WILLY (*Smiling*)   Well, I figure, what the hell, life is short, a couple of jokes. (*To himself*) I joke too much!

(*The smile goes*)

LINDA   Why? You're—

WILLY   I'm fat. I'm very—foolish to look at, Linda. I didn't tell you, but Christmas time I happened to be calling on F. H. Stewarts, and a salesman I know, as I was going in to see the buyer I heard him say something about—walrus. And I—I cracked him right across the face. I won't take that. I simply will not take that. But they do laugh at me. I know that.

LINDA   Darling . . .

WILLY   I gotta overcome it. I know I gotta overcome it. I'm not dressing to advantage, maybe.

LINDA   Willy, darling, you're the handsomest man in the world—

WILLY   Oh, no, Linda.

LINDA   To me you are. (*Slight pause*) The handsomest.

(*From the darkness is heard the laughter of a woman.* WILLY *doesn't turn to it, but it continues through* LINDA's *lines*)

LINDA   And the boys, Willy. Few men are idolized by their children the way you are.

(*Music is heard as behind a scrim, to the left of the house,* THE WOMAN, *dimly seen, is dressing*)

WILLY (*With great feeling*)   You're the best there is, Linda, you're a pal, you know that? On the road—on the road I want to grab you sometimes and just kiss the life outa you.

(*The laughter is loud now, and he moves into a brightening area at the left, where* THE WOMAN *has come from behind the scrim and is standing, putting on her hat, looking into a "mirror" and laughing*)

WILLY 'Cause I get so lonely—especially when business is bad and there's nobody to talk to. I get the feeling that I'll never sell anything again, that I won't make a living for you, or a business, a business for the boys. (*He talks through* THE WOMAN's *subsiding laughter;* THE WOMAN *primps at the "mirror"*) There's so much I want to make for—

THE WOMAN Me? You didn't make me, Willy. I picked you.

WILLY (*Pleased*) You picked me?

THE WOMAN (*Who is quite proper-looking,* WILLY's *age*) I did. I've been sitting at that desk watching all the salesmen go by, day in, day out. But you've got such a sense of humor, and we do have such a good time together, don't we?

WILLY Sure, sure. (*He takes her in his arms*) Why do you have to go now?

THE WOMAN It's two o'clock . . .

WILLY No, come on in!
(*He pulls her*)

THE WOMAN . . . my sisters'll be scandalized. When'll you be back?

WILLY Oh, two weeks about. Will you come up again?

THE WOMAN Sure thing. You do make me laugh. It's good for me. (*She squeezes his arm, kisses him*) And I think you're a wonderful man.

WILLY You picked me, heh?

THE WOMAN Sure. Because you're so sweet. And such a kidder.

WILLY Well, I'll see you next time I'm in Boston.

THE WOMAN I'll put you right through to the buyers.

WILLY (*Slapping her bottom*) Right. Well, bottoms up!

THE WOMAN (*Slaps him gently and laughs*) You just kill me, Willy. (*He suddenly grabs her and kisses her roughly*) You kill me. And thanks for the stockings. I love a lot of stockings. Well, good night.

WILLY Good night. And keep your pores open!

THE WOMAN Oh, Willy!
(THE WOMAN *bursts out laughing, and* LINDA's *laughter blends in.* THE WOMAN *disappears into the dark. Now the area at the kitchen table brightens.* LINDA *is sitting where she was at the kitchen table, but now is mending a pair of her silk stockings*)

LINDA You are, Willy. The handsomest man. You've got no reason to feel that—

WILLY (*Coming out of* THE WOMAN's *dimming area and going over to* LINDA) I'll make it all up to you, Linda, I'll—

LINDA There's nothing to make up, dear. You're doing fine, better than—

WILLY (*Noticing her mending*) What's that?

LINDA Just mending my stockings. They're so expensive—

WILLY (*Angrily, taking them from her*) I won't have you mending stockings in this house! Now throw them out!

(LINDA *puts the stockings in her pocket*)

BERNARD (*Entering on the run*) Where is he? If he doesn't study!

WILLY (*Moving to the forestage, with great agitation*) You'll give him the answers!

BERNARD I do, but I can't on a Regents! That's a state exam! They're liable to arrest me!

WILLY Where is he? I'll whip him, I'll whip him!

LINDA And he'd better give back that football, Willy, it's not nice.

WILLY Biff! Where is he? Why is he taking everything?

LINDA He's too rough with the girls, Willy. All the mothers are afraid of him!

WILLY I'll whip him!

BERNARD He's driving the car without a license!

(THE WOMAN's *laugh is heard*)

WILLY Shut up!

LINDA All the mothers—

WILLY Shut up!

BERNARD (*Backing quietly away and out*) Mr. Birnbaum says he's stuck up.

WILLY Get outa here!

BERNARD If he doesn't buckle down he'll flunk math!

(*He goes off*)

LINDA He's right, Willy, you've gotta—

WILLY (*Exploding at her*) There's nothing the matter with him! You want him to be a worm like Bernard? He's got spirit, personality . . .

(*As he speaks,* LINDA, *almost in tears, exits into the living-room.* WILLY *is alone in the kitchen, wilting and staring. The leaves are gone. It is night again, and the apartment houses look down from behind*)

WILLY Loaded with it. Loaded! What is he stealing? He's giving it back, isn't he? Why is he stealing? What did I tell him? I never in my life told him anything but decent things.

(HAPPY *in pajamas has come down the stairs;* WILLY *suddenly becomes aware of* HAPPY's *presence*)

HAPPY   Let's go now, come on.

WILLY   (*Sitting down at the kitchen table*)   Huh! Why did she have to wax the floors herself? Every time she waxes the floors she keels over. She knows that!

HAPPY   Shh! Take it easy. What brought you back tonight?

WILLY   I got an awful scare. Nearly hit a kid in Yonkers. God! Why didn't I go to Alaska with my brother Ben that time! Ben! That man was a genius, that man was success incarnate! What a mistake! He begged me to go.

HAPPY   Well, there's no use in—

WILLY   You guys! There was a man started with the clothes on his back and ended up with diamond mines!

HAPPY   Boy, someday I'd like to know how he did it.

WILLY   What's the mystery? The man knew what he wanted and went out and got it! Walked into a jungle, and comes out, the age of twenty-one, and he's rich! The world is an oyster, but you don't crack it open on a mattress!

HAPPY   Pop, I told you I'm gonna retire you for life.

WILLY   You'll retire me for life on seventy goddam dollars a week? And your women and your car and your apartment, and you'll retire me for life! Christ's sake, I couldn't get past Yonkers today! Where are you guys, where are you? The woods are burning! I can't drive a car!

(CHARLEY *has appeared in the doorway. He is a large man, slow of speech, laconic, immovable. In all he says, despite what he says, there is pity, and, now, trepidation. He has a robe over pajamas, slippers on his feet. He enters the kitchen*)

CHARLEY   Everything all right?

HAPPY   Yeah, Charley, everything's . . .

WILLY   What's the matter?

CHARLEY   I heard some noise. I thought something happened. Can't we do something about the walls? You sneeze in here, and in my house hats blow off.

HAPPY   Let's go to bed, Dad. Come on.

(CHARLEY *signals to* HAPPY *to go*)

WILLY   You go ahead, I'm not tired at the moment.

HAPPY   (*To* WILLY)   Take it easy, huh?

(*He exits*)

WILLY   What're you doin' up?

CHARLEY   (*Sitting down at the kitchen table opposite* WILLY) Couldn't sleep good. I had a heartburn.

WILLY   Well, you don't know how to eat.

CHARLEY   I eat with my mouth.

WILLY   No, you're ignorant. You gotta know about vitamins and things like that.

CHARLEY   Come on, let's shoot. Tire you out a little.

WILLY (*Hesitantly*)   All right. You got cards?

CHARLEY (*Taking a deck from his pocket*)   Yeah, I got them. Someplace. What is it with those vitamins?

WILLY (*Dealing*)   They build up your bones. Chemistry.

CHARLEY   Yeah, but there's no bones in a heartburn.

WILLY   What are you talkin' about? Do you know the first thing about it?

CHARLEY   Don't get insulted.

WILLY   Don't talk about something you don't know anything about. (*They are playing. Pause*)

CHARLEY   What're you doin' home?

WILLY   A little trouble with the car.

CHARLEY   Oh. (*Pause*) I'd like to take a trip to California.

WILLY   Don't say.

CHARLEY   You want a job?

WILLY   I got a job, I told you that. (*After a slight pause*) What the hell are you offering me a job for?

CHARLEY   Don't get insulted.

WILLY   Don't insult me.

CHARLEY   I don't see no sense in it. You don't have to go on this way.

WILLY   I got a good job. (*Slight pause*) What do you keep comin' in here for?

CHARLEY   You want me to go?

WILLY (*After a pause, withering*)   I can't understand it. He's going back to Texas again. What the hell is that?

CHARLEY   Let him go.

WILLY   I got nothin' to give him, Charley, I'm clean, I'm clean.

CHARLEY   He won't starve. None a them starve. Forget about him.

WILLY   Then what have I got to remember?

CHARLEY   You take it too hard. To hell with it. When a deposit bottle is broken you don't get your nickel back.

WILLY   That's easy enough for you to say.

CHARLEY   That ain't easy for me to say.

WILLY   Did you see the ceiling I put up in the living-room?

CHARLEY Yeah, that's a piece of work. To put up a ceiling is a mystery to me. How do you do it?

WILLY What's the difference?

CHARLEY Well, talk about it.

WILLY You gonna put up a ceiling?

CHARLEY How could I put up a ceiling?

WILLY Then what the hell are you bothering me for?

CHARLEY You're insulted again.

WILLY A man who can't handle tools is not a man. You're disgusting.

CHARLEY Don't call me disgusting, Willy.

(UNCLE BEN, *carrying a valise and an umbrella, enters the forestage from around the right corner of the house. He is a stolid man, in his sixties, with a mustache and an authoritative air. He is utterly certain of his destiny, and there is an aura of far places about him. He enters exactly as* WILLY *speaks*)

WILLY I'm getting awfully tired, Ben.

(BEN's *music is heard.* BEN *looks around at everything*)

CHARLEY Good, keep playing; you'll sleep better. Did you call me Ben?

(BEN *looks at his watch*)

WILLY That's funny. For a second there you reminded me of my brother Ben.

BEN I only have a few minutes.

(*He strolls, inspecting the place.* WILLY *and* CHARLEY *continue playing*)

CHARLEY You never heard from him again, heh? Since that time?

WILLY Didn't Linda tell you? Couple of weeks ago we got a letter from his wife in Africa. He died.

CHARLEY That so.

BEN (*Chuckling*) So this is Brooklyn, eh?

CHARLEY Maybe you're in for some of his money.

WILLY Naa, he had seven sons. There's just one opportunity I had with that man . . .

BEN I must make a train, William. There are several properties I'm looking at in Alaska.

WILLY Sure, sure! If I'd gone with him to Alaska that time, everything would've been totally different.

CHARLEY Go on, you'd froze to death up there.

WILLY What're you talking about?

BEN   Opportunity is tremendous in Alaska, William. Surprised you're not up there.

WILLY   Sure, tremendous.

CHARLEY   Heh?

WILLY   There was the only man I ever met who knew the answers.

CHARLEY   Who?

BEN   How are you all?

WILLY   (*Taking a pot, smiling*)   Fine, fine.

CHARLEY   Pretty sharp tonight.

BEN   Is Mother living with you?

WILLY   No, she died a long time ago.

CHARLEY   Who?

BEN   That's too bad. Fine specimen of a lady, Mother.

WILLY   (*To* CHARLEY)   Heh?

BEN   I'd hoped to see the old girl.

CHARLEY   Who died?

BEN   Heard anything from Father, have you?

WILLY   (*Unnerved*)   What do you mean, who died?

CHARLEY   (*Taking a pot*)   What're you talkin' about?

BEN   (*Looking at his watch*)   William, it's half-past eight!

WILLY   (*As though to dispel his confusion he angrily stops* CHARLEY'S *hand*)   That's my build!

CHARLEY   I put the ace—

WILLY   If you don't know how to play the game I'm not gonna throw my money away on you!

CHARLEY   (*Rising*)   It was my ace, for God's sake!

WILLY   I'm through, I'm through!

BEN   When did Mother die?

WILLY   Long ago. Since the beginning you never knew how to play cards.

CHARLEY   (*Picks up the cards and goes to the door*)   All right! Next time I'll bring a deck with five aces.

WILLY   I don't play that kind of game!

CHARLEY   (*Turning to him*)   You ought to be ashamed of yourself!

WILLY   Yeah?

CHARLEY   Yeah!

(*He goes out*)

WILLY   (*Slamming the door after him*)   Ignoramus!

BEN   (*As* WILLY *comes toward him through the wall-line of the kitchen*)   So you're William.

WILLY (*Shaking* BEN's *hand*) Ben! I've been waiting for you so long! What's the answer? How did you do it?

BEN Oh, there's a story in that.

(LINDA *enters the forestage, as of old, carrying the wash basket*)

LINDA Is this Ben?

BEN (*Gallantly*) How do you do, my dear.

LINDA Where've you been all these years? Willy's always wondered why you—

WILLY (*Pulling* BEN *away from her impatiently*) Where is Dad? Didn't you follow him? How did you get started?

BEN Well, I don't know how much you remember.

WILLY Well, I was just a baby, of course, only three or four years old—

BEN Three years and eleven months.

WILLY What a memory, Ben!

BEN I have many enterprises, William, and I have never kept books.

WILLY I remember I was sitting under the wagon in—was it Nebraska?

BEN It was South Dakota, and I gave you a bunch of wild flowers.

WILLY I remember you walking away down some open road.

BEN (*Laughing*) I was going to find Father in Alaska.

WILLY Where is he?

BEN At that age I had a very faulty view of geography, William. I discovered after a few days that I was heading due south, so instead of Alaska, I ended up in Africa.

LINDA Africa!

WILLY The Gold Coast!

BEN Principally diamond mines.

LINDA Diamond mines!

BEN Yes, my dear. But I've only a few minutes—

WILLY No! Boys! Boys! (YOUNG BIFF *and* HAPPY *appear*) Listen to this. This is your Uncle Ben, a great man! Tell my boys, Ben!

BEN Why, boys, when I was seventeen I walked into the jungle, and when I was twenty-one I walked out. (*He laughs*) And by God I was rich.

WILLY (*To the boys*) You see what I been talking about? The greatest things can happen!

BEN (*Glancing at his watch*) I have an appointment in Ketchikan Tuesday week.

WILLY No, Ben! Please tell about Dad. I want my boys to hear.

I want them to know the kind of stock they spring from. All I remember is a man with a big beard, and I was in Mamma's lap, sitting around a fire, and some kind of high music.

BEN   His flute. He played the flute.

WILLY   Sure, the flute, that's right!

(*New music is heard, a high, rollicking tune*)

BEN   Father was a very great and a very wild-hearted man. We would start in Boston, and he'd toss the whole family into the wagon, and then he'd drive the team right across the country; through Ohio, and Indiana, Michigan, Illinois, and all the Western states. And we'd stop in the towns and sell the flutes that he'd made on the way. Great inventor, Father. With one gadget he made more in a week than a man like you could make in a lifetime.

WILLY   That's just the way I'm bringing them up, Ben—rugged, well liked, all-around.

BEN   Yeah? (*To* BIFF) Hit that, boy—hard as you can.

(*He pounds his stomach*)

BIFF   Oh, no, sir!

BEN (*Taking boxing stance*)   Come on, get to me!

(*He laughs*)

WILLY   Go to it, Biff! Go ahead, show him!

BIFF   Okay!

(*He cocks his fists and starts in*)

LINDA (*To* WILLY)   Why must he fight, dear?

BEN (*Sparring with* BIFF)   Good boy! Good boy!

WILLY   How's that, Ben, heh?

HAPPY   Give him the left, Biff!

LINDA   Why are you fighting?

BEN   Good boy!

(*Suddenly comes in, trips* BIFF, *and stands over him, the point of his umbrella poised over* BIFF's *eye*)

LINDA   Look out, Biff!

BIFF   Gee!

BEN (*Patting* BIFF's *knee*)   Never fight fair with a stranger, boy. You'll never get out of the jungle that way. (*Taking* LINDA's *hand and bowing*) It was an honor and a pleasure to meet you, Linda.

LINDA (*Withdrawing her hand coldly, frightened*)   Have a nice—trip.

BEN (*To* WILLY)   And good luck with your—what do you do?

WILLY   Selling.

BEN   Yes. Well . . .

(*He raises his hand in farewell to all*)

WILLY   No, Ben, I don't want you to think . . . (*He takes* BEN's *arm to show him*) It's Brooklyn, I know, but we hunt too.

BEN   Really, now.

WILLY   Oh, sure, there's snakes and rabbits and—that's why I moved out here. Why, Biff can fell any one of these trees in no time! Boys! Go right over to where they're building the apartment house and get some sand. We're gonna rebuild the entire front stoop right now! Watch this, Ben!

BIFF   Yes, sir! On the double, Hap!

HAPPY (*As he and* BIFF *run off*)   I lost weight, Pop, you notice?

(CHARLEY *enters in knickers, even before the boys are gone*)

CHARLEY   Listen, if they steal any more from that building the watchman'll put the cops on them!

LINDA (*To* WILLY)   Don't let Biff . . .

(BEN *laughs lustily*)

WILLY   You shoulda seen the lumber they brought home last week. At least a dozen six-by-tens worth all kinds a money.

CHARLEY   Listen, if that watchman—

WILLY   I gave them hell, understand. But I got a couple of fearless characters there.

CHARLEY   Willy, the jails are full of fearless characters.

BEN (*Clapping* WILLY *on the back, with a laugh at* CHARLEY)   And the stock exchange, friend!

WILLY (*Joining in* BEN's *laughter*)   Where are the rest of your pants?

CHARLEY   My wife bought them.

WILLY   Now all you need is a golf club and you can go upstairs and go to sleep. (*To* BEN) Great athlete! Between him and his son Bernard they can't hammer a nail!

BERNARD (*Rushing in*)   The watchman's chasing Biff!

WILLY (*Angrily*)   Shut up! He's not stealing anything!

LINDA (*Alarmed, hurrying off left*)   Where is he? Biff, dear!

(*She exits*)

WILLY (*Moving toward the left, away from* BEN)   There's nothing wrong. What's the matter with you?

BEN   Nervy boy. Good!

WILLY (*Laughing*)   Oh, nerves of iron, that Biff!

CHARLEY   Don't know what it is. My New England man comes back and he's bleedin', they murdered him up there.

WILLY   It's contacts, Charley, I got important contacts!

CHARLEY (*Sarcastically*) Glad to hear it, Willy. Come in later,
we'll shoot a little casino. I'll take some of your Portland money.
(*He laughs at* WILLY *and exits*)

WILLY (*Turning to* BEN) Business is bad, it's murderous. But not
for me, of course.

BEN   I'll stop by on my way back to Africa.

WILLY (*Longingly*) Can't you stay a few days? You're just what
I need, Ben, because I—I have a fine position here, but I—well,
Dad left when I was such a baby and I never had a chance to
talk to him and I still feel—kind of temporary about myself.

BEN   I'll be late for my train.

(*They are at opposite ends of the stage*)

WILLY   Ben, my boys—can't we talk? They'd go into the jaws of
hell for me, see, but I—

BEN   William, you're being first-rate with your boys. Outstanding,
manly chaps!

WILLY (*Hanging on to his words*) Oh, Ben, that's good to hear!
Because sometimes I'm afraid that I'm not teaching them the
right kind of— Ben, how should I teach them?

BEN (*Giving great weight to each word, and with a certain vicious
audacity*) William, when I walked into the jungle, I was seventeen. When I walked out I was twenty-one. And, by God, I was
rich!

(*He goes off into darkness around the right corner of the house*)

WILLY   . . . was rich! That's just the spirit I want to imbue them
with! To walk into a jungle! I was right! I was right! I was right!
(BEN *is gone, but* WILLY *is still speaking to him as* LINDA, *in
nightgown and robe, enters the kitchen, glances around for*
WILLY, *then goes to the door of the house, looks out and sees
him. Comes down to his left. He looks at her*)

LINDA   Willy, dear? Willy?

WILLY   I was right!

LINDA   Did you have some cheese? (*He can't answer*) It's very
late, darling. Come to bed, heh?

WILLY (*Looking straight up*) Gotta break your neck to see a star
in this yard.

LINDA   You coming in?

WILLY   Whatever happened to that diamond watch fob? Remember? When Ben came from Africa that time? Didn't he give me
a watch fob with a diamond in it?

LINDA   You pawned it, dear. Twelve, thirteen years ago. For Biff's radio correspondence course.

WILLY   Gee, that was a beautiful thing. I'll take a walk.

LINDA   But you're in your slippers.

WILLY   (*Starting to go around the house at the left*)   I was right! I was! (*Half to* LINDA, *as he goes, shaking his head*) What a man! There was a man worth talking to. I was right!

LINDA   (*Calling after* WILLY)   But in your slippers, Willy!

(WILLY *is almost gone when* BIFF, *in his pajamas, comes down the stairs and enters the kitchen*)

BIFF   What is he doing out there?

LINDA   Sh!

BIFF   God Almighty, Mom, how long has he been doing this?

LINDA   Don't, he'll hear you.

BIFF   What the hell is the matter with him?

LINDA   It'll pass by morning.

BIFF   Shouldn't we do anything?

LINDA   Oh, my dear, you should do a lot of things, but there's nothing to do, so go to sleep.

(HAPPY *comes down the stair and sits on the steps*)

HAPPY   I never heard him so loud, Mom.

LINDA   Well, come around more often; you'll hear him.

(*She sits down at the table and mends the lining of* WILLY's *jacket*)

BIFF   Why didn't you ever write me about this, Mom?

LINDA   How would I write to you? For over three months you had no address.

BIFF   I was on the move. But you know I thought of you all the time. You know that, don't you, pal?

LINDA   I know, dear, I know. But he likes to have a letter. Just to know that there's still a possibility for better things.

BIFF   He's not like this all the time, is he?

LINDA   It's when you come home he's always the worst.

BIFF   When I come home?

LINDA   When you write you're coming, he's all smiles, and talks about the future, and—he's just wonderful. And then the closer you seem to come, the more shaky he gets, and then, by the time you get here, he's arguing, and he seems angry at you. I think it's just that maybe he can't bring himself to—to open up to you. Why are you so hateful to each other? Why is that?

BIFF   (*Evasively*)   I'm not hateful, Mom.

LINDA But you no sooner come in the door than you're fighting!

BIFF I don't know why. I mean to change. I'm tryin', Mom, you understand?

LINDA Are you home to stay now?

BIFF I don't know. I want to look around, see what's doin'.

LINDA Biff, you can't look around all your life, can you?

BIFF I just can't take hold, Mom. I can't take hold of some kind of a life.

LINDA Biff, a man is not a bird, to come and go with the springtime.

BIFF Your hair . . . (*He touches her hair*) Your hair got so gray.

LINDA Oh, it's been gray since you were in high school. I just stopped dyeing it, that's all.

BIFF Dye it again, will ya? I don't want my pal looking old. (*He smiles*)

LINDA You're such a boy! You think you can go away for a year and . . . You've got to get it into your head now that one day you'll knock on this door and there'll be strange people here—

BIFF What are you talking about? You're not even sixty, Mom.

LINDA But what about your father?

BIFF (*Lamely*) Well, I meant him too.

HAPPY He admires Pop.

LINDA Biff, dear, if you don't have any feeling for him, then you can't have any feeling for me.

BIFF Sure I can, Mom.

LINDA No. You can't just come to see me, because I love him. (*With a threat, but only a threat, of tears*) He's the dearest man in the world to me, and I won't have anyone making him feel unwanted and low and blue. You've got to make up your mind now, darling, there's no leeway any more. Either he's your father and you pay him that respect, or else you're not to come here. I know he's not easy to get along with—nobody knows that better than me—but . . .

WILLY (*From the left, with a laugh*) Hey, hey, Biffo!

BIFF (*Starting to go out after* WILLY) What the hell is the matter with him? (*HAPPY stops him*)

LINDA Don't—don't go near him!

BIFF Stop making excuses for him! He always, always wiped the floor with you. Never had an ounce of respect for you.

HAPPY He's always had respect for—

BIFF   What the hell do you know about it?

HAPPY (*Surlily*)   Just don't call him crazy!

BIFF   He's got no character— Charley wouldn't do this. Not in his own house—spewing out that vomit from his mind.

HAPPY   Charley never had to cope with what he's got to.

BIFF   People are worse off than Willy Loman. Believe me, I've seen them!

LINDA   Then make Charley your father, Biff. You can't do that, can you? I don't say he's a great man. Willy Loman never made a lot of money. His name was never in the paper. He's not the finest character that ever lived. But he's a human being, and a terrible thing is happening to him. So attention must be paid. He's not to be allowed to fall into his grave like an old dog. Attention, attention must be finally paid to such a person. You called him crazy—

BIFF   I didn't mean—

LINDA   No, a lot of people think he's lost his—balance. But you don't have to be very smart to know what his trouble is. The man is exhausted.

HAPPY   Sure!

LINDA   A small man can be just as exhausted as a great man. He works for a company thirty-six years this March, opens up unheard-of territories to their trademark, and now in his old age they take his salary away.

HAPPY (*Indignantly*)   I didn't know that, Mom.

LINDA   You never asked, my dear! Now that you get your spending money someplace else you don't trouble your mind with him.

HAPPY   But I gave you money last—

LINDA   Christmas time, fifty dollars! To fix the hot water it cost ninety-seven fifty! For five weeks he's been on straight commission, like a beginner, an unknown!

BIFF   Those ungrateful bastards!

LINDA   Are they any worse than his sons? When he brought them business, when he was young, they were glad to see him. But now his old friends, the old buyers that loved him so and always found some order to hand him in a pinch—they're all dead, retired. He used to be able to make six, seven calls a day in Boston. Now he takes his valises out of the car and puts them back and takes them out again and he's exhausted. Instead of walking he talks now. He drives seven hundred miles, and when he gets there no one knows him any more, no one welcomes him. And what goes through a man's mind, driving seven hundred miles home without having earned a cent? Why shouldn't he talk to himself? Why? When he has to go to Charley and borrow fifty dollars a week and pretend to me that it's his pay? How long can that go on? How long? You see what I'm sitting here and waiting for? And you tell me he has no character? The man who never worked a day but for your benefit? When does he get the medal for that? Is this his reward—to turn around at the age of sixty-three and find his sons, who he loved better than his life, one a philandering bum—

HAPPY   Mom!

LINDA   That's all you are, my baby! (*To* BIFF) And you! What happened to the love you had for him? You were such pals! How you used to talk to him on the phone every night! How lonely he was till he could come home to you!

BIFF   All right, Mom. I'll live here in my room, and I'll get a job. I'll keep away from him, that's all.

LINDA   No, Biff. You can't stay here and fight all the time.

BIFF   He threw me out of this house, remember that.

LINDA   Why did he do that? I never knew why.

BIFF   Because I know he's a fake and he doesn't like anybody around who knows!

LINDA   Why a fake? In what way? What do you mean?

BIFF   Just don't lay it all at my feet. It's between me and him—that's all I have to say. I'll chip in from now on. He'll settle for half my pay check. He'll be all right. I'm going to bed.

(*He starts for the stairs*)

LINDA   He won't be all right.

BIFF   (*Turning on the stairs, furiously*)   I hate this city and I'll stay here. Now what do you want?

LINDA   He's dying, Biff.

(HAPPY *turns quickly to her, shocked*)

BIFF   (*After a pause*)   Why is he dying?

LINDA   He's been trying to kill himself.

BIFF   (*With great horror*)   How?

LINDA   I live from day to day.

BIFF   What're you talking about?

LINDA   Remember I wrote you that he smashed up the car again? In February?

BIFF   Well?

LINDA   The insurance inspector came. He said that they have evidence. That all these accidents in the last year—weren't—weren't —accidents.

HAPPY   How can they tell that? That's a lie.

LINDA   It seems there's a woman . . .

(*She takes a breath as*)

⌠BIFF (*Sharply but contained*)   What woman?
⌡LINDA (*Simultaneously*)   . . . and this woman . . .

LINDA   What?

BIFF   Nothing. Go ahead.

LINDA   What did you say?

BIFF   Nothing. I just said what woman?

HAPPY   What about her?

LINDA   Well, it seems she was walking down the road and saw his car. She says that he wasn't driving fast at all, and that he didn't skid. She says he came to that little bridge, and then deliberately smashed into the railing, and it was only the shallowness of the water that saved him.

BIFF   Oh, no, he probably just fell asleep again.

LINDA   I don't think he fell asleep.

BIFF   Why not?

LINDA   Last month . . . (*With great difficulty*) Oh, boys, it's so hard to say a thing like this! He's just a big stupid man to you, but I tell you there's more good in him than in many other people. (*She chokes, wipes her eyes*) I was looking for a fuse. The lights blew out, and I went down the cellar. And behind the fuse box— it happened to fall out—was a length of rubber pipe—just short.

HAPPY   No kidding?

LINDA   There's a little attachment on the end of it. I knew right away. And sure enough, on the bottom of the water heater there's a new little nipple on the gas pipe.

HAPPY (*Angrily*)   That—jerk.

BIFF   Did you have it taken off?

LINDA   I'm—I'm ashamed to. How can I mention it to him? Every day I go down and take away that little rubber pipe. But, when he comes home, I put it back where it was. How can I insult him that way? I don't know what to do. I live from day to day, boys. I tell you, I know every thought in his mind. It sounds so old-fashioned and silly, but I tell you he put his whole life into you and you've turned your backs on him. (*She is bent over in the chair, weeping, her face in her hands*) Biff, I swear to God! Biff, his life is in your hands!

HAPPY (*To* BIFF) How do you like that damned fool!

BIFF (*Kissing her*) All right, pal, all right. It's all settled now. I've been remiss. I know that, Mom. But now I'll stay, and I swear to you, I'll apply myself. (*Kneeling in front of her, in a fever of self-reproach*) It's just—you see, Mom, I don't fit in business. Not that I won't try. I'll try, and I'll make good.

HAPPY Sure you will. The trouble with you in business was you never tried to please people.

BIFF I know, I—

HAPPY Like when you worked for Harrison's. Bob Harrison said you were tops, and then you go and do some damn fool thing like whistling whole songs in the elevator like a comedian.

BIFF (*Against* HAPPY) So what? I like to whistle sometimes.

HAPPY You don't raise a guy to a responsible job who whistles in the elevator!

LINDA Well, don't argue about it now.

HAPPY Like when you'd go off and swim in the middle of the day instead of taking the line around.

BIFF (*His resentment rising*) Well, don't you run off? You take off sometimes, don't you? On a nice summer day?

HAPPY Yeah, but I cover myself!

LINDA Boys!

HAPPY If I'm going to take a fade the boss can call any number where I'm supposed to be and they'll swear to him that I just left. I'll tell you something that I hate to say, Biff, but in the business world some of them think you're crazy.

BIFF (*Angered*) Screw the business world!

HAPPY All right, screw it! Great, but cover yourself!

LINDA Hap, Hap!

BIFF I don't care what they think! They've laughed at Dad for years, and you know why? Because we don't belong in this nuthouse of a city! We should be mixing cement on some open plain, or—or carpenters. A carpenter is allowed to whistle!

(WILLY *walks in from the entrance of the house, at left*)

WILLY Even your grandfather was better than a carpenter. (*Pause. They watch him*) You never grew up. Bernard does not whistle in the elevator, I assure you.

BIFF (*As though to laugh* WILLY *out of it*) Yeah, but you do, Pop.

WILLY I never in my life whistled in an elevator! And who in the business world thinks I'm crazy?

BIFF   I didn't mean it like that, Pop. Now don't make a whole thing out of it, will ya?

WILLY   Go back to the West! Be a carpenter, a cowboy, enjoy yourself!

LINDA   Willy, he was just saying—

WILLY   I heard what he said!

HAPPY (*Trying to quiet* WILLY)   Hey, Pop, come on now . . .

WILLY (*Continuing over* HAPPY's *line*)   They laugh at me, heh? Go to Filene's, go to the Hub, go to Slattery's, Boston. Call out the name Willy Loman and see what happens! Big shot!

BIFF   All right, Pop.

WILLY   Big!

BIFF   All right!

WILLY   Why do you always insult me?

BIFF   I didn't say a word. (*To* LINDA) Did I say a word?

LINDA   He didn't say anything, Willy.

WILLY (*Going to the doorway of the living-room*)   All right, good night, good night.

LINDA   Willy, dear, he just decided . . .

WILLY (*To* BIFF)   If you get tired hanging around tomorrow, paint the ceiling I put up in the living-room.

BIFF   I'm leaving early tomorrow.

HAPPY   He's going to see Bill Oliver, Pop.

WILLY (*Interestedly*)   Oliver? For what?

BIFF (*With reserve, but trying, trying*)   He always said he'd stake me. I'd like to go into business, so maybe I can take him up on it.

LINDA   Isn't that wonderful?

WILLY   Don't interrupt. What's wonderful about it? There's fifty men in the City of New York who'd stake him. (*To* BIFF) Sporting goods?

BIFF   I guess so. I know something about it and—

WILLY   He knows something about it! You know sporting goods better than Spalding, for God's sake! How much is he giving you?

BIFF   I don't know, I didn't even see him, yet, but—

WILLY   Then what're you talkin' about?

BIFF (*Getting angry*)   Well, all I said was I'm gonna see him, that's all!

WILLY (*Turning away*)   Ah, you're counting your chickens again.

BIFF (*Starting left for the stairs*)   Oh, Jesus, I'm going to sleep!

WILLY (*Calling after him*)   Don't curse in this house!

BIFF (*Turning*)   Since when did you get so clean?

HAPPY (*Trying to stop them*) Wait a . . .

WILLY Don't use that language to me! I won't have it!

HAPPY (*Grabbing* BIFF, *shouts*) Wait a minute! I got an idea. I got a feasible idea. Come here, Biff, let's talk this over now, let's talk some sense here. When I was down in Florida last time, I thought of a great idea to sell sporting goods. It just came back to me. You and I, Biff—we have a line, the Loman Line. We train a couple of weeks, and put on a couple of exhibitions, see?

WILLY That's an idea!

HAPPY Wait! We form two basketball teams, see? Two waterpolo teams. We play each other. It's a million dollars' worth of publicity. Two brothers, see? The Loman Brothers. Displays in the Royal Palms—all the hotels. And banners over the ring and the basketball court: "Loman Brothers." Baby, we could sell sporting goods!

WILLY That is a one-million-dollar idea!

LINDA Marvelous!

BIFF I'm in great shape as far as that's concerned.

HAPPY And the beauty of it is, Biff, it wouldn't be like a business. We'd be out playin' ball again . . .

BIFF (*Enthused*) Yeah, that's . . .

WILLY Million-dollar . . .

HAPPY And you wouldn't get fed up with it, Biff. It'd be the family again. There'd be the old honor, and comradeship, and if you wanted to go off for a swim or somethin'—well, you'd do it! Without some smart cooky gettin' up ahead of you!

WILLY Lick the world! You guys together could absolutely lick the civilized world.

BIFF I'll see Oliver tomorrow. Hap, if we could work that out . . .

LINDA Maybe things are beginning to—

WILLY (*Wildly enthused, to* LINDA) Stop interrupting! (*To* BIFF) But don't wear sport jacket and slacks when you see Oliver.

BIFF No, I'll—

WILLY A business suit, and talk as little as possible, and don't crack any jokes.

BIFF He did like me. Always liked me.

LINDA He loved you!

WILLY (*To* LINDA) Will you stop! (*To* BIFF) Walk in very serious. You are not applying for a boy's job. Money is to pass. Be quiet, fine, and serious. Everybody likes a kidder, but nobody lends him money.

HAPPY I'll try to get some myself, Biff. I'm sure I can.

WILLY I see great things for you kids, I think your troubles are over. But remember, start big and you'll end big. Ask for fifteen. How much you gonna ask for?

BIFF Gee, I don't know—

WILLY And don't say "Gee." "Gee" is a boy's word. A man walking in for fifteen thousand dollars does not say "Gee!"

BIFF Ten, I think, would be top though.

WILLY Don't be so modest. You always started too low. Walk in with a big laugh. Don't look worried. Start off with a couple of your good stories to lighten things up. It's not what you say, it's how you say it—because personality always wins the day.

LINDA Oliver always thought the highest of him—

WILLY Will you let me talk?

BIFF Don't yell at her, Pop, will ya?

WILLY (*Angrily*) I was talking, wasn't I?

BIFF I don't like you yelling at her all the time, and I'm tellin' you, that's all.

WILLY What're you, takin' over this house?

LINDA Willy—

WILLY (*Turning on her*) Don't take his side all the time, goddammit!

BIFF (*Furiously*) Stop yelling at her!

WILLY (*Suddenly pulling on his cheek, beaten down, guilt ridden*) Give my best to Bill Oliver—he may remember me.

(*He exits through the living-room doorway*)

LINDA (*Her voice subdued*) What'd you have to start that for? (BIFF *turns away*) You see how sweet he was as soon as you talked hopefully? (*She goes over to* BIFF) Come up and say good night to him. Don't let him go to bed that way.

HAPPY Come on, Biff, let's buck him up.

LINDA Please, dear. Just say good night. It takes so little to make him happy. Come. (*She goes through the living-room doorway, calling upstairs from within the living-room*) Your pajamas are hanging in the bathroom, Willy!

HAPPY (*Looking toward where* LINDA *went out*) What a woman! They broke the mold when they made her. You know that, Biff?

BIFF He's off salary. My God, working on commission!

HAPPY Well, let's face it: he's no hot-shot selling man. Except that sometimes, you have to admit, he's a sweet personality.

BIFF (*Deciding*) Lend me ten bucks, will ya? I want to buy some new ties.

HAPPY I'll take you to a place I know. Beautiful stuff. Wear one of my striped shirts tomorrow.

BIFF She got gray. Mom got awful old. Gee, I'm gonna go in to Oliver tomorrow and knock him for a—

HAPPY Come on up. Tell that to Dad. Let's give him a whirl. Come on.

BIFF (*Steamed up*) You know, with ten thousand bucks, boy!

HAPPY (*As they go into the living-room*) That's the talk, Biff, that's the first time I've heard the old confidence out of you! (*From within the living-room, fading off*) You're gonna live with me, kid, and any babe you want just say the word . . .

(*The last lines are hardly heard. They are mounting the stairs to their parents' bedroom*)

LINDA (*Entering her bedroom and addressing* WILLY, *who is in the bathroom. She is straightening the bed for him*) Can you do anything about the shower? It drips.

WILLY (*From the bathroom*) All of a sudden everything falls to pieces! Goddam plumbing, oughta be sued, those people. I hardly finished putting it in and the thing . . .

(*His words rumble off*)

LINDA I'm just wondering if Oliver will remember him. You think he might?

WILLY (*Coming out of the bathroom in his pajamas*) Remember him? What's the matter with you, you crazy? If he'd've stayed with Oliver he'd be on top by now! Wait'll Oliver gets a look at him. You don't know the average caliber any more. The average young man today—(*He is getting into bed*)—is got a caliber of zero. Greatest thing in the world for him was to bum around.

(BIFF *and* HAPPY *enter the bedroom. Slight pause*)

WILLY (*Stops short, looking at* BIFF) Glad to hear it, boy.

HAPPY He wanted to say good night to you, sport.

WILLY (*To* BIFF) Yeah. Knock him dead, boy. What'd you want to tell me?

BIFF Just take it easy, Pop. Good night.

(*He turns to go*)

WILLY (*Unable to resist*) And if anything falls off the desk while you're talking to him—like a package or something—don't you pick it up. They have office boys for that.

LINDA I'll make a big breakfast—

WILLY   Will you let me finish? (*To* BIFF) Tell him you were in the business in the West. Not farm work.

BIFF   All right, Dad.

LINDA   I think everything—

WILLY   (*Going right through her speech*) And don't undersell yourself. No less than fifteen thousand dollars.

BIFF   (*Unable to bear him*) Okay. Good night, Mom.

(*He starts moving*)

WILLY   Because you got a greatness in you, Biff, remember that. You got all kinds a greatness . . .

(*He lies back, exhausted.* BIFF *walks out*)

LINDA   (*Calling after* BIFF) Sleep well, darling!

HAPPY   I'm gonna get married, Mom. I wanted to tell you.

LINDA   Go to sleep, dear.

HAPPY   (*Going*) I just wanted to tell you.

WILLY   Keep up the good work. (HAPPY *exits*) God . . . remember that Ebbets Field game? The championship of the city?

LINDA   Just rest. Should I sing to you?

WILLY   Yeah. Sing to me. (LINDA *hums a soft lullaby*) When that team came out—he was the tallest, remember?

LINDA   Oh, yes. And in gold.

(BIFF *enters the darkened kitchen, takes a cigarette, and leaves the house. He comes downstage into a golden pool of light. He smokes, staring at the night*)

WILLY   Like a young god. Hercules—something like that. And the sun, the sun all around him. Remember how he waved to me? Right up from the field, with the representatives of three colleges standing by? And the buyers I brought, and the cheers when he came out—Loman, Loman, Loman! God Almighty, he'll be great yet. A star like that, magnificent, can never really fade away!

(*The light on* WILLY *is fading. The gas heater begins to glow through the kitchen wall, near the stairs, a blue flame beneath red coils*)

LINDA   (*Timidly*) Willy dear, what has he got against you?

WILLY   I'm so tired. Don't talk any more.

(BIFF *slowly returns to the kitchen. He stops, stares toward the heater*)

LINDA   Will you ask Howard to let you work in New York?

WILLY   First thing in the morning. Everything'll be all right.

(BIFF *reaches behind the heater and draws out a length of rubber tubing. He is horrified and turns his head toward* WILLY's *room, still dimly lit, from which the strains of* LINDA's *desperate but monotonous humming rise)*

WILLY (*Staring through the window into the moonlight*) Gee, look at the moon moving between the buildings!

(BIFF *wraps the tubing around his hand and quickly goes up the stairs*)

Curtain

ACT TWO

Music is heard, gay and bright. The curtain rises as the music fades away. WILLY, *in shirt sleeves, is sitting at the kitchen table, sipping coffee, his hat in his lap.* LINDA *is filling his cup when she can.*

WILLY   Wonderful coffee. Meal in itself.

LINDA   Can I make you some eggs?

WILLY   No. Take a breath.

LINDA   You look so rested, dear.

WILLY   I slept like a dead one. First time in months. Imagine, sleeping till ten on a Tuesday morning. Boys left nice and early, heh?

LINDA   They were out of here by eight o'clock.

WILLY   Good work!

LINDA   It was so thrilling to see them leaving together. I can't get over the shaving lotion in this house!

WILLY (*Smiling*)   Mmm—

LINDA   Biff was very changed this morning. His whole attitude seemed to be hopeful. He couldn't wait to get downtown to see Oliver.

WILLY   He's heading for a change. There's no question, there simply are certain men that take longer to get—solidified. How did he dress?

LINDA   His blue suit. He's so handsome in that suit. He could be a —anything in that suit!

(WILLY *gets up from the table.* LINDA *holds his jacket for him*)

WILLY   There's no question, no question at all. Gee, on the way home tonight I'd like to buy some seeds.

LINDA (*Laughing*)   That'd be wonderful. But not enough sun gets back there. Nothing'll grow any more.

WILLY   You wait, kid, before it's all over we're gonna get a little place out in the country, and I'll raise some vegetables, a couple of chickens . . .

LINDA   You'll do it yet, dear.

(WILLY *walks out of his jacket.* LINDA *follows him*)

WILLY   And they'll get married, and come for a weekend. I'd build a little guest house. 'Cause I got so many fine tools, all I'd need would be a little lumber and some peace of mind.

LINDA   (*Joyfully*)   I sewed the lining . . .

WILLY   I could build two guest houses, so they'd both come. Did he decide how much he's going to ask Oliver for?

LINDA   (*Getting him into the jacket*)   He didn't mention it, but I imagine ten or fifteen thousand. You going to talk to Howard today?

WILLY   Yeah. I'll put it to him straight and simple. He'll just have to take me off the road.

LINDA   And Willy, don't forget to ask for a little advance, because we've got the insurance premium. It's the grace period now.

WILLY   That's a hundred . . . ?

LINDA   A hundred and eight, sixty-eight. Because we're a little short again.

WILLY   Why are we short?

LINDA   Well, you had the motor job on the car . . .

WILLY   That goddam Studebaker!

LINDA   And you got one more payment on the refrigerator . . .

WILLY   But it just broke again!

LINDA   Well, it's old, dear.

WILLY   I told you we should've bought a well-advertised machine. Charley bought a General Electric and it's twenty years old and it's still good, that son-of-a-bitch.

LINDA   But, Willy—

WILLY   Whoever heard of a Hastings refrigerator? Once in my life I would like to own something outright before it's broken! I'm always in a race with the junkyard! I just finished paying for the car and it's on its last legs. The refrigerator consumes belts like a goddam maniac. They time those things. They time them so when you finally paid for them, they're used up.

LINDA   (*Buttoning up his jacket as he unbuttons it*)   All told, about two hundred dollars would carry us, dear. But that includes the last payment on the mortgage. After this payment, Willy, the house belongs to us.

WILLY   It's twenty-five years!

LINDA   Biff was nine years old when we bought it.

WILLY Well, that's a great thing. To weather a twenty-five year mortgage is—

LINDA It's an accomplishment.

WILLY All the cement, the lumber, the reconstruction I put in this house! There ain't a crack to be found in it any more.

LINDA Well, it served its purpose.

WILLY What purpose? Some stranger'll come along, move in, and that's that. If only Biff would take this house, and raise a family . . . (*He starts to go*) Good-by, I'm late.

LINDA (*Suddenly remembering*) Oh, I forgot! You're supposed to meet them for dinner.

WILLY Me?

LINDA At Frank's Chop House on Forty-eighth near Sixth Avenue.

WILLY Is that so! How about you?

LINDA No, just the three of you. They're gonna blow you to a big meal!

WILLY Don't say! Who thought of that?

LINDA Biff came to me this morning, Willy, and he said, "Tell Dad, we want to blow him to a big meal." Be there six o'clock. You and your two boys are going to have dinner.

WILLY Gee whiz! That's really somethin'. I'm gonna knock Howard for a loop, kid. I'll get an advance, and I'll come home with a New York job. Goddammit, now I'm gonna do it!

LINDA Oh, that's the spirit, Willy!

WILLY I will never get behind a wheel the rest of my life!

LINDA It's changing, Willy, I can feel it changing!

WILLY Beyond a question. G'by, I'm late.

(*He starts to go again*)

LINDA (*Calling after him as she runs to the kitchen table for a handkerchief*) You got your glasses?

WILLY (*Feels for them, then comes back in*) Yeah, yeah, got my glasses.

LINDA (*Giving him the handkerchief*) And a handkerchief.

WILLY Yeah, handkerchief.

LINDA And your saccharine?

WILLY Yeah, my saccharine.

LINDA Be careful on the subway stairs.

(*She kisses him, and a silk stocking is seen hanging from her hand.* WILLY *notices it*)

WILLY Will you stop mending stockings? At least while I'm in the house. It gets me nervous. I can't tell you. Please.

(LINDA *hides the stocking in her hand as she follows* WILLY *across the forestage in front of the house*)

LINDA Remember, Frank's Chop House.

WILLY (*Passing the apron*) Maybe beets would grow out there.

LINDA (*Laughing*) But you tried so many times.

WILLY Yeah. Well, don't work hard today.

(*He disappears around the right corner of the house*)

LINDA Be careful!

(*As* WILLY *vanishes,* LINDA *waves to him. Suddenly the phone rings. She runs across the stage and into the kitchen and lifts it*)

LINDA Hello? Oh, Biff! I'm so glad you called, I just . . . Yes, sure, I just told him. Yes, he'll be there for dinner at six o'clock, I didn't forget. Listen, I was just dying to tell you. You know that little rubber pipe I told you about? That he connected to the gas heater? I finally decided to go down the cellar this morning and take it away and destroy it. But it's gone! Imagine? He took it away himself, it isn't there! (*She listens*) When? Oh, then you took it. Oh—nothing, it's just that I'd hoped he'd taken it away himself. Oh, I'm not worried, darling, because this morning he left in such high spirits, it was like the old days! I'm not afraid any more. Did Mr. Oliver see you? . . . Well, you wait there then. And make a nice impression on him, darling. Just don't perspire too much before you see him. And have a nice time with Dad. He may have big news too! . . . That's right, a New York job. And be sweet to him tonight, dear. Be loving to him. Because he's only a little boat looking for a harbor. (*She is trembling with sorrow and joy*) Oh, that's wonderful, Biff, you'll save his life. Thanks, darling. Just put your arm around him when he comes into the restaurant. Give him a smile. That's the boy . . . Good-by, dear. . . . You got your comb? . . . That's fine. Good-by, Biff dear.

(*In the middle of her speech, Howard Wagner, thirty-six, wheels on a small typewriter table on which is a wire-recording machine and proceeds to plug it in. This is on the left forestage. Light slowly fades on Linda as it rises on Howard. Howard is intent on threading the machine and only glances over his shoulder as Willy appears*)

WILLY Pst! Pst!

HOWARD Hello, Willy, come in.

WILLY Like to have a little talk with you, Howard.

HOWARD Sorry to keep you waiting. I'll be with you in a minute.

WILLY   What's that, Howard?

HOWARD   Didn't you ever see one of these? Wire recorder.

WILLY   Oh. Can we talk a minute?

HOWARD   Records things. Just got delivery yesterday. Been driving me crazy, the most terrific machine I ever saw in my life. I was up all night with it.

WILLY   What do you do with it?

HOWARD   I bought it for dictation, but you can do anything with it. Listen to this. I had it home last night. Listen to what I picked up. The first one is my daughter. Get this. (*He flicks the switch and "Roll out the Barrel" is heard being whistled*) Listen to that kid whistle.

WILLY   That is lifelike, isn't it?

HOWARD   Seven years old. Get that tone.

WILLY   Ts, ts, Like to ask a little favor if you . . .

(*The whistling breaks off, and the voice of* HOWARD's *daughter is heard*)

HIS DAUGHTER   "Now you, Daddy."

HOWARD   She's crazy for me! (*Again the same song is whistled*) That's me! Ha!

(*He winks*)

WILLY   You're very good!

(*The whistling breaks off again. The machine runs silent for a moment*)

HOWARD   Sh! Get this now, this is my son.

HIS SON   "The capital of Alabama is Montgomery; the capital of Arizona is Phoenix; the capital of Arkansas is Little Rock; the capital of California is Sacramento . . ."

(*And on, and on*)

HOWARD   (*Holding up five fingers*)   Five years old, Willy!

WILLY   He'll make an announcer some day!

HIS SON   (*Continuing*)   "The capital . . ."

HOWARD   Get that—alphabetical order! (*The machine breaks off suddenly*) Wait a minute. The maid kicked the plug out.

WILLY   It certainly is a—

HOWARD   Sh, for God's sake!

HIS SON   "It's nine o'clock, Bulova watch time. So I have to go to sleep."

WILLY   That really is—

HOWARD   Wait a minute! The next is my wife.

(*They wait*)

HOWARD'S VOICE "Go on, say something." (*Pause*) "Well, you gonna talk?"

HIS WIFE "I can't think of anything."

HOWARD'S VOICE "Well, talk—it's turning."

HIS WIFE (*Shyly, beaten*) "Hello." (*Silence*) "Oh, Howard, I can't talk into this . . ."

HOWARD (*Snapping the machine off*) That was my wife.

WILLY That is a wonderful machine. Can we—

HOWARD I tell you, Willy, I'm gonna take my camera, and my bandsaw, and all my hobbies, and out they go. This is the most fascinating relaxation I ever found.

WILLY I think I'll get one myself.

HOWARD Sure, they're only a hundred and a half. You can't do without it. Supposing you wanna hear Jack Benny, see? But you can't be at home at that hour. So you tell the maid to turn the radio on when Jack Benny comes on, and this automatically goes on with the radio . . .

WILLY And when you come home you . . .

HOWARD You can come home twelve o'clock, one o'clock, any time you like, and you get yourself a Coke and sit yourself down, throw the switch, and there's Jack Benny's program in the middle of the night!

WILLY I'm definitely going to get one. Because lots of time I'm on the road, and I think to myself, what I must be missing on the radio!

HOWARD Don't you have a radio in the car?

WILLY Well, yeah, but who ever thinks of turning it on?

HOWARD Say, aren't you supposed to be in Boston?

WILLY That's what I want to talk to you about, Howard. You got a minute?

(*He draws a chair in from the wing*)

HOWARD What happened? What're you doing here?

WILLY Well . . .

HOWARD You didn't crack up again, did you?

WILLY Oh, no. No . . .

HOWARD Geez, you had me worried there for a minute. What's the trouble?

WILLY Well, tell you the truth, Howard. I've come to the decision that I'd rather not travel any more.

HOWARD Not travel! Well, what'll you do?

WILLY Remember, Christmas time, when you had the party here? You said you'd try to think of some spot for me here in town.

HOWARD With us?

WILLY Well, sure.

HOWARD Oh, yeah, yeah. I remember. Well, I couldn't think of anything for you, Willy.

WILLY I tell ya, Howard. The kids are all grown up, y'know. I don't need much any more. If I could take home—well, sixty-five dollars a week, I could swing it.

HOWARD Yeah, but Willy, see I—

WILLY I tell ya why, Howard. Speaking frankly and between the two of us, y'know—I'm just a little tired.

HOWARD Oh, I could understand that, Willy. But you're a road man, Willy, and we do a road business. We've only got a half-dozen salesmen on the floor here.

WILLY God knows, Howard, I never asked a favor of any man. But I was with the firm when your father used to carry you in here in his arms.

HOWARD I know that, Willy, but—

WILLY Your father came to me the day you were born and asked me what I thought of the name of Howard, may he rest in peace.

HOWARD I appreciate that, Willy, but there just is no spot here for you. If I had a spot I'd slam you right in, but I just don't have a single solitary spot.

(*He looks for his lighter.* WILLY *has picked it up and gives it to him. Pause*)

WILLY (*With increasing anger*) Howard, all I need to set my table is fifty dollars a week.

HOWARD But where am I going to put you, kid?

WILLY Look, it isn't a question of whether I can sell merchandise, is it?

HOWARD No, but it's business, kid, and everybody's gotta pull his own weight.

WILLY (*Desperately*) Just let me tell you a story, Howard—

HOWARD 'Cause you gotta admit, business is business.

WILLY (*angrily*) Business is definitely business, but just listen for a minute. You don't understand this. When I was a boy—eighteen, nineteen—I was already on the road. And there was a question in my mind as to whether selling had a future for me. Because in those days I had a yearning to go to Alaska. See, there were three gold strikes in one month in Alaska, and I felt like going out. Just for the ride, you might say.

HOWARD (*Barely interested*) Don't say.

WILLY Oh, yeah, my father lived many years in Alaska. He was an adventurous man. We've got quite a little streak of self-reliance in our family. I thought I'd go out with my older brother and try to locate him, and maybe settle in the North with the old man. And I was almost decided to go, when I met a salesman in the Parker House. His name was Dave Singleman. And he was eighty-four years old, and he'd drummed merchandise in thirty-one states. And old Dave, he'd go up to his room, y'understand, put on his green velvet slippers—I'll never forget—and pick up his phone and call the buyers, and without ever leaving his room, at the age of eighty-four, he made his living. And when I saw that, I realized that selling was the greatest career a man could want. 'Cause what could be more satisfying than to be able to go, at the age of eighty-four, into twenty or thirty different cities, and pick up a phone, and be remembered and loved and helped by so many different people? Do you know? when he died—and by the way he died the death of a salesman, in his green velvet slippers in the smoker of the New York, New Haven and Hartford, going into Boston—when he died, hundreds of salesmen and buyers were at his funeral. Things were sad on a lotta trains for months after that. (*He stands up.* HOWARD *has not looked at him*) In those days there was personality in it, Howard. There was respect, and comradeship, and gratitude in it. Today, it's all cut and dried, and there's no chance for bringing friendship to bear—or personality. Yet see what I mean? They don't know me any more.

HOWARD (*Moving away, to the right*) That's just the thing, Willy.

WILLY If I had forty dollars a week—that's all I'd need. Forty dollars, Howard.

HOWARD Kid, I can't take blood from a stone, I—

WILLY (*Desperation is on him now*) Howard, the year Al Smith was nominated, your father came to me and—

HOWARD (*Starting to go off*) I've got to see some people, kid.

WILLY (*Stopping him*) I'm talking about your father! There were promises made across this desk! You mustn't tell me you've got people to see—I put thirty-six years into this firm, Howard, and now I can't pay my insurance! You can't eat the orange and throw the peel away—a man is not a piece of fruit! (*After a pause*) Now pay attention. Your father—in 1928 I had a big year. I averaged a hundred and seventy dollars a week in commissions.

HOWARD (*Impatiently*)   Now, Willy, you never averaged—

WILLY (*Banging his hand on the desk*)   I averaged a hundred and seventy dollars a week in the year of 1928! And your father came to me—or rather, I was in the office here—it was right over this desk—and he put his hand on my shoulder—

HOWARD (*Getting up*)   You'll have to excuse me, Willy, I gotta see some people. Pull yourself together. (*Going out*) I'll be back in a little while.

(*On* HOWARD's *exit, the light on his chair grows very bright and strange*)

WILLY   Pull myself together! What the hell did I say to him? My God, I was yelling at him! How could I! (WILLY *breaks off, staring at the light, which occupies the chair, animating it. He approaches this chair, standing across the desk from it*) Frank, Frank, don't you remember what you told me that time? How you put your hand on my shoulder, and Frank . . .

(*He leans on the desk and as he speaks the dead man's name he accidentally switches on the recorder, and instantly*)

HOWARD'S SON   ". . . of New York is Albany. The capital of Ohio is Cincinnati, the capital of Rhode Island is . . ."

(*The recitation continues*)

WILLY (*Leaping away with fright, shouting*)   Ha! Howard! Howard! Howard!

HOWARD (*Rushing in*)   What happened?

WILLY (*Pointing at the machine, which continues nasally, childishly, with the capital cities*)   Shut it off! Shut it off!

HOWARD (*Pulling the plug out*)   Look, Willy . . .

WILLY (*Pressing his hands to his eyes*)   I gotta get myself some coffee. I'll get some coffee . . .

(WILLY *starts to walk out.* HOWARD *stops him*)

HOWARD (*Rolling up the cord*)   Willy, look . . .

WILLY   I'll go to Boston.

HOWARD   Willy, you can't go to Boston for us.

WILLY   Why can't I go?

HOWARD   I don't want you to represent us. I've been meaning to tell you for a long time now.

WILLY   Howard, are you firing me?

HOWARD   I think you need a good long rest, Willy.

WILLY   Howard—

HOWARD   And when you feel better, come back, and we'll see if we can work something out.

WILLY   But I gotta earn money, Howard. I'm in no position to—

HOWARD   Where are your sons? Why don't your sons give you a hand?

WILLY   They're working on a very big deal.

HOWARD   This is no time for false pride, Willy. You go to your sons and you tell them that you're tired. You've got two great boys, haven't you?

WILLY   Oh, no question, no question, but in the meantime . . .

HOWARD   Then that's that, heh?

WILLY   All right, I'll go to Boston tomorrow.

HOWARD   No, no.

WILLY   I can't throw myself on my sons. I'm not a cripple!

HOWARD   Look, kid, I'm busy this morning.

WILLY   (*Grasping* HOWARD's *arm*)   Howard, you've got to let me go to Boston!

HOWARD   (*Hard, keeping himself under control*)   I've got a line of people to see this morning. Sit down, take five minutes, and pull yourself together, and then go home, will ya? I need the office, Willy. (*He starts to go, turns, remembering the recorder, starts to push off the table holding the recorder*) Oh, yeah. Whenever you can this week, stop by and drop off the samples. You'll feel better, Willy, and then come back and we'll talk. Pull yourself together, kid, there's people outside.

(HOWARD *exits, pushing the table off left.* WILLY *stares into space, exhausted. Now the music is heard*—BEN's *music—first distantly, then closer, closer. As* WILLY *speaks,* BEN *enters from the right. He carries valise and umbrella*)

WILLY   Oh, Ben, how did you do it? What is the answer? Did you wind up the Alaska deal already?

BEN   Doesn't take much time if you know what you're doing. Just a short business trip. Boarding ship in an hour. Wanted to say good-by.

WILLY   Ben, I've got to talk to you.

BEN   (*Glancing at his watch*)   Haven't the time, William.

WILLY   (*Crossing the apron to* BEN)   Ben, nothing's working out. I don't know what to do.

BEN   Now, look here, William. I've bought timberland in Alaska and I need a man to look after things for me.

WILLY   God, timberland! Me and my boys in those grand outdoors!

BEN   You've a new continent at your doorstep, William. Get out of these cities, they're full of talk and time payments and courts of law. Screw on your fists and you can fight for a fortune up there.

WILLY   Yes, yes! Linda, Linda!

(LINDA *enters as of old, with the wash*)

LINDA   Oh, you're back?

BEN   I haven't much time.

WILLY   No, wait! Linda, he's got a proposition for me in Alaska.

LINDA   But you've got— (*To* BEN) He's got a beautiful job here.

WILLY   But in Alaska, kid, I could—

LINDA   You're doing well enough, Willy!

BEN (*To* LINDA)   Enough for what, my dear?

LINDA (*Frightened of* BEN *and angry at him*)   Don't say those things to him! Enough to be happy right here, right now. (*To* WILLY, *while* BEN *laughs*) Why must everybody conquer the world? You're well liked, and the boys love you, and someday— (*To* BEN)—why, old man Wagner told him just the other day that if he keeps it up he'll be a member of the firm, didn't he, Willy?

WILLY   Sure, sure. I am building something with this firm, Ben, and if a man is building something he must be on the right track, mustn't he?

BEN   What are you building? Lay your hand on it. Where is it?

WILLY (*Hesitantly*)   That's true, Linda, there's nothing.

LINDA   Why? (*To* BEN) There's a man eighty-four years old—

WILLY   That's right, Ben, that's right. When I look at that man I say, what is there to worry about?

BEN   Bah!

WILLY   It's true, Ben. All he has to do is go into any city, pick up the phone, and he's making his living and you know why?

BEN (*Picking up his valise*)   I've got to go.

WILLY (*Holding* BEN *back*)   Look at this boy!

(BIFF, *in his high school sweater, enters carrying suitcase.* HAPPY *carries* BIFF's *shoulder guards, gold helmet, and football pants*)

WILLY   Without a penny to his name, three great universities are begging for him, and from there the sky's the limit, because it's not what you do, Ben. It's who you know and the smile on your face! It's contacts, Ben, contacts! The whole wealth of Alaska passes over the lunch table at the Commodore Hotel, and that's the wonder, the wonder of this country, that a man can end with diamonds here on the basis of being liked! (*He turns to* BIFF) And that's why when you get out on that field today it's important. Because thousands of people will be rooting for you and loving you. (*To* BEN, *who has again begun to leave*) And Ben! when he walks into a business office his name will sound out like a bell and all the doors will open to him! I've seen it, Ben, I've seen it a thousand times! You can't feel it with your hand like timber, but it's there!

BEN   Good-by, William.

WILLY   Ben, am I right? Don't you think I'm right? I value your advice.

BEN   There's a new continent at your doorstep, William. You could walk out rich. Rich!

(*He is gone*)

WILLY   We'll do it here, Ben! You hear me? We're gonna do it here!

(*Young* BERNARD *rushes in. The gay music of the* BOYS *is heard*)

BERNARD   Oh, gee, I was afraid you left already!

WILLY   Why? What time is it?

BERNARD   It's half-past one!

WILLY   Well, come on, everybody! Ebbets Field next stop! Where's the pennants?

(*He rushes through the wall-line of the kitchen and out into the living-room*)

LINDA (*To* BIFF)   Did you pack fresh underwear?

BIFF (*Who has been limbering up*)   I want to go!

BERNARD   Biff, I'm carrying your helmet, ain't I?

HAPPY   No, I'm carrying the helmet.

BERNARD   Oh, Biff, you promised me.

HAPPY   I'm carrying the helmet.

BERNARD   How am I going to get in the locker room?

LINDA   Let him carry the shoulder guards.

(*She puts her coat and hat on in the kitchen*)

BERNARD   Can I, Biff? 'Cause I told everybody I'm going to be in the locker room.

HAPPY   In Ebbets Field it's the clubhouse.

BERNARD   I meant the clubhouse. Biff!

HAPPY   Biff!

BIFF (*Grandly, after a slight pause*)   Let him carry the shoulder guards.

HAPPY (*As he gives* BERNARD *the shoulder guards*)   Stay close to us now.

(WILLY *rushes in with the pennants*)

WILLY (*Handing them out*) Everybody wave when Biff comes out on the field. (HAPPY *and* BERNARD *run off*) You set now, boy? (*The music has died away*)

BIFF Ready to go, Pop. Every muscle is ready.

WILLY (*At the edge of the apron*) You realize what this means?

BIFF That's right, Pop.

WILLY (*Feeling* BIFF's *muscles*) You're comin' home this afternoon captain of the All-Scholastic Championship Team of the City of New York.

BIFF I got it, Pop. And remember, pal, when I take off my helmet, that touchdown is for you.

WILLY Let's go! (*He is starting out, with his arm around* BIFF, *when* CHARLEY *enters, as of old, in knickers*) I got no room for you, Charley.

CHARLEY Room? For what?

WILLY In the car.

CHARLEY You goin' for a ride? I wanted to shoot some casino.

WILLY (*Furiously*) Casino! (*Incredulously*) Don't you realize what today is?

LINDA Oh, he knows, Willy. He's just kidding you.

WILLY That's nothing to kid about!

CHARLEY No, Linda, what's goin' on?

LINDA He's playing in Ebbets Field.

CHARLEY Baseball in this weather?

WILLY Don't talk to him. Come on, come on! (*He is pushing them out*)

CHARLEY Wait a minute, didn't you hear the news?

WILLY What?

CHARLEY Don't you listen to the radio? Ebbets Field just blew up.

WILLY You go to hell! (CHARLEY *laughs. Pushing them out*) Come on, come on! We're late.

CHARLEY (*As they go*) Knock a homer, Biff, knock a homer!

WILLY (*The last to leave, turning to* CHARLEY) I don't think that was funny, Charley. This is the greatest day of his life.

CHARLEY Willy, when are you going to grow up?

WILLY Yeah, heh? When this game is over, Charley, you'll be laughing out of the other side of your face. They'll be calling him another Red Grange. Twenty-five thousand a year.

CHARLEY (*Kidding*) Is that so?

WILLY Yeah, that's so.

CHARLEY Well, then, I'm sorry, Willy. But tell me something.

WILLY   What?

CHARLEY   Who is Red Grange?

WILLY   Put up your hands. Goddam you, put up your hands!

(CHARLEY, *chuckling, shakes his head and walks away, around the left corner of the stage.* WILLY *follows him. The music rises to a mocking frenzy*)

WILLY   Who the hell do you think you are, better than everybody else? You don't know everything, you big, ignorant, stupid . . . Put up your hands!

(*Light rises, on the right side of the forestage, on a small table in the reception room of* CHARLEY'S *office. Traffic sounds are heard.* BERNARD, *now mature, sits whistling to himself. A pair of tennis rackets and an overnight bag are on the floor beside him*)

WILLY   (*Offstage*)   What are you walking away for? Don't walk away! If you're going to say something say it to my face! I know you laugh at me behind my back. You'll laugh out of the other side of your goddam face after this game. Touchdown! Touchdown! Eighty thousand people! Touchdown! Right between the goal posts.

(BERNARD *is a quiet, earnest, but self-assured young man.* WILLY'S *voice is coming from right upstage now.* BERNARD *lowers his feet off the table and listens.* JENNY, *his father's secretary, enters*)

JENNY   (*Distressed*)   Say, Bernard, will you go out in the hall?

BERNARD   What is that noise? Who is it?

JENNY   Mr. Loman. He just got off the elevator.

BERNARD   (*Getting up*)   Who's he arguing with?

JENNY   Nobody. There's nobody with him. I can't deal with him any more, and your father gets all upset everytime he comes. I've got a lot of typing to do, and your father's waiting to sign it. Will you see him?

WILLY   (*Entering*)   Touchdown! Touch— (*He sees* JENNY) Jenny, Jenny, good to see you. How're ya? Workin'? Or still honest?

JENNY   Fine. How've you been feeling?

WILLY   Not much any more, Jenny. Ha, ha!

(*He is surprised to see the rackets*)

BERNARD   Hello, Uncle Willy.

WILLY   (*Almost shocked*)   Bernard! Well, look who's here!

(*He comes quickly, guiltily, to* BERNARD *and warmly shakes his hand*)

BERNARD   How are you? Good to see you.

WILLY   What are you doing here?

BERNARD   Oh, just stopped by to see Pop. Get off my feet till my train leaves. I'm going to Washington in a few minutes.

WILLY   Is he in?

BERNARD   Yes, he's in his office with the accountant. Sit down.

WILLY (*Sitting down*)   What're you going to do in Washington?

BERNARD   Oh, just a case I've got there, Willy.

WILLY   That so? (*Indicating the rackets*) You going to play tennis there?

BERNARD   I'm staying with a friend who's got a court.

WILLY   Don't say. His own tennis court. Must be fine people, I bet.

BERNARD   They are, very nice. Dad tells me Biff's in town.

WILLY (*With a big smile*)   Yeah, Biff's in. Working on a very big deal, Bernard.

BERNARD   What's Biff doing?

WILLY   Well, he's been doing very big things in the West. But he decided to establish himself here. Very big. We're having dinner. Did I hear your wife had a boy?

BERNARD   That's right. Our second.

WILLY   Two boys! What do you know!

BERNARD   What kind of a deal has Biff got?

WILLY   Well, Bill Oliver—very big sporting-goods man—he wants Biff very badly. Called him in from the West. Long distance, carte blanche, special deliveries. Your friends have their own private tennis court?

BERNARD   You still with the old firm, Willy?

WILLY (*After a pause*)   I'm—I'm overjoyed to see how you made the grade, Bernard, overjoyed. It's an encouraging thing to see a young man really—really— Looks very good for Biff—very— (*He breaks off, then*) Bernard—

(*He is so full of emotion, he breaks off again*)

BERNARD   What is it, Willy?

WILLY (*Small and alone*)   What—what's the secret?

BERNARD   What secret?

WILLY   How—how did you? Why didn't he ever catch on?

BERNARD   I wouldn't know that, Willy.

WILLY (*Confidentially, desperately*)   You were his friend, his boyhood friend. There's something I don't understand about it. His life ended after that Ebbets Field game. From the age of seventeen nothing good ever happened to him.

BERNARD   He never trained himself for anything.

WILLY   But he did, he did. After high school he took so many cor-

respondence courses. Radio mechanics; television; God knows
what, and never made the slightest mark.

BERNARD (*Taking off his glasses*) Willy, do you want to talk can-
didly?

WILLY (*Rising, faces* BERNARD) I regard you as a very brilliant
man, Bernard. I value your advice.

BERNARD Oh, the hell with the advice, Willy. I couldn't advise you.
There's just one thing I've always wanted to ask you. When he
was supposed to graduate, and the math teacher flunked him—

WILLY Oh, that son-of-a-bitch ruined his life.

BERNARD Yeah, but, Willy, all he had to do was go to summer
school and make up that subject.

WILLY That's right, that's right.

BERNARD Did you tell him not to go to summer school?

WILLY Me? I begged him to go. I ordered him to go!

BERNARD Then why wouldn't he go?

WILLY Why? Why! Bernard, that question has been trailing me
like a ghost for the last fifteen years. He flunked the subject, and
laid down and died like a hammer hit him!

BERNARD Take it easy, kid.

WILLY Let me talk to you—I got nobody to talk to. Bernard,
Bernard, was it my fault? Y'see? It keeps going around in my
mind, maybe I did something to him. I got nothing to give him.

BERNARD Don't take it so hard.

WILLY Why did he lay down? What is the story there? You were
his friend!

BERNARD Willy, I remember, it was June, and our grades came out.
And he'd flunked math.

WILLY That son-of-a-bitch!

BERNARD No, it wasn't right then. Biff just got very angry, I remember, and he was ready to enroll in summer school.

WILLY (*Surprised*) He was?

BERNARD He wasn't beaten by it at all. But then, Willy, he disappeared from the block for almost a month. And I got the idea
that he'd gone up to New England to see you. Did he have a talk
with you then?

(WILLY *stares in silence*)

BERNARD Willy?

WILLY (*With a strong edge of resentment in his voice*) Yeah, he
came to Boston. What about it?

BERNARD Well, just that when he came back—I'll never forget this, it always mystifies me. Because I'd thought so well of Biff, even though he'd always taken advantage of me. I loved him, Willy, y'know? And he came back after that month and took his sneakers —remember those sneakers with "University of Virginia" printed on them? He was so proud of those, wore them every day. And he took them down in the cellar, and burned them up in the furnace. We had a fist fight. It lasted at least half an hour. Just the two of us, punching each other down the cellar, and crying right through it. I've often thought of how strange it was that I knew he'd given up his life. What happened in Boston, Willy?

(WILLY *looks at him as at an intruder*)

BERNARD   I just bring it up because you asked me.

WILLY (*Angrily*)   Nothing. What do you mean, "What happened?" What's that got to do with anything?

BERNARD   Well, don't get sore.

WILLY   What are you trying to do, blame it on me? If a boy lays down is that my fault?

BERNARD   Now, Willy, don't get—

WILLY   Well, don't—don't talk to me that way! What does that mean, "What happened?"

(CHARLEY *enters. He is in his vest, and he carries a bottle of bourbon*)

CHARLEY   Hey, you're going to miss that train.

(*He waves the bottle*)

BERNARD   Yeah, I'm going. (*He takes the bottle*) Thanks, Pop. (*He picks up his rackets and bag*) Good-by, Willy, and don't worry about it. You know, "If at first you don't succeed . . ."

WILLY   Yes, I believe in that.

BERNARD   But sometimes, Willy, it's better for a man just to walk away.

WILLY   Walk away?

BERNARD   That's right.

WILLY   But if you can't walk away?

BERNARD (*After a slight pause*)   I guess that's when it's tough. (*Extending his hand*) Good-by, Willy.

WILLY (*Shaking* BERNARD'S *hand*)   Good-by, boy.

CHARLEY (*An arm on* BERNARD'S *shoulder*)   How do you like this kid? Gonna argue a case in front of the Supreme Court.

BERNARD (*Protesting*)   Pop!

WILLY (*Genuinely shocked, pained, and happy*)   No! The Supreme Court!

BERNARD   I gotta run. 'By, Dad!

CHARLEY   Knock 'em dead, Bernard!

(BERNARD *goes off*)

WILLY (*As* CHARLEY *takes out his wallet*)   The Supreme Court! And he didn't even mention it!

CHARLEY (*Counting out money on the desk*)   He don't have to—he's gonna do it.

WILLY   And you never told him what to do, did you? You never took any interest in him.

CHARLEY   My salvation is that I never took any interest in anything. There's some money—fifty dollars. I got an accountant inside.

WILLY   Charley, look . . . (*With difficulty*) I got my insurance to pay. If you can manage it—I need a hundred and ten dollars.

(CHARLEY *doesn't reply for a moment; merely stops moving*)

WILLY   I'd draw it from my bank but Linda would know, and I . . .

CHARLEY   Sit down, Willy.

WILLY (*Moving toward the chair*)   I'm keeping an account of everything, remember. I'll pay every penny back.

(*He sits*)

CHARLEY   Now listen to me, Willy.

WILLY   I want you to know I appreciate . . .

CHARLEY (*Sitting down on the table*)   Willy, what're you doin'? What the hell is goin' on in your head?

WILLY   Why? I'm simply . . .

CHARLEY   I offered you a job. You can make fifty dollars a week. And I won't send you on the road.

WILLY   I've got a job.

CHARLEY   Without pay? What kind of a job is a job without pay? (*He rises*) Now, look, kid, enough is enough. I'm no genius but I know when I'm being insulted.

WILLY   Insulted!

CHARLEY   Why don't you want to work for me?

WILLY   What's the matter with you? I've got a job.

CHARLEY   Then what're you walkin' in here every week for?

WILLY (*Getting up*)   Well, if you don't want me to walk in here—

CHARLEY   I am offering you a job.

WILLY   I don't want your goddam job!

CHARLEY   When the hell are you going to grow up?

WILLY (*Furiously*)   You big ignoramus, if you say that to me again I'll rap you one! I don't care how big you are!

(*He's ready to fight. Pause*)

CHARLEY (*Kindly, going to him*) How much do you need, Willy?

WILLY Charley, I'm strapped, I'm strapped. I don't know what to do. I was just fired.

CHARLEY Howard fired you?

WILLY That snotnose. Imagine that? I named him. I named him Howard.

CHARLEY Willy, when're you gonna realize that them things don't mean anything? You named him Howard, but you can't sell that. The only thing you got in this world is what you can sell. And the funny thing is that you're a salesman, and you don't know that.

WILLY I've always tried to think otherwise, I guess. I always felt that if a man was impressive, and well liked, that nothing—

CHARLEY Why must everybody like you? Who liked J. P. Morgan? Was he impressive? In a Turkish bath he'd look like a butcher. But with his pockets on he was very well liked. Now listen, Willy, I know you don't like me, and nobody can say I'm in love with you, but I'll give you a job because—just for the hell of it, put it that way. Now what do you say?

WILLY I—I just can't work for you, Charley.

CHARLEY What're you, jealous of me?

WILLY I can't work for you, that's all, don't ask me why.

CHARLEY (*Angered, takes out more bills*) You been jealous of me all your life, you damned fool! Here, pay your insurance.

(*He puts the money in* WILLY's *hand*)

WILLY I'm keeping strict accounts.

CHARLEY I've got some work to do. Take care of yourself. And pay your insurance.

WILLY (*Moving to the right*) Funny, y'know? After all the highways, and the trains, and the appointments, and the years, you end up worth more dead than alive.

CHARLEY Willy, nobody's worth nothin' dead. (*After a slight pause*) Did you hear what I said?

(WILLY *stands still, dreaming*)

CHARLEY Willy!

WILLY Apologize to Bernard for me when you see him. I didn't mean to argue with him. He's a fine boy. They're all fine boys, and they'll end up big—all of them. Someday they'll all play tennis together. Wish me luck, Charley. He saw Bill Oliver today.

CHARLEY Good luck.

WILLY (*On the verge of tears*) Charley, you're the only friend I got. Isn't that a remarkable thing?

(*He goes out*)

CHARLEY   Jesus!

(CHARLEY *stares after him a moment and follows. All light blacks out. Suddenly raucous music is heard, and a red glow rises behind the screen at right.* STANLEY, *a young waiter, appears, carrying a table, followed by* HAPPY, *who is carrying two chairs*)

STANLEY (*Putting the table down*)   That's all right, Mr. Loman, I can handle it myself.

(*He turns and takes the chairs from* HAPPY *and places them at the table*)

HAPPY (*Glancing around*)   Oh, this is better.

STANLEY   Sure, in the front there you're in the middle of all kinds a noise. Whenever you got a party, Mr. Loman, you just tell me and I'll put you back here. Y'know, there's a lotta people they don't like it private, because when they go out they like to see a lotta action around them because they're sick and tired to stay in the house by theirself. But I know you, you ain't from Hackensack. You know what I mean?

HAPPY (*Sitting down*)   So how's it coming, Stanley?

STANLEY   Ah, it's a dog's life. I only wish during the war they'd a took me in the Army. I coulda been dead by now.

HAPPY   My brother's back, Stanley.

STANLEY   Oh, he come back, heh? From the Far West.

HAPPY   Yeah, big cattle man, my brother, so treat him right. And my father's coming too.

STANLEY   Oh, your father too!

HAPPY   You got a couple of nice lobsters?

STANLEY   Hundred per cent, big.

HAPPY   I want them with the claws.

STANLEY   Don't worry, I don't give you no mice. (HAPPY *laughs*) How about some wine? It'll put a head on the meal.

HAPPY   No. You remember, Stanley, that recipe I brought you from overseas? With the champagne in it?

STANLEY   Oh, yeah, sure. I still got it tacked up yet in the kitchen. But that'll have to cost a buck apiece anyways.

HAPPY   That's all right.

STANLEY   What'd you, hit a number or somethin'?

HAPPY   No, it's a little celebration. My brother is—I think he pulled off a big deal today. I think we're going into business together.

STANLEY   Great! That's the best for you. Because a family business, you know what I mean?—that's the best.

HAPPY   That's what I think.

STANLEY   'Cause what's the difference? Somebody steals? It's in the

family. Know what I mean? (*Sotto voce*) Like this bartender
here. The boss is goin' crazy what kinda leak he's got in the cash
register. You put it in but it don't come out.

HAPPY (*Raising his head*) Sh!

STANLEY What?

HAPPY You notice I wasn't lookin' right or left, was I?

STANLEY No.

HAPPY And my eyes are closed.

STANLEY So what's the—?

HAPPY Strudel's comin'.

STANLEY (*Catching on, looks around*) Ah, no, there's no—
  (*He breaks off as a furred, lavishly dressed girl enters and sits at
  the next table. Both follow her with their eyes*)

STANLEY Geez, how'd ya know?

HAPPY I got radar or something. (*Staring directly at her profile*)
  Oooooooo . . . Stanley.

STANLEY I think that's for you, Mr. Loman.

HAPPY Look at that mouth. Oh, God. And the binoculars.

STANLEY Geez, you got a life, Mr. Loman.

HAPPY Wait on her.

STANLEY (*Going to the* GIRL's *table*) Would you like a menu,
  ma'am?

GIRL I'm expecting someone, but I'd like a—

HAPPY Why don't you bring her—excuse me, miss, do you mind?
  I sell champagne, and I'd like you to try my brand. Bring her a
  champagne, Stanley.

GIRL That's awfully nice of you.

HAPPY Don't mention it. It's all company money.
  (*He laughs*)

GIRL That's a charming product to be selling, isn't it?

HAPPY Oh, gets to be like everything else. Selling is selling, y'know.

GIRL I suppose.

HAPPY You don't happen to sell, do you?

GIRL No, I don't sell.

HAPPY Would you object to a compliment from a stranger? You
  ought to be on a magazine cover.

GIRL (*Looking at him a little archly*) I have been.
  (STANLEY *comes in with a glass of champagne*)

HAPPY What'd I say before, Stanley? You see? She's a cover girl.

STANLEY Oh, I could see, I could see.

HAPPY (*To the* GIRL) What magazine?

GIRL   Oh, a lot of them. (*She takes the drink*) Thank you.

HAPPY   You know what they say in France, don't you? "Champagne is the drink of the complexion"—Hya, Biff!

(BIFF *has entered and sits with* HAPPY)

BIFF   Hello, kid. Sorry I'm late.

HAPPY   I just got here. Uh, Miss—?

GIRL   Forsythe.

HAPPY   Miss Forsythe, this is my brother.

BIFF   Is Dad here?

HAPPY   His name is Biff. You might've heard of him. Great football player.

GIRL   Really? What team?

HAPPY   Are you familiar with football?

GIRL   No, I'm afraid I'm not.

HAPPY   Biff is quarterback with the New York Giants.

GIRL   Well, that is nice, isn't it? (*She drinks*)

HAPPY   Good health.

GIRL   I'm happy to meet you.

HAPPY   That's my name. Hap. It's really Harold, but at West Point they called me Happy.

GIRL (*Now really impressed*)   Oh, I see. How do you do? (*She turns her profile*)

BIFF   Isn't Dad coming?

HAPPY   You want her?

BIFF   Oh, I could never make that.

HAPPY   I remember the time that idea would never come into your head. Where's the old confidence, Biff?

BIFF   I just saw Oliver—

HAPPY   Wait a minute. I've got to see that old confidence again. Do you want her? She's on call.

BIFF   Oh, no. (*He turns to look at the* GIRL)

HAPPY   I'm telling you. Watch this. (*Turning to the* GIRL) Honey? (*She turns to him*) Are you busy?

GIRL   Well, I am . . . but I could make a phone call.

HAPPY   Do that, will you, honey? And see if you can get a friend. We'll be here for a while. Biff is one of the greatest football players in the country.

GIRL (*Standing up*)   Well, I'm certainly happy to meet you.

HAPPY   Come back soon.

GIRL   I'll try.

HAPPY   Don't try, honey, try hard.

(*The* GIRL *exits.* STANLEY *follows, shaking his head in bewildered admiration*)

HAPPY   Isn't that a shame now? A beautiful girl like that? That's why I can't get married. There's not a good woman in a thousand. New York is loaded with them, kid!

BIFF   Hap, look—

HAPPY   I told you she was on call!

BIFF (*Strangely unnerved*)   Cut it out, will ya? I want to say something to you.

HAPPY   Did you see Oliver?

BIFF   I saw him all right. Now look, I want to tell Dad a couple of things and I want you to help me.

HAPPY   What? Is he going to back you?

BIFF   Are you crazy? You're out of your goddam head, you know that?

HAPPY   Why? What happened?

BIFF (*Breathlessly*)   I did a terrible thing today, Hap. It's been the strangest day I ever went through. I'm all numb, I swear.

HAPPY   You mean he wouldn't see you?

BIFF   Well, I waited six hours for him, see? All day. Kept sending my name in. Even tried to date his secretary so she'd get me to him, but no soap.

HAPPY   Because you're not showin' the old confidence, Biff. He remembered you, didn't he?

BIFF (*Stopping* HAPPY *with a gesture*)   Finally, about five o'clock, he comes out. Didn't remember who I was or anything. I felt like such an idiot, Hap.

HAPPY   Did you tell him my Florida idea?

BIFF   He walked away. I saw him for one minute. I got so mad I could've torn the walls down! How the hell did I ever get the idea I was a salesman there? I even believed myself that I'd been a salesman for him! And then he gave me one look and—I realized what a ridiculous lie my whole life has been! We've been talking in a dream for fifteen years. I was a shipping clerk.

HAPPY   What'd you do?

BIFF (*With great tension and wonder*)   Well, he left, see. And the secretary went out. I was all alone in the waiting-room. I don't know what came over me, Hap. The next thing I know I'm in his office—paneled walls, everything. I can't explain it. I—Hap, I took his fountain pen.

HAPPY Geez, did he catch you?

BIFF I ran out. I ran down all eleven flights. I ran and ran and ran.

HAPPY That was an awful dumb—what'd you do that for?

BIFF (*Agonized*) I don't know, I just—wanted to take something, I don't know. You gotta help me, Hap, I'm gonna tell Pop.

HAPPY You crazy? What for?

BIFF Hap, he's got to understand that I'm not the man somebody lends that kind of money to. He thinks I've been spiting him all these years and it's eating him up.

HAPPY That's just it. You tell him something nice.

BIFF I can't.

HAPPY Say you got a lunch date with Oliver tomorrow.

BIFF So what do I do tomorrow?

HAPPY You leave the house tomorrow and come back at night and say Oliver is thinking it over. And he thinks it over for a couple of weeks, and gradually it fades away and nobody's the worse.

BIFF But it'll go on forever!

HAPPY Dad is never so happy as when he's looking forward to something!

(*WILLY enters*)

HAPPY Hello, scout!

WILLY Gee, I haven't been here in years!

(*STANLEY has followed WILLY in and sets a chair for him. STANLEY starts off but HAPPY stops him*)

HAPPY Stanley!

(*STANLEY stands by, waiting for an order*)

BIFF (*Going to WILLY with guilt, as to an invalid*) Sit down, Pop. You want a drink?

WILLY Sure, I don't mind.

BIFF Let's get a load on.

WILLY You look worried.

BIFF N-no. (*To STANLEY*) Scotch all around. Make it doubles.

STANLEY Doubles, right.

(*He goes*)

WILLY You had a couple already, didn't you?

BIFF Just a couple, yeah.

WILLY Well, what happened, boy? (*Nodding affirmatively, with a smile*) Everything go all right?

BIFF (*Takes a breath, then reaches out and grasps WILLY's hand*)

Pal . . . (*He is smiling bravely, and* WILLY *is smiling too*) I had an experience today.

HAPPY Terrific, Pop.

WILLY That so? What happened?

BIFF (*High, slightly alcoholic, above the earth*) I'm going to tell you everything from first to last. It's been a strange day. (*Silence. He looks around, composes himself as best he can, but his breath keeps breaking the rhythm of his voice*) I had to wait quite a while for him, and—

WILLY Oliver?

BIFF Yeah, Oliver. All day, as a matter of cold fact. And a lot of —instances—facts, Pop, facts about my life came back to me. Who was it, Pop? Who ever said I was a salesman with Oliver?

WILLY Well, you were.

BIFF No, Dad, I was a shipping clerk.

WILLY But you were practically—

BIFF (*With determination*) Dad, I don't know who said it first, but I was never a salesman for Bill Oliver.

WILLY What're you talking about?

BIFF Let's hold on to the facts tonight, Pop. We're not going to get anywhere bullin' around. I was a shipping clerk.

WILLY (*Angrily*) All right, now listen to me—

BIFF Why don't you let me finish?

WILLY I'm not interested in stories about the past or any crap of that kind because the woods are burning, boys, you understand? There's a big blaze going on all around. I was fired today.

BIFF (*Shocked*) How could you be?

WILLY I was fired, and I'm looking for a little good news to tell your mother, because the woman has waited and the woman has suffered. The gist of it is that I haven't got a story left in my head, Biff. So don't give me a lecture about facts and aspects. I am not interested. Now what've you got to say to me?

(STANLEY *enters with three drinks. They wait until he leaves*)

WILLY Did you see Oliver?

BIFF Jesus, Dad!

WILLY You mean you didn't go up there?

HAPPY Sure he went up there.

BIFF I did. I—saw him. How could they fire you?

WILLY (*On the edge of his chair*) What kind of a welcome did he give you?

BIFF He won't even let you work on commission?

WILLY   I'm out! (*Driving*) So tell me, he gave you a warm welcome?

HAPPY   Sure, Pop, sure!

BIFF (*Driven*)   Well, it was kind of—

WILLY   I was wondering if he'd remember you. (*To* HAPPY) Imagine, man doesn't see him for ten, twelve years and gives him that kind of a welcome!

HAPPY   Damn right!

BIFF (*Trying to return to the offensive*)   Pop, look—

WILLY   You know why he remembered you, don't you? Because you impressed him in those days.

BIFF   Let's talk quietly and get this down to the facts, huh?

WILLY (*As though* BIFF *had been interrupting*)   Well, what happened? It's great news, Biff. Did he take you into his office or'd you talk in the waiting-room?

BIFF   Well, he came in, see, and—

WILLY (*With a big smile*)   What'd he say? Betcha he threw his arm around you.

BIFF   Well, he kinda—

WILLY   He's a fine man. (*To* HAPPY) Very hard man to see, y'know.

HAPPY (*Agreeing*)   Oh, I know.

WILLY (*To* BIFF)   Is that where you had the drinks?

BIFF   Yeah, he gave me a couple of—no, no!

HAPPY (*Cutting in*)   He told him my Florida idea.

WILLY   Don't interrupt. (*To* BIFF) How'd he react to the Florida idea?

BIFF   Dad, will you give me a minute to explain?

WILLY   I've been waiting for you to explain since I sat down here! What happened? He took you into his office and what?

BIFF   Well—I talked. And—and he listened, see.

WILLY   Famous for the way he listens, y'know. What was his answer?

BIFF   His answer was— (*He breaks off, suddenly angry*) Dad, you're not letting me tell you what I want to tell you!

WILLY (*Accusing, angered*)   You didn't see him, did you?

BIFF   I did see him!

WILLY   What'd you insult him or something? You insulted him, didn't you?

BIFF   Listen, will you let me out of it, will you just let me out of it!

HAPPY   What the hell!

WILLY Tell me what happened!

BIFF (*To* HAPPY) I can't talk to him!

(*A single trumpet note jars the ear. The light of green leaves stains the house, which holds the air of night and a dream.* YOUNG BERNARD *enters and knocks on the door of the house*)

YOUNG BERNARD (*Frantically*) Mrs. Loman, Mrs. Loman!

HAPPY Tell him what happened!

BIFF (*To* HAPPY) Shut up and leave me alone!

WILLY No, no! You had to go and flunk math!

BIFF What math? What're you talking about?

YOUNG BERNARD Mrs. Loman, Mrs. Loman!

(LINDA *appears in the house, as of old*)

WILLY (*Wildly*) Math, math, math!

BIFF Take it easy, Pop!

YOUNG BERNARD Mrs. Loman!

WILLY (*Furiously*) If you hadn't flunked you'd've been set by now!

BIFF Now, look, I'm gonna tell you what happened, and you're going to listen to me.

YOUNG BERNARD Mrs. Loman!

BIFF I waited six hours—

HAPPY What the hell are you saying?

BIFF I kept sending in my name but he wouldn't see me. So finally he . . .

(*He continues unheard as light fades low on the restaurant*)

YOUNG BERNARD Biff flunked math!

LINDA No!

YOUNG BERNARD Birnbaum flunked him! They won't graduate him!

LINDA But they have to. He's gotta go to the university. Where is he? Biff! Biff!

YOUNG BERNARD No, he left. He went to Grand Central.

LINDA Grand— You mean he went to Boston!

YOUNG BERNARD Is Uncle Willy in Boston?

LINDA Oh, maybe Willy can talk to the teacher. Oh, the poor, poor boy!

(*Light on house area snaps out*)

BIFF (*At the table, now audible, holding up a gold fountain pen*) . . . so I'm washed up with Oliver, you understand? Are you listening to me?

WILLY (*At a loss*) Yeah, sure. If you hadn't flunked—

BIFF Flunked what? What're you talking about?

WILLY Don't blame everything on me! I didn't flunk math—you did! What pen?

HAPPY That was awful dumb, Biff, a pen like that is worth—

WILLY (*Seeing the pen for the first time*) You took Oliver's pen?

BIFF (*Weakening*) Dad, I just explained it to you.

WILLY You stole Bill Oliver's fountain pen!

BIFF I didn't exactly steal it! That's just what I've been explaining to you!

HAPPY He had it in his hand and just then Oliver walked in, so he got nervous and stuck it in his pocket!

WILLY My God, Biff!

BIFF I never intended to do it, Dad!

OPERATOR'S VOICE Standish Arms, good evening!

WILLY (*Shouting*) I'm not in my room!

BIFF (*Frightened*) Dad, what's the matter?
(*He and* HAPPY *stand up*)

OPERATOR Ringing Mr. Loman for you!

WILLY I'm not there, stop it!

BIFF (*Horrified, gets down on one knee before* WILLY) Dad, I'll make good, I'll make good. (WILLY *tries to get to his feet.* BIFF *holds him down*) Sit down now.

WILLY No, you're no good, you're no good for anything.

BIFF I am, Dad, I'll find something else, you understand? Now don't worry about anything. (*He holds up* WILLY's *face*) Talk to me, Dad.

OPERATOR Mr. Loman does not answer. Shall I page him?

WILLY (*Attempting to stand, as though to rush and silence the* OPERATOR) No, no, no!

HAPPY He'll strike something, Pop.

WILLY No, no . . .

BIFF (*Desperately, standing over* WILLY) Pop, listen! Listen to me! I'm telling you something good. Oliver talked to his partner about the Florida idea. You listening? He—he talked to his partner, and he came to me . . . I'm going to be all right, you hear? Dad, listen to me, he said it was just a question of the amount!

WILLY Then you . . . got it?

HAPPY He's gonna be terrific, Pop!

WILLY (*Trying to stand*) Then you got it, haven't you? You got it! You got it!

BIFF (*Agonized, holds* WILLY *down*) No, no. Look, Pop. I'm supposed to have lunch with them tomorrow. I'm just telling you this

so you'll know that I can still make an impression, Pop. And I'll
make good somewhere, but I can't go tomorrow, see?

WILLY   Why not? You simply—

BIFF   But the pen, Pop!

WILLY   You give it to him and tell him it was an oversight!

HAPPY   Sure, have lunch tomorrow!

BIFF   I can't say that—

WILLY   You were doing a crossword puzzle and accidentally used
his pen!

BIFF   Listen, kid, I took those balls years ago, now I walk in with
his fountain pen? That clinches it, don't you see? I can't face him
like that! I'll try elsewhere.

PAGE'S VOICE   Paging Mr. Loman!

WILLY   Don't you want to be anything?

BIFF   Pop, how can I go back?

WILLY   You don't want to be anything, is that what's behind it?

BIFF   (*Now angry at* WILLY *for not crediting his sympathy*)   Don't
take it that way! You think it was easy walking into that office
after what I'd done to him? A team of horses couldn't have
dragged me back to Bill Oliver!

WILLY   Then why'd you go?

BIFF   Why did I go? Why did I go! Look at you! Look at what's
become of you!
(*Off left,* THE WOMAN *laughs*)

WILLY   Biff, you're going to go to that lunch tomorrow, or—

BIFF   I can't go. I've got no appointment!

HAPPY   Biff, for . . . !

WILLY   Are you spiting me?

BIFF   Don't take it that way! Goddammit!

WILLY   (*Strikes* BIFF *and falters away from the table*)   You rotten
little louse! Are you spiting me?

THE WOMAN   Someone's at the door, Willy!

BIFF   I'm no good, can't you see what I am?

HAPPY   (*Separating them*)   Hey, you're in a restaurant! Now cut
it out, both of you! (*The girls enter*) Hello, girls, sit down.
(THE WOMAN *laughs, off left*)

MISS FORSYTHE   I guess we might as well. This is Letta.

THE WOMAN   Willy, are you going to wake up?

BIFF   (*Ignoring* WILLY)   How're ya, miss, sit down. What do you
drink?

MISS FORSYTHE   Letta might not be able to stay long.

LETTA   I gotta get up very early tomorrow. I got jury duty. I'm so excited! Were you fellows ever on a jury?

BIFF   No, but I been in front of them! (*The girls laugh*) This is my father.

LETTA   Isn't he cute? Sit down with us, Pop.

HAPPY   Sit him down, Biff!

BIFF   (*Going to him*) Come on, slugger, drink us under the table. To hell with it! Come on, sit down, pal.

(*On* BIFF's *last insistence,* WILLY *is about to sit*)

THE WOMAN   (*Now urgently*) Willy, are you going to answer the door!

(THE WOMAN's *call pulls* WILLY *back. He starts right, befuddled*)

BIFF   Hey, where are you going?

WILLY   Open the door.

BIFF   The door?

WILLY   The washroom . . . the door . . . where's the door?

BIFF   (*Leading* WILLY *to the left*) Just go straight down.

(WILLY *moves left*)

THE WOMAN   Willy, Willy, are you going to get up, get up, get up, get up?

(WILLY *exits left*)

LETTA   I think it's sweet you bring your daddy along.

MISS FORSYTHE   Oh, he isn't really your father!

BIFF   (*At left, turning to her resentfully*) Miss Forsythe, you've just seen a prince walk by. A fine, troubled prince. A hard-working, unappreciated prince. A pal, you understand? A good companion. Always for his boys.

LETTA   That's so sweet.

HAPPY   Well, girls, what's the program? We're wasting time. Come on, Biff. Gather round. Where would you like to go?

BIFF   Why don't you do something for him?

HAPPY   Me!

BIFF   Don't you give a damn for him, Hap?

HAPPY   What're you talking about? I'm the one who—

BIFF   I sense it, you don't give a good goddam about him. (*He takes the rolled-up hose from his pocket and puts it on the table in front of* HAPPY) Look what I found in the cellar, for Christ's sake. How can you bear to let it go on?

HAPPY   Me? Who goes away? Who runs off and—

BIFF   Yeah, but he doesn't mean anything to you. You could help him—I can't! Don't you understand what I'm talking about? He's going to kill himself, don't you know that?

HAPPY   Don't I know it! Me!

BIFF   Hap, help him! Jesus . . . help him . . . Help me, help me, I can't bear to look at his face!

(*Ready to weep, he hurries out, up right*)

HAPPY (*Starting after him*)   Where are you going?

MISS FORSYTHE   What's he so mad about?

HAPPY   Come on, girls, we'll catch up with him.

MISS FORSYTHE (*As* HAPPY *pushes her out*)   Say, I don't like that temper of his!

HAPPY   He's just a little overstrung, he'll be all right!

WILLY (*Off left, as* THE WOMAN *laughs*)   Don't answer! Don't answer!

LETTA   Don't you want to tell your father—

HAPPY   No, that's not my father. He's just a guy. Come on, we'll catch Biff, and, honey, we're going to paint this town! Stanley, where's the check! Hey, Stanley!

(*They exit.* STANLEY *looks toward left*)

STANLEY (*Calling to* HAPPY *indignantly*)   Mr. Loman! Mr. Loman! (STANLEY *picks up a chair and follows them off. Knocking is heard off left.* THE WOMAN *enters, laughing.* WILLY *follows her. She is in a black slip; he is buttoning his shirt. Raw, sensuous music accompanies their speech*)

WILLY   Will you stop laughing? Will you stop?

THE WOMAN   Aren't you going to answer the door? He'll wake the whole hotel.

WILLY   I'm not expecting anybody.

THE WOMAN   Whyn't you have another drink, honey, and stop being so damn self-centered?

WILLY   I'm so lonely.

THE WOMAN   You know you ruined me, Willy? From now on, whenever you come to the office, I'll see that you go right through to the buyers. No waiting at my desk any more, Willy. You ruined me.

WILLY   That's nice of you to say that.

THE WOMAN   Gee, you are self-centered! Why so sad? You are the saddest, self-centeredest soul I ever did see-saw. (*She laughs. He kisses her*) Come on inside, drummer boy. It's silly to be dressing in the middle of the night. (*As knocking is heard*) Aren't you going to answer the door?

WILLY   They're knocking on the wrong door.

THE WOMAN   But I felt the knocking. And he heard us talking in here. Maybe the hotel's on fire!

WILLY   (*His terror rising*)   It's a mistake.

THE WOMAN   Then tell him to go away!

WILLY   There's nobody there.

THE WOMAN   It's getting on my nerves, Willy. There's somebody standing out there and it's getting on my nerves!

WILLY   (*Pushing her away from him*)   All right, stay in the bathroom here, and don't come out. I think there's a law in Massachusetts about it, so don't come out. It may be that new room clerk. He looked very mean. So don't come out. It's a mistake, there's no fire.

(*The knocking is heard again. He takes a few steps away from her, and she vanishes into the wing. The light follows him, and now he is facing* YOUNG BIFF, *who carries a suitcase.* BIFF *steps toward him. The music is gone*)

BIFF   Why didn't you answer?

WILLY   Biff! What are you doing in Boston?

BIFF   Why didn't you answer? I've been knocking for five minutes, I called you on the phone—

WILLY   I just heard you. I was in the bathroom and had the door shut. Did anything happen home?

BIFF   Dad—I let you down.

WILLY   What do you mean?

BIFF   Dad . . .

WILLY   Biffo, what's this about? (*Putting his arm around* BIFF) Come on, let's go downstairs and get you a malted.

BIFF   Dad, I flunked math.

WILLY   Not for the term?

BIFF   The term. I haven't got enough credits to graduate.

WILLY   You mean to say Bernard wouldn't give you the answers?

BIFF   He did, he tried, but I only got a sixty-one.

WILLY   And they wouldn't give you four points?

BIFF   Birnbaum refused absolutely. I begged him, Pop, but he won't give me those points. You gotta talk to him before they close the school. Because if he saw the kind of man you are, and you just talked to him in your way, I'm sure he'd come through for me. The class came right before practice, see, and I didn't go enough. Would you talk to him? He'd like you, Pop. You know the way you could talk.

WILLY   You're on. We'll drive right back.

BIFF   Oh, Dad, good work! I'm sure he'll change it for you!

WILLY   Go downstairs and tell the clerk I'm checkin' out. Go right down.

BIFF   Yes, sir! See, the reason he hates me, Pop—one day he was late for class so I got up at the blackboard and imitated him. I crossed my eyes and talked with a lithp.

WILLY (*Laughing*)   You did? The kids like it?

BIFF   They nearly died laughing!

WILLY   Yeah! What'd you do?

BIFF   The thquare root of thixthy twee is . . . (WILLY *bursts out laughing;* BIFF *joins him*) And in the middle of it he walked in!

   (WILLY *laughs and* THE WOMAN *joins in offstage*)

WILLY (*Without hesitation*)   Hurry downstairs and—

BIFF   Somebody in there?

WILLY   No, that was next door.

   (THE WOMAN *laughs offstage*)

BIFF   Somebody got in your bathroom!

WILLY   No, it's the next room, there's a party—

THE WOMAN (*Enters, laughing. She lisps this*)   Can I come in? There's something in the bathtub, Willy, and it's moving!

   (WILLY *looks at* BIFF, *who is staring open-mouthed and horrified at* THE WOMAN)

WILLY   Ah—you better go back to your room. They must be finished painting by now. They're painting her room so I let her take a shower here. Go back, go back . . .

   (*He pushes her*)

THE WOMAN (*Resisting*)   But I've got to get dressed, Willy, I can't—

WILLY   Get out of here! Go back, go back . . . (*Suddenly striving for the ordinary*) This is Miss Francis, Biff, she's a buyer. They're painting her room. Go back, Miss Francis, go back . . .

THE WOMAN   But my clothes, I can't go out naked in the hall!

WILLY (*Pushing her offstage*)   Get outa here! Go back, go back!

   (BIFF *slowly sits down on his suitcase as the argument continues offstage*)

THE WOMAN   Where's my stockings? You promised me stockings, Willy!

WILLY   I have no stockings here!

THE WOMAN   You had two boxes of size nine sheers for me, and I want them!

WILLY   Here, for God's sake, will you get outa here!

THE WOMAN (*Enters holding a box of stockings*)   I just hope there's nobody in the hall. That's all I hope. (*To* BIFF) Are you football or baseball?

BIFF   Football.

THE WOMAN (*Angry, humiliated*)   That's me too. G'night.

(*She snatches her clothes from* WILLY, *and walks out*)

WILLY (*After a pause*)   Well, better get going. I want to get to the school first thing in the morning. Get my suits out of the closet. I'll get my valise. (BIFF *doesn't move*) What's the matter? (BIFF *remains motionless, tears falling*) She's a buyer. Buys for J. H. Simmons. She lives down the hall—they're painting. You don't imagine— (*He breaks off. After a pause*) Now listen, pal, she's just a buyer. She sees merchandise in her room and they have to keep it looking just so . . . (*Pause. Assuming command*) All right, get my suits. (BIFF *doesn't move*) Now stop crying and do as I say. I gave you an order. Biff, I gave you an order! Is that what you do when I give you an order? How dare you cry! (*Putting his arm around* BIFF) Now look, Biff, when you grow up you'll understand about these things. You mustn't—you mustn't overemphasize a thing like this. I'll see Birnbaum first thing in the morning.

BIFF   Never mind.

WILLY (*Getting down beside* BIFF)   Never mind! He's going to give you those points. I'll see to it.

BIFF   He wouldn't listen to you.

WILLY   He certainly will listen to me. You need those points for the U. of Virginia.

BIFF   I'm not going there.

WILLY   Heh? If I can't get him to change that mark you'll make it up in summer school. You've got all summer to—

BIFF (*His weeping breaking from him*)   Dad . . .

WILLY (*Infected by it*)   Oh, my boy . . .

BIFF   Dad . . .

WILLY   She's nothing to me, Biff. I was lonely, I was terribly lonely.

BIFF   You—you gave her Mama's stockings!

(*His tears break through and he rises to go*)

WILLY (*Grabbing for* BIFF)   I gave you an order!

BIFF   Don't touch me, you—liar!

WILLY   Apologize for that!

BIFF   You fake! You phony little fake! You fake!

(*Overcome, he turns quickly and weeping fully goes out with his suitcase.* WILLY *is left on the floor on his knees*)

WILLY I gave you an order! Biff, come back here or I'll beat you! Come back here! I'll whip you!

(STANLEY *comes quickly in from the right and stands in front of* WILLY)

WILLY (*Shouts at* STANLEY) I gave you an order . . .

STANLEY Hey, let's pick it up, pick it up, Mr. Loman. (*He helps* WILLY *to his feet*) Your boys left with the chippies. They said they'll see you home.

(*A second waiter watches some distance away*)

WILLY But we were supposed to have dinner together.

(*Music is heard,* WILLY's *theme*)

STANLEY Can you make it?

WILLY I'll—sure, I can make it. (*Suddenly concerned about his clothes*) Do I—I look all right?

STANLEY Sure, you look all right.

(*He flicks a speck off* WILLY's *lapel*)

WILLY Here—here's a dollar.

STANLEY Oh, your son paid me. It's all right.

WILLY (*Putting it in* STANLEY's *hand*) No, take it. You're a good boy.

STANLEY Oh, no, you don't have to . . .

WILLY Here—here's some more, I don't need it any more. (*After a slight pause*) Tell me—is there a seed store in the neighborhood?

STANLEY Seeds? You mean like to plant?

(*As* WILLY *turns,* STANLEY *slips the money back into his jacket pocket*)

WILLY Yes. Carrots, peas . . .

STANLEY Well, there's hardware stores on Sixth Avenue, but it may be too late now.

WILLY (*Anxiously*) Oh, I'd better hurry. I've got to get some seeds. (*He starts off to the right*) I've got to get some seeds, right away. Nothing's planted. I don't have a thing in the ground.

(WILLY *hurries out as the light goes down.* STANLEY *moves over to the right after him, watches him off. The other waiter has been staring at* WILLY)

STANLEY (*To the waiter*) Well, whatta you looking at?

(*The waiter picks up the chairs and moves off right.* STANLEY *takes the table and follows him. The light fades on this area. There is a long pause, the sound of the flute coming over. The light gradually rises on the kitchen, which is empty.* HAPPY *appears at the door of the house, followed by* BIFF. HAPPY *is carrying a large bunch of long-stemmed roses. He enters the kitchen, looks around for* LINDA. *Not seeing her, he turns to* BIFF, *who is just outside the house door, and makes a gesture with his hands, indicating "Not here, I guess." He looks into the living-room and freezes. Inside,* LINDA, *unseen, is seated,* WILLY's *coat on her lap. She rises ominously and quietly and moves toward* HAPPY, *who backs up into the kitchen, afraid)*

HAPPY   Hey, what're you doing up? (LINDA *says nothing but moves toward him implacably)* Where's Pop? (*He keeps backing to the right, and now* LINDA *is in full view in the doorway to the living-room)* Is he sleeping?

LINDA   Where were you?

HAPPY (*Trying to laugh it off)* We met two girls, Mom, very fine types. Here, we brought you some flowers. (*Offering them to her)* Put them in your room, Ma.

(She knocks them to the floor at BIFF's *feet. He has now come inside and closed the door behind him. She stares at* BIFF, *silent)*

HAPPY   Now what'd you do that for? Mom, I want you to have some flowers—

LINDA (*Cutting* HAPPY *off, violently to* BIFF) Don't you care whether he lives or dies?

HAPPY (*Going to the stairs)* Come upstairs, Biff.

BIFF (*With a flare of disgust, to* HAPPY) Go away from me! (*To* LINDA) What do you mean, lives or dies? Nobody's dying around here, pal.

LINDA   Get out of my sight! Get out of here!

BIFF   I wanna see the boss.

LINDA   You're not going near him!

BIFF   Where is he?

(He moves into the living-room and LINDA *follows)*

LINDA (*Shouting after* BIFF) You invite him for dinner. He looks forward to it all day—(BIFF *appears in his parents' bedroom, looks around, and exits)*—and then you desert him there. There's no stranger you'd do that to!

HAPPY   Why? He had a swell time with us. Listen, when I—(LINDA *comes back into the kitchen)*—desert him I hope I don't outlive the day!

LINDA   Get out of here!

HAPPY   Now look, Mom . . .

LINDA   Did you have to go to women tonight? You and your lousy rotten whores!

(BIFF *re-enters the kitchen*)

HAPPY   Mom, all we did was follow Biff around trying to cheer him up! (*To* BIFF) Boy, what a night you gave me!

LINDA   Get out of here, both of you, and don't come back! I don't want you tormenting him any more. Go on now, get your things together! (*To* BIFF) You can sleep in his apartment. (*She starts to pick up the flowers and stops herself*) Pick up this stuff, I'm not your maid any more. Pick it up, you bum, you!

(HAPPY *turns his back to her in refusal.* BIFF *slowly moves over and gets down on his knees, picking up the flowers*)

LINDA   You're a pair of animals! Not one, not another living soul would have had the cruelty to walk out on that man in a restaurant!

BIFF (*Not looking at her*)   Is that what he said?

LINDA   He didn't have to say anything. He was so humiliated he nearly limped when he came in.

HAPPY   But, Mom, he had a great time with us—

BIFF (*Cutting him off violently*)   Shut up!

(*Without another word,* HAPPY *goes upstairs*)

LINDA   You! You didn't even go in to see if he was all right!

BIFF (*Still on the floor in front of* LINDA, *the flowers in his hand; with self-loathing*)   No. Didn't. Didn't do a damned thing. How do you like that, heh? Left him babbling in a toilet.

LINDA   You louse. You . . .

BIFF   Now you hit it on the nose! (*He gets up, throws the flowers in the wastebasket*) The scum of the earth, and you're looking at him!

LINDA   Get out of here!

BIFF   I gotta talk to the boss, Mom. Where is he?

LINDA   You're not going near him. Get out of this house!

BIFF (*With absolute assurance, determination*)   No. We're gonna have an abrupt conversation, him and me.

LINDA   You're not talking to him!

(*Hammering is heard from outside the house, off right.* BIFF *turns toward the noise*)

LINDA (*Suddenly pleading*)   Will you please leave him alone?

BIFF   What's he doing out there?

LINDA   He's planting the garden!

BIFF (*Quietly*)   Now? Oh, my God!

(BIFF *moves outside,* LINDA *following. The light dies down on them and comes up on the center of the apron as* WILLY *walks into it. He is carrying a flashlight, a hoe, and a handful of seed packets. He raps the top of the hoe sharply to fix it firmly, and then moves to the left, measuring off the distance with his foot. He holds the flashlight to look at the seed packets, reading off the instructions. He is in the blue of night*)

WILLY Carrots . . . quarter-inch apart. Rows . . . one-foot rows. (*He measures it off*) One foot. (*He puts down a package and measures off*) Beets. (*He puts down another package and measures again*) Lettuce. (*He reads the package, puts it down*) One foot— (*He breaks off as* BEN *appears at the right and moves slowly down to him*) What a proposition, ts, ts. Terrific, terrific. 'Cause she's suffered, Ben, the woman has suffered. You understand me? A man can't go out the way he came in, Ben, a man has got to add up to something. You can't, you can't. (BEN *moves toward him as though to interrupt*) You gotta consider, now. Don't answer so quick. Remember, it's a guaranteed twenty-thousand-dollar proposition. Now look, Ben, I want you to go through the ins and outs of this thing with me. I've got nobody to talk to, Ben, and the woman has suffered, you hear me?

BEN (*Standing still, considering*) What's the proposition?

WILLY It's twenty thousand dollars on the barrelhead. Guaranteed, gilt-edged, you understand?

BEN You don't want to make a fool of yourself. They might not honor the policy.

WILLY How can they dare refuse? Didn't I work like a coolie to meet every premium on the nose? And now they don't pay off? Impossible!

BEN It's called a cowardly thing, William.

WILLY Why? Does it take more guts to stand here the rest of my life ringing up a zero?

BEN (*Yielding*) That's a point, William. (*He moves, thinking, turns*) And twenty thousand—that *is* something one can feel with the hand, it is there.

WILLY (*Now assured, with rising power*) Oh, Ben, that's the whole beauty of it! I see it like a diamond, shining in the dark, hard and rough, that I can pick up and touch in my hand. Not like—like an appointment! This would not be another damned-fool appointment, Ben, and it changes all the aspects. Because he thinks I'm nothing, see, and so he spites me. But the funeral— (*Straightening *up*) Ben, *that* funeral will be massive! They'll come from Maine, Massachusetts, Vermont, New Hampshire! All the old-timers with the strange license plates—that boy will be thunder-struck, Ben, because he never realized—I am known! Rhode Island, New York, New Jersey—I am known, Ben, and he'll see it with his eyes once and for all. He'll see what I am, Ben! He's in for a shock, that boy!

BEN (*Coming down to the edge of the garden*) He'll call you a coward.

WILLY (*Suddenly fearful*) No, that would be terrible.

BEN Yes. And a damned fool.

WILLY No, no, he mustn't, I won't have that!
(*He is broken and desperate*)

BEN He'll hate you, William.
(*The gay music of the* BOYS *is heard*)

WILLY Oh, Ben, how do we get back to all the great times? Used to be so full of light, and comradeship, the sleigh-riding in winter, and the ruddiness on his cheeks. And always some kind of good news coming up, always something nice coming up ahead. And never even let me carry the valises in the house, and simonizing, simonizing that little red car! Why, why can't I give him something and not have him hate me?

BEN Let me think about it. (*He glances at his watch*) I still have a little time. Remarkable proposition, but you've got to be sure you're not making a fool of yourself.
(BEN *drifts off upstage and goes out of sight.* BIFF *comes down from the left*)

WILLY (*Suddenly conscious of* BIFF, *turns and looks up at him, then begins picking up the packages of seeds in confusion*) Where the hell is that seed? (*Indignantly*) You can't see nothing out here! They boxed in the whole goddam neighborhood!

BIFF There are people all around here. Don't you realize that?

WILLY I'm busy. Don't bother me.

BIFF (*Taking the hoe from* WILLY) I'm saying good-by to you, Pop. (WILLY *looks at him, silent, unable to move*) I'm not coming back any more.

WILLY You're not going to see Oliver tomorrow?

BIFF I've got no appointment, Dad.

WILLY He put his arm around you, and you've got no appointment?

BIFF Pop, get this now, will you? Everytime I've left it's been a fight that sent me out of here. Today I realized something about myself and I tried to explain it to you and I—I think I'm just not smart enough to make any sense out of it for you. To hell with whose fault it is or anything like that. (*He takes* WILLY's *arm*) Let's just wrap it up, heh? Come on in, we'll tell Mom.

(*He gently tries to pull* WILLY *to left*)

WILLY (*Frozen, immobile, with guilt in his voice*) No, I don't want to see her.

BIFF Come on!

(*He pulls again, and* WILLY *tries to pull away*)

WILLY (*Highly nervous*) No, no, I don't want to see her.

BIFF (*Tries to look into* WILLY's *face, as if to find the answer there*) Why don't you want to see her?

WILLY (*More harshly now*) Don't bother me, will you?

BIFF What do you mean, you don't want to see her? You don't want them calling you yellow, do you? This isn't your fault; it's me, I'm a bum. Now come inside! (WILLY *strains to get away*) Did you hear what I said to you?

(WILLY *pulls away and quickly goes by himself into the house.* BIFF *follows*)

LINDA (*To* WILLY) Did you plant, dear?

BIFF (*At the door, to* LINDA) All right, we had it out. I'm going and I'm not writing any more.

LINDA (*Going to* WILLY *in the kitchen*) I think that's the best way, dear. 'Cause there's no use drawing it out, you'll just never get along.

(WILLY *doesn't respond*)

BIFF People ask where I am and what I'm doing, you don't know, and you don't care. That way it'll be off your mind and you can start brightening up again. All right? That clears it, doesn't it? (WILLY *is silent, and* BIFF *goes to him*) You gonna wish me luck, scout? (*He extends his hand*) What do you say?

LINDA Shake his hand, Willy.

WILLY (*Turning to her, seething with hurt*) There's no necessity to mention the pen at all, y'know.

BIFF (*Gently*) I've got no appointment, Dad.

WILLY (*Erupting fiercely*) He put his arm around . . . ?

BIFF Dad, you're never going to see what I am, so what's the use of arguing? If I strike oil I'll send you a check. Meantime forget I'm alive.

WILLY (*To* LINDA) Spite, see?

BIFF   Shake hands, Dad.

WILLY   Not my hand.

BIFF   I was hoping not to go this way.

WILLY   Well, this is the way you're going. Good-by.

(BIFF *looks at him a moment, then turns sharply and goes to the stairs*)

WILLY (*Stops him with*)   May you rot in hell if you leave this house!

BIFF (*Turning*)   Exactly what is it that you want from me?

WILLY   I want you to know, on the train, in the mountains, in the valleys, wherever you go, that you cut down your life for spite!

BIFF   No, no.

WILLY   Spite, spite, is the word of your undoing! And when you're down and out, remember what did it. When you're rotting somewhere beside the railroad tracks, remember, and don't you dare blame it on me!

BIFF   I'm not blaming it on you!

WILLY   I won't take the rap for this, you hear?

(HAPPY *comes down the stairs and stands on the bottom step, watching*)

BIFF   That's just what I'm telling you!

WILLY (*Sinking into a chair at the table, with full accusation*) You're trying to put a knife in me—don't think I don't know what you're doing!

BIFF   All right, phony! Then let's lay it on the line.

(*He whips the rubber tube out of his pocket and puts it on the table*)

HAPPY   You crazy—

LINDA   Biff!

(*She moves to grab the hose, but* BIFF *holds it down with his hand*)

BIFF   Leave it there! Don't move it!

WILLY (*Not looking at it*)   What is that?

BIFF   You know goddam well what that is.

WILLY (*Caged, wanting to escape*)   I never saw that.

BIFF   You saw it. The mice didn't bring it into the cellar! What is this supposed to do, make a hero out of you? This supposed to make me sorry for you?

WILLY   Never heard of it.

BIFF   There'll be no pity for you, you hear it? No pity!

WILLY (*To* LINDA)   You hear the spite!

BIFF   No, you're going to hear the truth—what you are and what I am!

LINDA   Stop it!

WILLY   Spite!

HAPPY   (*Coming down toward* BIFF)   You cut it now!

BIFF   (*To* HAPPY)   The man don't know who we are! The man is gonna know! (*To* WILLY) We never told the truth for ten minutes in this house!

HAPPY   We always told the truth!

BIFF   (*Turning on him*)   You big blow, are you the assistant buyer? You're one of the two assistants to the assistant, aren't you?

HAPPY   Well, I'm practically—

BIFF   You're practically full of it! We all are! And I'm through with it. (*To* WILLY) Now hear this, Willy, this is me.

WILLY   I know you!

BIFF   You know why I had no address for three months? I stole a suit in Kansas City and I was in jail. (*To* LINDA, *who is sobbing*) Stop crying. I'm through with it.

(LINDA *turns away from them, her hands covering her face*)

WILLY   I suppose that's my fault!

BIFF   I stole myself out of every good job since high school!

WILLY   And whose fault is that?

BIFF   And I never got anywhere because you blew me so full of hot air I could never stand taking orders from anybody! That's whose fault it is!

WILLY   I hear that!

LINDA   Don't, Biff!

BIFF   It's goddam time you heard that! I had to be boss big shot in two weeks, and I'm through with it!

WILLY   Then hang yourself! For spite, hang yourself!

BIFF   No! Nobody's hanging himself, Willy! I ran down eleven flights with a pen in my hand today. And suddenly I stopped, you hear me? And in the middle of that office building, do you hear this? I stopped in the middle of that building and I saw—the sky. I saw the things that I love in this world. The work and the food and time to sit and smoke. And I looked at the pen and said to myself, what the hell am I grabbing this for? Why am I trying to become what I don't want to be? What am I doing in an office, making a contemptuous, begging fool of myself, when all I want is out there, waiting for me the minute I say I know who I am! Why can't I say that, Willy?

(*He tries to make* WILLY *face him, but* WILLY *pulls away and moves to the left*)

WILLY (*With hatred, threateningly*)   The door of your life is wide open!

BIFF   Pop! I'm a dime a dozen, and so are you!

WILLY (*Turning on him now in an uncontrolled outburst*)   I am not a dime a dozen! I am Willy Loman, and you are Biff Loman! (BIFF *starts for* WILLY, *but is blocked by* HAPPY. *In his fury,* BIFF *seems on the verge of attacking his father*)

BIFF   I am not a leader of men, Willy, and neither are you. You were never anything but a hard-working drummer who landed in the ash can like all the rest of them! I'm one dollar an hour, Willy! I tried seven states and couldn't raise it. A buck an hour! Do you gather my meaning? I'm not bringing home any prizes any more, and you're going to stop waiting for me to bring them home!

WILLY (*Directly to* BIFF)   You vengeful, spiteful mut!

(BIFF *breaks from* HAPPY. WILLY, *in fright, starts up the stairs.* BIFF *grabs him*)

BIFF (*At the peak of his fury*)   Pop, I'm nothing! I'm nothing, Pop. Can't you understand that? There's no spite in it any more. I'm just what I am, that's all.

(BIFF's *fury has spent itself, and he breaks down, sobbing, holding on to* WILLY, *who dumbly fumbles for* BIFF's *face*)

WILLY (*Astonished*)   What're you doing? What're you doing? (*To* LINDA)   Why is he crying?

BIFF (*Crying, broken*)   Will you let me go, for Christ's sake? Will you take that phony dream and burn it before something happens? (*Struggling to contain himself, he pulls away and moves to the stairs*)   I'll go in the morning. Put him—put him to bed. (*Exhausted,* BIFF *moves up the stairs to his room*)

WILLY (*After a long pause, astonished, elevated*)   Isn't that—isn't that remarkable? Biff—he likes me!

LINDA   He loves you, Willy!

HAPPY (*Deeply moved*)   Always did, Pop.

WILLY   Oh, Biff! (*Staring wildly*)   He cried! Cried to me. (*He is choking with his love, and now cries out his promise*)   That boy—that boy is going to be magnificent!

(BEN *appears in the light just outside the kitchen*)

BEN   Yes, outstanding, with twenty thousand behind him.

LINDA (*Sensing the racing of his mind, fearfully, carefully*)   Now come to bed, Willy. It's all settled now.

WILLY (*Finding it difficult not to rush out of the house*) Yes, we'll sleep. Come on. Go to sleep, Hap.

BEN And it does take a great kind of a man to crack the jungle.

(*In accents of dread,* BEN's *idyllic music starts up*)

HAPPY (*His arm around* LINDA) I'm getting married, Pop, don't forget it. I'm changing everything. I'm gonna run that department before the year is up. You'll see, Mom.

(*He kisses her*)

BEN The jungle is dark but full of diamonds, Willy.

(WILLY *turns, moves, listening to* BEN)

LINDA Be good. You're both good boys, just act that way, that's all.

HAPPY 'Night, Pop.

(*He goes upstairs*)

LINDA (*To* WILLY) Come, dear.

BEN (*With greater force*) One must go in to fetch a diamond out.

WILLY (*To* LINDA, *as he moves slowly along the edge of the kitchen, toward the door*) I just want to get settled down, Linda. Let me sit alone for a little.

LINDA (*Almost uttering her fear*) I want you upstairs.

WILLY (*Taking her in his arms*) In a few minutes, Linda. I couldn't sleep right now. Go on, you look awful tired.

(*He kisses her*)

BEN Not like an appointment at all. A diamond is rough and hard to the touch.

WILLY Go on now. I'll be right up.

LINDA I think this is the only way, Willy.

WILLY Sure, it's the best thing.

BEN Best thing!

WILLY The only way. Everything is gonna be—go on, kid, get to bed. You look so tired.

LINDA Come right up.

WILLY Two minutes.

(LINDA *goes into the living-room, then reappears in her bedroom.* WILLY *moves just outside the kitchen door*)

WILLY Loves me. (*Wonderingly*) Always loved me. Isn't that a remarkable thing? Ben, he'll worship me for it!

BEN (*With promise*) It's dark there, but full of diamonds.

WILLY Can you imagine that magnificence with twenty thousand dollars in his pocket?

LINDA (*Calling from her room*) Willy! Come up!

WILLY (*Calling into the kitchen*) Yes! Yes. Coming! It's very smart, you realize that, don't you, sweetheart? Even Ben sees it. I gotta go, baby. 'By! 'By! (*Going over to* BEN, *almost dancing*) Imagine? When the mail comes he'll be ahead of Bernard again!

BEN   A perfect proposition all around.

WILLY   Did you see how he cried to me? Oh, if I could kiss him, Ben!

BEN   Time, William, time!

WILLY   Oh, Ben, I always knew one way or another we were gonna make it, Biff and I!

BEN   (*Looking at his watch*)   The boat. We'll be late.

(*He moves slowly off into the darkness*)

WILLY   (*Elegiacally, turning to the house*)   Now when you kick off, boy, I want a seventy-yard boot, and get right down the field under the ball, and when you hit, hit low and hit hard, because it's important, boy. (*He swings around and faces the audience*) There's all kinds of important people in the stands, and the first thing you know . . . (*Suddenly realizing he is alone*) Ben! Ben, where do I . . . ? (*He makes a sudden movement of search*) Ben, how do I . . . ?

LINDA   (*Calling*)   Willy, you coming up?

WILLY   (*Uttering a gasp of fear, whirling about as if to quiet her*) Sh! (*He turns around as if to find his way; sounds, faces, voices, seem to be swarming in upon him and he flicks at them, crying*) Sh! Sh! (*Suddenly music, faint and high, stops him. It rises in intensity, almost to an unbearable scream. He goes up and down on his toes, and rushes off around the house*) Shhh!

LINDA   Willy?

(*There is no answer.* LINDA *waits.* BIFF *gets up off his bed. He is still in his clothes.* HAPPY *sits up.* BIFF *stands listening*)

LINDA   (*With real fear*)   Willy, answer me! Willy!

(*There is the sound of a car starting and moving away at full speed*)

LINDA   No!

BIFF   (*Rushing down the stairs*)   Pop!

(*As the car speeds off, the music crashes down in a frenzy of sound, which becomes the soft pulsation of a single cello string.* BIFF *slowly returns to his bedroom. He and* HAPPY *gravely don their jackets.* LINDA *slowly walks out of her room. The music has developed into a dead march. The leaves of day are appearing over everything.* CHARLEY *and* BERNARD, *somberly dressed, appear and knock on the kitchen door.* BIFF *and* HAPPY *slowly descend the stairs to the kitchen as* CHARLEY *and* BERNARD *enter. All stop a moment when* LINDA, *in clothes of mourning, bearing a little bunch of roses, comes through the draped doorway into the kitchen. She goes to* CHARLEY *and takes his arm. Now all move toward the audience, through the wall-line of the kitchen. At the limit of the apron,* LINDA *lays down the flowers, kneels, and sits back on her heels. All stare down at the grave)*

REQUIEM

CHARLEY It's getting dark, Linda.

(LINDA *doesn't react. She stares at the grave*)

BIFF How about it, Mom? Better get some rest, heh? They'll be closing the gate soon.

(LINDA *makes no move. Pause*)

HAPPY (*Deeply angered*) He had no right to do that. There was no necessity for it. We would've helped him.

CHARLEY (*Grunting*) Hmmm.

BIFF Come along, Mom.

LINDA Why didn't anybody come?

CHARLEY It was a very nice funeral.

LINDA But where are all the people he knew? Maybe they blame him.

CHARLEY Naa. It's a rough world, Linda. They wouldn't blame him.

LINDA I can't understand it. At this time especially. First time in thirty-five years we were just about free and clear. He only needed a little salary. He was even finished with the dentist.

CHARLEY No man only needs a little salary.

LINDA I can't understand it.

BIFF There were a lot of nice days. When he'd come home from a trip; or on Sundays, making the stoop; finishing the cellar; putting on the new porch; when he built the extra bathroom; and put up the garage. You know something, Charley, there's more of him in that front stoop than in all the sales he ever made.

CHARLEY Yeah. He was a happy man with a batch of cement.

LINDA He was so wonderful with his hands.

BIFF He had the wrong dreams. All, all, wrong.

HAPPY (*Almost ready to fight* BIFF) Don't say that!

BIFF He never knew who he was.

CHARLEY (*Stopping* HAPPY'S *movement and reply. To* BIFF) Nobody dast blame this man. You don't understand: Willy was a salesman. And for a salesman, there is no rock bottom to the life.

He don't put a bolt to a nut, he don't tell you the law or give you medicine. He's a man way out there in the blue, riding on a smile and a shoeshine. And when they start not smiling back—that's an earthquake. And then you get yourself a couple of spots on your hat, and you're finished. Nobody dast blame this man. A salesman is got to dream, boy. It comes with the territory.

BIFF Charley, the man didn't know who he was.

HAPPY (*Infuriated*) Don't say that!

BIFF Why don't you come with me, Happy?

HAPPY I'm not licked that easily. I'm staying right in this city, and I'm gonna beat this racket! (*He looks at* BIFF, *his chin set*) The Loman Brothers!

BIFF I know who I am, kid.

HAPPY All right, boy. I'm gonna show you and everybody else that Willy Loman did not die in vain. He had a good dream. It's the only dream you can have—to come out number-one man. He fought it out here, and this is where I'm gonna win it for him.

BIFF (*With a hopeless glance at* HAPPY, *bends toward his mother*) Let's go, Mom.

LINDA I'll be with you in a minute. Go on, Charley. (*He hesitates*) I want to, just for a minute. I never had a chance to say good-by. (CHARLEY *moves away, followed by* HAPPY. BIFF *remains a slight distance up and left of* LINDA. *She sits there, summoning herself. The flute begins, not far away, playing behind her speech*)

LINDA Forgive me, dear. I can't cry. I don't know what it is, but I can't cry. I don't understand it. Why did you ever do that? Help me, Willy, I can't cry. It seems to me that you're just on another trip. I keep expecting you. Willy, dear, I can't cry. Why did you do it? I search and search and I search, and I can't understand it, Willy. I made the last payment on the house today. Today, dear. And there'll be nobody home. (*A sob rises in her throat*) We're free and clear. (*Sobbing more fully, released*) We're free. (BIFF *comes slowly toward her*) We're free . . . We're free . . .

(BIFF *lifts her to her feet and moves out up right with her in his arms.* LINDA *sobs quietly.* BERNARD *and* CHARLEY *come together and follow them, followed by* HAPPY. *Only the music of the flute is left on the darkening stage as over the house the hard towers of the apartment buildings rise into sharp focus*)

Curtain

Mister Roberts

BY

Thomas Heggen
and
Joshua Logan

For Nedda

Characters

CHIEF JOHNSON

LIEUTENANT AJG) ROBERTS

DOC

DOWDY

THE CAPTAIN

INSIGNA

MANNION

LINDSTROM

STEFANOWSKI

WILEY

SCHLEMMER

REBER

ENSIGN PULVER

DOLAN

GERHART

PAYNE

LIEUTENANT ANN GIRARD

SHORE PATROLMAN

MILITARY POLICEMAN

SHORE PATROL OFFICER

SEAMEN, FIREMEN AND OTHERS

Synopsis of Scenes

Aboard the U.S. Navy Cargo Ship, *AK 601*, operating
in the back areas of the Pacific

Time: A few weeks before V-E Day until a few weeks
before V-J Day

NOTE: In the U.S. Navy, all officers below the rank of Commander
are addressed as "Mister."

ACT ONE

SCENE I

The curtain rises on the main set, which is the amidships section of a navy cargo ship. The section of the ship shown is the house, and the deck immediately forward of the house. Dominating center stage is a covered hatch. The house extends on an angle to the audience from downstage left to upstage right. At each side is a passageway leading to the after part of the ship. Over the passageways on each side are twenty-millimeter gun tubs; ladders lead up to each tub. In each passageway and hardly visible to the audience is a steep ladder leading up to a bridge. Downstage right is a double bitt. At the left end of the hatch cover is an opening. This is the entrance to the companionway which leads to the crew's compartment below. The lower parts of two kingposts are shown against the house. A life raft is also visible. A solid metal rail runs from stage right and disappears behind the house. Upstage center is the door to the Captain's cabin. The pilothouse with its many portholes is indicated on the bridge above. On the flying bridge are the usual nautical furnishings, a searchlight and two ventilators. Over the door is a loudspeaker. There is a porthole to the left of the door and two portholes to the right. These last two look into the Captain's cabin.

The only object which differentiates this ship from any other navy cargo ship is a small scrawny palm tree, potted in a five-gallon can, standing to the right of the Captain's cabin door. On the container, painted in large white letters, is the legend: "PROP.T OF CAPTAIN, KEEP AWAY."

At rise, the lighting indicates that it is shortly after dawn. The stage is empty and there is no indication of life other than the sound of snoring from below.

CHIEF JOHNSON, *a bulging man about forty, enters through pas-*

sageway upstage left. He wears dungaree shirt and pants and a chief petty officer's cap. He is obviously chewing tobacco, and he starts down the hatchway, notices the palm tree, crosses to the Captain's door cautiously, peering into the porthole to see that he is not being watched, then deliberately spits into the palm tree container. He wipes his mouth smugly and shuffles over to the hatch. There he stops, takes out his watch and looks at it, then disappears down the hatchway. A shrill whistle is heard.

JOHNSON (*Offstage—in a loud singsong voice which is obviously just carrying out a ritual*) Reveille . . . Hit the deck . . . Greet the new day . . . (*The whistle is heard again*) Reveille . . .

INSIGNA (*Offstage*) Okay, Chief, you done your duty—now get your big fat can out of here!

(JOHNSON *reappears at the head of hatchway calling back*)

JOHNSON Just thought you'd like to know about reveille. And you're going to miss chow again.

STEFANOWSKI (*Offstage*) Thanks, Chief. Now go back to bed and stop bothering us.

(*His duty done,* JOHNSON, *still chewing, shuffles across the stage and disappears. There is a brief moment of silence, then the snoring is resumed below. After a moment,* ROBERTS *enters from the passageway at right. He wears khaki shirt and trousers and an officer's cap. On each side of his collar he wears the silver bar indicating the rank of Lieutenant (junior grade). He carries a rumpled piece of writing paper in his left hand, on which there is a great deal of writing and large black marks indicating that much has been scratched out. He walks slowly to the bitt, concentrating, then stands a moment looking out right. He suddenly gets an idea and goes to hatch cover, sitting and writing on the paper.* DOC *enters from the left passageway.* DOC *is between thirty-five and forty and he wears khakis and an officer's fore-and-aft cap; he wears medical insignia and the bars of Lieutenant (senior grade) on his collar. A stethoscope sticks out of his hip pocket. He is wiping the sweat off his neck with his handkerchief as he crosses above hatch cover. He stops as he sees* ROBERTS)

DOC That you, Doug?

ROBERTS (*Wearily, looking up*) Hello, Doc. What are you doing up?

DOC I heard you were working cargo today so I thought I'd get ready. On days when there's any work to be done I can always count on a big turnout at sick call.

ROBERTS (*Smiles*) Oh, yeah.

DOC I attract some very rare diseases on cargo days. That day they knew you were going to load five ships I was greeted by six more cases of beriberi—double beriberi this time. So help me, I'm going down to the ship's library and throw that old copy of *Moby Dick* overboard!

(*He sits on hatch cover*)

ROBERTS What are you giving them these days for double beriberi?

DOC Aspirin—what else? (*He looks at* ROBERTS) Is there something wrong, Doug?

ROBERTS (*Preoccupied*) No.

DOC (*Lying back on the hatch*) We missed you when you went on watch last night. I gave young Ensign Pulver another drink of alcohol and orange juice and it inspired him to relate further sexual feats of his. Some of them bordered on the supernatural!

ROBERTS I don't doubt it. Did he tell you how he conquered a forty-five-year-old virgin by the simple tactic of being the first man in her life to ask her a direct question?

DOC No. Last night he was more concerned with quantity. It seems that on a certain cold and wintry night in November, 1939—a night when most of us mortal men would have settled for a cup of cocoa—he rendered pregnant three girls in Washington, D. C., caught the 11:45 train, and an hour later performed the same service for a young lady in Baltimore.

ROBERTS (*Laughing*) Oh, my God!

DOC I'm not sure what to do with young Pulver. I'm thinking of reporting his record to the American Medical Association.

ROBERTS Why don't you just get him a job as a fountain in Radio City?

DOC Don't be too hard on him, Doug. He thinks you are approximately God. . . . Say, there *is* something wrong, isn't there?

ROBERTS I've been up all night, Doc.

DOC What is it? What's the matter?

ROBERTS I saw something last night when I was on watch that just about knocked me out.

DOC (*Alarmed*) What happened?

ROBERTS (*With emotion*) I was up on the bridge. I was just standing there looking out to sea. I couldn't bear to look at that island any more. All of a sudden I noticed something. Little black specks crawling over the horizon. I looked through the glasses and it was a formation of our ships that stretched for miles! Carriers and battleships and cans—a whole task force, Doc!

DOC   Why didn't you break me out? I've never seen a battleship!

ROBERTS   They came on and they passed within half a mile of that reef! Carriers so big they blacked out half the sky! And battle-wagons sliding along—dead quiet! I could see the men on the bridges. And this is what knocked me out, Doc. Somehow—I thought I was on those bridges—I thought I was riding west across the Pacific. I watched them until they were out of sight, Doc—and I was right there on those bridges all the time.

DOC   I know how that must have hurt, Doug.

ROBERTS   And then I looked down from our bridge and saw our Captain's palm tree! (*Points at palm tree, then bitterly*) Our trophy for superior achievement! The Admiral John J. Finchley award for delivering more toothpaste and toilet paper than any other Navy cargo ship in the safe area of the Pacific. (*Taking letter from pocket and handing it to* DOC) Read this, Doc—see how it sounds.

DOC   What is it?

ROBERTS   My application for transfer. I've been rewriting it ever since I got off watch last night.

DOC   O God, not another one!

ROBERTS   This one's different—I'm trying something new, Doc—a stronger wording. Read it carefully.

(DOC *looks for a moment skeptically, then noticing the intensity in his face decides to read the letter*)

DOC (*Reading*)   "From: Lieutenant (jg) Douglas Roberts

To: Bureau of Naval Personnel

16 April 1945

Subject: Change of Duty, Request for . . ."

(*He looks up*) Boy, this is sheer poetry.

ROBERTS (*Rises nervously*)   Go on, Doc.

DOC (*Reads on*)   "For two years and four months I have served aboard this vessel as Cargo Officer. I feel that my continued service aboard can only reduce my own usefulness to the Navy and increase disharmony aboard this ship."

(*He looks at* ROBERTS *and rises.* ROBERTS *looks back defiantly*)

ROBERTS   How about *that*!

DOC (*Whistles softly, then continues*)   "It is therefore urgently requested that I be ordered to combat duty, preferably aboard a destroyer."

ROBERTS (*Tensely, going to* DOC) What do you say, Doc? I've got a chance, haven't I?

DOC Listen, Doug, you've been sending in a letter every week for God knows how long . . .

ROBERTS Not like this . . .

DOC . . . and every week the Captain has screamed like a stuck pig, *dis*approved your letters and forwarded them that way. . . .

ROBERTS That's just my point, Doc. He *does* forward them. They go through the chain of command all the way up to the Bureau . . . Just because the Captain doesn't . . .

DOC Doug, the Captain of a Navy ship is the most absolute monarch left in this world!

ROBERTS I know that.

DOC If he endorsed your letter "approved" you'd get your orders in a minute . . .

ROBERTS Naturally, but I . . .

(*Turns away from* DOC)

DOC . . . but "disapproved," you haven't got a prayer. You're stuck on this old bucket, Doug. Face it!

ROBERTS (*Turns quickly back*) Well, grant me this much, Doc. That one day I'll find the perfect wording and one human guy way up on top will read those words and say, "Here's a poor son-of-a-bitch screaming for help. Let's put him on a fighting ship!"

DOC (*Quietly*) Sure . . .

ROBERTS (*After a moment*) I'm not kidding myself, am I, Doc? I've got a chance, haven't I?

DOC Yes, Doug, you've got a chance. It's about the same chance as putting your letter in a bottle and dropping it in the ocean . . .

ROBERTS (*Snatching letter from* DOC) But it's still a chance, goddammit! It's still a chance!

(ROBERTS *stands looking out to sea.* DOC *watches him for a moment then speaks gently*)

DOC I wish you hadn't seen that task force, Doug. (*Pauses*) Well, I've got to go down to my hypochondriacs.

(*He goes off slowly through passageway.* ROBERTS *is still staring out as* DOWDY *enters from the hatchway. He is a hard-bitten man between thirty-five and forty and is wearing dungarees and no hat. He stands by hatchway with a cup of coffee in his hand*)

DOWDY   Morning, Mister Roberts.

ROBERTS   Good morning, Dowdy.

DOWDY   Jeez, it's even hotter up here than down in that mess hall!
(*He looks off*) Look at that cruddy island . . . smell it! It's so
hot it *already* smells like a hog pen. Think we'll get out of here
today, sir?
(ROBERTS *takes* DOWDY's *cup as he speaks and drinks from it, then
hands it back*)

ROBERTS   I don't know, Dowdy. There's one LCT coming alongside
for supplies . . . (*Goes to hatchway, looks down*) Are they getting up yet?

DOWDY (*Also looking down hatch*)   Yeah, they're starting to stumble around down there—the poor punch-drunk bastards. Mister
Roberts, when are you going to the Captain again and ask him
to give this crew a liberty? These guys ain't been off the ship for
over a year except on duty.

ROBERTS   Dowdy, the last time I asked him was last night.

DOWDY   What'd he say?

ROBERTS   He said "No."

DOWDY   We gotta get these guys ashore! They're going Asiatic!
(*Pause*) Will you see him anyhow, Mister Roberts—just once
more?

ROBERTS   You know I will, Dowdy. (*Hands* DOWDY *the letter*) In
the meantime, have Dolan type that up for me.
(*He starts off right*)

DOWDY (*Descending hatchway*)   Oh, your letter. Yes, sir!

ROBERTS (*Calling over his shoulder*)   Then will you bring a couple
of men back aft?
(*He exits through passageway*)

DOWDY   Okay, Mister Roberts. (*He disappears down hatchway. He
is heard below*) All right, you guys in there. Finish your coffee
and get up on deck. Stefanowski, Insigna, off your tails . . .
(*After a moment the center door opens and the* CAPTAIN *appears wearing pajamas and bathrobe and his officer's cap. He is
carrying water in an engine-room oil can. He waters the palm
tree carefully, looks at it for a moment tenderly and goes back
into his cabin. After a moment,* DOWDY's *voice is heard from the
companionway and he appears followed by members of the crew*)

DOWDY   All right, let's go! Bring me those glasses, Schlemmer.
(SCHLEMMER *exits by ladder to the bridge. Other men appear
from the hatchway. They are* INSIGNA, STEFANOWSKI, MANNION,

WILEY, REBER *and* LINDSTROM—*all yawning, buttoning pants, tucking in shirts and, in general, being comatose. The men do not appear to like one another very much at this hour—least of all* INSIGNA *and* MANNION) All right, I got a little recreation for you guys. Stefanowski, you take these guys and get this little rust patch here. (*He hands* STEFANOWSKI *an armful of scrapers and wire brushes, indicating a spot on the deck.* STEFANOWSKI *looks at instruments dully, then distributes them to the men standing near him.* SCHLEMMER *returns from the bridge, carrying four pairs of binoculars and a spy glass. He drops them next to* INSIGNA *who is sitting on the hatch*) Insigna, I got a real special job for you. You stay right here and clean these glasses.

INSIGNA Ah, let me work up forward, Dowdy. I don't want to be around this crud, Mannion.

MANNION Yeah, Dowdy. Take Insigna with you!

DOWDY Shut up, I'm tired of you two bellyaching! (*Nodding to others to follow him*) All right, let's go, Reber . . . Schlemmer. (DOWDY, REBER *and* SCHLEMMER *leave through passageway right. The others sit in sodden silence.* LINDSTROM *wanders slowly over to* INSIGNA. *He picks up spy glass and examines it. He holds the large end toward him and looks into it*)

LINDSTROM Hey, look! I can see myself!

STEFANOWSKI Terrifying, ain't it?

(INSIGNA *takes the spy glass from him and starts polishing it.* LINDSTROM *removes his shoe and feels inside it, then puts it back on*)

MANNION (*After a pause*) Hey, what time is it in San Francisco?

INSIGNA (*Scornfully*) When?

MANNION Anybody ask you? (*Turns to* WILEY) What time would it be there?

WILEY I don't know. I guess about midnight last night.

STEFANOWSKI (*Studying scraper in his hand*) I wonder if you could get sent back to the States if you cut off a finger.
(*Nobody answers*)

INSIGNA (*Looking offstage*) Hey, they got a new building on that island. Fancy—two stories . . .
(*Nobody shows any curiosity*)

MANNION You know, I had a girl in San Francisco wore flowers in her hair—instead of hats. Never wore a hat . . .
(*Another sodden pause*)

INSIGNA (*Holding spy glass*) Hey, Stefanowski! Which end of this you look through?

STEFANOWSKI It's optional, Sam. Depends on what size eyeball you've got.

(INSIGNA *idly looks through spy glass at something out right. Another pause*)

INSIGNA Hey, the Japs must've took over this island—there's a red and white flag on that new building.

MANNION Japs! We never been within five thousand miles of a Jap! Japs! You hear that, Wiley?

WILEY Yeah, smart, ain't he?

MANNION Japs! That's a hospital flag!

INSIGNA Anybody ask you guys? (*Nudging* LINDSTROM *and pointing to the other group*) The goldbrick twins! (*Looks through spy glass*) Hey, they got a fancy hospital . . . big windows and . . . (*Suddenly rises, gasping at what he sees*)

STEFANOWSKI What's the matter, Sam?

INSIGNA Oh, my God! She's bare-assed!

STEFANOWSKI *She!*

INSIGNA Taking a shower . . . in that bathroom . . . that nurse . . . upstairs window!

(*Instantly the others rush to hatch cover, grab binoculars and stand looking out right*)

WILEY She's a blonde—see!

LINDSTROM I never seen such a beautiful girl!

MANNION She's sure taking a long time in that shower!

WILEY Yeah, honey, come on over here by the window!

INSIGNA Don't you do it, honey! You take your time!

STEFANOWSKI There's another one over by the washbasin—taking a shampoo.

INSIGNA (*Indignantly*) Yeah. But why the hell don't she take her bathrobe off! That's a stupid goddamn way to take a shampoo!

(*For a moment the men watch in silent vigilance*)

STEFANOWSKI Ah-hah!

WILEY She's coming out of the shower!

MANNION She's coming over to the window! (*A pause*) Kee-ri-mi-ny!

(*For a moment the men stand transfixed, their faces radiant. They emit rapturous sighs. That is all*)

LINDSTROM Aw, she's turning around the other way!

MANNION What's that red mark she's got . . . there?

INSIGNA (*Authoritatively*)   That's a birthmark!

MANNION (*Scornfully*)   Birthmark!

INSIGNA   What do you think it is, wise guy?

MANNION   Why, that's paint! She's sat in some red paint!

INSIGNA   Sat in some red paint! I'm tellin' you, that's a birthmark!

MANNION   Did you ever see a birthmark down there?

INSIGNA (*Lowers his spy glass, turns to* MANNION)   Why, you
stupid jerk! I had an uncle once had a birthmark right down . . .

WILEY   Aww!

(INSIGNA *and* MANNION *return quickly to their glasses*)

STEFANOWSKI (*Groaning*)   She's put her bathrobe on!

MANNION   Hey, she's got the same color bathrobe as that stupid bag
taking the shampoo!

(*The four men notice something and exclaim in unison*)

INSIGNA   Bag, hell! Look at her now with her head out of the
water . . .

LINDSTROM   She's just as beautiful as the other one . . .

STEFANOWSKI   They look exactly alike with those bathrobes on.
Maybe they're twins.

MANNION   That's my girl on the right—the one with the red birthmark.

INSIGNA   You stupid crud, the one with the birthmark's on the left!

MANNION   The hell she is . . .

(MANNION *and* INSIGNA *again lower their glasses*)

INSIGNA   The hell she ain't . . .

WILEY   Awwww!

(MANNION *and* INSIGNA *quickly drop their argument and look*)

STEFANOWSKI   They're both leaving the bathroom together. . . .

(*The men are dejected again*)

LINDSTROM   Hey, there ain't no one in there now!

STEFANOWSKI (*Lowering his glasses*)   Did you figure that out all
by yourself?

(*He looks through his glasses again*)

MANNION (*After a pause*)   Come on, girls, let's go!

WILEY   Yeah. Who's next to take a nice zippy shower?

INSIGNA (*After a pause*)   They must think we got nothing better
to do than stand here!

LINDSTROM   These glasses are getting heavy!

STEFANOWSKI   Yeah. We're wasting manpower. Let's take turns,
okay? (*The others agree*) All right, Mannion, you take it first.

(MANNION *nods, crosses and sits on bitt, keeping watch with his binoculars. The others pick up their scrapers and wire brushes)*

INSIGNA (*Watching* MANNION) I don't trust that crud.

LINDSTROM Gee, I wish we was allowed to get over to that island. We could get a closer look.

STEFANOWSKI No, Lindstrom. They'd see us and pull the shades down.

LINDSTROM No, they wouldn't. We could cover ourselves with leaves and make out like we was bushes—and sneak up on them —like them Japs we seen in that movie . . .

(*He starts to sneak around front of hatch, holding his wire brush before his face.* STEFANOWSKI *hears a noise from the* CAPTAIN'S *cabin and quickly warns the others)*

STEFANOWSKI Flash Red! (*The men immediately begin working in earnest as the* CAPTAIN, *now in khaki, enters. He stands for a moment, looking at them, and then wanders over to the group scraping the rust patch to inspect their work. Then, satisfied that they are actually working, he starts toward passageway. He sees* MANNION, *sitting on the bitt, looking through his glasses and smiling. The* CAPTAIN *goes over and stands beside him, looking off in the same direction.* STEFANOWSKI *tries frantically to signal a warning to* MANNION *by beating out code with his scraper.* MAN-NION *suddenly sees the* CAPTAIN *and quickly lowers his glasses and pretends to clean them, alternately wiping the lenses and holding them up to his eyes to see that they are clean. The* CAP-TAIN *watches him suspiciously for a moment, then he exits by the ladder to the bridge.* STEFANOWSKI *rises and looks up ladder to make certain the* CAPTAIN *has gone)* Flash White! (*He turns and looks at* MANNION) Hey, Mannion. Anyone in there yet?

MANNION (*Watching something happily through glasses*) No, not yet!

INSIGNA (*Picks up spy glass and looks, and rises quickly*) Why, you dirty, miserable cheat!

(*Instantly all the men are at the glasses)*

LINDSTROM There's one in there again!

STEFANOWSKI The hell with her—she's already got her clothes on!

INSIGNA And there she goes! (*Slowly lowers his glass, turning to* MANNION *threateningly*) Why, you lousy, cheating crud!

MANNION (*Idly swinging his glasses*) That ain't all. I seen three!

STEFANOWSKI You lowdown Peeping Tom!

LINDSTROM (*Hurt*) Mannion, that's a real dirty trick.

INSIGNA What's the big idea?

MANNION   Who wants to know?

INSIGNA   *I* want to know! And you're damn well going to tell me!

MANNION   You loud-mouthed little bastard! Why don't you make me?

INSIGNA   You're damn right I will. Right now!

(*He swings on* MANNION *as* LINDSTROM *steps clumsily between them*)

LINDSTROM   Hey, fellows! Fellows!

INSIGNA   No wonder you ain't got a friend on this ship . . . except this crud, Wiley.

(*He jerks his head in direction of* WILEY *who stands behind him on hatch cover.* WILEY *takes him by shoulder and whirls him around*)

WILEY   What'd you say?

STEFANOWSKI   (*Shoving* WILEY)   You heard him!

(MANNION *jumps on hatch cover to protect* WILEY *from* STEFA- NOWSKI. INSIGNA *rushes at* MANNION *and for a moment they are all in a clinch.* LINDSTROM *plows up on the hatch and breaks them apart. The men have suddenly formed into two camps—*MANNION *and* WILEY *on one side,* INSIGNA *and* STEFANOWSKI *facing them.* LINDSTROM *is just an accessory, but stands prepared to intervene if necessary*)

MANNION   (*To* WILEY)   Look at them two! Everybody on the ship hates their guts! The two moochingest, no-good loudmouths on the ship!

(STEFANOWSKI *starts for* MANNION *but* INSIGNA *pulls him back and steps menacingly toward* MANNION)

INSIGNA   Why, you slimy, lying son-of-a-bitch!

(*Suddenly* MANNION *hits* INSIGNA, *knocking him down. He jumps on* INSIGNA *who catches* MANNION *in the chest with his feet and hurls him back.* WILEY *and* STEFANOWSKI *start fighting with* LIND- STROM, *attempting to break them apart.* MANNION *rushes back at* INSIGNA. INSIGNA *sidesteps* MANNION's *lunge and knocks him to the deck.* INSIGNA *falls on him. They wrestle to their feet and stand slugging. At this point* ROBERTS *and* DOWDY *run on from passage- way.* ROBERTS *flings* INSIGNA *and* MANNION *apart.* DOWDY *separates the others*)

ROBERTS   Break it up! Break it up, I tell you!

(INSIGNA *and* MANNION *rush at each other.* ROBERTS *and* DOWDY *stop them*)

DOWDY   Goddamn you guys, break it up!

ROBERTS   All right! What's going on?

INSIGNA (*Pointing at* MANNION)   This son-of-a-bitch here . . .

ROBERTS   Did you hear me?

MANNION (*To* INSIGNA)   Shut your mouth!

DOWDY   Shut up, both of you!

INSIGNA   Slimy son-of-a-bitch!

(*Picks up scraper and lunges at* MANNION *again.* ROBERTS *throws him back*)

ROBERTS   I said to cut it out! Did you hear me? (*Wheels on* MAN-NION) That goes for you too! (*Includes entire group*) I'm going to give it to the first one who opens his mouth! (*The men stand subdued, breathing hard from the fight*) Now get to work! All of you! (*They begin to move sullenly off right*) Mannion, you and the rest get to work beside number two! And, Insigna, take those glasses way up to the bow and work on them! Stefanowski, keep those two apart.

STEFANOWSKI   Yes, sir.

(*The men exit.* ROBERTS *and* DOWDY *look after them*)

DOWDY (*Tightly*)   You seen that, Mister Roberts. Well, last night down in the compartment I stopped three of them fights—worse than that. They've got to have a liberty, Mister Roberts.

ROBERTS   They sure do. Dowdy, call a boat for me, will you? I'm going ashore.

DOWDY   What are you going to do?

ROBERTS   I just got a new angle.

DOWDY   Are you going over the Captain's head?

ROBERTS   No, I'm going around his end—I hope. Get the lead out, Dowdy.

(*He exits left as* DOWDY *goes off right and the lights*

Fade Out

(*During the darkness, voices can be heard over the squawkbox saying*)

Now hear this . . . now hear this. Sweepers, man your brooms. Clean sweep-down fore and aft. Sweep-down all ladders and all passageways. Do *not* throw trash over the fantail.

Now, all men on report will see the master-at-arms for assignment to extra duty.

Now hear this . . . now hear this. Because in violation of the Captain's orders, a man has appeared on deck without a shirt on, there will be no movies again tonight—by order of the Captain.

SCENE II

The lights dim up revealing the stateroom of PULVER *and* ROBERTS. *Two lockers are shown, one marked "Ensign F. T. Pulver," the other marked "Lt. (jg) D. A. Roberts." There is a double bunk along the bulkhead right. A desk with its end against the bulkhead left has a chair at either side. There is a porthole in the bulkhead above it. Up center, right of* PULVER's *locker is a washbasin over which is a shelf and a medicine chest. The door is up center.*

An officer is discovered with his head inside ROBERTS' *locker, throwing skivvy shirts over his shoulder as he searches for something.* DOLAN, *a young, garrulous, rash yeoman, second class, enters. He is carrying a file folder.*

DOLAN Here's your letter, Mister Roberts. (*He goes to the desk, taking fountain pen from his pocket*) I typed it up. Just sign your old John Henry here and I'll take it in to the Captain . . . then hold your ears. (*No answer*) Mister Roberts! (PULVER's *head appears from the locker*) Oh, it's only you, Mister Pulver. What are you doing in Mister Roberts' locker?

PULVER (*Hoarsely*) Dolan, look in there, will you? I know there's a shoe box in there, but I can't find it.

(DOLAN *looks in the locker*)

DOLAN There ain't no shoe box in there, Mister Pulver.

PULVER They've stolen it! There's nothing they'll stop at now. They've broken right into the sanctity of a man's own locker.

(*He sits in chair at desk*)

DOLAN (*Disinterested*) Ain't Mister Roberts back from the island yet?

PULVER No.

DOLAN Well, as soon as he gets back, will you ask him to sign this baby?

PULVER What is it?

DOLAN What is it! It's the best damn letter Mister Roberts writ yet. It's going to blow the Old Man right through the overhead. And them big shots at the Bureau are going to drop their drawers too. This letter is liable to get him transferred.

PULVER Yeah, lemme see it.

DOLAN (*Handing letter to* PULVER) Get a load of that last paragraph. Right here.

PULVER (*Reading with apprehension*) ". . . increase disharmony aboard this ship . . ."

DOLAN (*Interrupting gleefully*) Won't that frost the Old Man's knockers? I can't wait to jab this baby in the Old Man's face. Mister Pulver, you know how he get sick to his stomach when he gets extra mad at Mister Roberts—well, when I deliver this letter I'm going to take along a wastebasket! Let me know when Mister Roberts gets back.

(DOLAN *exits.* PULVER *continues reading the letter with great dismay. He hears* ROBERTS *and* DOC *talking in the passageway, offstage, and quickly goes to his bunk and hides the letter under a blanket. He goes to the locker and is replacing skivvy shirts as* ROBERTS *and* DOC *enter*)

ROBERTS . . . so after the fight I figured I had to do something and do it quick!

DOC What did you do over on the island, Doug?

ROBERTS (*Sitting in chair and searching through desk drawer*) Hey, Frank, has Dolan been in here yet with my letter?

PULVER (*Innocently*) I don't know, Doug boy. I just came in here myself.

DOC You don't know anybody on the island, do you, Doug?

ROBERTS Yes. The Port Director—the guy who decides where to send this ship next. He confided to me that he used to drink a quart of whiskey every day of his life. So this morning when I broke up that fight it came to me that he might just possibly sell his soul for a quart of Scotch.

PULVER (*Rises*) Doug, you didn't give that shoe box to the Port Director!

ROBERTS I did. "Compliments of the Captain."

DOC You've had a quart of Scotch in a shoe box?

ROBERTS Johnny Walker! I was going to break it out the day I got off this ship—Resurrection Day!

PULVER Oh, my God! It's really gone!

(*He sinks to the bunk*)

DOC Well, did the Port Director say he'd send us to a Liberty Port?

ROBERTS Hell, no. He took the Scotch and said, "Don't bother me, Roberts. I'm busy." The rummy!

PULVER How could you do it!

DOC Well, where there's a rummy, there's hope. Maybe when he gets working on that Scotch he'll mellow a little.

PULVER You gave that bottle to a goddamn *man!*

ROBERTS Man! Will you name me another sex within a thousand miles . . . (PULVER, *dejected, goes up to porthole*) What the hell's eating you anyway, Frank?

(DOC *crosses to bunk. He sees two fancy pillows on bottom bunk, picks up one and tosses it to* ROBERTS. *He picks up the other*)

DOC Well, look here. Somebody seems to be expecting company!

ROBERTS Good Lord!

DOC (*Reads lettering on pillowcase*) "Toujours l'amour . . . Souvenir of San Diego . . . Oh, you kid!"

ROBERTS (*Reading from his pillowcase*) "Tonight or never . . . Compliments of Allis-Chalmers, Farm Equipment . . . We plow deep while others sleep." (*He looks at* DOC, *then rises*) Doc—that new hospital over there hasn't got nurses, has it?

DOC Nurses! It didn't have yesterday!

PULVER (*Turning from porthole*) It has today!

DOC But how did you find out they were there?

PULVER (*Trying to recall*) Now let me think . . . it just came to me all of a sudden. This morning it was so hot I was just lying on my bunk—thinking . . . There wasn't a breath of air. And then, all of a sudden, a funny thing happened. A little breeze came up and I took a big deep breath and said to myself, "Pulver boy, there's women on that island."

ROBERTS Doc, a thing like this could make a bird dog self-conscious as hell.

PULVER (*Warming up*) They just flew in last night. There's eighteen of them—all brunettes except for two beautiful blondes—twin sisters! I'm working on one of those. I asked her out to the ship for lunch and she said she was kind of tired. So then I got kind of desperate and turned on the old personality—and I said, "Ain't there anything in the world that'll make you come out to the ship with me?" And she said, "Yes, there is, one thing and one thing only—" (*Crosses to* ROBERTS, *looks at him accusingly*) "A good stiff drink of Scotch!"

(*He sinks into the chair*)

ROBERTS (*After a pause*) I'm sorry, Frank. I'm really sorry. Your first assignment in a year.

(*He pats* PULVER *on the shoulder*)

PULVER I figured I'd bring her in here . . . I fixed it up real cozy

. . . (*Fondling pillow on desk*) . . . and then I was going to throw a couple of fast slugs of Scotch into her and . . . but, hell, without the Scotch, she wouldn't . . . she just wouldn't, that's all.

ROBERTS (*After a pause*)   Doc, let's make some Scotch!

DOC   Huh?

ROBERTS   As naval officers we're supposed to be resourceful. Frank here's got a great opportunity and I've let him down. Let's fix him up!

DOC   Right! (*He goes to desk.* ROBERTS *begins removing bottles from medicine chest*)   Frank, where's the rest of that alcohol we were drinking last night?

PULVER (*Pulling a large vinegar bottle half filled with colorless liquid from the wastebasket and handing it to* DOC)   Hell, that ain't even the right color.

DOC (*Taking the bottle*)   Quiet! (*Thinks deeply*) Color . . . (*With sudden decision*) Coca-Cola! Have you got any?

ROBERTS   I haven't seen a Coke in four months—no, by God, it's five months!

PULVER   Oh, what the hell! (*He rises, crosses to bunk, reaches under mattress of top bunk and produces a bottle of Coca-Cola. The others watch him.* DOC *snatches the bottle.* PULVER *says apologetically*)   I forgot I had it.
(DOC *opens the bottle and is about to pour the Coca-Cola into the vinegar bottle when he suddenly stops*)

DOC   Oh—what shade would you like? Cutty Sark . . . Haig and Haig . . . Vat 69 . . .

PULVER (*Interested*)   I told her Johnny Walker.

DOC   Johnny Walker it is!
(*He pours some of the Coca-Cola into the bottle*)

ROBERTS (*Looking at color of the mixture*)   Johnny Walker Red Label!

DOC   Red Label!

PULVER   It may look like it—but it won't taste like it!

ROBERTS   Doc, what does Scotch taste like?

DOC   Well, it's a little like . . . uh . . . it tastes like . . .

ROBERTS   Do you know what it's always tasted a little like to me? Iodine.

DOC (*Shrugs as if to say "Of course" and rises. He takes dropper from small bottle of iodine and flicks a drop in the bottle*)   One drop of iodine—for taste.
(*Shakes the bottle and pours some in glass*)

PULVER   Lemme taste her, Doc!

DOC   (*Stops him with a gesture*)   No. This calls for a medical opinion.

(*Takes a ceremonial taste while the others wait for his verdict*)

PULVER   How about it?

DOC   We're on the right track! (*Sets glass down. Rubs hands professionally*)   Now we need a little something extra—for age! What've you got there, Doug?

ROBERTS   (*Reading labels of bottles on desk*)   Bromo-Seltzer . . . Wildroot Wave Set . . . Eno Fruit Salts . . . Kreml Hair Tonic . . .

DOC   Kreml! It has a coal-tar base! And it'll age the hell out of it! (*Pours a bit of Kreml into mixture. Shakes bottle solemnly*)   One drop Kreml for age. (*Sets bottle on desk, looks at wrist watch for a fraction of a second*)   That's it!

(*Pours drink into glass.* PULVER *reaches for it.* ROBERTS *pushes his arm aside and tastes it*)

ROBERTS   By God, it does taste a little like Scotch!

(PULVER *again reaches for glass.* DOC *pushes his arm aside and takes a drink*)

DOC   By God, it does!

(PULVER *finally gets glass and takes a quick sip*)

PULVER   It's delicious. That dumb little blonde won't know the difference.

DOC   (*Hands the bottle to* PULVER)   Here you are, Frank. Doug and I have made the Scotch. The *nurse* is your department.

(PULVER *takes the bottle and hides it under the mattress, then replaces the pillows*)

PULVER   (*Singing softly*)   Won't know the difference . . . won't know the difference. (DOC *starts to drink from Coca-Cola bottle as* PULVER *comes over and snatches it from his hand*)   Thanks, Doc. (*Puts cap on the bottle and hides it under the mattress. Turns and faces the others*)   Thanks, Doug. Jeez, you guys are wonderful to me.

ROBERTS   (*Putting bottles back in medicine chest*)   Don't mention it, Frank. I think you almost deserve it.

PULVER   You do—really? Or are you just giving me the old needle again? What do you really think of me, Doug—honestly?

ROBERTS   (*Turning slowly to face* PULVER)   Frank, I like you. No one can get around the fact that you're a hell of a likable guy.

PULVER (*Beaming*) Yeah—yeah . . .

ROBERTS *But* . . .

PULVER But what?

ROBERTS But I also think you are the most hapless . . . lazy . . . disorganized . . . and, in general, the most lecherous person I've ever known in my life.

PULVER I am not.

ROBERTS Not what?

PULVER I'm not disorganized—for one thing.

ROBERTS Have you ever in your life finished anything you started out to do? You sleep sixteen hours a day. You pretend you want me to improve your mind and you've never even finished a book I've given you to read!

PULVER I finished *God's Little Acre*, Doug boy!

ROBERTS I didn't give you that! (*To* DOC) He's been reading *God's Little Acre* for over a year! (*Takes dog-eared book from* PULVER'S *bunk*) He's underlined every erotic passage, and added exclamation points—and after a certain pornographic climax, he's inserted the words "well written." (*To* PULVER) You're the Laundry and Morale Officer and I doubt if you've ever seen the Laundry.

PULVER I was down there only last week.

ROBERTS And you're scared of the Captain.

PULVER I'm not scared of the Captain.

ROBERTS Then why do you hide in the passageway every time you see him coming? I doubt if he even knows you're on board. You're scared of him.

PULVER I am not. I'm scared of myself—I'm scared of what I might do to him.

ROBERTS (*Laughing*) What you might do to him! Doc, he lies in his sack all day long and bores me silly with great moronic plots against the Captain and he's never carried out one.

PULVER I haven't, huh.

ROBERTS No, Frank, you haven't. What happened to your idea of plugging up the line of the Captain's sanitary system? "I'll make it overflow," you said. "I'll make a backwash that'll lift him off the throne and knock him clean across the room."

PULVER I'm workin' on that. I thought about it for half an hour—yesterday.

ROBERTS Half an hour! There's only one thing you've thought about for half an hour in your life! And what about those marbles that you were going to put in the Captain's overhead—so they'd roll around at night and keep him awake?

PULVER Now you've gone too far. Now you've asked for it. (*Goes to bunk and produces small tin box from under mattress. Crosses to* ROBERTS *and shakes it in his face. Opens it*) What does that look like? Five marbles! I'm collecting marbles all the time. I've got one right here in my pocket! (*Takes marble from pocket, holds it close to* ROBERTS' *nose, then drops it in box. Closes box*) Six marbles! (*Puts box back under mattress, turns defiantly to* ROBERTS) I'm looking for marbles all day long!

ROBERTS Frank, you asked me what I thought of you. Well, I'll tell you! The day you finish one thing you've started out to do, the day you actually put those marbles in the Captain's overhead, and then have the guts to knock on his door and say, "Captain, I put those marbles there," that's the day I'll have some respect for you —that's the day I'll look up to you as a man. Okay?

PULVER (*Belligerently*) Okay!

(ROBERTS *goes to the radio and turns it up. While he is listening,* DOC *and* PULVER *exchange worried looks*)

RADIO VOICE . . . intersecting thirty miles north of Hanover. At the same time, General George S. Patton's Third Army continues to roll unchecked into Southern Germany. The abrupt German collapse brought forth the remark from a high London official that the end of the war in Europe is only weeks away—maybe days . . .

(ROBERTS *turns off radio*)

ROBERTS Where the hell's Dolan with that letter! (*Starts toward the door*) I'm going to find him.

PULVER Hey, Doug, wait! Listen! (ROBERTS *pauses at the door*) I wouldn't send in that letter if I were you!

ROBERTS What do you mean—*that* letter!

PULVER (*Hastily*) I mean any of those letters you been writin'. What are you so nervous about anyway?

ROBERTS Nervous!

PULVER I mean about getting off this ship. Hell, this ain't such a bad life. Look, Doug. We're a threesome, aren't we—you and Doc and me? Share and share alike! Now look, I'm not going to keep those nurses all to myself. Soon as I get my little nursie organized today, I'm going to start working on her twin sister—for you.

ROBERTS All right, Frank.

PULVER   And then I'm going to scare up something for you too, Doc. And in the meantime you've got a lot of work to do, Doug boy— improvin' my mind and watching my grammar. And speaking of grammar, you better watch your grammar. You're going to get in trouble, saying things like "disharmony aboard this ship!" (ROBERTS *looks at* PULVER *quickly.* PULVER *catches himself*) I mean just in case you ever said anything like "disharmony aboard this ship" . . . or . . . uh . . . "harmony aboard this ship" or . . .

ROBERTS   Where's that letter?

PULVER   I don't know, Doug boy . . . (*As* ROBERTS *steps toward him, he quickly produces the letter from the blanket*) Here it is, Doug.

ROBERTS   (*Snatching the letter*)   What's the big idea!

(ROBERTS *goes to desk, reading and preparing to sign the letter.* PULVER *follows him*)

PULVER   I just wanted to talk to you before you signed it. You can't send it in that way—it's too strong! Don't sign that letter, Doug, please don't! They'll transfer you and you'll get your ass shot off. You're just running a race with death, isn't he, Doc? It's stupid to keep asking for it like that. The Doc says so too. Tell him what you said to me last night, Doc—about how stupid he is.

ROBERTS   (*Coldly, to* DOC)   Yes, Doc, maybe you'd like to tell me to my face.

DOC   (*Belligerently*)   Yes, I would. Last night I asked you why you wanted to fight this war. And you said: anyone who doesn't fight it is only half-alive. Well, I thought that over and I've decided that's just a crock, Doug—just a crock.

ROBERTS   I take it back, Doc. After seeing my task force last night I don't even feel half-alive.

DOC   You are stupid! And I can prove it! You quit medical school to get into this thing when you could be saving lives today. Why? Do you even know yourself?

ROBERTS   Has it ever occurred to you that the guys who fight this war might also be saving lives . . . yours and mine, for instance! Not just putting men together again, but *keeping* them together! Right now I'd rather practice that kind of medicine—Doctor!

DOC   (*Rising*)   Well, right now, that's exactly what you're doing.

ROBERTS   What, for God's sake!

DOC   Whether you like it or not, this sorry old bucket does a necessary job. And you're the guy who keeps her lumbering along. You keep this crew working cargo, and more than that—you keep them *alive.* It might just be that right here, on this bucket, you're deeper and more truly in this war than you ever would be any-where else.

ROBERTS Oh, Jesus, Doc. In a minute, you'll start quoting Emerson.

DOC *That* is a lousy thing to say!

ROBERTS We've got nothing to do with the war. Maybe that's why we're on this ship—because we're not good enough to fight. (*Then quietly with emotion*) Maybe there's some omniscient son-of-a-bitch who goes down the line of all the servicemen and picks out the ones to send into combat, the ones whose glands secrete enough adrenalin, or whose great-great-grandfathers weren't afraid of the dark or something. The rest of us are packed off to ships like this where we can't do any harm.

DOC What is it you want to be—a hero or something?

ROBERTS (*Shocked*) Hero! My God, Doc! You haven't heard a word I said! Look, Doc, the war's way out there! I'm here. I don't want to be here—I want to be out there. I'm sick and tired of being a lousy spectator. I just happen to believe in this thing. I've got to feel I'm *good* enough to be in it—to *participate!*

DOC Good enough! Doug, you're good enough! You just don't have the opportunity. That's mostly what physical heroism is—opportunity. It's a reflex. I think seventy-five out of a hundred young males have that reflex. If you put any one of them—say, even Frank Thurlow Pulver, here—in a B-29 over Japan, do you know what you'd have?

ROBERTS No, by God, I don't.

DOC You'd have Pulver, the Congressional Medal of Honor winner! You'd have Pulver, who, singlehanded, shot down twenty-three attacking Zeroes, then with his bare hands held together the severed wing struts of his plane, and with his bare feet success-fully landed the mortally wounded plane on his home field. (PUL-VER *thinks this over*) Hell, it's a reflex. It's like the knee jerk. Strike the patella tendon of any human being and you produce the knee jerk. Look.

(*He illustrates on* PULVER. *There is no knee jerk. He strikes again —still no reaction*)

PULVER What's the matter, Doc?

DOC Nothing. But stay out of B-29's, will you, Frank?

ROBERTS You've made your point very vividly, Doc. But I still want to get into this thing. I've got to get into it! And I'm going to keep on sending in these letters until I do.

DOC I know you are, Doug.

ROBERTS (*Signs the letter. Then to* DOC) I haven't got much time. I found that out over on the island. That task force I saw last night is on its way to start our last big push in the Pacific. And it went by me, Doc. I've got to catch it.

(*He exits*)

PULVER (*After a pause*) Doc, what are you going to give Doug on his birthday?

DOC I hadn't thought of giving him anything.

PULVER You know what? I'm gonna show him he's got old Pulver figured out all wrong. (*Pulls small cardboard roll from under mattress*) Doc, what does that look like?

DOC Just what it is—the cardboard center of a roll of toilet paper.

PULVER I suppose it doesn't look like a firecracker.

DOC Not a bit like a firecracker.

PULVER (*Taking a piece of string from the bunk*) I suppose that doesn't look like a fuse.

DOC (*Rising and starting off*) No, that looks like a piece of string. (*He walks slowly out of the room.* PULVER *goes on*)

PULVER Well, you just wait till old Pulver gets through with it! I'm going to get me some of that black powder from the gunner's mate. No, by God, this isn't going to be any peanut firecracker— I'm going to pack this old thing full of that stuff they use to blow up bridges, that fulminate of mercury stuff. And then on the night of Doug's birthday, I'm going to throw it under the Old Man's bunk. Bam—bam—bam! (*Knocks on* ROBERTS' *locker, opens it*) Captain, it is I, Ensign Pulver. I just threw that firecracker under your goddamn bunk.

(*He salutes as the lights*

Fade Out

(*In the darkness we hear the sound of a winch and shouted orders*)

LCT OFFICER On the AK—where do you want us?

AK VOICE Starboard side, up for'd—alongside number two!

LCT OFFICER Shall we use our fenders or yours?

AK VOICE No, we'll use ours! Stand off till we finish with the barge!

SCENE III

The curtain rises and the lights dim up on the deck. ROBERTS *stands on the hatch cover.* SCHLEMMER, GERHART *and another seaman are sitting on the hatch cover. They are tired and hot. A cargo net, filled with crates, is disappearing off right. Offstage we hear the shouts of men working cargo. Two officers walk across the stage. Everyone's shirt is wet with perspiration.*

ROBERTS (*Calling through megaphone*) Okay—take it away—that's all for the barge. On the LCT—I'll give you a bow line.

LCT OFFICER (*Offstage*) Okay, Lieutenant.

ROBERTS (*To crew*) Get a line over!

DOWDY (*Offstage*) Yes, sir!

REBER (*Off right*) Heads up on the LCT!

ROBERTS That's good. Make it fast.

(PAYNE, *wearing the belt of a messenger, enters from companionway as* DOWDY *enters from right*)

PAYNE Mister Roberts, the Captain says not to give this LCT any fresh fruit. He says he's going to keep what's left for his own mess.

ROBERTS Okay, okay . . .

PAYNE Hold your hat, Mister Roberts. I just saw Dolan go in there with your letter.

(*He grins and exits as* ROBERTS *smiles at* DOWDY)

DOWDY Here's the list of what the LCT guy wants.

ROBERTS (*Reading rapidly*) One ton dry stores . . . quarter-ton frozen food . . . one gross dungarees . . . twenty cartons toothpaste . . . two gross skivvy shirts . . . Okay, we can give him all that.

DOWDY Can these guys take their shirts off while we're working?

ROBERTS Dowdy, you know the Captain has a standing order . . .

DOWDY Mister Roberts, Corcoran just passed out from the heat.

ROBERTS (*Looks at men who wait for his decision*) Hell, yes, take 'em off. (DOWDY *exits.* SCHLEMMER, REBER *and seaman remove shirts saying* "Thanks, MISTER ROBERTS" *and exit right.* ROBERTS *calls through megaphone*) LCT, want to swap movies? We've got a new one.

LCT (*Offstage*) What's that?

ROBERTS *Charlie Chan at the Opera.*

LCT (*Offstage*)   No, thanks, we've seen that three times!

ROBERTS   What you got?

LCT (*Offstage*)   Hoot Gibson in *Riders of the Range*.

ROBERTS   Sorry I brought the subject up.

DOWDY (*Entering from right*)   All set, Mister Roberts.

LCT (*Offstage*)   Lieutenant, one thing I didn't put on my list because I wanted to ask you—you couldn't spare us any fresh fruit,
could you?

ROBERTS   You all out?

LCT (*Offstage*)   We haven't seen any for two months.

ROBERTS (*To* DOWDY)   Dowdy, give 'em a couple of crates of
oranges.

DOWDY   Yes, sir.

ROBERTS   Compliments of the Captain.

DOWDY   Aye-aye, sir.

   (*He exits*)

ROBERTS (*To* LCT)   Here comes your first sling-load! (*There is the
grinding sound of a winch. With hand-signals* ROBERTS *directs
placing of the sling-load. Then he shouts*) Watch that line!

   (DOWDY's *voice is heard offstage*)

DOWDY   Slack off, you dumb bastards! Slack off!

   (PAYNE *enters.* ROBERTS *turns to him sharply*)

ROBERTS   What!

PAYNE   The Captain wants to see you, Mister Roberts.

DOWDY (*Offstage*)   Goddammit, there it goes! You've parted the
line!

ROBERTS   Get a fender over! Quick! (*To* PAYNE) You go tell the
Captain I'm busy! (PAYNE *exits.* ROBERTS *calls offstage*) Get a line
over—his bow's coming in!

REBER (*Offstage*)   Heads up!

GERHART (*Offstage*)   Where shall we secure?

DOWDY (*Offstage*)   Secure here!

ROBERTS   No. Take it around the bitt!

DOWDY (*Offstage*)   Around the bitt!

ROBERTS   That's too much! Give him some slack this time! (*Watches
intently*) That's good. Okay, let's give him the rest of his cargo.

GERHART (*Entering quickly and pointing toward companionway*)
Flash Red!

   (*He exits. The* CAPTAIN *enters, followed by* PAYNE *and* DOLAN)

CAPTAIN   All right, Mister! Let's have this out right here and now!
What do you mean—telling me you're busy!

ROBERTS   We parted a line, Captain. You didn't want me to leave the deck with this ship coming in on us?

CAPTAIN   You're damn right I want you to leave the deck. When I tell you I want to see you, I mean *now*, Mister! I mean jump! Do you understand?

(*At this point a group of men, attracted by the noise, crowd in. They are naked to the waist. They pretend they are working, but actually they are listening to the* CAPTAIN's *fight with* ROBERTS)

ROBERTS   Yes, Captain. I'll remember that next time.

CAPTAIN   You're damn right you'll remember it! Don't *ever* tell me you're too busy to see me! Ever! (ROBERTS *doesn't answer. The* CAPTAIN *points to the letter he is carrying*) By God, you think you're pretty cute with this letter, don't you? You're trying to get me in bad with the Admiral, ain't you? Ain't you?

ROBERTS   No, I'm not, Captain.

CAPTAIN   Then what do you mean by writing "disharmony aboard this ship"?

ROBERTS   Because it's true, Captain.

(*The men grin at each other*)

CAPTAIN   Any disharmony on this ship is my own doing!

ROBERTS   That's true too, Captain.

CAPTAIN   Damn right it's true. And it ain't gonna be in any letter that leaves this ship. Any criticism of this ship stays on this ship. I got a reputation with the Admiral and I ain't gonna lose it on account of a letter written by some smart-alec college officer. Now you retype that letter and leave out that disharmony crap and I'll send it in. But this is the last one, understand?

ROBERTS   Captain, every man in the Navy has the right to send in a request for transfer . . . and no one can change the wording. That's in Navy regs.

CAPTAIN (*After a pause*)   How about that, Dolan?

DOLAN   That's what it says, sir.

CAPTAIN   This goddamn Navy! I never put up with crap like that in the merchant service. All right, I'll send this one in as it is— *dis*approved, like I always do. But there's one thing I don't have to do and that's send in a letter that ain't been written. And, Mister, I'm tellin' you here and now—you ain't gonna write any more. You bring one next week and you'll regret it the rest of your life. You got a job right here and, Mister, you ain't *never* going to leave this ship. Now get on with your work. (*He looks around and notices the men. He shouts*) Where are your shirts?

ROBERTS   Captain, I . . .

CAPTAIN   Shut up! *Answer me, where are your shirts?* (*They stare at him*) Get those shirts on in a goddamn quick hurry.

(*The men pick up their shirts, then pause, looking at* ROBERTS)

ROBERTS   Captain, it was so hot working cargo, I . . .

CAPTAIN   (*Shouting louder*) I told you to shut up! (*To the men*) I'm giving you an order: get those shirts on!

(*The men do not move*)

ROBERTS   (*Quietly*) I'm sorry. Put your shirts on.

(*The men put on their shirts. There is a pause while the* CAPTAIN *stares at the men. Then he speaks quietly*)

CAPTAIN   Who's the Captain of this ship? By God, that's the rankest piece of insubordination I've seen. You've been getting pretty smart playing grab-ass with Roberts here . . . but now you've gone too far. I'm givin' you a little promise—I ain't never gonna forget this. And in the meantime, every one of you men who disobeyed my standing order and appeared on deck without a shirt —every one—is on report, do you hear? On report!

ROBERTS   Captain, you're not putting these men on report.

CAPTAIN   What do you mean—I'm not!

ROBERTS   I'm responsible. I gave them permission.

CAPTAIN   You disobeyed my order?

ROBERTS   Yes, sir. It was too hot working cargo in the sun. One man passed out.

CAPTAIN   I don't give a damn if fifty men passed out. I gave an order and you disobeyed it.

LCT   (*Offstage*) Thanks a million for the oranges, Lieutenant.

CAPTAIN   (*To* ROBERTS) Did you give that LCT fresh fruit?

ROBERTS   Yes, sir. We've got plenty, Captain. They've been out for two months.

CAPTAIN   I've taken all the crap from you that I'm going to. You've just got yourself ten days in your room. Ten days, Mister! Ten days!

ROBERTS   Very well, Captain. Do you relieve me here?

CAPTAIN   You're damn right, I relieve you. You can go to your room for ten days! See how you like that!

LCT   (*Offstage*) We're waiting on you, Lieutenant. We gotta shove off.

ROBERTS *gives the megaphone to the* CAPTAIN *and starts off. The* CAPTAIN *looks in direction of the* LCT *then calls to* ROBERTS)

CAPTAIN   Where do you think you're going?

ROBERTS (*Pretending surprise*)   To my room, Captain!

CAPTAIN   Get back to that cargo! I'll let you know when you have ten days in your room and you'll damn well know it! You're going to stay right here and do your job! (ROBERTS *crosses to the crew. The* CAPTAIN *slams the megaphone into* ROBERTS' *stomach.* PULVER *enters around the corner of the house, sees the* CAPTAIN *and starts to go back. The* CAPTAIN *sees* PULVER *and shouts*) Who's that? Who's that officer there?

PULVER (*Turning*)   Me, sir?

CAPTAIN   Yes, you. Come here, boy. (PULVER *approaches in great confusion and can think of nothing better to do than salute. This visibly startles the* CAPTAIN) Why, you're one of my officers!

PULVER   Yes, sir.

CAPTAIN   What's your name again?

PULVER   Ensign Pulver, sir.

(*He salutes again. The* CAPTAIN, *amazed, returns the salute, then says for the benefit of* ROBERTS *and the crew*)

CAPTAIN   By God, I'm glad to see one on this ship knows how to salute. (*Then to* PULVER) Pulver . . . oh, yes . . . Pulver. How is it I never see you around?

PULVER (*Terrified*)   I've wondered about that myself, sir.

CAPTAIN   What's your job?

PULVER (*Trembling*)   Officer in charge of laundry and morale, sir.

CAPTAIN   How long you been aboard?

PULVER   Fourteen months, sir.

CAPTAIN   Fourteen months! You spend most of your time down in the laundry, eh?

PULVER   Most of the time, sir. Yes, sir.

(ROBERTS *turns his face to hide his laughter*)

CAPTAIN   Well, you do a good job, Pulver, and . . . you know I'd like to see more of you. Why don't you have lunch with me in my cabin today?

PULVER   Oh, I can't today.

CAPTAIN   Can't? Why not?

PULVER   I'm on my way over to the hospital on the island. I've got to go pick up a piece . . . of medical equipment.

ROBERTS (*Calling over*)   Why, I'll take care of that, Frank.

CAPTAIN   That's right, Roberts. You finish here and you go over and fetch it.

ROBERTS   Yes, sir.

(*He nods and turns away grinning*)

CAPTAIN (*To* PULVER)   Well, how about it?

PULVER   This is something I've got to take care of myself, sir. If you don't mind, sir.

CAPTAIN   Well, some other time then.

PULVER   Yes, sir. Thank you, sir.

CAPTAIN   Okay, Pulver.

(*The* CAPTAIN *baits another salute from* PULVER, *then exits.* PULVER *watches him go, then starts to sneak off*)

ROBERTS (*Grinning and mimicking the* CAPTAIN)   Oh, boy! (PULVER *stops uneasily.* ROBERTS *salutes him*) I want to see more of you, Pulver!

PULVER (*Furiously*)   That son-of-a-bitch! Pretending he doesn't know me!

(*He looks at watch and exits.* ROBERTS *turns laughing to the crew who are standing rather solemnly*)

DOWDY (*Quietly*)   Nice going, Mister Roberts.

SCHLEMMER   It was really beautiful the way you read the Old Man off!

GERHART   Are you going to send in that letter next week, Mister Roberts?

ROBERTS   Are we, Dolan?

DOLAN   You're damn right we are! And I'm the baby who's going to deliver it!

SCHLEMMER   He said he'd fix you good. What do you think he'll do?

REBER   You got a promotion coming up, haven't you?

SCHLEMMER   Yeah. Could he stop that or something?

DOLAN   Promotion! This is Mister Roberts. You think he gives a good hoot-in-hell about another lousy stripe?

ALL   Yeah.

GERHART   Hey, Mister Roberts, can I take the letter in next week?

DOLAN (*Indignantly*)   You can like hell! That's my job—isn't it, Mister Roberts?

GERHART   Can I, Mister Roberts?

ROBERTS   I'm afraid I've promised that job to Dolan.

DOLAN (*Pushing* GERHART *away*)   You heard him. (*To* ROBERTS) We gotta write a really hot one next week.

ROBERTS   Got any asbestos paper?

(*He starts off, the men follow happily as the lights*

Fade Out

SCENE IV

The lights come up immediately on the main set. REBER *and* GERHART *enter from right passageway. As they get around the corner of the house, they break into a run.* REBER *dashes off through left passageway.*

GERHART (*Excitedly, descending hatchway*) Hey, Schlemmer! Schlemmer!
 (MISS GIRARD, *a young, attractive, blonde Army nurse, and* PULVER *enter from right passageway*)
PULVER Well, here it is.
MISS GIRARD This is a ship?
PULVER Unh-hunh.
MISS GIRARD My sister and I flew over some warships on our way out from the States and they looked so busy—men running around like mad.
PULVER It's kinda busy sometimes up on deck.
MISS GIRARD Oh, you mean you've seen a lot of action?
PULVER Well, I sure as hell haven't had much in the last year . . . Oh, battle action! Yeah . . . Yeah . . .
MISS GIRARD Then you must have a lot of B.F. on here.
PULVER Hunh?
MISS GIRARD You know—battle fatigue?
PULVER Yeah, we have a lot of that.
MISS GIRARD Isn't that too bad! But they briefed us to expect a lot of that out here. (*Pause*) Say, you haven't felt any yourself, have you?
PULVER I guess I had a little touch of it . . . just a scratch.
MISS GIRARD You know what you should do then? You should sleep more.
PULVER Yeah.
MISS GIRARD What's your job on the ship?
PULVER Me? I'm . . . Executive Officer . . .
MISS GIRARD But I thought that Executive Officers had to be at least a . . .
PULVER Say, you know what I was thinking? That we should have that little old drink of Scotcharoo right now—

MISS GIRARD   I think so too. You know, I just love Scotch. I've just learned to drink it since I've joined the Army. But I'm already an absolute connoisseur.

PULVER (*Dismayed*)   Oh, you are?

MISS GIRARD   My twin sister has a nickname for me that's partly because I like a particular brand of Scotch . . . (*Giggles*) and partly because of a little personal thing about me that you wouldn't understand. Do you know what she calls me? "Red Label!" (*They both laugh*) What are you laughing at? You don't know what I'm talking about—and what's more you never will.

PULVER   What I was laughing about is—that's the kind I've got.

MISS GIRARD   Red Label! Oh, you're God's gift to a thirsty nurstie! But where can we drink it? This is a Navy ship . . . isn't it?

PULVER   Oh, yeah, yeah, we'll have to be careful . . . We mustn't be seen . . . Lemme see, where shall we go . . . (*Considers*) I have it! We'll go back to my cabin. Nobody'd bother us there.

MISS GIRARD   Oh, you're what our outfit calls an operator. But you look harmless to me.

PULVER   Oh, I don't know about that.

MISS GIRARD   What's your first name—Harmless?

PULVER   Frank.

MISS GIRARD   Hello, Frank. Mine's Ann.

PULVER   Hello, Ann.

MISS GIRARD   All right. We'll have one nice little sip in your room.

PULVER   Right this way. (*They start off toward left passageway.* INSIGNA, MANNION, STEFANOWSKI, WILEY *and* LINDSTROM *enter from right, carrying the spy glass and binoculars.* STEFANOWSKI *trips on hatch cover.* MISS GIRARD *and* PULVER *turn*) Hello, Mannion . . . Insigna . . . Stefanowski . . .

MANNION (*Hoarsely*)   Hello, Mister Pulver . . .

PULVER   This is—Lieutenant Girard.

(*The men murmur a greeting*)

MISS GIRARD   What're you all doing with those glasses?

INSIGNA   We're . . . cleaning them.

(*Suddenly pulls out shirt tail and begins lamely polishing spy glass. The others follow his example. More men crowd onto the stage*)

PULVER   Well, don't work too hard . . . (*They turn to leave, but find themselves hemmed in by the men*) It's getting a little stuffy up here, I guess we better . . .

(ROBERTS *enters, very excited, carrying a piece of paper and a small book*)

ROBERTS (*Entering*) Hey, Insigna . . . Mannion . . . get a load of this . . . Hey, Frank . . .

(*He stops short seeing* MISS GIRARD)

PULVER Hiya, Doug boy! This is Ann Girard—Doug Roberts.

ROBERTS How do you do?

MISS GIRARD (*Beaming*) How do you do? You're Frank's roommate. He's told me all about you.

ROBERTS Really?

MISS GIRARD What are you doing on this ship?

ROBERTS Now there you've got me.

MISS GIRARD No, I mean what's your job? Like Frank here is Executive Officer.

ROBERTS Oh, I'm just the Laundry and Morale Officer.

MISS GIRARD Why, that's wonderful—I've just been made Laundry and Morale Officer in our outfit!

PULVER Oh, for Christ's sake!

(MANNION *and* INSIGNA *begin an argument in whispers*)

MISS GIRARD Maybe we can get together and compare notes.

ROBERTS I'd enjoy that very much.

PULVER (*Attempting to usher* MISS GIRARD *off*) Look, Doug. Will you excuse us? We're going down to have a little drink.

MISS GIRARD Frank, I don't think that's very nice. Aren't you going to ask Doug to join us?

PULVER Hell, no—I mean—he doesn't like Scotch.

ROBERTS That's right, Miss Girard. I stay true to alcohol and orange juice.

PULVER Come on, Ann . . .

MISS GIRARD Wait a minute! A lot of the girls at the hospital swear by alcohol and orange juice. We ought to all get together and have a party in our new dayroom.

INSIGNA (*To* MANNION) I bet you fifty bucks . . .

(STEFANOWSKI *moves* INSIGNA *and* MANNION *away from* MISS GIRARD)

MISS GIRARD Seems to be an argument.

PULVER Yeah.

MISS GIRARD Well, anyhow, we're fixing up a new dayroom. (*She looks offstage*) Look, you can see it! The hospital! And there's our new dormitory! That first window . . .

(PULVER *takes glasses from* WILEY *to look at island*)

INSIGNA (*To* MANNION, *his voice rising*)   All right, I got a *hundred* bucks says that's the one with the birthmark on her ass.

(*There is a terrible silence.* MISS GIRARD, *after a moment, takes the glasses from* PULVER *and looks at the island. After a moment she lowers the glasses and speaks to* PULVER)

MISS GIRARD   Frank, I won't be able to have lunch with you after all. Would you call the boat, please? (*To* ROBERTS) Good-bye, Doug. It was nice knowing you. You see, I promised the girls I'd help them hang some curtains and I think we'd better get started right away. Good-bye, everybody. (*To* MANNION) Oh, what's your name again?

INSIGNA   Mine?

MISS GIRARD   No. Yours.

MANNION   Mine? (MISS GIRARD *nods*) Mannion.

MISS GIRARD   Well, Mannion. I wouldn't take that bet if I were you because you'd lose a hundred bucks. (*To* PULVER) Come on, Harmless.

(*She exits, followed by a bewildered* PULVER. *The men watch her off.* STEFANOWSKI *throws his cap down in anger*)

MANNION (*To* INSIGNA)   You loud-mouthed little bastard! Now you've gone and done it!

ROBERTS   Shut up! Insigna, how did you . . .

INSIGNA   We seen her taking a bath.

LINDSTROM   Through these glasses, Mister Roberts! We could see everything!

STEFANOWSKI (*Furious*)   You heard what she said—she's going to hang some curtains.

MANNION   Yeah . . .

LINDSTROM   Gee, them nurses was pretty to look at.

(*He sighs. There is a little tragic moment*)

ROBERTS   She's got a ten-minute boat ride. You've still got ten minutes.

WILEY   It wouldn't be any fun when you know you're going to be rushed.

LINDSTROM   This was the first real good day this ship has ever had. But it's all over now.

ROBERTS   Well, maybe you've got time then to listen to a little piece of news . . . (*He reads from the paper in his hands*) "When in all respects ready for sea, on or about 1600 today, the *AK 601* will proceed at ten knots via points X-Ray, Yolk and Zebra to

Elysium Island, arriving there in seven days and reporting to the Port Director for cargo assignment." (*Emphatically*) "During its stay in Elysium, the ship will make maximum use of the recreational facilities of this port."

(*The men look up in slow surprise and disbelief*)

STEFANOWSKI But that means liberty!

LINDSTROM That don't mean liberty, Mister Roberts?

ROBERTS That's exactly what it means!

INSIGNA (*Dazed*) Somebody must've been drunk to send us to a Liberty Port!

(ROBERTS *nods*)

LINDSTROM Has the Old Man seen them orders?

ROBERTS He saw them before I did.

(*Now the men are excited*)

WILEY Elysium! Where's that?

MANNION Yeah! Where's that, Mister Roberts?

(*The men crowd around* ROBERTS *as he sits on the hatch*)

ROBERTS (*Reading from guide-book*) "Elysium is the largest of the Limbo Islands. It is often referred to as the 'Polynesian Paradise.' Vanilla, sugar, cocoa, coffee, copra, mother-of-pearl, phosphates and rum are the chief exports."

INSIGNA Rum! Did you hear that?

(*He gooses* LINDSTROM)

LINDSTROM Cut that out!

(DOLAN *gooses* INSIGNA)

INSIGNA Cut that out!

MANNION Shut up!

ROBERTS "Elysium City, its capital, is a beautiful metropolis of palm-lined boulevards, handsome public buildings and colorful stucco homes. Since 1900, its population has remained remarkably constant at approximately 30,000.

INSIGNA I'll fix that!

(*The men shout him down*)

ROBERTS That's all there is here. If you want the real dope on Elysium, there's one man on this ship who's been there.

STEFANOWSKI Who's that?

MANNION Who?

ROBERTS Dowdy!

(*The men run off wildly in every direction, shouting for* DOWDY. *The call is taken up all over the ship.* ROBERTS *listens to them happily, then notices a pair of binoculars. He looks toward the island for a moment, shrugs and is lifting the binoculars to his eyes as the lights*

Fade Out

SCENE V

During the darkness we can hear the exciting strains of Polynesian music.

The lights come up slowly through a porthole, casting a strong late-afternoon shaft of light onto motionless white figures. It is the enlisted men's compartment below decks. Except for a few not yet fully dressed, the men are all in white uniforms. The compartment is a crowded place with three-tiered bunks against the bulkheads. Most of the men are crowded around the porthole, downstage left. The men who cannot see are listening to the reports of INSIGNA, *who is standing on a bench, looking out the porthole. The only man who is not galvanized with excitement is* DOWDY, *who sits calmly on a bench, downstage center, reading a magazine—*True Detective.

GERHART (*To* INSIGNA) What do you see now, Sam?

INSIGNA There's a lot of little boats up forward—up around the bow.

PAYNE What kind of boats?

INSIGNA They're little sort of canoes and they're all filled up with flowers and stuff. And there's women in them boats, paddling them . . .

PAYNE Are they coming down this way?

INSIGNA Naw. They're sticking around the bow.

STEFANOWSKI Sam, where's that music coming from?

INSIGNA There's a great big canoe up there and it's all filled with fat bastards with flowers in their ears playing little old gittars . . .

SCHLEMMER Why the hell can't we go up on deck? That's what I'd like to know!

LINDSTROM When are we going ashore! That's what I'd like to know!

(INSIGNA *suddenly laughs*)

PAYNE What is it, Sam?

INSIGNA   I wish you could see this . . .

(CHIEF JOHNSON *enters, looking knowingly at the men, shakes his head and addresses* DOWDY)

JOHNSON   Same story in here, eh? Every porthole this side of the ship!

DOWDY   They're going to wear themselves down to a nub before they ever get over there . . .

LINDSTROM   (*Takes coin from pocket and thrusts it at* INSIGNA)   Hey, Sam, here's another penny. Make them kids down below dive for it.

INSIGNA   (*Impatiently*)   All right! (*Throws coin out the port*) Heads up, you little bastards!

(*The men watch tensely*)

LINDSTROM   Did he get that one too?

INSIGNA   Yeah . . .

(*The men relax somewhat*)

LINDSTROM   Them kids don't ever miss!

INSIGNA   Hey, Dowdy—where's that little park again? Where you said all the good-looking women hang out?

DOWDY   For the last time—you see that big hill over there to the right . . .

INSIGNA   Yeah.

DOWDY   You see a big church . . . with a street running off to the left of it.

INSIGNA   Yeah.

DOWDY   Well, you go up that street three blocks . . .

INSIGNA   Yeah, I'm there.

DOWDY   That's the park.

INSIGNA   Well, I'll be damned . . .

LINDSTROM   Hey, show me that park, Sam?

(*The other men gather around* INSIGNA, *asking to see the park*)

INSIGNA   (*The authority now*)   All right, you bastards, line up. I'll show you where the women hang out.

(*The men form a line and each steps up to the porthole where* INSIGNA *points out the park*)

JOHNSON   (*To* DOWDY)   Smell that shoe polish? These guys have gone nuts!

DOWDY   I went down the ship's store the other day to buy a bar of soap and, do you know, they been sold out for a week! No soap, no Listerine, no lilac shaving lotion—hell, they even sold eighteen

jars of Mum! Now these bastards are bootlegging it! They're
gettin' ten bucks for a used jar of Mum!

(REBER, *wearing the messenger's belt, enters. The men greet him
excitedly*)

STEFANOWSKI   What's the word on liberty, Reber? Is the Old Man
still asleep?

MANNION   Yeah, what's the word?

REBER   I just peeked in on him. He's snoring like a baby.

GERHART   Jeez, how any guy can sleep at a time like this!

INSIGNA   I'll get him up! I'm going up there and tap on his door!
(*Picks up a heavy lead pipe*)

DOWDY (*Grabbing INSIGNA*)   Like hell you are! You're going to stay
right here and pray. You're going to pray that he wakes up feeling
good and decides he's kept you guys sweating long enough!

MANNION   That's telling the little crud!

(INSIGNA *and* MANNION *threaten each other*)

REBER   Hey, Lindstrom. I got good news for you. You can take them
whites off.

LINDSTROM   I ain't got the duty *tonight?*

REBER   That's right. You and Mister Roberts got the duty tonight—
the twelve to four watch. The Exec just posted the list . . . (*He
is interrupted by the sound of static on the squawk box. Instantly
all men turn toward it eagerly*)

DOLAN (*On squawk box*)   Now hear this! Now hear this!

WILEY   Here we go! Here we go!

STEFANOWSKI (*Imitating the squawk box*)   Liberty . . . will commence . . . immediately!

GERHART   Quiet!

DOLAN (*On squawk box*)   Now hear this! The Captain's messenger
will report to the Captain's cabin on the double!

REBER   My God! He's awake!
(*He runs out*)

PAYNE   Won't be long now!

WILEY   Get going, Mannion! Get into those whites! We're going to
be the first ones over the side!

MANNION   Hell, yes! Give me a hand!
(*Now there is a general frenzy of preparation—the men put the
last-minute touches to shoes, hair, uniforms*)

GERHART (*Singing to the tune of "California, Here I Come"*)   Ee-
liss-*ee*-um, here I come! . . . Ta-ta-ta-ta-*ta*-da-tah . . .

SCHLEMMER (*To* GERHART) Watch where you're going! You stepped on my shine!

INSIGNA Schlemmer . . . Stef . . . Gerhart . . . come here! (*These men gather around him.* LINDSTROM *remains unhappily alone*) Now listen! Stefanowski and me are going to work alone for the first hour and a half! But if you pick up something first . . . (*Produces small map from his pocket*) We'll be working up and down this street here . . .

(*They study the map. Now the squawk box is clicked on again. All the men stand rigid, listening*)

DOLAN (*On squawk box*) Now hear this! Now hear this! The Captain is now going to make a personal announcement.

(*Sound of squawk-box switch*)

CAPTAIN (*On squawk box*) Goddammit, how does this thing work? (*Sound of squawk-box switch again*) This is the Captain speaking. I just woke up from a little nap and I got a surprise. I found out there were men on this ship who were expecting liberty. (*At this point, the lights start dimming until the entire scene is blacked out. The speech continues throughout the darkness. Under the* CAPTAIN's *speech the strains of Polynesian music can be heard*) Now I don't know how such a rumor got around, but I'd like to clear it up right now. You see, it's like this. Because of cargo requirements and security conditions which has just come to my personal attention there will be no liberty as long as we're in this here port. And one other thing—as long as we're here, no man will wear white uniforms. Now I would like to repeat for the benefit of complete understanding and clearness, NO LIBERTY. That is all.

SCENE VI

The lights come up on the CAPTAIN's *cabin. Against the left bulkhead is a settee. A chair is placed center. Up center is the only door. The* CAPTAIN *is seated behind his desk, holding a watch in one hand and the microphone in the other, in an attitude of waiting. Just over the desk and against the right bulkhead is a ship's intercommunication board. There is a wall-safe in the right bulkhead. After a moment there is a knock on the door.*

CAPTAIN   Come in, Mister Roberts. (*As* ROBERTS *enters, the* CAPTAIN *puts the microphone on the desk*) Thirty-eight seconds. Pretty good time! You see, I been expectin' you ever since I made my little announcement.

ROBERTS   Well, as long as you're expecting me, what about it—when does this crew get liberty?

CAPTAIN   Well, in the first place, just kinda hold your tongue. And in the second place, sit down.

ROBERTS   There's no time to sit down. When are you going to let this crew go ashore?

CAPTAIN   I'm not. This wasn't my idea—coming to a Liberty Port. One of my officers arranged it with a certain Port Director—gave him a bottle of Scotch whiskey—compliments of the Captain. And the Port Director was kind enough to send me a little thank-you note along with our orders. Sit down, Mister Roberts. (ROBERTS *sits*) Don't worry about it. I'm not going to make trouble about that wasted bottle of Scotch. I'll admit I was a little pre-voked about not being consulted. Then I got to thinking maybe we oughta come to this port anyway so's you and me could have a little talk.

ROBERTS   You can make all the trouble you want, Captain, but let's quit wasting time. Don't you hear that music? Don't you know it's tearing those guys apart? They're breakable, Captain! I promise you!

CAPTAIN   That's enough! I've had enough of your fancy educated talk. (*Rises, goes to* ROBERTS) Now you listen to me. I got two things I want to show you. (*He unlocks the wall-safe, opens it and takes out a commander's cap with gold braid "scrambled eggs" on the visor*) You see that? That's the cap of a full commander. I'm gonna wear that cap some day and you're going to help me. (*Replaces cap in safe, goes back to* ROBERTS) I guess there's no harm in telling you that you helped me get that palm tree by working cargo. Now don't let this go to your head, but when Admiral Finchley gave me that award, he said, "You got a good Cargo Officer, Morton; keep him at it, you're going places." So I went out and bought that hat. There's nothing gonna stand between me and that hat—certainly not you. Now last week you wrote a letter that said "disharmony aboard this ship." I told you there wasn't going to be any more letters. But what do I find on my desk this morning . . . (*Taking letter from desk*) Another

one. It says "friction between myself and the Commanding Officer." That ain't gonna go in, Mister.

ROBERTS   How are you going to stop it, Captain?

CAPTAIN   I ain't, you are. (*Goes to his chair and sits*) Just how
much do you want this crew to have a liberty anyhow? Enough
to stop this "disharmony"? To stop this "friction"? (*Leans forward*) Enough to get out of the habit of writing letters ever?
Because that's the only way this crew is ever gonna get ashore.
(*Leans back*) Well, we've had our little talk. What do you say?

ROBERTS   (*After a moment*)   How did you get in the Navy? How
did you get on our side? You're what I joined to fight *against*.
You ignorant, arrogant, ambitious . . . (*Rises*) jackass! Keeping
a hundred and sixty-seven men in prison because you got a palm
tree for the work *they* did. I don't know which I hate worse—
you or that other malignant growth that stands outside your door!

CAPTAIN   Why, you goddamn . . .

ROBERTS   How did you ever get command of a ship? I realize that
in wartime they have to scrape the bottom of the barrel, but
where the hell did they ever scrape you up?

CAPTAIN   (*Shouting*)   There's just one thing left for you, by God—
a general court-martial.

ROBERTS   That suits me fine. Court-martial me!

CAPTAIN   By God, you've got it!

ROBERTS   I'm asking for it!

CAPTAIN   You don't have to ask for it, you've got it now!

ROBERTS   If I can't get transferred off here, I'll get court-martialed
off! I'm fed up! But you'll need a witness. Send for your messenger. He's down below. I'll say it all again in front of him. (*Pauses*)
Go on, call in Reber! (*The* CAPTAIN *doesn't move*) Go on, call
him. (*Still the* CAPTAIN *doesn't move*) Do you want me to call
him?

CAPTAIN   No. (*He walks upstage, then turns to* ROBERTS) I think
you're a pretty smart boy. I may not talk very good, Mister, but
I know how to take care of smart boys. Let me tell you something.
Let me tell you a little secret. I hate your guts, you college son-
of-a-bitch! You think you're better than I am! You think you're
better because you've had everything handed to you! Let me tell
you something, Mister—I've worked since I was ten years old, and
all my life I've known you superior bastards. I knew you people
when I was a kid in Boston and I worked in eating-places and
you ordered me around. . . . "Oh, bus-boy! My friend here seems

to have thrown up on the table. Clean it up, please." I started
going to sea as a steward and I worked for you then . . . "Steward, take my magazine out to the deck chair!" . . . "Steward, I
don't like your looks. Please keep out of my way as much as
possible!" Well, I took that crap! I took that for years from
pimple-faced bastards who weren't good enough to wipe my
nose! And now I don't have to take it any more! There's a war
on, by God, and I'm the Captain and you can wipe my nose! The
worst thing I can do to you is to keep you on this ship! And that's
where you're going to stay! Now get out of here!

(*He goes to his chair and sits.* ROBERTS *moves slowly toward the
door. He hears the music, goes to the porthole and listens. Then
he turns to the* CAPTAIN)

ROBERTS   Can't you hear that music, Captain?

CAPTAIN   Yeah, I hear it.

(*Busies himself at desk, ignoring* ROBERTS)

ROBERTS   Don't you know those guys below can hear it too? Oh, my
God.

CAPTAIN   Get out of here.

(*After a moment,* ROBERTS *turns from the porthole and slumps
against the* CAPTAIN's *locker. His face is strained*)

ROBERTS   What do you want for liberty, Captain?

CAPTAIN   I want plenty. You're through writin' letters—ever.

ROBERTS   Okay.

CAPTAIN   That's not all. You're through givin' me trouble. You're
through talkin' back to me in front of the crew. You ain't even
gonna open your mouth—except in civil answer. (ROBERTS *doesn't
answer*) Mister Roberts, you know that if you don't take my terms
I'll let you out that door and that's the end of any hope for liberty.

ROBERTS   Is that all, Captain?

CAPTAIN   No. Anyone know you're in here?

ROBERTS   No one.

CAPTAIN   Then you won't go blabbin' about this to anyone ever.
It might not sound so good. And besides I don't want you to take
credit for gettin' this crew ashore.

ROBERTS   Do you think I'm doing this for credit? Do you think I'd
let anyone know about this?

CAPTAIN   I gotta be sure.

ROBERTS   You've got my word, that's all.

CAPTAIN   (*After a pause*)   Your word. Yes, you college fellas make
a big show about keeping your word.

ROBERTS How about it, Captain. Is it a deal?

CAPTAIN Yeah. (ROBERTS *picks up the microphone, turns on a switch and thrusts the microphone at the* CAPTAIN) Now hear this. This is the Captain speaking. I've got some further word on security conditions in this port and so it gives me great pleasure to tell you that liberty, for the starboard section . . .

ROBERTS (*Covering the microphone with his hand*) For the entire crew, goddammit.

CAPTAIN Correction: Liberty for the entire crew will commence immediately.

(ROBERTS *turns off the microphone. After a moment we hear the shouts of the crew.* ROBERTS *goes up to porthole. The* CAPTAIN *leans back on his chair. A song, "Roll Me Over," is started by someone and is soon taken up by the whole crew*)

ROBERTS (*Looking out of the porthole. He is excited and happy*) Listen to those crazy bastards. Listen to them.

(*The crew continues to sing with increasing volume. Now the words can be distinguished:*

Roll me over in the clover,
Roll me over, lay me down
And do it again.)

Curtain

ACT TWO

SCENE I

The curtain rises on the main set. It is now 3:45 A.M. The night is pitch-black, but we can see because of a light over the head of the gangway, where a temporary desk has been rigged; a large ship's logbook lies open on this desk. A small table on which are hospital supplies is at left of the door.

At rise, ROBERTS, DOC, LINDSTROM, JOHNSON *and four* SEAMEN *are discovered onstage.* LINDSTROM, *in web belt, is writing in the log.* ROBERTS *is standing with a pile of yellow slips in his hand; he wears the side-arms of the Officer of the Deck.* JOHNSON *and a* SEAMAN *are standing near the hatchway, holding the inert body of another* SEAMAN, *who has court plaster on his face. Two more* SEAMEN *lie on the hatch cover where* DOC *is kneeling, bandaging one of them. As the curtain rises we hear the sound of a siren off right. Everyone turns and looks—that is, everyone who is conscious.*

LINDSTROM   Here's another batch, Mister Roberts—a whole paddy wagon full. And this one's an Army paddy wagon.

ROBERTS   We haven't filed away this batch yet. (*To* DOC) Hurry up, Doc.

JOHNSON (*To* DOC, *indicating body he is carrying*)   Where do we put number twenty-three here, Doc? Sick bay or what?

DOC   Just put him to bed. His condition's only critical.

JOHNSON (*Carrying* SEAMAN *off*)   They just roll out of their bunks, Doc. Now I'm stacking 'em on the deck down there—I'm on the third layer already.

VOICE (*Offstage*)   Okay, Lieutenant! All set down here! You ready?

ROBERTS (*Calling offstage—and giving hand signal*)   Okay! (*To* DOC) Here they come, Doc! Heads up!

SHORE PATROLMAN'S VOICE (*Offstage*)   Lieutenant!

ROBERTS   Oh, not you again!

SHORE PATROLMAN'S VOICE (*Offstage*)   I got a bunch of real beauties for you this time.

ROBERTS (*Calling offstage*)   Can they walk?

SHORE PATROLMAN'S VOICE (*Offstage*)   Just barely!

ROBERTS (*Calling*)   Then send 'em up.

LINDSTROM   Man, oh, man, what a liberty! We got the record now, Mister Roberts! This makes the seventh batch since we went on watch!

(*The sound of a cargo winch and a voice offstage singing the Army Air Corps song are heard.* ROBERTS *is looking offstage*)

ROBERTS (*Signaling*)   Looks like a real haul this time. Schlemmer, look out!

LINDSTROM   Schlemmer, look out!

ROBERTS   Okay, Doc. (DOC *and* ROBERTS *lift the two bodies from the hatch cover and deposit them farther upstage. At this moment, the cargo net appears, loaded with bodies in once-white uniforms and leis. Riding on top of the net is* SCHLEMMER, *wearing a lei and singing "Off We Go into the Wild Blue Yonder"*) Let her in easy . . .

LINDSTROM   Let her in easy . . .

(*The net is lowered onto the hatch cover and* LINDSTROM *detaches it from the hook. All start untangling bodies*)

ROBERTS   Well, they're peaceful anyhow.

(*At this point a* SHORE PATROLMAN *enters from the gangway*)

SHORE PATROLMAN (*Handing* ROBERTS *a sheaf of yellow slips*)   For your collection. (*Points down gangway*) Take a look at them.

ROBERTS (*Looks offstage*)   My God, what did they do?

SHORE PATROLMAN   They done all right, Lieutenant. Six of them busted into a formal dance and took on a hundred and twenty-eight Army bastards. (*Calls off*) All right, let's go!

(STEFANOWSKI, REBER, WILEY, PAYNE *and* MANNION, *with his arm around* INSIGNA, *straggle on—a frightening sight—followed by a* MILITARY POLICEMAN. INSIGNA'S *uniform is torn to shreds.* MANNION *is clad in a little diaper of crepe paper. All have bloody faces and uniforms. A few bear souvenirs—a Japanese lantern, leis, Army caps, a Shore Patrol band, etc. They throw perfunctory salutes to the colors, then murmur a greeting to* ROBERTS)

MILITARY POLICEMAN   Duty Officer?

ROBERTS   That's right.

MILITARY POLICEMAN (*Salutes*)   Colonel Middleton presents his compliments to the Captain and wishes him to know that these men made a shambles out of the Colonel's testimonial dinner-dance.

ROBERTS   Is this true, Insigna?

INSIGNA   That's right, Mister Roberts. A shambles. (*To* MANNION) Ain't that right, Killer?

MANNION   That's right, Mister Roberts.

ROBERTS   You men crashed a dance for Army personnel?

MANNION   Yes, sir! And they made us feel unwelcome! (*To* IN-SIGNA) Didn't they, Slugger?

ROBERTS   Oh, they started a fight, eh?

WILEY   No, sir! *We* started it!

STEFANOWSKI   We finished it too! (*To* MILITARY POLICEMAN) Tell Mister Roberts how many of you Army bastards are in the hospital.

MANNION   Go on.

MILITARY POLICEMAN   Thirty-eight soldiers of the United States Army have been hospitalized. And the Colonel himself has a very bad bruise on his left shin!

PAYNE   *I* did that, Mister Roberts.

MILITARY POLICEMAN   And that isn't all, Lieutenant. There were young ladies present—fifty of them. Colonel Middleton had been lining them up for a month, from the best families of Elysium. And he had personally guaranteed their safety this evening. Well, sir . . .

ROBERTS   Well?

MILITARY POLICEMAN   Two of those young ladies got somewhat mauled, one actually got a black eye, six of them got their clothes torn off and then went screaming off into the night and they haven't been heard from since. What are you going to do about it, Lieutenant?

ROBERTS   Well, I'm due to get relieved here in fifteen minutes—I'll be glad to lead a search party.

MILITARY POLICEMAN   No, sir. The Army's taking care of that end. The Colonel will want to know what punishment you're going to give these men.

ROBERTS   Tell the Colonel that I'm sure our Captain will think of something.

MILITARY POLICEMAN   But . . .

ROBERTS   That's all, Sergeant.

MILITARY POLICEMAN   (*Salutes*)   Thank you, sir.

(*He goes off*)

SHORE PATROLMAN Lieutenant, I been pretty sore at your guys up till now—we had to put on ten extra Shore Patrolmen on account of this ship. But if you knew Colonel "Chicken" Middleton—well, I'd be willing to do this every night. (*To the men*) So long, fellows!

(*The men call "So long."* SHORE PATROLMAN *exits, saluting* ROBERTS *and quarter-deck*)

ROBERTS Well, what've you got to say for yourselves?

STEFANOWSKI (*After a moment*) Okay if we go ashore again, Mister Roberts?

ROBERTS (*To* LINDSTROM) Is this the first time for these guys?

LINDSTROM (*Showing log*) Yes, sir, they got a clean record—they only been brought back once.

ROBERTS What do you say, Doc?

(*The men turn eagerly to* DOC)

DOC Anybody got a fractured skull?

MEN No.

DOC Okay, you pass the physical.

ROBERTS Go down and take a shower first and get into some clothes.

(*The men rush to the hatchway*)

STEFANOWSKI We still got time to get back to that dance!

(*As they descend hatchway,* INSIGNA *pulls crepe paper from around* MANNION *as he is halfway down the hatchway*)

ROBERTS How you feeling, Doc?

DOC These alcohol fumes are giving me a cheap drunk—otherwise pretty routine. When do you get relieved, Doug? (*Takes box from table and gestures for men to remove table. They carry it off*)

ROBERTS Soon as Carney gets back from the island. Any minute now.

DOC What are you grinning like a skunk for?

ROBERTS Nothing. I always grin like a skunk. What have you got in the box?

DOC (*Descending hatchway—holding up small packet he has taken from the box*) Little favors from the Doc. I'm going to put one in each man's hand and when he wakes up he'll find pinned to his shirt full instructions for its use. I think it'll save me a lot of work later on.

(*His head disappears*)

LINDSTROM   I wish Gerhart would get back here and relieve me. I've got to get over to that island before it runs out of women.

(DOLAN *enters from gangway*)

DOLAN   Howdy, Mister Roberts! I'm drunk as a goat! (*Pulls a goat aboard*) Show him how drunk I am. Mister Roberts, when I first saw her she was eatin', and you know, she just eat her way into my heart. She was eatin' a little old palm tree and I thought to myself, our ship needs a mascot. (*He points out palm tree to goat*) There you are, kid. Chow!

(ROBERTS *blocks his way*)

ROBERTS   Wait a minute . . . wait a minute. What's her name?

DOLAN   I don't know, sir.

ROBERTS   She's got a name plate.

DOLAN   Oh, so she has . . . her name is . . . (*Reads from tag on goat's collar*) . . . Property Of.

ROBERTS   What's her last name?

DOLAN   Her last name . . . (*Reads again*) Rear Admiral Wentworth.

(*Approaching siren is heard offstage*)

ROBERTS   Okay, Dolan, hit the sack. I'll take care of her.

DOLAN   Okay, Mister Roberts. (*Descends hatchway*) See that she gets a good square meal.

(*He points to the* CAPTAIN's *palm tree and winks, then disappears.* GERHART *enters from gangway*)

LINDSTROM   Gerhart!

(LINDSTROM *frantically removes his web belt and shoves it at* GERHART)

GERHART   Okay, okay—you're relieved.

LINDSTROM   (*Tosses a fast salute to* ROBERTS *and says in one breath*) Requestpermissiontogoashore!

(*He hurries down gangway.* SHORE PATROLMAN *enters from gangway*)

SHORE PATROLMAN   Lieutenant, has one of your men turned up with a . . . (*Sees goat and takes leash*) Oh, Thanks. (*To goat*) Come on, come on, your papa over there is worried about you.

(*Pulls goat down gangway*)

GERHART   Where's your relief, Mister Roberts?

ROBERTS   (*Sitting on hatch*) He'll be along any minute. How was your liberty, Gerhart?

(GERHART *grins. So does* ROBERTS. DOC *enters from hatchway*)

DOC   What are you looking so cocky about anyway?

ROBERTS Am I looking cocky? Maybe it's because for the first time since I've been on this ship, I'm seeing a crew.

DOC What do you think you've been living with all this time?

ROBERTS Just a hundred and sixty-seven separate guys. There's a big difference, Doc. Now these guys are bound together. You saw Insigna and Mannion. Doc, I think these guys are strong enough now to take all the miserable, endless days ahead of us. I only hope I'm strong enough.

DOC Doug, tomorrow you and I are going over there and take advantage of the groundwork that's been laid tonight. You and I are going to have ourselves a liberty.

(PULVER *enters slowly from the gangway and walks across the stage.* DOC *calls* ROBERTS' *attention to him*)

ROBERTS Hello, Frank. How was your liberty?

(PULVER *half turns, shrugs and holds up seven fingers, then exits. A* SHORE PATROL OFFICER *enters from the gangway and calls offstage. He speaks with a Southern accent*)

SHORE PATROL OFFICER That's your post and that's your post. You know what to do. (*He salutes the quarter-deck, then* ROBERTS) Officer of the Deck? (ROBERTS *nods. The* SHORE PATROL OFFICER *hesitates a moment*) I hope you don't mind but I've stationed two of my men at the foot of the gangway. I'm sorry but this ship is restricted for the rest of its stay in Elysium. Your Captain is to report to the Island Commander at seven o'clock this morning. I'd recommend that he's there on time. The Admiral's a pretty tough cookie when he's mad, and he's madder now than I've ever seen him.

ROBERTS What in particular did this?

SHORE PATROL LIEUTENANT A little while ago six men from your ship broke into the home of the French Consul and started throwing things through the plate-glass living-room window. We found some of the things on the lawn: a large world globe, a small love seat, a lot of books and a bust of Balzac—the French writer. We also found an Army private first class who was unconscious at the time. He claims they threw him too.

ROBERTS Through the window?

SHORE PATROL LIEUTENANT That's right! It seems he took them there for a little joke. He didn't tell them it was the Consul's house; he said it was a—what we call in Alabama—a cat-house. (ROBERTS *and* DOC *nod*) Be sure that your Captain is there at seven o'clock sharp. If it makes you feel any better, Admiral Wentworth says

this is the worst ship he's ever seen in his entire naval career.
(*Laughs, then salutes*) Good night, Lieutenant.

ROBERTS (*Returning salute*)   Good night.

(*The* SHORE PATROL LIEUTENANT *exits down gangway—saluting the quarter-deck*)

GERHART   Well, there goes the liberty. That was sure a wham-bam-thank you, ma'am!

DOC   Good night.

(*He exits through left passageway*)

GERHART   But, by God, it was worth it. That liberty was worth anything!

ROBERTS   I think you're right, Gerhart.

GERHART   Hunh?

ROBERTS   I think you're right.

GERHART   Yeah.

(*He smiles.* ROBERTS *looks over the log.* GERHART *whistles softly to himself "Roll Me Over" as the lights slowly*

Fade Out

(*During the darkness we hear* JOHNSON *shouting*)

JOHNSON   All right, fall in for muster. Form two ranks. And pipe down.

SCENE II

The lights come up, revealing the deck. Morning sunlight. A group of men, right and left, in orderly formation. They are talking.

JOHNSON   'Ten-shun!

(*The command is relayed through the ship. The* CAPTAIN *enters from his cabin, followed by* ROBERTS. *The* CAPTAIN *steps up on the hatch cover.* ROBERTS *starts to fall in with the men*)

CAPTAIN (*Calling to* ROBERTS *and pointing to a place beside himself on hatch cover*)   Over here, Roberts. (ROBERTS *takes his place left of* CAPTAIN) We're being kicked out of this port. I had a feeling this liberty was a bad idea. That's why we'll never have one again. We're going to erase this blot from my record if we have to work twenty-four hours a day. We're going to move even more cargo than we've ever moved before. And if there ain't enough cargo work, Mister Roberts here is gonna find some. Isn't that right, Mister Roberts? (ROBERTS *doesn't answer*) Isn't that right, Mister Roberts?

ROBERTS Yes, sir.

CAPTAIN I'm appointing Mister Roberts here and now to see that you men toe the line. And I can't think of a more honorable man for the job. He's a man who keeps his word no matter what. (*Turns to* ROBERTS) Now, Roberts, if you do a good job—and if the Admiral begins to smile on us again—there might be something in it for you. What would you say if that little silver bar on your collar got a twin brother some day? (ROBERTS *is startled. The* CAPTAIN *calls offstage*) Officer of the Deck!

OFFSTAGE VOICE Yes, sir!

CAPTAIN (*To* ROBERTS) You wasn't expectin' that, was you? (*Calling offstage*) Get ready to sail!

OFFSTAGE VOICE Aye-aye, sir!

CAPTAIN You men are dismissed!

JOHNSON Fall out!

(*The men fall out. Some exit. A little group forms downstage*)

CAPTAIN Wait a minute! Wait a minute! Roberts, take these men here back aft to handle lines. And see that they work up a sweat. (ROBERTS *and men look at him*) Did you hear me, Roberts? I gave you an order!

ROBERTS (*Carefully*) Yes, Captain. I heard you.

CAPTAIN How do you answer when I give an order?

ROBERTS (*After a pause*) Aye-aye, sir.

CAPTAIN That's more like it . . . that's more like it!

(*He exits into his cabin*)

STEFANOWSKI What'd he mean, Mister Roberts?

ROBERTS I don't know. Just what he said, I guess.

GERHART What'd you let him give you all that guff for?

DOLAN (*Stepping up on hatch, carrying a file folder*) Because he's tired, that's why. He had the mid-watch last night. Your tail'd be dragging too if you had to handle all them customers.

ROBERTS Come on. Let's get going . . .

DOLAN Wait a minute, Mister Roberts. Something come for you in the mail this morning—a little love letter from the Bureau. (*Pulls out paper from file folder*) Get a load of this! (*Reads*) "To All Ships and Stations: Heightened war offensive has created urgent need aboard combat ships for experienced officers. (*He clicks his teeth and winks at* ROBERTS) All commanding officers are hereby directed to forward with their endorsements all applications for transfer from officers with twenty-four months' sea duty." (ROB-ERTS *grabs the directive and reads it.* DOLAN *looks at* ROBERTS *and smiles*) You got twenty-nine months—you're the only officer aboard that has. Mister Roberts, the Old Man is hanging on the ropes from the working-over the Admiral give him. All he needs to flatten him is one more little jab. And here it is. Your letter. I typed it up. (*He pulls out triplicate letters from file cover—then a fountain pen which he offers to* ROBERTS) Sign it and I'll take it in—

MANNION   Go on, sign it, Mister Roberts. He'll take off like a bird.

DOLAN   What're you waitin' for, Mister Roberts?

ROBERTS   (*Handing directive back to* DOLAN) I'll want to look it over first, Dolan. Come on, let's get going.

DOLAN   There's nothing to look over. This is the same letter we wrote yesterday—only quoting this new directive.

ROBERTS   Look, Dolan, I'm tired. And I told you I wanted—

DOLAN   You ain't too tired to sign your name!

ROBERTS   (*Sharply*) Take it easy, Dolan. I'm not going to sign it. So take it easy! (*Turns to exit right, finds himself blocked by crew*) Did you hear me? Let's get going!
(*Exits*)

STEFANOWSKI   What the hell's come over him?
(*They look at one another*)

INSIGNA   Aye-aye, sir—for Christ's sake!

MANNION   (*After a moment*)   Come on. Let's get going.

DOLAN   (*Bitterly*)   "Take it easy . . . take it easy!"
(*The men start to move off slowly as the lights*)

Fade Out

(*During the darkness we hear a radio. There is considerable static*)

AMERICAN BROADCASTER   Still, of course, we have no official word from the Headquarters of the Supreme Allied Command in Europe. I repeat, there is no official announcement yet. The report that the war in Europe has ended has come from only one correspondent. It has not been confirmed by other correspondents or by SHAEF headquarters. But here is one highly intriguing fact—that report has not been denied either in Washington or in

SHAEF headquarters in Europe. IT HAS NOT BEEN DENIED. Right now in those places the newsmen are crowded, waiting to flash to the world the announcement of V-E Day.

SCENE III

The lights come up on ROBERTS' *and* PULVER'S *cabin.* DOC, *at the desk, and* PULVER, *up in his bunk, are listening to the radio.*

PULVER Turn that damn thing off, Doc. Has Doug ever said anything to you about wanting a promotion?

DOC Of course not. I doubt if he's even conscious of what rank he is.

PULVER You can say that again!

DOC I doubt if he's even conscious of what rank he is.

PULVER That's what I said. He doesn't even think about a promotion. The only thing he thinks about is the war news—up in the radio shack two weeks now—all day long—listening with a headset, reading all the bulletins . . . Anyone who says he's bucking for another stripe is a dirty liar.

DOC Who says he is, Frank?

PULVER Insigna, Mannion and some of the other guys. I heard them talking outside the porthole. They were talking loud on purpose so I could hear them—they must've guessed I was lying here on my bunk. What's happened to Doug anyway, Doc?

DOC How would I know! He's spoken about ten words to me in as many days. But I'm damn well going to find out.

PULVER He won't talk, Doc. This morning I followed him all around the room while he was shaving. I begged him to talk to me. I says, "You're a fellow who needs a friend and here I am." And I says, "What's all this trouble you're having with the crew? You tell me and I'll fix it up like that." And then I give him some real good advice—I says, "Keep your chin up," and things like that. And then do you know what he did? He walked out of the room just as though I wasn't here.

(*There is a knock on the door*)

DOC Come in.

(DOWDY *enters*)

DOWDY Doc, Mister Pulver—could we see you officers a minute?

DOC   Sure. (GERHART *and* LINDSTROM *enter, closing the door*) What is it?

DOWDY   Tell them what happened, Gerhart.

GERHART   Well, sir, I sure don't like to say this but . . . Mister Roberts just put Dolan on report.

LINDSTROM   Me and Gerhart seen him.

PULVER   On report!

GERHART   Yes, sir. Tomorrow morning Dolan has to go up before the Captain—on account of Mister Roberts.

LINDSTROM   On account of Mister Roberts.

GERHART   And we was wondering if you officers could get him to take Dolan off report before . . . well, before—

DOC   Before what, Gerhart?

GERHART   Well, you see, the guys are all down in the compartment, talking about it. And they're saying some pretty rough things about Mister Roberts. Nobody just ever expected to see him put a man on report and . . .

LINDSTROM   He ain't gonna turn out to be like an officer, is he, Doc?

DOWDY   Lindstrom . . .

LINDSTROM   Oh, I didn't mean you, Doc . . . or even you, Mister Pulver!

DOC   That's all right, Lindstrom. What was this trouble with Dolan?

DOWDY   This letter business again!

GERHART   Yes, sir. Dolan was just kiddin' him about not sending in any more letters. And all of a sudden Mister Roberts turned just white and yelled, "Shut up, Dolan. Shut your goddamn mouth. I've had enough." And Dolan naturally got snotty back at him and Mister Roberts put him right on report.

LINDSTROM   Right on report.

  (ROBERTS *enters*)

PULVER   Hello, Doug boy. Aren't you listening to the war news?

DOWDY   All right, Doctor. We'll get that medical store room cleaned out tomorrow.

  (DOWDY, GERHART *and* LINDSTROM *leave*)

PULVER   We thought you were up in the radio shack.

ROBERTS   (*To* PULVER)   Don't you want to go down to the wardroom and have a cup of coffee?

PULVER   (*Jumping down from bunk*)   Sure. I'll go with you.

ROBERTS   I don't want any. Why don't you go ahead?

PULVER   Nah.

  (*He sits back on bunk. There is another little pause*)

ROBERTS   Will you go on out anyway? I want to talk to Doc.

PULVER (*Rising and crossing to door*) All right, I will. I'm going for a cup of coffee. (*Stops, turns and gets cap from top of locker*) No! I'm going up to the radio shack. You aren't the only one interested in the war news.

(*He exits*)

ROBERTS (*With emotion*) Doc, transfer me, will you? (DOC *looks at him*) Transfer me to the hospital on this next island! You can do it. You don't need the Captain's approval! Just put me ashore for examination—say there's something wrong with my eyes or my feet or my head, for Christ's sake! You can trump up something!

DOC What good would that do?

ROBERTS Plenty! I could lie around that hospital for a couple of weeks. The ship would have sailed—I'd have missed it! I'd be off this ship. Will you do it, Doc?

DOC Doug, why did you put Dolan on report just now?

ROBERTS (*Angrily*) I gave him an order and he didn't carry it out fast enough to suit me. (*Glares at* DOC, *who just studies him.* ROBERTS *rises and paces right*) No, that's not true. It was the war. I just heard the news. The war is ending and I couldn't get to it and there was Dolan giving me guff about something—and all of a sudden I hated him. I hated all of them. I was sick of the sullen bastards staring at me as though I'd sold them down the river or something. If they think I'm bucking for a promotion—if they're stupid enough to think I'd walk ten feet across the room to get anything from that Captain, then I'm through with the whole damn ungrateful mob!

DOC Does this crew owe you something?

ROBERTS What the hell do you mean by that?

DOC You talk as if they did.

(ROBERTS *rises and crosses to bunk*)

ROBERTS (*Quietly*) That's exactly how I'm talking. I didn't realize it but that's exactly the way I've been feeling. Oh, Jesus, that shows you how far gone I am, Doc. I've been taking something out on them. I've been blaming them for something that . . .

DOC What, Doug? Something what? You've made some sort of an agreement with the Captain, haven't you, Doug!

ROBERTS (*Turns*) Agreement? I don't know what you mean. Will you transfer me, Doc?

DOC Not a chance, Doug. I could never get away with it—you know that.

ROBERTS Oh, my God!

PULVER (*Offstage*) Doug! Doc! (*Entering*) Listen to the radio, you uninformed bastards! Turn it up!

(ROBERTS *reaches over and turns up the radio. The excited voice of an announcer can be heard*)

ANNOUNCER . . . this broadcast to bring you a special news flash! The war is over in Europe! THE WAR IS OVER IN EUROPE! (ROBERTS *grasps* DOC's *arm in excitement*) Germany has surrendered unconditionally to the Allied Armies. The surrender was signed in a schoolhouse in the city of Rheims . . .

(ROBERTS *stands staring.* DOC *turns off the radio. For a moment there is silence, then*)

DOC I would remind you that there's still a minor skirmish here in the Pacific.

ROBERTS I'll miss that one too. But to hell with me. This is the greatest day in the world. We're going to celebrate. How about it, Frank?

PULVER Yeah, Doug. We've got to celebrate!

DOC (*Starting to pull alcohol from waste basket*) What'll it be—alcohol and orange juice or orange juice and alcohol?

ROBERTS No, that's not good enough.

PULVER Hell, no, Doc!

(*He looks expectantly at* ROBERTS)

ROBERTS We've got to think of something that'll lift this ship right out of the water and turn it around the other way.

(PULVER *suddenly rises to his feet*)

PULVER (*Shouting*) Doug! Oh, my God, why didn't I think of this before. Doug! Doc! You're going to blow your tops when you hear the idea I got! Oh, Jesus, what a wonderful idea! It's the only thing to do. It's the only thing in the whole world to do! That's all! Doug, you said I never had any ideas. You said I never finished anything I started. Well, you're wrong—tonight you're wrong! I thought of something and I finished it. I was going to save it for your birthday, but I'm going to give it to you tonight, because we gotta celebrate . . .

ROBERTS (*Waves his hands in* PULVER's *face for attention*) Wait a minute, Frank! What is it?

PULVER A firecracker, by God. (*He reaches under his mattress and pulls out a large, wobbly firecracker which has been painted red*) We're gonna throw a firecracker under the Old Man's bunk. Bam-bam-bam! Wake up, you old son-of-a-bitch, IT'S V-E DAY!

ROBERTS (*Rising*) Frank!

PULVER Look at her, Doc. Ain't it a beauty? Ain't that the greatest hand-made, hand-painted, hand-packed firecracker you ever saw?

ROBERTS (*Smiling and taking firecracker*) Yes, Frank. That's the most beautiful firecracker I ever saw in my life. But will it work?

PULVER Sure it'll work. At least, I think so.

ROBERTS Haven't you tested it? It's got to work, Frank, it's just got to work!

PULVER I'll tell you what I'll do. I'll take it down to the laundry and test it—that's my laboratory, the laundry. I got all the fixings down there—powder, fuses, everything, all hid behind the soapflakes. And if this one works, I can make another one in two minutes.

ROBERTS Okay, Frank. Take off. We'll wait for you here. (PULVER *starts off*) Be sure you got enough to make it loud. What'd you use for powder?

PULVER Loud! This ain't a popgun. This is a firecracker. I used fulminate of mercury. I'll be right back.
(*He runs out*)

ROBERTS Fulminate of mercury! That stuff's murder! Do you think he means it?

DOC (*Taking alcohol bottle from waste basket*) Of course not. Where could he get fulminate of mercury?

ROBERTS I don't know. He's pretty resourceful. Where did he get the clap last year?

DOC How about a drink, Doug?
(*He pours alcohol and orange juice into two glasses*)

ROBERTS Right! Doc, I been living with a genius. This makes it all worth while—the whole year and a half he spent in his bunk. How else could you celebrate V-E Day? A firecracker under the Old Man's bunk! The silly little son-of-a-bitch!

DOC (*Handing* ROBERTS *a drink*) Here you are, Doug. (DOC *holds the drink up in a toast*) To better days!

ROBERTS Okay. And to a great American, Frank Thurlowe Pulver . . . Soldier . . . Statesman . . . Scientist . . .

DOC Friend of the Working Girl . . .
(*Suddenly there is a tremendous explosion.* DOC *and* ROBERTS *clutch at the desk*)

ROBERTS Oh, my God!

DOC He wasn't kidding! That's fulminate of mercury!

CAPTAIN (*Offstage*) What was that?
(ROBERTS *and* DOC *rush to porthole, listening*)

JOHNSON (*Offstage*)   I don't know, Captain. I'll find out!
(*We hear the sounds of running feet*)

ROBERTS   Doc, we've got to go down and get him.

DOC   This may be pretty bad, Doug.

(*They turn to start for the door when suddenly a figure hurtles into the room and stops. For a moment it looks like a combination scarecrow and snowman but it is* PULVER—*his uniform tattered; his knees, arms and face blackened; he is covered with soapsuds and his eyes are shining with excitement.* ROBERTS *stares in amazement*)

PULVER   Jeez, that stuff's terrific!

DOC   Are you all right?

PULVER   I'm great! Gee, you should've been there!

ROBERTS   You aren't burned—or anything?

PULVER   Hell, no. But the laundry's kinda beat up. The mangle's on the other side of the room now. And there's a new porthole on the starboard side where the electric iron went through. And I guess a steam-line must've busted or something—I was up to my ass in lather. And soapflakes flyin' around—it was absolutely beautiful!

(*During these last lines,* DOC *has been making a brisk, professional examination*)

DOC   It's a miracle. He isn't even scratched!

PULVER   Come on down and see it, Doug. It's a Winter Wonderland!

CAPTAIN (*Offstage*)   Johnson!

ROBERTS   Quiet!

JOHNSON (*Offstage*)   Yes, sir.

CAPTAIN (*Offstage*)   What was it?

JOHNSON (*Offstage*)   The laundry, Captain. A steam-line must've blew up.

PULVER (*Explaining*)   Steam-line came right out of the bulkhead. (*He demonstrates*) Whish!

CAPTAIN (*Offstage*)   How much damage?

JOHNSON (*Offstage*)   We can't tell yet, Captain. We can't get in there—the passageway is solid soapsuds.

PULVER   Solid soapsuds.

(*He pantomimes walking blindly through soapsuds*)

CAPTAIN (*Offstage*)   Tell those men to be more careful.

ROBERTS (*Excitedly*)   Frank, our celebration is just getting started. The night is young and our duty's clear.

PULVER   Yeah? What're we gonna do now, Doug?

ROBERTS   Get cleaned up, and come with me.

PULVER   Where we goin' now, Doug?

ROBERTS   We're going down and get the rest of your stuff. You proved it'd work—you just hit the wrong target, that's all. We're going to make another firecracker, and put it where it really belongs.

PULVER   (*Who has slowly wilted during* ROBERTS' *speech*)   The rest of my stuff was—in the laundry, Doug. It all went up. There isn't any more. I'm sorry, Doug. I'm awful sorry.

ROBERTS   (*Sinks into chair*)   That's all right, Frank.

PULVER   Maybe I can scrounge some more tomorrow.

ROBERTS   Sure.

PULVER   You aren't sore at me, are you, Doug?

ROBERTS   What for?

PULVER   For spoilin' our celebration?

ROBERTS   Of course not.

PULVER   It was a good idea though, wasn't it, Doug?

ROBERTS   Frank, it was a great idea. I'm proud of you. It just didn't work, that's all.

(*He starts for the door*)

DOC   Where are you going, Doug?

ROBERTS   Out on deck.

PULVER   Wait'll I get cleaned up and I'll come with you.

ROBERTS   No, I'm going to turn in after that. (*To* PULVER) It's okay, Frank.

(*He exits.* PULVER *turns pleadingly to* DOC)

PULVER   He was happy there for a minute though, wasn't he, Doc? Did you see him laughing? He was happy as hell. (*Pause*) We gotta do something for that guy, Doc. He's in bad shape. What's the matter with him anyhow, Doc. Did you find out?

DOC   No, he wouldn't tell me. But I know one thing he's feeling tonight and that's panic. Tonight he feels his war is dying before he can get to it.

(DOC *goes to radio and turns up volume*)

PULVER   I let him down. He wanted to celebrate and I let him down.

(*He drops his head.* ANNOUNCER'S VOICE *on radio comes up as the lights*

Fade Out

(*During the darkness and under the first part of Scene IV we hear the voice of a British broadcaster*)

BRITISH BROADCASTER . . . we hope that the King and Queen will come out. The crowds are cheering—listen to them—and at any second now we hope to see Their Majesties. The color here is tremendous—everywhere rosettes, everywhere gay, red-white-and-blue hats. All the girls in their summer frocks on this lovely, mild, historic May evening. And although we celebrate with joyous heart the great victory, perhaps the greatest victory in the history of mankind, the underlying mood is a mood of thanksgiving. And now, I believe, they're coming. They haven't appeared but the crowd in the center are cheering madly. Handkerchiefs, flags, hands waving—HERE THEY COME! First, Her Majesty, the Queen, has come into view. Then the King in the uniform of an Admiral of the Fleet. The two Princesses standing on the balcony—listen to the crowd—

(*Sound of wild cheering. This broadcast continues throughout the blackout and the next scene. Several times the station is changed, from a broadcast of the celebration in San Francisco to the speaker in New York and the band playing "The Stars and Stripes Forever" in Times Square*)

SCENE IV

The lights dim up on the main set. It is a few minutes later, and bright moonlight. The ship is under way—this is indicated by the apparent movement of the stars, slowly up and down. A group of men are sitting on the hatch cover in a late bull session. They are INSIGNA, MANNION, DOLAN *and* STEFANOWSKI. GERHART *stands over them; he has obviously just returned from some mission for the group.*

GERHART I'm telling you, that's all it was. A steam pipe busted in the laundry—they're cleaning it up now. It ain't worth going to see. (*The others make way for him and he sits down beside them.* INSIGNA *cocks his head toward the sound of the radio*)

INSIGNA What the hell's all the jabbering on the radio now?

MANNION I don't know. Something about the King and Queen . . .

(The men listen for a moment without curiosity; then, as the radio fades, they settle back in indolent positions)

INSIGNA Well, anyhow, like I was telling you, this big sergeant in Elysium was scared to fight me! Tell 'em how big he was, Killer.

MANNION Six foot seven or eight . . .

STEFANOWSKI That sergeant's grown eight inches since we left Elysium . . . Did you see me when I swiped that Shore Patrol band and went around arresting guys? That Shore Patrol Lieutenant said I was the best man he had. I arrested forty-three guys . . .

MANNION *(Smiles at DOLAN who is looking depressed)* Come on, Dolan, don't let him get you down.

INSIGNA Yeah, come on, Dolan.

(ROBERTS enters. He looks at the men, who have their backs turned, hesitates, then goes slowly over to them)

GERHART *(Idly)* What was them croquette things we had for chow tonight?

(STEFANOWSKI looks up and notices ROBERTS. Instantly he sits upright)

STEFANOWSKI Flash Red!

(The men sit up. There is an embarrassed silence)

ROBERTS Good evening. *(The men smile politely. ROBERTS is very embarrassed)* Did you hear the news? The war's over in Europe.

MANNION *(Smiling)* Yes, sir. We heard.

STEFANOWSKI *(Helping out the conversation)* Sure. Maybe somebody'll get on the ball out here now . . .

(DOLAN rises, starts down hatchway)

ROBERTS Dolan, I guess I kind of blew my top tonight. I'm sorry. I'm taking you off report.

DOLAN Whatever you want, sir . . . *(He looks ostentatiously at his watch and yawns)* Well, I guess I'll hit the old sack . . .

(He goes down hatchway)

MANNION Yeah, me too . . .

INSIGNA Yeah . . .

GERHART It's late as hell.

STEFANOWSKI I didn't realize how late it was . . .

(All the men get up, then go down the hatchway. ROBERTS stands looking after them. Now the radio is heard again. ROBERTS goes to hatchway and sits listening)

SPEAKER . . . Our boys have won this victory today. But the rest is up to you. You and you alone must recognize our enemies: the forces of ambition, cruelty, arrogance and stupidity. You must recognize them, you must destroy them, you must tear them out as you would a malignant growth! And cast them from the surface of the earth!

(*The end of the speech is followed by a band playing "The Stars and Stripes Forever."* ROBERTS' *face lights up and a new determination is in it. He repeats the words "malignant growth." The band music swells. He marches to the palm tree, salutes it, rubs his hands together and, as the music reaches a climax, he jerks the palm tree, earth and all, from the container and throws it over the side. Then, as the music continues, loud and climactic, he brushes his hands together, shrugs, and walks casually off left singing the tune to himself. For a moment the stage is empty. Then the lights go up in the* CAPTAIN'S *cabin. The door to the* CAPTAIN'S *cabin opens and the* CAPTAIN *appears. He is in pajamas and bathrobe, and in one hand he carries his watering can. He discovers the empty container. He looks at it, then plunges into his cabin. After a moment, the General Alarm is heard. It is a terrible clanging noise designed to rouse the dead. When the alarm stops, the* CAPTAIN'S *voice is heard, almost hysterical, over the squawk box*)

CAPTAIN   General Quarters! General Quarters! Every man to his battle station on the double!

(JOHNSON, *in helmet and life jacket, scurries from hatchway into the* CAPTAIN'S *cabin.* WILEY *enters from right passageway and climbs into the right gun tub. Now men appear from all directions in various degrees of dress. The stage is filled with men frantically running everywhere, all wearing helmets and life preservers*)

INSIGNA   (*Appearing from hatchway*)   What happened? (*He runs up the ladder and into the left gun tub.* PAYNE *enters from left and starts to climb up to left gun tub*) Get the hell out of here, Payne. This ain't your gun—your gun's over there!

DOLAN   (*Also trying to climb the ladder with* PAYNE)   Over there . . . over there . . .

(PAYNE *crosses to right gun tub*)

REBER   (*Entering from hatchway*)   What the hell happened?

SCHLEMMER   Are *we* in an air raid?

PAYNE   Submarine . . . must be a submarine!

GERHART   Hey, Wiley, what happened?

DOWDY   (*Calling to someone on life raft*)   Hey, get away from that life raft. He didn't say abandon ship!

(*During the confusion,* STEFANOWSKI, *bewildered, emerges from the hatchway and wanders over to right gun tub*)

STEFANOWSKI Hey, Wiley, Wiley—you sure you're supposed to be up there?

WILEY Yeah.

STEFANOWSKI (*Crossing to left gun tub*) Hey, Sam. Are you supposed to be up there?

INSIGNA Yeah, we was here last year!

STEFANOWSKI Hey, Dowdy. Where the hell's my battle station?

DOWDY I don't know where your battle station is! Look around!

(STEFANOWSKI *wanders aimlessly about.* WILEY, *in the gun tub right, is receiving reports of battle readiness from various parts of the ship*)

WILEY Twenty millimeters manned and ready. (*Pause*) Engine room manned and ready. (*Pause*) All battle stations manned and ready.

STEFANOWSKI (*Sitting on corner of hatch*) Yeah, all but mine . . .

JOHNSON'S VOICE (*In* CAPTAIN'S *cabin*) All battle stations manned and ready, Captain.

CAPTAIN'S VOICE Give me that thing.

JOHNSON'S VOICE (*"On mike"—that is, speaking directly into squawk-box microphone. "Off mike" means speaking unintentionally into this live microphone*) Attention . . . Attention . . . The Captain wishes to . . .

CAPTAIN'S VOICE (*Off mike*) Give me that thing! (*On mike*) All right, who did it? Who did it? You're going to stay here all night until someone confesses. You're going to stay at those battle stations until hell freezes over until I find out who did it. It's an insult to the honor of this ship, by God! The symbol of our cargo record has been destroyed and I'm going to find out who did it if it takes all night! (*Off mike*) Johnson, read me that muster list!

JOHNSON'S VOICE (*Reading muster list off mike*) Abernathy . . .

MANNION	CAPTAIN'S VOICE
Symbol of our cargo record? What the hell's that?	No, not Abernathy . . .
	JOHNSON'S VOICE
	Baker . . .
(STEFANOWSKI *rises, sees empty container, kneels and ceremoniously bows to it*)	CAPTAIN'S VOICE
	No . . .

DOWDY

For God's sake, Stefanowski, find some battle station!

(STEFANOWSKI *points to empty container.* DOWDY *sees it and spreads the news to the men on left.* SCHLEMMER *sees it and tells the other men. Now from all parts of the ship men enter and jubilantly look at the empty container. Bits of soil fly into the air as the men group around the empty can*)

JOHNSON'S VOICE

Bartholomew . . . Becker . . . Billings . . .
Carney . . . Daniels . . .
Dexter . . .
Ellison . . .
Everman . . .
Jenkins . . .
Kelly . . .
Kevin . . .
Martin . . .
Olsen . . .
O'Neill . . .

CAPTAIN'S VOICE

No, not O'Neill . . .

JOHNSON'S VOICE

Pulver . . .

CAPTAIN'S VOICE

No, not Pulver. He hasn't the guts . . .

JOHNSON'S VOICE

Roberts . . .

CAPTAIN'S VOICE (*Roaring, off mike*) Roberts! He's the one! Get him up here!

JOHNSON'S VOICE (*On mike*) Mister Roberts will report to the Captain's cabin on the double!

(*The men rush back to their battle stations*)

CAPTAIN'S VOICE Get him up here, I tell you! Get him up here . . .

JOHNSON'S VOICE (*On mike*) Mister Roberts will report to the Captain's cabin on the . . .

CAPTAIN (*Off mike*) Give me that thing. (*On mike*) Roberts, you get up here in a goddamn quick hurry. Get up here! Roberts, I'm giving you an order—get the lead out of your pants.

(ROBERTS *appears from left passageway and, walking slowly, enters the* CAPTAIN'S *cabin. The men move onstage and* LINDSTROM *gets to a position on the ladder where he can look through the porthole of the* CAPTAIN'S *cabin*)

ROBERTS' VOICE   Did you want to see me, Captain?

CAPTAIN'S VOICE   You did it. You did it. Don't lie to me. Don't stand there and lie to me. Confess it!

ROBERTS' VOICE   Confess what, Captain? I don't know what you're talking about.

CAPTAIN'S VOICE   You know damn well what I'm talkin' about because you did it. You've doublecrossed me—you've gone back on your word!

ROBERTS' VOICE   No, I haven't, Captain.

CAPTAIN   Yes, by God, you have. I kept my part of the bargain! I gave this crew liberty—I gave this crew liberty, by God, but you've gone back on *your* word.

(DOWDY *takes off his helmet and looks at the men*)

ROBERTS' VOICE   I don't see how you can say that, Captain. I haven't sent in any more letters.

(DOLAN, *on gun tub ladder, catches* INSIGNA's *eye*)

CAPTAIN'S VOICE   I'm not talkin' about your goddamn sons-a-bitchin' letters. I'm talkin' about what you did tonight.

ROBERTS' VOICE   Tonight? I don't understand you, Captain. What do you think I did?

CAPTAIN   Quit saying that, goddammit, quit saying that. You know damn well what you did. You stabbed me in the back. You stabbed me in the back . . . aaa . . . aa . . .

JOHNSON'S VOICE   Captain! Get over to the washbasin, Captain!

CAPTAIN'S VOICE   Aaaaaaa . . .

INSIGNA   What the hell happened?

DOLAN   Quiet!

JOHNSON   (*On mike*)   Will the Doctor please report to the Captain's cabin on the double?

(DOC *appears from left, pushing his way through the crowd, followed by two* MEDICAL CORPSMEN *wearing Red Cross brassards and carrying first-aid kits and a stretcher.* DOC *walks slowly; he is idly attaching a brassard and smoking a cigarette. He wears his helmet sloppily*)

DOC   Gangway . . . gangway . . .

DOWDY   Hey, Doc, tell us what's going on.

DOC   Okay. Okay.

(*He enters the* CAPTAIN's *cabin followed by the* CORPSMEN *who leave stretcher leaning against the bulkhead. The door closes. There is a tense pause. The men gather around the cabin again.* LINDSTROM *is at the porthole*)

REBER   Hey, Lindstrom, where's the Old Man?

LINDSTROM   He's sittin' in the chair—leaning way forward.

PAYNE   What's the Doc doin'?

LINDSTROM   He's holdin' the waste basket.

REBER   What waste basket?

LINDSTROM   The one the Old Man's got his head in. And he needs it too. (*Pause*) They're helpin' him over to the couch. (*Pause*) He's lying down there and they're takin' off his shoes. (*Pause*) Look out, here they come.

(*The men break quickly and rush back to their battle stations. The door opens and* ROBERTS, DOC *and the* CORPSMEN *come out*)

DOC (*To* CORPSMEN)   We won't need that stretcher. Sorry. (*Calls*) Dowdy! Come here.

(DOWDY *comes down to* DOC. *He avoids* ROBERTS' *eyes*)

ROBERTS   Dowdy, pass the word to the crew to secure from General Quarters.

DOC   And tell the men not to make any noise while they go to their bunks. The Captain's resting quietly now, and I think that's desirable.

ROBERTS   Pass the word, will you, Dowdy?

DOWDY   Yes, Mister Roberts.

(*He passes the word to the crew who slowly start to leave their battle stations. They are obviously stalling*)

DOC (*To* ROBERTS)   Got a cigarette? (ROBERTS *reaches in his pocket and offers* DOC *a cigarette. Then he lights* DOC's *cigarette.* DOC *notices the men stalling*) Well, guess I'd better get back inside. I'll be down to see you after I get through.

(*He enters cabin and stands there watching. The men move off-stage, very slowly, saying "Good night, Mister Roberts," "Good night, sir." Suddenly* ROBERTS *notices that all the men are saying good night to him*)

DOLAN (*Quietly*)   Good night, Mister Roberts. (ROBERTS *does not hear him*) Good night, Mister Roberts.

ROBERTS   Good night, Dolan.

(DOLAN *smiles and exits down hatch.* ROBERTS *steps toward hatch, removes helmet, looks puzzled as the lights*

Fade Out

(*During the darkness, over the squawk box the following announcements are heard*)

FIRST VOICE Now hear this . . . Now hear this . . . C, E and S Divisions and all Pharmacist's Mates will air bedding today—positively!

SECOND VOICE There is now available at the ship's store a small supply of peanut brittle. Ship's store will be open from 1300 to 1315.

THIRD VOICE Now, Dolan, Yeoman Second Class, report to the radio shack immediately.

SCENE V

The lights come up on the stateroom of ROBERTS *and* PULVER. PULVER *is lying in the lower bunk.* DOC *is sitting at the desk with a glass and a bottle of grain alcohol in front of him.* ROBERTS *is tying up a sea bag. A small suitcase stands beside it. His locker is open and empty.* WILEY *picks up the sea bag.*

WILEY Okay, Mister Roberts. I'll take these down to the gangway. The boat from the island should be out here any minute for you. I'll let you know.

ROBERTS Thanks, Wiley.

WILEY (*Grinning*) That's okay, Mister Roberts. Never thought you'd be taking this ride, did you?
(*He exits with the bags*)

ROBERTS I'm going to be off this bucket before I even wake up.

DOC They flying you all the way to the *Livingston*?

ROBERTS I don't know. The radio dispatch just said I was transferred and travel by air if possible. I imagine it's all the way though. They're landing planes at Okinawa now and that's where my can is probably running around. (*Laughs a little*) Listen to me, Doc—my can!

PULVER (*Studying map by* ROBERTS' *bunk*) Okinawa! Jeez, you be might-y careful, Doug.

ROBERTS Okay, Frank. This is *too* much to take, Doc. I even got a destroyer! The *Livingston*! That's one of the greatest cans out there.

PULVER I know a guy on the *Livingston*. He don't think it's so hot.

DOLAN (*Entering. He has a file folder under his arm*) Here you are, Mister Roberts. I typed up three copies of the radio dispatch.

I've got to keep a copy and here's two for you. You're now officially detached from this here bucket. Let me be the first.

ROBERTS   Thanks, Dolan. (*They shake hands.* ROBERTS *takes papers, and looks at them*) Dolan, how about these orders? I haven't sent in a letter for a month!

DOLAN (*Carefully*)   You know how the Navy works, Mister Roberts.

ROBERTS   Yeah, I know, but it doesn't seem . . .

DOLAN   Listen, Mister Roberts, I can tell you exactly what happened. Those guys at the Bureau need men for combat duty awful bad and they started looking through all the old letters and they just come across one of yours.

ROBERTS   Maybe—but still you'd think . . .

DOLAN   Listen, Mister Roberts. We can't stand here beating our gums! You better get cracking! You seen what it said there, "Proceed immediately." And the Old Man says if you ain't off of here in an hour, by God, he's going to throw you off!

ROBERTS   Is that all he said?

DOLAN   That's all he said.

ROBERTS (*Grinning at* DOC)   After fighting this for two years you'd think he'd say more than that . . .

CAPTAIN'S VOICE (*Offstage*)   Be careful of that one. Put it down easy.

DOC   What's that?

DOLAN   A new enlarged botanical garden. That's why he can't even be bothered about you today, Mister Roberts. Soon as we anchored this morning he sent Olsen over with a special detail—they dug up two palm trees . . . He's busy as a mother skunk now and you know what he's done—he's already set a twenty-four-hour watch on these new babies with orders to shoot to kill. (*To* PULVER) That reminds me, Mister Pulver. The Captain wants to see you right away.

PULVER   Yeah? What about?

DOLAN   I don't know, sir. (*To* ROBERTS) I'll be back to say good-bye, Mister Roberts. Come on, Mister Pulver.
    (*He exits*)

PULVER (*Following* DOLAN *out*)   What the hell did I do with his laundry this week?
    (ROBERTS *smiles as he starts putting on his black tie*)

DOC   You're a happy son-of-a-bitch, aren't you?

ROBERTS   Yep. You're happy about it too, aren't you, Doc?

DOC   I think it's the only thing for you. (*Casually*) What do you
think of the crew now, Doug?

ROBERTS   We're all right now. I think they're nice guys—all of them.

DOC   Unh-hunh. And how do you think they feel about you?

ROBERTS   I think they like me all right . . . till the next guy comes
along.

DOC   You don't think you're necessary to them?

ROBERTS   (*Sitting on bunk*)   Hell, no. No officer's necessary to the
crew, Doc.

DOC   Are you going to leave this ship believing that?

ROBERTS   That's nothing against them. A crew's too busy looking
after themselves to care about anyone else.

DOC   Well, take a good, deep breath, Buster. (*He drinks some alcohol*) What do you think got you your orders? Prayer and fast-
ing? Sending in enough Wheatie box tops?

ROBERTS   My orders? Why, what Dolan said—one of my old letters
turned up . . .

DOC   Bat crap! This crew got you transferred. They were so busy
looking out for themselves that they took a chance of landing in
prison for five years—any one of them. Since you couldn't send
in a letter for transfer, they sent one in for you. Since they knew
the Captain wouldn't sign it approved, they didn't bother him—
they signed it for him.

ROBERTS   What do you mean? They forged the Captain's name?

DOC   That's right.

ROBERTS   (*Rising*)   Doc! Who did? Which one of them?

DOC   That would be hard to say. You see, they had a mass meeting
down in the compartment. They put guards at every door. They
called it the Captain's-Name-Signing contest. And every man in
this crew—a hundred and sixty-seven of them—signed the Captain's name on a blank sheet of paper. And then there were judges
who compared these signatures with the Captain's and selected
the one to go in. At the time there was some criticism of the
decision on the grounds that the judges were drunk, but apparently, from the results, they chose well.

ROBERTS   How'd you find out about this, Doc?

DOC   Well, it was a great honor. I am the only officer aboard who
does know. I was a contestant. I was also a judge. This double
honor was accorded me because of my character, charm, good
looks and because the medical department contributed four gal-
lons of grain alcohol to the contest. (*Pauses*) It was quite a thing

to see, Doug. A hundred and sixty-seven guys with only one idea in their heads—to do something for Mister Roberts.

ROBERTS (*After a moment*) I wish you hadn't told me, Doc. It makes me look pretty silly after what I just said. But I didn't mean it, Doc. I was afraid to say what I really feel. I love those bastards, Doc. I think they're the greatest guys on this earth. All of a sudden I feel that there's something wrong—something terribly wrong—about leaving them. God, what can I say to them?

DOC You won't say anything—you don't even know. When you're safely aboard your new ship I'm supposed to write and tell you about it. And at the bottom of the letter, I'm supposed to say, "Thanks for the liberty, Mister Roberts. Thanks for everything."

ROBERTS Jesus!

(PULVER *enters, downcast*)

PULVER I'm the new Cargo Officer. And that's not all—I got to have dinner with him tonight. He *likes* me!

(*There is a polite rap on the door*)

DOC Come in. (*Enter* PAYNE, REBER, GERHART, SCHLEMMER, DOLAN *and* INSIGNA, *all carrying canteen cups except* INSIGNA *whose cup is in his belt. He carries a large, red fire extinguisher*) What's this?

INSIGNA Fire and rescue party. Heard you had a fire in here.

(*All are looking at* ROBERTS)

ROBERTS No, but—since you're here—I—

INSIGNA Hell, we got a false alarm then. Happens all the time. (*Sets extinguisher on desk*) In that case, we might as well drink this stuff. Give me your glass, Mister Roberts, and I'll put a head on it—yours too, Doc. I got one for you, Mister Pulver.

(*He fills their glasses from the fire extinguisher*)

ROBERTS What's in that, a new batch of jungle juice?

INSIGNA Yeah, in the handy, new, portable container. Everybody loaded?

(*All nod*)

DOLAN Go ahead, Sam.

INSIGNA (*To* ROBERTS) There's a story going around that you're leaving us. That right?

ROBERTS (*Carefully*) That's right, Sam. And I . . .

INSIGNA Well, we didn't want you to get away without having a little drink with us and we thought we ought to give you a little sort of going-away present. The fellows made it down in the machine shop. It ain't much but we hope you like it. (REBER *prompts*

Mister Roberts

him) We all sincerely hope you like it. (*Calls offstage*) All right, you bastards, you can come in now.

(*Enter* LINDSTROM, MANNION, DOWDY *and* STEFANOWSKI. MANNION *is carrying a candy box. He walks over to* ROBERTS *shyly and hands him the box*)

ROBERTS What is it?

SCHLEMMER Open it.

(ROBERTS *opens the box. There is a deep silence*)

PULVER What is it, Doug?

(ROBERTS *holds up the box. In it is a brass medal shaped like a palm tree attached to a piece of gaudy ribbon*)

LINDSTROM It's a palm tree, see.

DOLAN It was Dowdy's idea.

DOWDY Mannion here made it. He cut it out of sheet brass down in the machine shop.

INSIGNA Mannion drilled the words on it too.

MANNION Stefanowski thought up the words.

STEFANOWSKI (*Shoving* LINDSTROM *forward*) Lindstrom gets credit for the ribbon from a box of candy that his sister-in-law sent him. Read the words, Mister Roberts.

ROBERTS (*With difficulty*) "Order . . . order of . . ."

(*He hands the medal to* DOC)

DOC (*Rises and reads solemnly*) "Order of the palm. To Lieutenant (jg) Douglas Roberts for action against the enemy, above and beyond the call of duty on the night of eight May 1945."

(*He passes the medal back to* ROBERTS)

ROBERTS (*After a moment—smiling*) It's very nice but I'm afraid you've got the wrong guy.

(*The men turn to* DOWDY, *grinning*)

DOWDY We know that, but we'd kinda like for you to have it anyway.

ROBERTS All right, I'll keep it.

(*The men beam. There is an awkward pause*)

GERHART Stefanowski thought up the words.

ROBERTS They're fine words.

(WILEY *enters*)

WILEY The boat's here, Mister Roberts. I put your gear in. They want to shove off right away.

ROBERTS (*Rising*) Thanks. We haven't had our drink yet.

REBER No, we ain't.

(*All get to their feet.* ROBERTS *picks up his glass, looks at the crew, and everyone drinks*)

ROBERTS   Good-bye, Doc.

DOC   Good-bye, Doug.

ROBERTS   And thanks, Doc.

DOC   Okay.

ROBERTS   Good-bye, Frank.

PULVER   Good-bye, Doug.

ROBERTS   Remember, I'm counting on you.

(PULVER *nods.* ROBERTS *turns to the crew and looks at them for a moment. Then he takes the medal from the box, pins it on his shirt, shows it to them, then gives a little gestured salute and exits as the lights*

Fade Out

(*During the darkness we hear voices making announcements over the squawk box*)

FIRST VOICE   Now hear this . . . now hear this . . . Sweepers, man your brooms. Clean sweep-down fore and aft!

SECOND VOICE   Now hear this! All men put on report today will fall in on the quarter-deck—and form three ranks!

THIRD VOICE   Now hear this! All divisions will draw their mail at 1700—in the mess hall.

SCENE VI

The lights come up showing the main set at sunset. DOC *is sitting on the hatch, reading a letter.* MANNION, *wearing sidearms, is pacing up and down in front of the* CAPTAIN's *cabin. On each side of the door is a small palm tree in a five-gallon can—on one can is painted in large white letters, "Keep Away"; on the other, "This Means You." After a moment* PULVER *enters from the left passageway, carrying a small packet of letters.*

PULVER   Hello, Mannion. Got your mail yet?

MANNION   No. I've got the palm tree watch.

PULVER   Oh. (*To* DOC) What's your news, Doc?

DOC My wife got some new wallpaper for the living room.

(PULVER *sits on hatch cover.* DOWDY *enters wearing work gloves*)

DOWDY Mister Pulver, we'll be finished with the cargo in a few minutes.

PULVER How'd it go?

DOWDY Not bad. I've got to admit you were right about Number Three hold. It worked easier out of there. Mister Pulver, I just found out what the Captain decided—he ain't going to show a movie again tonight.

PULVER Why not?

DOWDY He's still punishing us because he caught Reber without a shirt on two days ago. You've got to go in and see him.

PULVER I did. I asked him to show a movie yesterday.

DOWDY Mister Pulver, what the hell good does that do us today? You've got to keep needlin' that guy—I'm tellin' you.

PULVER Don't worry. I'll take care of it in my own way.

DOWDY (*Going off, but speaking loud enough to be heard*) Oh, God, no movie again tonight.

(*He exits.* PULVER *starts looking at his packet of mail*)

PULVER (*Looking at first letter*) This is from my mother. All she ever says is stay away from Japan. (*He drops it on the hatch cover*) This is from Alabama. (*Puts it in his pocket and pats it. Looks at third letter*) Doc! This is from Doug!

DOC Yeah? (PULVER *rips open the envelope*) What does he say?

PULVER (*Reading*) "This will be short and sweet, as we're shoving off in about two minutes . . ." (*Pauses and remarks*) This is dated three weeks ago.

DOC Does he say where he is?

PULVER Yeah. He says: "My guess about the location of this ship was just exactly right." (*Looks up*) That means he's around Okinawa all right! (*Reads on and chuckles*) He's met Fornell. That's that friend of mine . . . a guy named Fornell I went to college with. Listen to this: "Fornell says that you and he used to load up your car with liquor in Omaha and then sell it at an indecent profit to the fraternity boys at Iowa City. How about that?" We did too. (*Smiles happily*) "This part is for Doc." (DOC *gestures for him to read it*) "I've been aboard this destroyer for two weeks now and we've already been through four air attacks. I'm in the war at last, Doc. I've caught up with that task force that passed me by. I'm glad to be here. I had to be here, I guess. But I'm thinking now of you, Doc, and you, Frank, and Dolan and Dowdy and Insigna and everyone else on that bucket—all the guys every-where who sail from Tedium to Apathy and back again—with an occasional side trip to Monotony. This is a tough crew on here, and they have a wonderful battle record. But I've discovered, Doc, that the most terrible enemy of this war is the boredom that eventually becomes a faith and, therefore, a sort of suicide—and I know now that the ones who refuse to surrender to it are the strongest of all.

"Right now, I'm looking at something that's hanging over my desk: a preposterous hunk of brass attached to the most bilious piece of ribbon I've ever seen. I'd rather have it than the Con-gressional Medal of Honor. It tells me what I'll always be proudest of—that at a time in the world when courage counted most, I lived among a hundred and sixty-seven brave men.

"So, Doc, and especially you, Frank, don't let those guys down. Of course, I know that by this time they must be very happy be-cause the Captain's overhead is filled with marbles and . . ." (*He avoids* DOC's *eyes*) "Oh, hell, here comes the mail orderly. This has to go now. I'll finish it later. Meanwhile you bastards can write too, can't you?

"Doug."

DOC   Can I see that, Frank?
(PULVER *hands him the letter, looks at the front of his next letter and says quietly*)
PULVER   Well, for God's sake, this is from Fornell!
DOC   (*Reading* ROBERTS' *letter to himself*) ". . . I'd rather have it than the Congressional Medal of Honor." I'm glad he found that out. (*He looks at* PULVER, *sensing something wrong*) What's the matter? (PULVER *does not answer*) What's the matter, Frank? (PULVER *looks at him slowly as* DOWDY *enters*)
DOWDY   All done, Mister Pulver. We've secured the hatch cover. No word on the movie, I suppose.
DOC (*Louder, with terror*)   Frank, what is it?
PULVER   Mister Roberts is dead. (*Looks at letter*) This is from For-nell . . . They took a Jap suicide plane. It killed everyone in a twin-forty battery and then it went on through and killed Doug and another officer in the wardroom. (*Pause*) They were drinking coffee when it hit.
DOWDY (*Quietly*)   Mister Pulver, can I please give that letter to the crew?
DOC   No. (*Holding out* ROBERTS' *letter*) Give them this one. It's

theirs. (DOWDY *removes gloves and takes the letter from* DOC *and goes off*) Coffee . . .

(PULVER *gets up restlessly.* DOC *stares straight ahead.* PULVER *straightens. He seems to grow. He walks casually over to* MANNION)

PULVER (*In a friendly voice*) Go on down and get your mail. I'll stand by for you.

MANNION (*Surprised*) You will? Okay, thanks, Mister Pulver.

(MANNION *disappears down hatch. As soon as he exits* PULVER *very calmly jerks the rooted palms, one by one, from their containers and throws them over the side.* DOC *looks up to see* PULVER *pull second tree.* DOC *ducks as tree goes past him. Then* PULVER *knocks loudly on the* CAPTAIN's *door*)

CAPTAIN (*Offstage. His voice is very truculent*) Yeah. Who is it?

PULVER Captain, this is Ensign Pulver. I just threw your palm trees overboard. Now what's all this crap about no movie tonight?

(*He throws the door open, banging it against the bulkhead, and is entering the* CAPTAIN's *cabin*)

Curtain

Come Back, Little Sheba

B Y

William Inge

For Phyllis Anderson

COME BACK, LITTLE SHEBA *was first presented by The Theatre Guild at the Booth Theatre, New York City, on February 15, 1950, with the following cast:*

(In order of appearance)

DOC	*Sidney Blackmer*
MARIE	*Joan Lorring*
LOLA	*Shirley Booth*
TURK	*Lonny Chapman*
POSTMAN	*Daniel Reed*
MRS. COFFMAN	*Olga Fabian*
MILKMAN	*John Randolph*
MESSENGER	*Arnold Schulman*
BRUCE	*Robert Cunningham*
ED ANDERSON	*Wilson Brooks*
ELMO HUSTON	*Paul Krauss*

Directed by Daniel Mann
Setting and lighting designed by Howard Bay
Costumes by Lucille Little
Production under the supervision of Lawrence Langner and Theresa Helburn
Associate Producer, Phyllis Anderson

Synopsis of Scenes

An old house in a run-down neighborhood of a Midwestern city.

ACT ONE

SCENE I   Morning in late spring.

SCENE II   The same evening, after supper.

ACT TWO

SCENE I   The following morning.

SCENE II   Late afternoon the same day.

SCENE III   5:30 the next morning.

SCENE IV   Morning, a week later.

ACT ONE

SCENE I

The stage is empty.

It is the downstairs of an old house in one of those semi-respectable neighborhoods in a Midwestern city. The stage is divided into two rooms, the living room at right and the kitchen at left, with a stairway and a door between. At the foot of the stairway is a small table with a telephone on it. The time is about 8:00 A.M., a morning in the late spring.

At rise of curtain the sun hasn't come out in full force and outside the atmosphere is a little gray. The house is extremely cluttered and even dirty. The living room somehow manages to convey the atmosphere of the twenties, decorated with cheap pretense at niceness and respectability. The general effect is one of fussy awkwardness. The furniture is all heavy and rounded-looking, the chairs and davenport being covered with a shiny mohair. The davenport is littered and there are lace antimacassars on all the chairs. In such areas, houses are so close together, they hide each other from the sunlight. What sun could come through the window, at right, is dimmed by the smoky glass curtains. In the kitchen there is a table, center. On it are piled dirty dishes from supper the night before. Woodwork in the kitchen is dark and grimy. No industry whatsoever has been spent in making it one of those white, cheerful rooms that we commonly think kitchens should be. There is no action on stage for several seconds.

DOC comes downstairs and turns into the kitchen, looking rather regretful at the disarray he always finds there. He hangs his suit coat on the back of a chair and then puts the water on the stove for coffee. Time is his own now, and he kneels reverently before the kitchen table and says a prayer, mumbling the words inaudibly but with deep feeling and humility. When the prayer is finished, he can smile, and set about getting his breakfast with a light heart.

A young college student, MARIE, *rents a bedroom just off the living room downstairs. She pops out of the door suddenly, wearing a dainty but respectable negligee, and skips into the kitchen with the ebullience that only youth can feel in the morning. She speaks to* DOC *as though he were someone she took pleasantly for granted, and he appears happy to see her.*

MARIE (*Goes to chair, opens pocketbook there*)   Hi!

DOC   Well, well, how is our star boarder this morning?

MARIE   Fine.

DOC   Want your breakfast now?

MARIE   Just my fruit juice. I'll drink it while I dress and have my breakfast later.

DOC (*Places two glasses on table*)   Up a little early, aren't you?

MARIE   I have to get to the library and check out some books before anyone else gets them.

DOC   Yes, you want to study hard, Marie, learn to be a fine artist some day. Paint lots of beautiful pictures. I remember a picture my mother had over the mantelpiece at home, a picture of a cathedral in a sunset, one of those big cathedrals in Europe somewhere. Made you feel religious just to look at it.

MARIE   These books aren't for art, they're for biology. I have an exam.

DOC   Biology? Why do they make you take biology?

MARIE (*Laughs*)   It's required. Didn't you have to take biology when you were in college?

DOC   Well . . . yes, but I was preparing to study medicine, so of course I *had* to take biology and things like that. You see—I was going to be a real doctor then—only I left college my third year.

MARIE   What's the matter? Didn't you like the pre-med course?

DOC   Yes, of course . . . I had to give it up.

MARIE   Why?

DOC (*Goes to stove with roll on plate—evasive*)   I'll put your sweet roll in now, Marie, so it will be nice and warm for you when you want it.

MARIE   Dr. Delaney, I hope my husband is as nice as you are. Most husbands would never think of getting their own breakfast.

DOC (*Accepting it as a compliment*)   . . . uh . . . you might as well sit down now and . . . yes, sit here and I'll serve you your breakfast now, Marie, and we can eat it together, the two of us.

MARIE (*A light little laugh as she dances away from him*)   No, I like to bathe first and feel that I'm all fresh and clean to start the day. I'm going to hop into the tub now. See you later.

(*She goes upstairs*)

DOC (*The words appeal to him*)   Yes, fresh and clean—

(DOC *now goes on in businesslike way setting his breakfast on the table*)

MARIE (*Offstage*)   Mrs. Delaney.

LOLA (*Offstage*)   'Mornin', honey.

(LOLA *comes downstairs. She is a contrast to* DOC's *neat cleanliness, and* MARIE's *scrubbed youthfulness. Over a nightdress she wears a lumpy kimono. Her eyes are dim with a morning expression of disillusionment, as though she had had a beautiful dream during the night and found on waking none of it was true. On her feet are worn dirty comfies*)

LOLA (*With some self-pity*)   I can't sleep late like I used to. It used to be I could sleep till noon if I wanted to, but I can't any more. I don't know why.

DOC   Habits change. Here's your fruit juice.

LOLA (*Taking it*)   I oughta be gettin' your breakfast, Doc, instead of you gettin' mine.

DOC   I have to get up anyway, Baby.

LOLA (*Sadly*)   I had another dream last night.

DOC (*Pours coffee*)   About Little Sheba?

LOLA (*With sudden animation*)   It was just as real. I dreamt I put her on a leash and we walked downtown—to do some shopping. All the people on the street turned around to admire her, and I felt so proud. Then we started to walk, and the blocks started going by so fast that Little Sheba couldn't keep up with me. Suddenly, I looked around and Little Sheba was gone. Isn't that funny? I looked everywhere for her but I couldn't find her. And I stood there feeling sort of afraid. (*Pause*) Do you suppose that means anything?

DOC   Dreams are funny.

LOLA   Do you suppose it means Little Sheba is going to come back?

DOC   I don't know, Baby.

LOLA (*Petulant*)   I miss her so, Doc. She was such a cute little puppy. Wasn't she cute?

DOC (*Smiles with the reminiscence*)   Yes, she was cute.

LOLA   Remember how white and fluffy she used to be after I gave her a bath? And how her little hind-end wagged from side to side when she walked?

DOC (*An appealing memory*) I remember.

LOLA She was such a cute little puppy. I hated to see her grow old, didn't you, Doc?

DOC Yah. Little Sheba should have stayed young forever. Some things should never grow old. That's what it amounts to, I guess.

LOLA She's been gone for such a long time. What do you suppose ever happened to her?

DOC You can't ever tell.

LOLA (*With anxiety*) Do you suppose she got run over by a car? Or do you think that old Mrs. Coffman next door poisoned her? I wouldn't be a bit surprised.

DOC No, Baby. She just disappeared. That's all we know.

LOLA (*Redundantly*) Just vanished one day . . . vanished into thin air.

(*As though in a dream*)

DOC I told you I'd find you another one, Baby.

LOLA (*Pessimistically*) You couldn't ever find another puppy as cute as Little Sheba.

DOC (*Back to reality*) Want an egg?

LOLA No. Just this coffee. (*He pours coffee and sits down to breakfast.* LOLA, *suddenly*) Have you said your prayer, Doc?

DOC Yes, Baby.

LOLA And did you ask God to be with you—all through the day, and keep you strong?

DOC Yes, Baby.

LOLA Then God will be with you, Docky. He's been with you almost a year now and I'm so proud of you.

DOC (*Preening a little*) Sometimes I feel sorta proud of myself.

LOLA Say your prayer, Doc. I like to hear it.

DOC (*Matter-of-factly*) God grant me the serenity to accept the things I cannot change, courage to change the things I can, and wisdom always to tell the difference.

LOLA That's nice. That's so pretty. When I think of the way you used to drink, always getting into fights, we had so much trouble. I was so scared! I never knew what was going to happen.

DOC That was a long time ago, Baby.

LOLA I know it, Daddy. I know how you're going to be when you come home now.

(*She kisses him lightly*)

DOC *I* don't know what I would have done without you.

LOLA And now you've been sober almost a year.

DOC Yep. A year next month.

(*He rises and goes to the sink with coffee cup and two glasses, rinsing them*)

LOLA Do you have to go to the meeting tonight?

DOC No. No meeting tonight.

LOLA Oh, good! Then you can take me to a movie.

DOC Sorry, Baby. I'm going out on some Twelfth Step work with Ed Anderson.

LOLA What's that?

DOC (*Drying the glasses*) I showed you that list of twelve steps the Alcoholics Anonymous have to follow. This is the final one. After you learn to stay dry yourself, then you go out and help other guys that need it.

LOLA Oh!

DOC When we help others, we help ourselves.

LOLA I know what you mean. Whenever I help Marie in some way, it makes me feel good.

DOC Yes. (LOLA *takes her cup to* DOC *and he washes it*) Yes, but this is a lot different, Baby. When I go out to help some poor drunk, I have to give him courage—to stay sober like I've stayed sober. Most alcoholics are disappointed men. . . . They need courage . . .

LOLA You weren't ever disappointed, were you, Daddy?

DOC (*After another evasive pause*) The important thing is to forget the past and live for the present. And stay sober doing it.

LOLA Who do you have to help tonight?

DOC Some guy they picked up on Skid Row last night. (*Gets his coat from back of chair*) They got him at the City Hospital. I kinda dread it.

LOLA I thought you said it helped you.

DOC (*Puts on coat*) It does, if you can stand it. I did some Twelfth Step work down there once before. They put alcoholics right in with the crazy people. It's horrible—these men all twisted and shaking—eyes all foggy and full of pain. Some guy there with his fists clamped together, so he couldn't kill anyone. There was a young man, just a *young* man, had scratched his eyes out.

LOLA (*Cringing*) Don't, Daddy. Seems a shame to take a man there just 'cause he got drunk.

DOC Well, they'll sober a man up. That's the important thing. Let's not talk about it any more.

LOLA (*With relief*) Rita Hayworth's on tonight, out at the Plaza. Don't you want to see it?

DOC Maybe Marie will go with you.

LOLA Oh, no. She's probably going out with Turk tonight.

DOC She's too nice a girl to be going out with a guy like Turk.

LOLA I don't know why, Daddy. Turk's nice.

DOC A guy like that doesn't have any respect for *nice* young girls. You can tell that by looking at him.

LOLA I never saw Marie object to any of the love-making.

DOC A big, brawny bozo like Turk, he probably forces her to kiss him.

LOLA Daddy, that's not so at all. I came in the back way once when they were in the living room, and she was kissing him like he was Rudolph Valentino.

DOC (*An angry denial*) Marie is a nice girl.

LOLA I know she's nice. I just said she and Turk were doing some tall spooning. It wouldn't surprise me any if . . .

DOC Honey, I don't want to hear any more about it.

LOLA You try to make out like every young girl is Jennifer Jones in the *Song of Bernadette*.

DOC I do not. I just like to believe that young people like her are clean and decent. . . .

(MARIE *comes downstairs*)

MARIE Hi!

(*Gets cup and saucer from drainboard*)

LOLA (*At stove*) There's an extra sweet roll for you this morning, honey. I didn't want mine.

MARIE One's plenty, thank you.

DOC How soon do you leave this morning?

(LOLA *brings coffee*)

MARIE (*Eating*) As soon as I finish my breakfast.

DOC Well, I'll wait and we can walk to the corner together.

MARIE Oh, I'm sorry, Doc. Turk's coming by. He has to go to the library, too.

DOC Oh, well, I'm not going to be competition with a football player. (*To* LOLA) It's a nice spring morning. Wanta walk to the office with me?

LOLA I look too terrible, Daddy. I ain't even dressed.

DOC Kiss Daddy good-bye.

LOLA (*Gets up and kisses him softly*) Bye, bye, Daddy. If you get hungry, come home and I'll have something for you.

MARIE (*Joking*) Aren't you going to kiss *me*, Dr. Delaney?

DOC (*Startled, hesitates, forces himself to realize she is only joking and manages to answer*) Can't spend my time kissing *all* the girls.

(MARIE *laughs.* DOC *goes into living room while* LOLA *and* MARIE *continue talking.* MARIE's *scarf is tossed over his hat on chair, so he picks it up, then looks at it fondly, holding it in the air gazing through its transparent loveliness. Suddenly, he drops it back on chair and starts out*)

MARIE I think Dr. Delaney is so nice.

LOLA (*She is by the closet now, where she keeps a few personal articles. She is getting into a more becoming smock*) When did you say Turk was coming by?

MARIE Said he'd be here about 9:30. (DOC *exits, hearing the line about* TURK) That's a pretty smock.

LOLA (*Goes to table, sits in chair and changes shoes*) It'll be better to work around the house in.

MARIE (*Not sounding exactly cheerful*) Mrs. Delaney, I'm expecting a telegram this morning. Would you leave it on my dresser for me when it comes?

LOLA Sure, honey. No bad news, I hope.

MARIE Oh, no! It's from Bruce.

LOLA (MARIE's *boy friends are one of her liveliest interests*) Oh, your boy friend in Cincinnati. Is he coming to see you?

MARIE I guess so.

LOLA I'm just dying to meet him.

MARIE (*Changing the subject*) Really, Mrs. Delaney, you and Doc have been so nice to me. I just want you to know I appreciate it.

LOLA Thanks, honey.

MARIE You've been like a father and mother to me. I appreciate it.

LOLA Thanks, honey.

MARIE Turk was saying just the other night what good sports you both are.

LOLA (*Brushing hair*) That so?

MARIE Honest. He said it was just as much fun being with you as with kids our own age.

LOLA (*Couldn't be more flattered*) Oh, I like that Turk. He reminds me of a boy I used to know in high school, Dutch McCoy. Where did you ever meet him?

MARIE In art class.

LOLA   Turk take art?

MARIE   (*Laughs*)   No. It was in a life class. He was modeling. Lots of the athletes do that. It pays them a dollar an hour.

LOLA   That's nice.

MARIE   Mrs. Delaney? I've got some corrections to make in some of my drawings. Is it all right if I bring Turk home this morning to pose for me? It'll just take a few minutes.

LOLA   Sure, honey.

MARIE   There's a contest on now. They're giving a prize for the best drawing to use for advertising the Spring Relays.

LOLA   And you're going to do a picture of Turk? That's nice. (*A sudden thought*) Doc's gonna be gone tonight. You and Turk can have the living room if you want to. (*A little secretively*)

MARIE   (*This is a temptation*)   O.K. Thanks. (*Exits to bedroom*)

LOLA   Tell me more about Bruce. (*Follows her to bedroom door*)

MARIE   (*Offstage in bedroom*)   Well, he comes from one of the best families in Cincinnati. And they have a great big house. And they have a maid, too. And he's got a wonderful personality. He makes $300 a month.

LOLA   That so?

MARIE   And he stays at the best hotels. His company insists on it. (*Returns to living room*)

LOLA   Do you like him as well as Turk?

MARIE   (*Evasive*)   Bruce is so dependable, and . . . he's a gentleman, too.

LOLA   Are you goin' to marry him, honey?

MARIE   Maybe, after I graduate from college and he feels he can support a wife and children. I'm going to have lots and lots of children.

LOLA   I wanted children, too. When I lost my baby and found out I couldn't have any more, I didn't know what to do with myself. I wanted to get a job, but Doc wouldn't hear of it.

MARIE   Bruce is going to come into a lot of money some day. His uncle made a fortune in men's garters.

LOLA   Doc was a rich boy when I married him. His mother left him $25,000 when she died. (*Disillusioned*) It took him a lot to get his office started and everything . . . then, he got sick. (*She makes a futile gesture*) But Doc's always good to me . . . *now.*

MARIE (*Re-enters*) O, Doc's a peach.

LOLA I used to be pretty, something like you. (*She gets her picture from table*) I was Beauty Queen of the senior class in high school. My dad was awful strict, though. Once he caught me holding hands with that good-looking Dutch McCoy. Dad sent Dutch home, and wouldn't let me go out after supper for a whole month. Daddy would never let me go out with boys much. Just because I was pretty. He was afraid all the boys would get the wrong idea—*you* know. I never had any fun at all until I met Doc.

MARIE Sometimes I'm glad I didn't know my father. Mom always let me do pretty much as I please.

LOLA Doc was the first boy my dad ever let me go out with. We got married that spring.

(*Replaces picture.* MARIE *sits on couch, puts on shoes and socks*)

MARIE What did your father think of that?

LOLA We came right to the city then. And, well, Doc gave up his pre-med course and went to Chiropractor School instead.

MARIE You must have been married awful young.

LOLA Oh, yes. Eighteen.

MARIE That must have made your father really mad.

LOLA Yes, it did. I never went home after that, but my mother comes down here from Green Valley to visit me sometimes.

TURK (*Bursts into the front room from outside. He is a young, good-looking boy, nineteen or twenty. He has the openness, vigor and health of youth. He wears faded dungarees and a T-shirt. He always enters unannounced*) Hey, Marie! Ready?

MARIE (*Calling. Runs and exits into bedroom, closing door*) Just a minute, Turk.

LOLA (*Confidentially*) I'll entertain him until you're ready. (*She is by nature coy and kittenish with any attractive man. Picks up papers—stuffs them under table*) The house is such a mess, Turk! I bet you think I'm an awful housekeeper. Some day I'll surprise you. But you're like one of the family now. (*Pause*) My, you're an early caller.

TURK Gotta get to the library. Haven't cracked a book for a biology exam and Marie's gotta help me.

LOLA (*Unconsciously admiring his stature*) My, I'd think you'd be chilly running around in just that thin little shirt.

TURK Me? I go like this in the middle of winter.

LOLA Well, you're a big husky man.

TURK (*Laughs*) Oh, I'm a brute, *I* am.

LOLA You should be out in Hollywood making those Tarzan movies.

TURK (*Calling*) Hey, Marie, hurry up.

MARIE Oh, be patient, Turk.

TURK (*To* LOLA) She doesn't realize how busy I am. I'll only have a half hour to study at most. I gotta report to the coach at 10:30.

LOLA What are you in training for now?

TURK Spring track. They got me throwing the javelin.

LOLA The javelin? What's that?

TURK (*Laughs at her ignorance*) It's a big, long lance. (*Assumes the stance*) You hold it like this, erect—then you let go and it goes singing through the air, and lands yards away, if you're any good at it, and sticks in the ground, quivering like an arrow. I won the State championship last year.

LOLA (*She has watched as though fascinated*) My!

TURK (*Very generous*) Get Marie to take you to the track field some afternoon, and you can watch me.

LOLA That would be thrilling.

MARIE (*Comes dancing in*) Hi, Turk.

TURK Hi, juicy.

LOLA (*As the young couple move to the doorway*) Remember, Marie, you and Turk can have the front room tonight. All to yourselves. You can play the radio and dance and make a plate of fudge, or anything you want.

MARIE (*To* TURK) O.K.?

TURK Sure.

MARIE Let's go.

(*Exits*)

LOLA 'Bye, kids.

TURK 'Bye, Mrs. Delaney. (*Gives her a chuck under the chin*) You're a swell skirt.

(LOLA *couldn't be more flattered. For a moment she is breathless. They speed out the door and* LOLA *stands, sadly watching them depart. Then a sad, vacant look comes over her face. Her arms drop in a gesture of futility. Slowly she walks out on the front porch and calls*)

LOLA Little Sheba! Come, Little She-ba. Come back . . . come back, Little Sheba! (*She waits for a few moments, then comes wearily back into the house, closing the door behind her. Now the morning has caught up with her. She goes to the kitchen, kicks off her pumps and gets back into comfies. The sight of the dishes on the drainboard depresses her. Clearly she is bored to death. Then the telephone rings with the promise of relieving her. She answers it)* Hello— Oh, no, you've got the wrong number— Oh, that's all right. *(Again it looks hopeless. She hears the* POSTMAN. *Now her spirits are lifted. She runs to the door, opens it and awaits him. When he's within distance, she lets loose a barrage of welcome)* 'Morning, Mr. Postman.

POSTMAN 'Morning, ma'am.

LOLA You better have something for me today. Sometimes I think you don't even know I live here. You haven't left me anything for two whole weeks. If you can't do better than that, I'll just have to get a new postman.

POSTMAN *(On the porch)* You'll have to get someone to write you some letters, lady. Nope, nothing for you.

LOLA Well, I was only joking. You knew I was joking, didn't you? I bet you're thirsty. You come right in here and I'll bring you a glass of cold water. Come in and sit down for a few minutes and rest your feet awhile.

POSTMAN I'll take you up on that, lady. I've worked up quite a thirst.

(Coming in)

LOLA You sit down. I'll be back in just a minute.

(Goes to kitchen, gets pitcher out of refrigerator and brings it back)

POSTMAN Spring is turnin' into summer awful soon.

LOLA You feel free to stop here and ask me for a drink of water any time you want to. *(Pouring drink)* That's what we're all here for, isn't it? To make each other comfortable?

POSTMAN Thank you, ma'am.

LOLA *(Clinging, not wanting to be left alone so soon; she hurries her conversation to hold him)* You haven't been our postman very long, have you?

POSTMAN *(She stands holding pitcher as he drinks)* No.

LOLA You postmen have things pretty nice, don't you? I hear you get nice pensions after you been working for the government twenty years. I think that's dandy. It's a *good* job, too. *(Pours him a second glass)* You may get tired but I think it's good for a man to be outside and get a lot of exercise. Keeps him strong and healthy. My husband, he's a doctor, a *chiro*practor; he has to stay inside his office all day long. The only exercise he gets is rubbin' people's backbones. *(They laugh)* It makes his hands strong, but he's got a poor digestion. I keep tellin' him he oughta get some fresh air once in a while and some exercise. (POSTMAN *rises as if to go, and this hurries her into a more absorbing monologue*) You know what? My husband is an Alcoholics Anonymous. He doesn't care if I tell you that 'cause he's proud of it. He hasn't touched a drop in almost a year. All that time we've had a quart of whiskey in the pantry for company and he hasn't even gone near it. Doesn't even want to. You know, alcoholics can't drink like ordinary people; they're *allergic* to it. It affects them different. They get started drinking and can't stop. Liquor transforms them. Sometimes they get mean and violent and wanta fight, but if they let liquor alone, they're perfectly all right, just like you and me. (POSTMAN *tries to leave*) You should have seen Doc before he gave it up. He lost all his patients, wouldn't even go to the office; just wanted to stay drunk all day long and he'd come home at night and . . . (*Decides against saying more*) You just wouldn't believe it if you saw him now. He's got his patients all back, and he's just doing fine.

POSTMAN Sure, I know Dr. Delaney. I deliver his office mail. He's a fine man.

LOLA Oh, thanks. You don't ever drink, do you?

POSTMAN Oh, a few beers once in a while.

(*He is ready to go*)

LOLA Well, I guess that stuff doesn't do any of us any good.

POSTMAN No. (*Crosses down for mail on floor center*) Well, good day, ma'am.

LOLA Say, you got any kids?

POSTMAN Three grandchildren.

LOLA (*Getting it from console table*) We don't have any kids, and we got this toy in a box of breakfast food. Why don't you take it home to them?

POSTMAN Why, that's very kind of you, ma'am.

(*He takes it, and goes*)

LOLA Good-bye, Mr. Postman.

POSTMAN (*On porch*) Good-bye, ma'am.

LOLA (*Left alone, she turns on radio. Then she goes to kitchen to start dishes, showing her boredom in the half-hearted way she washes them. She spies* MRS. COFFMAN *hanging baby clothes on lines just outside kitchen door. She calls*) My, you're a busy woman this morning, Mrs. Coffman.

MRS. COFFMAN (*A German woman, she speaks with a little accent, appearing briefly at the window*) Being busy is being happy.

LOLA   I guess so.

MRS. COFFMAN   I don't have it as easy as you. When you got seven kids to look after, you got no time to sit around the house, Mrs. Delaney.

LOLA   I s'pose not.

MRS. COFFMAN   But you don't hear me complain.

LOLA   Oh, no. You never complain. (*Pause*) I guess my little doggie's gone for good, Mrs. Coffman. I sure miss her.

MRS. COFFMAN   The only way to keep from missing one dog is to get another.

LOLA   (*Goes to sink, turns off water*) Oh, I never could find another doggie as cute as Little Sheba.

MRS. COFFMAN   Did you put an ad in the paper?

LOLA   For two whole weeks. No one answered it. It's just like she vanished—into thin air. (*She likes this metaphor*) Every day, though, I go out on the porch and call her. You can't tell; she might be around. Don't you think?

MRS. COFFMAN   You should get busy and forget her. You should get busy, Mrs. Delaney.

LOLA   Yes, I'm going to. I'm going to start my spring housecleaning one of these days real soon. Why don't you come in and have a cup of coffee with me, Mrs. Coffman, and we can chat awhile?

MRS. COFFMAN   I got work to do, Mrs. Delaney. I got work.

(*Exit.* LOLA *turns from the window, annoyed at her rejection. She is about to start on the dishes again when the* MILKMAN *arrives. She opens the back door and detains him*)

MILKMAN   'Morning, Mrs. Coffman.

MRS. COFFMAN   'Morning.

LOLA   (*Brightly*) Hello there, Mr. Milkman. How are you today?

MILKMAN   'Morning, Lady.

LOLA   I think I'm going to want a few specials today. Can you come in a minute?

(*Goes to icebox*)

MILKMAN   (*Coming in*) What'll it be?

(*He probably is used to her. He is not a handsome man but husky and attractive in his uniform*)

LOLA   (*At refrigerator*) Well, now, let's see. You got any cottage cheese?

MILKMAN   We always got cottage cheese, Lady. (*Showing her card*) All you gotta do is check the items on the card and we leave 'em. Now I gotta go back to the truck.

LOLA   Now, don't scold me. I always mean to do that but you're always here before I think of it. Now, I guess I'll need some coffee cream, too—half a pint.

MILKMAN   Coffee cream. O.K.

LOLA   Now let me see . . . Oh, yes, I want a quart of buttermilk. My husband has liked buttermilk ever since he stopped drinking. My husband's an alcoholic. Had to give it up. Did I ever tell you? (*Starts out. Stops at sink*)

MILKMAN   Yes, Lady.
(*Starts to go. She follows*)

LOLA   Now he can't get enough to eat. Eats six times a day. He comes home in the middle of the morning, and I fix him a snack. In the middle of the afternoon he has a malted milk with an egg in it. And then another snack before he goes to bed.

MILKMAN   What'd ya know?

LOLA   Keeps his energy up.

MILKMAN   I'll bet. Anything else, Lady?

LOLA   No, I guess not.

MILKMAN (*Going out*)   Be back in a jiffy.
(*Gives her slip*)

LOLA   I'm just so sorry I put you to so much extra work. (*He goes. Returns shortly with dairy products*) After this I'm going to do my best to remember to check the card. I don't think it's right to put people to extra work.
(*Goes to icebox, puts things away*)

MILKMAN (*Smiles, is willing to forget*)   That's all right, Lady.

LOLA   Maybe you'd like a piece of cake or a sandwich. Got some awfully good cold cuts in the icebox.

MILKMAN   No, thanks, Lady.

LOLA   Or maybe you'd like a cup of coffee.

MILKMAN   No, thanks.
(*He's checking the items, putting them on the bill*)

LOLA   You're just a young man. You oughta be going to college. I think everyone should have an education. Do you like your job?

MILKMAN   It's O.K.
(*Looks at* LOLA)

LOLA   You're a husky young man. You oughta be out in Hollywood making those Tarzan movies.

MILKMAN (*Steps back. Feels a little flattered*)   When I first began on this job I didn't get enough exercise, so I started working out on the bar-bell.

LOLA Bar-bells?

MILKMAN Keeps you in trim.

LOLA (*Fascinated*) Yes, I imagine.

MILKMAN I sent my picture in to *Strength and Health* last month. (*Proudly*) It's a physique study! If they print it, I'll bring you a copy.

LOLA Oh, will you? I think we should all take better care of ourselves, don't you?

MILKMAN If you ask me, Lady, that's what's wrong with the world today. We're not taking care of ourselves.

LOLA I wouldn't be surprised.

MILKMAN Every morning, I do forty push-ups before I eat my breakfast.

LOLA Push-ups?

MILKMAN Like this. (*He spreads himself on the floor and demonstrates, doing three rapid push-ups.* LOLA *couldn't be more fascinated. Then he springs to his feet*) That's good for shoulder development. Wanta feel my shoulders?

LOLA Why . . . why, yes. (*He makes one arm tense and puts her hand on his shoulder*) Why, it's just like a rock.

MILKMAN I can do seventy-nine without stopping.

LOLA Seventy-nine!

MILKMAN Now feel my arm.

LOLA (*Does so*) Goodness!

MILKMAN You wouldn't believe what a puny kid I was. Sickly, no appetite.

LOLA Is that a fact? And, my! Look at you now.

MILKMAN (*Very proud*) Shucks, any man could do the same . . . if he just takes care of himself.

LOLA Oh, sure, sure.

(*A horn is heard offstage*)

MILKMAN There's my partner. I gotta beat it. (*Picks up his things, shakes hands, leaves hurriedly*) See you tomorrow, Lady.

LOLA 'Bye.

(*She watches him from kitchen window until he gets out of sight. There is a look of some wonder on her face, an emptiness, as though she were unable to understand anything that ever happened to her. She looks at clock, runs into living room, turns on*)

radio. *A pulsating tom-tom is heard as a theme introduction. Then
the* ANNOUNCER)

ANNOUNCER (*In dramatic voice*) TA-BOOoooo! (*Now in a very
soft, highly personalized voice.* LOLA *sits on couch, eats candy*)
It's Ta-boo, radio listeners, your fifteen minutes of temptation.
(*An alluring voice*) Won't you join me? (LOLA *swings feet up*)
Won't you leave behind your routine, the dull cares that make
up your day-to-day existence, the little worries, the uncertainties,
the confusions of the work-a-day world, and follow *me* where
pagan spirits hold sway, where lithe natives dance on a moon-
enchanted isle, where palm trees sway with the restless ocean
tide, restless surging on the white shore? Won't you come along?
(*More tom-tom. Now in an oily voice*) But remember, it's TA-
BOOOOOooooo-OOO!

(*Now the tom-tom again, going into a sensual, primitive rhythm
melody.* LOLA *has been transfixed from the beginning of the program. She lies down on the davenport, listening, then slowly,
growing more and more comfortable*)

WESTERN UNION BOY (*Appears suddenly in the open door*) Telegram for Miss Marie Buckholder.

LOLA (*Startled*) Oh! she's not here.

WESTERN UNION BOY Sign here.

(LOLA *signs, then she closes the door and brings the envelope
into the house, looking at it wonderingly. This is a major temptation for her. She puts the envelope on the table but can't resist
looking at it. Finally she gives in and takes it to the kitchen to
steam it open. Then* MARIE *and* TURK *burst into the room.* LOLA,
confused, wonders what to do with the telegram)

MARIE Mrs. Delaney! (*Turns off radio.* LOLA *embarrassedly slips
the message into her apron pocket and runs in to greet them*)
Mind if we turn your parlor into an art studio?

LOLA Sure, go right ahead. Hi, Turk.

(TURK *gives a wave of his arm*)

MARIE (*To* TURK, *indicating her bedroom*) You can change in
there, Turk.

(*Exit to bedroom*)

LOLA (*Puzzled*) Change?

MARIE He's gotta take off his clothes.

LOLA Huh?

(*Closes door*)

MARIE These drawings are for my life class.

LOLA (*Consoled but still mystified*) Oh.

MARIE (*Sits on couch*) Turk's the best male model we've had all year. Lotsa athletes pose for us 'cause they've all got muscles.

LOLA You mean . . . he's gonna pose *naked?*

MARIE (*Laughs*) No. The women do, but the men are always more proper. Turk's going to pose in his track suit.

LOLA Oh. (*Almost to herself*) The women pose naked but the men don't. (*This strikes her as a startling inconsistency*) If it's all right for a woman, it oughta be for a man.

MARIE (*Businesslike*) The man always keeps covered. (*Calling to* TURK) Hurry up, Turk.

TURK (*With all his muscles in place, he comes out. He is not at all self-conscious about his semi-nudity. His body is something he takes very much for granted.* LOLA *is a little dazed by the spectacle of flesh*) How do you want this lovely body? Same pose I took in Art Class?

MARIE Yah. Over there where I can get more light on you.

TURK (*Opens door. Starts pose*) Anything in the house I can use for a javelin?

MARIE Is there, Mrs. Delaney?

LOLA How about the broom?

TURK O.K.

(LOLA *runs out to get it.* TURK *goes to her in kitchen, takes it, returns to living room and resumes pose*)

MARIE (*From her sofa, studying* TURK *in relation to her sketch-pad*) Your left foot a little more this way. (*Studying it*) O.K., hold it. (*Starts sketching rapidly and industriously*)

LOLA (*Starts unwillingly into the kitchen, changes her mind and returns to the scene of action.* MARIE *and* TURK *are too busy to comment.* LOLA *looks at sketch, inspecting it*) Well . . . that's real pretty, Marie. (MARIE *is intent.* LOLA *moves closer to look at the drawing*) It . . . it's real artistic. (*Pause*) I wish *I* was artistic.

TURK Baby, I can't hold this pose very long at a time.

MARIE Rest whenever you feel like it.

TURK O.K.

MARIE (*To* LOLA) If I make a good drawing, they'll use it for the posters for the Spring Relays.

LOLA Ya. You told me.

MARIE (*To* TURK) After I'm finished with these sketches I won't have to bother you any more.

TURK   No bother. (*Rubs his shoulder—he poses*) Hard pose, though. Gets me in the shoulder.

(MARIE *pays no attention.* LOLA *peers at him so closely, he becomes a little self-conscious and breaks pose. This also breaks* LOLA's *concentration*)

LOLA   I'll heat you up some coffee.

(*A little embarrassed, she goes to kitchen*)

TURK   (*Softly to* MARIE)   Hey, can't you keep her out of here? She makes me feel naked.

MARIE   (*Laughs*)   I can't keep her out of her own house, can I?

TURK   Didn't she ever see a man before?

MARIE   Not a big, beautiful man like you, Turky. (TURK *smiles, is flattered by any recognition of his physical worth, takes it as an immediate invitation to lovemaking. Pulling her up, he kisses her as* DOC *comes up on porch.* MARIE *pushes* TURK *away*) Turk, get back in your corner.

(DOC *comes in from outside*)

DOC   (*Cheerily*)   Hi, everyone.

MARIE   Hi.

TURK   Hi, Doc. (DOC *then sees* TURK, *feels immediate resentment. Goes into kitchen to* LOLA) What's goin' on here?

LOLA   (*Getting cups*)   Oh, hello, Daddy. Marie's doin' a drawin'.

DOC   (*Trying to size up the situation.* MARIE *and* TURK *are too busy to speak*)   Oh.

LOLA   I've just heated up the coffee, want some?

DOC   Yeah. What happened to Turk's clothes?

LOLA   Marie's doing some drawings for her *life* class, Doc.

DOC   Can't she draw him with his clothes on?

LOLA   (*Very professional now*)   No, Doc, it's not the same. See, it's a *life* class. They draw bodies. They all do it, right in the classroom.

DOC   Why, Marie's just a young girl; she shouldn't be drawing things like that. I don't care if they do teach it at college. It's not right.

LOLA   (*Disclaiming responsibility*)   I don't know, Doc.

TURK   (*Turns*)   I'm tired.

MARIE   (*Squats at his feet*)   Just let me finish the foot.

DOC   Why doesn't she draw something else, a bowl of flowers or a cathedral . . . or a sunset?

LOLA   All she told me, Doc, was if she made a good drawing of Turk, they'd use it for the posters for the Spring Relay. (*Pause*) So I guess they don't want sunsets.

DOC   What if someone walked into the house now? What would they think?

LOLA   Daddy, Marie just asked me if it was all right if Turk came and posed for her. Now that's all she said, and I said O.K. But if you think it's wrong I won't let them do it again.

DOC   I just don't like it.

MARIE   Hold it a minute more.

TURK   O.K.

LOLA   Well, then you speak to Marie about it if . . .

DOC   (*He'd never mention anything disapprovingly to* MARIE)   No, Baby. I couldn't do that.

LOLA   Well, then . . .

DOC   Besides, it's not her fault. If those college people make her do drawings like that, I suppose she has to do them. I just don't think it's right she should have to, that's all.

LOLA   Well, if you think it's wrong . . .

DOC   (*Ready to dismiss it*)   Never mind.

LOLA   I don't see any harm in it, Daddy.

DOC   Forget it.

LOLA   (*Goes to icebox*)   Would you like some buttermilk?

DOC   Thanks.

   (MARIE *finishes sketch*)

MARIE   O.K. That's all I can do for today.

TURK   Is there anything I can do for *you*?

MARIE   Yes—get your clothes on.

TURK   O.K., Coach.

   (TURK *exits*)

LOLA   You know what Marie said, Doc? She said that the women pose naked, but the men don't.

DOC   Why, of course, honey.

LOLA   Why is that?

DOC   (*Stumped*)   Well . . .

LOLA   If it's all right for a woman it oughta be for a man. But the man always keeps covered. That's what she said.

DOC   Well, that's the way it should be, honey. A man, after all, is a man, and he . . . well, he has to protect himself.

LOLA   And a woman doesn't?

DOC   It's different, honey.

LOLA   Is it? (*She doesn't understand, so she changes the subject*) I've got a secret, Doc, Bruce is coming.

DOC   Is that so?

LOLA (*After a glum silence*) You know, Marie's boy friend from Cincinnati. I promised Marie a long time ago, when her fiancé came to town, dinner was on me. So I'm getting out the best china and cooking the best meal you ever sat down to.

DOC When did she get the news?

LOLA The telegram came this morning.

DOC That's fine. That Bruce sounds to me like just the fellow for her. I think I'll go in and congratulate her.

LOLA (*Nervous*) Not now, Doc.

DOC Why not?

LOLA Well, Turk's there. It might make him feel embarrassed.

DOC Well, why doesn't Turk clear out now that Bruce is coming? What's he hanging around for? She's engaged to marry Bruce, isn't she?

(TURK *enters from bedroom and goes to* MARIE, *starting to make advances*)

LOLA Marie's just doing a picture of him, Doc.

DOC You always stick up for him. You encourage him.

LOLA Shhh, Daddy. Don't get upset.

DOC (*Angrily*) Who says I'm upset?

LOLA (*Cautiously*) Well . . . you are, Doc. Just a little.

DOC (*Angry and embarrassed*) Why *should* I be? Why should I?

LOLA I don't know, Doc, but . . .

DOC (*Stamping out of kitchen*) You imagine things.

(*He hurries upstairs as though to avoid further disclosure of his feelings.* LOLA *remains in kitchen almost in tears, she is so dismayed.* TURK, *knowing he is unobserved, grabs* MARIE *in his arms and she is ready to let him kiss her. They are unobserved*)

Curtain

SCENE II

The same evening, after supper. Outside it is dark. There has been an almost miraculous transformation of the entire house. LOLA, *apparently, has been working hard and fast all day. The rooms are spotlessly clean and there are such additions as new lampshades, fresh curtains, etc. In the kitchen all the enamel surfaces glisten, and piles of junk that have lain around for months have been disposed of.* LOLA *and* DOC *are in the kitchen, he washing up the dishes and she puttering around putting the finishing touches on her housecleaning.*

LOLA (*At stove*) There's still some beans left. Do you want them, Doc?

DOC I had enough.

LOLA I hope you got enough to eat tonight, Daddy. I been so busy cleaning I didn't have time to fix you much.

DOC I wasn't very hungry.

LOLA (*At table, cleaning up*) You know what? Mrs. Coffman said I could come over and pick all the lilacs I wanted for my centerpiece tomorrow. Isn't that nice? I don't think she poisoned Little Sheba, do you?

DOC I never did think so, Baby. Where'd you get the new curtains?

LOLA I went out and bought them this afternoon. Aren't they pretty? Be careful of the woodwork, it's been varnished.

DOC How come, honey?

LOLA (*Gets broom and dustpan from closet*) Bruce is comin'. I figured I had to do my spring housecleaning *some* time.

DOC You got all this done in one day? The house hasn't looked like this in years.

LOLA I can be a good housekeeper when I want to be, can't I, Doc?

DOC (*Holding dustpan for* LOLA) I never had any complaints. Where's Marie now?

LOLA I don't know, Doc. I haven't seen her since she left here this morning with Turk.

DOC Well! I'm not going to say anything more about that.

LOLA Daddy, Marie can take care of herself. Don't worry.
(*Returns broom to closet*)

DOC (*Goes into living room*) 'Bout time for Fibber McGee and Molly.

LOLA (*At the back door, before going out*) Daddy, I'm gonna run over to Mrs. Coffman's and see if she's got any silver polish. I'll be right back. (*At the radio* DOC *starts twisting the dial. He rejects one noisy program after another, then very unexpectedly he comes across a rendition of Shubert's famous "Ave Maria," sung in a high soprano voice. Probably he has encountered the piece before somewhere, but it is now making its first impression on him. Gradually he is transported into a world of ethereal beauty which he never knew existed. He listens intently. The music has expressed some ideal of beauty he never fully realized. Then* LOLA *returns through the back door, letting it slam, breaking the spell, and announcing in a loud, energetic voice)* Isn't it funny? I'm not a bit tired tonight. You'd think after working so hard all day I'd be pooped.

DOC (*In the living room; he cringes*) Baby, don't use that word.

LOLA (*Sets silver polish on kitchen table and joins* DOC) I'm sorry, Doc. I hear Marie and Turk say it all the time, and I thought it was kinda cute.

DOC It . . . it sounds vulgar.

LOLA (*Kisses* DOC) I won't say it again, Daddy. Where's Fibber McGee?

DOC Not quite time yet.

LOLA Let's get some peppy music.

DOC (*Tuning in a sentimental dance band*) That what you want?

LOLA That's O.K. (DOC *takes a pack of cards off radio and starts shuffling them, very deftly*) I love to watch you shuffle cards, Daddy. You use your hands so gracefully. (*She watches closely*) Do me one of your card tricks.

DOC Baby, you've seen them all.

LOLA But I never get tired of them.

DOC O.K. Take a card. (LOLA *does*) Keep it now. Don't tell me what it is.

LOLA I won't.

DOC (*Shuffling cards again*) Now put it back in the deck. I won't look.

(*He closes his eyes*)

LOLA (*With childish delight*) All right.

DOC Put it back.

LOLA Uh-huh.

DOC O.K. (*Shuffles cards again, cutting them, taking top half off, exposing* LOLA's *card to her astonishment*) That your card?

LOLA (*Unbelievingly*) Daddy, how did you do it?

DOC Baby, I've pulled that trick on you dozens of times.

LOLA But I never understand how you do it.

DOC Very simple.

LOLA Docky, show me how you do that.

DOC (*You can forgive him a harmless feeling of superiority*) Try it for yourself.

LOLA Doc, you're clever. I never could do it.

DOC Nothing to it.

LOLA There is *too*. Show me how you do it, Doc.

DOC And give away all my secrets? It's a gift, honey. A magic gift.

LOLA Can't you give it to me?

DOC (*Picks up newspaper*) A man has to keep some things to himself.

LOLA It's not a gift at all, it's just some trick you *learned*.

DOC O.K., Baby, any way you want to look at it.

LOLA Let's have some music. How soon do you have to meet Ed Anderson?

(DOC *tunes radio*)

DOC I still got a little time.

(*Pleased*)

LOLA We'll have a real party for Marie and Bruce, won't we, Doc? And maybe you'll do your card tricks.

DOC Sure.

LOLA And then we'll make sure they get a chance to be alone a while, won't we, Doc?

DOC I . . . I suppose. After all, they're engaged.

LOLA There were times when *we* wanted to be alone. Remember, Doc?

DOC . . . Yes.

LOLA And we wouldn't wanta act like *my* folks used to. We had to *steal* all the good times we used to have, didn't we, Doc? Remember the dances we used to go to, without ever telling Mama and Daddy?

DOC Yes, Baby.

LOLA Remember the homecoming dance, when Charlie Kettlekamp and I won the Charleston contest?

DOC (*He'd like to forget it*) Please, honey, I'm trying to read.

LOLA And you got mad at him 'cause he thought he should take me home afterwards.

DOC I did not.

LOLA Yes, you did— Charlie was all right, Doc, really he was. You were just jealous.

DOC I *wasn't* jealous.

LOLA (*She has become very coy and flirtatious now, an old dog playing old tricks*) You got jealous every time we went out any place and I even looked at another boy. There was never anything between Charlie and me; there never was.

DOC That was a long time ago . . .

LOLA Lots of other boys called me up for dates . . . Sammy Knight . . . Hank Biderman . . . Dutch McCoy.

DOC Sure, Baby. You were the "it" girl.

LOLA (*Pleading for his attention now*) But I saved all my dates for *you*, didn't I, Doc?

DOC (*Trying to joke*) As far as *I* know, Baby.

LOLA (*Hurt*) Daddy, I did. You *got* to believe that. I never took a date with any other boy but you.

DOC (*A little weary and impatient*) That's all forgotten now.
(*Turns off radio*)

LOLA How can you talk that way, Doc? That was the happiest time of our lives. I'll never forget it.

DOC (*Disapprovingly*) Honey!

LOLA (*At the window*) That was a lovely spring. The trees were so heavy and green and the air smelled so sweet. Remember the walks we used to take, down to the old chapel, where it was so quiet and still?
(*Sits on couch*)

DOC In the spring a young man's fancy turns . . . pretty fancy.

LOLA (*In the same tone of reverie*) I was pretty then, wasn't I, Doc? Remember the first time you kissed me? You were scared as a young girl, I believe, Doc; you trembled so. (*She is being very soft and delicate. Caught in the reverie, he chokes a little and cannot answer*) We'd been going together all year and you were always so shy. Then for the first time you grabbed me and kissed me. Tears came to your eyes, Doc, and you said you'd love me forever and ever. Remember? You said . . . if I didn't marry you, you wanted to die . . . I remember 'cause it scared me for anyone to say a thing like that.

DOC (*In a repressed tone*) Yes, Baby.

LOLA And when the evening came on, we stretched out on the cool grass and you kissed me all night long.

DOC (*Opens doors*) Baby, you've got to forget those things. That was twenty years ago.

LOLA I'll soon be forty. Those years have just vanished—vanished into thin air.

DOC Yes.

LOLA Just disappeared—like Little Sheba. (*Pause*) Maybe you're sorry you married me now. You didn't know I was going to get old and fat and sloppy . . .

DOC Oh, Baby!

LOLA It's the truth. That's what I am. But I didn't know it, either. Are you sorry you married me, Doc?

DOC Of course not.

LOLA I mean, are you sorry you *had* to marry me?

DOC (*Goes to porch*) We were never going to talk about that, Baby.

LOLA (*Following* DOC *out*) You *were* the first one, Daddy, the *only* one. I'd just die if you didn't believe that.

DOC (*Tenderly*) I know, Baby.

LOLA You were so nice and so proper, Doc; I thought nothing we could do together could ever be wrong—or make us unhappy. Do you think we did wrong, Doc?

DOC (*Consoling*) No, Baby, of course I don't.

LOLA I don't think anyone knows about it except my folks, do you?

DOC Of course not, Baby.

LOLA (*Follows him in*) I wish the baby had lived, Doc. I don't think that woman knew her business, do you, Doc?

DOC I guess not.

LOLA If we'd gone to a doctor, she would have lived, don't you think?

DOC Perhaps.

LOLA A doctor wouldn't have known we'd just got married, would he? Why were we so afraid?

DOC (*Sits on couch*) We were just kids. Kids don't know how to look after things.

LOLA (*Sits on couch*) If we'd had the baby she'd be a young girl now; then maybe you'd have *saved* your money, Doc, and she could be going to college—like Marie.

DOC Baby, what's done is done.

LOLA It must make you feel bad at times to think you had to give up being a doctor and to think you don't have any money like you used to.

DOC No . . . no, Baby. We should never feel bad about what's past. What's in the past can't be helped. You . . . you've got to forget it and live for the present. If you can't forget the past, you stay in it and never get out. I might be a big M.D. today, instead of a chiropractor; we might have had a family to raise and be with us now; I might still have a lot of money if I'd used my head and invested it carefully, instead of gettin' drunk every night. We might have a nice house, and comforts, and friends. But we don't have any of those things. So what! We gotta keep on living, don't we? I can't stop just 'cause I made a few mistakes. I gotta keep goin' . . . somehow.

LOLA   Sure, Daddy.

DOC   (*Sighs and wipes brow*) I . . . I wish you wouldn't ask me questions like that, Baby. Let's not talk about it any more. I gotta keep goin', and not let things upset me, or . . . or . . .

LOLA   I'm sorry, Doc. I didn't mean to upset you.

DOC   I'm not upset.

LOLA   What time'll you be home tonight?

DOC   'Bout eleven o'clock.

LOLA   I wish you didn't have to go tonight. I feel kinda lonesome.

DOC   Some time soon, we'll go *out* together. I kinda hate to go to those night clubs and places since I stopped drinking, but some night I'll take you out to dinner.

LOLA   Oh, will you, Daddy?

DOC   We'll get dressed up and go to the Windermere and have a fine dinner and dance between courses.

LOLA   (*Eagerly*) Let's do, Daddy. I got a little money saved up. I got about forty dollars out in the kitchen. We can take that if you need it.

DOC   I'll have plenty of money the first of the month.

LOLA   (*She has made a quick response to the change of mood, seeing a future evening of carefree fun*) What are we sitting round here so serious for? (*Turns to radio*) Let's have some music. (*LOLA gets a lively foxtrot on the radio, dances with DOC. They begin dancing vigorously as though to dispense with the sadness of the preceding dialogue, but slowly it winds them and leaves LOLA panting*) We oughta go dancing . . . all the time, Docky . . . It'd be good for us. Maybe if I danced more often, I'd lose . . . some of . . . this fat. I remember . . . I used to be able to dance like this . . . all night . . . and not even notice . . . it. (*LOLA breaks into a Charleston routine as of yore*) Remember the Charleston, Daddy?

(*DOC is clapping his hands in rhythm. Then MARIE bursts in through the front door, the personification of the youth that LOLA is trying to recapture*)

DOC   Hi, Marie.

MARIE   What are you trying to do, a jig, Mrs. Delaney? (*MARIE doesn't intend her remark to be cruel, but it wounds LOLA. LOLA stops abruptly in her dancing, losing all the fun she has been able to create for herself. She feels she might cry; so to hide her feel-*

ings she hurries quietly out to kitchen, but DOC *and* MARIE *do not notice.* MARIE *notices the change in atmosphere*) Hey, what's been happening around here?

DOC Lola got to feeling industrious. You oughta see the kitchen.

MARIE (*Running to kitchen, where she is too observant of the changes to notice* LOLA *weeping in corner.* LOLA, *of course, straightens up as soon as* MARIE *enters*) What got into you, Mrs. Delaney? You've done wonders with the house. It looks marvelous.

LOLA (*Quietly*) Thanks, Marie.

MARIE (*Darting back into living room*) I can hardly believe I'm in the same place.

DOC Think your boy friend'll like it?

(*Meaning* BRUCE)

MARIE (*Thinking of* TURK) You know how men are. Turk never notices things like that.

(*Starts into her room blowing a kiss to* DOC *on her way.* LOLA *comes back in, dabbing at her eyes*)

DOC Turk?

(MARIE *is gone*)

LOLA I didn't want her to see me dancing that way. I feel sorta silly.

DOC Does she know we're having *Bruce* to dinner? Not Turk!

LOLA (*Nervous*) Let's not argue any more, Daddy.

MARIE (*Jumps back into the room with her telegram*) My telegram's here. When did it come?

LOLA It came about an hour ago, honey.

(LOLA *looks nervously at* DOC. DOC *looks puzzled and a little sore*)

MARIE Bruce is coming! "Arriving tomorrow 5:00 P.M. CST, Flight 22, Love, Bruce." When did the telegram come?

DOC (*Looking hopelessly at* LOLA) So it came an hour ago.

LOLA (*Nervously*) Isn't it nice I got the house all cleaned? Marie, you bring Bruce to dinner with us tomorrow night. It'll be a sort of wedding present.

MARIE That would be wonderful, Mrs. Delaney, but I don't want you to go to any trouble.

LOLA No trouble at all. Now I insist. (*Front doorbell rings*) That must be Turk.

MARIE (*Whisper*) Don't tell *him*. (*Goes to door.* LOLA *scampers to kitchen*) Hi, Turk. Come on in.

TURK (*Entering. Stalks her*) Hi.

(*Looks around to see if anyone is present, then takes her in his arms and starts to kiss her*)

LOLA I'm sorry, Doc. I'm sorry about the telegram.

DOC Baby, people don't do things like that. Don't you understand? *Nice* people don't.

MARIE Stop it!

TURK What's the matter?

MARIE They're in the kitchen.

(TURK *sits with book*)

DOC Why didn't you give it to her when it came?

LOLA Turk was posing for Marie this morning and I couldn't give it to her while he was here.

(TURK *listens at door*)

DOC Well, it just isn't nice to open other people's mail.

(TURK *goes to* MARIE's *door*)

LOLA I guess I'm not nice then. That what you mean?

MARIE Turk, will you get away from that door?

DOC No, Baby, but . . .

LOLA I don't see any harm in it, Doc. I steamed it open and sealed it back. (TURK *at switch in living room*) She'll never know the difference. I don't see any harm in that, Doc.

DOC (*Gives up*) O.K., Baby, if you don't see any harm in it, I guess I can't explain it.

(*Starts getting ready to go*)

LOLA I'm sorry, Doc. Honest, I'll never do it again. Will you forgive me?

DOC (*Giving her a peck of a kiss*) I forgive you.

MARIE (*Comes back with book*) Let's look like we're studying.

TURK Biology? Hot dog!

LOLA (*After* MARIE *leaves her room*) Now I feel better. Do you have to go now?

(TURK *sits by* MARIE *on the couch*)

DOC Yah.

LOLA Before you go, why don't you show your tricks to Marie?

DOC (*Reluctantly*) Not now.

LOLA Oh, please do. They'd be crazy about them.

DOC (*With pride*) O.K. (*Preens himself a little*) If you think they'd enjoy them . . . (LOLA, *starting to living room, stops suddenly upon seeing* MARIE *and* TURK *spooning behind a book. A broad, pleased smile breaks on her face and she stands silently watching.* DOC *is at sink*) Well . . . what's the matter, Baby?

LOLA (*In a soft voice*) Oh . . . nothing . . . nothing . . . Doc.

DOC Well, do you want me to show 'em my tricks or don't you?

LOLA (*Coming back to center kitchen; in a secretive voice with a little giggle*) I guess they wouldn't be interested now.

DOC (*With injured pride. A little sore*) Oh, very well.

LOLA Come and look, Daddy.

DOC (*Shocked and angry*) No!

LOLA Just one little look. They're just kids, Daddy. It's sweet. (*Drags him by arm*)

DOC (*Jerking loose*) Stop it, Baby. I won't do it. It's not decent to snoop around spying on people like that. It's cheap and mischievous and mean.

LOLA (*This had never occurred to her*) Is it?

DOC Of course it is.

LOLA I don't spy on Marie and Turk to be mischievous and mean.

DOC Then why *do* you do it?

LOLA You watch young people make love in the movies, don't you, Doc? There's nothing wrong with that. And I *know* Marie and I like her, and Turk's nice, too. They're both so young and pretty. Why shouldn't I watch them?

DOC I give up.

LOLA Well, why shouldn't I?

DOC I don't know, Baby, but it's not nice.

(TURK *kisses* MARIE's *ear*)

LOLA (*Plaintive*) I think it's one of the nicest things I know.

DOC It's not right for Marie to do that, particularly since Bruce is coming. We shouldn't allow it.

LOLA Oh, they don't do any harm, Doc. I think it's all right.

DOC It's not all right. I don't know why you encourage that sort of thing.

LOLA I don't encourage it.

DOC You do, too. You like that fellow Turk. You said so. And I say he's no good. Marie's sweet and innocent; she doesn't understand guys like him. I think I oughta run him outa the house.

LOLA Daddy, you wouldn't do that.

DOC (*Very heated*) Then you talk to her and tell her how we feel.

LOLA Hush, Daddy. They'll hear you.

DOC I don't care if they do hear me.

LOLA (*To* DOC *at stove*) Don't get upset, Daddy. Bruce is coming and Turk won't be around any longer. I promise you.

DOC All right. I better go.

LOLA   I'll go with you, Doc. Just let me run up and get a sweater. Now wait for me.

DOC   Hurry, Baby.

(LOLA *hurries upstairs.* DOC *stands in the center of the kitchen where he can hear, from the living room, the cautious murmur of intimate laughter shared by* MARIE *and* TURK. *To* DOC, *the laughter suggests something a little obscene and he bristles with indignation. But when he hears* LOLA's *voice, he finds composure again*)

LOLA   I'm coming, Doc. (*She hurries downstairs.* DOC *turns out kitchen lights and joins her at foot of stairs.* LOLA *speaks to* TURK *and* MARIE) I'm walking Doc to the bus. (TURK *has been studying a youthful picture of* LOLA *which* DOC, *rather rudely, takes from his hands. Eager to prevent any possible conflict,* LOLA *hurries* DOC *out the front door. When he is outside, she turns back to* MARIE *and speaks very privately*) Then I'm going for a long, long walk in the moonlight. You kids have a good time.

(*She goes out*)

MARIE   'Bye, Mrs. Delaney.

(*Exits*)

TURK   He hates my guts.

(*Goes to front door*)

MARIE   Oh, he does not.

(*Follows* TURK, *blocks his exit in door*)

TURK   Yes, he does. If you ask me, he's jealous.

MARIE   Jealous?

TURK   I've always thought he had a crush on you.

MARIE   Now, Turk, don't be silly. Doc is nice to me. It's just in a few little things he does, like fixing my breakfast, but he's nice to everyone.

TURK   He ever make a pass?

MARIE   No.

TURK   He better not.

MARIE   Turk, don't be ridiculous. Doc's such a nice, quiet man; if he gets any fun out of being nice to me, why not?

TURK   He's got a wife of his own, hasn't he? Why doesn't he make a few passes at her?

MARIE   Things like that are none of our business.

TURK   O.K. How about a snuggle, lovely?

MARIE   (*A little prim*)   No more for tonight, Turk.

TURK   Why's tonight different from any other night?

MARIE   I think we should make it a rule, every once in a while, just to sit and talk.

(*Starts to sit on couch, but goes to chair*)

TURK   (*Restless, sits on couch*)   O.K. What'll we talk about?

MARIE   Well . . . there's lotsa things.

TURK   O.K. Start in.

MARIE   A person doesn't start a conversation that way.

TURK   Start it any way you want to.

MARIE   Two people should have something to talk about, like politics or psychology or religion.

TURK   How 'bout sex?

MARIE   Turk!

TURK   Have you read the Kinsey Report, Miss Buckholder?

MARIE   I should say not.

TURK   How old were you when you had your first affair, Miss Buckholder? And did you ever have relations with your grandfather?

MARIE   Turk, stop it.

TURK   You wanted to talk about something; I was only trying to please. Let's have a kiss.

MARIE   Not tonight.

TURK   Who you savin' it up for?

MARIE   Don't talk that way.

TURK   (*Gets up, yawns*)   Well, thanks, Miss Buckholder, for a nice evening. It's been a most enjoyable talk.

MARIE   (*Anxious*)   Turk, where are you going?

TURK   I guess I'm a man of action, Baby.

MARIE   Turk, don't go.

TURK   Why not? I'm not doin' any good here.

MARIE   Don't go.

TURK   (*Returns and she touches him. They sit on couch*)   Now why didn't you think of this before? C'mon, let's get to work.

MARIE   Oh, Turk, this is all we ever do.

TURK   Are you complaining?

MARIE   (*Weakly*)   No.

TURK   Then what do you want to put on such a front for?

MARIE   It's not a front.

TURK   What else is it? (*Mimicking*) Oh, no, Turk. Not tonight, Turk. I want to talk about philosophy, Turk. (*Himself again*) When all the time you know that if I went outa here without givin' you a good lovin' up you'd be sore as hell . . . Wouldn't you?

MARIE (*She has to admit to herself it's true; she chuckles*)   Oh . . .
   Turk . . .

TURK   It's true, isn't it?

MARIE   Maybe.

TURK   How about tonight, lovely; going to be lonesome?

MARIE   Turk, you're in training.

TURK   What of it? I can throw that old javelin any old time, *any
   old time.* C'mon, Baby, we've got by with it before, haven't we?

MARIE   I'm not so sure.

TURK   What do you mean?

MARIE   Sometimes I think Mrs. Delaney knows.

TURK   Well, bring her along. I'll take care of her, too, if it'll keep
   her quiet.

MARIE (*A pretense of being shocked*)   Turk!

TURK   What makes you think so?

MARIE   Women just sense those things. She asks so many questions.

TURK   She ever *say* anything?

MARIE   No.

TURK   Now *you're* imagining things.

MARIE   Maybe.

TURK   Well, stop it.

MARIE   O.K.

(*Now they engage in a little rough-house, he cuffing her like an
affectionate bear, she responding with "Stop it," "Turk, that hurt,"
etc. And she slaps him playfully. Then they laugh together at
their own pretense. Now* LOLA *enters the back way very quietly,
tiptoeing through the dark kitchen, standing by the doorway
where she can peek at them. There is a quiet, satisfied smile on
her face. She watches every move they make, alertly*)

TURK   Now, Miss Buckholder, what is your opinion of the psycho-
   dynamic pressure of living in the atomic age?

MARIE (*Playfully*)   Turk, don't make fun of me.

TURK   Tonight?

MARIE (*Her eyes dance as she puts him off just a little longer*)
   Well.

TURK   Tonight will never come again. (*This is true. She smiles*)
   O.K.?

MARIE (*They embrace and start to dance*)   Let's go out somewhere
   first and have a few beers. We can't come back till they're asleep.

TURK   O.K.

(They dance slowly out the door. Then LOLA *moves quietly into the living room and out onto the porch. There she can be heard calling plaintively in a lost voice)*

LOLA   Little Sheba . . . Come back . . . Come back, Little Sheba. Come back.

Curtain

ACT TWO

SCENE I

The next morning. LOLA *and* DOC *are at breakfast again.* LOLA *is rambling on while* DOC *sits meditatively, his head down, his face in his hands.*

LOLA (*In a light, humorous way, as though the faults of youth were as blameless as the uncontrollable actions of a puppy. Chuckles*) Then they danced for a while and went out together, arm in arm. . . .

DOC (*Sitting at table, very nervous and tense*) I don't wanta hear any more about it, Baby.

LOLA What's the matter, Docky?

DOC Nothing.

LOLA You look like you didn't feel very good.

DOC I didn't sleep well last night.

LOLA You didn't take any of those sleeping pills, did you?

DOC No.

LOLA Well, don't. The doctors say they're terrible for you.

DOC I'll feel better after a while.

LOLA Of course you will.

DOC What time did Marie come in last night?

LOLA I don't know, Doc. I went to bed early and went right to sleep. Why?

DOC Oh . . . nothing.

LOLA You musta slept if you didn't hear her.

DOC I heard her; it was after midnight.

LOLA Then what did you ask me for?

DOC I wasn't sure it was her.

LOLA What do you mean?

DOC I thought I heard a man's voice.

LOLA Turk probably brought her inside the door.

DOC (*Troubled*) I thought I heard someone laughing. A man's laugh . . . I guess I was just hearing things.

LOLA Say your prayer?

DOC (*Gets up*) Yes.

LOLA Kiss me 'bye. (*He leans over and kisses her, then puts on his coat and starts to leave*) Do you think you could get home a little early? I want you to help me entertain Bruce. Marie said he'd be here about 5:30. I'm going to have a lovely dinner: stuffed pork chops, twice-baked potatoes, and asparagus, and for dessert a big chocolate cake and maybe ice cream . . .

DOC Sounds fine.

LOLA So you get home and help me.

DOC O.K.

(DOC *leaves kitchen and goes into living room. Again on the chair is* MARIE's *scarf. He picks it up as before and fondles it. Then there is the sound of* TURK's *laughter, soft and barely audible. It sounds like the laugh of a sated Bacchus.* DOC's *body stiffens. It is a sickening fact he must face and it has been revealed to him in its ugliest light. The lyrical grace, the spiritual ideal of Ave Maria is shattered. He has been fighting the truth, maybe suspecting all along that he was deceiving himself. Now he looks sick, with all his blind confusion inside him. With an immobile expression of blankness on his face, he stumbles into the table above the sofa*)

LOLA (*Still in kitchen*) Haven't you gone yet, Docky?

DOC (*Dazed*) No . . . no, Baby.

LOLA (*In doorway*) Anything the matter?

DOC No . . . no. I'm all right now. (*Drops scarf, takes hat, exits. He has managed to sound perfectly natural. He braces himself and goes out.* LOLA *stands a moment, looking after him with a little curiosity. Then* MRS. COFFMAN *sticks her head in back door*)

MRS. COFFMAN Anybody home?

LOLA (*Turning*) 'Morning, Mrs. Coffman.

MRS. COFFMAN (*Inspecting the kitchen's new look*) So this is what you've been up to, Mrs. Delaney.

LOLA (*Proud*) Yes, I been busy.

(MARIE's *door opens and closes.* MARIE *sticks her head out of her bedroom door to see if the coast is clear, then sticks her head back in again to whisper to* TURK *that he can leave without being observed*)

MRS. COFFMAN Busy? Good Lord, I never seen such activity. What got into you, Lady?

LOLA Company tonight. I thought I'd fix things up a little.

MRS. COFFMAN You mean you done all this in one day?

LOLA (*With simple pride*) I said I been busy.

MRS. COFFMAN Dear God, you done your spring housecleaning all in one day.

(TURK *appears in living room*)

LOLA (*Appreciating this*) I fixed up the living room a little, too.

MRS. COFFMAN I must see it. (*Goes into living room.* TURK *overhears her and ducks back into* MARIE's *room, shutting the door behind himself and* MARIE) I declare! Overnight you turn the place into something really swanky.

LOLA Yes, and I bought a few new things, too.

MRS. COFFMAN Neat as a pin, and so warm and cozy. I take my hat off to you, Mrs. Delaney. I didn't know you had it in you. All these years, now, I been sayin' to myself, "That Mrs. Delaney is a good for nothing, sits around the house all day, and never so much as shakes a dust mop." I guess it just shows, we never really know what people are like.

LOLA I still got some coffee.

MRS. COFFMAN Not now, Mrs. Delaney. Seeing your house so clean makes me feel ashamed. I gotta get home and get to work.

(*Goes to kitchen*)

LOLA (*Follows*) I hafta get busy, too. I got to get out all the silver and china. I like to set the table early, so I can spend the rest of the day looking at it.

(*Both laugh*)

MRS. COFFMAN Good day, Mrs. Delaney.

(*Exits. Hearing the screen door slam,* MARIE *guards the kitchen door and* TURK *slips out the front. But neither has counted on* DOC's *reappearance. After seeing that* TURK *is safe,* MARIE *blows a good-bye kiss to him and joins* LOLA *in the kitchen. But* DOC *is coming in the front door just as* TURK *starts to go out. There is a moment of blind embarrassment, during which* DOC *only looks stupefied and* TURK, *after mumbling an unintelligible apology, runs out. First* DOC *is mystified, trying to figure it all out. His face looks more and more troubled. Meanwhile,* MARIE *and* LOLA *are talking in the kitchen*)

MARIE Boo! (*Sneaking up behind* LOLA *at back porch*)

LOLA (*Jumping around*) Heavens! You scared me, Marie. You up already?

MARIE Yah.

LOLA This is Saturday. You could sleep as late as you wanted.

MARIE (*Pouring a cup of coffee*) I thought I'd get up early and help you.

LOLA Honey, I'd sure appreciate it. You can put up the table in the living room, after you've had your breakfast. That's where we'll eat. Then you can help me set it.

(DOC *closes door*)

MARIE O.K.

LOLA Want a sweet roll?

MARIE I don't think so. Turk and I had so much beer last night. He got kinda tight.

LOLA He shouldn't do that, Marie.

MARIE (*Starts for living room*) Just keep the coffee hot for me. I'll want another cup in a minute. (*Stops on seeing* DOC) Why, Dr. Delaney! I thought you'd gone.

DOC (*Trying to sustain his usual manner*) Good morning, Marie. (*But not looking at her*)

MARIE (*She immediately wonders*) Why . . . why . . . how long have you been here, Doc?

DOC Just got here, just this minute.

LOLA (*Comes in*) That you, Daddy?

DOC It's me.

LOLA What are you doing back?

DOC I . . . I just thought maybe I'd feel better . . . if I took a glass of soda water . . .

LOLA I'm afraid you're not well, Daddy.

DOC I'm all right.

(*Starts for kitchen*)

LOLA (*Helping* MARIE *with table*) The soda's on the drainboard. (DOC *goes to kitchen, fixes some soda, and stands a moment, just thinking. Then he sits sipping the soda, as though he were trying to make up his mind about something*) Marie, would you help me move the table? It'd be nice now if we had a dining room, wouldn't it? But if we had a dining room, I guess we wouldn't have you, Marie. It was my idea to turn the dining room into a bedroom and rent it. I thought of lots of things to do for extra money . . . a few years ago . . . when Doc was so . . . so sick.

(*They set up table—*LOLA *gets cloth from cabinet*)

MARIE This is a lovely tablecloth.

LOLA Irish linen. Doc's mother gave it to us when we got married. She gave us all our silver and china, too. The china's Havelin. I'm so proud of it. It's the most valuable possession we own. I just washed it. . . . Will you help me bring it in? (*Getting china from kitchen*) Doc was sortuva Mama's boy. He was an only child and his mother thought the sun rose and set in him. Didn't she, Docky? She brought Doc up like a real gentleman.

MARIE Where are the napkins?

LOLA Oh, I forgot them. They're so nice I keep them in my bureau drawer with my handkerchiefs. Come upstairs and we'll get them.

(LOLA *and* MARIE *go upstairs. Then* DOC *listens to be sure* LOLA *and* MARIE *are upstairs, looks cautiously at the whiskey bottle on pantry shelf but manages to resist several times. Finally he gives in to temptation, grabs bottle off shelf, then starts wondering how to get past* LOLA *with it. Finally, it occurs to him to wrap it inside his trench coat which he gets from pantry and carries over his arm.* LOLA *and* MARIE *are heard upstairs. They return to the living room and continue setting table as* DOC *enters from kitchen on his way out*)

LOLA (*Coming downstairs*) Did you ever notice how nice he keeps his fingernails? Not many men think of things like that. And he used to take his mother to church every Sunday.

MARIE (*At table*) Oh, Doc's a real gentleman.

LOLA Treats women like they were all beautiful angels. We went together a whole year before he even kissed me. (DOC *comes through the living room with coat and bottle, going to front door*) On your way back to the office now, Docky?

DOC (*His back to them*) Yes.

LOLA Aren't you going to kiss me good-bye before you go, Daddy? (*She goes to him and kisses him.* MARIE *catches* DOC's *eye and smiles. Then she exits to her room, leaving door open*) Get home early as you can. I'll need you. We gotta give Bruce a royal welcome.

DOC Yes, Baby.

LOLA Feeling all right?

DOC Yes.

LOLA (*In doorway,* DOC *is on porch*) Take care of yourself.

DOC (*In a toneless voice*) Good-bye.

(*He goes*)

LOLA (*Coming back to table with pleased expression, which changes to a puzzled look, calls to* MARIE)   Now that's funny. Why did Doc take his raincoat? It's a beautiful day. There isn't a cloud in sight.

Curtain

SCENE II

It is now 5:30. The scene is the same as the preceding except that more finishing touches have been added and the two women, still primping the table, lighting the tapers, are dressed in their best. LOLA *is arranging the centerpiece.*

LOLA (*Above table, fixing flowers*)   I just love lilacs, don't you, Marie? (*Takes one and studies it*) Mrs. Coffman was nice; she let me have all I wanted. (*Looks at it very closely*) Aren't they pretty? And they smell so sweet. I think they're the nicest flower there is.

MARIE   They don't last long.

LOLA (*Respectfully*)   No. Just a few days. Mrs. Coffman's started blooming just day before yesterday.

MARIE   By the first of the week they'll all be gone.

LOLA   Vanish . . . they'll vanish into thin air. (*Gayer now*) Here, honey, we have them to spare *now*. Put this in your hair. There. (MARIE *does*) Mrs. Coffman's been so nice lately. I didn't use to like her. Now where could Doc be? He promised he'd get here early. He didn't even come home for lunch.

MARIE (*Gets two chairs from bedroom*)   Mrs. Delaney, you're a peach to go to all this trouble.

LOLA (*Gets salt and pepper*)   Shoot, I'm gettin' more fun out of it than you are. Do you think Bruce is going to like us?

MARIE   If he doesn't, I'll never speak to him again.

LOLA (*Eagerly*)   I'm just dying to meet him. But I feel sorta bad I never got to do anything nice for Turk.

MARIE (*Carefully prying*)   Did . . . Doc ever say anything to you about Turk . . . and me?

LOLA   About Turk and you? No, honey. Why?

MARIE (*She seems to feel a little guilty*) I just wondered.

LOLA What if Bruce finds out that you've been going with some-one else?

MARIE Bruce and I had a very businesslike understanding before I left for school that we weren't going to sit around lonely just because we were separated.

LOLA Aren't you being kind of mean to Turk?

MARIE I don't think so.

LOLA How's he going to feel when Bruce comes?

MARIE He may be sore for a little while, but he'll get over it.

LOLA Won't he feel bad?

MARIE He's had his eye on a pretty little Spanish girl in his his-tory class for a long time. I like Turk, but I wouldn't think of marrying him.

LOLA No! Really?

(LOLA, *with a look of sad wonder on her face, sits on arm of couch. It's been a serious disillusionment*)

MARIE What's the matter?

LOLA I . . . I don't know.

MARIE Did I say anything that upset you?

LOLA Well . . . I guess I thought you and Turk kind of *cared* for each other. You know what I mean.

(MARIE *gives an irresponsible little laugh*)

MARIE You're a sentimentalist, Mrs. Delaney.

LOLA (*With sad realization*) Yes . . . I suppose I am.

(*The doorbell rings and* MARIE *jumps to answer it*)

MARIE That must be Bruce. (*Opens the door and greets him*) Bruce!

BRUCE (*Steps inside, taking* MARIE *in his arms*) How are you, sweetheart?

(*He is an efficient-looking young businessman*)

MARIE Wonderful.

BRUCE Did you get my wire?

MARIE Sure.

BRUCE You're looking swell.

MARIE Thanks. What took you so long to get here?

BRUCE Well, honey, I had to go to my hotel and take a shower.

MARIE Bruce, this is Mrs. Delaney.

BRUCE (*Now he gets the cozy quality out of his voice*) How do you do, ma'am?

LOLA How d'ya do?

BRUCE   Marie has said some very nice things about you in her letters.

MARIE   Mrs. Delaney has fixed the grandest dinner for us.

BRUCE   Now that was to be my treat. I have a big expense account now, honey. I thought we could all go down to the hotel and have dinner there, and celebrate first with a few cocktails.

LOLA   Oh, we can have cocktails, too. Excuse me, just a minute. (*She hurries to the kitchen and starts looking for the whiskey.* BRUCE *kisses* MARIE)

MARIE   (*Whispers*) Now, Bruce, she's been working on this dinner all day. She even cleaned the house for you.

BRUCE   (*With a surveying look*) Did she?

MARIE   And Doc's joining us. You'll like Doc.

BRUCE   Honey, are we going to have to stay here the whole evening?

MARIE   We just can't eat and run. We'll get away as soon as we can.

BRUCE   I hope so. I got the raise, sweetheart. They're giving me new territory.

(LOLA *is frantic in the kitchen, having found the bottle missing. She hurries back into the living room*)

LOLA   You kids are going to have to entertain yourselves awhile 'cause I'm going to be busy in the kitchen. Why don't you turn on the radio, Marie? Get some dance music. I'll shut the door so . . . so I won't disturb you.

(LOLA *does so, then goes to the telephone*)

MARIE   Come and see my room, Bruce. I've fixed it up just darling. And I've got your picture in the prettiest frame right on my dresser.

(*They exit and their voices are heard from the bedroom while* LOLA *is phoning*)

LOLA   (*At the phone*) This is Mrs. Delaney. Is . . . Doc there? Well, then, is Ed Anderson there? Well, would you give me Ed Anderson's telephone number? You see, he sponsored Doc into the club and helped him . . . you know . . . and . . . and I was a little worried tonight. . . . Oh, thanks. Yes, I've got it. (*She writes down number*) Could you have Ed Anderson call me if he comes in? Thank you. (*She hangs up. On her face is a dismal expression of fear, anxiety and doubt. She searches flour bin, icebox, closet. Then she goes into the living room, calling to* MARIE *and* BRUCE *as she comes*) I . . . I guess we'll go ahead without Doc, Marie.

MARIE   (*Enters from her room*) What's the matter with Doc, Mrs. Delaney?

LOLA Well . . . he got held up at the office . . . just one of those
things, you know. It's too bad. It would have to happen when I
needed him most.

MARIE Sure you don't need any help?

LOLA Huh? Oh, no. I'll make out. Everything's ready. I tell you
what I'm going to do. Three's a crowd, so I'm going to be the
butler and serve the dinner to you two young lovebirds . . . (*The
telephone rings*) Pardon me . . . pardon me just a minute. (*She
rushes to phone, closing the door behind her*) Hello? Ed? Have
you seen Doc? He went out this morning and hasn't come back.
We're having company for dinner and he was supposed to be
home early. . . . That's not all. All this time we've had a quart
of whiskey in the kitchen and Doc's never gone near it. I went
to get it tonight. I was going to serve some cocktails. It was *gone*.
Yes, I saw it there yesterday. No, I don't think so. . . . He said
this morning he had an upset stomach but . . . Oh, would you?
. . . Thank you, Mr. Anderson. Thank you a million times. And
you let me know when you find out anything. Yes, I'll be here
. . . yes. (*Hangs up and crosses back to living room*) Well, I
guess we're all ready.

BRUCE Aren't you going to look at your present?

MARIE Oh, sure, let's get some scissors.

(*Their voices continue in bedroom*)

MARIE (*Enters with* BRUCE) Mrs. Delaney, we think you should
eat with us.

LOLA Oh, no, honey, I'm not very hungry. Besides, this is the first
time you've been together in months and I think you should be
alone. Marie, why don't you light the candles? Then we'll have
just the right atmosphere.

(*She goes into kitchen, gets tomato-juice glasses from icebox
while* BRUCE *lights the candles*)

BRUCE Do we have to eat by candlelight? I won't be able to see.

(LOLA *returns*)

LOLA Now, Bruce, you sit here. (*He and* MARIE *sit*) Isn't that going
to be cozy? Dinner for two. Sorry we won't have time for cocktails.
Let's have a little music.

(*She turns on the radio and a Viennese waltz swells up as the
curtain falls*)

Curtain

SCENE III

Funereal atmosphere. It is about 5:30 the next morning. The sky is just beginning to get light outside, while inside the room the shadows still cling heavily to the corners. The remains of last night's dinner clutter the table in the living room. The candles have guttered down to stubs amid the dirty dinner plates, and the lilacs in the centerpiece have wilted. LOLA *is sprawled on the davenport, sleeping. Slowly she awakens and regards the morning light. She gets up and looks about strangely, beginning to show despair for the situation she is in. She wears the same spiffy dress she had on the night before but it is wrinkled now, and her marcelled coiffure is awry. One silk stocking has twisted loose and falls around her ankle. When she is sufficiently awake to realize her situation, she rushes to the telephone and dials a number.*

LOLA (*At telephone. She sounds frantic*) Mr. Anderson? Mr. Anderson, this is Mrs. Delaney again. I'm sorry to call you so early, but I just *had* to. . . . Did you find Doc? . . . No, he's not home yet. I don't suppose he'll come home till he's drunk all he can hold and wants to sleep. . . . I don't know what else to think, Mr. Anderson. I'm scared, Mr. Anderson. I'm awful scared. Will you come right over? . . . Thanks, Mr. Anderson. (*She hangs up and goes to kitchen to make coffee. She finds some left from the night before, so turns on the fire to warm it up. She wanders around vaguely, trying to get her thoughts in order, jumping at every sound. Pours herself a cup of coffee, then takes it to living room, sits and sips it. Very quietly* DOC *enters through the back way into the kitchen. He carries a big bottle of whiskey which he carefully places back in the pantry, not making a sound, hangs up trench coat, then puts suit coat on back of chair. Starts to go upstairs, but* LOLA *speaks*) Doc? That you, Doc?
(*Then* DOC *quietly walks in from kitchen. He is staggering drunk, but he is managing for a few minutes to appear as though he were perfectly sober and nothing had happened. His steps, however, are not too sure and his eyes are like blurred ink spots.* LOLA *is too frightened to talk. Her mouth is gaping and she is breathless with fear*)

DOC   Good morning, honey.

LOLA   Doc! You all right?

DOC   The morning paper here? I wanta see the morning paper.

LOLA   Doc, we don't get a morning paper. *You* know that.

DOC   Oh, then I suppose I'm drunk or something. That what you're trying to say?

LOLA   No, Doc . . .

DOC   Then give me the morning paper.

LOLA   (*Scampering to get last night's paper from console table*) Sure, Doc. Here it is. Now just sit there and be quiet.

DOC   (*Resistance rising*)   Why shouldn't I be quiet?

LOLA   Nothin', Doc . . .

DOC   (*Has trouble unfolding paper. He places it before his face in order not to be seen. But he is too blind even to see*)   Nothing, Doc.
(*Mockingly*)

LOLA   (*Cautiously, after a few minutes' silence*)   Doc, are you all right?

DOC   Of course, I'm all right. Why shouldn't I be all right?

LOLA   Where you been?

DOC   What's it your business where I been? I been to London to see the Queen. What do you think of that? (*Apparently she doesn't know what to think of it*) Just let me alone. That's all I ask. I'm all right.

LOLA   (*Whimpering*)   Doc, what made you do it? You said you'd be home last night . . . 'cause we were having company. Bruce was here and I had a big dinner fixed . . . and you never came. What was the matter, Doc?

DOC   (*Mockingly*)   We had a big dinner for *Bruce*.

LOLA   Doc, it was for you, too.

DOC   Well . . . I don't want it.

LOLA   Don't get mad, Doc.

DOC   (*Threateningly*)   Where's Marie?

LOLA   I don't know, Doc. She didn't come in last night. She was out with Bruce.

DOC   (*Back to audience*)   I suppose you tucked them in bed together and peeked through the keyhole and applauded.

LOLA   (*Sickened*)   Doc, don't talk that way. Bruce is a nice boy. They're gonna get married.

DOC   He probably *has* to marry her, the poor bastard. Just 'cause she's pretty and he got amorous one day . . . Just like I had to marry *you.*

LOLA   Oh, Doc!

DOC   You and Marie are both a couple of sluts.

LOLA   Doc, please don't talk like that.

DOC   What are you good for? You can't even get up in the morning and cook my breakfast.

LOLA (*Mumbling*)   I will, Doc. I will after this.

DOC   You won't even sweep the floors, till some bozo comes along to make love to Marie, and then you fix things up like Buckingham Palace or a Chinese whorehouse with perfume on the lampbulbs, and flowers, and the gold-trimmed china *my mother* gave us. We're not going to use these any more. My mother didn't buy those dishes for whores to eat off of.

(*He jerks the cloth off the table, sending the dishes rattling to the floor*)

LOLA   Doc! Look what you done.

DOC   Look what I *did*, not *done.* I'm going to get me a drink.

(*Goes to kitchen*)

LOLA (*Follows to platform*)   Oh, no, Doc! You know what it does to you!

DOC   You're damn right I know what it does to me. It makes me willing to come home here and look at you, you two-ton old heifer. (*Takes a long swallow*) There! And pretty soon I'm going to have another, then another.

LOLA (*With dread*)   Oh, Doc! (LOLA *takes phone.* DOC *sees this, rushes for the butcher-knife from kitchen-cabinet drawer. Not finding it, he gets a hatchet from the back porch*) Mr. Anderson? Come quick, Mr. Anderson. He's back. He's *back!* He's got a hatchet!

DOC   God damn you! Get away from that telephone. (*He chases her into living room where she gets the couch between them*) That's right, phone! Tell the world I'm drunk. Tell the whole damn world. Scream your head off, you fat slut. Holler till all the neighbors think I'm beatin' hell outuv you. Where's Bruce now— under Marie's bed? You got all fresh and pretty for him, didn't you? Combed your hair for once—you even washed the back of your neck and put on a girdle. You were willing to harness all that fat into one bundle.

LOLA (*About to faint under the weight of the crushing accusations*) Doc, don't say any more . . . I'd rather you hit me with an axe,

Doc. . . . Honest I would. But I can't stand to hear you talk like that.

DOC   I oughta hack off all that fat, and then wait for Marie and chop off those pretty ankles she's always dancing around on . . . then start lookin' for Turk and fix him too.

LOLA   Daddy, you're talking crazy!

DOC   I'm making sense for the first time in my life. You didn't know I knew about it, did you? But I saw him coming outa there, I saw him. You knew about it all the time and thought you were hidin' something . . .

LOLA   Daddy, I didn't know anything about it at all. Honest, Daddy.

DOC   Then *you're* the one that's crazy, if you think I didn't know. You were running a regular house, weren't you? It's probably been going on for years, ever since we were married.

(*He lunges for her. She breaks for kitchen. They struggle in front of sink*)

LOLA   Doc, it's not so; it's not so. You gotta believe me, Doc.

DOC   You're lyin'. But none a that's gonna happen any more. I'm gonna fix you now, once and for all. . . .

LOLA   Doc . . . don't do that to me. (LOLA, *in a frenzy of fear, clutches him around the neck holding arm with axe by his side*) Remember, Doc. It's *me*, Lola! You said I was the prettiest girl you ever saw. Remember, Doc! It's me! Lola!

DOC   (*The memory has overpowered him. He collapses, slowly mumbling*)   Lola . . . my pretty Lola.

(*He passes out on the floor.* LOLA *stands now, as though in a trance. Quietly* MRS. COFFMAN *comes creeping in through the back way*)

MRS. COFFMAN   (*Calling softly*)   Mrs. Delaney! (LOLA *doesn't even hear.* MRS. COFFMAN *comes in*) Mrs. Delaney! Here you are, Lady. I heard screaming and I was frightened for you.

LOLA   I . . . I'll be all right . . . some men are comin' pretty soon; everything'll be all right.

MRS. COFFMAN   I'll stay until they get here.

LOLA   (*Feeling a sudden need*)   Would you . . . would you *please*, Mrs. Coffman?

(*Breaks into sobs*)

MRS. COFFMAN   Of course, Lady. (*Regarding* DOC) The doctor got "sick" again?

LOLA   (*Mumbling*)   Some men . . . 'll be here pretty soon . . .

MRS. COFFMAN   I'll try to straighten things up before they get here. . . .

(*She rights chair, hangs up telephone and picks up the axe, which she is holding when* ED ANDERSON *and* ELMO HUSTON *enter unannounced. They are experienced AA's. Neatly dressed businessmen approaching middle-age*)

ED   Pardon us for walking right in, Mrs. Delaney, but I didn't want to waste a second.

(*Kneels by* DOC)

LOLA (*Weakly*)   It's all right. . . .

(*Both men observe* DOC *on the floor, and their expressions hold understanding mixed with a feeling of irony. There is even a slight smile of irony on* ED's *face. They have developed the surgeon's objectivity*)

ED   Where is the hatchet? (*To* ELMO *as though appraising* DOC's *condition*) What do you think, Elmo?

ELMO   We can't leave him here if he's gonna play around with hatchets.

ED   Give me a hand, Elmo. We'll get him to sit up and then try to talk some sense into him. (*They struggle with the lumpy body,* DOC *grunting his resistance*) Come on, Doc, old boy. It's Ed and Elmo. We're going to take care of you.

(*They seat him at table*)

DOC (*Through a thick fog*)   Lemme alone.

ED   Wake up. We're taking you away from here.

DOC   Lemme 'lone, God damn it.

(*Falls forward, head on table*)

ELMO (*To* MRS. COFFMAN)   Is there any coffee?

MRS. COFFMAN   I think so, I'll see.

(*Goes to stove with cup from drainboard. Lights fire under coffee and waits for it to get heated*)

ED   He's way beyond coffee.

ELMO   It'll help some. Get something hot into his stomach.

ED   If we could get him to eat. How 'bout some hot food, Doc?

(DOC *makes a hideous face*)

ELMO   City Hospital, Ed?

ED   I guess that's what it will have to be.

LOLA   Where you going to take him?

(ELMO *goes to phone; speaks quietly to City Hospital*)

ED   Don't know. Wanta talk to him first.

MRS. COFFMAN (*Coming in with the coffee*)   Here's the coffee.

ED (*Taking cup*) Hold him, Elmo, while I make him swallow this.

ELMO Come on, Doc, drink your coffee.

(DOC *only blubbers*)

DOC (*After the coffee is down*) Uh . . . what . . . what's goin' on here?

ED It's me, Doc. Your old friend Ed. I got Elmo with me.

DOC (*Twisting his face painfully*) Get out, both of you. Lemme 'lone.

ED (*With certainty*) We're takin' you with us, Doc.

DOC Hell you are. I'm all right. I just had a little slip. We all have slips. . . .

ED Sometimes, Doc, but we gotta get over 'em.

DOC I'll be O.K. Just gimme a day to sober up. I'll be as good as new.

ED Remember the last time, Doc? You said you'd be all right in the morning and we found you with a broken collar bone. Come on.

DOC Boys, I'll be all right. Now lemme alone.

ED How much has he had, Mrs. Delaney?

LOLA I don't know. He had a quart when he left here yesterday and he didn't get home till now.

ED He's probably been through a *couple* of quarts. He's been dry for a long time. It's going to hit him pretty hard. Yah, he'll be a pretty sick man for a few days. (*Louder to* DOC, *as though he were talking to a deaf man*) Wanta go to the City Hospital, Doc?

DOC (*This has a sobering effect on him. He looks about him furtively for possible escape*) No . . . no, boys. Don't take me there. That's a torture chamber. No, Ed. You wouldn't do that to me.

ED They'll sober you up.

DOC Ed, I been there; I've seen the place. That's where they take the crazy people. You can't do that to me, Ed.

ED Well, *you're* crazy aren't you? Goin' after your wife with a hatchet.

(*They lift* DOC *to his feet.* DOC *looks with dismal pleading in his eyes at* LOLA, *who has her face in her hands*)

DOC (*So plaintive, a sob in his voice*) Honey! Honey! (LOLA *can't look at him. Now* DOC *tries to make a getaway, bolting blindly into the living room before the two men catch him and hold him in front of living-room table*) Honey, don't let 'em take me there. They'll believe *you*. Tell 'em you won't *let* me take a drink.

LOLA Isn't there any place else you could take him?

ED Private sanitariums cost a lotta dough.

LOLA I got forty dollars in the kitchen.

ED That won't be near enough.

DOC I'll be at the meeting tomorrow night sober as you are now.

ED (*To* LOLA) All the king's horses couldn't keep him from takin' another drink now, Mrs. Delaney. He got himself into this; he's gotta sweat it out.

DOC I won't go to the City Hospital. That's where they take the crazy people.

(*Stumbles into chair*)

ED (*Using all his patience now*) Look, Doc. Elmo and I are your friends. You know that. Now if you don't come along peacefully, we're going to call the cops and you'll have to wear off this jag in the cooler. How'd you like that? (DOC *is as though stunned*) The important thing is for you to get sober.

DOC I don't wanna go.

ED The City Hospital or the City Jail. Take your choice. We're not going to leave you here. Come on, Elmo.

(*They grab hold of him*)

DOC (*Has collected himself and now given in*) O.K., boys. Gimme another drink and I'll go.

LOLA Oh, no, Doc.

ED Might as well humor him, ma'am. Another drink couldn't make much difference now. (MRS. COFFMAN *runs for bottle and glass in pantry and comes right back with them. She hands them to* LOLA) O.K., Doc, we're goin' to give you a drink. Take a good one; it's gonna be your last for a long, long time to come. (ED *takes the bottle, removes the cork and gives* DOC *a glass of whiskey.* DOC *takes his fill, straight, coming up once or twice for air. Then* ED *takes the bottle from him and hands it to* LOLA. *To* LOLA) They'll keep him three or four days, Mrs. Delaney; then he'll be home again, good as new. (*Modestly*) I . . . I don't want to pry into personal affairs, ma'am . . . but he'll need you then, pretty bad . . . Come on, Doc. Let's go.

(ED *has a hold of* DOC's *coat sleeve trying to maneuver him. A faraway look is in* DOC's *eyes, a dazed look containing panic and fear. He gets to his feet*)

DOC (*Struggling to sound reasonable*) Just a minute, boys . . .

ED What's the matter?

DOC I . . . I wanta glass of water.

ED You'll get a glass of water later. Come on.

DOC (*Beginning to twist a little in* ED's *grasp*) . . . a glass of water
. . . that's all . . .

(*One furious, quick twist of his body and he eludes* ED)

ED   Quick, Elmo.

(ELMO *acts fast and they get* DOC *before he gets away. Then* DOC *struggles with all his might, kicking and screaming like a pampered child,* ED *and* ELMO *holding him tightly to usher him out*)

DOC (*As he is led out*)   Don't let 'em take me there. Don't take me there. Stop them, somebody. Stop them. That's where they take the crazy people. Oh, God, stop them, somebody. Stop them.

(LOLA *looks on blankly while* ED *and* ELMO *depart with* DOC. *Now there are several moments of deep silence*)

MRS. COFFMAN (*Clears up. Very softly*)   Is there anything more I can do for you now, Mrs. Delaney?

LOLA   I guess not.

MRS. COFFMAN (*Puts a hand on* LOLA's *shoulder*)   Get busy, Lady. Get busy and forget it.

LOLA   Yes . . . I'll get busy right away. Thanks, Mrs. Coffman.

MRS. COFFMAN   I better go. I've got to make breakfast for the children. If you want me for anything, let me know.

LOLA   Yes . . . yes . . . good-bye, Mrs. Coffman.

(MRS. COFFMAN *exits.* LOLA *is too exhausted to move from the big chair. At first she can't even cry; then the tears come slowly, softly. In a few moments* BRUCE *and* MARIE *enter, bright and merry.* LOLA *turns her head slightly to regard them as creatures from another planet*)

MARIE (*Springing into room.* BRUCE *follows*)   Congratulate me, Mrs. Delaney.

LOLA   Huh?

MARIE   We're going to be married.

LOLA   Married? (*It barely registers*)

MARIE (*Showing ring*)   Here it is. My engagement ring.

(MARIE *and* BRUCE *are too engrossed in their own happiness to notice* LOLA's *stupor*)

LOLA   That's lovely . . . lovely.

MARIE   We've had the most wonderful time. We danced all night and then drove out to the lake and saw the sun rise.

LOLA   That's nice.

MARIE   We've made all our plans. I'm quitting school and flying back to Cincinnati with Bruce this afternoon. His mother has invited me to visit them before I go home. Isn't that wonderful?

LOLA   Yes . . . yes, indeed.

MARIE   Going to miss me?

LOLA   Yes, of course, Marie. We'll miss you very much . . . uh . . . congratulations.

MARIE   Thanks, Mrs. Delaney. (*Goes to bedroom door*) Come on, Bruce, help me get my stuff. (*To* LOLA) Mrs. Delaney, would you throw everything into a big box and send it to me at home? We haven't had breakfast yet. We're going down to the hotel and celebrate.

BRUCE   I'm sorry we're in such a hurry, but we've got a taxi waiting. (*They go into* MARIE'S *room*)

LOLA   (*Goes to telephone, dials*) Long-distance? I want to talk to Green Valley 223. Yes. This is Delmar 1887. (*She hangs up.* MARIE *comes from bedroom, followed by* BRUCE, *who carries suitcase*)

MARIE   Mrs. Delaney, I sure hate to say good-bye to you. You've been so wonderful to me. But Bruce says I can come and visit you once in a while, didn't you, Bruce?

BRUCE   Sure thing.

LOLA   You're going?

MARIE   We're going downtown and have our breakfast, then do a little shopping and catch our plane. And thanks for everything, Mrs. Delaney.

BRUCE   It was very nice of you to have us to dinner.

LOLA   Dinner? Oh, don't mention it.

MARIE   (*To* LOLA) There isn't much time for good-bye now, but I just want you to know Bruce and I wish you the best of everything. You and Doc both. Tell Doc good-bye for me, will you, and remember I think you're both a coupla peaches.

BRUCE   Hurry, honey.

MARIE   'Bye, Mrs. Delaney! (*She goes out*)

BRUCE   'Bye, Mrs. Delaney. Thanks for being nice to my girl. (*They make a hurried exit*)

LOLA   (LOLA *stands a moment in the doorway, automatically waving farewell. Then the telephone rings and she makes a rush to answer it*) Hello. Hello, Mom. It's Lola, Mom. How are you? Mom, Doc's sick again. Do you think Dad would let me come home for a while? I'm awfully unhappy, Mom. Do you think . . . just till I made up my mind? . . . All right. No, I guess it wouldn't do any good for you to come here . . . I . . . I'll let you know what I decide to do. That's all, Mom. Thanks. Tell Daddy hello. (*She hangs up and doesn't move, but sits looking emptily before her*)

Curtain

SCENE IV

It is morning, a week later. The house is neat again. LOLA *is dusting in the living room as* MRS. COFFMAN *enters.*

MRS. COFFMAN   Mrs. Delaney! Good morning, Mrs. Delaney.

LOLA   Come in, Mrs. Coffman.

MRS. COFFMAN (*Coming in*)   It's a fine day for the games. I've got a box lunch ready, and I'm taking all the kids to the Stadium. My boy's got a ticket for you, too. You better get dressed and come with us.

LOLA   Thanks, Mrs. Coffman, but I've got work to do.

MRS. COFFMAN   But it's a big day. The Spring Relays . . . All the athletes from the colleges are supposed to be there.

LOLA   Oh, yes. You know that boy, Turk, who used to come here to see Marie—he's one of the big stars.

MRS. COFFMAN   Is that so? Come on . . . do. We've got a ticket for you. . . .

LOLA   Oh, no, I have to stay here and clean up the house. Doc may be coming home today. I talked to him on the phone. He wasn't sure what time they'd let him out, but I wanta have the place all nice for him.

MRS. COFFMAN   Well, I'll tell you all about it when I come home. Everybody and his brother will be there.

LOLA   Have a good time.

MRS. COFFMAN   'Bye, Mrs. Delaney.

LOLA   'Bye.

(MRS. COFFMAN *leaves, and* LOLA *goes into kitchen. The* MAILMAN *comes onto porch and leaves a letter, but* LOLA *doesn't even know he's there. Then the* MILKMAN *knocks on the kitchen door*)

LOLA   Come in.

MILKMAN (*Entering with armful of bottles, etc.*) I see you checked the list, lady. You've got a lot of extras.

LOLA Ya— I think my husband's coming home.

MILKMAN (*He puts the supplies on table, then pulls out magazine*) Remember, I told you my picture was going to appear in *Strength and Health.* (*Showing her magazine*) Well, see that pile of muscles? That's me.

LOLA My goodness. You got your picture in a magazine.

MILKMAN Yes, ma'am. See what it says about my chest development? For the greatest self-improvement in a three months' period.

LOLA Goodness sakes. You'll be famous, won't you?

MILKMAN If I keep busy on these bar-bells. I'm working now for "muscular separation."

LOLA That's nice.

MILKMAN (*Cheerily*) Well, good day, ma'am.

LOLA You forgot your magazine.

MILKMAN That's for you.

(*Exits.* LOLA *puts away the supplies in the icebox. Then* DOC *comes in the front door, carrying the little suitcase she previously packed for him. His quiet manner and his serious demeanor are the same as before.* LOLA *is shocked by his sudden appearance*)

LOLA Docky!

(*Without thinking she assumes an attitude of fear.* DOC *observes this and it obviously pains him*)

DOC Good morning, honey.

(*Pause*)

LOLA Are . . . are you all right, Doc?

DOC Yes, I'm all right. (*An awkward pause. Then* DOC *tries to reassure her*) Honest, I'm all right, honey. Please don't stand there like that . . . like I was gonna . . . gonna . . .

LOLA (*Tries to relax*) I'm sorry, Doc.

DOC How you been?

LOLA Oh, I been all right, Doc. Fine.

DOC Any news?

LOLA I told you about Marie—over the phone.

DOC Yah.

LOLA He was a very nice boy, Doc. Very nice.

DOC That's good. I hope they'll be happy.

LOLA (*Trying to sound bright*) She said . . . maybe she'd come back and visit us some time. That's what she *said.*

DOC She . . . seemed like such a sweet young girl.

LOLA Honest, Doc, I didn't know what she and Turk were up to, all that time. I knew they spooned a lot, and I might have guessed at other things, but I didn't know.

DOC I know you didn't, honey.

LOLA I guess . . . I've always thought that . . . you and I were the only people . . . in all the world . . . that ever did anything wrong.

DOC (*Takes her hand consolingly*) Now, now. Now, now. Let's forget it, shall we? (*He looks around the room contentedly*) It's *good* to be home.

LOLA Is it, Daddy?

DOC Yah.

(*Beginning to choke up, just a little*)

LOLA Did everything go all right . . . I mean . . . did they treat you well and . . .

DOC (*Now loses control of his feelings. Tears in his eyes, he all but lunges at her, gripping her arms, drilling his head into her bosom*) Honey, don't ever leave me. *Please* don't ever leave me. If you do, they'd have to keep me down at that place all the time. I don't know what I said to you or what I did, I can't remember hardly anything. But please forgive me . . . please . . . please . . . And I'll try to make everything up.

LOLA (*There is surprise on her face and new contentment. She becomes almost angelic in demeanor. Tenderly she places a soft hand on his head*) Daddy! Why, of course I'll never leave you. (*A smile of satisfaction*) You're all I've got. You're all I ever had. (*Very tenderly he kisses her*)

DOC (*Collecting himself now.* LOLA *sits beside* DOC) I . . . I feel better . . . already.

LOLA (*Almost gay*) So do I. Have you had your breakfast?

DOC No. The food there was terrible. When they told me I could go this morning, I decided to wait and fix myself breakfast here.

LOLA (*Happily*) Come on out in the kitchen and I'll get you a nice, big breakfast. I'll scramble some eggs and . . . You see I've got the place all cleaned up just the way you like it. (DOC *goes to kitchen*) Now you sit down here and I'll get your fruit juice. (*He sits and she gets fruit juice from refrigerator*) I've got bacon this morning, too. My, it's expensive now. And I'll light the oven and make you some toast, and here's some orange marmalade, and . . .

DOC (*With a new feeling of control*) Fruit juice. I'll need lots of fruit juice for a while. The doctor said it would restore the vitamins. You see, that damn whiskey kills all the vitamins in your system, eats up all the sugar in your kidneys. They came around every morning and shot vitamins in my arm. Oh, it didn't hurt. And the doctor told me to drink a quart of fruit juice every day. And you better get some candy bars for me at the grocery this morning. Doctor said to eat lots of candy, try to replace the sugar.

LOLA   I'll do that, Doc. Here's another glass of grapefruit juice now. I'll get some candy bars first thing.

DOC   The doctor said I should have a hobby. Said I should go out more. That's all that's wrong with me. I thought maybe I'd go hunting once in a while.

LOLA   Yes, Doc. And bring home lots of good things to eat.

DOC   I'll get a big bird dog, too. Would you like a sad-looking old bird dog around the house?

LOLA   Of course, I would. (*All her life and energy have been restored*) You know what, Doc? I had another dream last night.

DOC   About Little Sheba?

LOLA   Oh, it was about everyone and everything. (*In a raptured tone. She gets bacon from icebox and starts to cook it*) Marie and I were going to the Olympics back in our old high school stadium. There were thousands of people there. There was Turk out in the center of the field throwing the javelin. Every time he threw it, the crowd would roar . . . and you know who the man in charge was? It was my father. Isn't that funny? . . . But Turk kept changing into someone else all the time. And then my father disqualified him. So he had to sit on the sidelines . . . and guess who took his place, Daddy? You! You came trotting out there on the field just as big as you please . . .

DOC (*Smilingly*)   How did I do, Baby?

LOLA   Fine. You picked the javelin up real careful, like it was awful heavy. But you threw it, Daddy, clear, *clear* up into the sky. And it never came down again. (*DOC looks very pleased with himself.* LOLA *goes on*) Then it started to rain. And I couldn't find Little Sheba. I almost went crazy looking for her and there were so many people, I didn't even know where to look. And you were waiting to take me home. And we walked and walked through the slush and mud, and people were hurrying all around us and . . . and . . . (*Leaves stove and sits. Sentimental tears come to her eyes*) But this part is sad, Daddy. All of a sudden I saw Little Sheba . . . she was lying in the middle of the field . . . dead. . . .

It made me cry, Doc. No one paid any attention . . . I cried and cried. It made me feel so bad, Doc. That sweet little puppy . . . her curly white fur all smeared with mud, and no one to stop and take care of her . . .

DOC Why couldn't *you?*

LOLA I wanted to, but you wouldn't let me. You kept saying, "We can't stay here, honey; we gotta go on. We gotta go on." (*Pause*) Now, isn't that strange?

DOC Dreams are funny.

LOLA I don't think Little Sheba's ever coming back, Doc. I'm not going to call her any more.

DOC Not much point in it, Baby. I guess she's gone for good.

LOLA I'll fix your eggs.

(*She gets up, embraces* DOC, *and goes to stove.* DOC *remains at table sipping his fruit juice. The curtain comes slowly down*)

Look Back
in Anger

B Y

John Osborne

For my Father

LOOK BACK IN ANGER *was first presented by the English Stage Company at the Royal Court Theatre, Sloane Square, London, May 8, 1956 with the following cast:*

(In order of appearance)

JIMMY PORTER	*Kenneth Haigh*
CLIFF LEWIS	*Alan Bates*
ALISON PORTER	*Mary Ure*
HELENA CHARLES	*Helena Hughes*
COLONEL REDFERN	*John Welsh*

Directed by Tony Richardson
Décor by Alan Tagg

Synopsis of Scenes

The action throughout takes place in the Porters' one-room flat in the Midlands. The time is the present.

ACT ONE
Early Evening. April.

ACT TWO
SCENE 1   Two weeks later.
SCENE 2   The following evening.

ACT THREE
SCENE 1   Several months later.
SCENE 2   A few minutes later.

ACT ONE

The Porters' one-room flat in a large Midland town. Early evening. April.

The scene is a fairly large attic room, at the top of a large Victorian house. The ceiling slopes down quite sharply. Down R. are two small low windows. In front of these is a dark oak dressing table. Most of the furniture is simple, and rather old. Up R. is a double bed, running the length of most of the back wall, the rest of which is taken up with a shelf of books. Down R. below the bed is a heavy chest of drawers, covered with books, neckties and odds and ends, including a large, tattered toy teddy bear and soft, woolly squirrel. Up L. is a door. Below this a small wardrobe. Most of the wall L. is taken up with a high, oblong window. This looks out on to the landing, but light comes through it from a skylight beyond. Below the wardrobe is a gas stove, and, beside this, a wooden food cupboard, on which is a small, portable radio. Down C. is a sturdy dining table and three chairs, and, below this, L. and R., two deep, shabby leather armchairs.

At rise of curtain, JIMMY and CLIFF are seated in the two armchairs R. and L., respectively. All that we can see of either of them is two pairs of legs, sprawled way out beyond the newspapers which hide the rest of them from sight. They are both reading. Beside them, and between them, is a jungle of newspapers and weeklies. When we do eventually see them, we find that JIMMY is a tall, thin young man about twenty-five, wearing a very worn tweed jacket and flannels. Clouds of smoke fill the room from the pipe he is smoking. He is a disconcerting mixture of sincerity and cheerful malice, of tenderness and freebooting cruelty; restless, importunate, full of pride, a combination which alienates the sensitive and insensitive alike. Blistering honesty, or apparent honesty, like his, makes few friends. To many he may seem sensitive to the point of vulgarity. To others, he is simply a loudmouth. To be as vehement as he is is to be almost non-committal. CLIFF *is the same age, short, dark, big boned, wearing a pullover and grey, new, but very creased trousers. He is easy and relaxed, almost to lethargy, with the rather sad, natural intelligence of the self-taught. If* JIMMY *alienates love,* CLIFF *seems to exact it—demonstrations of it, at least, even from the cautious. He is a soothing, natural counterpoint to* JIMMY.

Standing L., below the food cupboard, is ALISON. *She is leaning over an ironing board. Beside her is a pile of clothes. Hers is the most elusive personality to catch in the uneasy polyphony of these three people. She is turned in a different key, a key of well-bred malaise that is often drowned in the robust orchestration of the other two. Hanging over the grubby, but expensive, skirt she is wearing is a cherry red shirt of* JIMMY'S, *but she manages somehow to look quite elegant in it. She is roughly the same age as the men. Somehow, their combined physical oddity makes her beauty more striking than it really is. She is tall, slim, dark. The bones of her face are long and delicate. There is a surprising reservation about her eyes, which are so large and deep they should make equivocation impossible. The room is still, smoke filled. The only sound is the occasional thud of* ALISON'S *iron on the board. It is one of those chilly Spring evenings, all cloud and shadows. Presently,* JIMMY *throws his paper down.*

JIMMY   Why do I do this every Sunday? Even the book reviews seem to be the same as last week's. Different books—same reviews. Have you finished that one yet?

CLIFF   Not yet.

JIMMY   I've just read three whole columns on the English Novel. Half of it's in French. Do the Sunday papers make *you* feel ignorant?

CLIFF   Not 'arf.

JIMMY   Well, you *are* ignorant. You're just a peasant. (*To* ALISON) What about you? You're not a peasant are you?

ALISON   (*Absently*)   What's that?

JIMMY   I said do the papers make you feel you're not so brilliant after all?

ALISON   Oh—I haven't read them yet.

JIMMY   I didn't ask you that. I said—

CLIFF   Leave the poor girlie alone. She's busy.

JIMMY   Well, she can talk, can't she? You can talk, can't you? You can express an opinion. Or does the White Woman's Burden make it impossible to think?

ALISON   I'm sorry. I wasn't listening properly.

JIMMY   You bet you weren't listening. Old Porter talks, and everyone turns over and goes to sleep. And Mrs. Porter gets 'em all going with the first yawn.

CLIFF   Leave her alone, I said.

JIMMY   (*Shouting*) All right, dear. Go back to sleep. It was only me talking. You know? Talking? Remember? I'm sorry.

CLIFF   Stop yelling. I'm trying to read.

JIMMY   Why do you bother? You can't understand a word of it.

CLIFF   Uh huh.

JIMMY   You're too ignorant.

CLIFF   Yes, and uneducated. Now shut up, will you?

JIMMY   Why don't you get my wife to explain it to you? She's educated. (*To her*) That's right, isn't it?

CLIFF   (*Kicking out at him from behind his paper*) Leave her alone, I said.

JIMMY   Do that again, you Welsh ruffian, and I'll pull your ears off. (*He bangs* CLIFF's *paper out of his hands*)

CLIFF   (*Leaning forward*) Listen—I'm trying to better myself. Let me get on with it, you big, horrible man. Give it me. (*Puts his hand out for paper*)

ALISON   Oh, give it to him, Jimmy, for heaven's sake! I can't think!

CLIFF   Yes, come on, give me the paper. She can't think.

JIMMY   Can't think! (*Throws the paper back at him*) She hasn't had a thought for years! Have you?

ALISON   No.

JIMMY   (*Picks up a weekly*) I'm getting hungry.

ALISON   Oh no, not already!

CLIFF   He's a bloody pig.

JIMMY   I'm not a pig. I just like food—that's all.

CLIFF   Like it! You're like a sexual maniac—only with you it's food. You'll end up in the *News of the World*, boyo, you wait. James Porter, aged twenty-five, was bound over last week after pleading guilty to interfering with a small cabbage and two tins of beans on his way home from the Builder's Arms. The accused said he hadn't been feeling well for some time, and had been having black-outs. He asked for his good record as an air-raid warden, second class, to be taken into account.

JIMMY (*Grins*) Oh, yes, yes, yes. I like to eat. I'd like to live too. Do you mind?

CLIFF Don't see any use in your eating at all. You never get any fatter.

JIMMY People like me don't get fat. I've tried to tell you before. We just burn everything up. Now shut up while I read. You can make me some more tea.

CLIFF Good God, you've just had a great potful! I only had one cup.

JIMMY Like hell! Make some more.

CLIFF (*To* ALISON) Isn't that right? Didn't I only have one cup?

ALISON (*Without looking up*) That's right.

CLIFF There you are. And she only had one cup too. I saw her. You guzzled the lot.

JIMMY (*Reading his weekly*) Put the kettle on.

CLIFF Put it on yourself. You've creased up my paper.

JIMMY I'm the only one who knows how to treat a paper, or anything else, in this house. (*Picks up another paper*) Girl here wants to know whether her boy friend will lose all respect for her if she gives him what he asks for. Stupid bitch.

CLIFF Just let me get at her, that's all.

JIMMY Who buys this damned thing? (*Throws it down*) Haven't you read the other posh paper yet?

CLIFF Which?

JIMMY Well, there are only two posh papers on a Sunday—the one you're reading, and this one. Come on, let me have that one, and you take this.

CLIFF Oh, all right. (*They exchange*) I was only reading the Bishop of Bromley. (*Puts out his hand to* ALISON) How are you, dullin'?

ALISON All right thank you, dear.

CLIFF (*Grasping her hand*) Why don't you leave all that, and sit down for a bit? You look tired.

ALISON (*Smiling*) I haven't much more to do.

CLIFF (*Kisses her hand, and puts her fingers in his mouth*) She's a beautiful girl, isn't she?

JIMMY That's what they all tell me.

(*His eyes meet hers*)

CLIFF It's a lovely, delicious paw you've got. Ummmmm. I'm going to bite it off.

ALISON Don't! I'll burn his shirt.

JIMMY   Give her her finger back, and don't be so sickening. What's the Bishop of Bromley say?

CLIFF (*Letting go of* ALISON)   Oh, it says here that he makes a very moving appeal to all Christians to do all they can to assist in the manufacture of the H-Bomb.

JIMMY   Yes, well, that's quite moving, I suppose. (*To* ALISON) Are you moved, my darling?

ALISON   Well, naturally.

JIMMY   There you are: even my wife is moved. I ought to send the Bishop a subscription. Let's see. What else does he say. Dumdidumdidumdidum. Ah yes. He's upset because someone has suggested that he supports the rich against the poor. He says he denies the difference of class distinctions. "This idea has been persistently and wickedly fostered by—the working classes!" Well! (*He looks up at both of them for reaction, but* CLIFF *is reading, and* ALISON *is intent on her ironing*)

JIMMY (*To* CLIFF)   Did you read that bit?

CLIFF   Um?

(*He has lost them, and he knows it, but he won't leave it*)

JIMMY (*To* ALISON)   You don't suppose your father could have written it, do you?

ALISON   Written what?

JIMMY   What I just read out, of course.

ALISON   Why should my father have written it?

JIMMY   Sounds rather like Daddy, don't you think?

ALISON   Does it?

JIMMY   Is the Bishop of Bromley his nom de plume, do you think?

CLIFF   Don't take any notice of him. He's being offensive. And it's so easy for him.

JIMMY (*Quickly*)   Did you read about the woman who went to the mass meeting of a certain American evangelist at Earls Court? She went forward, to declare herself for love or whatever it is, and, in the rush of converts to get to the front, she broke four ribs and got kicked in the head. She was yelling her head off in agony, but with 50,000 people putting all they'd got into "Onward Christian Soldiers", nobody even knew she was there. (*He looks up sharply for a response, but there isn't any*) Sometimes, I wonder if there isn't something wrong with me. What about that tea?

CLIFF (*Still behind the paper*)   What tea?

JIMMY   Put the kettle on.

(ALISON *looks up at him*)

ALISON   Do you want some more tea?

JIMMY   I don't know. No, I don't think so.

ALISON   Do you want some, Cliff?

JIMMY   No, he doesn't. How much longer will you be doing that?

ALISON   Won't be long.

JIMMY   God, how I hate Sundays! It's always so depressing, always the same. We never seem to get any further, do we? Always the same ritual. Reading the papers, drinking tea, ironing. A few more hours, and another week gone. Our youth is slipping away. Do you know that?

CLIFF (*Throws down the paper*)   What's that?

JIMMY (*Casually*)   Oh, nothing, nothing. Damn you, damn both of you, damn them all.

CLIFF   Let's go to the pictures. (*To* ALISON)   What do you say, lovely?

ALISON   I don't think I'll be able to. Perhaps Jimmy would like to go. (*To* JIMMY)   Would you like to?

JIMMY   And have my enjoyment ruined by the Sunday night yobs in the front row? No, thank you. (*Pause*)   Did you read Priestley's piece this week? Why on earth I ask, I don't know. I know damned well you haven't. Why do I spend ninepence on that damned paper every week? Nobody reads it except me. Nobody can be bothered. No one can raise themselves out of their delicious sloth. You two will drive me round the bend soon—I know it, as sure as I'm sitting here. I know you're going to drive me mad. Oh heavens, how I long for a little ordinary human enthusiasm. Just enthusiasm—that's all. I want to hear a warm, thrilling voice cry out Hallelujah! (*He bangs his breast theatrically*)   Hallelujah! I'm alive! I've an idea. Why don't we have a little game? Let's pretend that we're human beings, and that we're actually alive. Just for a while. What do you say? Let's pretend we're human. (*He looks from one to the other*)   Oh, brother, it's such a long time since I was with anyone who got enthusiastic about anything.

CLIFF   What did he say?

JIMMY (*Resentful of being dragged away from his pursuit of* ALISON)   What did who say?

CLIFF   Mr. Priestley.

JIMMY   What he always says, I suppose. He's like Daddy—still casting well-fed glances back to the Edwardian twilight from his comfortable, disenfranchised wilderness. What the devil have you done to those trousers?

CLIFF Done?

JIMMY Are they the ones you bought last week-end? Look at them. Do you see what he's done to those new trousers?

ALISON You are naughty, Cliff. They look dreadful.

JIMMY You spend good money on a new pair of trousers, and then sprawl about in them like a savage. What do you think you're going to do when I'm not around to look after you? Well, what are you going to do? Tell me?

CLIFF (*Grinning*) I don't know. (*To* ALISON) What am I going to do, lovely?

ALISON You'd better take them off.

JIMMY Yes, go on. Take 'em off. And I'll kick your behind for you.

ALISON I'll give them a press while I've got the iron on.

CLIFF O.K. (*Starts taking them off*) I'll just empty the pockets. (*He takes out keys, matches, handkerchief*)

JIMMY Give me those matches, will you?

CLIFF Oh, you're not going to start up that old pipe again, are you? It stinks the place out. (*To* ALISON) Doesn't it smell awful?
(JIMMY *grabs the matches, and lights up*)

ALISON I don't mind it. I've got used to it.

JIMMY She's a great one for getting used to things. If she were to die, and wake up in paradise—after the first five minutes, she'd have got used to it.

CLIFF (*Hands her the trousers*) Thank you, lovely. Give me a cigarette, will you?

JIMMY Don't give him one.

CLIFF I can't stand the stink of that old pipe any longer. I must have a cigarette.

JIMMY I thought the doctor said no cigarettes?

CLIFF Oh, why doesn't he shut up?

JIMMY All right. They're your ulcers. Go ahead, and have a belly-ache, if that's what you want. I give up. I give up. I'm sick of doing things for people. And all for what? (ALISON *gives* CLIFF *a cigarette. They both light up, and she goes on with her ironing*) Nobody thinks, nobody cares. No beliefs, no convictions and no enthusiasm. Just another Sunday evening. (CLIFF *sits down again, in his pullover and shorts*) Perhaps there's a concert on. (*Picks up* Radio Times) Ah. (*Nudges* CLIFF *with his foot*) Make some more tea. (CLIFF *grunts. He is reading again*) Oh, yes. There's a

Vaughan Williams. Well, that's something, anyway. Something strong, something simple, something English. I suppose people like me aren't supposed to be very patriotic. Somebody said— what was it—we get our cooking from Paris (that's a laugh), our politics from Moscow, and our morals from Port Said. Something like that, anyway. Who was it? (*Pause*) Well, you wouldn't know anyway. I hate to admit it, but I think I can understand how her Daddy must have felt when he came back from India, after all those years away. The old Edwardian brigade do make their brief little world look pretty tempting. All homemade cakes and croquet, bright ideas, bright uniforms. Always the same picture: high summer, the long days in the sun, slim volumes of verse, crisp linen, the smell of starch. What a romantic picture. Phoney too, of course. It must have rained sometimes. Still, even I regret it somehow, phoney or not. If you've no world of your own, it's rather pleasant to regret the passing of someone else's. I must be getting sentimental. But I must say it's pretty dreary living in the American Age—unless you're an American of course. Perhaps all our children will be Americans. That's a thought isn't it? (*He gives* CLIFF *a kick, and shouts at him*) I said that's a thought!

CLIFF   You did?

JIMMY   You sit there like a lump of dough. I thought you were going to make me some tea. (CLIFF *groans.* JIMMY *turns to* ALISON) Is your friend Webster coming tonight?

ALISON   He might drop in. You know what he is.

JIMMY   Well, I hope he doesn't. I don't think I could take Webster tonight.

ALISON   I thought you said he was the only person who spoke your language.

JIMMY   So he is. Different dialect but same language. I like him. He's got bite, edge, drive——

ALISON   Enthusiasm.

JIMMY   You've got it. When he comes here, I begin to feel exhilarated. He doesn't like me, but he gives me something, which is more than I get from most people. Not since——

ALISON   Yes, we know. Not since you were living with Madeline. (*She folds some of the clothes she has already ironed, and crosses to the bed with them*)

CLIFF (*Behind paper again*)   Who's Madeline?

ALISON   Oh, wake up, dear. You've heard about Madeline enough times. She was his mistress. Remember? When he was fourteen. Or was it thirteen?

JIMMY Eighteen.

ALISON He owes just about everything to Madeline.

CLIFF I get mixed up with all your women. Was she the one all those years older than you?

JIMMY Ten years.

CLIFF Proper little Marchbanks, you are!

JIMMY What time's that concert on?

(*He checks the paper*)

CLIFF (*Yawns*) Oh, I feel so sleepy. Don't feel like standing behind that blinking sweet-stall again tomorrow. Why don't you do it on your own, and let me sleep in?

JIMMY I've got to be at the factory first thing, to get some more stock, so you'll have to put it up on your own. Another five minutes. (ALISON *has returned to her ironing board. She stands with her arms folded, smoking, staring thoughtfully*) She had more animation in her little finger than you two put together.

CLIFF Who did?

ALISON Madeline.

JIMMY Her curiosity about things, and about people was staggering. It wasn't just a naïve nosiness. With her, it was simply the delight of being awake, and watching.

(ALISON *starts to press* CLIFF's *trousers*)

CLIFF (*Behind the paper*) Perhaps I will make some tea, after all.

JIMMY (*Quietly*) Just to be with her was an adventure. Even to sit on the top of a bus with her was like setting out with Ulysses.

CLIFF Wouldn't have said Webster was much like Ulysses. He's an ugly little devil.

JIMMY I'm not talking about Webster, stupid. He's all right though, in his way. A sort of female Emily Brontë. He's the only one of your friends (*To* ALISON) who's worth tuppence, anyway. I'm surprised you get on with him.

ALISON So is he, I think.

JIMMY (*Going to the window, and looking out*) He's not only got guts, but sensitivity as well. That's about the rarest combination I can think of. None of your other friends have got either.

ALISON (*Very quietly and earnestly*) Jimmy, please—don't go on. (*He turns and looks at her. The tired appeal in her voice has pulled him up suddenly. But he soon gathers himself for a new assault. He walks behind* CLIFF, *and stands, looking down at his head)*

JIMMY   Your friends—there's a shower for you.

CLIFF (*Mumbling*)   Dry up. Let her get on with my trousers.

JIMMY (*Musingly*)   Don't think I could provoke her. Nothing I could do would provoke her. Not even if I were to drop dead.

CLIFF   Then drop dead.

JIMMY   They're either militant like her Mummy and Daddy. Militant, arrogant and full of malice. Or vague. She's somewhere between the two.

CLIFF   Why don't you listen to that concert of yours? And don't stand behind me. That blooming droning on behind me gives me a funny feeling down the spine. (JIMMY *gives his ears a twist and* CLIFF *roars with pain.* JIMMY *grins back at him*) That hurt, you rotten sadist! (*To* ALISON) I wish you'd kick his head in for him.

JIMMY (*Moving in between them*)   Have you ever seen her brother? Brother Nigel? The straight-backed, chinless wonder from Sandhurst? I only met him once myself. He asked me to step outside when I told his mother she was evil minded.

CLIFF   And did you?

JIMMY   Certainly not. He's a big chap. Well, you've never heard so many well-bred commonplaces come from beneath the same bowler hat. The Platitude from Outer Space—that's brother Nigel. He'll end up in the Cabinet one day, make no mistake. But somewhere at the back of that mind is the vague knowledge that he and his pals have been plundering and fooling everybody for generations. (*Going upstage, and turning*) Now Nigel is just about as vague as you can get without being actually invisible. And invisible politicians aren't much use to anyone—not even to *his* supporters! And nothing is more vague about Nigel than his knowledge. His knowledge of life and ordinary human beings is so hazy, he really deserves some sort of decoration for it—a medal inscribed "For Vaguery in the Field." But it wouldn't do for him to be troubled by any stabs of conscience, however vague. (*Moving down again*) Besides, he's a patriot and an Englishman, and he doesn't like the idea that he may have been selling out his countryman all these years, so what does he do? The only thing he *can* do—seek sanctuary in his own stupidity. The only way to keep things as much like they always have been as possible, is to make any alternative too much for your poor, tiny brain to grasp. It takes some doing nowadays. It really does. But they knew all about character building at Nigel's school, and he'll make it all right. Don't you worry, he'll make it. And, what's more, he'll do it better than anybody else! (*There is no sound, only the plod of* ALISON's *iron. Her eyes are fixed on what she is doing.* CLIFF *stares at the floor. His cheerfulness has deserted him for the moment.* JIMMY *is rather shakily triumphant. He cannot allow himself to look at either of them to catch their response to his rhetoric, so he moves across to the window, to recover himself, and look out*) It's started to rain. That's all it needs. This room and the rain. (*He's been cheated out of his response, but he's got to draw blood somehow. Conversationally*) Yes, that's the little woman's family. You know Mummy and Daddy, of course. And don't let the Marquess of Queensberry manner fool you. They'll kick you in the groin while you're handing your hat to the maid. As for Nigel and Alison—(*In a reverent, Stuart Hibberd voice*) Nigel and Alison. They're what they sound like: sycophantic, phlegmatic and pusillanimous.

CLIFF   I'll bet that concert's started by now. Shall I put it on?

JIMMY   I looked up that word the other day. It's one of those words I've never been quite sure of, but always thought I knew.

CLIFF   What was that?

JIMMY   I told you—pusillanimous. Do you know what it means? (CLIFF *shakes his head*) Neither did I really. All this time, I have been married to this woman, this monument to non-attachment, and suddenly I discover that there is actually a word that sums her up. Not just an adjective in the English language to describe her with—it's her name! Pusillanimous! It sounds like some fleshy Roman matron, doesn't it? The Lady Pusillanimous seen here with her husband Sextus, on their way to the Games. (CLIFF *looks troubled, and glances uneasily at* ALISON) Poor old Sextus! If he were put into a Hollywood film, he's so unimpressive, they'd make some poor British actor play the part. He doesn't know it, but those beefcake Christians will make off with his wife in the wonder of stereophonic sound before the picture's over. (ALISON *leans against the board, and closes her eyes*) The Lady Pusillanimous has been promised a brighter easier world than old Sextus can ever offer her. Hi, Pusey! What say we get the hell down to the Arena, and maybe feed ourselves to a couple of lions, huh?

John Osborne

ALISON   God help me, if he doesn't stop, I'll go out of my mind in a minute.

JIMMY   Why don't you? That would be something, anyway. (*Crosses to the chest of drawers*) But I haven't told you what it means yet, have I? (*Picks up the dictionary*) I don't have to tell her—she knows. In fact, if my pronunciation is at fault, she'll probably wait for a suitably public moment to correct it. Here it is. I quote: Pusillanimous. Adjective. Wanting of firmness of mind, of small courage, having a little mind, mean spirited, cowardly, timid of mind. From the Latin pusillus, very little, and animus, the mind. (*Slams the book shut*) That's my wife! That's *her* isn't it? Behold the Lady Pusillanimous. (*Shouting hoarsely*) Hi, Pusey! When's your next picture?

(JIMMY *watches her, waiting for her to break. For no more than a flash,* ALISON's *face seems to contort, and it looks as though she might throw her head back, and scream. But it passes in a moment. She is used to these carefully rehearsed attacks, and it doesn't look as though he will get his triumph tonight. She carries on with her ironing.* JIMMY *crosses, and switches on the radio. The Vaughan Williams concert has started. He goes back to his chair, leans back in it, and closes his eyes*)

ALISON   (*Handing* CLIFF *his trousers*) There you are, dear. They're not very good, but they'll do for now.

(CLIFF *gets up and puts them on*)

CLIFF   Oh, that's lovely.

ALISON   Now try and look after them. I'll give them a real press later on.

CLIFF   Thank you, you beautiful, darling girl.

(*He puts his arms round her waist, and kisses her. She smiles, and gives his nose a tug.* JIMMY *watches from his chair*)

ALISON   (*To* CLIFF) Let's have a cigarette, shall we?

CLIFF   That's a good idea. Where are they?

ALISON   On the stove. Do you want one Jimmy?

JIMMY   No thank you, I'm trying to listen. Do you mind?

CLIFF   Sorry, your lordship.

(*He puts a cigarette in* ALISON's *mouth, and one in his own, and lights up.* CLIFF *sits down, and picks up his paper.* ALISON *goes back to her board.* CLIFF *throws down paper, picks up another, and thumbs through that*)

JIMMY   Do you have to make all that racket?

CLIFF   Oh, sorry.

JIMMY   It's quite a simple thing, you know—turning over a page. Anyway, that's my paper.

(*He snatches it away*)

CLIFF   Oh, don't be so mean!

JIMMY   Price ninepence, obtainable from any newsagent's. Now let me hear the music, for God's sake. (*Pause. To* ALISON) Are you going to be much longer doing that?

ALISON   Why?

JIMMY   Perhaps you haven't noticed it, but it's interfering with the radio.

ALISON   I'm sorry. I shan't be much longer. (*A pause. The iron mingles with the music.* CLIFF *shifts restlessly in his chair,* JIMMY *watches* ALISON, *his foot beginning to twitch dangerously. Presently, he gets up quickly, crossing below* ALISON *to the radio, and turns it off*) What did you do that for?

JIMMY   I wanted to listen to the concert, that's all.

ALISON   Well, what's stopping you?

JIMMY   Everyone's making such a din—that's what's stopping me.

ALISON   Well, I'm very sorry, but I can't just stop everything because you want to listen to music.

JIMMY   Why not?

ALISON   Really, Jimmy, you're like a child.

JIMMY   Don't try and patronise me. (*Turning to* CLIFF) She's so clumsy. I watch for her to do the same things every night. The way she jumps on the bed, as if she were stamping on someone's face, and draws the curtains back with a great clatter, in that casually destructive way of hers. It's like someone launching a battleship. Have you ever noticed how noisy women are? (*He crosses below chairs to L.C.*) Have you? The way they kick the floor about, simply walking over it? Or have you watched them sitting at their dressing tables, dropping their weapons and banging down their bits of boxes and brushes and lipsticks? (*He faces her dressing table*) I've watched her doing it night after night. When you see a woman in front of her bedroom mirror, you realise what a refined sort of a butcher she is. (*Turns in*) Did you ever see some dirty old Arab, sticking his fingers into some mess of lamb fat and gristle? Well, she's just like that. Thank God they don't have many women surgeons! Those primitive hands would have your guts out in no time. Flip! Out it comes, like the powder out of its box. Flop! Back it goes, like the powder puff on the table.

CLIFF (*Grimacing cheerfully*)   Ugh! Stop it!

JIMMY (*Moving upstage*)   She'd drop your guts like hair clips and fluff all over the floor. You've got to be fundamentally insensitive to be as noisy and as clumsy as that. (*He moves C., and leans against the table*) I had a flat underneath a couple of girls once. You heard every damned thing those bastards did, all day and night. The most simple, everyday actions were a sort of assault course on your sensibilities. I used to plead with them. I even got to screaming the most ingenious obscenities I could think of, up the stairs at them. But nothing, nothing, would move them. With those two, even a simple visit to the lavatory sounded like a medieval siege. Oh, they beat me in the end—I had to go. I expect they're still at it. Or they're probably married by now, and driving some other poor devils out of their minds. Slamming their doors, stamping their high heels, banging their irons and saucepans—the eternal flaming racket of the female.

(*Church bells start ringing outside*)

JIMMY   Oh, hell! Now the bloody bells have started! (*He rushes to the window*) Wrap it up, will you? Stop ringing those bells! There's somebody going crazy in here! I don't want to hear them!

ALISON   Stop shouting! (*Recovering immediately*) You'll have Miss Drury up here.

JIMMY   I don't give a damn about Miss Drury—that mild old gentlewoman doesn't fool me, even if she takes in you two. She's an old robber. She gets more than enough out of us for this place every week. Anyway, she's probably in church (*Points to the window*), swinging on those bloody bells!

(CLIFF *goes to the window, and closes it*)

CLIFF   Come on now, be a good boy. I'll take us all out, and we'll have a drink.

JIMMY   They're not open yet. It's Sunday. Remember? Anyway, it's raining.

CLIFF   Well, shall we dance? (*He pushes* JIMMY *round the floor, who is past the mood for this kind of fooling*) Do you come here often?

JIMMY   Only in the mating season. All right, all right, very funny. (*He tries to escape, but* CLIFF *holds him like a vice*) Let me go.

CLIFF   Not until you've apologised for being nasty to everyone. Do you think bosoms will be in or out, this year?

JIMMY   Your teeth will be out in a minute, if you don't let go!

(*He makes a great effort to wrench himself free, but* CLIFF *hangs on. They collapse to the floor below the table, struggling.* ALISON *carries on with her ironing. This is routine, but she is getting close to breaking point, all the same.* CLIFF *manages to break away, and finds himself in front of the ironing board.* JIMMY *springs up. They grapple*)

ALISON Look out, for heaven's sake! Oh, it's more like a zoo every day!

(JIMMY *makes a frantic, deliberate effort, and manages to push* CLIFF *on to the ironing board, and into* ALISON. *The board collapses.* CLIFF *falls against her, and they end up in a heap on the floor.* ALISON *cries out in pain.* JIMMY *looks down at them, dazed and breathless*)

CLIFF (*Picking himself up*) She's hurt. Are you all right?

ALISON Well, does it look like it!

CLIFF She's burnt her arm on the iron.

JIMMY Darling, I'm sorry.

ALISON Get out!

JIMMY I'm sorry, believe me. You think I did it on pur——

ALISON (*Her head shaking helplessly*) Clear out of my *sight!*

(*He stares at her uncertainly.* CLIFF *nods to him, and he turns and goes out of the door*)

CLIFF Come and sit down. (*He leads her to the armchair*) You look a bit white. Are you all right?

ALISON Yes. I'm all right now.

CLIFF Let's have a look at your arm. (*Examines it*) Yes, it's quite red. That's going to be painful. What should I do with it?

ALISON Oh, it's nothing much. A bit of soap on it will do. I never can remember what you do with burns.

CLIFF I'll just pop down to the bathroom and get some. Are you sure you're all right?

ALISON Yes.

CLIFF (*Crossing to the door*) Won't be a minute.

(*He exits. She leans back in the chair, and looks up at the ceiling. She breathes in deeply, and brings her hands up to her face. She winces as she feels the pain in her arm, and she lets it fall. She runs her hand through her hair*)

ALISON (*In a clenched whisper*) Oh, God!

(CLIFF *re-enters with a bar of soap*)

CLIFF It's this scented muck. Do you think it'll be all right?

ALISON That'll do.

CLIFF Here we are then. Let's have your arm. (*He kneels down be-*

side her, and she holds out her arm) I've put it under the tap. It's quite soft. I'll do it ever so gently. (*Very carefully, he rubs the soap over the burn*) All right? (*She nods*) You're a brave girl.

ALISON   I don't feel very brave. (*Tears harshening her voice*) I really don't, Cliff. I don't think I can take much more. (*Turns her head away*) I think I feel rather sick.

CLIFF   All over now. (*Puts the soap down*) Would you like me to get you something? (*She shakes her head. He sits on the arm of the chair, and puts his arm round her. She leans her head back on to him*) Don't upset yourself, lovely.

(*He massages the back of her neck, and she lets her head fall forward*)

ALISON   Where is he?

CLIFF   In my room.

ALISON   What's he doing?

CLIFF   Lying on the bed. Reading, I think. (*Stroking her neck*) That better?

(*She leans back, and closes her eyes again*)

ALISON   Bless you.

(*He kisses the top of her head*)

CLIFF   I don't think I'd have the courage to live on my own again —in spite of everything. I'm pretty rough, and pretty ordinary really, and I'd seem worse on my own. And you get fond of people too, worse luck.

ALISON   I don't think I want anything more to do with love. Any more. I can't take it on.

CLIFF   You're too young to start giving up. Too young, and too lovely. Perhaps I'd better put a bandage on that—do you think so?

ALISON   There's some on my dressing table. (CLIFF *crosses to the dressing table*) I keep looking back, as far as I remember, and I can't think what it was to feel young, really young. Jimmy said the same thing to me the other day. I pretended not to be listening—because I knew that would hurt him, I suppose. And—of course—he got savage, like tonight. But I knew just what he meant. I suppose it would have been so easy to say "Yes, darling, I know just what you mean. I know what you're feeling." (*Shrugs*) It's those easy things that seem to be so impossible with us.

(CLIFF *stands, holding the bandage, his back to her*)

CLIFF   I'm wondering how much longer I can go on watching you two tearing the insides out of each other. It looks pretty ugly sometimes.

ALISON You wouldn't seriously think of leaving us, would you?

CLIFF I suppose not.

(*He crosses to her*)

ALISON I think I'm frightened. If only I knew what was going to happen.

CLIFF (*Kneeling on the arm of her chair*) Give it here. (*She holds out her arm*) Yell out if I hurt you.

(*He bandages it for her*)

ALISON (*Staring at her outstretched arm*) Cliff——

CLIFF Um? (*Slight pause*) What is it, lovely?

ALISON Nothing.

CLIFF I said: what is it?

ALISON You see——(*Hesitates*) I'm pregnant.

CLIFF (*After a few moments*) I'll need some scissors.

ALISON They're over there.

CLIFF (*Crossing to the dressing table*) That is something, isn't it? When did you find this out?

ALISON Few days ago. It was a bit of a shock.

CLIFF Yes, I dare say.

ALISON After three years of married life, I have to get caught out now.

CLIFF None of us infallible, I suppose. (*Crosses to her*) Must say I'm surprised though.

ALISON It's always been out of the question. What with—this place, and no money, and oh—everything. He's resented it, I know. What can you do?

CLIFF You haven't told him yet.

ALISON Not yet.

CLIFF What are you going to do?

ALISON I've no idea.

CLIFF (*Having cut her bandage, he starts tying it*) That too tight?

ALISON Fine, thank you.

(*She rises, goes to the ironing board, folds it up, and leans it against the food cupboard*)

CLIFF Is it . . . Is it . . . ?

ALISON Too late to avert the situation? (*Places the iron on the rack of the stove*) I'm not certain yet. Maybe not. If not, there won't be any problem, will there?

CLIFF   And if it is too late? (*Her face is turned away from him.
She simply shakes her head*) Why don't you tell him now? (*She
kneels down to pick up the clothes on the floor, and folds them
up*) After all, he does love you. You don't need me to tell you
that.

ALISON   Can't you see? He'll suspect my motives at once. He never
stops telling himself that I know how vulnerable he is. Tonight
it might be all right—we'd make love. But later, we'd both lie
awake, watching for the light to come through that little window,
and dreading it. In the morning, he'd feel hoaxed, as if I were
trying to kill him in the worst way of all. He'd watch me growing
bigger every day, and I wouldn't dare to look at him.

CLIFF   You may have to face it, lovely.

ALISON   Jimmy's got his own private morality, as you know. What
my mother calls "loose." It is pretty free, of course, but it's very
harsh too. You know, it's funny, but we never slept together before we were married.

CLIFF   It certainly is—knowing him!

ALISON   We knew each other such a short time, everything moved
at such a pace, we didn't have much opportunity. And, afterwards, he actually taunted me with my virginity. He was quite
angry about it, as if I had deceived him in some strange way.
He seemed to think an untouched woman would defile him.

CLIFF   I've never heard you talking like this about him. He'd be
quite pleased.

ALISON   Yes, he would. (*She gets up, the clothes folded over her
arm*) Do you think he's right?

CLIFF   What about?

ALISON   Oh—everything.

CLIFF   Well, I suppose he and I think the same about a lot of
things, because we're alike in some ways. We both come from
working people, if you like. Oh I know some of his mother's relatives are pretty posh, but he hates them as much as he hates
yours. Don't quite know why. Anyway, he gets on with me because I'm common. (*Grins*) Common as dirt, that's me.
(*She puts her hand on his head, and strokes it thoughtfully*)

ALISON   You think I should tell him about the baby?
(*He gets up, and puts his arm round her*)

CLIFF   It'll be all right—you see. Tell him. (*He kisses her. Enter
JIMMY. He looks at them curiously, but without surprise. They
are both aware of him, but make no sign of it. He crosses to the*

armchair and sits down next to them. He picks up a paper, and starts looking at it. CLIFF *glances at him,* ALISON's *head against his cheek*) There you are, you old devil, you! Where have you been?

JIMMY You know damn well where I've been. (*Without looking at her*) How's your arm?

ALISON Oh, it's all right. It wasn't much.

CLIFF She's beautiful, isn't she?

JIMMY You seem to think so.

(CLIFF *and* ALISON *still have their arms round one another*)

CLIFF Why the hell she married you, I'll never know.

JIMMY You think she'd have been better off with you?

CLIFF I'm not her type. Am I, dullin'?

ALISON I'm not sure what my type is.

JIMMY Why don't you both get into bed, and have done with it.

ALISON You know, I think he really means that.

JIMMY I do. I can't concentrate with you two standing there like that.

CLIFF He's just an old Puritan at heart.

JIMMY Perhaps I am, at that. Anyway, you both look pretty silly slobbering over each other.

CLIFF I think she's beautiful. And so do you, only you're too much of a pig to say so.

JIMMY You're just a sexy little Welshman, and you know it! Mummy and Daddy turn pale, and face the east every time they remember she's married to me. But if they saw all this going on, they'd collapse. Wonder what they would do, incidentally. Send for the police I expect. (*Genuinely friendly*) Have you got a cigarette?

ALISON (*Disengaging*) I'll have a look.

(*She goes to her handbag on the table*)

JIMMY (*Pointing at* CLIFF) He gets more like a little mouse every day, doesn't he? (*He is trying to re-establish himself*) He really does look like one. Look at those ears, and that face, and the little short legs.

ALISON (*Looking through her bag*) That's because he *is* a mouse.

CLIFF Eek! Eek! I'm a mouse.

JIMMY A randy little mouse.

CLIFF (*Dancing round the table, and squeaking*) I'm a mouse, I'm a mouse, I'm a randy little mouse. That's a mourris dance.

JIMMY A what?

CLIFF A *Mourris Dance*. That's a Morris Dance strictly for mice.

JIMMY You stink. You really do. Do you know that?

CLIFF Not as bad as you, you horrible old bear. (*Goes over to him, and grabs his foot*) You're a stinking old bear, you hear me?

JIMMY Let go of my foot, you whimsy little half-wit. You're making my stomach heave. I'm resting! If you don't let go, I'll cut off your nasty, great, slimy tail!

(CLIFF *gives him a tug, and* JIMMY *falls to the floor.* ALISON *watches them, relieved and suddenly full of affection*)

ALISON I've run out of cigarettes.

(CLIFF *is dragging* JIMMY *along the floor by his feet*)

JIMMY (*Yelling*) Go out and get me some cigarettes, and stop playing the fool!

CLIFF O.K.

(*He lets go of* JIMMY's *legs suddenly, who yells again as his head bangs on the floor*)

ALISON Here's half a crown. (*Giving it him*) The shop on the corner will be open.

CLIFF Right you are. (*Kisses her on the forehead quickly*) Don't forget.

(*He crosses upstage to the door*)

JIMMY Now get to hell out of here!

CLIFF (*At the door*) Hey, shorty!

JIMMY What do you want?

CLIFF Make a nice pot of tea.

JIMMY (*Getting up*) I'll kill you first.

CLIFF (*Grinning*) That's my boy!

(*He exits.* JIMMY *is now beside* ALISON, *who is still looking through her handbag. She becomes aware of his nearness, and, after a few moments, closes it. He takes hold of her bandaged arm*)

JIMMY How's it feeling?

ALISON Fine. It wasn't anything.

JIMMY All this fooling about can get a bit dangerous. (*He sits on the edge of the table, holding her hand*) I'm sorry.

ALISON I know.

JIMMY I mean it.

ALISON There's no need.

JIMMY I did it on purpose.

ALISON Yes.

JIMMY There's hardly a moment when I'm not—watching and

wanting you. I've got to hit out somehow. Nearly four years of being in the same room with you, night and day, and I still can't stop my sweat breaking out when I see you doing—something as ordinary as leaning over an ironing board. (*She strokes his head, not sure of herself yet. Sighing*) Trouble is—Trouble is you get used to people. Even their trivialities become indispensable to you. Indispensable, and a little mysterious. (*He slides his head forward, against her, trying to catch his thoughts*) I think . . . I must have a lot of—old stock. . . . Nobody wants it. . . . (*He puts his face against her belly. She goes on stroking his head, still on guard a little. Then he lifts his head, and they kiss passionately*) What are we going to do tonight?

ALISON What would you like to do? Drink?

JIMMY I know what I want now.

(*She takes his head in her hands and kisses him*)

ALISON Well, you'll have to wait till the proper time.

JIMMY There's no such thing.

ALISON Cliff will be back in a minute.

JIMMY What did he mean by "don't forget"?

ALISON Something I've been meaning to tell you.

JIMMY (*Kissing her again*) You're fond of him, aren't you?

ALISON Yes, I am.

JIMMY He's the only friend I seem to have left now. People go away. You never see them again. I can remember lots of names —men and women. When I was at school—Watson, Roberts, Davies. Jenny, Madeline, Hugh . . . (*Pause*) And there's Hugh's mum, of course. I'd almost forgotten her. She's been a good friend to us, if you like. She's even letting me buy the sweet-stall off her in my own time. She only bought it for us, anyway. She's so fond of you. I can never understand why you're so—distant with her.

ALISON (*Alarmed at this threat of a different mood*) Jimmy—please no!

JIMMY (*Staring at her anxious face*) You're very beautiful. A beautiful, great-eyed squirrel. (*She nods brightly, relieved*) Hoarding, nut-munching squirrel. (*She mimes this delightedly*) With highly polished, gleaming fur, and an ostrich feather of a tail.

ALISON Wheeeeeeeeee!

JIMMY How I envy you.

(*He stands, her arms around his neck*)

ALISON   Well, you're a jolly super bear, too. A really soooooooooo-ooooooper, marvellous bear.

JIMMY   Bears and squirrels *are* marvellous.

ALISON   Marvellous *and* beautiful. (*She jumps up and down excitedly, making little "paw gestures"*) Oooooooooh! Oooooooooh!

JIMMY   What the hell's that?

ALISON   That's a dance squirrels do when they're happy.

(*They embrace again*)

JIMMY   What makes you think you're happy?

ALISON   Everything just seems all right suddenly. That's all. Jimmy——

JIMMY   Yes?

ALISON   You know I told you I'd something to tell you?

JIMMY   Well?

(CLIFF *appears in the doorway*)

CLIFF   Didn't get any further than the front door. Miss Drury hadn't gone to church after all. I couldn't get away from her. (*To* ALISON) Someone on the phone for you.

ALISON   On the phone? Who on earth is it?

CLIFF   Helena something.

(JIMMY *and* ALISON *look at each other quickly*)

JIMMY (*To* CLIFF)   Helena Charles?

CLIFF   That's it.

ALISON   Thank you, Cliff. (*Moves upstage*) I won't be a minute.

CLIFF   You will. Old Miss Drury will keep you down there forever. She doesn't think we keep this place clean enough. (*Comes and sits in the armchair*) Thought you were going to make me some tea, you rotter. (JIMMY *makes no reply*) What's the matter, boyo?

JIMMY (*Slowly*)   That bitch.

CLIFF   Who?

JIMMY (*To himself*)   Helena Charles.

CLIFF   Who is this Helena?

JIMMY   One of her old friends. And one of my natural enemies. You're sitting on my chair.

CLIFF   Where are we going for a drink?

JIMMY   I don't know.

CLIFF   Well, you were all for it earlier on.

JIMMY   What does she want? What would make her ring up? It can't be for anything pleasant. Oh well, we shall soon know. (*He settles on the table*) Few minutes ago things didn't seem so bad either. I've just about had enough of this "expense of spirit" lark, as far as women are concerned. Honestly, it's enough to make you become a scoutmaster or something isn't it? Sometimes I almost envy old Gide and the Greek Chorus boys. Oh, I'm not saying that it mustn't be hell for them a lot of the time. But, at least, they do seem to have a cause—not a particularly good one, it's true. But plenty of them do seem to have a revolutionary fire about them, which is more than you can say for the rest of us. Like Webster, for instance. He doesn't like me—they hardly ever do. (*He is talking for the sake of it, only half listening to what he is saying*) I dare say he suspects me because I refuse to treat him either as a clown or as a tragic hero. He's like a man with a strawberry mark—he keeps thrusting it in your face because he can't believe it doesn't interest or horrify you particularly. (*Picks up* ALISON's *handbag thoughtfully, and starts looking through it*) As if I give a damn which way he likes his meat served up. I've got my own strawberry mark—only it's in a different place. No, as far as the Michaelangelo Brigade's concerned, I must be a sort of right-wing deviationist. If the Revolution ever comes, I'll be the first to be put up against the wall, with all the other poor old liberals.

CLIFF (*Indicating* ALISON's *handbag*) Wouldn't you say that that was her private property?

JIMMY You're quite right. But do you know something? Living night and day with another human being has made me predatory and suspicious. I know that the only way of finding out exactly what's going on is to catch them when they don't know you're looking. When she goes out, I go through everything—trunks, cases, drawers, bookcase, everything. Why? To see if there is something of me somewhere, a reference to me. I want to know if I'm being betrayed.

CLIFF You look for trouble, don't you?

JIMMY Only because I'm pretty certain of finding it. (*Brings out a letter from the handbag*) Look at that! Oh, I'm such a fool. This is happening every five minutes of the day. She gets letters. (*He holds it up*) Letters from her mother, letters in which I'm not mentioned at all because my name is a dirty word. And what does she do? (*Enter* ALISON. *He turns to look at her*) She writes long letters back to Mummy, and never mentions me at all, because I'm just a dirty word to her too. (*He throws the letter down at her feet*) Well, what did your friend want?

ALISON She's at the station. She's—coming over.

JIMMY I see. She said "Can I come over?" And you said "My husband, Jimmy—if you'll forgive me using such a dirty word, will
be delighted to see you. He'll kick your face in!"

(*He stands up, unable to sustain his anger, poised on the table*)

ALISON (*Quietly*) She's playing with the company at the Hip-
podrome this week, and she's got no digs. She can't find anywhere to stay——

JIMMY That I don't believe!

ALISON So I said she could come here until she fixes something
else. Miss Drury's got a spare room downstairs.

JIMMY Why not have her in here? Did you tell her to bring her
armour? Because she's going to need it!

ALISON (*Vehemently*) Oh why don't you shut up, please!

JIMMY Oh, my dear wife, you've got so much to learn. I only hope
you learn it one day. If only something—something would happen to you, and wake you out of your beauty sleep! (*Coming in
close to her*) If you could have a child, and it would die. Let it
grow, let a recognisable human face emerge from that little mass
of indiarubber and wrinkles. (*She retreats away from him*)
Please—if only I could watch you face that. I wonder if you might
even become a recognisable human being yourself. But I doubt
it. (*She moves away, stunned, and leans on the gas stove. He
stands rather helplessly on his own*) Do you know I have never
known the great pleasure of lovemaking when I didn't desire it
myself. Oh, it's not that she hasn't her own kind of passion. She
has the passion of a python. She just devours me whole every
time, as if I were some over-large rabbit. That's me. That bulge
around her navel—if you're wondering what it is—it's me. Me,
buried alive down there, and going mad, smothered in that peaceful looking coil. Not a sound, not a flicker from her—she doesn't
even rumble a little. You'd think that this indigestible mess would
stir up some kind of tremor in those distended, overfed tripes—
but not her! (*Crosses to the door*) She'll go on sleeping and de-
vouring until there's nothing left of me.

(*He exits.* ALISON's *head goes back as if she were about to make
some sound. But her mouth remains open and trembling, as* CLIFF
looks on)

Curtain

ACT TWO

SCENE I

Two weeks later. Evening. ALISON *is standing over the gas stove, pouring water from the kettle into a large teapot. She is only wearing a slip, and her feet are bare. In the room across the hall,* JIMMY *is playing on his jazz trumpet, in intermittent bursts.* ALISON *takes the pot to the table, which is laid for four people. The Sunday paper jungle around the two armchairs is as luxuriant as ever. It is late afternoon, the end of a hot day. She wipes her forehead. She crosses to the dressing table, takes out a pair of stockings from one of the drawers, and sits down on the small chair beside it to put them on. While she is doing this, the door opens and* HELENA *enters. She is the same age as* ALISON, *medium height, carefully and expensively dressed. Now and again, when she allows her rather judicial expression of alertness to soften, she is very attractive. Her sense of matriarchal authority makes most men who meet her anxious, not only to please but impress, as if she were the gracious representative of visiting royalty. In this case, the royalty of that middle-class womanhood, which is so eminently secure in its divine rights, that it can afford to tolerate the parliament, and reasonably free assembly of its menfolk. Even from other young women, like* ALISON, *she receives her due of respect and admiration. In* JIMMY, *as one would expect, she arouses all the rabble-rousing instincts of his spirit. And she is not accustomed to having to defend herself against catcalls. However, her sense of modestly exalted responsibility enables her to behave with an impressive show of strength and dignity, although the strain of this is beginning to tell on her a little. She is carrying a large salad colander.*

ALISON Did you manage all right?

HELENA   Of course. I've prepared most of the meals in the last week, you know.

ALISON   Yes, you have. It's been wonderful having someone to help. Another woman, I mean.

HELENA   (*Crossing*)   I'm enjoying it. Although I don't think I shall ever get used to having to go down to the bathroom every time I want some water for something.

ALISON   It is primitive, isn't it?

HELENA   Yes. It is rather. (*She starts tearing up green salad on to four plates, which she takes from the food cupboard*) Looking after one man is really enough, but two is rather an undertaking.

ALISON   Oh, Cliff looks after himself, more or less. In fact, he helps me quite a lot.

HELENA   Can't say I'd noticed it.

ALISON   You've been doing it instead, I suppose.

HELENA   I see.

ALISON   You've settled in so easily somehow.

HELENA   Why shouldn't I?

ALISON   It's not exactly what you're used to, is it?

HELENA   And are you used to it?

ALISON   Everything seems very different here now—with you here.

HELENA   Does it?

ALISON   Yes. I was on my own before——

HELENA   Now you've got me. So you're not sorry you asked me to stay?

ALISON   Of course not. Did you tell him his tea was ready?

HELENA   I banged on the door of Cliff's room, and yelled. He didn't answer, but he must have heard. I don't know where Cliff is.

ALISON   (*Leaning back in her chair*)   I thought I'd feel cooler after a bath, but I feel hot again already. God, I wish he'd lose that damned trumpet.

HELENA   I imagine that's for my benefit.

ALISON   Miss Drury will ask us to go soon, I know it. Thank goodness she isn't in. Listen to him.

HELENA   Does he drink?

ALISON   Drink? (*Rather startled*) He's not an alcoholic, if that's what you mean. (*They both pause, listening to the trumpet*) He'll have the rest of the street banging on the door next.

HELENA   (*Pondering*)   It's almost as if he wanted to kill someone with it. And me in particular. I've never seen such hatred in someone's eyes before. It's slightly horrifying. Horrifying (*Crossing to the food cupboard for tomatoes, beetroot and cucumber*) and oddly exciting.

(ALISON *faces her dressing mirror, and brushes her hair*)

ALISON He had his own jazz band once. That was when he was still a student, before I knew him. I rather think he'd like to start another, and give up the stall altogether.

HELENA Is Cliff in love with you?

ALISON (*Stops brushing for a moment*) No . . . I don't think so.

HELENA And what about you? You look as though I've asked you a rather peculiar question. The way things are, you might as well be frank with me. I only want to help. After all, your behaviour together is a little strange—by most people's standards, to say the least.

ALISON You mean you've seen us embracing each other?

HELENA Well, it doesn't seem to go on as much as it did, I admit. Perhaps he finds my presence inhibiting—even if Jimmy's isn't.

ALISON We're simply fond of each other—there's no more to it than that.

HELENA Darling, really! It can't be as simple as that.

ALISON You mean there must be something physical too? I suppose there is, but it's not exactly a consuming passion with either of us. It's just a relaxed, cheerful sort of thing, like being warm in bed. You're too comfortable to bother about moving for the sake of some other pleasure.

HELENA I find it difficult to believe anyone's that lazy!

ALISON I think *we* are.

HELENA And what about Jimmy? After all, he is your husband. Do you mean to say he actually approves of it?

ALISON It isn't easy to explain. It's what he would call a question of allegiances, and he expects you to be pretty literal about them. Not only about himself and all the things he believes in, his present and his future, but his past as well. All the people he admires and loves, and has loved. The friends he used to know, people I've never even known—and probably wouldn't have liked. His father, who died years ago. Even the other women he's loved. Do you understand?

HELENA Do you?

ALISON I've tried to. But I still can't bring myself to feel the way he does about things. I can't believe that he's right somehow.

HELENA Well, that's something, anyway.

ALISON If things have worked out with Cliff, it's because he's kind and lovable, and I've grown genuinely fond of him. But it's been a fluke. It's worked because Cliff is such a nice person anyway. With Hugh, it was quite different.

HELENA Hugh?

ALISON Hugh Tanner. He and Jimmy were friends almost from childhood. Mrs. Tanner is his mother——

HELENA Oh yes—the one who started him off in the sweet business.

ALISON That's right. Well, after Jimmy and I were married, we'd no money—about eight pounds ten in actual fact—and no home. He didn't even have a job. He'd only left the university about a year. (*Smiles*) No—left. I don't think one "comes down" from Jimmy's university. According to him, it's not even red brick, but white tile. Anyway, we went off to live in Hugh's flat. It was over a warehouse in Poplar.

HELENA Yes. I remember seeing the postmark on your letters.

ALISON Well, that was where I found myself on my wedding night. Hugh and I disliked each other on sight, and Jimmy knew it. He was so proud of us both, so pathetically anxious that we should take to each other. Like a child showing off his toys. We had a little wedding celebration, and the three of us tried to get tight on some cheap port they'd brought in. Hugh got more and more subtly insulting—he'd a rare talent for that. Jimmy got steadily depressed, and I just sat there, listening to their talk, looking and feeling very stupid. For the first time in my life, I was cut off from the kind of people I'd always known, my family, my friends, everybody. And I'd burnt my boats. After all those weeks of brawling with Mummy and Daddy about Jimmy, I knew I couldn't appeal to them without looking foolish and cheap. It was just before the General Election, I remember, and Nigel was busy getting himself into Parliament. He didn't have time for anyone but his constituents. Oh, he'd have been sweet and kind, I know.

HELENA Darling, why didn't you come to me?

ALISON You were away on tour in some play, I think.

HELENA So I was.

ALISON Those next few months at the flat in Poplar were a nightmare. I suppose I must be soft and squeamish, and snobbish, but I felt as though I'd been dropped in a jungle. I couldn't believe that two people, two educated people could be so savage, and so—so uncompromising. Mummy has always said that Jimmy is utterly ruthless, but she hasn't met Hugh. He takes the first prize for ruthlessness—from all comers. Together, they were frightening.

They both came to regard me as a sort of hostage from those sections of society they had declared war on.

HELENA   How were you living all this time?

ALISON   I had a tiny bit coming in from a few shares I had left, but it hardly kept us. Mummy had made me sign everything else over to her, in trust, when she knew I was really going to marry Jimmy.

HELENA   Just as well, I imagine.

ALISON   They soon thought of a way out of that. A brilliant campaign. They started inviting themselves—through me—to people's houses, friends of Nigel's and mine, friends of Daddy's, oh everyone: The Arksdens, the Tarnatts, the Wains—

HELENA   Not the Wains?

ALISON   Just about everyone I'd ever known. Your people must have been among the few we missed out. It was just enemy territory to them, and, as I say, they used me as a hostage. We'd set out from headquarters in Poplar, and carry out our raids on the enemy in W.1., S.W.1., S.W.3. and W.8. In my name, we'd gate-crash everywhere—cocktails, week-ends, even a couple of house-parties. I used to hope that one day, somebody would have the guts to slam the door in our faces, but they didn't. They were too well-bred, and probably sorry for me as well. Hugh and Jimmy despised them for it. So we went on plundering them, wolfing their food and drinks, and smoking their cigars like ruffians. Oh, they enjoyed themselves.

HELENA   Apparently.

ALISON   Hugh fairly revelled in the role of the barbarian invader. Sometimes I thought he might even dress the part—you know, furs, spiked helmet, sword. He even got a fiver out of old Man Wain once. Blackmail, of course. People would have signed almost anything to get rid of us. He told him that we were about to be turned out of our flat for not paying the rent. At least it was true.

HELENA   I don't understand you. You must have been crazy.

ALISON   Afraid more than anything.

HELENA   But letting them do it! Letting them get away with it! You managed to stop them stealing the silver, I suppose?

ALISON   Oh, they knew their guerrilla warfare better than that. Hugh tried to seduce some fresh-faced young girl at the Arksdens' once, but that was the only time we were more or less turned out.

HELENA It's almost unbelievable. I don't understand your part in it at all. Why? That's what I don't see. Why did you——

ALISON Marry him? There must be about six different answers. When the family came back from India, everything seemed, I don't know—unsettled? Anyway, Daddy seemed remote and rather irritable. And Mummy—well, you know Mummy. I didn't have much to worry about. I didn't know I was born as Jimmy says. I met him at a party. I remember it so clearly. I was almost twenty-one. The men there all looked as though they distrusted him, and as for the women, they were all intent on showing their contempt for this rather odd creature, but no one seemed quite sure how to do it. He'd come to the party on a bicycle, he told me, and there was oil all over his dinner jacket. It had been such a lovely day, and he'd been in the sun. Everything about him seemed to burn, his face, the edges of his hair glistened and seemed to spring off his head, and his eyes were so blue and full of the sun. He looked so young and frail, in spite of the tired line of his mouth. I knew I was taking on more than I was ever likely to be capable of bearing, but there never seemed to be any choice. Well, the howl of outrage and astonishment went up from the family, and that did it. Whether or no he was in love with me, that did it. He made up his mind to marry me. They did just about everything they could think of to stop us.

HELENA Yes, it wasn't a very pleasant business. But you can see their point.

ALISON Jimmy went into battle with his axe swinging round his head—frail, and so full of fire. I had never seen anything like it. The old story of the knight in shining armour—except that his armour didn't really shine very much.

HELENA And what about Hugh?

ALISON Things got steadily worse between us. He and Jimmy even went to some of Nigel's political meetings. They took bunches of their Poplar cronies with them, and broke them up for him.

HELENA He's really a savage, isn't he?

ALISON Well, Hugh was writing some novel or other, and he made up his mind he must go abroad—to China, or some God-forsaken place. He said that England was finished for us, anyway. All the old gang was back—Dame Alison's Mob, as he used to call it. The only real hope was to get out, and try somewhere else. He wanted us to go with him, but Jimmy refused to go. There was a terrible, bitter row over it. Jimmy accused Hugh of giving up, and he thought it was wrong of him to go off forever, and leave his mother all on her own. He was upset by the whole idea. They quarrelled for days over it. I almost wished they'd both go, and leave me behind. Anyway, they broke up. A few months later we came up here, and Hugh went off to find the New Millennium on his own. Sometimes, I think Hugh's mother blames me for it all. Jimmy too, in a way, although he's never said so. He never mentions it. But whenever that woman looks at me, I can feel her thinking "If it hadn't been for you, everything would have been all right. We'd have all been happy." Not that I dislike her—I don't. She's very sweet, in fact. Jimmy seems to adore her principally because she's been poor almost all her life, and she's frankly ignorant. I'm quite aware how snobbish that sounds, but it happens to be the truth.

HELENA Alison, listen to me. You've got to make up your mind what you're going to do. You're going to have a baby, and you have a new responsibility. Before, it was different—there was only yourself at stake. But you can't go on living in this way any longer. (*To her*)

ALISON I'm so tired. I dread him coming into the room.

HELENA Why haven't you told him you're going to have a child?

ALISON I don't know. (*Suddenly anticipating* HELENA's *train of thought*) Oh, it's his all right. There couldn't be any doubt of that. You see—— (*She smiles*) I've never really wanted anyone else.

HELENA Listen, darling—you've got to tell him. Either he learns to behave like anyone else, and looks after you——

ALISON Or?

HELENA Or you must get out of this mad-house. (*Trumpet crescendo*) This menagerie. He doesn't seem to know what love or anything else means.

ALISON (*Pointing to chest of drawers up* R.) You see that bear, and that squirrel? Well, that's him, and that's me.

HELENA Meaning?

ALISON The game we play: bears and squirrels, squirrels and bears. (HELENA *looks rather blank*) Yes, it's quite mad, I know. Quite mad. (*Picks up the two animals*) That's him. . . . And that's me. . . .

HELENA I didn't realise he was a bit fey, as well as everything else!

ALISON Oh, there's nothing fey about Jimmy. It's just all we seem to have left. Or had left. Even bears and squirrels seem to have gone their own ways now.

HELENA   Since I arrived?

ALISON   It started during those first months we had alone together —after Hugh went abroad. It was the one way of escaping from everything—a sort of unholy priesthole of being animals to one another. We could become little furry creatures with little furry brains. Full of dumb, uncomplicated affection for each other. Playful, careless creatures in their own cosy zoo for two. A silly symphony for people who couldn't bear the pain of being human beings any longer. And now, even they are dead, poor little silly animals. They were all love, and no brains.

(She puts them back)

HELENA   *(Gripping her arm)*   Listen to me. You've got to fight him. Fight, or get out. Otherwise, he *will* kill you.

(CLIFF enters)

CLIFF   There you are, dullin'. Hullo, Helena. Tea ready?

ALISON   Yes, dear, it's all ready. Give Jimmy a call, will you?

CLIFF   Right. *(Yelling back through door)* Hey, you horrible man! Stop that bloody noise, and come and get your tea! *(Coming in)* Going out?

HELENA   Yes.

CLIFF   Pictures?

HELENA   No. *(Pause)* Church.

CLIFF   *(Really surprised)* Oh! I see. Both of you?

HELENA   Yes. Are you coming?

CLIFF   Well. . . . I—I haven't read the papers properly yet. Tea, tea, tea! Let's have some tea, shall we? *(He sits at the upstage end of the table.* HELENA *puts the four plates of salad on it, sits down, and they begin the meal.* ALISON *is making up her face at her dressing table. Presently,* JIMMY *enters. He places his trumpet on the bookcase, and comes above the table)* Hullo, boyo. Come and have your tea. That blinkin' trumpet—why don't you stuff it away somewhere?

JIMMY   You like it all right. Anyone who doesn't like real jazz, hasn't any feeling either for music or people.

(He sits at the end of the table)

HELENA   Rubbish.

JIMMY   *(To CLIFF)* That seems to prove my point for you. Did you know that Webster played the banjo?

CLIFF   No, does he really?

HELENA He said he'd bring it along next time he came.

ALISON (*Muttering*) Oh, no!

JIMMY Why is it that nobody knows how to treat the papers in this place? Look at them. I haven't even glanced at them yet—not the posh ones, anyway.

CLIFF By the way, can I look at your *New*——

JIMMY No, you can't! (*Loudly*) You want anything, you pay for it. Like I have to. Price——

CLIFF Price ninepence, obtainable from any bookstall! You're a mean old man, that's what you are.

JIMMY What do you want to read it for, anyway? You've no intellect, no curiosity. It all just washes over you. Am I right?

CLIFF Right.

JIMMY What are you, you Welsh trash?

CLIFF Nothing, that's what I am.

JIMMY Nothing are you? Blimey you ought to be Prime Minister. You must have been talking to some of my wife's friends. They're a very intellectual set, aren't they? I've seen 'em. (CLIFF *and* HELENA *carry on with their meal*) They all sit around feeling very spiritual, with their mental hands on each other's knees, discussing sex as if it were the Art of Fugue. If you don't want to be an emotional old spinster, just you listen to your dad! (*He starts eating. The silent hostility of the two women has set him off on the scent, and he looks quite cheerful, although the occasional, thick edge of his voice belies it*) You know your trouble, son? Too anxious to please.

HELENA Thank heavens somebody is!

JIMMY You'll end up like one of those chocolate meringues my wife is so fond of. My wife—that's the one on the tom-toms behind me. Sweet and sticky on the outside, and sink your teeth in it (*Savouring every word*), inside, all white, messy and disgusting. (*Offering the teapot sweetly to Helena*) Tea?

HELENA Thank you.

(*He smiles, and pours out a cup for her*)

JIMMY That's how you'll end up, my boy—black hearted, evil minded and vicious.

HELENA (*Taking the cup*) Thank you.

JIMMY And those old favourites, your friends and mine: sycophantic, phlegmatic, and, of course, top of the bill—pusillanimous.

HELENA (*To* ALISON) Aren't you going to have your tea?

ALISON Won't be long.

JIMMY Thought of the title for a new song today. It's called "You can quit hanging round my counter Mildred 'cos you'll find my position is closed." (*Turning to* ALISON *suddenly*) Good?

ALISON Oh, very good.

JIMMY Thought you'd like it. If I can slip in a religious angle, it should be a big hit. (*To* HELENA) Don't you think so? I was thinking you might help me there. (*She doesn't reply*) It might help you if I recite the lyrics. Let's see now, it's something like this:

I'm so tired of necking,
of pecking, home wrecking,
of empty bed blues—
just pass me the booze.
I'm tired of being hetero
Rather ride on the metero
Just pass me the booze.
This perpetual whoring
Gets quite dull and boring
So avoid that old python coil
And pass me the celibate oil.
You can quit etc.

No?

CLIFF Very good, boyo.

JIMMY Oh, yes, and I know what I meant to tell you—I wrote a poem while I was at the market yesterday. If you're interested, which you obviously are. (*To* HELENA) It should appeal to you, in particular. It's soaked in the theology of Dante, with a good slosh of Eliot as well. It starts off "There are no dry cleaners in Cambodia!"

CLIFF What do you call it?

JIMMY "The Cess Pool." Myself being a stone dropped in it, you see——

CLIFF You should be dropped in it, all right.

HELENA (*To* JIMMY) Why do you try so hard to be unpleasant? (*He turns very deliberately, delighted that she should rise to the bait so soon—he's scarcely in his stride yet*)

JIMMY What's that?

HELENA Do you have to be so offensive?

JIMMY You mean now? You think I'm being offensive? You underestimate me. (*Turning to* ALISON) Doesn't she?

HELENA I think you're a very tiresome young man.

(*A slight pause as his delight catches up with him. He roars with laughter*)

JIMMY Oh dear, oh dear! My wife's friends! Pass Lady Bracknell the cucumber sandwiches, will you? (*He returns to his meal, but his curiosity about* ALISON's *preparations at the mirror won't be denied any longer. He turns round casually, and speaks to her*) Going out?

ALISON That's right.

JIMMY On a Sunday evening in this town? Where on earth are you going?

ALISON (*Rising*) I'm going out with Helena.

JIMMY That's not a direction—that's an affliction. (*She crosses to the table, and sits down. He leans forward, and addresses her again*) I didn't ask you what was the matter with you. I asked you where you were going.

HELENA (*Steadily*) She's going to church.

(*He has been prepared for some plot, but he is as genuinely surprised by this as* CLIFF *was a few minutes earlier*)

JIMMY You're doing what? (*Silence*) Have you gone out of your mind or something? (*To* HELENA) You're determined to win her, aren't you? So it's come to this now! How feeble can you get? (*His rage mounting within*) When I think of what I did, what I endured, to get you out——

ALISON (*Recognising an onslaught on the way, starts to panic*) Oh yes, we all know what you did for me! You rescued me from the wicked clutches of my family, and all my friends! I'd still be rotting away at home, if you hadn't ridden up on your charger, and carried me off!

(*The wild note in her voice has re-assured him. His anger cools and hardens. His voice is quite calm when he speaks*)

JIMMY The funny thing is, you know, I really did have to ride up on a white charger—off white, really. Mummy locked her up in their eight bedroomed castle, didn't she? There is no limit to what the middle-aged mummy will do in the holy crusade against ruffians like me. Mummy and I took one quick look at each other, and, from then on, the age of chivalry was dead. I knew that, to protect her innocent young, she wouldn't hesitate to cheat, lie, bully and blackmail. Threatened with me, a young man without money, background or even looks, she'd bellow like a rhinoceros in labour—enough to make every male rhino for miles turn white, and pledge himself to celibacy. But even I under-estimated her strength. Mummy may look over-fed and a bit flabby on the out-side, but don't let that well-bred guzzler fool you. Underneath all that, she's armour plated—— (*He clutches wildly for something to shock* HELENA *with*) She's as rough as a night in a Bombay brothel, and as tough as a matelot's arm. She's probably in that bloody cistern, taking down every word we say. (*Kicks cistern*) Can you 'ear me, mother. (*Sits on it, beats like bongo drums*) Just about get her in there. Let me give you an example of this lady's tactics. You may have noticed that I happen to wear my hair rather long. Now, if my wife is honest, or concerned enough to ex-plain, she could tell you that this is not due to any dark, unnatural instincts I possess, but because (a) I can usually think of better things than a haircut to spend two bob on, and (b) I prefer long hair. But that obvious, innocent explanation didn't appeal to Mummy at all. So she hires detectives to watch me, to see if she can't somehow get me into the *News of the World.* All so that I shan't carry off her daughter on that poor old charger of mine, all tricked out and caparisoned in discredited passions and ideals! The old grey mare that actually once led the charge against the old order—well, she certainly ain't what she used to be. It was all she could do to carry me, but your weight (*To* ALISON) was too much for her. She just dropped dead on the way.

CLIFF (*Quietly*) Don't let's brawl, boyo. It won't do any good.

JIMMY Why *don't* we brawl? It's the only thing left I'm any good at.

CLIFF Jimmy, boy——

JIMMY (*To* ALISON) You've let this genuflecting sin jobber win you over, haven't you? She's got you back, hasn't she?

HELENA Oh for heaven's sake, don't be such a bully! You've no right to talk about her mother like that!

JIMMY (*Capable of anything now*) I've got every right. That old bitch should be dead! (*To* ALISON) Well? Aren't I right? (CLIFF *and* HELENA *look at* ALISON *tensely, but she just gazes at her plate*) I said she's an old bitch, and should be dead! What's the matter with you? Why don't you leap to her defense!

(CLIFF *gets up quickly, and takes his arm*)

CLIFF Jimmy, don't!

(JIMMY *pushes him back savagely, and he sits down helplessly, turning his head away on to his hand*)

JIMMY If someone said something like that about me, she'd react soon enough—she'd spring into her well known lethargy, and say nothing! I say she ought to be dead. (*He brakes for a fresh spurt later. He's saving his strength for the knock-out*) My God, those worms will need a good dose of salts the day they get through her! Oh what a bellyache you've got coming to you, my little wormy ones! Alison's mother is on the way! (*In what he intends to be a comic declamatory voice*) She will pass away, my friends, leaving a trail of worms gasping for laxatives behind her—from purgatives to purgatory. (*He smiles down at* ALISON, *but still she hasn't broken.* CLIFF *won't look at them. Only* HELENA *looks at him. Denied the other two, he addresses her*) Is anything the matter?

HELENA I feel rather sick, that's all. Sick with contempt and loathing.

(*He can feel her struggling on the end of his line, and he looks at her rather absently*)

JIMMY One day, when I'm no longer spending my days running a sweet-stall, I may write a book about us all. It's all here. (*Slapping his forehead*) Written in flames a mile high. And it won't be recollected in tranquillity either, picking daffodils with Auntie Wordsworth. It'll be recollected in fire, and blood. My blood.

HELENA (*Thinking patient reasonableness may be worth a try*) She simply said that she's going to church with me. I don't see why that calls for this incredible outburst.

JIMMY Don't you? Perhaps you're not as clever as I thought.

HELENA You think the world's treated you pretty badly, don't you?

ALISON (*Turning her face away*) Oh, don't try and take his suffering away from him—he'd be lost without it.

(*He looks at her in surprise, but he turns back to* HELENA. ALISON *can have her turn again later*)

JIMMY I thought this play you're touring in finished up on Saturday week?

HELENA That's right.

JIMMY Eight days ago, in fact.

HELENA Alison wanted me to stay.

JIMMY What are you plotting?

HELENA Don't you think we've had enough of the heavy villain?

JIMMY (*To* ALISON) You don't believe in all that stuff. Why you don't believe in anything. You're just doing it to be vindictive, aren't you? Why—why are you letting her influence you like this?

ALISON (*Starting to break*) Why, why, why, why! (*Putting her hands over her ears*) That word's pulling my head off!

JIMMY And as long as you're around, I'll go on using it.

(*He crosses down to the armchair, and seats himself on the back of it. He addresses* HELENA's *back*)

JIMMY The last time she was in a church was when she was married to me. I expect that surprises you, doesn't it? It was expediency, pure and simple. We were in a hurry, you see. (*The comedy of this strikes him at once, and he laughs*) Yes, we were actually in a hurry! Lusting for the slaughter! Well, the local registrar was a particular pal of Daddy's, and we knew he'd spill the beans to the Colonel like a shot. So we had to seek out some local vicar who didn't know him quite so well. But it was no use. When my best man—a chap I'd met in the pub that morning—and I turned up, Mummy and Daddy were in the church already. They'd found out at the last moment, and had come to watch the execution carried out. How I remember looking down at them, full of beer for breakfast, and feeling a bit buzzed. Mummy was slumped over her pew in a heap—the noble, female rhino, poleaxed at last! And Daddy sat beside her, upright and unafraid, dreaming of his days among the Indian Princes, and unable to believe he'd left his horsewhip at home. Just the two of them in that empty church—them and me. (*Coming out of his remembrance suddenly*) I'm not sure what happened after that. We must have been married, I suppose. I think I remember being sick in the vestry. (*To* ALISON) Was I?

HELENA Haven't you finished?

(*He can smell blood again, and he goes on calmly, cheerfully*)

JIMMY (*To* ALISON) Are you going to let yourself be taken in by this saint in Dior's clothing? I will tell you the simple truth about her. (*Articulating with care*) She is a cow. I wouldn't mind that so much, but she seems to have become a sacred cow as well!

CLIFF You've gone too far, Jimmy. Now dry up!

HELENA Oh, let him go on.

JIMMY (*To* CLIFF) I suppose you're going over to that side as well. Well, why don't you? Helena will help to make it pay off for you. She's an expert in the New Economics—the Economics of the Supernatural. It's all a simple matter of payments and penalties. (*Rises*) She's one of those apocalyptic share pushers who are spreading all those rumours about a transfer of power. (*His imagination is racing, and the words pour out*) Reason and Progress, the old firm, is selling out! Everyone get out while the going's good. Those forgotten shares you had in the old traditions, the old beliefs are going up—up and up and up. (*Moves up*) There's going to be a change over. A new Board of Directors, who are going to see that the dividends are always attractive, and that they go to the right people. (*Facing them*) Sell out everything you've got: all those stocks in the old, free inquiry. (*Crosses to the table*) The Big Crash is coming, you can't escape it, so get in on the ground floor with Helena and her friends while there's still time. And there isn't much of it left. Tell me, what could be more gilt-edged than the next world! It's a capital gain, and it's all yours. (*He moves round the table, back to his chair*) You see, I know Helena and her kind so very well. In fact, her kind are everywhere, you can't move for them. They're a romantic lot. They spend their time mostly looking forward to the past. The only place they can see the light is the Dark Ages. She's moved long ago into a lovely little cottage of the soul, cut right off from the ugly problems of the twentieth century altogether. She prefers to be cut off from all the conveniences we've fought to get for centuries. She'd rather go down to the ecstatic little shed at the bottom of the garden to relieve her sense of guilt. Our Helena is full of ecstatic wind— (*He leans across the table at her*) aren't you?

(*He waits for her to reply*)

HELENA (*Quite calmly*) It's a pity you've been so far away all this time. I would probably have slapped your face. (*They look into each other's eyes across the table. He moves slowly up, above* CLIFF, *until he is beside her*) You've behaved like this ever since I first came.

JIMMY Helena, have you ever watched somebody die? (*She makes a move to rise*) No, don't move away. (*She remains seated, and looks up at him*) It doesn't look dignified enough for you.

HELENA (*Like ice*) If you come any nearer, I will slap your face. (*He looks down at her, a grin smouldering round his mouth*)

JIMMY I hope you won't make the mistake of thinking for one moment that I am a gentleman.

HELENA I'm not very likely to do that.

JIMMY (*Bringing his face close to hers*) I've no public school scruples about hitting girls. (*Gently*) If you slap my face—by God, I'll lay you out!

HELENA You probably would. You're the type.

JIMMY You bet I'm the type. I'm the type that detests physical violence. Which is why, if I find some woman trying to cash in on what she thinks is my defenceless chivalry by lashing out with her frail little fists, I lash back at her.

HELENA Is that meant to be subtle, or just plain Irish?

(*His grin widens*)

JIMMY I think you and I understand one another all right. But you haven't answered my question. I said: have you watched somebody die?

HELENA No, I haven't.

JIMMY Anyone who's never watched somebody die is suffering from a pretty bad case of virginity. (*His good humour of a moment ago deserts him, as he begins to remember*) For twelve months, I watched my father dying—when I was ten years old. He'd come back from the war in Spain, you see. And certain god-fearing gentlemen there had made such a mess of him, he didn't have long left to live. Everyone knew it—even I knew it. But, you see, I was the only one who cared. (*Turns to the window*) His family were embarrassed by the whole business. Embarrassed and irritated. (*Looking out*) As for my mother, all she could think about was the fact that she had allied herself to a man who seemed to be on the wrong side in all things. My mother was all for being associated with minorities, provided they were the smart, fashionable ones. (*He moves up again*) We all of us waited for him to die. The family sent him a cheque every month, and hoped he'd get on with it quietly, without too much vulgar fuss. My mother looked after him without complaining, and that was about all. Perhaps she pitied him. I suppose she was capable of that. (*With a kind of appeal in his voice*) But I was the only one who cared! (*He moves behind the armchair*) Every time I sat on the edge of his bed, to listen to him talking or reading to me, I had to fight back my tears. At the end of twelve months, I was a veteran. (*He leans forward on the back of the armchair*) All that that feverish failure of a man had to listen to him was a small, frightened boy. I spent hour upon hour in that tiny bedroom. He would talk to me for hours, pouring out all that was left of his life to one, lonely, bewildered little boy, who could barely understand half of what he said. All he could feel was the despair and the bitterness, the sweet, sickly smell of a dying man. (*He moves around the chair*) You see, I learnt at an early age what it was to be angry—angry and helpless. And I can never forget it. (*Sits*) I knew more about—love . . . betrayal . . . and death, when I was ten years old than you will probably ever know all your life. (*They all sit silently. Presently,* HELENA *rises*)

HELENA   Time we went. (ALISON *nods*) I'll just get my things together. (*Crosses to the door*) I'll see you downstairs. (*She exits. A slight pause*)

JIMMY   (*Not looking at her, almost whispering*)   Doesn't it matter to you—what people do to me? What are you trying to do to me? I've given you just everything. Doesn't it mean *anything* to you? (*Her back stiffens. His axe-swinging bravado has vanished, and his voice crumples in disabled rage*) You Judas! You phlegm! She's taking you with her, and you're so bloody feeble, you'll let her do it!

(ALISON *suddenly takes hold of her cup, and hurls it on the floor. He's drawn blood at last. She looks down at the pieces on the floor, and then at him. Then she crosses, takes out a dress on a hanger, and slips it on. As she is zipping up the side, she feels giddy, and she has to lean against the wardrobe for support. She closes her eyes*)

ALISON   (*Softly*)   All I want is a little peace.

JIMMY   Peace! God! She wants peace! (*Hardly able to get his words out*) My heart is so full, I feel ill—and she wants peace! (*She crosses to the bed to put on her shoes.* CLIFF *gets up from the table, and sits in the armchair. He picks up a paper, and looks at that.* JIMMY *has recovered slightly, and manages to sound almost detached*) I rage, and shout my head off, and everyone thinks "poor chap!" or "what an objectionable young man!" But that girl there can twist your arm off with her silence. I've sat in this chair in the dark for hours. And, although she knows I'm feeling as I feel now, she's turned over, and gone to sleep. (*He gets up and faces* CLIFF, *who doesn't look up from his paper*) One of us is crazy. One of us is mean and stupid and crazy. Which is it? Is it me? Is it me, standing here like an hysterical girl, hardly able to get my words out? Or is it her? Sitting there, putting on her shoes to go out with that— (*But inspiration has deserted him by now*) Which is it? (CLIFF *is still looking down at his paper*) I wish to heaven you'd try loving her, that's all. (*He moves up, watching her look for her gloves*) Perhaps, one day, you may want to come back. I shall wait for that day. I want to stand up in your tears, and splash about in them, and sing. I want to be there when you grovel. I want to be there, I want to watch it, I want the front seat. (HELENA *enters, carrying two prayer books*) I want to see your face rubbed in the mud—that's all I can hope for. There's nothing else I want any longer.

HELENA (*After a moment*) There's a phone call for you.

JIMMY (*Turning*) Well, it can't be anything good, can it?

(*He goes out*)

HELENA All ready?

ALISON Yes—I think so.

HELENA You feel all right, don't you? (*She nods*) What's he been raving about now? Oh, what does it matter? He makes me want to claw his hair out by the roots. When I think of what you will be going through in a few months' time—and all for him! It's as if you'd done *him* wrong! These *men!* (*Turning on* CLIFF) And all the time you just sit there, and do nothing!

CLIFF (*Looking up slowly*) That's right—I just sit here.

HELENA What's the matter with you? What sort of a man are you?

CLIFF I'm not the District Commissioner, you know. Listen, Helena—I don't feel like Jimmy does about you, but I'm not exactly on your side either. And since you've been here, everything's certainly been worse than it's ever been. This has always been a battlefield, but I'm pretty certain that if I hadn't been here, everything would have been over between these two long ago. I've been a—a no-man's land between them. Sometimes, it's been still and peaceful, no incidents, and we've all been reasonably happy. But most of the time, it's simply a very narrow strip of plain hell. But where I come from, we're used to brawling and excitement. Perhaps I even enjoy being in the thick of it. I love these two people very much. (*He looks at her steadily, and adds simply*) And I pity all of us.

HELENA Are you including me in that? (*But she goes on quickly to avoid his reply*) I don't understand him, you or any of it. All I know is that none of you seems to know how to behave in a decent, civilised way. (*In command now*) Listen, Alison—I've sent your father a wire.

ALISON (*Numbed and vague by now*) Oh?

(HELENA *looks at her, and realizes quickly that everything now will have to depend on her own authority. She tries to explain patiently*)

HELENA Look, dear—he'll get it first thing in the morning. I thought it would be better than trying to explain the situation over the phone. I asked him to come up, and fetch you home tomorrow.

ALISON What did you say?

HELENA Simply that you wanted to come home, and would he come up for you.

ALISON I see.

HELENA I knew that would be quite enough. I told him there was nothing to worry about, so they won't worry and think there's been an accident or anything. I had to do something, dear. (*Very gently*) You didn't mind, did you?

ALISON No, I don't mind. Thank you.

HELENA And you will go when he comes for you?

ALISON (*Pause*) Yes. I'll go.

HELENA (*Relieved*) I expect he'll drive up. He should be here about tea-time. It'll give you plenty of time to get your things together. And, perhaps, after you've gone—Jimmy (*Saying the word almost with difficulty*) will come to his senses, and face up to things.

ALISON Who was on the phone?

HELENA I didn't catch it properly. It rang after I'd sent the wire off—just as soon as I put the receiver down almost. I had to go back down the stairs again. Sister somebody, I think.

ALISON Must have been a hospital or something. Unless he knows someone in a convent—*that* doesn't seem very likely, does it? Well, we'll be late, if we don't hurry.

(*She puts down one of the prayer books on the table. Enter* JIMMY. *He comes down between the two women*)

CLIFF All right, boyo?

JIMMY (*To* ALISON) It's Hugh's mum. She's—had a stroke.

(*Slight pause*)

ALISON I'm sorry.

(JIMMY *sits on the bed*)

CLIFF How bad is it?

JIMMY They didn't say much. But I think she's dying.

CLIFF Oh dear. . . .

JIMMY (*Rubbing his fist over his face*) It doesn't make any sense at all. Do you think it does?

ALISON I'm sorry—I really am.

CLIFF Anything I can do?

JIMMY The London train goes in half an hour. You'd better order me a taxi.

CLIFF Right. (*He crosses to the door, and stops*) Do you want me to come with you, boy?

JIMMY No thanks. After all, you hardly knew her. It's not for you to go. (HELENA *looks quickly at* ALISON) She may not even remember me, for all I know.

CLIFF   O.K.

(*He exits*)

JIMMY   I remember the first time I showed her your photograph —just after we were married. She looked at it, and the tears just welled up in her eyes, and she said: "But she's so beautiful! She's so beautiful!" She kept repeating it as if she couldn't believe it. Sounds a bit simple and sentimental when you repeat it. But it was pure gold the way she said it. (*He looks at her. She is standing by the dressing table, her back to him*) She got a kick out of you, like she did out of everything else. Hand me my shoes, will you? (*She kneels down, and hands them to him. Looking down at his feet*) You're coming with me, aren't you? She (*He shrugs*) hasn't got anyone else now. I . . . need you . . . to come with me.

(*He looks into her eyes, but she turns away, and stands up. Outside, the church bells start ringing.* HELENA *moves up to the door, and waits watching them closely.* ALISON *stands quite still,* JIMMY'S *eyes burning into her. Then, she crosses in front of him to the table where she picks up the prayer book, her back to him. She wavers, and seems about to say something, but turns upstage instead, and walks quickly to the door*)

ALISON (*Hardly audible*)   Let's go.

(*She goes out,* HELENA *following.* JIMMY *gets up, looks about him unbelievingly, and leans against the chest of drawers. The teddy bear is close to his face, and he picks it up gently, looks at it quickly, and throws it downstage. It hits the floor with a thud, and it makes a rattling, groaning sound—as guaranteed in the advertisement.* JIMMY *falls forward on to the bed, his face buried in the covers*)

Curtain

SCENE II

The following evening. When the curtain rises, ALISON *is discovered going from her dressing table to the bed, and packing her things into a suitcase. Sitting is her father,* COLONEL REDFERN, *a large hand-some man, about sixty. Forty years of being a soldier sometimes conceals the essentially gentle, kindly man underneath. Brought up to command respect, he is often slightly withdrawn and uneasy now that he finds himself in a world where his authority has lately become less and less unquestionable. His wife would relish the present situation, but he is only disturbed and bewildered by it. He looks around him, discreetly scrutinising everything.*

COLONEL *(Partly to himself)* I'm afraid it's all beyond me. I sup-pose it always will be. As for Jimmy—he just speaks a different language from any of us. Where did you say he'd gone?

ALISON He's gone to see Mrs. Tanner.

COLONEL Who?

ALISON Hugh Tanner's mother.

COLONEL Oh, I see.

ALISON She's been taken ill—a stroke. Hugh's abroad, as you know, so Jimmy's gone to London to see her. *(He nods)* He wanted me to go with him.

COLONEL Didn't she start him off in this sweet-stall business?

ALISON Yes.

COLONEL What is she like? Nothing like her son, I trust?

ALISON Not remotely. Oh—how can you describe her? Rather—ordinary. What Jimmy insists on calling working class. A Char-woman who married an actor, worked hard all her life, and spent most of it struggling to support her husband and her son. Jimmy and she are very fond of each other.

COLONEL So you didn't go with him?

ALISON No.

COLONEL Who's looking after the sweet-stall?

ALISON Cliff. He should be in soon.

COLONEL Oh yes, of course—Cliff. Does he live here too?

ALISON Yes. His room is just across the landing.

COLONEL Sweet-stall. It does seem an extraordinary thing for an educated young man to be occupying himself with. Why should he want to do that, of all things. I've always thought he must be quite clever in his way.

ALISON *(No longer interested in this problem)* Oh, he tried so many things—journalism, advertising, even vacuum cleaners for a few weeks. He seems to have been as happy doing this as any-thing else.

COLONEL I've often wondered what it was like—where you were living, I mean. You didn't tell us very much in your letters.

ALISON There wasn't a great deal to tell you. There's not much social life here.

COLONEL Oh, I know what you mean. You were afraid of being disloyal to your husband.

ALISON Disloyal! (*She laughs*) He thought it was high treason of me to write to you at all! I used to have to dodge downstairs for the post, so that he wouldn't see I was getting letters from home. Even then I had to hide them.

COLONEL He really does hate us doesn't he?

ALISON Oh yes—don't have any doubts about that. He hates all of us.

COLONEL (*Sighs*) It seems a great pity. It was all so unfortunate —unfortunate and unnecessary. I'm afraid I can't help feeling that he must have had a certain amount of right on his side.

ALISON (*Puzzled by this admission*) Right on his side?

COLONEL It's a little late to admit it, I know, but your mother and I weren't entirely free from blame. I have never said anything— there was no point afterwards—but I have always believed that she went too far over Jimmy. Of course, she was extremely upset at the time—we both were—and that explains a good deal of what happened. I did my best to stop her, but she was in such a state of mind, there was simply nothing I could do. She seemed to have made up her mind that if he was going to marry you, he must be a criminal, at the very least. All those inquiries, the private detectives—the accusations. I hated every moment of it.

ALISON I suppose she was trying to protect me—in a rather heavy-handed way, admittedly.

COLONEL I must confess I find that kind of thing rather horrifying. Anyway, I try to think now that it never happened. I didn't approve of Jimmy at all, and I don't suppose I ever should, but, looking back on it, I think it would have been better, for all concerned, if we had never attempted to interfere. At least, it would have been a little more dignified.

ALISON It wasn't your fault.

COLONEL I don't know. We were all to blame, in our different ways. No doubt Jimmy acted in good faith. He's honest enough, whatever else he may be. And your mother—in her heavy-handed way, as you put it—acted in good faith as well. Perhaps you and I were the ones most to blame.

ALISON   You and I!

COLONEL   I think you may take after me a little, my dear. You like to sit on the fence because it's comfortable and more peaceful.

ALISON   Sitting on the fence! I married him, didn't I.

COLONEL   Oh yes, you did.

ALISON   In spite of all the humiliating scenes and the threats! What did you say to me at the time? Wasn't I letting you down, turning against you, how could I do this to you et cetera?

COLONEL   Perhaps it might have been better if you hadn't written letters to us—knowing how we felt about your husband, and after everything that had happened. (*He looks at her uncomfortably*) Forgive me, I'm a little confused, what with everything—the telegram, driving up here suddenly. . . .

   (*He trails off rather helplessly. He looks tired. He glances at her nervously, a hint of accusation in his eyes, as if he expected her to defend herself further. She senses this, and is more confused than ever*)

ALISON   Do you know what he said about Mummy? He said she was an overfed, overprivileged old bitch. "A good blow-out for the worms" was his expression, I think.

COLONEL   I see. And what does he say about me?

ALISON   Oh, he doesn't seem to mind you so much. In fact, I think he rather likes you. He likes you because he can feel sorry for you. (*Conscious that what she says is going to hurt him*) "Poor old Daddy—just one of those sturdy old plants left over from the Edwardian Wilderness that can't understand why the sun isn't shining any more." (*Rather lamely*) Something like that, anyway.

COLONEL   He has quite a turn of phrase, hasn't he? (*Simply, and without malice*) Why did you ever have to meet this young man?

ALISON   Oh, Daddy, please don't put me on trial now. I've been on trial every day and night of my life for nearly four years.

COLONEL   But why should he have married you, feeling as he did about everything?

ALISON   That is the famous American question—you know, the sixty-four dollar one! Perhaps it was revenge. (*He looks up uncomprehendingly*) Oh yes. Some people do actually marry for revenge. People like Jimmy, anyway. Or perhaps he should have been another Shelley, and can't understand now why I'm not another Mary, and you're not William Godwin. He thinks he's got a sort of genius for love and friendship—on his own terms. Well, for twenty years, I'd lived a happy, uncomplicated life, and suddenly, this—this spiritual barbarian—throws down the gauntlet at me. Perhaps only another woman could understand what a challenge like that means—although I think Helena was as mystified as you are.

COLONEL   I am mystified. (*He rises, and crosses to the window*) Your husband has obviously taught you a great deal, whether you realise it or not. What any of it means, I don't know. I always believed that people married each other because they were in love. That always seemed a good enough reason to me. But apparently, that's too simple for young people nowadays. They have to talk about challenges and revenge. I just can't believe that love between men and women is really like that.

ALISON   Only some men and women.

COLONEL   But why you? My daughter. . . . No. Perhaps Jimmy is right. Perhaps I am a—what was it? an old plant left over from the Edwardian Wilderness. And I can't understand why the sun isn't shining any more. You can see what he means, can't you? It was March, 1914, when I left England, and, apart from leaves every ten years or so, I didn't see much of my own country until we all came back in '47. Oh, I knew things had changed, of course. People told you all the time the way it was going—going to the dogs, as the Blimps are supposed to say. But it seemed very unreal to me, out there. The England I remembered was the one I left in 1914, and I was happy to go on remembering it that way. Besides, I had the Maharajah's army to command—that was my world, and I loved it, all of it. At the time, it looked like going on forever. When I think of it now, it seems like a dream. If only it could have gone on forever. Those long, cool evenings up in the hills, everything purple and golden. Your mother and I were so happy then. It seemed as though we had everything we could ever want. I think the last day the sun shone was when that dirty little train steamed out of that crowded, suffocating Indian station, and the battalion band playing for all it was worth. I knew in my heart it was all over then. Everything.

ALISON   You're hurt because everything is changed. Jimmy is hurt because everything is the same. And neither of you can face it. Something's gone wrong somewhere, hasn't it?

COLONEL   It looks like it, my dear. (*She picks up the squirrel from the chest of drawers, is about to put it in her suitcase, hesitates, and then puts it back. The* COLONEL *turns and looks at her. She moves down toward him, her head turned away. For a few mo-*

ments, she seems to be standing on the edge of choice. The choice made, her body wheels round suddenly, and she is leaning against him, weeping softly. Presently) This is a big step you're taking. You've made up your mind to come back with me? Is that really what you want?

(HELENA *enters*)

HELENA   I'm sorry. I came in to see if I could help you pack, Alison. Oh, you look as though you've finished.

(ALISON *leaves her father, and moves to the bed, pushing down the lid of her suitcase*)

ALISON   All ready.

HELENA   Have you got everything?

ALISON   Well, no. But Cliff can send the rest on sometime, I expect. He should have been back by now. Oh, of course, he's had to put the stall away on his own today.

COLONEL   (*Crossing and picking up the suitcase*)   Well, I'd better put this in the car then. We may as well get along. Your mother will be worried, I know. I promised her I'd ring her when I got here. She's not very well.

HELENA   I hope my telegram didn't upset her too much. Perhaps I shouldn't have——

COLONEL   Not at all. We were very grateful that you did. It was very kind of you, indeed. She tried to insist on coming with me, but I finally managed to talk her out of it. I thought it would be best for everyone. What about your case, Helena? If you care to tell me where it is, I'll take it down with this one.

HELENA   I'm afraid I shan't be coming tonight.

ALISON   (*Very surprised*)   Aren't you coming with us?

(CLIFF *enters*)

HELENA   I'd like to, but the fact is I've an appointment tomorrow in Birmingham—about a job. They've just sent me a script. It's rather important, and I don't want to miss it. So it looks as though I shall have to stay here tonight.

ALISON   Oh, I see. Hullo, Cliff.

CLIFF   Hullo there.

ALISON   Daddy—this is Cliff.

COLONEL   How do you do, Cliff.

CLIFF   How do you do, sir.

(*A slight pause*)

COLONEL   Well, I'd better put this in the car, hadn't I? Don't be long, Alison. Good-bye, Helena. I expect we shall be seeing you again soon, if you're not busy.

HELENA   Oh, yes, I shall be back in a day or two.

(CLIFF *takes off his jacket*)

COLONEL   Well, then—good-bye, Cliff.

CLIFF   Good-bye, sir. (*The* COLONEL *goes out*) You're really going then?

ALISON   Really going.

CLIFF   I should think Jimmy would be back pretty soon. You won't wait?

ALISON   No, Cliff.

CLIFF   Who's going to tell him?

HELENA   I can tell him. That is, if I'm here when he comes back.

CLIFF   (*Quietly*) You'll be here. (*To* ALISON) Don't you think you ought to tell him yourself? (*She hands him an envelope from her handbag. He takes it*) Bit conventional, isn't it?

ALISON   I'm a conventional girl.

(*He crosses to her, and puts his arms round her*)

CLIFF   (*Back over his shoulder, to* HELENA) I hope you're right, that's all.

HELENA   What do you mean? You hope *I'm* right?

CLIFF   (*To* ALISON)   The place is going to be really cock-eyed now. You know that, don't you?

ALISON   Please, Cliff—— (*He nods. She kisses him*) I'll write to you later.

CLIFF   Good-bye, lovely.

ALISON   Look after him.

CLIFF   We'll keep the old nut-house going somehow.

(*She crosses in between the two of them, glances quickly at the two armchairs, the papers still left around them from yesterday.* HELENA *kisses her on the cheek, and squeezes her hand*)

HELENA   See you soon. (ALISON *nods, and goes out quickly.* CLIFF *and* HELENA *are left looking at each other*) Would you like me to make you some tea?

CLIFF   No, thanks.

HELENA   Think I might have some myself, if you don't mind.

CLIFF   So you're staying?

HELENA   Just for tonight. Do you object?

CLIFF   Nothing to do with me. (*Against the table*) Of course, he may not be back until later on.

(*She crosses to the window, and lights a cigarette*)

HELENA What do you think he'll do? Perhaps he'll look out one of his old girl friends. What about this Madeline?

CLIFF What about her?

HELENA Isn't she supposed to have done a lot for him? Couldn't he go back to her?

CLIFF I shouldn't think so.

HELENA What happened?

CLIFF She was nearly old enough to be his mother. I expect that's something to do with it! Why the hell should I know!

(*For the first time in the play, his good humour has completely deserted him. She looks surprised*)

HELENA You're his friend, aren't you? Anyway, he's not what you'd call reticent about himself, is he? I've never seen so many souls stripped to the waist since I've been here.

(*He turns to go*)

HELENA Aren't you staying?

CLIFF No, I'm not. There was a train in from London about five minutes ago. And, just in case he may have been on it, I'm going out.

HELENA Don't you think you ought to be here when he comes?

CLIFF I've had a hard day, and I don't think I want to see anyone hurt until I've had something to eat first, and perhaps a few drinks as well. I think I might pick up some nice, pleasant little tart in a milk bar, and sneak her in past old mother Drury. Here! (*Tossing the letter at her*) You give it to him! (*Crossing to door*) He's all yours. (*At the door*) And I hope he rams it up your nostrils! (*He exits. She crosses to the table, and stubs out her cigarette. The front door downstairs is heard to slam. She moves to the wardrobe, opens it idly. It is empty, except for one dress, swinging on a hanger. She goes over to the dressing table, now cleared but for a framed photograph of* JIMMY. *Idly, she slams the empty drawers open and shut. She turns upstage to the chest of drawers, picks up the toy bear, and sits on the bed, looking at it. She lays her head back on the pillow, still holding the bear. She looks up quickly as the door crashes open, and* JIMMY *enters. He stands looking at her, then taking off his raincoat and throwing it over the table. He is almost giddy with anger, and has to steady himself on the chair. He looks up*)

JIMMY That old bastard nearly ran me down in his car! Now, if he'd killed me, that really would have been ironical. And how right and fitting that my wife should have been a passenger. A passenger! What's the matter with everybody? (*Crossing up to her*) Cliff practically walked into me, coming out of the house. He belted up the other way, and pretended not to see me. Are you the only one who's not afraid to stay? (*She hands him* ALISON's *note. He takes it*) Oh, it's one of these, is it? (*He rips it open. He reads a few lines, and almost snorts with disbelief*) Did you write this for her! Well, listen to this then! (*Reading*) "My dear—I must get away. I don't suppose you will understand, but please try. I need peace so desperately, and, at the moment, I am willing to sacrifice everything just for that. I don't know what's going to happen to us. I know you will be feeling wretched and bitter, but try to be a little patient with me. I shall always have a deep, loving need of you—Alison." Oh, how could she be so bloody wet! Deep loving need! That makes me puke! She couldn't say "You rotten bastard! I hate your guts, I'm clearing out, and I hope you rot!" No, she has to make a polite, emotional mess out of it! (*Seeing the dress in the wardrobe, he rips it out, and throws it in the corner*) Deep, loving need! I never thought she was capable of being as phoney as that! What is that—a line from one of those plays you've been in? What are you doing here anyway? You'd better keep out of my way, if you don't want your head kicked in.

HELENA (*Calmly*) If you'll stop thinking about yourself for one moment, I'll tell you something I think you ought to know. Your wife is going to have a baby. (*He just looks at her*) Well? Doesn't that mean anything? Even to you?

(*He is taken aback, but not so much by the news, as by her*)

JIMMY All right—yes. I am surprised. I give you that. But, tell me. Did you honestly expect me to go soggy at the knees, and collapse with remorse! (*Leaning nearer*) Listen, if you'll stop breathing your female wisdom all over me, I'll tell you something: I don't care. (*Beginning quietly*) I don't care if she's going to have a baby. I don't care if it has two heads! (*He knows her fingers are itching*) Do I disgust you? Well, go on—slap my face. But remember what I told you before, will you? For eleven hours, I have been watching someone I love very much going through the sordid process of dying. She was alone, and I was the only one with her. And when I have to walk behind that coffin on Thursday, I'll be on my own again. Because that bitch won't even send her a bunch of flowers—I know! She made the great mistake of all her kind. She thought that because Hugh's mother was a deprived

and ignorant old woman, who said all the wrong things in all the wrong places, she couldn't be taken seriously. And you think I should be overcome with awe because that cruel, stupid girl is going to have a baby! (*Anguish in his voice*) I can't believe it! I can't. (*Grabbing her shoulder*) Well, the performance is over. Now leave me alone, and *get out*, you evil-minded little virgin.
(*She slaps his face savagely. An expression of horror and disbelief floods his face. But it drains away, and all that is left is pain. His hand goes up to his head, and a muffled cry of despair escapes him.* HELENA *tears his hand away, and kisses him passionately, drawing him down beside her*)

Curtain

ACT THREE

SCENE I

Several months later. A Sunday evening. ALISON's *personal belongings, such as her make-up things on the dressing table, for example, have been replaced by* HELENA's. *At rise of curtain, we find* JIMMY *and* CLIFF *sprawled in their respective armchairs, immersed in the Sunday newspapers.* HELENA *is leaning over the ironing board, a small pile of clothes beside her. She looks more attractive than before, for the setting of her face is more relaxed. She still looks quite smart, but in an unpremeditated, careless way; she wears an old shirt of* JIMMY's.

CLIFF   That stinking old pipe!

   (*A pause*)

JIMMY   Shut up.

CLIFF   Why don't you do something with it?

JIMMY   Why do I spend half of Sunday reading the papers?

CLIFF (*Kicks him without lowering his paper*)   It stinks!

JIMMY   So do you, but I'm not singing an aria about it. (*Turns to the next page*) The dirty ones get more and more wet round the mouth, and the posh ones are more pompous than ever. (*Lowering paper, and waving pipe at* HELENA) Does this bother you?

HELENA   No. I quite like it.

JIMMY (*To* CLIFF)   There you are—she likes it! (*He returns to his paper.* CLIFF *grunts*) Have you read about the grotesque and evil practices going on in the Midlands?

CLIFF   Read about the what?

JIMMY   Grotesque and evil practices going on in the Midlands.

CLIFF   No, what about 'em?

JIMMY   Seems we don't know the old place. It's all in here. Startling Revelations this week! Pictures too. Reconstructions of midnight invocations to the Coptic Goddess of fertility.

HELENA Sounds madly depraved.

JIMMY Yes, it's rather us, isn't it? My gosh, look at 'em! Snarling themselves silly. Next week a well-known debutante relates how, during an evil orgy in Market Harborough, she killed and drank the blood of a white cockerel. Well—I'll bet Fortnums must be doing a roaring line in sacrificial cocks! (*Thoughtful*) Perhaps that's what Miss Drury does on Sunday evenings. She puts in a stint as evil high priestess down at the Y.W.—probably having a workout at this very moment. (*To* HELENA) You never dabbled in this kind of thing, did you?

HELENA (*Laughs*) Not lately!

JIMMY Sounds rather your cup of tea—cup of blood, I should say. (*In an imitation of a Midlands accent*) Well, I mean, it gives you something to do, doesn't it? After all, it wouldn't do if we was all alike, would it? It'd be a funny world if we was all the same, that's what *I* always say! (*Resuming in his normal voice*) All I know is that somebody's been sticking pins into *my* wax image for years. (*Suddenly*) Of course: Alison's mother! Every Friday, the wax arrives from Harrods, and all through the week-end, she's stabbing away at it with a hatpin! Ruined her bridge game, I dare say.

HELENA Why don't *you* try it?

JIMMY Yes, it's an idea. (*Pointing to* CLIFF) Just for a start, we could roast him over the gas stove. Have we got enough shillings for the meter? It seems to be just the thing for these Autumn evenings. After all the whole point of a sacrifice is that you give up something you never really wanted in the first place. You know what I mean? People are doing it around you all the time. They give up their careers, say—or their beliefs—or sex. And everyone thinks to themselves: how wonderful to be able to do that. If only I were capable of doing that! But the truth of it is that they've been kidding themselves, and they've been kidding you. It's not awfully difficult—giving up something you were incapable of ever really wanting. We shouldn't be admiring them. We should feel rather sorry for them. (*Coming back from this sudden, brooding excursion, and turning to* CLIFF) You'll make an admirable sacrifice.

CLIFF (*Mumbling*) Dry up! I'm trying to read.

JIMMY Afterwards, we can make a loving cup from his blood. Can't say I fancy that so much. I've seen it—it looks like cochineal, ever so common. (*To* HELENA) Yours would be much better—pale

Cambridge blue, I imagine. No? And afterwards, we could make invocations to the Coptic Goddess of fertility. Got any idea how you do that? (*To* CLIFF) Do you know?

CLIFF   Shouldn't have thought *you* needed to make invocations to the Coptic whatever-she-is!

JIMMY   Yes, I see what you mean. (*To* HELENA) Well, we don't want to *ask* for trouble, do we? Perhaps it might appeal to the lady here—she's written a long letter all about artificial insemination. It's headed: Haven't we tried God's patience enough! (*Throws the paper down*) Let's see the other posh one.

CLIFF   Haven't finished yet.

JIMMY   Well, hurry up. I'll have to write and ask them to put hyphens in between the syllables for you. There's a particularly savage correspondence going on in there about whether Milton wore braces or not. I just want to see who gets shot down this week.

CLIFF   Just read that. Don't know what it was about, but a Fellow of All Souls seems to have bitten the dust, and the Athenaeum's going up in flames, so the Editor declares that this correspondence is now closed.

JIMMY   I think you're actually acquiring yourself a curiosity, my boy. Oh yes, and then there's an American professor from Yale or somewhere, who believes that when Shakespeare was writing *The Tempest,* he changed his sex. Yes, he was obliged to go back to Stratford because the other actors couldn't take him seriously any longer. This professor chap is coming over here to search for certain documents which will prove that poor old W.S. ended up in someone else's second best bed—a certain Warwickshire farmer's, whom he married after having three children by him. (HELENA *laughs.* JIMMY *looks up quizzically*) Is anything the matter?

HELENA   No, nothing. I'm only beginning to get used to him. I never (*This is to* CLIFF) used to be sure when he was being serious, or when he wasn't.

CLIFF   Don't think he knows himself half the time. When in doubt, just mark it down as an insult.

JIMMY   Hurry up with that paper, and shut up! What are we going to do tonight? There isn't even a decent concert on. (*To* HELENA) Are you going to church?

HELENA   (*Rather taken aback*) No. I don't think so. Unless you want to.

JIMMY   Do I detect a growing, satanic glint in her eyes lately? Do

you think it's living in sin with me that does it? (*To* HELENA) Do
you feel very sinful my dear? Well? Do you? (*She can hardly
believe that this is an attack, and she can only look at him, uncertain of herself*) Do you feel sin crawling out of your ears, like
stored up wax or something? Are you wondering whether I'm
joking or not? Perhaps I ought to wear a red nose and funny hat.
I'm just curious, that's all. (*She is shaken by the sudden coldness
in his eyes, but before she has time to fully realise how hurt she
is, he is smiling at her, and shouting cheerfully at* CLIFF) Let's
have that paper, stupid!

CLIFF Why don't you drop dead!

JIMMY (*To* HELENA) Will you be much longer doing that?

HELENA Nearly finished.

JIMMY Talking of sin, wasn't that Miss Drury's Reverend friend
I saw you chatting with yesterday. Helena darling, I said wasn't
that. . . .

HELENA Yes it was.

JIMMY My dear, you don't have to be on the defensive you know.

HELENA I'm not on the defensive.

JIMMY After all, there's no reason why we shouldn't have the par-
son to tea up here. Why don't we? Did you find that you had much
in common?

HELENA No I don't think so.

JIMMY Do you think that some of this spiritual beefcake would
make a man of me? Should I go in for this moral weight lifting
and get myself some over-developed muscle? I was a liberal
skinny weakling. I too was afraid to strip down to my soul, but
now everyone looks at my superb physique in envy. I can perform
any kind of press there is without betraying the least sign of passion or kindliness.

HELENA All right Jimmy.

JIMMY Two years ago I couldn't even lift up my head—now I have
more uplift than a film starlet.

HELENA Jimmy, can we have one day, just one day, without tum-
bling over religion or politics?

CLIFF Yes, change the record old boy, or pipe down.

JIMMY (*Rising*) Thought of the title for a new song today. It's
called "My mother's in the madhouse—that's why I'm in love with
you." The lyrics are catchy too. I was thinking we might work it
into the act.

HELENA Good idea.

JIMMY I was thinking we'd scrub Jock and Day, and call ourselves something else. "And jocund day stands tiptoe on the misty mountain tops." It's too intellectual! Anyway, I shouldn't think people will want to be reminded of that peculiar man's plays after Harvard and Yale have finished with him. How about something bright and snappy? I know— What about—T. S. Eliot and Pam!

CLIFF (*Casually falling in with this familiar routine*) Mirth, mellerdy and madness!

JIMMY (*Sitting at the table and "strumming" it*) Bringing quips and strips for you! (*They sing together*)

"For we may be guilty, darling. . . .
But we're both insane as well!"

(JIMMY *stands up, and rattles his lines off at almost unintelligible speed*) Ladies and gentlemen, as I was coming to the theatre tonight, I was passing through the stage door, and a man comes up to me, and 'e says:

CLIFF 'Ere! Have you seen nobody?

JIMMY Have I seen who?

CLIFF Have you seen nobody?

JIMMY Of course, I haven't seen nobody! Kindly don't waste my time! Ladies and gentlemen, a little recitation entitled "She said she was called a little Gidding, but she was more like a gelding iron!" Thank you "She said she was called little Gidding—"

CLIFF Are you quite sure you haven't seen nobody?

JIMMY Are you still here?

CLIFF I'm looking for nobody!

JIMMY *Will* you kindly go away! "She said she was called little Gidding—"

CLIFF Well, I can't find nobody anywhere, and I'm supposed to give him this case!

JIMMY Will you kindly stop interrupting per*lease*! Can't you see I'm trying to entertain these ladies and gentlemen? Who is this nobody you're talking about?

CLIFF I was told to come here and give this case to nobody.

JIMMY You were told to come here and give this case to nobody.

CLIFF That's right. And when I gave it to him, nobody would give me a shilling.

JIMMY And when you gave it to him, nobody would give you a shilling.

CLIFF That's right.

JIMMY Well, what about it?

CLIFF Nobody's not here!

JIMMY   Now, let me get this straight: when you say nobody's here,
you don't mean nobody's here?

CLIFF   No.

JIMMY   No. You mean—nobody's here.

CLIFF   That's right.

JIMMY   Well, why didn't you say so before?

HELENA   (*Not quite sure if this is really her cue*)   Hey! You down
there!

JIMMY   Oh, it goes on for hours yet, but never mind. What is it, sir?

HELENA   (*Shouting*)   I think your sketch stinks! I say—I think your
sketch stinks!

JIMMY   He thinks it stinks. And, who, pray, might you be?

HELENA   Me? Oh—(*With mock modesty*) I'm nobody.

JIMMY   Then here's your bloody case!

(*He hurls a cushion at her, which hits the ironing board*)

HELENA   My ironing board!

(*The two men do a Flanagan and Allen, moving slowly in step,
as they sing*)

Now there's a certain little lady, and you all know who I
mean,

She may have been to Roedean, but to me she's still a
queen.

Someday I'm goin' to marry her,

When times are not so bad,

Her mother doesn't care for me

So I'll 'ave to ask 'er dad.

We'll build a little home for two,

And have some quiet menage,

We'll send our kids to public school

And live on bread and marge.

Don't be afraid to sleep with your sweetheart,

Just because she's better than you.

Those forgotten middle-classes may have fallen on their
noses,

But a girl who's true blue,

Will still have something left for you,

The angels up above, will know that you're in love

So don't be afraid to sleep with your sweetheart,

Just because she's better than you. . . .

They call me Sydney,

Just because she's better than you.

(*But* JIMMY *has had enough of this gag by now, and he pushes*
CLIFF *away*)

JIMMY　Your damned great feet! That's the second time you've
kicked my ankle! It's no good—Helena will have to do it. Go on,
go and make some tea, and we'll decide what we're going to do.

CLIFF　Make some yourself!

(*He pushes him back violently,* JIMMY *loses his balance, and falls
over*)

JIMMY　You rough bastard!

(*He leaps up, and they grapple, falling on to the floor with a
crash. They roll about, grunting and gasping.* CLIFF *manages to
kneel on* JIMMY's *chest*)

CLIFF　(*Breathing heavily*)　I want to read the papers!

JIMMY　You're a savage, a hooligan! You really are! Do you know
that! You don't deserve to live in the same house with decent,
sensitive people!

CLIFF　Are you going to dry up, or do I read the papers down here?

(JIMMY *makes a supreme effort, and* CLIFF *topples to the floor*)

JIMMY　You've made me wrench my guts!

(*He pushes the struggling* CLIFF *down*)

CLIFF　Look what you're doing! You're ripping my shirt. Get *off*!

JIMMY　Well, what do you want to wear a shirt for? (*Rising*) A
tough character like you! Now go and make me some tea.

CLIFF　It's the only clean one I've got. Oh, you big oaf! (*Getting up
from the floor, and appealing to* HELENA) Look! It's filthy!

HELENA　Yes, it is. He's stronger than he looks. If you like to take it
off now, I'll wash it through for you. It'll be dry by the time we
want to go out. (CLIFF *hesitates*) What's the matter, Cliff?

CLIFF　Oh, it'll be all right.

JIMMY　Give it to her, and quit moaning!

CLIFF　Oh, all right. (*He takes it off, and gives it to her*) Thanks,
Helena.

HELENA　(*Taking it*)　Right. I won't be a minute with it.

(*She goes out.* JIMMY *flops into his armchair*)

JIMMY　(*Amused*)　You look like Marlon Brando or something.
(*Slight pause*) You don't care for Helena, do you?

CLIFF　You didn't seem very keen yourself once. (*Hesitating, then
quickly*) It's not the same, is it?

JIMMY　(*Irritably*)　No, of course it's not the same, you idiot! It
never is! Today's meal is always different from yesterday's and

the last woman isn't the same as the one before. If you can't accept that, you're going to be pretty unhappy, my boy.

CLIFF (*Sits on the arm of his chair, and rubs his feet*) Jimmy—I don't think I shall stay here much longer.

JIMMY (*Rather casually*) Oh, why not?

CLIFF (*Picking up his tone*) Oh, I don't know. I've just thought of trying somewhere different. The sweet-stall's all right, but I think I'd like to try something else. You're highly educated, and it suits you, but I need something a bit better.

JIMMY Just as you like, my dear boy. It's your business, not mine.

CLIFF And another thing—I think Helena finds it rather a lot of work to do with two chaps about the place. It won't be so much for her if there's just the two of you. Anyway, I think I ought to find some girl who'll just look after me.

JIMMY Sounds like a good idea. Can't think who'd be stupid enough to team themselves up with you though. Perhaps Helena can think of somebody for you—one of her posh girl friends with lots of money, and no brains. That's what you want.

CLIFF Something like that.

JIMMY Any idea what you're going to do?

CLIFF Not much.

JIMMY That sounds like you all right! Shouldn't think you'll last five minutes without me to explain the score to you.

CLIFF (*Grinning*) Don't suppose so.

JIMMY You're such a scruffy little beast—I'll bet some respectable little madam from Pinner or Guildford gobbles you up in six months. She'll marry you, send you out to work, and you'll end up as clean as a new pin.

CLIFF (*Chuckling*) Yes, I'm stupid enough for that too!

JIMMY (*To himself*) I seem to spend my life saying good-bye.
(*A slight pause*)

CLIFF My feet hurt.

JIMMY Try washing your socks. (*Slowly*) It's a funny thing. You've been loyal, generous and a good friend. But I'm quite prepared to see you wander off, find a new home, and make out on your own. And all because of something I want from that girl downstairs, something I know in my heart she's incapable of giving. You're worth a half a dozen Helenas to me or to anyone. And, if you were in my place, you'd do the same thing. Right?

CLIFF Right.

JIMMY Why, why, why, why do we let these women bleed us to

death? Have you ever had a letter, and on it is franked "Please Give Your Blood Generously"? Well, the Postmaster-General does that, on behalf of all the women of the world. I suppose people of our generation aren't able to die for good causes any longer. We had all that done for us, in the thirties and the forties, when we were still kids. (*In his familiar, semi-serious mood*) There aren't any good, brave causes left. If the big bang does come, and we all get killed off, it won't be in aid of the old-fashioned, grand design. It'll just be for the Brave New-nothing-very-much-thank-you. About as pointless and inglorious as stepping in front of a bus. No, there's nothing left for it, me boy, but to let yourself be butchered by the women.

(HELENA *enters*)

HELENA (*Handing him the shirt*) Here you are, Cliff.

CLIFF Oh, thanks, Helena, very much. That's decent of you.

HELENA Not at all. I should dry it over the gas—the fire in your room would be better. There won't be much room for it over that stove.

CLIFF Right, I will.

(*He crosses to the door*)

JIMMY And hurry up about it, stupid. We'll all go out, and have a drink soon. (*To* HELENA) O.K.?

HELENA O.K.

JIMMY (*Shouting to* CLIFF *on his way out*) But make me some tea first, you madcap little Charlie. (*She crosses*) Darling, I'm sick of seeing you behind that damned ironing board!

HELENA (*Wryly*) Sorry.

JIMMY Get yourself glammed up, and we'll hit the town. See you've put a shroud over Mummy, I think you should have laid a Union Jack over it.

HELENA Is anything wrong?

JIMMY Oh, don't frown like that—you look like the presiding magistrate!

HELENA How should I look?

JIMMY As if your heart stirred a little when you looked at me.

HELENA Oh, it does that all right.

JIMMY Cliff tells me he's leaving us.

HELENA I know. He told me last night.

JIMMY Did he? I always seem to be at the end of the queue when they're passing information out.

HELENA I'm sorry he's going.

JIMMY   Yes, so am I. He's a sloppy, irritating bastard, but he's got a big heart. You can forgive somebody almost anything for that. He's had to learn how to take it, and he knows how to hand it out. Come here. (*He is sitting on the arm of his chair. She crosses to him, and they look at each other. Then she puts out her hand, and runs it over his head, fondling his ear and neck*) Right from that first night, you have always put out your hand to me first. As if you expected nothing, or worse than nothing, and didn't care. You made a good enemy, didn't you? What they call a worthy opponent. But then, when people put down their weapons, it doesn't mean they've necessarily stopped fighting.

HELENA (*Steadily*)   I love you.

JIMMY   I think perhaps you do. Yes, I think perhaps you do. Perhaps it means something to lie with your victorious general in your arms. Especially, when he's heartily sick of the whole campaign, tired out, hungry and dry. (*His lips find her fingers, and he kisses them. She presses his head against her*) You stood up, and came out to meet me. Oh, Helena—(*His face comes up to hers, and they embrace fiercely*) Don't let anything go wrong!

HELENA (*Softly*)   Oh, my darling—

JIMMY   Either you're with me or against me.

HELENA   I've always wanted you—always!

(*They kiss again*)

JIMMY   T. S. Eliot and Pam, we'll make a good double. If you'll help me. I'll close that damned sweet-stall, and we'll start everything from scratch. What do you say? We'll get away from this place.

HELENA (*Nodding happily*)   I say that's wonderful.

JIMMY (*Kissing her quickly*)   Put all that junk away, and we'll get out. We'll get pleasantly, joyfully tiddly, we'll gaze at each other tenderly and lecherously in "The Builder's Arms", and then we'll come back here, and I'll make such love to you, you'll not care about anything else at all.

(*She moves away after kissing his hand*)

HELENA   I'll just change out of your old shirt.

(*Folding the ironing board*)

JIMMY (*Moving toward the door*)   Right. I'll hurry up the little man.

(*But before he reaches the door, it opens and* ALISON *enters. She wears a raincoat, her hair is untidy, and she looks rather ill. There is a stunned pause*)

ALISON (*Quietly*)   Hullo.

JIMMY (*To* HELENA, *after a moment*)   Friend of yours to see you. (*He goes out quickly, and the two women are left looking at each other*)

Curtain

SCENE II

It is a few minutes later. From CLIFF's *room, across the landing, comes the sound of* JIMMY's *jazz trumpet. At the rise of the curtain,* HELENA *is standing next to the table, pouring out a cup of tea.* AL-ISON *is sitting on the armchair. She bends down and picks up* JIMMY's *pipe. Then she scoops up a little pile of ash from the floor, and drops it in the ashtray on the arm of the chair.*

ALISON   He still smokes this foul old stuff. I used to hate it at first, but you get used to it.

HELENA   Yes.

ALISON   I went to the pictures last week, and some old man was smoking it in front, a few rows away. I actually got up, and sat right behind him.

HELENA (*Coming down with cup of tea*)   Here, have this. It usually seems to help.

ALISON (*Taking it*)   Thanks.

HELENA   Are you sure you feel all right now?

ALISON (*Nods*)   It was just—oh, everything. It's my own fault—entirely. I must be mad, coming here like this. I'm sorry, Helena.

HELENA   Why should you be sorry—you of all people?

ALISON   Because it was unfair and cruel of me to come back. I'm afraid a sense of timing is one of the things I seem to have learnt from Jimmy. But it's something that can be in very bad taste. (*Sips her tea*) So many times, I've just managed to stop myself coming here—right at the last moment. Even today, when I went to the booking office at St. Pancras, it was like a charade, and I never believed that I'd let myself walk on to that train. And when I was on it, I got into a panic. I felt like a criminal. I told myself I'd turn round at the other end, and come straight back. I couldn't even believe that this place existed any more. But once I got here, there was nothing I could do. I had to convince myself that everything I remembered about this place had really happened to me once. (*She lowers her cup, and her foot plays with the newspapers on the floor*) How many times in these past few months I've thought of the evenings we used to spend here in this room. Suspended and rather remote. You make a good cup of tea.

HELENA (*Sitting near the table*) Something Jimmy taught *me*.

ALISON (*Covering her face*) Oh, why am I here! You must all wish me a thousand miles away!

HELENA I don't wish anything of the kind. You've more right to be here than I.

ALISON Oh, Helena, don't bring out the book of rules——

HELENA You are his wife, aren't you? Whatever I have done, I've never been able to forget that fact. You have all the rights——

ALISON Helena—even I gave up believing in the divine rights of marriage long ago. Even before I met Jimmy. They've got something different now—constitutional monarchy. You are where you are by consent. And if you start trying any strong arm stuff, you're out. And I'm out.

HELENA Is that something you learnt from him?

ALISON Don't make me feel like a blackmailer or something, please! I've done something foolish, and rather vulgar in coming here tonight. I regret it, and I detest myself for doing it. But I did not come here in order to gain anything. Whatever it was—hysteria or just macabre curiosity, I'd certainly no intention of making any kind of breach between you and Jimmy. You must believe that.

HELENA Oh, I believe it all right. That's why everything seems more wrong and terrible than ever. You didn't even reproach me. You should have been outraged, but you weren't. (*She leans back, as if she wanted to draw back from herself*) I feel so—*ashamed*.

ALISON You talk as though he were something you'd swindled me out of—

HELENA (*Fiercely*) And you talk as if he were a book or something you pass around to anyone who happens to want it for five minutes. What's the matter with you? You sound as though you were quoting *him* all the time. I thought you told me once you couldn't bring yourself to believe in him.

ALISON I don't think I ever believed in your way either.

HELENA At least, I still believe in right and wrong! Not even the months in this madhouse have stopped me doing that. Even though everything I have done is wrong, at least I have known it was wrong.

ALISON You loved him, didn't you? That's what you wrote, and told me.

HELENA And it was true.

ALISON It was pretty difficult to believe at the time. I couldn't understand it.

HELENA I could hardly believe it myself.

ALISON Afterwards, it wasn't quite so difficult. You used to say some pretty harsh things about him. Not that I was sorry to hear them—they were rather comforting then. But you even shocked me sometimes.

HELENA I suppose I was a little over-emphatic. There doesn't seem much point in trying to explain everything, does there?

ALISON Not really.

HELENA Do you know—I have discovered what is wrong with Jimmy? It's very simple really. He was born out of his time.

ALISON Yes. I know.

HELENA There's no place for people like that any longer—in sex, or politics, or anything. That's why he's so futile. Sometimes, when I listen to him, I feel he thinks he's still in the middle of the French Revolution. And that's where he ought to be, of course. He doesn't know where he is, or where he's going. He'll never do anything, and he'll never amount to anything.

ALISON I suppose he's what you'd call an Eminent Victorian. Slightly comic—in a way. . . . We seem to have had this conversation before.

HELENA Yes, I remember everything you said about him. It horrified me. I couldn't believe that you could have married someone like that. Alison—it's all over between Jimmy and me. I can see it now. I've got to get out. No—listen to me. When I saw you standing there tonight, I knew that it was all utterly wrong. That I didn't believe in any of this, and not Jimmy or anyone could make me believe otherwise. (*Rising*) How could I have ever thought I could get away with it! He wants one world and I want another, and lying in that bed won't ever change it! I believe in good and evil, and I don't have to apologise for that. It's quite a modern, scientific belief now, so they tell me. And,

by everything I have ever believed in, or wanted, what I have
been doing is wrong and evil.

ALISON Helena—you're not going to leave him?

HELENA Yes, I am. (*Before* ALISON *can interrupt, she goes on*) Oh,
I'm not stepping aside to let you come back. You can do what
you like. Frankly, I think you'd be a fool—but that's your own
business. I think I've given you enough advice.

ALISON But he—he'll have no one.

HELENA Oh, my dear, he'll find somebody. He'll probably hold
court here like one of the Renaissance popes. Oh, I know I'm
throwing the book of rules at you, as you call it, but, believe me,
you're never going to be happy without it. I tried throwing it
away all these months, but I know now it just doesn't work.
When you came in at that door, ill and tired and hurt, it was
all over for me. You see—I didn't know about the baby. It was
such a shock. It's like a judgment on us.

ALISON You saw me, and I had to tell you what had happened.
I lost the child. It's a simple fact. There is no judgment, there's
no blame——

HELENA Maybe not. But I feel it just the same.

ALISON But don't you see? It isn't logical!

HELENA No, it isn't. (*Calmly*) But I know it's right.

(*The trumpet gets louder*)

ALISON Helena (*Going to her*), you mustn't leave him. He needs
you, I know he needs you—

HELENA Do you think so?

ALISON Maybe you're not the right one for him—we're neither of
us right—

HELENA (*Moving upstage*) Oh, why doesn't he stop that damned
noise!

ALISON He wants something quite different from us. What it is
exactly I don't know—a kind of cross between a mother and a
Greek courtesan, a henchwoman, a mixture of Cleopatra and Bos-
well. But give him a little longer—

HELENA (*Wrenching the door open*) Please! Will you stop that!
I can't think! (*There is a slight pause, and the trumpet goes on.
She puts her hands to her head*) Jimmy, for God's sake! (*It
stops*) Jimmy, I want to speak to you.

JIMMY (*Off*) Is your friend still with you?

HELENA Oh, don't be an idiot, and come in here!

ALISON (*Rising*) He doesn't want to see me.

HELENA   Stay where you are, and don't be silly. I'm sorry. It won't be very pleasant, but I've made up my mind to go, and I've got to tell him now.

(JIMMY *enters*)

JIMMY   Is this another of your dark plots? (*He looks at* ALISON) Hadn't she better sit down? She looks a bit ghastly.

HELENA   I'm so sorry, dear. Would you like some more tea, or an aspirin or something? (ALISON *shakes her head, and sits. She can't look at either of them. To* JIMMY, *the old authority returning*) It's not very surprising, is it? She's been very ill, she's——

JIMMY   (*Quietly*)   You don't have to draw a diagram for me—I can see what's happened to her.

HELENA   And doesn't it mean anything to you?

JIMMY   I don't exactly relish the idea of anyone being ill, or in pain. It was my child too, you know. But (*He shrugs*) it isn't my first loss.

ALISON   (*On her breath*)   It was mine.

(*He glances at her, but turns back to* HELENA *quickly*)

JIMMY   What are you looking so solemn about? What's she doing here?

ALISON   I'm sorry, I'm——

(*Presses her hand over her mouth.* HELENA *crosses to* JIMMY *and grasps his hand*)

HELENA   Don't please. Can't you see the condition she's in? She's done nothing, she's said nothing, none of it's her fault.

(*He takes his hand away, and moves away a little downstage*)

JIMMY   What isn't her fault?

HELENA   Jimmy—I don't want a brawl, so please——

JIMMY   Let's hear it, shall we?

HELENA   Very well. I'm going downstairs to pack my things. If I hurry, I shall just catch the 7.15 to London. (*They both look at him, but he simply leans forward against the table, not looking at either of them*) This is not Alison's doing—you must understand that. It's my own decision entirely. In fact, she's just been trying to talk me out of it. It's just that suddenly, tonight, I see what I have really known all along. That you can't be happy when what you're doing is wrong, or is hurting someone else. I suppose it could never have worked, anyway, but I do love you, Jimmy. I shall never love anyone as I have loved you. (*Turns away*) But I can't go on. (*Passionately and sincerely*) I can't take part—in all this suffering. I can't! (*She appeals to him for some*

reaction, but he only looks down at the table, and nods. HELENA
recovers, and makes an effort to regain authority. To ALISON)
You probably won't feel up to making that journey again tonight,
but we can fix you up at an hotel before I go. There's about half
an hour. I'll just make it.

(*She turns up to the door, but* JIMMY's *voice stops her*)

JIMMY (*In a low, resigned voice*) They all want to escape from
the pain of being alive. And, most of all, from love. (*Crosses
to the dressing table*) I always knew something like this would
turn up—some problem, like an ill wife—and it would be too much
for those delicate, hot-house feelings of yours. (*He sweeps up*
HELENA's *things from the dressing table, and crosses over to the
wardrobe. Outside, the church bells start ringing*) It's no good
trying to fool yourself about love. You can't fall into it like a soft
job, without dirtying up your hands. (*Hands her the make-up
things, which she takes. He opens the wardrobe*) It takes muscle
and guts. And if you can't bear the thought (*Takes out a dress on
a hanger*) of messing up your nice, clean soul (*Crossing back to
her*), you'd better give up the whole idea of life, and become a
saint. (*Puts the dress in her arms*) Because you'll never make it as
a human being. It's either this world or the next. (*She looks at
him for a moment, and then goes out quickly. He is shaken, and
he avoids* ALISON's *eyes, crossing to the window. He rests against
it, then bangs his fist against the frame*) Oh, those bells!

(*The shadows are growing around them.* JIMMY *stands, his head
against the window pane.* ALISON *is huddled forward in the armchair. Presently, she breaks the stillness, and rises to above the
table*)

ALISON   I'm . . . sorry. I'll go now.

(*She starts to move upstage. But his voice pulls her up*)

JIMMY   You never even sent any flowers to the funeral. Not—a little
bunch of flowers. You had to deny me that too, didn't you? (*She
starts to move, but again he speaks*) The injustice of it is almost
perfect! The wrong people going hungry, the wrong people being loved, the wrong people dying! (*She moves to the gas stove.
He turns to face her*) Was I really wrong to believe that there's a
—a kind of—burning virility of mind and spirit that looks for something as powerful as itself? The heaviest, strongest creatures in
this world seem to be the loneliest. Like the old bear, following
his own breath in the dark forest. There's no warm pack, no herd
to comfort him. That voice that cries out doesn't *have* to be a

weakling's, does it? (*He moves in a little*) Do you remember that first night I saw you at that grisly party? You didn't really notice me, but I was watching you all the evening. You seemed to have a wonderful relaxation of spirit. I knew that was what I wanted. You've got to be really brawny to have that kind of strength— the strength to relax. It was only after we were married that I discovered that it wasn't relaxation at all. In order to relax, you've first got to sweat your guts out. And, as far as you were concerned, you'd never had a hair out of place, or a bead of sweat anywhere. (*A cry escapes from her, and her fist flies to her mouth. She moves down to below the table, leaning on it*) I may be a lost cause, but I thought if you loved me, it needn't matter.

(*She is crying silently. He moves down to face her*)

ALISON   It doesn't matter! I was wrong, I was wrong! I don't want to be neutral, I don't want to be a saint. I want to be a lost cause. I want to be corrupt and futile! (*All he can do is watch her helplessly. Her voice takes on a little strength, and rises*) Don't you understand? It's gone! It's gone! That—that helpless human being inside my body. I thought it was so safe, and secure in there. Nothing could take it from me. It was mine, my responsibility. But it's lost. (*She slides down against the leg of the table to the floor*) All I wanted was to die. I never knew what it was like. I didn't know it could be like that! I was in pain, and all I could think of was you, and what I'd lost. (*Scarcely able to speak*) I thought: if only—if only he could see me now, so stupid, and ugly and ridiculous. This is what he's been longing for me to feel. This is what he wants to splash about in! I'm in the fire, and I'm burning, and all I want is to die! It's cost him his child, and any others I might have had! But what does it matter —this is what he wanted from me! (*She raises her face to him*) Don't you see! I'm in the mud at last! I'm grovelling! I'm crawling! Oh, God—

(*She collapses at his feet. He stands, frozen for a moment, then he bends down and takes her shaking body in his arms. He shakes his head, and whispers*)

JIMMY   Don't. Please don't. . . . I can't——(*She gasps for her breath against him*) You're all right. You're all right now. Please, I—I. . . . Not any more. . . . (*She relaxes suddenly. He looks down at her, full of fatigue, and says with a kind of mocking, tender irony*) We'll be together in our bear's cave, and our squirrel's drey, and we'll live on honey, and nuts—lots and lots of nuts.

And we'll sing songs about ourselves—about warm trees and snug caves, and lying in the sun. And you'll keep those big eyes on my fur, and help me keep my claws in order, because I'm a bit of a soppy, scruffy sort of a bear. And I'll see that you keep that sleek, bushy tail glistening as it should, because you're a very beautiful squirrel, but you're none too bright either, so we've got to be careful. There are cruel steel traps lying about everywhere, just waiting for rather mad, slightly satanic, and very timid little animals. Right? (ALISON *nods, pathetically*) Poor squirrels!

ALISON (*With the same comic emphasis*)   Poor bears! (*She laughs a little. Then looks at him very tenderly, and adds very, very softly*) Oh, poor, poor bears!

(*She slides her arms around him*)

Curtain

A Raisin
in the Sun

BY

Lorraine Hansberry

To Mama:
in gratitude for the dream

A RAISIN IN THE SUN *was first presented by Philip Rose and David J. Cogan at the Ethel Barrymore Theatre, New York City, March 11, 1959, with the following cast:*

(*In order of appearance*)

RUTH YOUNGER	*Ruby Dee*
TRAVIS YOUNGER	*Glynn Turman*
WALTER LEE YOUNGER (BROTHER)	*Sidney Poitier*
BENEATHA YOUNGER	*Diana Sands*
LENA YOUNGER (MAMA)	*Claudia McNeil*
JOSEPH ASAGAI	*Ivan Dixon*
GEORGE MURCHISON	*Louis Gossett*
KARL LINDNER	*John Fiedler*
BOBO	*Lonne Elder III*
MOVING MEN	*Ed Hall, Douglas Turner*

Directed by Lloyd Richards
Designed and lighted by Ralph Alswang
Costumes by Virginia Volland

Synopsis of Scenes

The action of the play is set in Chicago's Southside, sometime between World War II and the present.

ACT ONE

ACT TWO

ACT THREE
An hour later.

What happens to a dream deferred?
Does it dry up
Like a raisin in the sun?
Or fester like a sore—
And then run?
Does it stink like rotten meat?
Or crust and sugar over—
Like a syrupy sweet?

Maybe it just sags
Like a heavy load.

Or does it explode?

—Langston Hughes

ACT ONE

SCENE 1

The YOUNGER *living room would be a comfortable and well-ordered room if it were not for a number of indestructible contradictions to this state of being. Its furnishings are typical and undistinguished and their pirmary feature now is that they have clearly had to accommodate the living of too many people for too many years—and they are tired. Still, we can see that at some time, a time probably no longer remembered by the family (except perhaps for* MAMA*), the furnishings of this room were actually selected with care and love and even hope—and brought to this apartment and arranged with taste and pride.*

That was a long time ago. Now the once loved pattern of the couch upholstery has to fight to show itself from under acres of crocheted doilies and couch covers which have themselves finally come to be more important than the upholstery. And here a table or a chair has been moved to disguise the worn places in the carpet; but the carpet has fought back by showing its weariness, with depressing uniformity, elsewhere on its surface.

Weariness has, in fact, won in this room. Everything has been polished, washed, sat on, used, scrubbed too often. All pretenses but living itself have long since vanished from the very atmosphere of this room.

Moreover, a section of this room, for it is not really a room unto itself, though the landlord's lease would make it seem so, slopes backward to provide a small kitchen area, where the family prepares the meals that are eaten in the living room proper, which must also serve as dining room. The single window that has been provided for these "two" rooms is located in this kitchen area. The sole natural light the family may enjoy in the course of a day is only that which fights its way through this little window.

At left, a door leads to a bedroom which is shared by MAMA *and her daughter,* BENEATHA. *At right, opposite, is a second room (which in the beginning of the life of this apartment was probably a break-fast room) which serves as a bedroom for* WALTER *and his wife,* RUTH.

Time: Sometime between World War II and the present.
Place: Chicago's Southside.
At Rise: It is morning dark in the living room. TRAVIS *is asleep on the make-down bed at center. An alarm clock sounds from within the bedroom at right, and presently* RUTH *enters from that room and closes the door behind her. She crosses sleepily toward the window. As she passes her sleeping son she reaches down and shakes him a little. At the window she raises the shade and a dusky Southside morning light comes in feebly. She fills a pot with water and puts it on to boil. She calls to the boy, between yawns, in a slightly muffled voice.*

RUTH *is about thirty. We can see that she was a pretty girl, even exceptionally so, but now it is apparent that life has been little that she expected, and disappointment has already begun to hang in her face. In a few years, before thirty-five even, she will be known among her people as a "settled woman."*

She crosses to her son and gives him a good, final, rousing shake.

RUTH   Come on now, boy, it's seven thirty! (*Her son sits up at last, in a stupor of sleepiness*) I say hurry up, Travis! You ain't the only person in the world got to use a bathroom! (*The child, a sturdy, handsome little boy of ten or eleven, drags himself out of the bed and almost blindly takes his towels and "today's clothes" from drawers and a closet and goes out to the bathroom, which is in an outside hall and which is shared by another family or families on the same floor.* RUTH *crosses to the bedroom door at right and opens it and calls in to her husband*) Walter Lee! . . . It's after seven thirty! Lemme see you do some waking up in there now! (*She waits*) You better get up from there, man! It's after seven thirty I tell you. (*She waits again*) All right, you just go ahead and lay there and next thing you know Travis be fin-ished and Mr. Johnson'll be in there and you'll be fussing and cussing round here like a mad man! And be late too! (*She waits, at the end of patience*) Walter Lee—it's time for you to get up!
(*She waits another second and then starts to go into the bedroom, but is apparently satisfied that her husband has begun to get up.*

She stops, pulls the door to, and returns to the kitchen area. She wipes her face with a moist cloth and runs her fingers through her sleep-disheveled hair in a vain effort and ties an apron around her housecoat. The bedroom door at right opens and her husband stands in the doorway in his pajamas, which are rumpled and mismated. He is a lean, intense young man in his middle thirties, inclined to quick nervous movements and erratic speech habits—and always in his voice there is a quality of indictment)

WALTER Is he out yet?

RUTH What you mean *out*? He ain't hardly got in there good yet.

WALTER (*Wandering in, still more oriented to sleep than to a new day*) Well, what was you doing all that yelling for if I can't even get in there yet? (*Stopping and thinking*) Check coming today?

RUTH They *said* Saturday and this is just Friday and I hopes to God you ain't going to get up here first thing this morning and start talking to me 'bout no money—'cause I 'bout don't want to hear it.

WALTER Something the matter with you this morning?

RUTH No—I'm just sleepy as the devil. What kind of eggs you want?

WALTER Not scrambled. (RUTH *starts to scramble eggs*) Paper come? (RUTH *points impatiently to the rolled up* Tribune *on the table, and he gets it and spreads it out and vaguely reads the front page*) Set off another bomb yesterday.

RUTH (*Maximum indifference*) Did they?

WALTER (*Looking up*) What's the matter with you?

RUTH Ain't nothing the matter with me. And don't keep asking me that this morning.

WALTER Ain't nobody bothering you. (*Reading the news of the day absently again*) Say Colonel McCormick is sick.

RUTH (*Affecting tea-party interest*) Is he now? Poor thing.

WALTER (*Sighing and looking at his watch*) Oh, me. (*He waits*) Now what is that boy doing in that bathroom all this time? He just going to have to start getting up earlier. I can't be being late to work on account of him fooling around in there.

RUTH (*Turning on him*) Oh, no he ain't going to be getting up no earlier no such thing! It ain't his fault that he can't get to bed no earlier nights 'cause he got a bunch of crazy good-for-nothing clowns sitting up running their mouths in what is supposed to be his bedroom after ten o'clock at night . . .

WALTER That's what you mad about, ain't it? The things I want to talk about with my friends just couldn't be important in your mind, could they?

(*He rises and finds a cigarette in her handbag on the table and crosses to the little window and looks out, smoking and deeply enjoying this first one*)

RUTH (*Almost matter of factly, a complaint too automatic to deserve emphasis*) Why you always got to smoke before you eat in the morning?

WALTER (*At the window*) Just look at 'em down there . . . Running and racing to work . . . (*He turns and faces his wife and watches her a moment at the stove, and then, suddenly*) You look young this morning, baby.

RUTH (*Indifferently*) Yeah?

WALTER Just for a second—stirring them eggs. It's gone now—just for a second it was—you looked real young again. (*Then, drily*) It's gone now—you look like yourself again.

RUTH Man, if you don't shut up and leave me alone.

WALTER (*Looking out to the street again*) First thing a man ought to learn in life is not to make love to no colored woman first thing in the morning. You all some evil people at eight o'clock in the morning.

(TRAVIS *appears in the hall doorway, almost fully dressed and quite wide awake now, his towels and pajamas across his shoulders. He opens the door and signals for his father to make the bathroom in a hurry*)

TRAVIS (*Watching the bathroom*) Daddy, come on!

(WALTER *gets his bathroom utensils and flies out to the bathroom*)

RUTH Sit down and have your breakfast, Travis.

TRAVIS Mama, this is Friday. (*Gleefully*) Check coming tomorrow, huh?

RUTH You get your mind off money and eat your breakfast.

TRAVIS (*Eating*) This is the morning we supposed to bring the fifty cents to school.

RUTH Well, I ain't got no fifty cents this morning.

TRAVIS Teacher say we have to.

RUTH I don't care what teacher say. I ain't got it. Eat your breakfast, Travis.

TRAVIS I *am* eating.

RUTH Hush up now and just eat!

(*The boy gives her an exasperated look for her lack of understanding, and eats grudgingly*)

TRAVIS You think Grandmama would have it?

RUTH No! And I want you to stop asking your grandmother for money, you hear me?

TRAVIS (*Outraged*) Gaaaleee! I don't ask her, she just gimme it sometimes!

RUTH Travis Willard Younger—I got too much on me this morning to be—

TRAVIS Maybe Daddy—

RUTH *Travis!*

(*The boy hushes abruptly. They are both quiet and tense for several seconds*)

TRAVIS (*Presently*) Could I maybe go carry some groceries in front of the supermarket for a little while after school then?

RUTH Just hush, I said. (*Travis jabs his spoon into his cereal bowl viciously, and rests his head in anger upon his fists*) If you through eating, you can get over there and make up your bed.

(*The boy obeys stiffly and crosses the room, almost mechanically, to the bed and more or less carefully folds the covering. He carries the bedding into his mother's room and returns with his books and cap*)

TRAVIS (*Sulking and standing apart from her unnaturally*) I'm gone.

RUTH (*Looking up from the stove to inspect him automatically*) Come here. (*He crosses to her and she studies his head*) If you don't take this comb and fix this here head, you better! (TRAVIS *puts down his books with a great sigh of oppression, and crosses to the mirror. His mother mutters under her breath about his "slubbornness"*) 'Bout to march out of here with that head looking just like chickens slept in it! I just don't know where you get your slubborn ways . . . And get your jacket, too. Looks chilly out this morning.

TRAVIS (*With conspicuously brushed hair and jacket*) I'm gone.

RUTH Get carfare and milk money—(*Waving one finger*)—and not a single penny for no caps, you hear me?

TRAVIS (*With sullen politeness*) Yes'm.

(*He turns in outrage to leave. His mother watches after him as in his frustration he approaches the door almost comically. When she speaks to him, her voice has become a very gentle tease*)

RUTH (*Mocking; as she thinks he would say it*) Oh, Mama makes me so mad sometimes, I don't know what to do! (*She waits and continues to his back as he stands stock-still in front of the door*)

I wouldn't kiss that woman good-bye for nothing in this world this morning! (*The boy finally turns around and rolls his eyes at her, knowing the mood has changed and he is vindicated; he does not, however, move toward her yet*) Not for nothing in this world! (*She finally laughs aloud at him and holds out her arms to him and we see that it is a way between them, very old and practiced. He crosses to her and allows her to embrace him warmly but keeps his face fixed with masculine rigidity. She holds him back from her presently and looks at him and runs her fingers over the features of his face. With utter gentleness—*) Now—whose little old angry man are you?

TRAVIS (*The masculinity and gruffness start to fade at last*) Aw gaalee—Mama . . .

RUTH (*Mimicking*) Aw—gaaaaalleeeee, Mama! (*She pushes him, with rough playfulness and finality, toward the door*) Get on out of here or you going to be late.

TRAVIS (*In the face of love, new aggressiveness*) Mama, could I *please* go carry groceries?

RUTH Honey, it's starting to get so cold evenings.

WALTER (*Coming in from the bathroom and drawing a make-believe gun from a make-believe holster and shooting at his son*) What is it he wants to do?

RUTH Go carry groceries after school at the supermarket.

WALTER Well, let him go . . .

TRAVIS (*Quickly, to the ally*) I *have* to—she won't gimme the fifty cents . . .

WALTER (*To his wife only*) Why not?

RUTH (*Simply, and with flavor*) 'Cause we don't have it.

WALTER (*To RUTH only*) What you tell the boy things like that for? (*Reaching down into his pants with a rather important gesture*) Here, son—

(*He hands the boy the coin, but his eyes are directed to his wife's. TRAVIS takes the money happily*)

TRAVIS Thanks, Daddy.

(*He starts out. RUTH watches both of them with murder in her eyes. WALTER stands and stares back at her with defiance, and suddenly reaches into his pocket again on an afterthought*)

WALTER (*Without even looking at his son, still staring hard at his wife*) In fact, here's another fifty cents . . . Buy yourself some fruit today—or take a taxi cab to school or something!

TRAVIS Whoopee—

(*He leaps up and clasps his father around the middle with his legs, and they face each other in mutual appreciation; slowly* WALTER LEE *peeks around the boy to catch the violent rays from his wife's eyes and draws his head back as if shot*)

WALTER   You better get down now—and get to school, man.

TRAVIS (*At the door*)   O.K. Good-bye.

(*He exits*)

WALTER (*After him, pointing with pride*)   That's *my* boy. (*She looks at him in disgust and turns back to her work*) You know what I was thinking 'bout in the bathroom this morning?

RUTH   No.

WALTER   How come you always try to be so pleasant!

RUTH   What is there to be pleasant 'bout!

WALTER   You want to know what I was thinking 'bout in the bathroom or not!

RUTH   I know what you was thinking 'bout.

WALTER (*Ignoring her*)   'Bout what me and Willy Harris was talking about last night.

RUTH (*Immediately—a refrain*)   Willy Harris is a good-for-nothing loud mouth.

WALTER   Anybody who talks to me has got to be a good-for-nothing loud mouth, ain't he? And what you know about who is just a good-for-nothing loud mouth? Charlie Atkins was just a "good-for-nothing loud mouth" too, wasn't he! When he wanted me to go in the dry-cleaning business with him. And now—he's grossing a hundred thousand a year. A hundred thousand dollars a year! You still call *him* a loud mouth!

RUTH (*Bitterly*)   Oh, Walter Lee . . .

(*She folds her head on her arms over on the table*)

WALTER (*Rising and coming to her and standing over her*)   You tired, ain't you? Tired of everything. Me, the boy, the way we live—this beat-up hole—everything. Ain't you? (*She doesn't look up, doesn't answer*) So tired—moaning and groaning all the time, but you wouldn't do nothing to help, would you? You couldn't be on my side that long for nothing, could you?

RUTH   Walter, please leave me alone.

WALTER   A man needs for a woman to back him up . . .

RUTH   Walter—

WALTER   Mama would listen to you. You know she listen to you more than she do me and Bennie. She think more of you. All you have to do is just sit down with her when you drinking your coffee one morning and talking 'bout things like you do and—(*He sits down beside her and demonstrates graphically what he thinks her methods and tone should be*)—you just sip your coffee, see, and say easy like that you been thinking 'bout that deal Walter Lee is so interested in, 'bout the store and all, and sip some more coffee, like what you saying ain't really that important to you— And the next thing you know, she be listening good and asking you questions and when I come home—I can tell her the details. This ain't no fly-by-night proposition, baby. I mean we figured it out, me and Willy and Bobo.

RUTH (*With a frown*) Bobo?

WALTER Yeah. You see, this little liquor store we got in mind cost seventy-five thousand and we figured the initial investment on the place be 'bout thirty thousand, see. That be ten thousand each. Course, there's a couple of hundred you got to pay so's you don't spend your life just waiting for them clowns to let your license get approved—

RUTH You mean graft?

WALTER (*Frowning impatiently*) Don't call it that. See there, that just goes to show you what women understand about the world. Baby, don't *nothing* happen for you in this world 'less you pay *somebody* off!

RUTH Walter, leave me alone! (*She raises her head and stares at him vigorously—then says, more quietly*) Eat your eggs, they gonna be cold.

WALTER (*Straightening up from her and looking off*) That's it. There you are. Man say to his woman: I got me a dream. His woman say: Eat your eggs. (*Sadly, but gaining in power*) Man say: I got to take hold of this here world, baby! And a woman will say: Eat your eggs and go to work. (*Passionately now*) Man say: I got to change my life, I'm choking to death, baby! And his woman say—(*In utter anguish as he brings his fists down on his thighs*)—Your eggs is getting cold!

RUTH (*Softly*) Walter, that ain't none of our money.

WALTER (*Not listening at all or even looking at her*) This morning, I was lookin' in the mirror and thinking about it . . . I'm thirty-five years old; I been married eleven years and I got a boy who sleeps in the living room—(*Very, very quietly*)—and all I got to give him is stories about how rich white people live . . .

RUTH Eat your eggs, Walter.

WALTER *Damn my eggs . . . damn all the eggs that ever was!*

RUTH   Then go to work.

WALTER   (*Looking up at her*) See—I'm trying to talk to you 'bout myself—(*Shaking his head with the repetition*)—and all you can say is eat them eggs and go to work.

RUTH   (*Wearily*) Honey, you never say nothing new. I listen to you every day, every night and every morning, and you never say nothing new. (*Shrugging*) So you would rather *be* Mr. Arnold than be his chauffeur. So—I would *rather* be living in Buckingham Palace.

WALTER   That is just what is wrong with the colored woman in this world . . . Don't understand about building their men up and making 'em feel like they somebody. Like they can do something.

RUTH   (*Drily, but to hurt*) There *are* colored men who do things.

WALTER   No thanks to the colored woman.

RUTH   Well, being a colored woman, I guess I can't help myself none.

(*She rises and gets the ironing board and sets it up and attacks a huge pile of rough-dried clothes, sprinkling them in preparation for the ironing and then rolling them into tight fat balls*)

WALTER   (*Mumbling*) We one group of men tied to a race of women with small minds.

(*His sister BENEATHA enters. She is about twenty, as slim and intense as her brother. She is not as pretty as her sister-in-law, but her lean, almost intellectual face has a handsomeness of its own. She wears a bright-red flannel nightie, and her thick hair stands wildly about her head. Her speech is a mixture of many things; it is different from the rest of the family's insofar as education has permeated her sense of English—and perhaps the Midwest rather than the South has finally—at last—won out in her inflection; but not altogether, because over all of it is a soft slurring and transformed use of vowels which is the decided influence of the Southside. She passes through the room without looking at either RUTH or WALTER and goes to the outside door and looks, a little blindly, out to the bathroom. She sees that it has been lost to the Johnsons. She closes the door with a sleepy vengeance and crosses to the table and sits down a little defeated*)

BENEATHA   I am going to start timing those people.

WALTER   You should get up earlier.

BENEATHA   (*Her face in her hands. She is still fighting the urge to go back to bed*) Really—would you suggest dawn? Where's the paper?

WALTER (*Pushing the paper across the table to her as he studies her almost clinically, as though he has never seen her before*) You a horrible-looking chick at this hour.

BENEATHA (*Drily*) Good morning, everybody.

WALTER (*Senselessly*) How is school coming?

BENEATHA (*In the same spirit*) Lovely. Lovely. And you know, biology is the greatest. (*Looking up at him*) I dissected something that looked just like you yesterday.

WALTER I just wondered if you've made up your mind and everything.

BENEATHA (*Gaining in sharpness and impatience*) And what did I answer yesterday morning—and the day before that?

RUTH (*From the ironing board, like someone disinterested and old*) Don't be so nasty, Bennie.

BENEATHA (*Still to her brother*) And the day before that and the day before that!

WALTER (*Defensively*) I'm interested in you. Something wrong with that? Ain't many girls who decide—

WALTER *and* BENEATHA (*In unison*) —"to be a doctor."
(*Silence*)

WALTER Have we figured out yet just exactly how much medical school is going to cost?

RUTH Walter Lee, why don't you leave that girl alone and get out of here to work?

BENEATHA (*Exits to the bathroom and bangs on the door*) Come on out of there, please!
(*She comes back into the room*)

WALTER (*Looking at his sister intently*) You know the check is coming tomorrow.

BENEATHA (*Turning on him with a sharpness all her own*) That money belongs to Mama, Walter, and it's for her to decide how she wants to use it. I don't care if she wants to buy a house or a rocket ship or just nail it up somewhere and look at it. It's hers. Not ours—*hers*.

WALTER (*Bitterly*) Now ain't that fine! You just got your mother's interest at heart, ain't you, girl? You such a nice girl—but if Mama got that money she can always take a few thousand and help you through school too—can't she?

BENEATHA I have never asked anyone around here to do anything for me!

WALTER   No! And the line between asking and just accepting when the time comes is big and wide—ain't it!

BENEATHA   (*With fury*)   What do you want from me, Brother—that I quit school or just drop dead, which!

WALTER   I don't want nothing but for you to stop acting holy 'round here. Me and Ruth done made some sacrifices for you—why can't you do something for the family?

RUTH   Walter, don't be dragging me in it.

WALTER   You are in it— Don't you get up and go work in somebody's kitchen for the last three years to help put clothes on her back?

RUTH   Oh, Walter—that's not fair . . .

WALTER   It ain't that nobody expects you to get on your knees and say thank you, Brother; thank you, Ruth; thank you, Mama—and thank you, Travis, for wearing the same pair of shoes for two semesters—

BENEATHA   (*Dropping to her knees*)   Well—I *do*—all right?—thank everybody . . . and forgive me for ever wanting to be anything at all . . . forgive me, forgive me!

RUTH   Please stop it! Your mama'll hear you.

WALTER   Who the hell told you you had to be a doctor? If you so crazy 'bout messing 'round with sick people—then go be a nurse like other women—or just get married and be quiet . . .

BENEATHA   Well—you finally got it said . . . It took you three years but you finally got it said. Walter, give up; leave me alone—it's Mama's money.

WALTER   *He was my father, too!*

BENEATHA   So what? He was mine, too—and Travis' grandfather—but the insurance money belongs to Mama. Picking on me is not going to make her give it to you to invest in any liquor stores— (*Underbreath, dropping into a chair*)—and I for one say, God bless Mama for that!

WALTER   (*To* RUTH)   See—did you hear? Did you hear!

RUTH   Honey, please go to work.

WALTER   Nobody in this house is ever going to understand me.

BENEATHA   Because you're a nut.

WALTER   Who's a nut?

BENEATHA   You—you are a nut. Thee is mad, boy.

WALTER   (*Looking at his wife and his sister from the door, very sadly*)   The world's most backward race of people, and that's a fact.

BENEATHA (*Turning slowly in her chair*) And then there are all those prophets who would lead us out of the wilderness—(WALTER *slams out of the house*)—into the swamps!

RUTH Bennie, why you always gotta be pickin' on your brother? Can't you be a little sweeter sometimes?

(*Door opens.* WALTER *walks in*)

WALTER (*To* RUTH) I need some money for carfare.

RUTH (*Looks at him, then warms; teasing, but tenderly*) Fifty cents? (*She goes to her bag and gets money*) Here, take a taxi.

(WALTER *exits.* MAMA *enters. She is a woman in her early sixties, full-bodied and strong. She is one of those women of a certain grace and beauty who wear it so unobtrusively that it takes a while to notice. Her dark-brown face is surrounded by the total whiteness of her hair, and, being a woman who has adjusted to many things in life and overcome many more, her face is full of strength. She has, we can see, wit and faith of a kind that keep her eyes lit and full of interest and expectancy. She is, in a word, a beautiful woman. Her bearing is perhaps most like the noble bearing of the women of the Hereros of Southwest Africa—rather as if she imagines that as she walks she still bears a basket or a vessel upon her head. Her speech, on the other hand, is as careless as her carriage is precise—she is inclined to slur everything—but her voice is perhaps not so much quiet as simply soft*)

MAMA Who that 'round here slamming doors at this hour?

(*She crosses through the room, goes to the window, opens it, and brings in a feeble little plant growing doggedly in a small pot on the window sill. She feels the dirt and puts it back out*)

RUTH That was Walter Lee. He and Bennie was at it again.

MAMA My children and they tempers. Lord, if this little old plant don't get more sun than it's been getting it ain't never going to see spring again. (*She turns from the window*) What's the matter with you this morning, Ruth? You looks right peaked. You aiming to iron all them things? Leave some for me. I'll get to 'em this afternoon. Bennie honey, it's too drafty for you to be sitting 'round half dressed. Where's your robe?

BENEATHA In the cleaners.

MAMA Well, go get mine and put it on.

BENEATHA I'm not cold, Mama, honest.

MAMA I know—but you so thin . . .

BENEATHA (*Irritably*) Mama, I'm not cold.

MAMA (*Seeing the make-down bed as* TRAVIS *has left it*) Lord have mercy, look at that poor bed. Bless his heart—he tries, don't he?

(*She moves to the bed* TRAVIS *has sloppily made up*)

RUTH No—he don't half try at all 'cause he knows you going to come along behind him and fix everything. That's just how come he don't know how to do nothing right now—you done spoiled that boy so.

MAMA Well—he's a little boy. Ain't supposed to know 'bout housekeeping. My baby, that's what he is. What you fix for his breakfast this morning?

RUTH (*Angrily*) I feed my son, Lena!

MAMA I ain't meddling—(*Underbreath; busy-bodyish*) I just noticed all last week he had cold cereal, and when it starts getting this chilly in the fall a child ought to have some hot grits or something when he goes out in the cold—

RUTH (*Furious*) I gave him hot oats—is that all right!

MAMA I ain't meddling. (*Pause*) Put a lot of nice butter on it? (RUTH *shoots her an angry look and does not reply*) He likes lots of butter.

RUTH (*Exasperated*) Lena—

MAMA (*To* BENEATHA. MAMA *is inclined to wander conversationally sometimes*) What was you and your brother fussing 'bout this morning?

BENEATHA It's not important, Mama.

(*She gets up and goes to look out at the bathroom, which is apparently free, and she picks up her towels and rushes out*)

MAMA What was they fighting about?

RUTH Now you know as well as I do.

MAMA (*Shaking her head*) Brother still worrying hisself sick about that money?

RUTH You know he is.

MAMA You had breakfast?

RUTH Some coffee.

MAMA Girl, you better start eating and looking after yourself better. You almost thin as Travis.

RUTH Lena—

MAMA Un-hunh?

RUTH What are you going to do with it?

MAMA Now don't you start, child. It's too early in the morning to be talking about money. It ain't Christian.

RUTH It's just that he got his heart set on that store—

MAMA You mean that liquor store that Willy Harris want him to invest in?

RUTH Yes—

MAMA We ain't no business people, Ruth. We just plain working folks.

RUTH Ain't nobody business people till they go into business. Walter Lee say colored people ain't never going to start getting ahead till they start gambling on some different kinds of things in the world—investments and things.

MAMA What done got into you, girl? Walter Lee done finally sold you on investing.

RUTH No. Mama, something is happening between Walter and me. I don't know what it is—but he needs something—something I can't give him any more. He needs this chance, Lena.

MAMA (*Frowning deeply*) But liquor, honey—

RUTH Well—like Walter say—I spec people going to always be drinking themselves some liquor.

MAMA Well—whether they drinks it or not ain't none of my business. But whether I go into business selling it to 'em *is*, and I don't want that on my ledger this late in life. (*Stopping suddenly and studying her daughter-in-law*) Ruth Younger, what's the matter with you today? You look like you could fall over right there.

RUTH I'm tired.

MAMA Then you better stay home from work today.

RUTH I can't stay home. She'd be calling up the agency and screaming at them, "My girl didn't come in today—send me somebody! My girl didn't come in!" Oh, she just have a fit . . .

MAMA Well, let her have it. I'll just call her up and say you got the flu—

RUTH (*Laughing*) Why the flu?

MAMA 'Cause it sounds respectable to 'em. Something white people get, too. They know 'bout the flu. Otherwise they think you been cut up or something when you tell 'em you sick.

RUTH I got to go in. We need the money.

MAMA Somebody would of thought my children done all but starved to death the way they talk about money here lately. Child, we got a great big old check coming tomorrow.

RUTH (*Sincerely, but also self-righteously*) Now that's your money. It ain't got nothing to do with me. We all feel like that—Walter and Bennie and me—even Travis.

MAMA (*Thoughtfully, and suddenly very far away*) Ten thousand dollars—

RUTH Sure is wonderful.

MAMA *Ten thousand dollars.*

RUTH You know what you should do, Miss Lena? You should take yourself a trip somewhere. To Europe or South America or someplace—

MAMA (*Throwing up her hands at the thought*) Oh, child!

RUTH I'm serious. Just pack up and leave! Go on away and enjoy yourself some. Forget about the family and have yourself a ball for once in your life—

MAMA (*Drily*) You sound like I'm just about ready to die. Who'd go with me? What I look like wandering 'round Europe by myself?

RUTH Shoot—these here rich white women do it all the time. They don't think nothing of packing up they suitcases and piling on one of them big steamships and—swoosh!—they gone, child.

MAMA Something always told me I wasn't no rich white woman.

RUTH Well—what are you going to do with it then?

MAMA I ain't rightly decided. (*Thinking. She speaks now with emphasis*) Some of it got to be put away for Beneatha and her schoolin'—and ain't nothing going to touch that part of it. Nothing. (*She waits several seconds, trying to make up her mind about something, and looks at* RUTH *a little tentatively before going on*) Been thinking that we maybe could meet the notes on a little old two-story somewhere, with a yard where Travis could play in the summertime, if we use part of the insurance for a down payment and everybody kind of pitch in. I could maybe take on a little day work again, few days a week—

RUTH (*Studying her mother-in-law furtively and concentrating on her ironing, anxious to encourage without seeming to*) Well, Lord knows, we've put enough rent into this here rat trap to pay for four houses by now . . .

MAMA (*Looking up at the words "rat trap" and then looking around and leaning back and sighing—in a suddenly reflective mood—*) "Rat trap"—yes, that's all it is. (*Smiling*) I remember just as well the day me and Big Walter moved in here. Hadn't been married but two weeks and wasn't planning on living here no more than a year. (*She shakes her head at the dissolved dream*) We was going to set away, little by little, don't you know, and buy a little place out in Morgan Park. We had even picked out the house. (*Chuckling a little*) Looks right dumpy today. But Lord, child, you should know all the dreams I had 'bout buying that house and fixing it up and making me a little garden in the back— (*She waits and stops smiling*) And didn't none of it happen.

(*Dropping her hands in a futile gesture*)

RUTH (*Keeps her head down, ironing*) Yes, life can be a barrel of disappointments, sometimes.

MAMA Honey, Big Walter would come in here some nights back then and slump down on that couch there and just look at the rug, and look at me and look at the rug and then back at me—and I'd know he was down then . . . really down. (*After a second very long and thoughtful pause; she is seeing back to times that only she can see*) And then, Lord, when I lost that baby—little Claude—I almost thought I was going to lose Big Walter too. Oh, that man grieved hisself! He was one man to love his children.

RUTH Ain't nothin' can tear at you like losin' your baby.

MAMA I guess that's how come that man finally worked hisself to death like he done. Like he was fighting his own war with this here world that took his baby from him.

RUTH He sure was a fine man, all right. I always liked Mr. Younger.

MAMA Crazy 'bout his children! God knows there was plenty wrong with Walter Younger—hard-headed, mean, kind of wild with women—plenty wrong with him. But he sure loved his children. Always wanted them to have something—be something. That's where Brother gets all these notions, I reckon. Big Walter used to say, he'd get right wet in the eyes sometimes, lean his head back with the water standing in his eyes and say, "Seem like God didn't see fit to give the black man nothing but dreams—but He did give us children to make them dreams seem worth while." (*She smiles*) He could talk like that, don't you know.

RUTH Yes, he sure could. He was a good man, Mr. Younger.

MAMA Yes, a fine man—just couldn't never catch up with his dreams, that's all.

(BENEATHA *comes in, brushing her hair and looking up to the ceiling, where the sound of a vacuum cleaner has started up*)

BENEATHA What could be so dirty on that woman's rugs that she has to vacuum them every single day?

RUTH I wish certain young women 'round here who I could name would take inspiration about certain rugs in a certain apartment I could also mention.

BENEATHA (*Shrugging*) How much cleaning can a house need, for Christ's sakes.

MAMA (*Not liking the Lord's name used thus*) Bennie!

RUTH Just listen to her—just listen!

BENEATHA Oh, God!

MAMA If you use the Lord's name just one more time—

BENEATHA (*A bit of a whine*) Oh, Mama—

RUTH Fresh—just fresh as salt, this girl!

BENEATHA (*Drily*) Well—if the salt loses its savor—

MAMA Now that will do. I just ain't going to have you 'round here reciting the scriptures in vain—you hear me?

BENEATHA How did I manage to get on everybody's wrong side by just walking into a room?

RUTH If you weren't so fresh—

BENEATHA Ruth, I'm twenty years old.

MAMA What time you be home from school today?

BENEATHA Kind of late. (*With enthusiasm*) Madeline is going to start my guitar lessons today.

(MAMA *and* RUTH *look up with the same expression*)

MAMA Your *what* kind of lessons?

BENEATHA Guitar.

RUTH Oh, Father!

MAMA How come you done taken it in your mind to learn to play the guitar?

BENEATHA I just want to, that's all.

MAMA (*Smiling*) Lord, child, don't you know what to do with yourself? How long it going to be before you get tired of this now—like you got tired of that little play-acting group you joined last year? (*Looking at Ruth*) And what was it the year before that?

RUTH The horseback-riding club for which she bought that fifty-five-dollar riding habit that's been hanging in the closet ever since!

MAMA (*To* BENEATHA) Why you got to flit so from one thing to another, baby?

BENEATHA (*Sharply*) I just want to learn to play the guitar. Is there anything wrong with that?

MAMA Ain't nobody trying to stop you. I just wonders sometimes why you has to flit so from one thing to another all the time. You ain't never done nothing with all that camera equipment you brought home—

BENEATHA I don't flit! I—I experiment with different forms of expression—

RUTH Like riding a horse?

BENEATHA —People have to express themselves one way or another.

MAMA What is it you want to express?

BENEATHA (*Angrily*) Me! (MAMA *and* RUTH *look at each other and burst into raucous laughter*) Don't worry—I don't expect you to understand.

MAMA (*To change the subject*) Who you going out with tomorrow night?

BENEATHA (*With displeasure*) George Murchison again.

MAMA (*Pleased*) Oh—you getting a little sweet on him?

RUTH You ask me, this child ain't sweet on nobody but herself—
(*Underbreath*) Express herself!
(*They laugh*)

BENEATHA Oh—I like George all right, Mama. I mean I like him enough to go out with him and stuff, but—

RUTH (*For devilment*) What does *and stuff* mean?

BENEATHA Mind your own business.

MAMA Stop picking at her now, Ruth. (*A thoughtful pause, and then a suspicious sudden look at her daughter as she turns in her chair for emphasis*) What *does* it mean?

BENEATHA (*Wearily*) Oh, I just mean I couldn't ever really be serious about George. He's—he's so shallow.

RUTH Shallow—what do you mean he's shallow? He's *rich!*

MAMA Hush, Ruth.

BENEATHA I know he's rich. He knows he's rich, too.

RUTH Well—what other qualities a man got to have to satisfy you, little girl?

BENEATHA You wouldn't even begin to understand. Anybody who married Walter could not possibly understand.

MAMA (*Outraged*) What kind of way is that to talk about your brother?

BENEATHA Brother is a flip—let's face it.

MAMA (*To* RUTH, *helplessly*) What's a flip?

RUTH (*Glad to add kindling*) She's saying he's crazy.

BENEATHA Not crazy. Brother isn't really crazy yet—he—he's an elaborate neurotic.

MAMA Hush your mouth!

BENEATHA As for George. Well. George looks good—he's got a beautiful car and he takes me to nice places and, as my sister-in-law says, he is probably the richest boy I will ever get to know and I even like him sometimes—but if the Youngers are sitting around waiting to see if their little Bennie is going to tie up the family with the Murchisons, they are wasting their time.

RUTH   You mean you wouldn't marry George Murchison if he asked you someday? That pretty, rich thing? Honey, I knew you was odd—

BENEATHA   No I would not marry him if all I felt for him was what I feel now. Besides, George's family wouldn't really like it.

MAMA   Why not?

BENEATHA   Oh, Mama—the Murchisons are honest-to-God-real-*live*-rich colored people, and the only people in the world who are more snobbish than rich white people are rich colored people. I thought everybody knew that. I've met Mrs. Murchison. She's a scene!

MAMA   You must not dislike people 'cause they well off, honey.

BENEATHA   Why not? It makes just as much sense as disliking people 'cause they are poor, and lots of people do that.

RUTH   (*A wisdom-of-the-ages manner. To* MAMA)   Well, she'll get over some of this—

BENEATHA   Get over it? What are you talking about, Ruth? Listen, I'm going to be a doctor. I'm not worried about who I'm going to marry yet—if I ever get married.

MAMA *and* RUTH   *If!*

MAMA   Now, Bennie—

BENEATHA   Oh, I probably will . . . but first I'm going to be a doctor, and George, for one, still thinks that's pretty funny. I couldn't be bothered with that. I am going to be a doctor and everybody around here better understand that!

MAMA   (*Kindly*)   'Course you going to be a doctor, honey, God willing.

BENEATHA   (*Drily*)   God hasn't got a thing to do with it.

MAMA   Beneatha—that just wasn't necessary.

BENEATHA   Well—neither is God. I get sick of hearing about God.

MAMA   Beneatha!

BENEATHA   I mean it! I'm just tired of hearing about God all the time. What has He got to do with anything? Does He pay tuition?

MAMA   You 'bout to get your fresh little jaw slapped!

RUTH   That's just what she needs, all right!

BENEATHA   Why? Why can't I say what I want to around here, like everybody else?

MAMA It don't sound nice for a young girl to say things like that
—you wasn't brought up that way. Me and your father went to
trouble to get you and Brother to church every Sunday.

BENEATHA Mama, you don't understand. It's all a matter of ideas,
and God is just one idea I don't accept. It's not important. I am
not going out and be immoral or commit crimes because I don't
believe in God. I don't even think about it. It's just that I get
tired of Him getting credit for all the things the human race
achieves through its own stubborn effort. There simply is no
blasted God—there is only man and it is he who makes miracles!
(MAMA *absorbs this speech, studies her daughter and rises
slowly and crosses to* BENEATHA *and slaps her powerfully across
the face. After, there is only silence and the daughter drops her
eyes from her mother's face, and* MAMA *is very tall before her*)

MAMA Now—you say after me, in my mother's house there is still
God. (*There is a long pause and* BENEATHA *stares at the floor
wordlessly.* MAMA *repeats the phrase with precision and cool
emotion*) In my mother's house there is still God.

BENEATHA In my mother's house there is still God.
(*A long pause*)

MAMA (*Walking away from* BENEATHA, *too disturbed for triumphant
posture. Stopping and turning back to her daughter*) There are
some ideas we ain't going to have in this house. Not long as I
am at the head of this family.

BENEATHA Yes, ma'am.
(MAMA *walks out of the room*)

RUTH (*Almost gently, with profound understanding*) You think
you a woman, Bennie—but you still a little girl. What you did
was childish—so you got treated like a child.

BENEATHA I see. (*Quietly*) I also see that everybody thinks it's
all right for Mama to be a tyrant. But all the tyranny in the world
will never put a God in the heavens!
(*She picks up her books and goes out*)

RUTH (*Goes to* MAMA's *door*) She said she was sorry.

MAMA (*Coming out, going to her plant*) They frightens me, Ruth.
My children.

RUTH You got good children, Lena. They just a little off sometimes—but they're good.

MAMA No—there's something come down between me and them
that don't let us understand each other and I don't know what it
is. One done almost lost his mind thinking 'bout money all the

time and the other done commence to talk about things I can't seem to understand in no form or fashion. What is it that's changing, Ruth?

RUTH (*Soothingly, older than her years*) Now . . . you taking it all too seriously. You just got strong-willed children and it takes a strong woman like you to keep 'em in hand.

MAMA (*Looking at her plant and sprinkling a little water on it*) They spirited all right, my children. Got to admit they got spirit —Bennie and Walter. Like this little old plant that ain't never had enough sunshine or nothing—and look at it . . .

(*She has her back to* RUTH, *who has had to stop ironing and lean against something and put the back of her hand to her forehead*)

RUTH (*Trying to keep* MAMA *from noticing*) You . . . sure . . . loves that little old thing, don't you? . . .

MAMA Well, I always wanted me a garden like I used to see sometimes at the back of the houses down home. This plant is close as I ever got to having one. (*She looks out of the window as she replaces the plant*) Lord, ain't nothing as dreary as the view from this window on a dreary day, is there? Why ain't you singing this morning, Ruth? Sing that "No Ways Tired." That song always lifts me up so—(*She turns at last to see that* RUTH *has slipped quietly into a chair, in a state of semiconsciousness*) Ruth! Ruth honey—what's the matter with you . . . Ruth!

Curtain

SCENE 2

It is the following morning; a Saturday morning, and house cleaning is in progress at the YOUNGERS. *Furniture has been shoved hither and yon and* MAMA *is giving the kitchen-area walls a washing down.* BENEATHA, *in dungarees, with a handkerchief tied around her face, is spraying insecticide into the cracks in the walls. As they work, the radio is on and a Southside disk-jockey program is inappropriately filling the house with a rather exotic saxophone blues.* TRAVIS, *the sole idle one, is leaning on his arms, looking out of the window.*

TRAVIS Grandmama, that stuff Bennie is using smells awful. Can
I go downstairs, please?

MAMA Did you get all them chores done already? I ain't seen you
doing much.

TRAVIS Yes'm—finished early. Where did Mama go this morning?

MAMA (*Looking at* BENEATHA) She had to go on a little errand.

TRAVIS Where?

MAMA To tend to her business.

TRAVIS Can I go outside then?

MAMA Oh, I guess so. You better stay right in front of the house,
though . . . and keep a good lookout for the postman.

TRAVIS Yes'm. (*He starts out and decides to give his* AUNT
BENEATHA *a good swat on the legs as he passes her*) Leave them
poor little old cockroaches alone, they ain't bothering you none.
(*He runs as she swings the spray gun at him both viciously and
playfully.* WALTER *enters from the bedroom and goes to the
phone*)

MAMA Look out there, girl, before you be spilling some of that
stuff on that child!

TRAVIS (*Teasing*) That's right—look out now!
(*He exits*)

BENEATHA (*Drily*) I can't imagine that it would hurt him—it has
never hurt the roaches.

MAMA Well, little boys' hides ain't as tough as Southside roaches.

WALTER (*Into phone*) Hello—Let me talk to Willy Harris.

MAMA You better get over there behind the bureau. I seen one
marching out of there like Napoleon yesterday.

WALTER Hello, Willy? It ain't come yet. It'll be here in a few
minutes. Did the lawyer give you the papers?

BENEATHA There's really only one way to get rid of them, Mama—

MAMA How?

BENEATHA Set fire to this building.

WALTER Good. Good. I'll be right over.

BENEATHA Where did Ruth go, Walter?

WALTER I don't know.
(*He exits abruptly*)

BENEATHA Mama, where did Ruth go?

MAMA (*Looking at her with meaning*) To the doctor, I think.

BENEATHA The doctor? What's the matter? (*They exchange
glances*) You don't think—

MAMA (*With her sense of drama*) Now I ain't saying what I think. But I ain't never been wrong 'bout a woman neither.

(*The phone rings*)

BENEATHA (*At the phone*) Hay-lo . . . (*Pause, and a moment of recognition*) Well—when did you get back! . . . And how was it? . . . Of course I've missed you—in my way . . . This morning? No . . . house cleaning and all that and Mama hates it if I let people come over when the house is like this . . . You *have?* Well, that's different . . . What is it— Oh, what the hell, come on over . . . Right, see you then.

(*She hangs up*)

MAMA (*Who has listened vigorously, as is her habit*) Who is that you inviting over here with this house looking like this? You ain't got the pride you was born with!

BENEATHA Asagai doesn't care how houses look, Mama—he's an intellectual.

MAMA Who?

BENEATHA Asagai—Joseph Asagai. He's an African boy I met on campus. He's been studying in Canada all summer.

MAMA What's his name?

BENEATHA Asagai, Joseph. Ah-sah-guy . . . He's from Nigeria.

MAMA Oh, that's the little country that was founded by slaves way back . . .

BENEATHA No, Mama—that's Liberia.

MAMA I don't think I never met no African before.

BENEATHA Well, do me a favor and don't ask him a whole lot of ignorant questions about Africans. I mean, do they wear clothes and all that—

MAMA Well, now, I guess if you think we so ignorant 'round here maybe you shouldn't bring your friends here—

BENEATHA It's just that people ask such crazy things. All anyone seems to know about when it comes to Africa is Tarzan—

MAMA (*Indignantly*) Why should I know anything about Africa?

BENEATHA Why do you give money at church for the missionary work?

MAMA Well, that's to help save people.

BENEATHA You mean save them from *heathenism*—

MAMA (*Innocently*) Yes.

BENEATHA I'm afraid they need more salvation from the British and the French.

(RUTH *comes in forlornly and pulls off her coat with dejection. They both turn to look at her*)

RUTH (*Dispiritedly*) Well, I guess from all the happy faces—everybody knows.

BENEATHA You pregnant?

MAMA Lord have mercy, I sure hope it's a little old girl. Travis ought to have a sister.

(BENEATHA *and* RUTH *give her a hopeless look for this grandmotherly enthusiasm*)

BENEATHA How far along are you?

RUTH Two months.

BENEATHA Did you mean to? I mean did you plan it or was it an accident?

MAMA What do you know about planning or not planning?

BENEATHA Oh, Mama.

RUTH (*Wearily*) She's twenty years old, Lena.

BENEATHA Did you plan it, Ruth?

RUTH Mind your own business.

BENEATHA It is my business—where is he going to live, on the *roof?* (*There is silence following the remark as the three women react to the sense of it*) Gee—I didn't mean that, Ruth, honest. Gee, I don't feel like that at all. I—I think it is wonderful.

RUTH (*Dully*) Wonderful.

BENEATHA Yes—really.

MAMA (*Looking at* RUTH, *worried*) Doctor say everything going to be all right?

RUTH (*Far away*) Yes—she says everything is going to be fine . . .

MAMA (*Immediately suspicious*) "She"— What doctor you went to?

(RUTH *folds over, near hysteria*)

MAMA (*Worriedly hovering over* RUTH) Ruth honey—what's the matter with you—you sick?

(RUTH *has her fists clenched on her thighs and is fighting hard to suppress a scream that seems to be rising in her*)

BENEATHA What's the matter with her, Mama?

MAMA (*Working her fingers in* RUTH's *shoulder to relax her*) She be all right. Women gets right depressed sometimes when they get her way. (*Speaking softly, expertly, rapidly*) Now you just relax. That's right . . . just lean back, don't think 'bout nothing at all . . . nothing at all—

RUTH I'm all right . . .

(*The glassy-eyed look melts and then she collapses into a fit of heavy sobbing. The bell rings*)

BENEATHA Oh, my God—that must be Asagai.

MAMA (*To* RUTH) Come on now, honey. You need to lie down and rest awhile . . . then have some nice hot food.

(*They exit,* RUTH's *weight on her mother-in-law.* BENEATHA, *herself profoundly disturbed, opens the door to admit a rather dramatic-looking young man with a large package*)

ASAGAI Hello, Alaiyo—

BENEATHA (*Holding the door open and regarding him with pleasure*) Hello . . . (*Long pause*) Well—come in. And please excuse everything. My mother was very upset about my letting anyone come here with the place like this.

ASAGAI (*Coming into the room*) You look disturbed too . . . Is something wrong?

BENEATHA (*Still at the door, absently*) Yes . . . we've all got acute ghetto-itus. (*She smiles and comes toward him, finding a cigarette and sitting*) So—sit down! How was Canada?

ASAGAI (*A sophisticate*) Canadian.

BENEATHA (*Looking at him*) I'm very glad you are back.

ASAGAI (*Looking back at her in turn*) Are you really?

BENEATHA Yes—very.

ASAGAI Why—you were quite glad when I went away. What happened?

BENEATHA You went away.

ASAGAI Ahhhhhhhh.

BENEATHA Before—you wanted to be so serious before there was time.

ASAGAI How much time must there be before one knows what one feels?

BENEATHA (*Stalling this particular conversation. Her hands pressed toegther, in a deliberately childish gesture*) What did you bring me?

ASAGAI (*Handing her the package*) Open it and see.

BENEATHA (*Eagerly opening the package and drawing out some records and the colorful robes of a Nigerian woman*) Oh, Asagai! . . . You got them for me! . . . How beautiful . . . and the records too! (*She lifts out the robes and runs to the mirror with them and holds the drapery up in front of herself*)

ASAGAI (*Coming to her at the mirror*) I shall have to teach you how to drape it properly. (*He flings the material about her for

the moment and stands back to look at her) Ah—*Oh-pay-gay-day,*
oh-gbah-mu-shay. (*A Yoruba exclamation for admiration*) You
wear it well . . . very well . . . mutilated hair and all.

BENEATHA (*Turning suddenly*) My hair—what's wrong with my
hair?

ASAGAI (*Shrugging*) Were you born with it like that?

BENEATHA (*Reaching up to touch it*) No . . . of course not.
(*She looks back to the mirror, disturbed*)

ASAGAI (*Smiling*) How then?

BENEATHA You know perfectly well how . . . as crinkly as yours
. . . that's how.

ASAGAI And it is ugly to you that way?

BENEATHA (*Quickly*) Oh, no—not ugly . . . (*More slowly, apologetically*) But it's so hard to manage when it's, well—raw.

ASAGAI And so to accommodate that—you mutilate it every
week?

BENEATHA It's not mutilation!

ASAGAI (*Laughing aloud at her seriousness*) Oh . . . please! I am
only teasing you because you are so very serious about these
things. (*He stands back from her and folds his arms across his
chest as he watches her pulling at her hair and frowning in the
mirror*) Do you remember the first time you met me at school?
. . . (*He laughs*) You came up to me and you said—and I thought
you were the most serious little thing I had ever seen—you said:
(*He imitates her*) "Mr. Asagai—I want very much to talk with
you. About Africa. You see, Mr. Asagai, I am looking for my
identity!"
(*He laughs*)

BENEATHA (*Turning to him, not laughing*) Yes—
(*Her face is quizzical, profoundly disturbed*)

ASAGAI (*Still teasing and reaching out and taking her face in his
hands and turning her profile to him*) Well . . . it is true that
this is not so much a profile of a Hollywood queen as perhaps
a queen of the Nile—(*A mock dismissal of the importance of the
question*) But what does it matter? Assimilationism is so popular
in your country.

BENEATHA (*Wheeling, passionately, sharply*) I am not an assimilationist!

ASAGAI (*The protest hangs in the room for a moment and* ASAGAI
studies her, his laughter fading) Such a serious one. (*There is*

a pause) So—you like the robes? You must take excellent care of them—they are from my sister's personal wardrobe.

BENEATHA (*With incredulity*) You—you sent all the way home—for me?

ASAGAI (*With charm*) For you—I would do much more . . . Well, that is what I came for. I must go.

BENEATHA Will you call me Monday?

ASAGAI Yes . . . We have a great deal to talk about. I mean about identity and time and all that.

BENEATHA Time?

ASAGAI Yes. About how much time one needs to know what one feels.

BENEATHA You never understood that there is more than one kind of feeling which can exist between a man and a woman—or, at least, there should be.

ASAGAI (*Shaking his head negatively but gently*) No. Between a man and a woman there need be only one kind of feeling. I have that for you . . . Now even . . . right this moment . . .

BENEATHA I know—and by itself—it won't do. I can find that anywhere.

ASAGAI For a woman it should be enough.

BENEATHA I know—because that's what it says in all the novels that men write. But it isn't. Go ahead and laugh—but I'm not interested in being someone's little episode in America or—(*With feminine vengeance*)—one of them! (ASAGAI *has burst into laughter again*) That's funny as hell, huh!

ASAGAI It's just that every American girl I have known has said that to me. White—black—in this you are all the same. And the same speech, too!

BENEATHA (*Angrily*) Yuk, yuk, yuk!

ASAGAI It's how you can be sure that the world's most liberated women are not liberated at all. You all talk about it too much!

(MAMA *enters and is immediately all social charm because of the presence of a guest*)

BENEATHA Oh—Mama—this is Mr. Asagai.

MAMA How do you do?

ASAGAI (*Total politeness to an elder*) How do you do, Mrs. Younger. Please forgive me for coming at such an outrageous hour on a Saturday.

MAMA Well, you are quite welcome. I just hope you understand that our house don't always look like this. (*Chatterish*) You must come again. I would love to hear all about—(*Not sure of the name*)—your country. I think it's so sad the way our American Negroes don't know nothing about Africa 'cept Tarzan and all that. And all that money they pour into these churches when they ought to be helping you people over there drive out them French and Englishmen done taken away your land.

(*The mother flashes a slightly superior look at her daughter upon completion of the recitation*)

ASAGAI (*Taken aback by this sudden and acutely unrelated expression of sympathy*)   Yes . . . yes . . .

MAMA (*Smiling at him suddenly and relaxing and looking him over*)   How many miles is it from here to where you come from?

ASAGAI   Many thousands.

MAMA (*Looking at him as she would* WALTER)   I bet you don't half look after yourself, being away from your mama either. I spec you better come 'round here from time to time and get yourself some decent home-cooked meals . . .

ASAGAI (*Moved*)   Thank you. Thank you very much. (*They are all quiet, then—*) Well . . . I must go. I will call you Monday, Alaiyo.

MAMA   What's that he call you?

ASAGAI   Oh—"Alaiyo." I hope you don't mind. It is what you would call a nickname, I think. It is a Yoruba word. I am a Yoruba.

MAMA (*Looking at* BENEATHA)   I—I thought he was from—

ASAGAI (*Understanding*)   Nigeria is my country. Yoruba is my tribal origin—

BENEATHA   You didn't tell us what Alaiyo means . . . for all I know, you might be calling me Little Idiot or something . . .

ASAGAI   Well . . . let me see . . . I do not know how just to explain it . . . The sense of a thing can be so different when it changes languages.

BENEATHA   You're evading.

ASAGAI   No—really it is difficult . . . (*Thinking*) It means . . . it means One for Whom Bread—Food—Is Not Enough. (*He looks at her*) Is that all right?

BENEATHA (*Understanding, softly*)   Thank you.

MAMA (*Looking from one to the other and not understanding any of it*)   Well . . . that's nice . . . You must come see us again— Mr.—

ASAGAI   Ah-sah-guy . . .

MAMA   Yes . . . Do come again.

ASAGAI   Good-bye.
   (*He exits*)
MAMA   (*After him*)   Lord, that's a pretty thing just went out here!
   (*Insinuatingly, to her daughter*)   Yes, I guess I see why we done
   commence to get so interested in Africa 'round here. Missionaries
   my aunt Jenny!
   (*She exits*)
BENEATHA   Oh, Mama! . . .
   (*She picks up the Nigerian dress and holds it up to her in front
   of the mirror again. She sets the headdress on haphazardly and
   then notices her hair again and clutches at it and then replaces
   the headdress and frowns at herself. Then she starts to wriggle
   in front of the mirror as she thinks a Nigerian woman might.* TRAVIS
   enters and regards her)
TRAVIS   You cracking up?
BENEATHA   Shut up.
   (*She pulls the headdress off and looks at herself in the mirror
   and clutches at her hair again and squinches her eyes as if trying
   to imagine something. Then, suddenly, she gets her raincoat and
   kerchief and hurriedly prepares for going out*)
MAMA   (*Coming back into the room*)   She's resting now. Travis,
   baby, run next door and ask Miss Johnson to please let me have
   a little kitchen cleanser. This here can is empty as Jacob's kettle.
TRAVIS   I just came in.
MAMA   Do as you told. (*He exits and she looks at her daughter*)
   Where you going?
BENEATHA   (*Halting at the door*)   To become a queen of the Nile!
   (*She exits in a breathless blaze of glory.* RUTH *appears in the bed-
   room doorway*)
MAMA   Who told you to get up?
RUTH   Ain't nothing wrong with me to be lying in no bed for. Where
   did Bennie go?
MAMA   (*Drumming her fingers*)   Far as I could make out—to Egypt.
   (RUTH *just looks at her*) What time is it getting to?
RUTH   Ten twenty. And the mailman going to ring that bell this
   morning just like he done every morning for the last umpteen
   years.
   (TRAVIS *comes in with the cleanser can*)
TRAVIS   She say to tell you that she don't have much.
MAMA   (*Angrily*)   Lord, some people I could name sure is tight-
   fisted! (*Directing her grandson*) Mark two cans of cleanser down

on the list there. If she that hard up for kitchen cleanser, I sure don't want to forget to get her none!

RUTH Lena—maybe the woman is just short on cleanser—

MAMA (*Not listening*) —Much baking powder as she done borrowed from me all these years, she could of done gone into the baking business!

(*The bell sounds suddenly and sharply and all three are stunned —serious and silent—mid-speech. In spite of all the other conversations and distractions of the morning, this is what they have been waiting for, even* TRAVIS, *who looks helplessly from his mother to his grandmother.* RUTH *is the first to come to life again*)

RUTH (*To* TRAVIS) Get down them steps, boy!

(TRAVIS *snaps to life and flies out to get the mail*)

MAMA (*Her eyes wide, her hand to her breast*) You mean it done really come?

RUTH (*Excited*) Oh, Miss Lena!

MAMA (*Collecting herself*) Well . . . I don't know what we all so excited about 'round here for. We known it was coming for months.

RUTH That's a whole lot different from having it come and being able to hold it in your hands . . . a piece of paper worth ten thousand dollars . . . (TRAVIS *bursts back into the room. He holds the envelope high above his head, like a little dancer, his face is radiant and he is breathless. He moves to his grandmother with sudden slow ceremony and puts the envelope into her hands. She accepts it, and then merely holds it and looks at it*) Come on! Open it . . . Lord have mercy, I wish Walter Lee was here!

TRAVIS Open it, Grandmama!

MAMA (*Staring at it*) Now you all be quiet. It's just a check.

RUTH Open it . . .

MAMA (*Still staring at it*) Now don't act silly . . . We ain't never been no people to act silly 'bout no money—

RUTH (*Swiftly*) We ain't never had none before—*open it!*

(MAMA *finally makes a good strong tear and pulls out the thin blue slice of paper and inspects it closely. The boy and his mother study it raptly over* MAMA's *shoulders*)

MAMA Travis! (*She is counting off with doubt*) Is that the right number of zeros.

TRAVIS Yes'm . . . ten thousand dollars. Gaalee, Grandmama, you rich.

MAMA (*She holds the check away from her, still looking at it. Slowly her face sobers into a mask of unhappiness*) Ten thousand dollars. (*She hands it to* RUTH) Put it away somewhere, Ruth. (*She does not look at* RUTH; *her eyes seem to be seeing something somewhere very far off*) Ten thousand dollars they give you. Ten thousand dollars.

TRAVIS (*To his mother, sincerely*) What's the matter with Grandmama—don't she want to be rich?

RUTH (*Distractedly*) You go on out and play now, baby. (TRAVIS *exits.* MAMA *starts wiping dishes absently, humming intently to herself.* RUTH *turns to her, with kind exasperation*) You've gone and got yourself upset.

MAMA (*Not looking at her*) I spec if it wasn't for you all . . . I would just put that money away or give it to the church or something.

RUTH Now what kind of talk is that. Mr. Younger would just be plain mad if he could hear you talking foolish like that.

MAMA (*Stopping and staring off*) Yes . . . he sure would. (*Sighing*) We got enough to do with that money, all right. (*She halts then, and turns and looks at her daughter-in-law hard;* RUTH *avoids her eyes and* MAMA *wipes her hands with finality and starts to speak firmly to* RUTH) Where did you go today, girl?

RUTH To the doctor.

MAMA (*Impatiently*) Now, Ruth . . . you know better than that. Old Doctor Jones is strange enough in his way but there ain't nothing 'bout him make somebody slip and call him "she"—like you done this morning.

RUTH Well, that's what happened—my tongue slipped.

MAMA You went to see that woman, didn't you?

RUTH (*Defensively, giving herself away*) What woman you talking about?

MAMA (*Angrily*) That woman who—
(WALTER *enters in great excitement*)

WALTER Did it come?

MAMA (*Quietly*) Can't you give people a Christian greeting before you start asking about money?

WALTER (*To* RUTH) Did it come? (RUTH *unfolds the check and lays it quietly before him, watching him intently with thoughts of her own.* WALTER *sits down and grasps it close and counts off the zeros*) Ten thousand dollars—(*He turns suddenly, frantically to his mother and draws some papers out of his breast pocket*) Mama —look. Old Willy Harris put everything on paper—

MAMA   Son—I think you ought to talk to your wife . . . I'll go on out and leave you alone if you want—

WALTER   I can talk to her later— Mama, look—

MAMA   Son—

WALTER   WILL SOMEBODY PLEASE LISTEN TO ME TODAY!

MAMA   (*Quietly*) I don't 'low no yellin' in this house, Walter Lee, and you know it—(WALTER *stares at them in frustration and starts to speak several times*) And there ain't going to be no investing in no liquor stores. I don't aim to have to speak on that again.

(*A long pause*)

WALTER   Oh—so you don't aim to have to speak on that again? So *you* have decided . . . (*Crumpling his papers*) Well, *you* tell that to my boy tonight when you put him to sleep on the living-room couch . . . (*Turning to* MAMA *and speaking directly to her*) Yeah —and tell it to my wife, Mama, tomorrow when she has to go out of here to look after somebody else's kids. And tell it to *me*, Mama, every time we need a new pair of curtains and I have to watch *you* go out and work in somebody's kitchen. Yeah, you tell me then!

(WALTER *starts out*)

RUTH   Where you going?

WALTER   I'm going out!

RUTH   Where?

WALTER   Just out of this house somewhere—

RUTH   (*Getting her coat*) I'll come too.

WALTER   I don't want you to come!

RUTH   I got something to talk to you about, Walter.

WALTER   That's too bad.

MAMA   (*Still quietly*) Walter Lee—(*She waits and he finally turns and looks at her*) Sit down.

WALTER   I'm a grown man, Mama.

MAMA   Ain't nobody said you wasn't grown. But you still in my house and my presence. And as long as you are—you'll talk to your wife civil. Now sit down.

RUTH   (*Suddenly*) Oh, let him go on out and drink himself to death! He makes me sick to my stomach!

(*She flings her coat against him*)

WALTER   (*Violently*) And you turn mine too, baby! (RUTH *goes into their bedroom and slams the door behind her*) That was my greatest mistake—

MAMA   (*Still quietly*) Walter, what is the matter with you?

WALTER Matter with me? Ain't nothing the matter with *me!*

MAMA Yes there is. Something eating you up like a crazy man. Something more than me not giving you this money. The past few years I been watching it happen to you. You get all nervous acting and kind of wild in the eyes—(WALTER *jumps up impatiently at her words*) I said sit there now, I'm talking to you!

WALTER Mama—I don't need no nagging at me today.

MAMA Seem like you getting to a place where you always tied up in some kind of knot about something. But if anybody ask you 'bout it you just yell at 'em and bust out the house and go out and drink somewheres. Walter Lee, people can't live with that. Ruth's a good, patient girl in her way—but you getting to be too much. Boy, don't make the mistake of driving that girl away from you.

WALTER Why—what she do for me?

MAMA She loves you.

WALTER Mama—I'm going out. I want to go off somewhere and be by myself for a while.

MAMA I'm sorry 'bout your liquor store, son. It just wasn't the thing for us to do. That's what I want to tell you about—

WALTER I got to go out, Mama— (*He rises*)

MAMA It's dangerous, son.

WALTER What's dangerous?

MAMA When a man goes outside his home to look for peace.

WALTER (*Beseechingly*) Then why can't there never be no peace in this house then?

MAMA You done found it in some other house?

WALTER No—there ain't no woman! Why do women always think there's a woman somewhere when a man gets restless. (*Coming to her*) Mama—Mama—I want so many things . . .

MAMA Yes, son—

WALTER I want so many things that they are driving me kind of crazy . . . Mama—look at me.

MAMA I'm looking at you. You a good-looking boy. You got a job, a nice wife, a fine boy and—

WALTER A job. (*Looks at her*) Mama, a job? I open and close car doors all day long. I drive a man around in his limousine and I say, "Yes, sir; no, sir; very good, sir; shall I take the Drive, sir?" Mama, that ain't no kind of job . . . that ain't nothing at all. (*Very quietly*) Mama, I don't know if I can make you understand.

MAMA Understand what, baby?

WALTER (*Quietly*) Sometimes it's like I can see the future stretched out in front of me—just plain as day. The future, Mama. Hanging over there at the edge of my days. Just waiting for me— a big, looming blank space—full of *nothing*. Just waiting for *me*. (*Pause*) Mama—sometimes when I'm downtown and I pass them cool, quiet-looking restaurants where them white boys are sitting back and talking 'bout things . . . sitting there turning deals worth millions of dollars . . . sometimes I see guys don't look much older than me—

MAMA   Son—how come you talk so much 'bout money?

WALTER (*With immense passion*)   Because it is life, Mama!

MAMA (*Quietly*)   Oh—(*Very quietly*) So now it's life. Money is life. Once upon a time freedom used to be life—now it's money. I guess the world really do change . . .

WALTER   No—it was always money, Mama. We just didn't know about it.

MAMA   No . . . something has changed. (*She looks at him*) You something new, boy. In my time we was worried about not being lynched and getting to the North if we could and how to stay alive and still have a pinch of dignity too . . . Now here come you and Beneatha—talking 'bout things we ain't never even thought about hardly, me and your daddy. You ain't satisfied or proud of nothing we done. I mean that you had a home; that we kept you out of trouble till you was grown; that you don't have to ride to work on the back of nobody's streetcar— You my children —but how different we done become.

WALTER   You just don't understand, Mama, you just don't understand.

MAMA   Son—do you know your wife is expecting another baby? (WALTER *stands, stunned, and absorbs what his mother has said*) That's what she wanted to talk to you about. (WALTER *sinks down into a chair*) This ain't for me to be telling—but you ought to know. (*She waits*) I think Ruth is thinking 'bout getting rid of that child.

WALTER (*Slowly understanding*)   No—no—Ruth wouldn't do that.

MAMA   When the world gets ugly enough—a woman will do anything for her family. *The part that's already living.*

WALTER   You don't know Ruth, Mama, if you think she would do that.

(RUTH *opens the bedroom door and stands there a little limp*)

RUTH (*Beaten*) Yes I would too, Walter. (*Pause*) I gave her a five-dollar down payment.

(*There is total silence as the man stares at his wife and the mother stares at her son*)

MAMA (*Presently*) Well—(*Tightly*) Well—son, I'm waiting to hear you say something . . . I'm waiting to hear how you be your father's son. Be the man he was . . . (*Pause*) Your wife say she going to destroy your child. And I'm waiting to hear you talk like him and say we a people who give children life, not who destroys them—(*She rises*) I'm waiting to see you stand up and look like your daddy and say we done give up one baby to poverty and that we ain't going to give up nary another one . . . I'm waiting.

WALTER Ruth—

MAMA If you a son of mine, tell her! (WALTER *turns, looks at her and can say nothing. She continues, bitterly*) You . . . you are a disgrace to your father's memory. Somebody get me my hat.

Curtain

ACT TWO

SCENE 1

Time: Later the same day.

At rise: RUTH *is ironing again. She has the radio going. Presently* BENEATHA's *bedroom door opens and* RUTH's *mouth falls and she puts down the iron in fascination.*

RUTH   What have we got on tonight!

BENEATHA   (*Emerging grandly from the doorway so that we can see her thoroughly robed in the costume Asagai brought*)   You are looking at what a well-dressed Nigerian woman wears—(*She parades for* RUTH, *her hair completely hidden by the headdress; she is coquettishly fanning herself with an ornate oriental fan, mistakenly more like Butterfly than any Nigerian that ever was*) Isn't it beautiful? (*She promenades to the radio and, with an arrogant flourish, turns off the good loud blues that is playing*) Enough of this assimilationist junk! (*RUTH follows her with her eyes as she goes to the phonograph and puts on a record and turns and waits ceremoniously for the music to come up. Then, with a shout—*) OCOMOGOSIAY!

(*RUTH jumps. The music comes up, a lovely Nigerian melody.* BENEATHA *listens, enraptured, her eyes far away—"back to the past." She begins to dance.* RUTH *is dumfounded*)

RUTH   What kind of dance is that?

BENEATHA   A folk dance.

RUTH (*Pearl Bailey*)   What kind of folks do that, honey?

BENEATHA   It's from Nigeria. It's a dance of welcome.

RUTH   Who you welcoming?

BENEATHA   The men back to the village.

RUTH   Where they been?

BENEATHA   How should I know—out hunting or something. Anyway, they are coming back now . . .

RUTH   Well, that's good.

BENEATHA   (*With the record*)

Alundi, alundi
Alundi alunya
Jop pu a jeepua
Ang gu sooooooooooo

Ai yai yae . . .
Ayehaye—alundi . . .

(WALTER *comes in during this performance; he has obviously been drinking. He leans against the door heavily and watches his sister, at first with distaste. Then his eyes look off—"back to the past"—as he lifts both his fists to the roof, screaming*)

WALTER   YEAH . . . AND ETHIOPIA STRETCH FORTH HER HANDS AGAIN! . . .

RUTH   (*Drily, looking at him*)   Yes—and Africa sure is claiming her own tonight.

(*She gives them both up and starts ironing again*)

WALTER   (*All in a drunken, dramatic shout*)   Shut up! . . . I'm digging them drums . . . them drums move me! . . . (*He makes his weaving way to his wife's face and leans in close to her*)   In my heart of hearts—(*He thumps his chest*)—I am much warrior!

RUTH   (*Without even looking up*)   In your heart of hearts you are much drunkard.

WALTER   (*Coming away from her and starting to wander around the room, shouting*)   Me and Jomo . . . (*Intently, in his sister's face. She has stopped dancing to watch him in this unknown mood*)   That's my man, Kenyatta. (*Shouting and thumping his chest*)   FLAMING SPEAR! HOT DAMN! (*He is suddenly in possession of an imaginary spear and actively spearing enemies all over the room*)   OCOMOGOSIAY . . . THE LION IS WAKING . . . OWIMOWEH! (*He pulls his shirt open and leaps up on a table and gestures with his spear. The bell rings.* RUTH *goes to answer*)

BENEATHA   (*To encourage* WALTER, *thoroughly caught up with this side of him*)   OCOMOGOSIAY, FLAMING SPEAR!

WALTER   (*On the table, very far gone, his eyes pure glass sheets. He sees what we cannot, that he is a leader of his people, a great chief, a descendant of Chaka, and that the hour to march has come*)   Listen, my black brothers—

BENEATHA   OCOMOGOSIAY!

WALTER   —Do you hear the waters rushing against the shores of the coastlands—

BENEATHA   OCOMOGOSIAY!

WALTER   —Do you hear the screeching of the cocks in yonder hills beyond where the chiefs meet in council for the coming of the mighty war—

BENEATHA   OCOMOGOSIAY!

WALTER   —Do you hear the beating of the wings of the birds flying low over the mountains and the low places of our land—

(RUTH *opens the door.* GEORGE MURCHISON *enters*)

BENEATHA   OCOMOGOSIAY!

WALTER   —Do you hear the singing of the women, singing the war songs of our fathers to the babies in the great houses . . . singing the sweet war songs? OH, DO YOU HEAR, MY BLACK BROTHERS!

BENEATHA (*Completely gone*)   We hear you, Flaming Spear—

WALTER   Telling us to prepare for the greatness of the time— (*To* GEORGE) Black Brother!

(*He extends his hand for the fraternal clasp*)

GEORGE   Black Brother, hell!

RUTH (*Having had enough, and embarrassed for the family*)   Beneatha, you got company—what's the matter with you? Walter Lee Younger, get down off that table and stop acting like a fool . . .

(WALTER *comes down off the table suddenly and makes a quick exit to the bathroom*)

RUTH   He's had a little to drink . . . I don't know what her excuse is.

GEORGE (*To* BENEATHA)   Look honey, we're going *to* the theatre—we're not going to be *in* it . . . so go change, huh?

RUTH   You expect this boy to go out with you looking like that?

BENEATHA (*Looking at* GEORGE)   That's up to George. If he's ashamed of his heritage—

GEORGE   Oh, don't be so proud of yourself, Bennie—just because you look eccentric.

BENEATHA   How can something that's natural be eccentric?

GEORGE   That's what being eccentric means—being natural. Get dressed.

BENEATHA I don't like that, George.

RUTH Why must you and your brother make an argument out of everything people say?

BENEATHA Because I hate assimilationist Negroes!

RUTH Will somebody please tell me what assimila-whoever means!

GEORGE Oh, it's just a college girl's way of calling people Uncle Toms—but that isn't what it means at all.

RUTH Well, what does it mean?

BENEATHA (*Cutting* GEORGE *off and staring at him as she replies to* RUTH) It means someone who is willing to give up his own culture and submerge himself completely in the dominant, and in this case, *oppressive* culture!

GEORGE Oh, dear, dear, dear! Here we go! A lecture on the African past! On our Great West African Heritage! In one second we will hear all about the great Ashanti empires; the great Songhay civilizations; and the great sculpture of Bénin—and then some poetry in the Bantu—and the whole monologue will end with the word *heritage!* (*Nastily*) Let's face it, baby, your heritage is nothing but a bunch of raggedy-assed spirituals and some grass huts!

BENEATHA *Grass huts!* (RUTH *crosses to her and forcibly pushes her toward the bedroom*) See there . . . you are standing there in your splendid ignorance talking about people who were the first to smelt iron on the face of the earth! (RUTH *is pushing her through the door*) The Ashanti were performing surgical operations when the English—(RUTH *pulls the door to, with* BENEATHA *on the other side, and smiles graciously at* GEORGE. BENEATHA *opens the door and shouts the end of the sentence defiantly at* GEORGE) —were still tattooing themselves with blue dragons . . . (*She goes back inside*)

RUTH Have a seat, George. (*They both sit.* RUTH *folds her hands rather primly on her lap, determined to demonstrate the civilization of the family*) Warm, ain't it? I mean for September. (*Pause*) Just like they always say about Chicago weather: If it's too hot or cold for you, just wait a minute and it'll change. (*She smiles happily at this cliché of clichés*) Everybody say it's got to do with them bombs and things they keep setting off. (*Pause*) Would you like a nice cold beer?

GEORGE No, thank you. I don't care for beer. (*He looks at his watch*) I hope she hurries up.

RUTH What time is the show?

GEORGE   It's an eight-thirty curtain. That's just Chicago, though. In New York standard curtain time is eight forty.

(*He is rather proud of this knowledge*)

RUTH (*Properly appreciating it*)   You get to New York a lot?

GEORGE (*Offhand*)   Few times a year.

RUTH   Oh—that's nice. I've never been to New York.

(WALTER *enters. We feel he has relieved himself, but the edge of unreality is still with him*)

WALTER   New York ain't got nothing Chicago ain't. Just a bunch of hustling people all squeezed up together—being "Eastern."

(*He turns his face into a screw of displeasure*)

GEORGE   Oh—you've been?

WALTER   *Plenty* of times.

RUTH (*Shocked at the lie*)   Walter Lee Younger!

WALTER (*Staring her down*)   Plenty! (*Pause*) What we got to drink in this house? Why don't you offer this man some refreshment. (*To* GEORGE) They don't know how to entertain people in this house, man.

GEORGE   Thank you—I don't really care for anything.

WALTER (*Feeling his head; sobriety coming*)   Where's Mama?

RUTH   She ain't come back yet.

WALTER (*Looking* MURCHISON *over from head to toe, scrutinizing his carefully casual tweed sports jacket over cashmere V-neck sweater over soft eyelet shirt and tie, and soft slacks, finished off with white buckskin shoes*) Why all you college boys wear them fairyish-looking white shoes?

RUTH   Walter Lee!

(GEORGE MURCHISON *ignores the remark*)

WALTER (*To* RUTH)   Well, they look crazy as hell—white shoes, cold as it is.

RUTH (*Crushed*)   You have to excuse him—

WALTER   No he don't! Excuse me for what? What you always excusing me for! I'll excuse myself when I needs to be excused! (*A pause*) They look as funny as them black knee socks Beneatha wears out of here all the time.

RUTH   It's the college *style*, Walter.

WALTER   Style, hell. She looks like she got burnt legs or something!

RUTH   Oh, Walter—

WALTER (*An irritable mimic*)   Oh, Walter! Oh, Walter! (*To* MURCHISON) How's your old man making out? I understand you all going to buy that big hotel on the Drive? (*He finds a beer in* the refrigerator, *wanders over to* MURCHISON, *sipping and wiping his lips with the back of his hand, and straddling a chair backwards to talk to the other man*) Shrewd move. Your old man is all right, man. (*Tapping his head and half winking for emphasis*) I mean he knows how to operate. I mean he thinks *big*, you know what I mean, I mean for a *home*, you know? But I think he's kind of running out of ideas now. I'd like to talk to him. Listen, man, I got some plans that could turn this city upside down. I mean I think like he does. *Big.* Invest big, gamble big, hell, lose *big* if you have to, you know what I mean. It's hard to find a man on this whole Southside who understands my kind of thinking—you dig? (*He scrutinizes* MURCHISON *again, drinks his beer, squints his eyes and leans in close, confidential, man to man*) Me and you ought to sit down and talk sometimes, man. Man, I got me some ideas . . .

MURCHISON (*With boredom*) Yeah—sometimes we'll have to do that, Walter.

WALTER (*Understanding the indifference, and offended*) Yeah—well, when you get the time, man. I know you a busy little boy.

RUTH Walter, please—

WALTER (*Bitterly, hurt*) I know ain't nothing in this world as busy as you colored college boys with your fraternity pins and white shoes . . .

RUTH (*Covering her face with humiliation*) Oh, Walter Lee—

WALTER I see you all all the time—with the books tucked under your arms—going to your (*British A—a mimic*) "clahsses." And for what! What the hell you learning over there? Filling up your heads—(*Counting off on his fingers*)—with the sociology and the psychology—but they teaching you how to be a man? How to take over and run the world? They teaching you how to run a rubber plantation or a steel mill? Naw—just to talk proper and read books and wear white shoes . . .

GEORGE (*Looking at him with distaste, a little above it all*) You're all wacked up with bitterness, man.

WALTER (*Intently, almost quietly, between the teeth, glaring at the boy*) And you—ain't you bitter, man? Ain't you just about had it yet? Don't you see no stars gleaming that you can't reach out and grab? You happy?—you contented son-of-a-bitch—you happy? You got it made? Bitter? Man, I'm a volcano. Bitter? Here I am a giant—surrounded by ants! Ants who can't even understand what it is the giant is talking about.

RUTH (*Passionately and suddenly*)   Oh, Walter—ain't you with no-body!

WALTER (*Violently*)   No! 'Cause ain't nobody with me! Not even my own mother!

RUTH   Walter, that's a terrible thing to say!

(BENEATHA *enters, dressed for the evening in a cocktail dress and earrings*)

GEORGE   Well—hey, you look great.

BENEATHA   Let's go, George. See you all later.

RUTH   Have a nice time.

GEORGE   Thanks. Good night. (*To* WALTER, *sarcastically*) Good night, *Prometheus.*

(BENEATHA *and* GEORGE *exit*)

WALTER (*To* RUTH)   Who is Prometheus?

RUTH   I don't know. Don't worry about it.

WALTER (*In fury, pointing after* GEORGE)   See there—they get to a point where they can't insult you man to man—they got to go talk about something ain't nobody never heard of!

RUTH   How you know it was an insult? (*To humor him*) Maybe Prometheus is a nice fellow.

WALTER   Prometheus! I bet there ain't even no such thing! I bet that simple-minded clown—

RUTH   Walter—

(*She stops what she is doing and looks at him*)

WALTER (*Yelling*)   Don't start!

RUTH   Start what?

WALTER   Your nagging! Where was I? Who was I with? How much money did I spend?

RUTH (*Plaintively*)   Walter Lee—why don't we just try to talk about it . . .

WALTER (*Not listening*)   I been out talking with people who understand me. People who care about the things I got on my mind.

RUTH (*Wearily*)   I guess that means people like Willy Harris.

WALTER   Yes, people like Willy Harris.

RUTH (*With a sudden flash of impatience*)   Why don't you all just hurry up and go into the banking business and stop talking about it!

WALTER   Why? You want to know why? 'Cause we all tied up in a race of people that don't know how to do nothing but moan, pray and have babies!

(*The line is too bitter even for him and he looks at her and sits down*)

RUTH Oh, Walter . . . (*Softly*) Honey, why can't you stop fighting me?

WALTER (*Without thinking*) Who's fighting you? Who even cares about you?

(*This line begins the retardation of his mood*)

RUTH Well—(*She waits a long time, and then with resignation starts to put away her things*) I guess I might as well go on to bed . . . (*More or less to herself*) I don't know where we lost it . . . but we have . . . (*Then, to him*) I—I'm sorry about this new baby, Walter. I guess maybe I better go on and do what I started . . . I guess I just didn't realize how bad things was with us . . . I guess I just didn't really realize—(*She starts out to the bedroom and stops*) You want some hot milk?

WALTER Hot milk?

RUTH Yes—hot milk.

WALTER Why hot milk?

RUTH 'Cause after all that liquor you come home with you ought to have something hot in your stomach.

WALTER I don't want no milk.

RUTH You want some coffee then?

WALTER No, I don't want no coffee. I don't want nothing hot to drink. (*Almost plaintively*) Why you always trying to give me something to eat?

RUTH (*Standing and looking at him helplessly*) What else can I give you, Walter Lee Younger?

(*She stands and looks at him and presently turns to go out again. He lifts his head and watches her going away from him in a new mood which began to emerge when he asked her "Who cares about you?"*)

WALTER It's been rough, ain't it, baby? (*She hears and stops but does not turn around and he continues to her back*) I guess between two people there ain't never as much understood as folks generally thinks there is. I mean like between me and you—(*She turns to face him*) How we gets to the place where we scared to talk softness to each other. (*He waits, thinking hard himself*) Why you think it got to be like that? (*He is thoughtful, almost as a child would be*) Ruth, what is it gets into people ought to be close?

RUTH I don't know, honey. I think about it a lot.

WALTER   On account of you and me, you mean? The way things are with us. The way something done come down between us.

RUTH   There ain't so much between us, Walter . . . Not when you come to me and try to talk to me. Try to be with me . . . a little even.

WALTER   (*Total honesty*) Sometimes . . . sometimes . . . I don't even know how to try.

RUTH   Walter—

WALTER   Yes?

RUTH   (*Coming to him, gently and with misgiving, but coming to him*) Honey . . . life don't have to be like this. I mean sometimes people can do things so that things are better . . . You remember how we used to talk when Travis was born . . . about the way we were going to live . . . the kind of house . . . (*She is stroking his head*) Well, it's all starting to slip away from us . . .

(MAMA *enters, and* WALTER *jumps up and shouts at her*)

WALTER   Mama, where have you been?

MAMA   My—them steps is longer than they used to be. Whew! (*She sits down and ignores him*) How you feeling this evening, Ruth? (RUTH *shrugs, disturbed some at having been prematurely interrupted and watching her husband knowingly*)

WALTER   Mama, where have you been all day?

MAMA   (*Still ignoring him and leaning on the table and changing to more comfortable shoes*) Where's Travis?

RUTH   I let him go out earlier and he ain't come back yet. Boy, is he going to get it!

WALTER   Mama!

MAMA   (*As if she has heard him for the first time*) Yes, son?

WALTER   Where did you go this afternoon?

MAMA   I went downtown to tend to some business that I had to tend to.

WALTER   What kind of business?

MAMA   You know better than to question me like a child, Brother.

WALTER   (*Rising and bending over the table*) Where were you, Mama? (*Bringing his fists down and shouting*) Mama, you didn't go do something with that insurance money, something crazy?

(*The front door opens slowly, interrupting him, and* TRAVIS *peeks his head in, less than hopefully*)

TRAVIS   (*To his mother*) Mama, I—

RUTH   "Mama I" nothing! You're going to get it, boy! Get on in that bedroom and get yourself ready!

TRAVIS   But I—

MAMA   Why don't you all never let the child explain hisself.

RUTH   Keep out of it now, Lena.

(MAMA *clamps her lips together, and* RUTH *advances toward her son menacingly*)

RUTH   A thousand times I have told you not to go off like that—

MAMA   (*Holding out her arms to her grandson*) Well—at least let me tell him something. I want him to be the first one to hear . . . Come here, Travis. (*The boy obeys, gladly*) Travis—(*She takes him by the shoulders and looks into his face*)—you know that money we got in the mail this morning?

TRAVIS   Yes'm—

MAMA   Well—what you think your grandmama gone and done with that money?

TRAVIS   I don't know, Grandmama.

MAMA   (*Putting her finger on his nose for emphasis*) She went out and she bought you a house! (*The explosion comes from* WALTER *at the end of the revelation and he jumps up and turns away from all of them in a fury.* MAMA *continues, to* TRAVIS) You glad about the house? It's going to be yours when you get to be a man.

TRAVIS   Yeah—I always wanted to live in a house.

MAMA   All right, gimme some sugar then—(TRAVIS *puts his arms around her neck as she watches her son over the boy's shoulder. Then, to* TRAVIS, *after the embrace*) Now when you say your prayers tonight, you thank God and your grandfather—'cause it was him who give you the house—in his way.

RUTH   (*Taking the boy from* MAMA *and pushing him toward the bedroom*) Now you get out of here and get ready for your beating.

TRAVIS   Aw, Mama—

RUTH   Get on in there—(*Closing the door behind him and turning radiantly to her mother-in-law*) So you went and did it!

MAMA   (*Quietly, looking at her son with pain*) Yes, I did.

RUTH   (*Raising both arms classically*) *Praise God!* (*Looks at* WALTER *a moment, who says nothing. She crosses rapidly to her husband*) Please, honey—let me be glad . . . you be glad too. (*She has laid her hands on his shoulders, but he shakes himself free of her roughly, without turning to face her*) Oh, Walter . . . a home . . . a home. (*She comes back to* MAMA) Well—where is it? How big is it? How much it going to cost?

MAMA   Well—

RUTH   When we moving?

MAMA (*Smiling at her*)   First of the month.

RUTH (*Throwing back her head with jubilance*)   *Praise God!*

MAMA (*Tentatively, still looking at her son's back turned against her and* RUTH)   It's—it's a nice house too . . . (*She cannot help speaking directly to him. An imploring quality in her voice, her manner, makes her almost like a girl now*)   Three bedrooms—nice big one for you and Ruth. . . . Me and Beneatha still have to share our room, but Travis have one of his own—and—(*With difficulty*) I figures if the—new baby—is a boy, we could get one of them double-decker outfits . . . And there's a yard with a little patch of dirt where I could maybe get to grow me a few flowers . . . And a nice big basement . . .

RUTH   Walter honey, be glad—

MAMA (*Still to his back, fingering things on the table*)   'Course I don't want to make it sound fancier than it is . . . It's just a plain little old house—but it's made good and solid—and it will be *ours*. Walter Lee—it makes a difference in a man when he can walk on floors that belong to *him* . . .

RUTH   Where is it?

MAMA (*Frightened at this telling*)   Well—well—it's out there in Clybourne Park—

(RUTH's *radiance fades abruptly, and* WALTER *finally turns slowly to face his mother with incredulity and hostility*)

RUTH   Where?

MAMA (*Matter-of-factly*)   Four o six Clybourne Street, Clybourne Park.

RUTH   Clybourne Park? Mama, there ain't no colored people living in Clybourne Park.

MAMA (*Almost idiotically*)   Well, I guess there's going to be some now.

WALTER (*Bitterly*)   So that's the peace and comfort you went out and bought for us today!

MAMA (*Raising her eyes to meet his finally*)   Son—I just tried to find the nicest place for the least amount of money for my family.

RUTH (*Trying to recover from the shock*)   Well—well—'course I ain't one never been 'fraid of no crackers, mind you—but—well, wasn't there no other houses nowhere?

MAMA   Them houses they put up for colored in them areas way out all seem to cost twice as much as other houses. I did the best I could.

RUTH (*Struck senseless with the news, in its various degrees of goodness and trouble, she sits a moment, her fists propping her chin
in thought, and then she starts to rise, bringing her fists down
with vigor, the radiance spreading from cheek to cheek again*)
Well—well!—All I can say is—if this is my time in life—*my time*—
to say good-bye—(*And she builds with momentum as she starts
to circle the room with an exuberant, almost tearfully happy release*)—to these God-damned cracking walls!—(*She pounds the
walls*)—and these marching roaches!—(*She wipes at an imaginary
army of marching roaches*)—and this cramped little closet which
ain't now or never was no kitchen! . . . then I say it loud and
good, *Hallelujah! and good-bye misery* . . . *I don't never want
to see your ugly face again!* (*She laughs joyously, having practically destroyed the apartment, and flings her arms up and lets
them come down happily, slowly, reflectively, over her abdomen,
aware for the first time perhaps that the life therein pulses with
happiness and not despair*) Lena?

MAMA (*Moved, watching her happiness*) Yes, honey?

RUTH (*Looking off*) Is there—is there a whole lot of sunlight?

MAMA (*Understanding*) Yes, child, there's a whole lot of sunlight.
(*Long pause*)

RUTH (*Collecting herself and going to the door of the room* TRAVIS
is in) Well—I guess I better see 'bout Travis. (*To* MAMA) Lord,
I sure don't feel like whipping nobody today!
(*She exits*)

MAMA (*The mother and son are left alone now and the mother
waits a long time, considering deeply, before she speaks*) Son
—you—you understand what I done, don't you? (WALTER *is silent
and sullen*) I—I just seen my family falling apart today . . . just
falling to pieces in front of my eyes . . . We couldn't of gone on
like we was today. We was going backwards 'stead of forwards—
talking 'bout killing babies and wishing each other was dead . . .
When it gets like that in life—you just got to do something different, push on out and do something bigger . . . (*She waits*) I
wish you say something, son . . . I wish you'd say how deep inside you you think I done the right thing—

WALTER (*Crossing slowly to his bedroom door and finally turning
there and speaking measuredly*) What you need me to say you
done right for? *You* the head of this family. You run our lives like
you want to. It was your money and you did what you wanted
with it. So what you need for me to say it was all right for? (*Bit-*

terly, to hurt her as deeply as he knows is possible) So you butchered up a dream of mine—you—who always talking 'bout your
children's dreams . . .

MAMA   Walter Lee—

(*He just closes the door behind him.* MAMA *sits alone, thinking
heavily*)

Curtain

SCENE 2

Time: Friday night. A few weeks later.

At rise: Packing crates mark the intention of the family to move.
BENEATHA *and* GEORGE *come in, presumably from an evening out
again.*

GEORGE   O.K. . . . O.K., whatever you say . . . (*They both sit on
the couch. He tries to kiss her. She moves away*) Look, we've
had a nice evening; let's not spoil it, huh? . . .

(*He again turns her head and tries to nuzzle in and she turns
away from him, not with distaste but with momentary lack of
interest; in a mood to pursue what they were talking about*)

BENEATHA   I'm *trying* to talk to you.

GEORGE   We always talk.

BENEATHA   Yes—and I love to talk.

GEORGE (*Exasperated; rising*)   I know it and I don't mind it sometimes . . . I want you to cut it out, see— The moody stuff, I mean.
I don't like it. You're a nice-looking girl . . . all over. That's all
you need, honey, forget the atmosphere. Guys aren't going to go
for the atmosphere—they're going to go for what they see. Be
glad for that. Drop the Garbo routine. It doesn't go with you. As
for myself, I want a nice—(*Groping*)—simple—(*Thoughtfully*)—
sophisticated girl . . . not a poet—O.K.?

(*She rebuffs him again and he starts to leave*)

BENEATHA   Why are you angry?

GEORGE   Because this is stupid! I don't go out with you to discuss
the nature of "quiet desperation" or to hear all about your

A Raisin in the Sun

thoughts—because the world will go on thinking what it thinks regardless—

BENEATHA Then why read books? Why go to school?

GEORGE (*With artificial patience, counting on his fingers*) It's simple. You read books—to learn facts—to get grades—to pass the course—to get a degree. That's all—it has nothing to do with thoughts.

(*A long pause*)

BENEATHA I see. (*A longer pause as she looks at him*) Good night, George.

(GEORGE *looks at her a little oddly, and starts to exit. He meets* MAMA *coming in*)

GEORGE Oh—hello, Mrs. Younger.

MAMA Hello, George, how you feeling?

GEORGE Fine—fine, how are you?

MAMA Oh, a little tired. You know them steps can get you after a day's work. You all have a nice time tonight?

GEORGE Yes—a fine time. Well, good night.

MAMA Good night. (*He exits.* MAMA *closes the door behind her*) Hello, honey. What you sitting like that for?

BENEATHA I'm just sitting.

MAMA Didn't you have a nice time?

BENEATHA No.

MAMA No? What's the matter?

BENEATHA Mama, George is a fool—honest. (*She rises*)

MAMA (*Hustling around unloading the packages she has entered with. She stops*) Is he, baby?

BENEATHA Yes.

(BENEATHA *makes up* TRAVIS' *bed as she talks*)

MAMA You sure?

BENEATHA Yes.

MAMA Well—I guess you better not waste your time with no fools. (BENEATHA *looks up at her mother, watching her put groceries in the refrigerator. Finally she gathers up her things and starts into the bedroom. At the door she stops and looks back at her mother*)

BENEATHA Mama—

MAMA Yes, baby—

BENEATHA Thank you.

MAMA For what?

BENEATHA For understanding me this time.

(*She exits quickly and the mother stands, smiling a little, looking at the place where* BENEATHA *just stood.* RUTH *enters*)

RUTH   Now don't you fool with any of this stuff, Lena—

MAMA   Oh, I just thought I'd sort a few things out.

(*The phone rings.* RUTH *answers*)

RUTH   (*At the phone*)   Hello—Just a minute. (*Goes to door*) Walter, it's Mrs. Arnold. (*Waits. Goes back to the phone. Tense*) Hello. Yes, this is his wife speaking . . . He's lying down now. Yes . . . well, he'll be in tomorrow. He's been very sick. Yes—I know we should have called, but we were so sure he'd be able to come in today. Yes—yes, I'm very sorry. Yes . . . Thank you very much. (*She hangs up.* WALTER *is standing in the doorway of the bedroom behind her*) That was Mrs. Arnold.

WALTER   (*Indifferently*)   Was it?

RUTH   She said if you don't come in tomorrow that they are getting a new man . . .

WALTER   Ain't that sad—ain't that crying sad.

RUTH   She said Mr. Arnold has had to take a cab for three days . . . Walter, you ain't been to work for three days! (*This is a revelation to her*) Where you been, Walter Lee Younger? (WALTER *looks at her and starts to laugh*) You're going to lose your job.

WALTER   That's right . . .

RUTH   Oh, Walter, and with your mother working like a dog every day—

WALTER   That's sad too— Everything is sad.

MAMA   What you been doing for these three days, son?

WALTER   Mama—you don't know all the things a man what got leisure can find to do in this city . . . What's this—Friday night? Well—Wednesday I borrowed Willy Harris' car and I went for a drive . . . just me and myself and I drove and drove . . . Way out . . . way past South Chicago, and I parked the car and I sat and looked at the steel mills all day long. I just sat in the car and looked at them big black chimneys for hours. Then I drove back and I went to the Green Hat. (*Pause*) And Thursday—Thursday I borrowed the car again and I got in it and I pointed it the other way and I drove the other way—for hours—way, way up to Wisconsin, and I looked at the farms. I just drove and looked at the farms. Then I drove back and I went to the Green Hat. (*Pause*) And today—today I didn't get the car. Today I just walked. All over the Southside. And I looked at the Negroes and they looked

at me and finally I just sat down on the curb at Thirty-ninth and
South Parkway and I just sat there and watched the Negroes go
by. And then I went to the Green Hat. You all sad? You all depressed? And you know where I am going right now—

(RUTH *goes out quietly*)

MAMA   Oh, Big Walter, is this the harvest of our days?

WALTER   You know what I like about the Green Hat? (*He turns
the radio on and a steamy, deep blues pours into the room*) I like
this little cat they got there who blows a sax . . . He blows. He
talks to me. He ain't but 'bout five feet tall and he's got a conked
head and his eyes is always closed and he's all music—

MAMA   (*Rising and getting some papers out of her handbag*)
Walter—

WALTER   And there's this other guy who plays the piano . . . and
they got a sound. I mean they can work on some music . . .
They got the best little combo in the world in the Green Hat
. . . You can just sit there and drink and listen to them three
men play and you realize that don't nothing matter worth a damn,
but just being there—

MAMA   I've helped do it to you, haven't I, son? Walter, I been
wrong.

WALTER   Naw—you ain't never been wrong about nothing, Mama.

MAMA   Listen to me, now. I say I been wrong, son. That I been
doing to you what the rest of the world been doing to you. (*She
stops and he looks up slowly at her and she meets his eyes pleadingly*) Walter—what you ain't never understood is that I ain't got
nothing, don't own nothing, ain't never really wanted nothing that
wasn't for you. There ain't nothing as precious to me . . . There
ain't nothing worth holding on to, money, dreams, nothing else—
if it means—if it means it's going to destroy my boy. (*She puts
her papers in front of him and he watches her without speaking
or moving*) I paid the man thirty-five hundred dollars down on
the house. That leaves sixty-five hundred dollars. Monday morning I want you to take this money and take three thousand dollars and put it in a savings account for Beneatha's medical schooling. The rest you put in a checking account—with your name on
it. And from now on any penny that come out of it or that go in it
is for you to look after. For you to decide. (*She drops her hands
a little helplessly*) It ain't much, but it's all I got in the world
and I'm putting it in your hands. I'm telling you to be the head of
this family from now on like you supposed to be.

WALTER (*Stares at the money*) You trust me like that, Mama?

MAMA   I ain't never stop trusting you. Like I ain't never stop loving you.
(*She goes out, and* WALTER *sits looking at the money on the table
as the music continues in its idiom, pulsing in the room. Finally,
in a decisive gesture, he gets up, and, in mingled joy and desperation, picks up the money. At the same moment,* TRAVIS *enters
for bed*)

TRAVIS   What's the matter, Daddy? You drunk?

WALTER (*Sweetly, more sweetly than we have ever known him*)
No, Daddy ain't drunk. Daddy ain't going to never be drunk
again. . . .

TRAVIS   Well, good night, Daddy.
(*The* FATHER *has come from behind the couch and leans over,
embracing his son*)

WALTER   Son, I feel like talking to you tonight.

TRAVIS   About what?

WALTER   Oh, about a lot of things. About you and what kind of
man you going to be when you grow up. . . . Son—son, what do
you want to be when you grow up?

TRAVIS   A bus driver.

WALTER (*Laughing a little*) A what? Man, that ain't nothing to
want to be!

TRAVIS   Why not?

WALTER   'Cause, man—it ain't big enough—you know what I mean.

TRAVIS   I don't know then. I can't make up my mind. Sometimes
Mama asks me that too. And sometimes when I tell you I just
want to be like you—she says she don't want me to be like that
and sometimes she says she does. . . .

WALTER (*Gathering him up in his arms*) You know what, Travis?
In seven years you going to be seventeen years old. And things is
going to be very different with us in seven years, Travis. . . . One
day when you are seventeen I'll come home—home from my office downtown somewhere—

TRAVIS   You don't work in no office, Daddy.

WALTER   No—but after tonight. After what your daddy gonna do
tonight, there's going to be offices—a whole lot of offices. . . .

TRAVIS   What you gonna do tonight, Daddy?

WALTER   You wouldn't understand yet, son, but your daddy's gonna
make a transaction . . . a business transaction that's going to
change our lives. . . . That's how come one day when you 'bout

seventeen years old I'll come home and I'll be pretty tired, you know what I mean, after a day of conferences and secretaries getting things wrong the way they do . . . 'cause an executive's life is hell, man—(*The more he talks the farther away he gets*) And I'll pull the car up on the driveway . . . just a plain black Chrysler, I think, with white walls—no—black tires. More elegant. Rich people don't have to be flashy . . . though I'll have to get something a little sportier for Ruth—maybe a Cadillac convertible to do her shopping in. . . . And I'll come up the steps to the house and the gardener will be clipping away at the hedges and he'll say, "Good evening, Mr. Younger." And I'll say, "Hello, Jefferson, how are you this evening?" And I'll go inside and Ruth will come downstairs and meet me at the door and we'll kiss each other and she'll take my arm and we'll go up to your room to see you sitting on the floor with the catalogues of all the great schools in America around you. . . . All the great schools in the world! And—and I'll say, all right son—it's your seventeenth birthday, what is it you've decided? . . . Just tell me where you want to go to school and you'll *go*. Just tell me, what it is you want to be—and you'll *be* it. . . . Whatever you want to be—Yessir! (*He holds his arms open for* TRAVIS) You just name it, son . . . (TRAVIS *leaps into them*) and I hand you the world!

(WALTER'S *voice has risen in pitch and hysterical promise and on the last line he lifts* TRAVIS *high*)

Blackout

SCENE 3

Time: Saturday, moving day, one week later.

Before the curtain rises, RUTH'S *voice, a strident, dramatic church alto, cuts through the silence.*

It is, in the darkness, a triumphant surge, a penetrating statement of expectation: "Oh, Lord, I don't feel no ways tired! Children, oh, glory hallelujah!"

As the curtain rises we see that RUTH *is alone in the living room, finishing up the family's packing. It is moving day. She is nailing crates and tying cartons.* BENEATHA *enters, carrying a guitar case, and watches her exuberant sister-in-law.*

RUTH   Hey!

BENEATHA (*Putting away the case*)   Hi.

RUTH (*Pointing at a package*)   Honey—look in that package there and see what I found on sale this morning at the South Center. (RUTH *gets up and moves to the package and draws out some curtains*) Lookahere—hand-turned hems!

BENEATHA   How do you know the window size out there?

RUTH (*Who hadn't thought of that*)   Oh— Well, they bound to fit something in the whole house. Anyhow, they was too good a bargain to pass up. (RUTH *slaps her head, suddenly remembering something*) Oh, Bennie—I meant to put a special note on that carton over there. That's your mama's good china and she wants 'em to be very careful with it.

BENEATHA   I'll do it.

(BENEATHA *finds a piece of paper and starts to draw large letters on it*)

RUTH   You know what I'm going to do soon as I get in that new house?

BENEATHA   What?

RUTH   Honey—I'm going to run me a tub of water up to here . . . (*With her fingers practically up to her nostrils*) And I'm going to get in it—and I am going to sit . . . and sit . . . and sit in that hot water and the first person who knocks to tell *me* to hurry up and come out—

BENEATHA   Gets shot at sunrise.

RUTH (*Laughing happily*)   You said it, sister! (*Noticing how large* BENEATHA *is absent-mindedly making the note*) Honey, they ain't going to read that from no airplane.

BENEATHA (*Laughing herself*)   I guess I always think things have more emphasis if they are big, somehow.

RUTH (*Looking up at her and smiling*)   You and your brother seem to have that as a philosophy of life. Lord, that man—done changed so 'round here. You know—you know what we did last night? Me and Walter Lee?

BENEATHA   What?

RUTH (*Smiling to herself*)   We went to the movies. (*Looking at* BENEATHA *to see if she understands*) We went to the movies. You know the last time me and Walter went to the movies together?

BENEATHA   No.

RUTH   Me neither. That's how long it been. (*Smiling again*) But we went last night. The picture wasn't much good, but that didn't seem to matter. We went—and we held hands.

BENEATHA   Oh, Lord!

RUTH   We held hands—and you know what?

BENEATHA   What?

RUTH   When we come out of the show it was late and dark and all the stores and things was closed up . . . and it was kind of chilly and there wasn't many people on the streets . . . and we was still holding hands, me and Walter.

BENEATHA   You're killing me.

(WALTER *enters with a large package. His happiness is deep in him; he cannot keep still with his new-found exuberance. He is singing and wiggling and snapping his fingers. He puts his package in a corner and puts a phonograph record, which he has brought in with him, on the record player. As the music comes up he dances over to* RUTH *and tries to get her to dance with him. She gives in at last to his raunchiness and in a fit of giggling allows herself to be drawn into his mood and together they deliberately burlesque an old social dance of their youth*)

BENEATHA   (*Regarding them a long time as they dance, then drawing in her breath for a deeply exaggerated comment which she does not particularly mean*)   Talk about—olddddddddddd-fashioneddddddddd—Negroes!

WALTER   (*Stopping momentarily*)   What kind of Negroes?

(*He says this in fun. He is not angry with her today, nor with anyone. He starts to dance with his wife again*)

BENEATHA   Old-fashioned.

WALTER   (*As he dances with* RUTH)   You know, when these *New Negroes* have their convention—(*Pointing at his sister*)—that is going to be the chairman of the Committee on Unending Agitation. (*He goes on dancing, then stops*) Race, race, race! . . . Girl, I do believe you are the first person in the history of the entire human race to successfully brainwash yourself. (BENEATHA *breaks up and he goes on dancing. He stops again, enjoying his tease*) Damn, even the N double A C P takes a holiday sometimes! (BENEATHA *and* RUTH *laugh. He dances with* RUTH *some more and starts to laugh and stops and pantomimes someone over an operating table*) I can just see that chick someday looking down at some poor cat on an operating table before she starts to slice him, saying . . . (*Pulling his sleeves back maliciously*) "By the way, what are your views on civil rights down there? . . ."

(*He laughs at her again and starts to dance happily. The bell sounds*)

BENEATHA   Sticks and stones may break my bones but . . . words will never hurt me!

(BENEATHA *goes to the door and opens it as* WALTER *and* RUTH *go on with the clowning.* BENEATHA *is somewhat surprised to see a quiet-looking middle-aged white man in a business suit holding his hat and a briefcase in his hand and consulting a small piece of paper*)

MAN   Uh—how do you do, miss. I am looking for a Mrs.—(*He looks at the slip of paper*) Mrs. Lena Younger?

BENEATHA (*Smoothing her hair with slight embarrassment*)   Oh— yes, that's my mother. Excuse me. (*She closes the door and turns to quiet the other two*) Ruth! Brother! Somebody's here. (*Then she opens the door. The man casts a curious quick glance at all of them*) Uh—come in please.

MAN (*Coming in*)   Thank you.

BENEATHA   My mother isn't here just now. Is it business?

MAN   Yes . . . well, of a sort.

WALTER (*Freely, the Man of the House*)   Have a seat. I'm Mrs. Younger's son. I look after most of her business matters.

(RUTH *and* BENEATHA *exchange amused glances*)

MAN (*Regarding* WALTER, *and sitting*)   Well— My name is Karl Lindner . . .

WALTER (*Stretching out his hand*)   Walter Younger. This is my wife—(RUTH *nods politely*)—and my sister.

LINDNER   How do you do.

WALTER (*Amiably, as he sits himself easily on a chair, leaning with interest forward on his knees and looking expectantly into the newcomer's face*)   What can we do for you, Mr. Lindner!

LINDNER (*Some minor shuffling of the hat and briefcase on his knees*)   Well—I am a representative of the Clybourne Park Improvement Association—

WALTER (*Pointing*)   Why don't you sit your things on the floor?

LINDNER   Oh—yes. Thank you. (*He slides the briefcase and hat under the chair*) And as I was saying—I am from the Clybourne Park Improvement Association and we have had it brought to our attention at the last meeting that you people—or at least your mother—has bought a piece of residential property at—(*He digs for the slip of paper again*)—four o six Clybourne Street . . .

WALTER   That's right. Care for something to drink? Ruth, get Mr. Lindner a beer.

LINDNER (*Upset for some reason*)   Oh—no, really. I mean thank you very much, but no thank you.

RUTH (*Innocently*)   Some coffee?

LINDNER   Thank you, nothing at all.

(BENEATHA *is watching the man carefully*)

LINDNER   Well, I don't know how much you folks know about our organization. (*He is a gentle man; thoughtful and somewhat labored in his manner*) It is one of these community organizations set up to look after—oh, you know, things like block upkeep and special projects and we also have what we call our New Neighbors Orientation Committee . . .

BENEATHA (*Drily*)   Yes—and what do they do?

LINDNER (*Turning a little to her and then returning the main force to* WALTER)   Well—it's what you might call a sort of welcoming committee, I guess. I mean they, we, I'm the chairman of the committee—go around and see the new people who move into the neighborhood and sort of give them the lowdown on the way we do things out in Clybourne Park.

BENEATHA (*With appreciation of the two meanings, which escape* RUTH *and* WALTER)   Un-huh.

LINDNER   And we also have the category of what the association calls—(*He looks elsewhere*)—uh—special community problems . . .

BENEATHA   Yes—and what are some of those?

WALTER   Girl, let the man talk.

LINDNER (*With understated relief*)   Thank you. I would sort of like to explain this thing in my own way. I mean I want to explain to you in a certain way.

WALTER   Go ahead.

LINDNER   Yes. Well. I'm going to try to get right to the point. I'm sure we'll all appreciate that in the long run.

BENEATHA   Yes.

WALTER   Be still now!

LINDNER   Well—

RUTH (*Still innocently*)   Would you like another chair—you don't look comfortable.

LINDNER (*More frustrated than annoyed*)   No, thank you very much. Please. Well—to get right to the point I—(*A great breath, and he is off at last*) I am sure you people must be aware of some of the incidents which have happened in various parts of the city when colored people have moved into certain areas—(BE-NEATHA *exhales heavily and starts tossing a piece of fruit up and down in the air*) Well—because we have what I think is going to be a unique type of organization in American community life—not only do we deplore that kind of thing—but we are trying to do something about it. (BENEATHA *stops tossing and turns with a new and quizzical interest to the man*) We feel—(*Gaining confidence in his mission because of the interest in the faces of the people he is talking to*)—we feel that most of the trouble in this world, when you come right down to it—(*He hits his knee for emphasis*)—most of the trouble exists because people just don't sit down and talk to each other.

RUTH (*Nodding as she might in church, pleased with the remark*) You can say that again, mister.

LINDNER (*More encouraged by such affirmation*) That we don't try hard enough in this world to understand the other fellow's problem. The other guy's point of view.

RUTH Now that's right.

(BENEATHA *and* WALTER *merely watch and listen with genuine interest*)

LINDNER Yes—that's the way we feel out in Clybourne Park. And that's why I was elected to come here this afternoon and talk to you people. Friendly like, you know, the way people should talk to each other and see if we couldn't find some way to work this thing out. As I say, the whole business is a matter of *caring* about the other fellow. Anybody can see that you are a nice family of folks, hard working and honest I'm sure. (BENEATHA *frowns slightly, quizzically, her head tilted regarding him*) Today everybody knows what it means to be on the outside of *something*. And of course, there is always somebody who is out to take the advantage of people who don't always understand.

WALTER What do you mean?

LINDNER Well—you see our community is made up of people who've worked hard as the dickens for years to build up that little community. They're not rich and fancy people; just hard-working, honest people who don't really have much but those little homes and a dream of the kind of community they want to raise their children in. Now, I don't say we are perfect and there is a lot wrong in some of the things they want. But you've got to admit that a man, right or wrong, has the right to want to have the neighborhood he lives in a certain kind of way. And at the moment the overwhelming majority of our people out there feel that people get along better, take more of a common interest in the life of the community, when they share a common background. I want you to believe me when I tell you that race prejudice simply doesn't enter into it. It is a matter of the people of Clybourne Park believing, rightly or wrongly, as I say, that for the happiness of all concerned that our Negro families are happier when they live in their *own* communities.

BENEATHA (*With a grand and bitter gesture*) This, friends, is the Welcoming Committee!

WALTER (*Dumfounded, looking at* LINDNER) Is this what you came marching all the way over here to tell us?

LINDNER Well, now we've been having a fine conversation. I hope you'll hear me all the way through.

WALTER (*Tightly*) Go ahead, man.

LINDNER You see—in the face of all things I have said, we are prepared to make your family a very generous offer . . .

BENEATHA Thirty pieces and not a coin less!

WALTER Yeah?

LINDNER (*Putting on his glasses and drawing a form out of the briefcase*) Our association is prepared, through the collective effort of our people, to buy the house from you at a financial gain to your family.

RUTH Lord have mercy, ain't this the living gall!

WALTER All right, you through?

LINDNER Well, I want to give you the exact terms of the financial arrangement—

WALTER We don't want to hear no exact terms of no arrangements. I want to know if you got any more to tell us 'bout getting together?

LINDNER (*Taking off his glasses*) Well—I don't suppose that you feel . . .

WALTER Never mind how I feel—you got any more to say 'bout how people ought to sit down and talk to each other? . . . Get out of my house, man.

(*He turns his back and walks to the door*)

LINDNER (*Looking around at the hostile faces and reaching and assembling his hat and briefcase*) Well—I don't understand why you people are reacting this way. What do you think you are going to gain by moving into a neighborhood where you just aren't wanted and where some elements—well—people can get awful worked up when they feel that their whole way of life and everything they've ever worked for is threatened.

WALTER   Get out.

LINDNER   (*At the door, holding a small card*)   Well—I'm sorry it went like this.

WALTER   Get out.

LINDNER   (*Almost sadly regarding* WALTER)   You just can't force people to change their hearts, son.

(*He turns and puts his card on a table and exits.* WALTER *pushes the door to with stinging hatred, and stands looking at it.* RUTH *just sits and* BENEATHA *just stands. They say nothing.* MAMA *and* TRAVIS *enter*)

MAMA   Well—this all the packing got done since I left out of here this morning. I testify before God that my children got all the energy of the dead. What time the moving men due?

BENEATHA   Four o'clock. You had a caller, Mama.

(*She is smiling, teasingly*)

MAMA   Sure enough—who?

BENEATHA   (*Her arms folded saucily*)   The Welcoming Committee.

(WALTER *and* RUTH *giggle*)

MAMA   (*Innocently*)   Who?

BENEATHA   The Welcoming Committee. They said they're sure going to be glad to see you when you get there.

WALTER   (*Devilishly*)   Yeah, they said they can't hardly wait to see your face.

(*Laughter*)

MAMA   (*Sensing their facetiousness*)   What's the matter with you all?

WALTER   Ain't nothing the matter with us. We just telling you 'bout the gentleman who came to see you this afternoon. From the Clybourne Park Improvement Association.

MAMA   What he want?

RUTH   (*In the same mood as* BENEATHA *and* WALTER)   To welcome you, honey.

WALTER   He said they can't hardly wait. He said the one thing they don't have, that they just *dying* to have out there is a fine family of colored people! (*To* RUTH *and* BENEATHA)   Ain't that right!

RUTH *and* BENEATHA (*Mockingly*) Yeah! He left his card in case—
(*They indicate the card, and* MAMA *picks it up and throws it on
the floor—understanding and looking off as she draws her chair up
to the table on which she has put her plant and some sticks and
some cord*)

MAMA Father, give us strength. (*Knowingly—and without fun*)
Did he threaten us?

BENEATHA Oh—Mama—they don't do it like that any more. He
talked Brotherhood. He said everybody ought learn how to sit
down and hate each other with good Christian fellowship.
(*She and* WALTER *shake hands to ridicule the remark*)

MAMA (*Sadly*) Lord, protect us . . .

RUTH You should hear the money those folks raised to buy the
house from us. All we paid and then some.

BENEATHA What they think we going to do—eat 'em?

RUTH No, honey, marry 'em.

MAMA (*Shaking her head*) Lord, Lord, Lord . . .

RUTH Well—that's the way the crackers crumble. Joke.

BENEATHA (*Laughingly noticing what her mother is doing*) Mama,
what are you doing?

MAMA Fixing my plant so it won't get hurt none on the way . . .

BENEATHA Mama, you going to take *that* to the new house?

MAMA Un-huh—

BENEATHA That raggedy-looking old thing?

MAMA (*Stopping and looking at her*) It expresses *me*.

RUTH (*With delight, to* BENEATHA) So there, Miss Thing!
(WALTER *comes to* MAMA *suddenly and bends down behind her
and squeezes her in his arms with all his strength. She is over-
whelmed by the suddenness of it and, though delighted, her
manner is like that of* RUTH *with* TRAVIS)

MAMA Look out now, boy! You make me mess up my thing here!

WALTER (*His face lit, he slips down on his knees beside her, his arms
still about her*) Mama . . . you know what it means to climb up
in the chariot?

MAMA (*Gruffly, very happy*) Get on away from me now . . .

RUTH (*Near the gift-wrapped package, trying to catch* WALTER's
eye) Psst—

WALTER What the old song say, Mama . . .

RUTH Walter— Now?
(*She is pointing at the package*)

WALTER (*Speaking the lines, sweetly, playfully, in his mother's face*)

I got wings . . . you got wings . . .
All God's children got wings . . .

MAMA   Boy—get out of my face and do some work . . .

WALTER

When I get to heaven gonna put on my wings,
Gonna fly all over God's heaven . . .

BENEATHA (*Teasingly, from across the room*)   Everybody talking 'bout heaven ain't going there!

WALTER (*To* RUTH, *who is carrying the box across to them*)   I don't know, you think we ought to give her that . . . Seems to me she ain't been very appreciative around here.

MAMA (*Eying the box, which is obviously a gift*)   What is that?

WALTER (*Taking it from* RUTH *and putting it on the table in front of* MAMA)   Well—what you all think. Should we give it to her?

RUTH   Oh—she was pretty good today.

MAMA   I'll good you—
(*She turns her eyes to the box again*)

BENEATHA   Open it, Mama.
(*She stands up, looks at it, turns and looks at all of them, and then presses her hands together and does not open the package*)

WALTER (*Sweetly*)   Open it, Mama. It's for you. (MAMA *looks in his eyes. It is the first present in her life without its being Christmas. Slowly she opens her package and lifts out, one by one, a brand-new sparkling set of gardening tools.* WALTER *continues, prodding*) Ruth made up the note—read it . . .

MAMA (*Picking up the card and adjusting her glasses*)   "To our own Mrs. Miniver—Love from Brother, Ruth and Beneatha." Ain't that lovely . . .

TRAVIS (*Tugging at his father's sleeve*)   Daddy, can I give her mine now?

WALTER   All right, son. (TRAVIS *flies to get his gift*) Travis didn't want to go in with the rest of us, Mama. He got his own. (*Somewhat amused*) We don't know what it is . . .

TRAVIS (*Racing back in the room with a large hatbox and putting it in front of his grandmother*)   Here!

MAMA   Lord have mercy, baby. You done gone and bought your grandmother a hat?

TRAVIS (*Very proud*) Open it!

(*She does and lifts out an elaborate, but very elaborate, wide gardening hat, and all the adults break up at the sight of it*)

RUTH Travis, honey, what is that?

TRAVIS (*Who thinks it is beautiful and appropriate*) It's a gardening hat! Like the ladies always have on in the magazines when they work in their gardens.

BENEATHA (*Giggling fiercely*) Travis—we were trying to make Mama Mrs. Miniver—not Scarlett O'Hara!

MAMA (*Indignantly*) What's the matter with you all! This here is a beautiful hat! (*Absurdly*) I always wanted me one just like it! (*She pops it on her head to prove it to her grandson, and the hat is ludicrous and considerably oversized*)

RUTH Hot dog! Go, Mama!

WALTER (*Doubled over with laughter*) I'm sorry, Mama—but you look like you ready to go out and chop you some cotton sure enough!

(*They all laugh except* MAMA, *out of deference to* TRAVIS' *feelings*)

MAMA (*Gathering the boy up to her*) Bless your heart—this is the prettiest hat I ever owned— (WALTER, RUTH *and* BENEATHA *chime in—noisily, festively and insincerely congratulating* TRAVIS *on his gift*) What are we all standing around here for? We ain't finished packin' yet. Bennie, you ain't packed one book.

(*The bell rings*)

BENEATHA That couldn't be the movers . . . it's not hardly two good yet—

(BENEATHA *goes into her room.* MAMA *starts for door*)

WALTER (*Turning, stiffening*) Wait—wait—I'll get it.

(*He stands and looks at the door*)

MAMA You expecting company, son?

WALTER (*Just looking at the door*) Yeah—yeah . . .

(MAMA *looks at* RUTH, *and they exchange innocent and unfrightened glances*)

MAMA (*Not understanding*) Well, let them in, son.

BENEATHA (*From her room*) We need some more string.

MAMA Travis—you run to the hardware and get me some string cord.

(MAMA *goes out and* WALTER *turns and looks at* RUTH. TRAVIS *goes to a dish for money*)

RUTH Why don't you answer the door, man?

WALTER (*Suddenly bounding across the floor to her*) 'Cause sometimes it hard to let the future begin! (*Stooping down in her face*)

I got wings! You got wings!
All God's children got wings!

(*He crosses to the door and throws it open. Standing there is a very slight little man in a not too prosperous business suit and with haunted frightened eyes and a hat pulled down tightly, brim up, around his forehead.* TRAVIS *passes between the men and exits.* WALTER *leans deep in the man's face, still in his jubilance*)

When I get to heaven gonna put on my wings,
Gonna fly all over God's heaven . . .

(*The little man just stares at him*)

Heaven—

(*Suddenly he stops and looks past the little man into the empty hallway*) Where's Willy, man?

BOBO   He ain't with me.

WALTER (*Not disturbed*)   Oh—come on in. You know my wife.

BOBO (*Dumbly, taking off his hat*)   Yes—h'you, Miss Ruth.

RUTH (*Quietly, a mood apart from her husband already, seeing* BOBO)   Hello, Bobo.

WALTER   You right on time today . . . Right on time. That's the way! (*He slaps* BOBO *on his back*) Sit down . . . lemme hear.

(RUTH *stands stiffly and quietly in back of them, as though somehow she senses death, her eyes fixed on her husband*)

BOBO (*His frightened eyes on the floor, his hat in his hands*)   Could I please get a drink a water, before I tell you about it, Walter Lee?

(WALTER *does not take his eyes off the man.* RUTH *goes blindly to the tap and gets a glass of water and brings it to* BOBO)

WALTER   There ain't nothing wrong, is there?

BOBO   Lemme tell you—

WALTER   Man—didn't nothing go wrong?

BOBO   Lemme tell you—Walter Lee. (*Looking at* RUTH *and talking to her more than to* WALTER) You know how it was. I got to tell you how it was. I mean first I got to tell you how it was all the way . . . I mean about the money I put in, Walter Lee . . .

WALTER (*With taut agitation now*) What about the money you put in?

BOBO Well—it wasn't much as we told you—me and Willy—(*He stops*) I'm sorry, Walter. I got a bad feeling about it. I got a real bad feeling about it . . .

WALTER Man, what you telling me about all this for? . . . Tell me what happened in Springfield . . .

BOBO Springfield.

RUTH (*Like a dead woman*) What was supposed to happen in Springfield?

BOBO (*To her*) This deal that me and Walter went into with Willy— Me and Willy was going to go down to Springfield and spread some money 'round so's we wouldn't have to wait so long for the liquor license . . . That's what we were going to do. Everybody said that was the way you had to do, you understand, Miss Ruth?

WALTER Man—what happened down there?

BOBO (*A pitiful man, near tears*) I'm trying to tell you, Walter.

WALTER (*Screaming at him suddenly*) THEN TELL ME, GOD-DAMNIT . . . WHAT'S THE MATTER WITH YOU?

BOBO Man . . . I didn't go to no Springfield, yesterday.

WALTER (*Halted, life hanging in the moment*) Why not?

BOBO (*The long way, the hard way to tell*) 'Cause I didn't have no reasons to . . .

WALTER Man, what are you talking about!

BOBO I'm talking about the fact that when I got to the train station yesterday morning—eight o'clock like we planned . . . Man— *Willy didn't never show up.*

WALTER Why . . . where was he . . . where is he?

BOBO That's what I'm trying to tell you . . . I don't know . . . I waited six hours . . . I called his house . . . and I waited . . . six hours . . . I waited in that train station six hours . . . (*Breaking into tears*) That was all the extra money I had in the world . . . (*Looking up at* WALTER *with the tears running down his face*) Man, *Willy is gone.*

WALTER Gone, what you mean Willy is gone? Gone where? You mean he went by himself. You mean he went off to Springfield by himself—to take care of getting the license—(*Turns and looks anxiously at* RUTH) You mean maybe he didn't want too many people in on the business down there? (*Looks to* RUTH *again, as before*) You know Willy got his own ways. (*Looks back to* BOBO)

Maybe you was late yesterday and he just went on down there without you. Maybe—maybe—he's been callin' you at home tryin' to tell you what happened or something. Maybe—maybe—he just got sick. He's somewhere—he's got to be somewhere. We just got to find him—me and you got to find him. (*Grabs* BOBO *senselessly by the collar and starts to shake him*) We got to!

BOBO (*In sudden angry, frightened agony*) What's the matter with you, Walter! *When a cat takes off with your money he don't leave you no maps!*

WALTER (*Turning madly, as though he is looking for* WILLY *in the very room*) Willy! . . . Willy . . . don't do it . . . Please don't do it . . . Man, not with that money . . . Man, please, not with that money . . . Oh, God . . . Don't let it be true . . . (*He is wandering around, crying out for* Willy *and looking for him or perhaps for help from God*) Man . . . I trusted you . . . Man, I put my life in your hands . . . (*He starts to crumple down on the floor as* RUTH *just covers her face in horror.* MAMA *opens the door and comes into the room, with* BENEATHA *behind her*) Man . . . (*He starts to pound the floor with his fists, sobbing wildly*) That money is made out of my father's flesh . . .

BOBO (*Standing over him helplessly*) I'm sorry, Walter . . . (*Only* WALTER's *sobs reply.* BOBO *puts on his hat*) I had my life staked on this deal, too . . .

(*He exits*)

MAMA (*To* WALTER) Son—(*She goes to him, bends down to him, talks to his bent head*) Son . . . Is it gone? Son, I gave you sixty-five hundred dollars. Is it gone? All of it? Beneatha's money too?

WALTER (*Lifting his head slowly*) Mama . . . I never . . . went to the bank at all . . .

MAMA (*Not wanting to believe him*) You mean . . . your sister's school money . . . you used that too . . . Walter? . . .

WALTER Yessss! . . . All of it . . . It's all gone . . .

(*There is total silence.* RUTH *stands with her face covered with her hands;* BENEATHA *leans forlornly against a wall, fingering a piece of red ribbon from the mother's gift.* MAMA *stops and looks at her son without recognition and then, quite without thinking about it, starts to beat him senselessly in the face.* BENEATHA *goes to them and stops it*)

BENEATHA Mama!

(MAMA *stops and looks at both of her children and rises slowly and wanders vaguely, aimlessly away from them*)

MAMA I seen . . . him . . . night after night . . . come in . . . and look at that rug . . . and then look at me . . . the red showing in his eyes . . . the veins moving in his head . . . I seen him grow thin and old before he was forty . . . working and working and working like somebody's old horse . . . killing himself . . . and you—you give it all away in a day . . .

BENEATHA Mama—

MAMA Oh, God . . . (*She looks up to Him*) Look down here—and show me the strength.

BENEATHA Mama—

MAMA (*Folding over*) Strength . . .

BENEATHA (*Plaintively*) Mama . . .

MAMA Strength!

Curtain

ACT THREE

An hour later.

At curtain, there is a sullen light of gloom in the living room, gray light not unlike that which began the first scene of Act One. At left we can see WALTER *within his room, alone with himself. He is stretched out on the bed, his shirt out and open, his arms under his head. He does not smoke, he does not cry out, he merely lies there, looking up at the ceiling, much as if he were alone in the world.*

In the living room BENEATHA *sits at the table, still surrounded by the now almost ominous packing crates. She sits looking off. We feel that this is a mood struck perhaps an hour before, and it lingers now, full of the empty sound of profound disappointment. We see on a line from her brother's bedroom the sameness of their attitudes. Presently the bell rings and* BENEATHA *rises without ambition or interest in answering. It is* ASAGAI, *smiling broadly, striding into the room with energy and happy expectation and conversation.*

ASAGAI   I came over . . . I had some free time. I thought I might help with the packing. Ah, I like the look of packing crates! A household in preparation for a journey! It depresses some people . . . but for me . . . it is another feeling. Something full of the flow of life, do you understand? Movement, progress . . . It makes me think of Africa.

BENEATHA   Africa!

ASAGAI   What kind of a mood is this? Have I told you how deeply you move me?

BENEATHA   He gave away the money, Asagai . . .

ASAGAI   Who gave away what money?

BENEATHA   The insurance money. My brother gave it away.

ASAGAI   Gave it away?

BENEATHA   He made an investment! With a man even Travis wouldn't have trusted.

ASAGAI And it's gone?

BENEATHA Gone!

ASAGAI I'm very sorry . . . And you, now?

BENEATHA Me? . . . Me? . . . Me I'm nothing . . . Me. When I was very small . . . we used to take our sleds out in the wintertime and the only hills we had were the ice-covered stone steps of some houses down the street. And we used to fill them in with snow and make them smooth and slide down them all day . . . and it was very dangerous you know . . . far too steep . . . and sure enough one day a kid named Rufus came down too fast and hit the sidewalk . . . and we saw his face just split open right there in front of us . . . And I remember standing there looking at his bloody open face thinking that was the end of Rufus. But the ambulance came and they took him to the hospital and they fixed the broken bones and they sewed it all up . . . and the next time I saw Rufus he just had a little line down the middle of his face . . . I never got over that . . .

ASAGAI What?

BENEATHA That that was what one person could do for another, fix him up—sew up the problem, make him all right again. That was the most marvelous thing in the world . . . I wanted to do that. I always thought it was the one concrete thing in the world that a human being could do. Fix up the sick, you know—and make them whole again. This was truly being God . . .

ASAGAI You wanted to be God?

BENEATHA No—I wanted to cure. It used to be so important to me. I wanted to cure. It used to matter. I used to care. I mean about people and how their bodies hurt . . .

ASAGAI And you've stopped caring?

BENEATHA Yes—I think so.

ASAGAI Why?

(WALTER *rises, goes to the door of his room and is about to open it, then stops and stands listening, leaning on the door jamb*)

BENEATHA Because it doesn't seem deep enough, close enough to what ails mankind—I mean this thing of sewing up bodies or administering drugs. Don't you understand? It was a child's reaction to the world. I thought that doctors had the secret to all the hurts. . . . That's the way a child sees things—or an idealist.

ASAGAI Children see things very well sometimes—and idealists even better.

BENEATHA I know that's what you think. Because you are still where I left off—you still care. This is what you see for the world, for Africa. You with the dreams of the future will patch up all Africa—you are going to cure the Great Sore of colonialism with Independence——

ASAGAI   Yes!

BENEATHA   Yes—and you think that one word is the penicillin of the human spirit: "Independence!" But then what?

ASAGAI   That will be the problem for another time. First we must get there.

BENEATHA   And where does it end?

ASAGAI   End? Who even spoke of an end? To life? To living?

BENEATHA   An end to misery!

ASAGAI   (Smiling)   You sound like a French intellectual.

BENEATHA   No! I sound like a human being who just had her future taken right out of her hands! While I was sleeping in my bed in there, things were happening in this world that directly concerned me—and nobody asked me, consulted me—they just went out and did things—and changed my life. Don't you see there isn't any real progress, Asagai, there is only one large circle that we march in, around and around, each of us with our own little picture—in front of us—our own little mirage that we think is the future.

ASAGAI   That is the mistake.

BENEATHA   What?

ASAGAI   What you just said—about the circle. It isn't a circle—it is simply a long line—as in geometry, you know, one that reaches into infinity. And because we cannot see the end—we also cannot see how it changes. And it is very odd but those who see the changes are called "idealists"—and those who cannot, or refuse to think, they are the "realists." It is very strange, and amusing too, I think.

BENEATHA   You—you are almost religious.

ASAGAI   Yes . . . I think I have the religion of doing what is necessary in the world—and of worshipping man—because he is so marvelous, you see.

BENEATHA   Man is foul! And the human race deserves its misery!

ASAGAI   You see: you have become the religious one in the old sense. Already, and after such a small defeat, you are worshipping despair.

BENEATHA   From now on, I worship the truth—and the truth is that people are puny, small and selfish. . . . And you cannot answer *it!* All your talk and dreams about Africa and Independence. Independence and then what? What about all the crooks and petty thieves and just plain idiots who will come into power to steal and plunder the same as before—only now they will be black and do it in the name of the new Independence— You cannot answer that.

ASAGAI (*Shouting over her*) *I live the answer!* (*Pause*) In my village at home it is the exceptional man who can even read a newspaper . . . or who ever *sees* a book at all. I will go home and much of what I will have to say will seem strange to the people of my village . . . But I will teach and work and things will happen, slowly and swiftly. At times it will seem that nothing changes at all . . . and then again . . . the sudden dramatic events which make history leap into the future. And then quiet again. Retrogression even. Guns, murder, revolution. And I even will have moments when I wonder if the quiet was not better than all that death and hatred. But I will look about my village at the illiteracy and disease and ignorance and I will not wonder long. And perhaps . . . perhaps I will be a great man . . . I mean perhaps I will hold on to the substance of truth and find my way always with the right course . . . and perhaps for it I will be butchered in my bed some night by the servants of empire . . .

BENEATHA *The martyr!*

ASAGAI . . . or perhaps I shall live to be a very old man respected and esteemed in my new nation . . . And perhaps I shall hold office and this is what I'm trying to tell you, Alaiyo; perhaps the things I believe now for my country will be wrong and outmoded, and I will not understand and do terrible things to have things my way or merely to keep my power. Don't you see that there will be young men and women, not British soldiers then, but my own black countrymen . . . to step out of the shadows some evening and slit my then useless throat? Don't you see they have always been there . . . that they always will be. And that such a thing as my own death will be an advance? They who might kill me even . . . actually replenish me!

BENEATHA Oh, Asagai, I know all that.

ASAGAI Good! Then stop moaning and groaning and tell me what you plan to do.

BENEATHA Do?

ASAGAI I have a bit of a suggestion.

BENEATHA What?

ASAGAI (*Rather quietly for him*) That when it is all over—that you come home with me—

BENEATHA (*Slapping herself on the forehead with exasperation born of misunderstanding*) Oh—Asagai—at this moment you decide to be romantic!

ASAGAI (*Quickly understanding the misunderstanding*) My dear, young creature of the New World—I do not mean across the city—I mean across the ocean; home—to Africa.

BENEATHA (*Slowly understanding and turning to him with murmured amazement*) To—to Nigeria?

ASAGAI Yes! . . . (*Smiling and lifting his arms playfully*) Three hundred years later the African Prince rose up out of the seas and swept the maiden back across the middle passage over which her ancestors had come—

BENEATHA (*Unable to play*) Nigeria?

ASAGAI Nigeria. Home. (*Coming to her with genuine romantic flippancy*) I will show you our mountains and our stars; and give you cool drinks from gourds and teach you the old songs and the ways of our people—and, in time, we will pretend that—(*Very softly*)—you have only been away for a day—

(*She turns her back to him, thinking. He swings her around and takes her full in his arms in a long embrace which proceeds to passion*)

BENEATHA (*Pulling away*) You're getting me all mixed up—

ASAGAI Why?

BENEATHA Too many things—too many things have happened today. I must sit down and think. I don't know what I feel about anything right this minute.

(*She promptly sits down and props her chin on her fist*)

ASAGAI (*Charmed*) All right, I shall leave you. No—don't get up. (*Touching her, gently, sweetly*) Just sit awhile and think . . . Never be afraid to sit awhile and think. (*He goes to door and looks at her*) How often I have looked at you and said, "Ah—so this is what the New World hath finally wrought . . ."

(*He exits. BENEATHA sits on alone. Presently WALTER enters from his room and starts to rummage through things, feverishly looking for something. She looks up and turns in her seat*)

BENEATHA (*Hissingly*) Yes—just look at what the New World hath wrought! . . . Just look! (*She gestures with bitter disgust*) There he is! *Monsieur le petit bourgeois noir*—himself! There he is— Symbol of a Rising Class! Entrepreneur! Titan of the system!

(WALTER *ignores her completely and continues frantically and destructively looking for something and hurling things to floor and tearing things out of their place in his search.* BENEATHA *ignores the eccentricity of his actions and goes on with the monologue of insult*) Did you dream of yachts on Lake Michigan, Brother? Did you see yourself on that Great Day sitting down at the Conference Table, surrounded by all the mighty bald-headed men in America? All halted, waiting, breathless, waiting for your pronouncements on industry? Waiting for you—Chairman of the Board? (WALTER *finds what he is looking for—a small piece of white paper—and pushes it in his pocket and puts on his coat and rushes out without ever having looked at her. She shouts after him*) I look at you and I see the final triumph of stupidity in the world!

(*The door slams and she returns to just sitting again.* RUTH *comes quickly out of* MAMA's *room*)

RUTH   Who was that?

BENEATHA   Your husband.

RUTH   Where did he go?

BENEATHA   Who knows—maybe he has an appointment at U.S. Steel.

RUTH   (*Anxiously, with frightened eyes*)   You didn't say nothing bad to him, did you?

BENEATHA   Bad? Say anything bad to him? No—I told him he was a sweet boy and full of dreams and everything is strictly peachy keen, as the ofay kids say!

(MAMA *enters from her bedroom. She is lost, vague, trying to catch hold, to make some sense of her former command of the world, but it still eludes her. A sense of waste overwhelms her gait; a measure of apology rides on her shoulders. She goes to her plant, which has remained on the table, looks at it, picks it up and takes it to the window sill and sits it outside, and she stands and looks at it a long moment. Then she closes the window, straightens her body with effort and turns around to her children*)

MAMA   Well—ain't it a mess in here, though? (*A false cheerfulness, a beginning of something*) I guess we all better stop moping around and get some work done. All this unpacking and everything we got to do. (RUTH *raises her head slowly in response to the sense of the line; and* BENEATHA *in similar manner turns very slowly to look at her mother*) One of you all better call the moving people and tell 'em not to come.

RUTH   Tell 'em not to come?

MAMA   Of course, baby. Ain't no need in 'em coming all the way here and having to go back. They charges for that too. (*She sits down, fingers to her brow, thinking*) Lord, ever since I was a little girl, I always remembers people saying, "Lena—Lena Eggleston, you aims too high all the time. You needs to slow down and see life a little more like it is. Just slow down some." That's what they always used to say down home—"Lord, that Lena Eggleston is a high-minded thing. She'll get her due one day!"

RUTH   No, Lena . . .

MAMA   Me and Big Walter just didn't never learn right.

RUTH   Lena, no! We gotta go. Bennie—tell her . . . (*She rises and crosses to* BENEATHA *with her arms outstretched.* BENEATHA *doesn't respond*) Tell her we can still move . . . the notes ain't but a hundred and twenty five a month. We got four grown people in this house—we can work . . .

MAMA (*To herself*) Just aimed too high all the time—

RUTH (*Turning and going to* MAMA *fast—the words pouring out with urgency and desperation*) Lena—I'll work . . . I'll work twenty hours a day in all the kitchens in Chicago . . . I'll strap my baby on my back if I have to and scrub all the floors in America and wash all the sheets in America if I have to—but we got to move . . . We got to get out of here . . .

(MAMA *reaches out absently and pats* RUTH's *hand*)

MAMA   No—I sees things differently now. Been thinking 'bout some of the things we could do to fix this place up some. I seen a second-hand bureau over on Maxwell Street just the other day that could fit right there. (*She points to where the new furniture might go.* RUTH *wanders away from her*) Would need some new handles on it and then a little varnish and then it look like something brand-new. And—we can put up them new curtains in the kitchen . . . Why this place be looking fine. Cheer us all up so that we forget trouble ever came . . . (*To* RUTH) And you could get some nice screens to put up in your room round the baby's bassinet . . . (*She looks at both of them, pleadingly*) Sometimes you just got to know when to give up some things . . . and hold on to what you got.

(WALTER *enters from the outside, looking spent and leaning against the door, his coat hanging from him*)

MAMA   Where you been, son?

WALTER (*Breathing hard*) Made a call.

MAMA To who, son?

WALTER To The Man.

MAMA What man, baby?

WALTER The Man, Mama. Don't you know who The Man is?

RUTH Walter Lee?

WALTER *The Man.* Like the guys in the streets say—The Man. Captain Boss—Mistuh Charley . . . Old Captain Please Mr. Bossman . . .

BENEATHA (*Suddenly*) Lindner!

WALTER That's right! That's good. I told him to come right over.

BENEATHA (*Fiercely, understanding*) For what? What do you want to see him for!

WALTER (*Looking at his sister*) We going to do business with him.

MAMA What you talking 'bout, son?

WALTER Talking 'bout life, Mama. You all always telling me to see life like it is. Well—I laid in there on my back today . . . and I figured it out. Life just like it is. Who gets and who don't get. (*He sits down with his coat on and laughs*) Mama, you know it's all divided up. Life is. Sure enough. Between the takers and the "tooken." (*He laughs*) I've figured it out finally. (*He looks around at them*) Yeah. Some of us always getting "tooken." (*He laughs*) People like Willy Harris, they don't never get "tooken." And you know why the rest of us do? 'Cause we all mixed up. Mixed up bad. We get to looking 'round for the right and the wrong; and we worry about it and cry about it and stay up nights trying to figure out 'bout the wrong and the right of things all the time . . . And all the time, man, them takers is out there operating, just taking and taking. Willy Harris? Shoot—Willy Harris don't even count. He don't even count in the big scheme of things. But I'll say one thing for old Willy Harris . . . he's taught me something. He's taught me to keep my eye on what counts in this world. Yeah— (*Shouting out a little*) Thanks, Willy!

RUTH What did you call that man for, Walter Lee?

WALTER Called him to tell him to come on over to the show. Gonna put on a show for the man. Just what he wants to see. You see, Mama, the man came here today and he told us that them people out there where you want us to move—well they so upset they willing to pay us not to move out there. (*He laughs again*) And —and oh, Mama—you would of been proud of the way me and Ruth and Bennie acted. We told him to get out . . . Lord have mercy! We told the man to get out. Oh, we was some proud folks this afternoon, yeah. (*He lights a cigarette*) We were still full of that old-time stuff . . .

RUTH (*Coming toward him slowly*)   You talking 'bout taking them people's money to keep us from moving in that house?

WALTER   I ain't just talking 'bout it, baby—I'm telling you that's what's going to happen.

BENEATHA   Oh, God! Where is the bottom! Where is the real honest-to-God bottom so he can't go any farther!

WALTER   See—that's the old stuff. You and that boy that was here today. You all want everybody to carry a flag and a spear and sing some marching songs, huh? You wanna spend your life looking into things and trying to find the right and the wrong part, huh? Yeah. You know what's going to happen to that boy someday—he'll find himself sitting in a dungeon, locked in forever—and the takers will have the key! Forget it, baby! There ain't no causes—there ain't nothing but taking in this world, and he who takes most is smartest—and it don't make a damn bit of difference *how.*

MAMA   You making something inside me cry, son. Some awful pain inside me.

WALTER   Don't cry, Mama. Understand. That white man is going to walk in that door able to write checks for more money than we ever had. It's important to him and I'm going to help him . . . I'm going to put on the show, Mama.

MAMA   Son—I come from five generations of people who was slaves and sharecroppers—but ain't nobody in my family never let nobody pay 'em no money that was a way of telling us we wasn't fit to walk the earth. We ain't never been that poor. (*Raising her eyes and looking at him*) We ain't never been that dead inside.

BENEATHA   Well—we are dead now. All the talk about dreams and sunlight that goes on in this house. All dead.

WALTER   What's the matter with you all! I didn't make this world! It was give to me this way! Hell, yes, I want me some yachts someday! Yes, I want to hang some real pearls 'round my wife's neck. Ain't she supposed to wear no pearls? Somebody tell me—tell me, who decides which women is suppose to wear pearls in this world. I tell you I am a *man*—and I think my wife should wear some pearls in this world!

(*This last line hangs a good while and* WALTER *begins to move about the room. The word "Man" has penetrated his conscious-*

ness; he mumbles it to himself repeatedly between strange agitated pauses as he moves about)

MAMA   Baby, how you going to feel on the inside?

WALTER   Fine! . . . Going to feel fine . . . a man . . .

MAMA   You won't have nothing left then, Walter Lee.

WALTER   (*Coming to her*)   I'm going to feel fine, Mama. I'm going to look that son-of-a-bitch in the eyes and say—(*He falters*)—and say, "All right, Mr. Lindner—(*He falters even more*)—that's your neighborhood out there. You got the right to keep it like you want. You got the right to have it like you want. Just write the check and—the house is yours." And, and I am going to say—(*His voice almost breaks*) And you—you people just put the money in my hand and you won't have to live next to this bunch of stinking niggers! . . . (*He straightens up and moves away from his mother, walking around the room*) Maybe—maybe I'll just get down on my black knees . . . (*He does so;* RUTH *and* BENNIE *and* MAMA *watch him in frozen horror*) Captain, Mistuh, Bossman. (*He starts crying*) A-hee-hee-hee! (*Wringing his hands in profoundly anguished imitation*) Yasssssuh! Great White Father, just gi' ussen de money, fo' God's sake, and we's ain't gwine come out deh and dirty up yo' white folks neighborhood . . .

(*He breaks down completely, then gets up and goes into the bedroom*)

BENEATHA   That is not a man. That is nothing but a toothless rat.

MAMA   Yes—death done come in this here house. (*She is nodding, slowly, reflectively*) Done come walking in my house. On the lips of my children. You what supposed to be my beginning again. You—what supposed to be my harvest. (*To* BENEATHA) You—you mourning your brother?

BENEATHA   He's no brother of mine.

MAMA   What you say?

BENEATHA   I said that that individual in that room is no brother of mine.

MAMA   That's what I thought you said. You feeling like you better than he is today? (BENEATHA *does not answer*) Yes? What you tell him a minute ago? That he wasn't a man? Yes? You give him up for me? You done wrote his epitaph too—like the rest of the world? Well, who give you the privilege?

BENEATHA   Be on my side for once! You saw what he just did, Mama! You saw him—down on his knees. Wasn't it you who taught me—to despise any man who would do that. Do what he's going to do.

MAMA Yes—I taught you that. Me and your daddy. But I thought I taught you something else too . . . I thought I taught you to love him.

BENEATHA Love him? There is nothing left to love.

MAMA There is always something left to love. And if you ain't learned that, you ain't learned nothing. (*Looking at her*) Have you cried for that boy today? I don't mean for yourself and for the family 'cause we lost the money. I mean for him; what he been through and what it done to him. Child, when do you think is the time to love somebody the most; when they done good and made things easy for everybody? Well then, you ain't through learning—because that ain't the time at all. It's when he's at his lowest and can't believe in hisself 'cause the world done whipped him so. When you starts measuring somebody, measure him right, child, measure him right. Make sure you done taken into account what hills and valleys he come through before he got to wherever he is.

(TRAVIS *bursts into the room at the end of the speech, leaving the door open*)

TRAVIS Grandmama—the moving men are downstairs! The truck just pulled up.

MAMA (*Turning and looking at him*) Are they, baby? They downstairs?

(*She sighs and sits.* LINDNER *appears in the doorway. He peers in and knocks lightly, to gain attention, and comes in. All turn to look at him*)

LINDNER (*Hat and briefcase in hand*) Uh—hello . . .

(RUTH *crosses mechanically to the bedroom door and opens it and lets it swing open freely and slowly as the lights come up on* WALTER *within, still in his coat, sitting at the far corner of the room. He looks up and out through the room to* LINDNER)

RUTH He's here.

(*A long minute passes and* WALTER *slowly gets up*)

LINDNER (*Coming to the table with efficiency, putting his briefcase on the table and starting to unfold papers and unscrew fountain pens*) Well, I certainly was glad to hear from you people. (WALTER *has begun the trek out of the room, slowly and awkwardly, rather like a small boy, passing the back of his sleeve across his mouth from time to time*) Life can really be so much simpler than people let it be most of the time. Well—with whom do I negotiate? You, Mrs. Younger, or your son here? (MAMA *sits with her hands folded on her lap and her eyes closed as* WALTER *advances.* TRAVIS *goes close to* LINDNER *and looks at the papers curiously*) Just some official papers, sonny.

RUTH   Travis, you go downstairs.

MAMA   (*Opening her eyes and looking into* WALTER's) No. Travis, you stay right here. And you make him understand what you doing, Walter Lee. You teach him good. Like Willy Harris taught you. You show where our five generations done come to. Go ahead, son—

WALTER   (*Looks down into his boy's eyes.* TRAVIS *grins at him merrily and* WALTER *draws him beside him with his arm lightly around his shoulder*) Well, Mr. Lindner. (BENEATHA *turns away*) We called you—(*There is a profound, simple groping quality in his speech*)—because, well, me and my family (*He looks around and shifts from one foot to the other*) Well—we are very plain people . . .

LINDNER   Yes—

WALTER   I mean—I have worked as a chauffeur most of my life—and my wife here, she does domestic work in people's kitchens. So does my mother. I mean—we are plain people . . .

LINDNER   Yes, Mr. Younger—

WALTER   (*Really like a small boy, looking down at his shoes and then up at the man*) And—uh—well, my father, well, he was a laborer most of his life.

LINDNER   (*Absolutely confused*) Uh, yes—

WALTER   (*Looking down at his toes once again*) My father almost beat a man to death once because this man called him a bad name or something, you know what I mean?

LINDNER   No, I'm afraid I don't.

WALTER   (*Finally straightening up*) Well, what I mean is that we come from people who had a lot of pride. I mean—we are very proud people. And that's my sister over there and she's going to be a doctor—and we are very proud—

LINDNER   Well—I am sure that is very nice, but—

WALTER   (*Starting to cry and facing the man eye to eye*) What I am telling you is that we called you over here to tell you that we are very proud and that this is—this is my son, who makes the sixth generation of our family in this country, and that we have all thought about your offer and we have decided to move into our house because my father—my father—he earned it. (MAMA *has her eyes closed and is rocking back and forth as though she were in church, with her head nodding the amen yes*) We don't want to make no trouble for nobody or fight no causes—but we will try to be good neighbors. That's all we got to say. (*He looks the man absolutely in the eyes*) We don't want your money.

(*He turns and walks away from the man*)

LINDNER (*Looking around at all of them*)   I take it then that you have decided to occupy.

BENEATHA   That's what the man said.

LINDNER (*To* MAMA *in her reverie*)   Then I would like to appeal to you, Mrs. Younger. You are older and wiser and understand things better I am sure . . .

MAMA (*Rising*)   I am afraid you don't understand. My son said we was going to move and there ain't nothing left for me to say. (*Shaking her head with double meaning*) You know how these young folks is nowadays, mister. Can't do a thing with 'em. Goodbye.

LINDNER (*Folding up his materials*)   Well—if you are that final about it . . . There is nothing left for me to say. (*He finishes. He is almost ignored by the family, who are concentrating on* WALTER LEE. *At the door* LINDNER *halts and looks around*) I sure hope you people know what you're doing.

(*He shakes his head and exits*)

RUTH (*Looking around and coming to life*)   Well, for God's sake— if the moving men are here—LET'S GET THE HELL OUT OF HERE!

MAMA (*Into action*)   Ain't it the truth! Look at all this here mess. Ruth put Travis' good jacket on him . . . Walter Lee, fix your tie and tuck your shirt in, you look just like somebody's hoodlum. Lord have mercy, where is my plant? (*She flies to get it amid the general bustling of the family, who are deliberately trying to ignore the nobility of the past moment*) You all start on down . . . Travis child, don't go empty-handed . . . Ruth, where did I put that box with my skillets in it? I want to be in charge of it myself . . . I'm going to make us the biggest dinner we ever ate tonight . . . Beneatha, what's the matter with them stockings? Pull them things up, girl . . .

(*The family starts to file out as two moving men appear and begin to carry out the heavier pieces of furniture, bumping into the family as they move about*)

BENEATHA Mama, Asagai—asked me to marry him today and go to Africa—

MAMA (*In the middle of her getting-ready activity*) He did? You ain't old enough to marry nobody—(*Seeing the moving men lifting one of her chairs precariously*) Darling, that ain't no bale of cotton, please handle it so we can sit in it again. I had that chair twenty-five years . . .

(*The movers sigh with exasperation and go on with their work*)

BENEATHA (*Girlishly and unreasonably trying to pursue the conversation*) To go to Africa, Mama—be a doctor in Africa . . .

MAMA (*Distracted*) Yes, baby—

WALTER Africa! What he want you to go to Africa for?

BENEATHA To practice there . . .

WALTER Girl, if you don't get all them silly ideas out your head! You better marry yourself a man with some loot . . .

BENEATHA (*Angrily, precisely as in the first scene of the play*) What have you got to do with who I marry!

WALTER Plenty. Now I think George Murchison—

(*He and* BENEATHA *go out yelling at each other vigorously;* BENEATHA *is heard saying that she would not marry* GEORGE MURCHISON *if he were Adam and she were Eve, etc. The anger is loud and real till their voices diminish.* RUTH *stands at the door and turns to* MAMA *and smiles knowingly*)

MAMA (*Fixing her hat at last*) Yeah—they something all right, my children . . .

RUTH Yeah—they're something. Let's go, Lena.

MAMA (*Stalling, starting to look around at the house*) Yes—I'm coming. Ruth—

RUTH Yes?

MAMA (*Quietly, woman to woman*) He finally come into his manhood today, didn't he? Kind of like a rainbow after the rain . . .

RUTH (*Biting her lip lest her own pride explode in front of* MAMA) Yes, Lena.

(WALTER's *voice calls for them raucously*)

MAMA (*Waving* RUTH *out vaguely*) All right, honey—go on down. I be down directly.

(RUTH *hesitates, then exits.* MAMA *stands, at last alone in the living room, her plant on the table before her as the lights start to come down. She looks around at all the walls and ceilings and suddenly, despite herself, while the children call below, a great heaving thing rises in her and she puts her fist to her mouth, takes a final desperate look, pulls her coat about her, pats her hat and goes out. The lights dim down. The door opens and she comes back in, grabs her plant, and goes out for the last time)*

Curtain

A Man
for All Seasons

BY

Robert Bolt

A Man for All Seasons *was first presented by Robert Whitehead and Roger L. Stevens at the ANTA Theatre, New York City, New York, on November 22, 1961, with the following cast:*

(*In order of appearance*)

THE COMMON MAN	George Rose
SIR THOMAS MORE	Paul Scofield
RICHARD RICH	William Redfield
THE DUKE OF NORFOLK	Albert Dekker
ALICE MORE	Carol Goodner
MARGARET MORE	Olga Bellin
CARDINAL WOLSEY	Jack Creley
THOMAS CROMWELL	Thomas Gomez
SIGÑOR CHAPUYS, the Spanish Ambassador	David J. Stewart
HIS ATTENDANT	John Colenback
WILLIAM ROPER	Peter Brandon
KING HENRY VIII	Keith Baxter
THE WOMAN	Sarah Burton
CRANMER, Archbishop of Canterbury	Lester Rawlins

Directed by Noel Willman
Settings and costumes by Motley
Lighting by Paul Morrison
Produced by arrangement with H. M. Tennent Ltd.

People In The Play

THE COMMON MAN: Late middle age. He wears from head to foot black tights which delineate his pot-bellied figure. His face is crafty, loosely benevolent, its best expression that of base humor.

SIR THOMAS MORE: Late forties. Pale, middle-sized, not robust. But the life of the mind in him is so abundant and debonair that it illuminates the body. His movements are open and swift but never wild, having a natural moderation. The face is intellectual and quickly delighted, the norm to which it returns serious and compassionate. Only in moments of high crisis does it become ascetic —though then freezingly.

RICHARD RICH: Early thirties. A good body unexercised. A studious unhappy face lit by the fire of banked-down appetite. He is an academic hounded by self-doubt to be in the world of affairs and longing to be rescued from himself.

DUKE OF NORFOLK: Late forties. Heavy, active, a sportsman and soldier held together by rigid adherence to the minimal code of conventional duty. Attractively aware of his moral and intellectual insignificance, but also a great nobleman, untouchably convinced that his acts and ideas are important because they are his.

ALICE MORE: Late forties. Born into the merchant class, now a great lady; she is absurd at a distance, impressive close to. Overdressed, coarsely fashioned, she worships society; brave, hot-hearted, she worships her husband. In consequence, troubled by and defiant towards both.

MARGARET MORE: Middle twenties. A beautiful girl of ardent moral fineness; she both suffers and shelters behind a reserved stillness which it is her father's care to mitigate.

CARDINAL WOLSEY: Old. A big decayed body in scarlet. An almost megalomaniac ambition unhappily matched by an excelling intellect, he now inhabits a lonely den of self-indulgence and contempt.

THOMAS CROMWELL: Late thirties. Subtle and serious; the face expressing not inner tension but the tremendous outgoing will of the renaissance. A self-conceit that can cradle gross crimes in the name of effective action. In short, an intellectual bully.

CHAPUYS: Sixties. A professional diplomat and lay ecclesiastic dressed in black. Much on his dignity as a man of the world, he in fact trots happily along a mental footpath as narrow as a peasant's.

CHAPUYS' ATTENDANT: An apprentice diplomat of good family.

WILLIAM ROPER: Early thirties; a stiff body and an immobile face. Little imagination, moderate brain, but an all-consuming rectitude which is his cross, his solace, and his hobby.

THE KING: *Not* the Holbein Henry, but a much younger man, clean-shaven, bright-eyed, graceful and athletic. The Golden Hope of the New Learning throughout Europe. Only the levity with which he handles his absolute power foreshadows his future corruption.

A WOMAN: Middle fifties. Self-opinionated, self-righteous, selfish, indignant.

CRANMER: Late forties. Sharp-minded, sharp-faced. He treats the Church as a job of administration, and theology as a set of devices, for he lacks personal religiosity.

SIR THOMAS MORE

More is a man of an angel's wit and singular learning; I know not his fellow. For where is the man of that gentleness, lowliness, and affability? And as time requireth a man of marvellous mirth and pastimes; and sometimes of as sad gravity: a man for all seasons.

Robert Whittinton

He was the person of the greatest virtue these islands ever produced.

Samuel Johnson

ACT ONE

When the curtain rises, the set is in darkness but for a single spot upon the COMMON MAN, *who sits on a big property basket.*

COMMON MAN (*Rises*) It is perverse! To start a play made up of Kings and Cardinals in speaking costumes and intellectuals with embroidered mouths, with me.

If a King or a Cardinal had done the prologue he'd have had the right materials. And an intellectual would have shown enough majestic meanings, colored propositions, and closely woven liturgical stuff to dress the House of Lords! But this!

Is this a costume? Does this say anything? It barely covers one man's nakedness! A bit of black material to reduce Old Adam to the Common Man.

Oh, if they'd let me come on naked, I could have shown you something of my own. Which would have told you without words—! Something I've forgotten . . . Old Adam's muffled up. (*Backing towards the basket*) Well, for a proposition of my own, I need a costume. (*Takes out and puts on the coat and hat of* STEWARD) Matthew! The Household Steward of Sir Thomas More! (*Lights come up swiftly on set. He takes from the basket five silver goblets, one larger than the others, and a jug with a lid, with which he furnishes the table. A burst of conversational merriment off; he pauses and indicates head of stairs*) There's company to dinner. (*He pours a cup of wine*) All right! A Common Man! A Sixteenth-Century Butler! (*He drinks from the cup*) All right—the Six——(*He breaks off, agreeably surprised by the quality of the liquor, regards the jug respectfully and drinks again from jug*) The Sixteenth Century is the Century of the Common Man. (*He puts down the jug*) Like all the other centuries. And that's my proposition.

(*During the last part of the speech, voices are heard off. Now, enter, at the head of the stairs,* SIR THOMAS MORE)

STEWARD   That's Sir Thomas More.

MORE   The wine please, Matthew?

STEWARD   It's there, Sir Thomas.

MORE (*Looking into the jug*)   Is it good?

STEWARD   Bless you, sir! I don't know.

MORE (*Mildly*)   Bless you too, Matthew.

(*Enter* RICH *at the head of the stairs*)

RICH (*Enthusiastically pursuing an argument*)   But every man has his price!

MORE   No-no-no—

STEWARD (*Contemptuously*)   Master Richard Rich.

RICH   But yes! In money too.

MORE (*With gentle impatience*)   No no no.

RICH   Or pleasure. Titles, women, bricks-and-mortar, there's always something.

MORE   Childish.

RICH   Well, in suffering, certainly.

MORE (*Interested*)   Buy a man with suffering?

RICH   Impose suffering, and offer him—escape.

MORE   Oh. For a moment I thought you were being profound.

(*He gives a cup to* RICH)

RICH (*To* STEWARD)   Good evening, Matthew.

STEWARD (*Snubbing*)   'Evening, sir.

RICH   No, not a bit profound; it then becomes a purely practical question of how to make him suffer sufficiently.

MORE   Mm . . . (*He takes him by the arm and walks with him*) And . . . who recommended you to read Signor Machiavelli? (RICH *breaks away laughing—a fraction too long.* MORE *smiles*) No, who? (*More laughter*) . . . Mm?

RICH   Master Cromwell.

MORE   Oh . . . (*He goes back to the wine jug and cups*) He's a very able man.

RICH   And so he is!

MORE   Yes, I say he is. He's very able.

RICH   And he will do something for me, he says.

MORE   I didn't know you knew him.

RICH   Pardon me, Sir Thomas, but how much do you know about me?

MORE   Whatever you've let me know.

RICH   I've let you know everything!

MORE   Richard, you should go back to Cambridge; you're deteriorating.

RICH   Well, I'm not used! . . . D'you know how much I have to show for seven months' work—

MORE   Work?

RICH   Work! Waiting's work when you wait as I wait, hard! . . . For seven months, that's two hundred days, I have to show: the acquaintance of the Cardinal's outer doorman, the indifference of the Cardinal's inner doorman, and the Cardinal's chamberlain's hand in my chest! . . . Oh—also one half of a Good Morning delivered at fifty paces by the Duke of Norfolk. Doubtless he mistook me for someone.

MORE   He was very affable at dinner.

RICH   Oh, everyone's affable *here* . . . (MORE *is pleased*) Also, of course, the friendship of Sir Thomas More. Or should I say acquaintance?

MORE   Say friendship.

RICH   Well, there! "A friend of Sir Thomas and still no office? There must be something wrong with him."

MORE   I thought we said friendship . . . (*He considers; then*) The Dean of St. Paul's offers you a post; with a house, a servant and fifty pounds a year.

RICH   What? What post?

MORE   At the new school.

RICH   (*Bitterly disappointed*)   A teacher!

MORE   A man should go where he won't be tempted. Look, Richard, see this. (*He hands him a silver cup*) Look . . . Look . . .

RICH   Beautiful.

MORE   Italian . . . Do you want it?

RICH   Why?

MORE   No joke; keep it; or sell it.

RICH   Well—Thank you, of course. Thank you! Thank you! But—

MORE   You'll sell it, won't you?

RICH   Well—I—Yes, I will.

MORE   And buy, what?

RICH   (*With sudden ferocity*)   Some decent clothes!

MORE   (*With sympathy*)   Ah.

RICH   I want a gown like yours.

MORE   You'll get several gowns for that I should think. It was sent to me a little while ago by some woman. Now she's put a lawsuit into the Court of Requests. It's a bribe, Richard.

RICH   Oh . . . (*Chagrined*) So you give it away, of course.

MORE   Yes!

RICH   To me?

MORE   Well, I'm not going to keep it, and you need it. Of course—if you feel it's contaminated . . .

RICH   No, no. I'll risk it.

(*They both smile*)

MORE   But, Richard, in office they offer you all sorts of things. I was once offered a whole village, with a mill, and a manor house, and heaven knows what else—a coat of arms, I shouldn't be surprised. Why not be a teacher? You'd be a fine teacher. Perhaps even a great one.

RICH   And if I was, who would know it?

MORE   You, your pupils, your friends, God. Not a bad public, that . . . Oh, and a *quiet* life.

RICH   (*Laughing*)   *You* say that!

MORE   Richard, I was commanded into office; it was inflicted on me . . . (RICH *regards him*) Can't you believe that?

RICH   It's hard.

MORE   (*Grimly*)   Be a teacher.

NORFOLK   (*Enters at the head of the stairs*)   It was magnificent!

STEWARD   (*To audience*)   The Duke of Norfolk. Earl Marshal of England.

NORFOLK   I tell you he stooped from the clouds! (*Breaks off; irritably*) Alice!

(ALICE *enters instantly at the head of the stairs*)

ALICE   (*Irritably*)   Here!

STEWARD   (*To audience*)   Lady Alice. My master's wife.

NORFOLK   I tell you he stooped—

ALICE   He didn't—

NORFOLK   Goddammit, he did—

ALICE   Couldn't—

NORFOLK   He *does*—

ALICE   Not possible—

NORFOLK   But *often*—

ALICE   Never.

NORFOLK   Well, damn my soul.

MORE   (*To* MARGARET, *who has appeared on the gallery*)   Come down, Meg.

STEWARD   (*Soapy; to audience*)   Lady Margaret, my master's daughter; lovely, really lovely.

ALICE (*Glances suspiciously at* STEWARD) Matthew, get about your business. (STEWARD *exits*) We'll settle this, my lord, we'll put it to Thomas. Thomas, no falcon could stoop from a cloud, could it?

MORE I don't know, my dear; it sounds unlikely. I have seen falcons do some very splendid things.

ALICE But how could he stoop from a cloud? He couldn't see where he was going.

NORFOLK You see, Alice—you're ignorant of the subject; a real falcon don't *care* where he's going! (*He takes some wine*) Thank you, Thomas. Anyway, I'm talking to Meg. (*A sportsman's story*) 'Twas the very first cast of the day, Meg; the sun was behind us. And from side to side of the valley like the roof of a tent was solid mist—

ALICE Oh, mist.

NORFOLK Well, mist is cloud, isn't it?

ALICE No.

RICH The opinion of Aristotle is that mists are an exhalation of the earth whereas clouds—

NORFOLK He stooped five hundred feet! Like that! Like an Act of God, isn't he, Thomas?

MORE He's tremendous.

NORFOLK (*To* ALICE) Tremendous.

MARGARET Did he kill the heron?

NORFOLK Oh, the *heron* was *clever*. (*Very evidently discreditable*) It was a royal stoop though. (*Slyly*) If you could ride, Alice, I'd show you.

ALICE (*Hotly*) I can ride, my lord!

MORE No, no, you'll make yourself ill.

ALICE And I'll bet—twenty-five—no, thirty shillings I see no falcon stoop from no cloud!

NORFOLK Done.

MORE Alice—you can't ride with *them*.

ALICE God's body, Thomas, remember who you are. Am I a city wife?

MORE No indeed, you've just lost thirty shillings, I think; there *are* such birds. And the heron got home to his chicks, Meg, so everything was satisfactory.

MARGARET (*Smiling*) Yes.

MORE What was that of Aristotle's, Richard?

RICHARD Nothing, Sir Thomas—'twas out of place.

NORFOLK (*To* RICH) I've never found much use in Aristotle myself, not practically. Great philosopher, of course. Wonderful mind.

RICH   Exactly, Your Grace!

NORFOLK (*Suspicious*) Eh?

MORE   Master Rich is newly converted to the doctrines of Machiavelli.

RICH   Oh *no* . . . !

NORFOLK   Oh, the Italian. Nasty book, from what I hear.

MARGARET   Very practical, Your Grace.

NORFOLK   You read it? Amazing girl, Thomas, but where are you going to find a husband for her?

MORE (MORE *and* MEG *exchange a glance*) Where indeed?

RICH   The doctrines of Machiavelli have been largely mistaken, I think; indeed, properly apprehended, he has no doctrine. Master Cromwell has the sense of it I think when he says—

NORFOLK   You know Cromwell?

RICH   . . . Slightly, Your Grace . . .

NORFOLK   The Cardinal's Secretary.

(*Exclamations of shock from* MORE, MARGARET *and* ALICE)

ALICE   Never—it can't be.

MARGARET   The Cardinal's—it's impossible.

MORE   Not possible!

NORFOLK   It's a fact.

MORE   When, Howard?

NORFOLK   Two, three days.

(*They move about uneasily*)

ALICE   A *farrier's* son?

NORFOLK   Well, the Cardinal's a butcher's son, isn't he?

ALICE   It'll be up quick and down quick with Master Cromwell.

(NORFOLK *grunts*)

MORE (*Quietly*) Did you know this?

RICH   No!

MARGARET   Do you *like* Master Cromwell, Master Rich?

ALICE   He's the only man in London if he does!

RICH   I think I do, Lady Alice!

MORE (*Pleased*) Good . . . Well, you don't need *my* help now.

RICH   Sir Thomas, if only you knew how much, much rather I'd yours than his!

(*Enter* STEWARD, *who gives a letter to* MORE, *who opens it and reads*)

MORE   Talk of the Cardinal's Secretary and the Cardinal appears. He wants me. Now.

ALICE   At this time of the night?

MORE (*Mildly*)   The King's business.

ALICE   The Queen's business.

NORFOLK   More than likely, Alice, more than likely.

MORE (*Cuts in sharply*)   What's the time?

STEWARD   Eleven o'clock, sir.

MORE   Is there a boat?

STEWARD   Waiting, sir.

MORE (*To* ALICE *and* MARGARET)   Go to bed. You'll excuse me, Your Grace? Richard? Now you'll go to bed . . .

   (*The* MORE *family, as a matter of routine, put their hands together*)

MORE, ALICE, MARGARET   Dear Lord, give us rest tonight, or if we must be wakeful, cheerful. Careful only for our soul's salvation. For Christ's sake. Amen.

MORE   And bless our Lord the King.

ALICE and MARGARET   And bless our Lord the King.

ALL   Amen.

   (*And then immediately a brisk leave-taking:* MORE *moving off below, the others mounting the stairs*)

MORE   Howard, are *you* at Richmond?

NORFOLK   No, down the river.

MORE   Then good night! (*He sees* RICH *disconsolate*) Oh, Your Grace, here's a young man desperate for employment. Something in the clerical line.

NORFOLK   Well, if you recommend him.

MORE   No. I don't recommend him; but I point him out. (*Moving off*) He's at the New Inn. Can you take him there?

NORFOLK (*To* RICH; *mounting the stairs*)   All right, come on.

RICH   My Lord.

NORFOLK   We'll hawk at Hounslow, Alice.

ALICE   Wherever you like.

   (ALICE *and* MARGARET *follow* NORFOLK)

RICH (*At foot of the stairs*)   Sir Thomas! . . . (MORE *turns*) Thank you.

MORE   Be a teacher. (*Moving off again*) Alice! The ground's hard at Hounslow!

NORFOLK   Eh? (*Delighted roar*) That's where the Cardinal crushed his bum!

MORE, NORFOLK, ALICE, RICH   Good night! Good night!

(*They process off along the gallery*)

MORE (*Softly*)   Margaret!

MARGARET   Yes?

MORE   Go to bed.

(MARGARET *exits above*, MORE *exits below. After a moment* RICH *walks swiftly back, picks up the goblet and is going off with it*)

STEWARD (*Takes goblet*)   Eh!

RICH   What—Oh . . . It's a gift, Matthew. Sir Thomas gave it to me.

(STEWARD *regards it silently*)   He gave it to me.

STEWARD (*Returns it*)   Very nice present, sir.

RICH (*Beginning to leave with it*)   Yes. Good night, Matthew.

STEWARD   Sir Thomas has taken quite a fancy to you, sir.

RICH   Er, here—

(*Gives him some money and goes*)

STEWARD   Thank you, sir . . . (*To audience*) That one'll come to nothing. (*Begins packing props into basket. Pauses with a cup in hand*) My master Thomas More would give anything to anyone. Some say that's good and some say that's bad, but I say he can't help it—and that's bad . . . because some day someone's going to ask him for something that he wants to keep; and he'll be out of practice. (*Puts a cloth, papers, pen and ink, and candles on the table*) There must be something that he wants to keep. That's only common sense.

(*Enter* WOLSEY. *He sits at the table and immediately commences writing, watched by* COMMON MAN, *who then exits. Enter* MORE)

WOLSEY (*Writing*)   It's half-past one. Where've you been?

(*A bell strikes one*)

MORE   One o'clock, Your Grace. I've been on the river.

(WOLSEY *writes in silence while* MORE *waits standing*)

WOLSEY (*Still writing, pushes paper across the table*)   Since you seemed so violently opposed to the dispatch for Rome, I thought you'd like to look it over.

MORE (*Touched*)   Thank you, Your Grace.

WOLSEY   Before it goes.

MORE (*Smiles*)   Your Grace is very kind. (*He takes it and reads*) Thank you.

WOLSEY   Well, what d'you think of it?

(*He is still writing*)

MORE   It seems very well phrased, Your Grace.

WOLSEY (*Permits himself a chuckle*) The devil it does! (*He sits back*) And apart from the style, Sir Thomas?

MORE (*Crisply*) It's addressed to Cardinal Campeggio.

WOLSEY Yes?

MORE Not to our ambassador.

WOLSEY Our ambassador's a ninny.

MORE (*A smile*) Your Grace appointed him.

WOLSEY (*Treats it at the level of humor, mock exasperation*) Yes I need a *ninny* in Rome! So that I can write to Cardinal Campeggio!

MORE (*Won't respond; with aesthetic distaste—not moral disapproval*) It's devious.

WOLSEY It's a devious situation!

MORE There must be something simple in the middle of it.
(*Again this is not a moral dictum; it is said rather wistfully, as of something he is beginning to doubt*)

WOLSEY (*After a pause, rather gently*) I believe you believe that. (*Briskly*) You're a constant regret to me, Thomas. If you could just see facts flat on, without that horrible moral squint; with just a little common sense, you could have been a statesman.

MORE (*After a little pause*) Oh, Your Grace flatters me.

WOLSEY Don't frivol . . . Thomas, are you going to help me?

MORE (*Hesitates, looks away*) If Your Grace will be specific.

WOLSEY Ach, you're a plodder! Take you altogether, Thomas, your scholarship, your experience, what are you? (*A single trumpet calls, distant, frosty and clear.* WOLSEY *gets up and goes and looks from the window*) Come here. (MORE *joins him*) The King.

MORE Yes.

WOLSEY Where has he been? D'you know?

MORE I, Your Grace?

WOLSEY Oh, spare me your discretion. He's been to play in the mud again.

MORE (*Coldly*) Indeed.

WOLSEY Indeed! Indeed! Are you going to oppose me? (*Trumpet sounds again.* WOLSEY *visibly relaxes*) He's gone in . . . (*He leaves the window*) All right, we'll plod. The King wants a son; what are you going to do about it?

MORE (*Dry murmur*) I'm very sure the King needs no advice from me on what to do about it.

WOLSEY (*From behind, grips his shoulder fiercely*) Thomas, we're alone. I give you my word. There's no one here.

MORE I didn't suppose there was, Your Grace.

WOLSEY   Oh. Sit down! (*He goes to the table, sits, signals* MORE *to sit.* MORE *unsuspectingly obeys. Then, deliberately loud*) Do you favor a change of dynasty, Sir Thomas? Thomas? D'you think two Tudors is sufficient?

MORE   (*Starting up in horrified alarm*) For God's sake, Your Grace—

WOLSEY   Then the King needs a son; I repeat, what are you going to do about it?

MORE   (*Steadily*) I pray for it daily.

WOLSEY   (*Softly*) God's death, he means it . . . That thing out there's at least fertile, Thomas.

MORE   But she's not his wife.

WOLSEY   No, Catherine's his wife and she's as barren as a brick. Are you going to pray for a miracle?

MORE   There *are* precedents.

WOLSEY   Yes. All right. Good. Pray. Pray by all means. But in addition to prayer there is effort. My effort's to secure a divorce. Have I your support or have I not?

MORE   (*Sits*) A dispensation was granted so that the King might marry Queen Catherine, for state reasons. Now we are to ask the Pope to—dispense with his dispensation, also for state reasons?

WOLSEY   I don't *like* plodding, Thomas, don't make me plod longer than I have to—Well?

MORE   Then clearly all we have to do is approach His Holiness and ask him.

(*The pace becomes rapid*)

WOLSEY   I think we might influence His Holiness' answer—

MORE   Like this?

(*Indicating the dispatch*)

WOLSEY   Like that and in other ways—

MORE   I've already expressed my opinion on this—

WOLSEY   Then, good night! Oh, your conscience is your own affair; but you're a statesman! Do you *remember* the Yorkist Wars?

MORE   Very clearly.

WOLSEY   Let him die without an heir and we'll have them back again. Let him die without an heir and this "peace" you think so much of will go out like that! (*He extinguishes the candle*) Very well then . . . England needs an heir; certain measures, perhaps regrettable, perhaps not— (*Pompous*) there is much in the Church that *needs* reformation, Thomas— (MORE *smiles*) All right, regrettable! But necessary, to get us an heir! Now explain how you as Councilor of England can obstruct those measures for the sake of your own, private, conscience.

MORE   Well . . . I believe, when statesmen forsake their own private conscience for the sake of their public duties . . . they lead their country by a short route to chaos. (*During this speech he relights the candle with another*) And we shall have my prayers to fall back on.

WOLSEY   You'd like that, wouldn't you? To govern the country by prayers?

MORE   Yes, I should.

WOLSEY   I'd like to be there when you try. Who *will*? (*He half lifts the chain from his shoulders*) Who will put his neck in this—after me? You? Tunstall? Suffolk?

MORE   Tunstall for me.

WOLSEY   Aye, but for the King. What about my Secretary, Master Cromwell?

MORE   Cromwell!

WOLSEY   You'd rather do it yourself?

MORE   Me rather than Cromwell.

WOLSEY   Then come down to earth, Thomas. (*He looks away*) And until you do, bear in mind you have an enemy!

MORE   (*Wishing to make sure, quietly*)   Where, Your Grace?

WOLSEY   (*Looks back at him, hard-faced, harsh; for the first time we see this is a carnivore*)   Here, Thomas.

MORE   As Your Grace pleases.

WOLSEY   As God wills!

MORE   Perhaps, Your Grace.

    (*Mounting stairs*)

WOLSEY   More! You should have been a cleric!

MORE   (*Amused, looking down from gallery*)   Like yourself, Your Grace?

    (*Exit* MORE. WOLSEY *is left staring, then exits through the lower arches with candle, taking most of the light from the stage as he does so. But the whole rear of the stage is now patterned with webbed reflections thrown from brightly moonlit water, so that the structure is thrown into black relief, while a strip of light descends along the front of the stage, which is to be the acting area for the next scene. An oar and a bundle of clothing are lowered into this area from above. Enter* COMMON MAN; *he unties the bundle and begins to don the coat and hat of* BOATMAN)

MORE   (*Off*)   Boat! Boat! (*Approaching*) Boat!

BOATMAN (*Donning coat and hat*) Here, sir!

MORE (*Off*) A boatman please!

BOATMAN Boat here, sir!

(*He seizes the oar. Enter* MORE)

MORE (*Peering*) Boatman?

BOATMAN Yes, sir. (*To audience, indicating oar*) A boatman.

MORE Take me home.

BOATMAN (*Pleasantly*) I was just going home myself, sir.

MORE Then find me another boat.

BOATMAN Bless you, sir—that's all right. (*Comfortably*) I expect you'll make it worth my while, sir.

CROMWELL (*Stepping from behind an arch*) Boatman, have you a license?

BOATMAN Eh? Bless you, sir, yes; I've got a license.

CROMWELL Then you know that the fares are fixed— (*Turns to* MORE. *Exaggerated pleasure*) Why, it's Sir Thomas!

MORE Good morning, Master Cromwell. You work very late.

CROMWELL I'm on my way to the Cardinal.

MORE (*Recollecting*) Ah yes, you are to be felicitated. Good morning, Master *Secretary*.

(*He smiles politely*)

CROMWELL (*Smiling*) Yes.

MORE If it *is* felicity to be busy in the night.

CROMWELL It is.

MORE Felicitations then.

(*They exchange a dry little bow*)

CROMWELL You have just left him, I think.

MORE Yes, I have.

CROMWELL You left him . . . in his laughing mood, I hope?

MORE On the whole I would say not. No, not laughing.

CROMWELL Oh, I'm sorry. (*Backing to exit*) I am one of your *multitudinous* admirers, Sir Thomas. A penny ha'penny to Chelsea, Boatman.

(*Exit* CROMWELL)

BOATMAN The coming man they say, sir.

MORE Do they? Well, where's your boat?

BOATMAN Just along the wharf, sir.

(*They are going when* CHAPUYS *and his* ATTENDANT *enter*)

CHAPUYS Sir Thomas More!

MORE Signor Chapuys? You're up very late, Your Excellency.

CHAPUYS (*Significantly*) So is the Cardinal, Sir Thomas.

MORE (*Closing up*) He sleeps very little.

CHAPUYS You have just left him, I think.

MORE You are correctly informed. As always.

CHAPUYS I will not ask you the subject of your conversation . . .
(*He waits*)

MORE No, of course not.

CHAPUYS Sir Thomas, I will be plain with you . . . plain, that is,
so far as the diplomatic decencies permit. (*Loudly*) My master
Charles, the King of Spain! (*Pulls* MORE *aside; discreetly*) My
master Charles, the King of Spain, feels himself concerned in
anything concerning his blood relations. He would feel himself
insulted by any insult offered to his mother's sister! I refer, of
course, to Queen Catherine. (*He regards* MORE *keenly*) The King
of Spain would feel himself insulted by any insult offered to
Queen Catherine.

MORE His feeling would be natural.

CHAPUYS (*Consciously shy*) Sir Thomas, may I ask if you and the
Cardinal parted, how shall I say, amicably?

MORE Amicably . . . Yes.

CHAPUYS (*A shade indignant*) In agreement?

MORE Amicably.

CHAPUYS (*Warmly*) Say no more, Sir Thomas; I understand.

MORE (*A bit worried*) I hope you do, Your Excellency.

CHAPUYS You are a good man.

MORE I don't see how you deduce that from what I told you.

CHAPUYS (*Holds up a hand*) A nod is as good as a wink to a blind
horse. I understand. You are a good man. (*He turns to exit*)
Dominus vobiscum.

(CHAPUYS *exits.* MORE *looks after him*)

MORE (*Abstracted*) . . . spiritu tuo . . .

BOATMAN (*Mournful; he is squatting on the ground*) Some people
think boats stay afloat on their own, sir, but the don't; they cost
money. (MORE *is abstractedly gazing over the audience*) Take
anchor rope, sir, you may not believe me, for a little skiff like
mine, but it's a penny a fathom. (MORE *is still abstracted*) And
with a young wife, sir, as you know . . .

MORE (*Abstracted*) I'll pay what I always pay you . . . The river
looks very black tonight. They say it's tilting up, is that so?

BOATMAN (*Joining him*) Not in the middle, sir. There's a channel
there getting deeper all the time.

MORE How is your wife?

BOATMAN   She's losing her shape, sir, losing it fast.

MORE   Well, so are we all.

BOATMAN   Oh yes, sir; it's common.

MORE   (*Going*)   Well, take me home.

   (*Exit* MORE)

BOATMAN   That I will, sir! (*Crossing to the basket and pulling it out*) From Richmond to Chelsea, a penny halfpenny . . . (*He goes for the tablecloth*) from Chelsea to Richmond, a penny halfpenny. From Richmond to Chelsea, it's a quiet float downstream, from Chelsea to Richmond, it's a hard pull upstream. And it's a penny halfpenny either way. Whoever makes the regulations doesn't row a boat. (*Puts the cloth into the basket, takes out slippers*) Home again.

   (*Lighting changes to* MORE'S *house.* MORE *enters, sits wearily. He takes off hat, half takes off coat but is too tired. A bell chimes three.* STEWARD *kneels to put on his slippers for him*)

MORE   Ah, Matthew . . . Is Lady Alice in bed?

STEWARD   Yes, sir.

MORE   Lady Margaret?

STEWARD   No, sir. Master Roper's here.

MORE   (*Surprised*)   At this hour? . . . Who let him in?

STEWARD   He's a hard man to keep out, sir.

MORE   Where are they?

   (MARGARET *and* ROPER *enter*)

MARGARET   Here, Father.

MORE   Thank you, Matthew. (STEWARD *exits.* MORE, *regarding them; resignedly*) Good morning, William. It's a little early for breakfast.

ROPER   (*Stolidly*)   I haven't come for breakfast, sir.

   (MORE *looks at him and sighs*)

MARGARET   Will wants to marry me, Father.

MORE   Well, he can't marry you.

ROPER   Sir Thomas, I'm to be called to the Bar.

MORE   (*Warmly*)   Oh, congratulations, Roper!

ROPER   My family may not be at the palace, sir, but in the City—

MORE   The Ropers were advocates when the Mores were selling pewter; there's nothing wrong with your family. There's nothing wrong with your fortune—there's nothing wrong with you— (*Sourly*) except you need a clock—

ROPER   I can buy a clock, sir.

MORE Roper, the answer's "no." (*Firmly*) And will be "no" so long as you're a heretic.

ROPER (*Firing*) That's a word I don't like, Sir Thomas!

MORE It's not a likable word. (*Coming to life*) It's not a likable thing!

(MARGARET *is alarmed, and from behind* MORE *tries to silence* ROPER)

ROPER The Church is heretical! Doctor Luther's proved that to my satisfaction!

MORE Luther's an excommunicate.

ROPER From a heretic Church! Church? It's a shop—Forgiveness by the florin! Job lots now in Germany! . . . Mmmm, and divorces.

MORE (*Expressionless*) Divorces?

ROPER Oh, half England's buzzing with that.

MORE "Half England." The Inns of Court may be buzzing, England doesn't buzz so easily.

ROPER It will. And is that a Church? Is that a Cardinal? Is that a Pope? Or Antichrist! (MORE *looks up angrily.* MARGARET *signals frantically*) Look, what I know I'll say!

MARGARET You've no sense of the *place!*

MORE (*Rueful*) He's no sense of the time.

ROPER I—

(*But* MORE *gently holds up his hand and he stops*)

MORE Listen, Roper. Two years ago you were a passionate Churchman; now you're a passionate—Lutheran. We must just pray that when your head's finished turning, your face is to the front again.

ROPER Don't lengthen your prayers with *me*, sir!

MORE Oh, one more or less . . . Is your horse here?

ROPER No, I walked.

MORE Well, take a horse from the stables and get back home. (ROPER *hesitates*) Go along.

ROPER May I come again?

(MORE *indicates* MARGARET)

MARGARET Yes. Soon.

ROPER Good night, sir.

(ROPER *exits*)

MARGARET Is that final, Father?

MORE As long as he's a heretic, Meg, that's absolute. (*Warmly*)

Nice boy . . . Terribly strong principles though. I thought I told
you to go to bed.

MARGARET   Yes, why?

MORE (*Lightly*)   Because I intended you to *go* to bed. You're very
pensive?

MARGARET   You're very gay. Did the Cardinal talk about the divorce?

MORE   Mm? You know I think we've been on the wrong track with
Will—It's no good arguing with a Roper—

MARGARET   Father, did he?

MORE   *Old* Roper was just the same. Now let him think he's going
with the current and he'll turn round and start swimming in the
opposite direction. What we want is a really substantial attack
on the Church.

MARGARET   We're going to get it, aren't we?

MORE   Margaret, I'll not have you talk treason . . . And I'll not
have you repeat lawyer's gossip. I'm a lawyer myself and I know
what it's worth.

ALICE (*Off. Indignant and excited*)   Thomas!

MORE   Now look what you've done.

(ALICE *enters at the head of the stairs in her nightgown*)

ALICE   Young Roper! I've just seen young Roper! On *my* horse.

MORE   He'll bring it back, dear. He's been to see Margaret.

ALICE   Oh—why you don't beat that girl!

MORE   No, no, she's full of education—and it's a delicate commodity.

ALICE   Mm! And more's the pity!

MORE   Yes, but it's there now and think what it cost.

(*He sneezes*)

ALICE (*Pouncing*)   Ah! Margaret—hot water.

(*Exit* MARGARET)

MORE   I'm sorry you were awakened, chick.

ALICE   I wasn't sleeping very deeply. Thomas—what did Wolsey
want?

MORE (*Innocently*)   Young Roper asked me for Margaret.

ALICE   What! Impudence!

MORE   Yes, wasn't it?

ALICE   Old fox! What did he want, Thomas?

MORE   He wanted me to read a dispatch.

ALICE   Was that all?

MORE   A Latin dispatch.

ALICE   Oh! You don't want to talk about it?

MORE *(Gently)* No.

(Enter MARGARET *with a cup, which she takes to* MORE*)*

ALICE   Norfolk was speaking for you as Chancellor before he left.

MORE   He's a dangerous friend then. Wolsey's Chancellor, God help him. We don't want another. *(*MARGARET *takes the cup to him; he sniffs it)* I don't want this.

ALICE   Drink it. Great men get colds in the head just the same as commoners.

MORE   That's dangerous, leveling talk, Alice. Beware of the Tower.

ALICE   Drink it!

MORE *(Rises)*   I will, I'll drink it in bed.

(They move to the stairs and ascend, talking)

MARGARET   Would you want to be Chancellor?

MORE   No.

MARGARET   That's what I said. But Norfolk said if Wolsey fell—

MORE *(No longer flippant)*   If Wolsey fell, the splash would swamp a few small boats like ours. There will be no new Chancellors while Wolsey lives.

(They exit above. The light is dimmed there and a bright spot descends below. Into this bright circle is thrown a great red robe and the Cardinal's hat. The COMMON MAN *enters and roughly piles them into his basket. He then takes from his pocket a pair of spectacles and from the basket a book)*

COMMON MAN *(Reading)*   "Whether we follow tradition in ascribing Wolsey's death to a broken heart, or accept Professor Larcomb's less feeling diagnosis of pulmonary pneumonia, its effective cause was the King's displeasure. He died at Leicester on 29 November, 1530, while on his way to the Tower under charge of High Treason.

"England's next Lord Chancellor was Sir Thomas More, a scholar and, by popular repute, a saint. His scholarship is supported by his writings; saintliness is a quality less easy to establish. But from his willful indifference to realities which were obvious to quite ordinary contemporaries, it seems all too probable that he had it."

(Exit COMMON MAN. *As he goes, lights come up and a screen is lowered depicting Hampton Court.* CROMWELL *is sitting halfway up the stairs.* RICH *enters)*

CROMWELL   Rich! *(*RICH *stops, sees him, and smiles willingly)* What brings you to Hampton?

RICH   I came with the Duke last night, Master Cromwell. They're hunting again.

CROMWELL   It's a kingly pastime, Master Rich. (*Both smile*) I'm glad you found employment. You're the Duke's Secretary, are you not?

RICH (*Flustered*)   My work is mostly secretarial.

CROMWELL (*As if making an effort of memory*)   Or is it his librarian you are?

RICH   I do look after His Grace's library, yes.

CROMWELL   Oh. Well, that's something. And I don't suppose you're bothered much by His Grace—in the library? (RICH *smiles uncertainly*) It's odd how differently men's fortunes flow. My late master, Wolsey, died in disgrace, and here I am in the King's own service. There you are in a *comparative* backwater—yet the new Lord Chancellor's an old friend of yours.

(*He looks at* RICH *directly*)

RICH (*Uncertain*)   He isn't really my *friend.* . . .

CROMWELL   Oh, I thought he was.

(*He gets up, prepares to go*)

RICH   In a sense he is.

CROMWELL (*Reproachful*)   Well, I always understood he set you up in life.

RICH   He recommended me to the Duke.

CROMWELL   Ah yes. Are you very attached to His Grace's library, or would you be free to accept an office?

RICH (*Suspicious*)   Have you offices in gift?

CROMWELL (*Deprecating*)   I am listened to by those who have.

RICH   Master Cromwell—what *is* it that you do for the King?

(*Enter* CHAPUYS)

CHAPUYS (*Roguish*)   Yes, *I* should like to know that, Master Cromwell.

CROMWELL   Ah, Signor Chapuys. You've met His Excellency, Rich? (*He indicates* CHAPUYS) The Spanish Ambassador. (*He indicates* RICH) The Duke of Norfolk's librarian.

CHAPUYS   But how should we introduce *you*, Master Cromwell, if we had the happiness?

CROMWELL   Oh, sly! Do you notice how sly he is, Rich? Well, I suppose you would call me (*He suddenly turns*) "The King's Ear" . . . (*A deprecating shrug*) It's a useful organ, the ear. But in fact it's even simpler than that. When the King wants something done, I do it.

CHAPUYS Ah. (*Mock interest*) But then why these Justices, Chancellors, Admirals?

CROMWELL Oh, *they* are the constitution. Our ancient, English constitution. I merely do things.

CHAPUYS For example, Master Cromwell. . . .

CROMWELL (*Admiring*) O-ho—beware these professional diplomats. Well now, for example; next week at Deptford we are launching the *Great Harry*—one thousand tons, four masts, sixty-six guns, an overall length of one hundred and seventy-five feet; it's expected to be very effective—all this you probably know. However, you may not know that the King himself will guide her down the river; yes, the King himself will be her pilot. He will have assistance, of course, but he himself will be her pilot. He will have a pilot's whistle upon which he will blow, and he will wear in every respect a common pilot's uniform. Except for the material, which will be cloth of gold. These innocent fancies require more preparation than you might suppose and someone has to do it. (*He spreads his hands*) Meanwhile, I do prepare myself for higher things. I stock my mind.

CHAPUYS Alas, Master Cromwell, don't we all? This ship for instance—it has fifty-six guns by the way, not sixty-six, and only forty of them heavy. After the launching, I understand, the King will take his barge to Chelsea.

(CROMWELL's *face darkens during this speech*)

CROMWELL (*Sharply*) Yes—

CHAPUYS To—

CROMWELL Sir Thomas More's.

CHAPUYS (*Sweetly*) Will you be there?

CROMWELL Oh no—they'll talk about the divorce. (*It is* CHAPUY's *turn to be shocked.* RICH *draws away uneasily*) The King will ask him for an answer.

CHAPUYS (*Ruffled*) He has given his answer!

CROMWELL The King will ask him for another.

CHAPUYS Sir Thomas is a good son of the Church!

CROMWELL Sir Thomas is a man.

(*Enter* STEWARD. *Both* CROMWELL *and* CHAPUYS *look towards him sharply, then back at one another*)

CHAPUYS (*Innocently*) Isn't that his Steward now?

CROMWELL I believe it is. Well, good day, Your Excellency.

CHAPUYS (*Eagerly*) Good day, Master Cromwell.

(*He expects him to go*)

CROMWELL (*Standing firm*)   Good day.

(*And* CHAPUYS *has to go.* CROMWELL *walks aside with furtive and urgent beckonings to* STEWARD *to follow.* RICH *follows but hangs off. Meanwhile* CHAPUYS *and his* ATTENDANT *have gone behind screen, beneath which their legs protrude clearly*)

STEWARD (*Conspiratorially*)   Sir, Sir Thomas doesn't talk about it. (*He waits but* CROMWELL *remains stony*) He doesn't talk about it to his wife, sir.
(*He waits again*)

CROMWELL   This is worth nothing.

STEWARD (*Significantly*)   But he doesn't talk about it to Lady Margaret—that's his daughter, sir.

CROMWELL   So?

STEWARD   So he's worried, sir . . . (CROMWELL *is interested*) Frightened . . . (CROMWELL *takes out a coin but pauses suspiciously*) Sir, he goes *white* when it's mentioned!

CROMWELL (*Hands him the coin*)   All right.

STEWARD (*Looks at the coin; reproachfully*)   Oh, *sir!*

CROMWELL (*Waves him away*)   Are you coming in my direction, Rich?

RICH (*Still hanging off*)   No no.

CROMWELL   I think you should, you know.

RICH   *I* can't tell you anything!
(*Exit* CROMWELL *and* RICH *in separate directions.* CHAPUYS *and* ATTENDANT *come from behind screen*)

CHAPUYS (*Beckons* STEWARD)   Well?

STEWARD   Sir Thomas rises at six, sir, and prays for an hour and a half.

CHAPUYS   Yes?

STEWARD   During Lent, sir, he lived entirely on bread and water.

CHAPUYS   Yes?

STEWARD   He goes to confession twice a week, sir. Parish priest. Dominican.

CHAPUYS   Ah. He is a true son of the Church.

STEWARD (*Soapy*)   That he is, sir.

CHAPUYS   What did Master Cromwell want?

STEWARD   Same as you, sir.

CHAPUYS   No man can serve two masters, Steward.

STEWARD   No indeed, sir; I serve *one*.
(*He pulls to the front an enormous cross until then hanging on*

his back on a length of string—a caricature of the ebony cross worn by CHAPUYS)

CHAPUYS Good, simple man. Here. (*Gives him a coin. Going*) Peace be with you.

STEWARD And with you, sir.

CHAPUYS Our Lord watch you.

STEWARD You too, sir. (*Exit* CHAPUYS *and* ATTENDANT) That's a very religious man.

(*Enter* RICH)

RICH Matthew! What does Signor Chapuys want?

STEWARD I've no idea, sir.

RICH (*Gives him a coin*) What did you tell him?

STEWARD I told him that Sir Thomas says his prayers and goes to confession.

RICH Why that?

STEWARD That's what he wanted to know, sir. I mean I could have told him any number of things about Sir Thomas—that he has rheumatism, prefers red wine to white, is easily seasick, fond of kippers, afraid of drowning. But that's what he wanted to know, sir.

RICH What did he say?

STEWARD He said that Sir Thomas is a good churchman, sir.

RICH (*Going*) Well, that's true, isn't it?

STEWARD I'm just telling you what he said, sir. Oh, uh, Master Cromwell went that way, sir.

RICH (*Furious*) Did I ask you which way Master Cromwell went? (RICH *exits in opposite direction*)

STEWARD (*To audience, thoughtfully*) The great thing's not to get out of your depth . . . What I can tell them's common knowledge! But now they've given money for it and everyone wants value for his money. They'll make a secret of it now to prove they've not been bilked . . . They'll make it a secret by making it dangerous . . . Mm . . . Oh, when I can't touch the bottom I'll go deaf, blind and dumb. (*He holds out coins*) And that's more than I *earn* in a fortnight!

(*A fanfare of trumpets; the rear of the stage becomes a source of glittering blue light; Hampton Court is hoisted out of sight, and a rosebay is lowered. As the fanfare ceases,* NORFOLK, ALICE, MARGARET *erupt onto the stage*)

ALICE (*With chain of office which she puts on table. Distressed*) No sign of him, my lord!

NORFOLK   God's body, Alice, he must be found!

ALICE (*To* MEG)   He *must* be in the house!

MARGARET   He's *not* in the house, Mother!

ALICE   Then he must be here in the garden!

   (*They "search" among the screens*)

NORFOLK   He takes things too far, Alice.

ALICE   Do I not know it?

NORFOLK   It will end badly for him!

ALICE   I know that too!

   (*They "notice" the* STEWARD)

NORFOLK   Where's your master?

MARGARET   Matthew! Where's my father?   } (*Together*)

ALICE   Where is Sir Thomas?

   (*Fanfare, shorter but nearer*)

NORFOLK (*Despairing*)   Oh, my God.

ALICE   Oh, Jesus!

STEWARD   My lady—the King?

NORFOLK   Yes, fool! (*Threatening*) And if the King arrives and the Chancellor's not here—

STEWARD   Sir, my lady, it's not *my* fault!

NORFOLK (*Quietly displeased*)   Lady Alice, Thomas'll get no good of it. This is not how Wolsey made himself great.

ALICE (*Stiffly*)   Thomas has his own way of doing things, my lord!

NORFOLK (*Testily*)   Yes yes, Thomas is unique; but where *is* Thomas?

   (STEWARD *swings onstage a small Gothic door. Plainsong is heard. All run to the door.* NORFOLK *opens it*)

ALICE   Thomas!

STEWARD   Sir!

MARGARET   Father!

NORFOLK (*Indignantly*)   My Lord Chancellor! (MORE *enters through the doorway. He blinks in the light. He is wearing a cassock; he shuts the door behind him*) What sort of fooling is this? Does the King visit you every day?

MORE   No, but I go to vespers most days.

NORFOLK   He's here!

MORE   But isn't this visit *meant* to be a surprise?

NORFOLK (*Grimly*)   For you, yes, not for him.

MARGARET   Father . . .

   (*She indicates his cassock*)

NORFOLK   Yes—d'you propose to meet the King disguised as a parish clerk? (*They fall upon him to drag the cassock over his head*) A parish clerk, my Lord Chancellor! You dishonor the King and his office!

MORE   (*Appearing momentarily from the folds of the cassock*) The service of God is not a dishonor to any office. (*The cassock is pulled off*) Believe me, my friend, I do not belittle the honor His Majesty is doing me. (*Briskly*) Well! That's a lovely dress, Alice; so's that, Margaret. (*He looks at* NORFOLK) I'm a dowdy bird, aren't I? (*Looks at* ALICE) Calm yourself. (STEWARD *swings the door offstage*) Alice, we're all ready now.

(*He turns about and we see that his gown is caught up behind him revealing his spindly legs in long hose laced up at the thighs*)

ALICE   Thomas!

(MARGARET *laughs*)

MORE   What's the matter?

(*He turns around again and his womenfolk pursue him to pull down the gown while* NORFOLK *throws his hands in the air. Expostulation, explanation, exclamation overlap in a babble*)

NORFOLK   By God, you can be harebrained!

MARGARET   *Be still!*

ALICE   Oh, Thomas! Thomas!

(MARGARET *spies chain of office, brings it to* MORE)

NORFOLK   What whim possessed you—

MORE   'Twas not a whim!

ALICE   Your second-best stockings!

MARGARET   (*Offering the chain*)   Father—

MORE   (*Refusing*)   No, no, no, no—

NORFOLK   Oh, enough's enough!

MORE   Haven't you done—

(*Fanfare—at the end of which* HENRY, *in a cloth of gold, runs out of the sunlight halfway down the steps and blows a blast on his pilot's whistle. All kneel. In the silence he descends slowly to their level, blowing softly*)

MORE   Your Majesty does my house more honor than I fear my household can bear.

HENRY   No ceremony, Thomas! No ceremony! (*They rise*) A passing fancy—I happened to be on the river. (*Holds out a shoe, proudly*) Look, mud.

MORE   We do it in better style, Your Grace, when we come by the road.

HENRY   Oh, the road! There's the road for me, Thomas, the river; *my* river . . . By heaven, what an evening! Lady Alice, I fear we come upon you unexpectedly.

ALICE (*Shocked*)   Oh no, Your Grace— (*Remembering*) that is yes, but we are ready for you—ready to entertain Your Grace, that is.

MORE   This is my daughter Margaret, sir. She has not had the honor to meet Your Grace.

(*She curtsies low*)

HENRY (*Looking her over*)   Why, Margaret, they told me you were a scholar.

(MARGARET *is confused*)

MORE   Answer, Margaret.

MARGARET   Among women I pass for one, Your Grace.

(NORFOLK *and* ALICE *exchange approving glances*)

HENRY   Antiquone modo Latine loqueris, an Oxoniensi?

[Is your Latin the old Latin, or Oxford Latin?]

MARGARET   Quem me docuit pater, Domine.

[My father's Latin, Sire.]

HENRY   Bene. Optimus est. Graecamne linguam quoque te docuit?

[Good. That is the best. And has he taught you Greek too?]

MARGARET   Graecam me docuit non pater meus sed mei patris amicus, Johannes Coletus, Sancti Pauli Decanus. In litteris Graecis tamen, non minus quam Latinis, ars magistri minuitur discipuli stultitia.

[Not my father, Sire, but my father's friend, John Colet, Dean of St. Paul's. But it is with the Greek as it is with the Latin; the skill of the master is lost in the pupil's lack of it.]

(*Her Latin is better than his; he is not altogether pleased*)

HENRY   Ho! (*He walks away from her, talking; she begins to rise from her curtsy;* MORE *gently presses her down again before* KING HENRY *turns*) Take care, Thomas: "too much learning is a weariness of the flesh, and there is no end to the making of books." (*Back to* MARGARET) Can you dance, too?

MARGARET   Not well, Your Grace.

HENRY   Well, *I* dance superlatively! (*He plants his leg before her face*) That's a dancer's *leg*, Margaret! (*She has the wit to look straight up and smile at him. All good humor, he pulls her to her feet, sees* NORFOLK *grinning the grin of a comrade*) Hey, Norfolk? (*Indicates* NORFOLK's *leg with much distaste*) Now *that's* a wrestler's leg. But I can throw him. (*Seizes* NORFOLK) Shall I show them, Howard? (NORFOLK *is alarmed for his dignity. To* MARGARET) Shall I?

MARGARET (*Looking at* NORFOLK; *gently*) No, Your Grace.

HENRY (*Releases* NORFOLK; *seriously*) You are gentle. (*To* MORE, *approvingly*) That's good. (*To* MARGARET) You shall read to me. (MARGARET *is about to demur*) No no, you shall read to me. Lady Alice, the river's given me an appetite.

ALICE If Your Grace would share a very simple supper.

HENRY It would please me to. (*Preparing to lead off, sees* MARGARET *again*) I'm something of a scholar too, Margaret, did you know?

MARGARET All the world knows Your Grace's book, asserting the seven sacraments of the Church.

HENRY Ah yes. Between ourselves, your father had a hand in that; eh, Thomas?

MORE Here and there, Your Grace. In a minor capacity.

HENRY (*Looking at him*) He seeks to shame me with his modesty . . . (*Turns to* ALICE) On second thought we'll follow, Lady Alice, Thomas and I will follow. (*He waves them off. They bow, withdraw to the steps and start up*) Wait! (*Raises whistle to lips*) Margaret, are you fond of music?

MARGARET Yes, Your Grace.

HENRY (*Beckons her to him; holds out whistle*) Blow. (*She is uncertain*) Blow. (*She does*) Louder! (*She does and at once music is heard without, stately and oversweet. Expressions of pleasure all round*) I brought them with me, Lady Alice; take them in! (*Exit all but* MORE *and* HENRY. *The music begins to recede*) Listen to this, Thomas. (*He walks about, the auditor, beating time*) Do you know it?

MORE No, Your Grace, I—

HENRY Sh! (MORE *is silent;* HENRY *goes on with his listening*) . . . I launched a ship today, Thomas.

MORE Yes, Your Grace, I—

HENRY Listen, man, listen . . . (*A pause*) . . . The *Great Harry* . . . I steered her, Thomas, under sail.

MORE You have many accomplishments, Your Grace.

HENRY (*Holds up a finger for silence. A pause*) A great experience. (MORE *keeps silent*) . . . A great experience, Thomas.

MORE Yes, Your Grace.

(*The music is growing fainter*)

HENRY I am a fool.

MORE   How so, Your Grace?

HENRY   (*A pause, during which the music fades to silence*) What
else but a fool to live in a Court, in a licentious mob—when I have
friends, with gardens.

MORE   Your Grace—

HENRY   No courtship, no ceremony, Thomas. Be seated. You *are*
my friend, are you not?
(MORE *sits*)

MORE   Your Majesty.

HENRY   (*Eyes lighting on the chain on the table by* MORE) And
thank God I have a friend for my Chancellor. (*Laughingly, but
implacably, he takes up the chain and lowers it over* MORE's *head*)
Readier to be friends, I trust, than he was to be Chancellor.

MORE   My own knowledge of my poor abilities—

HENRY   I will judge of your abilities, Thomas . . . Did you know
that Wolsey named you for Chancellor?

MORE   Wolsey!

HENRY   Aye, before he died. Wolsey named you and Wolsey was
no fool.

MORE   He was a statesman of incomparable ability, Your Grace.

HENRY   Was he? Was he so? (*He rises*) Then why did he fail me?
Be seated—it was villainy then! Yes, villainy. I was right to break
him; he was all pride, Thomas; a proud man; pride right through.
And he failed me! (MORE *opens his mouth*) He failed me in the
one thing that mattered! The one thing that matters, Thomas,
then or now. And why? He wanted to be Pope! Yes, he wanted
to be the Bishop of Rome. I'll tell you something, Thomas, and
you can check this for yourself—it was never merry in England
while we had Cardinals amongst us. (*He nods significantly at*
MORE, *who lowers his eyes*) But look now—(*Walking away*)—I
shall not forget the feel of that . . . great tiller under my hands
. . . I took her down to Dogget's Bank, went about and brought
her up in Tilbury Roads. A man could sail clean round the world
in that ship.

MORE   (*With affectionate admiration*) Some men could, Your
Grace.

HENRY   (*Offhand*) Touching this matter of my divorce, Thomas;
have you thought of it since we last talked?

MORE   Of little else.

HENRY   Then you see your way clear to me?

MORE   That you should put away Queen Catherine, Sire? Oh, alas.

(*He thumps the chair in distress*) As I think of it I see so clearly that I can *not* come with Your Grace, that my endeavor is not to think of it at all.

HENRY Then you have not thought enough! . . . (*With real appeal*) Great God, Thomas, why do you hold out against me in the desire of my heart—the very wick of my heart?

MORE (*Draws up his sleeve, baring his arm*) There is my right arm. (*A practical proposition*) Take your dagger and saw it from my shoulder, and I will laugh and be thankful, if by that means I can come with Your Grace with a clear conscience.

HENRY (*Uncomfortably pulls at the sleeve*) I know it, Thomas, I know . . .

MORE (*Rises, formally*) I crave pardon if I offend.

HENRY (*Suspiciously*) Speak then.

MORE When I took the Great Seal, Your Majesty promised not to pursue me on this matter.

HENRY Ha! So I break my word, Master More! No no, I'm joking . . . I joke roughly . . . (*He wanders away*) I often think I'm a rough fellow . . . Yes, a rough young fellow. (*He shakes his head indulgently*) Be seated . . . That's a rosebay. We have one like it at Hampton—not so red as that though. Ha—I'm in an excellent frame of mind. (*Glances at the rosebay*) Beautiful. (*Reasonable, pleasant*) You must consider, Thomas, that I stand in peril of my soul. It was no marriage; she was my brother's widow. Leviticus: "Thou shalt not uncover the nakedness of thy brother's wife." Leviticus, Chapter eighteen, Verse sixteen.

MORE Yes, Your Grace. But Deuteronomy—

HENRY (*Triumphant*) Deuteronomy's ambiguous!

MORE (*Bursting out*) Your Grace, I'm not fit to meddle in these matters—to me it seems a matter for the Holy See—

HENRY (*Reprovingly*) Thomas, Thomas, does a man need a Pope to tell him when he's sinned? It was a sin, Thomas; I admit it; I repent. And God has punished me; I have no son . . . Son after son she's borne me, Thomas, all dead at birth, or dead within the month; I never saw the hand of God so clear in anything . . . I have a daughter, she's a good child, a well-set child—But I have no son. (*He flares up*) It is my bounden *duty* to put away the Queen, and all the Popes back to St. Peter shall not come between me and my duty! How is it that you cannot see? Everyone else does.

MORE (*Eagerly*) Then why does Your Grace need my poor support?

HENRY Because you are honest. What's more to the purpose, you're known to be honest . . . There are those like Norfolk who follow me because I wear the crown, and there are those like Master Cromwell who follow me because they are jackals with sharp teeth and I am their lion, and there is a mass that follows me because it follows anything that moves—and there is you.

MORE I am sick to think how much I must displease Your Grace.

HENRY No, Thomas, I respect your sincerity. Respect? Oh, man, it's water in the desert . . . How did you like our music? That air they played, it had a certain—well, tell me what you thought of it.

MORE (*Relieved at this turn; smiling*) Could it have been Your Grace's own?

HENRY (*Smiles back*) Discovered! Now I'll never know your true opinion. And that's irksome, Thomas, for we artists, though we love praise, yet we love truth better.

MORE (*Mildly*) Then I will tell Your Grace truly what I thought of it.

HENRY (*A little disconcerted*) Speak then.

MORE To me it seemed—delightful.

HENRY Thomas—I chose the right man for Chancellor.

MORE I must in fairness add that my taste in music is reputedly deplorable.

HENRY Your taste in music is excellent. It exactly coincides with my own. Ah music! Music! Send them back without me, Thomas; I will live here in Chelsea and make music.

MORE My house is at Your Grace's disposal.

HENRY Thomas, you understand me; we will stay here together and make music.

MORE Will Your Grace honor my roof after dinner?

HENRY (*Walking away, blowing moodily on his whistle*) Mm? Yes, I expect I'll bellow for you . . .

MORE My wife will be more—

HENRY Yes, yes. (*He turns, his face set*) Touching this other business, mark you, Thomas, I'll have no opposition.

MORE (*Sadly*) Your Grace?

HENRY No opposition, I say! No opposition! Your conscience is your own affair; but you are my Chancellor! There, you have my word —I'll leave you out of it. But I don't take it kindly, Thomas, and

I'll have no opposition! I see how it will be; the bishops will oppose me. The full-fed hypocritical "Princes of the *Church*"! Ha! As for the Pope! Am I to burn in Hell because the Bishop of Rome, with the King of Spain's knife to his throat, mouths me Deuteronomy? Hypocrites! They're all hypocrites! Mind they do not take you in, Thomas! Lie low if you will, but I'll brook no opposition—no noise! No words, no signs, no letters, no pamphlets —Mind that, Thomas—no writings against me!

MORE Your Grace is unjust. I am Your Grace's loyal minister. If I cannot serve Your Grace in this great matter of the Queen—

HENRY I have no Queen! Catherine is not my wife and no priest can make her so, and they that say she is my wife are not only liars . . . but traitors! Mind it, Thomas!

MORE Am I a babbler, Your Grace?

(*But his voice is unsteady*)

HENRY You are stubborn . . . (*Wooingly*) If you could come with me, you are the man I would soonest raise—yes, with my own hand.

MORE (*Covers his face*) Oh, Your Grace overwhelms me!

(*A complicated chiming of little bells is heard*)

HENRY What's that?

MORE Eight o'clock, Your Grace.

HENRY (*Uneasily eying* MORE) Oh, lift yourself up, man—have I not promised? (MORE *braces*) Shall we eat?

MORE If Your Grace pleases. (*Recovering*) What will Your Grace sing for us?

HENRY Eight o'clock you said? Thomas, the tide will be changing. I was forgetting the tide. I'd better go.

MORE (*Gravely*) I'm sorry, Your Grace.

HENRY I must catch the tide or I'll not get back to Richmond till . . . No, don't come. Tell Norfolk. (*He has his foot on the stairs when* ALICE *enters above*) Oh, Lady Alice, I must go. (ALICE *descends, her face serious*) I want to catch the tide. To tell the truth, Lady Alice, I have forgotten in your haven here how time flows past outside. Affairs call me to court and so I give you my thanks and say good night.

(*He mounts*)

MORE *and* ALICE (*Bowing*) Good night, Your Grace.

(*Exit* HENRY, *above*)

ALICE What's this? You crossed him.

MORE Somewhat.

ALICE   Why?

ALICE   (*Angrily*) You're too nice altogether, Thomas!

MORE   Woman, mind your house.

ALICE   I *am* minding my house!

MORE   (*Taking in her anxiety*) Well, Alice. What would you *want* me to do?

ALICE   Be ruled! If you won't rule him, be ruled!

MORE   (*Quietly*) I neither could nor would rule my King. (*Pleasantly*) But there's a little . . . little, area . . . where I must rule myself. It's very little—less to him than a tennis court. (*Her face is still full of foreboding; he sighs*) Look; it was eight o'clock. At eight o'clock, Lady Anne likes to dance.

ALICE   (*Relieved*) Oh?

MORE   I think so.

ALICE   (*With irritation*) And *you* stand between them!

MORE   I? What stands between them is a sacrament of the Church. I'm less important than you think, Alice.

ALICE   (*Appealing*) Thomas, stay friends with him.

MORE   Whatever can be done by smiling, you may rely on me to do.

ALICE   You don't know *how* to flatter.

MORE   I flatter very well! My recipe's beginning to be widely

MORE   (*Apologetic*) I couldn't find the other way.
copied. It's the basic syrup with just a soupçon of discreet impudence . . .

ALICE   (*Still uneasy*) I wish he'd eaten here . . .

MORE   Yes—we shall be living on that "simple supper" of yours for a fortnight. (*She won't laugh*) Alice . . . (*She won't turn*) Alice . . . (*She turns*) Set your mind at rest—this (*Tapping himself*) is not the stuff of which martyrs are made.

(*Enter above, quickly,* ROPER)

ROPER   Sir Thomas!

MORE   (*Winces*) Oh, no . . .

(*Enter after* ROPER, MARGARET)

ALICE   Will Roper—what do you want?

MARGARET   William, I told you not to!

ROPER   I'm not easily "told," Meg.

MARGARET   I *asked* you not to.

ROPER   Meg, I'm full to here!

(*Indicates his throat*)

MARGARET   It's not convenient!

ROPER   Must everything be made convenient? I'm not a convenient man, Meg—I've got an inconvenient conscience!

(MARGARET *gestures helplessly to* MORE)

MORE   (*Laughs*)   Joshua's trumpet. One note on that brass conscience of yours and my daughter's walls are down.

ROPER (*Descending*)   You raised her, sir.

MORE (*A bit puzzled*)   How long have you been here? Are you in the King's party?

ROPER   No, sir, I am *not* in the King's party! (*Advancing*) It's of that I wish to speak to you. My spirit is perturbed.

MORE (*Suppressing a grin*)   It is, Will? Why?

ROPER   I've been offered a seat in the next Parliament. (MORE *looks up sharply*) Ought I to take it?

MORE   No . . . Well that depends. With your views on Church Reform I should have thought you could do yourself a lot of good in the next Parliament.

ROPER   My views on the Church, I must confess—Since last we met my views have somewhat modified. (MORE *and* MARGARET *exchange a smile*) I modify nothing concerning the *body* of the Church—the money-changers in the temple must be scourged from thence—with a scourge of fire if that is needed! But an attack on the Church herself! No, I see behind that an attack on God—

MORE   Roper—

ROPER   The Devil's work!

MORE   Roper!

ROPER   To be done by the Devil's ministers!

MORE   For heaven's sake remember my office!

ROPER   Oh, if you stand on your office—

MORE   I don't stand on it, but there are certain things I may not hear!

ROPER   Sophistication. It is what I was told. The Court has corrupted you, Sir Thomas; you are not the man you were; you have learned to study your "convenience"; you have learned to flatter!

MORE   There, Alice, you see? I have a reputation for it.

ALICE   God's Body, young man, if I was the Chancellor I'd have you whipped!

(*Enter* STEWARD)

STEWARD   Master Rich is here, Sir Thomas.

(RICH *follows him closely*)

RICH   Good evening, sir.

MORE   Ah, Richard?

RICH Good evening, Lady Alice. (ALICE *nods, noncommittally*) Lady Margaret.

MARGARET (*Quite friendly but very clear*) Good evening, Master Rich.

(*A pause*)

MORE Do you know—(*Indicates* ROPER) William Roper, the younger?

RICH By reputation, of course.

ROPER Good evening, Master . . .

RICH Rich.

ROPER Oh. (*Recollecting something*) Oh.

RICH (*Quickly and hostilely*) You have heard of me?

ROPER (*Shortly*) Yes.

RICH (*Excitedly*) In what connection? I don't know what you can have heard—(*He looks about; hotly*) I sense that I'm not welcome here!

(*He has jumped the gun; they are startled*)

MORE (*Gently*) Why, Richard, have you done something that should make you not welcome?

RICH Why, do you suspect me of it?

MORE I shall begin to.

RICH (*Drawing closer to him and speaking hurriedly*) Cromwell is asking questions. About you. About you particularly. (MORE *is unmoved*) He is continually collecting information about you!

MORE I know it. (STEWARD *begins to slide out*) Stay a minute, Matthew.

RICH (*Pointing*) That's one of his sources!

MORE Of course; that's one of my servants.

RICH (*Hurriedly, in a low voice again*) Signor Chapuys, the Spanish Ambassador—

MORE —collects information too. That's one of his functions.

(*He looks at* RICH *very gravely*)

RICH (*Voice cracking*) You look at me as though I were an enemy!

MORE (*Putting out a hand to steady him*) Why, Richard, you're shaking.

RICH I'm adrift. Help me.

MORE How?

RICH Employ me.

MORE No.

RICH (*Desperately*) Employ me!

MORE No!

RICH (*Moves swiftly to exit; turns*) I would be steadfast!

MORE Richard, you couldn't answer for yourself even so far as to-night.

(RICH *exits. All watch him; the others turn to* MORE, *their faces alert*)

ROPER Arrest him.

ALICE Yes!

MORE For what?

ALICE He's dangerous!

ROPER For libel; he's a spy.

ALICE He is! Arrest him!

MARGARET Father, that man's bad.

MORE There is no law against that.

ROPER There is! God's law!

MORE Then God can arrest him.

ROPER Sophistication upon sophistication!

MORE No, sheer simplicity. The law. Roper, the law. I know what's legal not what's right. And I'll stick to what's legal.

ROPER Then you set man's law above God's!

MORE No, far below; but let *me* draw your attention to a fact—I'm *not* God. The currents and eddies of right and wrong, which you find such plain sailing, I can't navigate. I'm no voyager. But in the thickets of the law, oh, there I'm a forester. I doubt if there's a man alive who could follow me there, thank God . . . (*He says this last to himself*)

ALICE (*Exasperated, pointing after* RICH) While you talk, he's gone!

MORE And go he should, if he was the Devil himself, until he broke the law!

ROPER So now you'd give the Devil benefit of law!

MORE Yes. What would you do? Cut a great road through the law to get after the Devil?

ROPER I'd cut down every law in England to do that!

MORE (*Roused and excited*) Oh? (*Advances on* ROPER) And when the last law was down, and the Devil turned round on you—where would you hide, Roper, the laws all being flat? (*He leaves him*) This country's planted thick with laws from coast to coast—man's laws, not God's—and if you cut them down—and you're just the man to do it—d'you really think you could stand upright in the winds that would blow then? (*Quietly*) Yes, I'd give the Devil benefit of law, for my own safety's sake.

ROPER   I have long suspected this; this is the golden calf; the law's your god.

MORE   (*Wearily*)   Oh, Roper, you're a fool, God's my god. . . . (*Rather bitterly*) But I find him rather too (*Very bitterly*) subtle . . . I don't know where he is nor what he wants.

ROPER   My god wants service, to the end and unremitting; nothing else!

MORE   (*Dryly*)   Are you sure that's God? He sounds like Moloch. But indeed it may be God—And whoever hunts for me, Roper, God or Devil, will find me hiding in the thickets of the law! And I'll hide my daughter with me! Not hoist her up the mainmast of your seagoing principles! They put about too nimbly!

(*Exit* MORE. *They all look after him.* MARGARET *touches* ROPER's *hand*)

MARGARET   Oh, that was harsh.

ROPER   (*Turning to her; seriously*)   What's happened here?

ALICE   (*Still with her back to them, her voice strained*)   He can't abide a fool, that's all! Be off!

ROPER   (*To* MARGARET)   Hide you. Hide you from what?

ALICE   (*Turning, near to tears*)   He said nothing about hiding me, you noticed! I've got too fat to hide, I suppose!

MARGARET   You know he meant us both.

ROPER   But from what?

ALICE   I don't know. I don't know if he knows. He's not said one simple, direct word to me since this divorce came up. It's not God who's gone subtle! It's him!

(*Enter* MORE, *a little sheepish. He goes to* ROPER)

MORE   (*Kindly*)   Roper, that was harsh: your principles are—(*He can't resist sending him up*) excellent—the very best quality. (ROPER *bridles. Contritely*) No, truly now, your principles are fine. (*Indicating the stairs, to all*) Look, we must make a start on all that food.

MARGARET   Father, can't you be plain with us?

MORE   (*Looks quickly from daughter to wife. Takes* ALICE's *hand*) I stand on the wrong side of no statute, and no common law. (*Takes* MEG's *hand too*) I have not disobeyed my sovereign. I truly believe no man in England is safer than myself. And I want my supper. (*He starts them up the stairs and goes to* ROPER) We shall need your assistance, Will. There's an excellent Burgundy—if your principles permit.

ROPER   They don't, sir.

MORE   Well, have some water in it.

ROPER   Just the water, sir.

MORE   My poor boy.

ALICE   (*Stopping at the head of the stairs, as if she will be answered*)   Why does Cromwell collect information about you?

MORE   I'm a prominent figure. Someone somewhere's collecting information about Cromwell. Now no more shirking; we must make a start. (*Shepherding* ROPER *up the stairs*) There's a stuffed swan if you please. (ALICE *and* MARGARET *exit above*) Will, I'd trust *you* with my life. But not your principles. (*They mount the stairs*) You see, we speak of being anchored to our principles. But if the weather turns nasty you up with an anchor and let it down where there's less wind, and the fishing's better. And "Look," we say, "look, I'm anchored!" (*Laughing, inviting* ROPER *to laugh with him*) "To my principles!"

(*Exit above,* MORE *and* ROPER. *Enter* COMMON MAN *pulling the basket. From it he takes an inn sign, which he hangs in the alcove. He inspects it*)

COMMON MAN   "The Loyal Subject" . . . (*To audience*) A pub. (*Takes from the basket and puts on a jacket, cap and napkin*) A publican. (*Places two stools at the table, and on it mugs and a candle, which he lights*) Oh, he's a deep one, that Sir Thomas More . . . Deep . . . It takes a lot of education to get a man as deep as that . . . (*Straight to audience*) And a deep nature to begin with too. (*Deadpan*) The likes of me can hardly be *expected* to follow the process of a man like that. . . . (*Slyly*) Can we? (*He inspects the pub*) Right, ready. (*He goes right*) Ready, sir!

(CROMWELL *enters, carrying a bottle*)

CROMWELL   Is this a *good* place for a conspiracy, innkeeper?

PUBLICAN (*Woodenly*)   You asked for a private room, sir.

CROMWELL (*Looking round*)   Yes, I want one without too many little dark corners.

PUBLICAN   I don't understand you, sir. Just the four corners as you see.

CROMWELL (*Sardonically*)   You don't understand me.

PUBLICAN   That's right, sir.

CROMWELL   Do you know who I am?

PUBLICAN (*Promptly*)   No, sir.

CROMWELL   Don't be too tactful, innkeeper.

PUBLICAN   I don't understand, sir.

RICH   Collector of Revenues for York.

CROMWELL   When the likes of you *are* too tactful, the likes of me

PUBLICAN   I just don't understand you, sir.

CROMWELL   (*Puts back his head and laughs silently*) The master statesman of us all. "I don't understand." (*Looks at* PUBLICAN *almost with hatred*) All right. Get out. (*Exit* PUBLICAN. CROMWELL *goes to the exit. Calling*) Come on. (*Enter* RICH. *He glances at the bottle in* CROMWELL's *hand and remains cautiously by the exit*) Yes, it may be that I am a little intoxicated. (*Leaves* RICH *standing*) But not with alcohol, I've a strong head for that. With success! And who has a strong head for success? None of us gets enough of it. Except Kings. And they're born drunk.

RICH   Success? What success?

CROMWELL   Guess.

CROMWELL   (*Amused*) You do keep your ear to the ground don't you? No.

RICH   What then?

CROMWELL   Sir Thomas Paget is—retiring.

RICH   Secretary to the Council!

CROMWELL   'Tis astonishing, isn't it?

RICH (*Hastily*)   Oh no—I mean—one sees, it's logical.

CROMWELL   No ceremony, no courtship. Be seated. (RICH *starts to sit*) As His Majesty would say. (RICH *jumps up—is pulled down, laughs nervously and involuntarily glances round*) Yes; see how I trust you.

RICH   Oh, I would never repeat or report a thing like that—

CROMWELL   (*Pouring the wine*) What kind of thing would you repeat or report?

RICH   Well, nothing said in friendship—may I say "friendship"?

CROMWELL   If you like. D'you believe that—that you would never repeat or report anything et cetera?

RICH   Yes!

CROMWELL   No, but seriously.

RICH   Why, yes!

CROMWELL   (*Puts down the bottle. Not sinister, but rather as a kindly teacher with a promising pupil*) Rich; seriously.

RICH (*Pauses, then bitterly*)   It would depend what I was offered.

CROMWELL   Don't say it just to please me.

RICH   It's true. It would depend what I was offered.

CROMWELL (*Patting his arm*) Everyone knows it; not many people can say it.

RICH There are *some* things one wouldn't do for anything. Surely.

CROMWELL Mm—that idea's like these life lines they have on the embankment: comforting, but you don't expect to have to use them. (*Briskly*) Well, congratulations!

RICH (*Suspiciously*) On what?

CROMWELL I think you'd make a good Collector of Revenues for York Diocese.

RICH (*Gripping himself*) Is it in your gift?

CROMWELL It will be.

RICH (*With conscious cynicism*) What do I have to do for it?

CROMWELL Nothing. (*He lectures*) It isn't like that, Rich. There are no rules. With rewards and penalties—so much wickedness purchases so much worldly prospering—(*Rises. He breaks off and stops, suddenly struck*) Are you sure you're not religious?

RICH Almost sure.

CROMWELL Get sure. (*Resumes pacing up steps*) No, it's not like that, it's much more a matter of convenience, administrative convenience. The normal aim of administration is to keep steady this factor of convenience—and Sir Thomas would agree. Now normally when a man wants to change his woman, you let him if it's convenient and prevent him if it's not—normally indeed it's of so little importance that you leave it to the priests. But the constant factor is this element of convenience.

RICH Whose convenience?

(CROMWELL *stops*)

CROMWELL (*Sits*) Oh, ours. But everybody's too. However, in the present instance the man who wants to change his woman is our Sovereign Lord, Harry, by the Grace of God, the Eighth of that name. Which is a quaint way of saying that if he wants to change his woman he will. (*He rises and walks back towards* RICH) So *that* becomes the constant factor. And our job as administrators is to make it as convenient as we can. I say "our" job, on the assumption that you'll take this post at York I've offered you?

(*Makes* RICH *move over*)

RICH Yes . . . yes, yes.

(*But he seems gloomy*)

CROMWELL (*Sits. Sharply*) It's a bad sign when people are depressed by their own good fortune.

RICH (*Defensively*) I'm not depressed!

CROMWELL   You look depressed.

RICH   (*Hastily buffooning*)   I'm lamenting. I've lost my innocence.

CROMWELL   You lost that some time ago. If you've only just noticed, it can't have been very important to you.

RICH   (*Much struck*)   That's true! Why that's true, it can't!

CROMWELL   We experience a sense of release, do we, Master Rich?
An unfamiliar freshness in the head, as of open air?

RICH   (*Takes the wine*)   Collector of Revenues isn't bad!

CROMWELL   Not bad for a start. (*He watches* RICH *drink*) Now our
present Lord Chancellor—*there's* an innocent man.

RICH   (*Indulgently*)   The odd thing is—he *is*.

CROMWELL   (*Looks at him with dislike*)   Yes, I say he is. (*With the
light tone again*) The trouble is, his innocence is tangled in this
proposition that you can't change your woman without a divorce,
and can't have a divorce unless the Pope says so. And although
his present Holiness is—judged even by the most liberal standards
—a strikingly corrupt old person, yet he still has this word "Pope"
attached to him. And from this quite meaningless circumstance
I fear some degree of . . .

RICH   (*Pleased, waving his cup*)   . . . Administrative inconvenience.

CROMWELL   (*Nodding as to a word-perfect pupil*)   Just so. (*Deadpan*) This goblet that he gave you, how much was it worth?
(RICH *looks down. Quite gently*) Come along, Rich, he gave you
a silver goblet. How much did you get for it?

RICH   Fifty shillings.

CROMWELL   Could you take me to the shop?

RICH   Yes.

CROMWELL   Where did he get it? (*No reply.* RICH *puts the cup
down*) It was a gift from a litigant, a woman, wasn't it?

RICH   Yes.

CROMWELL   Which court? Chancery? (*Takes the bottle; restrains*
RICH *from filling his glass*) No, don't get drunk. In which court
was this litigant's case?

RICH   Court of Requests.

CROMWELL   (*Grunts, his face abstracted. Becoming aware of* RICH's
regard, he smiles)   There, that wasn't too painful, was it?

RICH   (*Laughing a little and a little rueful*)   No!

CROMWELL   (*Spreading his hands*)   That's all there is. And you'll
find it easier next time.

RICH   (*Looks up briefly, unhappily*)   What application do they have,
these tidbits of information you collect?

CROMWELL None at all, usually.

RICH (*Stubbornly, not looking up*) But sometimes.

CROMWELL Well, there *are* these men—you know—"upright," "steadfast," men who want themselves to be the constant factor in the situation; which, of course, they can't be. The situation rolls forward in any case.

RICH (*Still stubbornly*) So what happens?

CROMWELL (*Not liking his tone, coldly*) If they've any sense they get out of its way.

RICH What if they haven't any sense?

CROMWELL (*Still coldly*) What, none at all? Well, then they're only fit for Heaven. But Sir Thomas has plenty of sense; he could be frightened.

RICH (*Looks up, his face nasty*) Don't forget he's an innocent, Master Cromwell.

CROMWELL I think we'll finish there for tonight. After all, he *is* the Lord Chancellor.
(*Going*)

RICH You wouldn't find him easy to frighten! (CROMWELL *exits. He calls after him*) You've mistaken your man this time! He doesn't know how to be frightened!

CROMWELL (*Returning.* RICH *rises at his approach*) Doesn't know how to be frightened? Why, then he never put his hand in a candle . . . Did he?
(*And seizing* RICH *by the wrist he holds his hand in the candle flame*)

RICH (*Screeches and darts back, hugging his hand in his armpit, regarding* CROMWELL *with horror*) You enjoyed that! (CROMWELL's *downturned face is amazed. Triumphantly*) You enjoyed it!

Curtain

ACT TWO

The scene is as for start of Act One. When the curtain rises the stage is in darkness save for a spot, in which stands the COMMON MAN. *He carries the book, a place marked by his finger, and wears his spectacles.*

COMMON MAN The interval started early in the year 1530 and it's now the middle of May, 1532. (*Explanatory*) Two years. During that time a lot of water's flowed under the bridge, and one of the things that have come floating along on it is . . . (*Reads*) "The Church of England, that finest flower of our Island genius for compromise; that system, peculiar to these shores, the despair of foreign observers, which deflects the torrents of religious passion down the canals of moderation." That's very well put. (*Returns to the book, approvingly*) "Typically, this great effect was achieved not by bloodshed but by simple Act of Parliament. Only an unhappy few were found to set themselves against the current of their times, and in so doing to court disaster. For we are dealing with an age less fastidious than our own. Imprisonment without trial, and even examination under torture, were common practice."

(Lights rise to show MORE, *seated, and* ROPER, *standing. Exit* COMMON MAN. ROPER *is dressed in black and wears a cross. He commences to walk up and down, watched by* MORE. *A pause*)

MORE Must you wear those clothes, Will?

ROPER Yes, I must.

MORE Why?

ROPER The time has come for decent men to declare their allegiance!

MORE And what allegiance are those designed to express?

ROPER My allegiance to the Church.

MORE Well, you *look* like a Spaniard.

ROPER   All credit to Spain then!

MORE   You wouldn't last six months in Spain. You'd have been burned alive in Spain, during your heretic period.

ROPER   I suppose you have the right to remind me of it. (*Points accusingly*) That chain of office that *you* wear is a degradation!

MORE   (*Glances down at it*)   I've told you. If the bishops in Convocation submitted this morning, I'll take it off . . . It's no degradation. Great men have worn this.

ROPER   When d'you expect to hear from the bishops?

MORE   About now. I was promised an immediate message.

ROPER   (*Recommences pacing*)   I don't see what difference Convocation can make. The Church is already a wing of the Palace, is it not? The King is already its "Supreme Head"! Is he not?

MORE   No.

ROPER   (*Startled*)   You are denying the Act of Supremacy!

MORE   No, I'm not; the Act states that the King—

ROPER   —is Supreme Head of the Church in England.

MORE   Supreme Head of the Church in England—(*Underlining the words*) "so far as the law of God allows." How far the law of God does allow it remains a matter of opinion, since the Act doesn't state it.

ROPER   A legal quibble.

MORE   Call it what you like, it's there, thank God.

ROPER   Very well; in your opinion how far does the law of God allow this?

MORE   I'll keep my opinion to myself, Will.

ROPER   Yes? I'll tell you mine—

MORE   Don't! If your opinion's what I think it is, it's High Treason, Roper! (*Enter* MARGARET *above, unseen*) Will you remember you've a wife now! And may have children!

MARGARET   Why must he remember that?

ROPER   To keep myself "discreet."

MARGARET   (*Smiling*)   Then I'd rather you forgot it.

MORE   (*Unsmiling*)   You are either idiots, or children.
   (*Enter* CHAPUYS, *above*)

CHAPUYS   (*Very sonorously*)   Or saints, my lord!

MARGARET   Oh, Father, Signor Chapuys has come to see you.

MORE   (*Rising*)   Your Excellency.

CHAPUYS   (*Strikes pose with* MARGARET *and* ROPER)   Or saints, my lord; or saints.

MORE   (*Grins maliciously at* ROPER)   That's it of course—saints!

Roper—turn your head a bit—yes, I think I do detect a faint radiance. (*Reproachfully*) You should have told us, Will.

CHAPUYS Come come, my lord; you too at this time are not free from some suspicion of saintliness.

MORE (*Quietly*) I don't like the sound of that, Your Excellency. What do you require of *me?* What, Your Excellency?

CHAPUYS (*Awkward beneath his sudden keen regard*) May I not come simply to pay my respects to the English Socrates—as I see your angelic friend Erasmus calls you.

MORE (*Wrinkles nose*) Yes, I'll think of something presently to call Erasmus. (*Checks*) Socrates! I've no taste for hemlock, Your Excellency, if that's what you require.

CHAPUYS (*With a display of horror*) Heaven forbid!

MORE (*Dryly*) Amen.

CHAPUYS (*Spreads hands*) Must I require anything? (*Sonorously*) After all, we are brothers in Christ, you and I!

MORE A characteristic we share with the rest of humanity. You live in Cheapside, Signor? To make contact with a brother in Christ you have only to open your window and empty a chamber-pot. There was no need to come to Chelsea. (CHAPUYS *titters nervously. Coldly*) William. The Spanish Ambassador is here on business. Would you mind?

(ROPER *and* MARGARET *begin to go*)

CHAPUYS (*Rising, unreal protestations*) Oh no! I protest!

MORE He is clearly here on business.

CHAPUYS No; but really, I protest! (*It is no more than token: when* ROPER *and* MARGARET *reach head of stairs he calls*) Dominus vobiscum filii mei!

ROPER (*Pompously*) Et cum spiritu tuo, excellencies!

(*Exit* ROPER *and* MARGARET)

CHAPUYS (*Approaching* MORE, *thrillingly*) And how much longer shall we hear that holy language in these shores?

MORE (*Alert, poker-faced*) 'Tisn't "holy," Your Excellency; just old. (CHAPUYS *sits with the air of one getting down to brass tacks*)

CHAPUYS My lord, I cannot believe you will allow yourself to be associated with the recent actions of King Henry! In respect of Queen Catherine.

MORE Subjects are associated with the actions of Kings willy-nilly.

CHAPUYS The Lord Chancellor is not an ordinary subject. He bears responsibility (*He lets the word sink in;* MORE *shifts*) for what is done.

MORE (*Agitation begins to show through*) Have you considered that what has been done badly, might have been done worse, with a different Chancellor.

CHAPUYS (*Mounting confidence, as* MORE's *attention is caught*) Believe me, Sir Thomas, your influence in these policies has been much searched for, and where it has been found it has been praised—*but* . . . There comes a point, does there not? . . .

MORE Yes. (*Agitated*) There does come such a point.

CHAPUYS When the sufferings of one unfortunate lady swell to an open attack on the religion of an entire country that point has been passed. Beyond that point, Sir Thomas, one is not merely "compromised," one is in truth corrupted.

MORE (*Stares at him*) What do you want?

CHAPUYS Rumor has it that if the Church in Convocation has submitted to the King, you will resign.

MORE (*Looks down and regains composure*) I see. (*Suavely*) Supposing rumor to be right. Would you approve of that?

CHAPUYS Approve, applaud, admire.

MORE (*Still looking down*) Why?

CHAPUYS Because it would show one man—and that man known to be temperate—unable to go further with this wickedness.

MORE And that man known to be Chancellor of England too.

CHAPUYS Believe me, my lord, such a signal would be seen—

MORE "Signal"?

CHAPUYS Yes, my lord; it would be seen and understood.

MORE (*Now positively silky*) By whom?

CHAPUYS By half of your fellow countrymen! (*Now* MORE *looks up sharply*) Sir Thomas, I have just returned from Yorkshire and Northumberland, where I have made a tour.

MORE (*Softly*) Have you indeed?

CHAPUYS Things are very different there, my lord. There they are ready.

MORE For what?

CHAPUYS Resistance!

MORE (*Softly, as before*) Resistance by what means? (*Suddenly his agitation must find expression, if only physical. He is galvanized from his seat and as he suddenly stops, with his back to* CHAPUYS, MORE's *face is electrically alert.* CHAPUYS *hears the excitement in:*) By force of arms?

CHAPUYS (*Almost sure the fish is hooked, leaning forward but play-*

ing it cool)   We are adjured by St. Paul to don the arms of God
when the occasion warrants.

MORE   Metaphorical arms. The breastplate of righteousness and
the helmet of salvation. Do you mean a metaphorical resistance?
(*Indignation and fear make his voice vibrate with the excitement
of enthusiasm*)

CHAPUYS (*Intones*)   "He shall flee the *iron* weapons, and the bow
of steel shall strike him through."

MORE (*There is a pause while his agile mind scans the full frightening implications of this for himself; it is almost with a start of
recollection that he remembers to answer* CHAPUYS *at all*)   I see.
(*Enter* ROPER, *above, excited*)

ROPER   Sir Thomas! (MORE *looks up angrily*) Excuse me, sir—(*Indicates off*) His Grace the Duke of Norfolk—(MORE *and* CHAPUYS
rise. ROPER *excitedly descends*) It's all over, sir, they've—
(*Enter* NORFOLK above, ALICE *and* MARGARET, *below*)

NORFOLK   One moment, Roper, I'll do this! Thomas—(*Sees* CHAPUYS)
Oh.
(*He stares at* CHAPUYS *hostilely*)

CHAPUYS   I was on the point of leaving, Your Grace. Just a personal
call. I have been trying . . . er, to borrow a book . . . but without
success—you're sure you have no copy, my lord? Then I'll leave
you. (*Bowing*) Gentlemen, ladies.
(*Going up the stairs, he stops unnoticed as* ROPER *speaks*)

ROPER   Sir Thomas—

NORFOLK   I'll do it, Roper! Convocation's knuckled under, Thomas.
They're to pay a fine of a hundred thousand pounds. And . . .
we've severed the connection with Rome.

MORE (*Smiling bitterly*)   "The connection with Rome" is nice. (*Bitterly*) "The connection with Rome."

ROPER (*Addressing Norfolk, but looking at* MORE)   Your Grace,
this is quite certain, is it?

NORFOLK   Yes. (MORE *puts his hand to his chain.* CHAPUYS *exits. All
turn*) Funny company, Thomas?

MORE   It's quite unintentional. He doesn't mean to be funny. (*He
fumbles with the chain*) Help me with this.

NORFOLK   Not I.

ROPER (*Takes a step forward. Then, subdued*)   Shall I, sir?

MORE   No thank you, Will. Alice?

ALICE   Hell's fire—God's Blood and Body, *no!* Sun and moon, Master More, you're taken for a wise man! Is this wisdom—to betray

your ability, abandon practice, forget your station and your duty to your kin and behave like a printed book!

MORE (*Listens gravely; then*) Margaret, will you?

MARGARET If you want.

MORE There's my clever girl.

(*She takes it from his neck*)

NORFOLK Well, Thomas, why? Make me understand—because I'll tell you now, from where I stand, this looks like cowardice!

MORE (*Excited and angry*) All right I will—this isn't "Reformation," this is war against the Church! . . . (*Indignant*) Our King, Norfolk, has declared war on the Pope—because the Pope will not declare that our Queen is not his wife.

NORFOLK And is she?

MORE (*With cunning*) I'll answer that question for one person only, the King. Aye, and that in private too.

NORFOLK (*Contemptuously*) Man, you're cautious.

MORE Yes, cautious. I'm not one of your hawks.

NORFOLK (*Walks away and turns*) All right—we're at war with the Pope! The Pope's a Prince, isn't he?

MORE He is.

NORFOLK And a bad one?

MORE Bad enough. But the theory is that he's also the Vicar of God, the descendant of St. Peter, our only link with Christ.

NORFOLK (*Sneering*) A tenuous link.

MORE Oh, tenuous indeed.

NORFOLK (*To the others*) Does this make sense? (*No reply; they look at* MORE) You'll forfeit all you've got—which includes the respect of your country—for a theory?

MORE (*Hotly*) The Apostolic Succession of the Pope is—(*Stops; interested*) . . . Why, it's a theory, yes; you can't see it; can't touch it; it's a theory. (*To* NORFOLK, *very rapidly but calmly*) But what matters to me is not whether it's true or not but that I believe it to be true, or rather, not that I *believe* it, but that *I* believe it . . . I trust I make myself obscure?

NORFOLK Perfectly.

MORE That's good. Obscurity's what I have need of now.

NORFOLK Thomas. This isn't Spain, you know.

MORE (*Looks at him, takes him aside; in a lowered voice*) Have I your word that what we say here is between us and has no existence beyond these walls?

NORFOLK (*Impatient*) Very well.

MORE (*Almost whispering*) And if the King should command you to repeat what I have said?

NORFOLK I should keep my word to you!

MORE Then what has become of your oath of obedience to the King?

NORFOLK (*Indignant*) You lay traps for me!

MORE (*Now grown calm*) No, I show you the times.

NORFOLK Why do you insult me with these lawyer's tricks?

MORE Because I am afraid.

NORFOLK And here's your answer. The King accepts your resignation very sadly; he is mindful of your goodness and past loyalty, and in any matter concerning your honor and welfare he will be your good lord. So much for your fear.

MORE (*Flatly*) You will convey my humble gratitude.

NORFOLK I will. Good day, Alice. (*Going*) I'd rather deal with you than your husband.

MORE (*Complete change of tone; briskly professional*) Oh, Howard! (*He stops him*) Signor Chapuys tells me he's just made a "tour" of the North Country. He thinks we shall have trouble there. So do I.

NORFOLK (*Stolid*) Yes? What kind of trouble?

MORE The Church—the old Church, not the new Church—is very strong up there. I'm serious, Howard, keep an eye on the border this next spring; and bear in mind the Old Alliance.

NORFOLK (*Looks at him*) We will. We do . . . As for the Spaniard, Thomas, it'll perhaps relieve your mind to know that one of Secretary Cromwell's agents made the tour with him.

MORE Oh. (*A flash of jealousy*) Of course if Master Cromwell has matters in hand—

NORFOLK He has.

MORE Yes, I can imagine.

NORFOLK But thanks for the information. (*Going upstairs*) It's good to know you still have . . . some vestige of patriotism.

MORE (*Angrily*) That's a remarkably stupid observation, Norfolk! (NORFOLK *exits*)

ALICE So there's an end of you. What will you do now—sit by the fire and make goslings in the ash?

MORE Not at all, Alice, I expect I'll write a bit. (*He woos them with unhappy cheerfulness*) I'll write, I'll read, I'll think. I think I'll learn to fish! I'll play with my grandchildren—when son Roper's done his duty. (*Eagerly*) Alice, shall I teach you to read?

ALICE   No, by God!

MORE   Son Roper, *you're* pleased with me I hope?

ROPER   (*Goes to him; moved*)   Sir, you've made a noble gesture.

MORE   (*Blankly*)   A gesture? (*Eagerly*) It wasn't possible to continue, Will. I was not *able* to continue. I would have if I could! I make no gesture! (*Apprehensive, looks after* NORFOLK) My God, I hope it's understood I make no gesture! (*He turns back to them*) Alice, you don't think I would do this to you for a gesture! *That's* a gesture! (*Thumbs his nose*) That's a gesture! (*Jerks up two fingers*) I'm no street acrobat to make gestures! I'm practical!

ROPER   You belittle yourself, sir, this was not practical; (*Resonantly*) this was moral!

MORE   Oh, now I understand you, Will. Morality's *not* practical. Morality's a gesture. A complicated gesture learned from books— that's what you say, Alice, isn't it? . . . And you, Meg?

MARGARET   It *is*, for most of us, Father.

MORE   Oh no, if you're going to plead humility! Oh, you're cruel. I have a cruel family.

ALICE   Yes, you can fit the cap on anyone you want, I know that well enough. If there's cruelty in this house, I know where to look for it.

MARGARET   No, Mother!

ALICE   Oh, you'd walk on the bottom of the sea and think yourself a crab if he suggested it! (*To* ROPER) And you! You'd dance him to the Tower—You'd dance him to the block! Like David with a harp! Scattering hymn books in his path! (*To* MORE) Poor silly man, d'you think they'll *leave* you here to learn to fish?

MORE   (*Straight at her*)   If we govern our tongues they will! Now listen, I have a word to say about that. I have made no statement. I've resigned, that's *all*. On the King's Supremacy, the King's divorce which he'll now grant himself, the marriage he'll then make—have you heard me make a statement?

ALICE   No—and if I'm to lose my rank and fall to housekeeping I want to know the reason; so make a statement now.

MORE   No— (ALICE *exhibits indignation*) Alice, it's a point of law! Accept it from me, Alice, that in silence is my safety under the law, but my silence must be absolute, it must extend to you.

ALICE   In short you don't trust us!

MORE   A man would need to be half-witted not to trust you—but— (*Impatiently*) Look—(*He advances on her*) I'm the Lord Chief Justice, I'm Cromwell, I'm the King's Head Jailer—and I take your hand (*He does so*) and I clamp it on the Bible, on the Blessed Cross (*Clamps her hand on his closed fist*) and I say: "Woman, has your husband made a statement on these matters?" Now—on peril of your soul remember—what's your answer?

ALICE   No.

MORE   And so it must remain. (*He looks around at their grave faces*) Oh, it's only a life line, we shan't have to use it but it's comforting to have. No, no, when they find I'm silent they'll ask nothing better than to leave me silent; you'll see.

(*Enter* STEWARD)

STEWARD   Sir, the household's in the kitchen. They want to know what's happened.

MORE   Oh. Yes. We must speak to them. Alice, they'll mostly have to go, my dear. (*To* STEWARD) But not before we've found them places.

ALICE   We can't find places for them all!

MORE   Yes, we can; yes, we can. Tell them so.

ALICE   God's death, it comes on us quickly . . .

(*Exit* ALICE, MARGARET *with the chain, and* ROPER)

MORE   What about you, Matthew? It'll be a smaller household now, and for you I'm afraid, a smaller wage. Will you stay?

STEWARD   Don't see how I could then, sir.

MORE   You're a single man.

STEWARD   (*Awkwardly*) Well, yes, sir, but I mean I've got my own—

MORE   (*Quickly*) Quite right, why should you? . . . I shall miss you, Matthew.

STEWARD   (*With man-to-man jocosity*) No-o-o. You never had much time for me, sir. You see through *me*, sir, I know that.

(*He almost winks*)

MORE   (*Gently insists*) I shall miss you, Matthew; I shall miss you.

(*Exit* MORE. STEWARD *snatches off his hat and hurls it to the floor*)

STEWARD   Now, damn me, isn't that them all over! (*He broods, face downturned*) Miss? . . . He . . . Miss? . . . *Miss* me? . . . What's *in* me *for him* to miss? . . . (*Suddenly he cries out like one who sees a danger at his very feet*) Wo-AH! (*Chuckling*) We-e-eyup! (*To audience*) I nearly fell for it. (*He walks away*) "Matthew, will you kindly take a cut in your wages?" "No, Sir Thomas, I will not." That's it and (*Fiercely*) that's all of it! (*Falls to thought again. Resentfully*) All right, so he's down on his luck! I'm sorry. I don't mind saying that: I'm sorry! Bad luck! If I'd any good luck to spare he could have some. I wish we could *all* have good luck, *all* the time! I wish we had wings! I wish rain water was beer! But it isn't! . . . And what with not having wings but walking—on two flat feet; and good luck and bad luck being just exactly even stevens; and rain being water—don't you complicate the job by putting things in me for me to miss! (*He takes off his steward's coat, picks up his hat; draws the curtain to the alcove. Chuckling*) I did, you know. I nearly fell for it.

(*Exit* COMMON MAN. NORFOLK *and* CROMWELL *enter to alcove*)

NORFOLK But he makes no noise, Mr. Secretary; he's silent, why not leave him silent?

CROMWELL (*Patiently*) Not being a man of letters, Your Grace, you perhaps don't realize the extent of his reputation. This "silence" of his is bellowing up and down Europe! Now may I recapitulate: He reported the Spaniard's conversation to you, informed on the Spaniard's tour of the North Country, warned against a possible rebellion there.

NORFOLK He did!

CROMWELL We may say, then, that he showed himself hostile to the hopes of Spain.

NORFOLK That's what I *say*!

CROMWELL (*Patiently*) Bear with me, Your Grace. Now if he opposes Spain, he supports us. Well, surely that follows? (*Sarcastically*) Or do you see some third alternative?

NORFOLK No no, that's the line-up all right. And I may say Thomas More—

CROMWELL Thomas More will line up on the right side.

NORFOLK Yes! Crank he may be, traitor he is not.

CROMWELL (*Spreading his hands*) And with a little pressure, he can be got to say so. And that's all we need—a brief declaration of his loyalty to the present administration.

NORFOLK I still say let sleeping dogs lie.

CROMWELL (*Heavily*) The King does not agree with you.

NORFOLK (*Glances at him, flickers, but then rallies*) What kind of "pressure" d'you think you can bring to bear?

CROMWELL I have evidence that Sir Thomas, during the period of his judicature, accepted bribes.

NORFOLK (*Incredulous*) What! Goddammit, he was the only judge since Cato who *didn't* accept bribes! When was there last a Chancellor whose possessions after three years in office totaled one hundred pounds and a gold chain.

CROMWELL *(Rings hand bell and calls)* Richard! It is, as you imply, common practice, but a practice may be common and remain an offense; this offense could send a man to the Tower.

NORFOLK *(Contemptuously)* I don't believe it.

(Enter a WOMAN *and* RICH, *who motions her to remain and approaches the table, where* CROMWELL *indicates a seat.* RICH *has acquired self-importance)*

CROMWELL Ah, Richard. You know His Grace, of course.

RICH *(Respectful affability)* Indeed yes, we're *old* friends.

NORFOLK *(Savage snub)* Used to look after my books or something, didn't you?

CROMWELL *(Clicks his fingers at* WOMAN) Come here. This woman's name is Catherine Anger; she comes from Lincoln. And she put a case in the Court of Requests in—

(Consults a paper)

WOMAN A property case, it was.

CROMWELL Be quiet. A property case in the Court of Requests in April, 1526.

WOMAN And got a wicked false judgment!

CROMWELL And got an impeccably correct judgment from our friend Sir Thomas.

WOMAN No, sir, it was not!

CROMWELL We're not concerned with the judgment but the gift you gave the judge. Tell this gentleman about that. The judgment, for what it's worth, was the right one.

WOMAN No, sir! (CROMWELL *looks at her; she hastily addresses* NORFOLK) I sent him a cup, sir, an Italian silver cup I bought in Lincoln for a hundred shillings.

NORFOLK Did Sir Thomas accept this cup?

WOMAN I sent it.

CROMWELL He did accept it, we can corroborate that. You can go. *(She opens her mouth)* Go!

(Exit WOMAN)

NORFOLK *(Scornfully)* Is that your witness?

CROMWELL No; by an odd coincidence this cup later came into the hands of Master Rich here.

NORFOLK How?

RICH He gave it to me.

NORFOLK *(Brutally)* Can you corroborate that?

CROMWELL I have a fellow outside who can; he was More's steward at that time. Shall I call him?

NORFOLK Don't bother, I know him. When did Thomas give you this thing?

RICH I don't exactly remember.

NORFOLK Well, make an effort. Wait! I can tell you! I can tell you— it was that spring—it was that night we were there together. You had a cup with you when we left; was that it?

(RICH *looks to* CROMWELL *for guidance but gets none*)

RICH It may have been.

NORFOLK Did he often give you cups?

RICH I don't suppose so, Your Grace.

NORFOLK That was it then. (*New realization*) And it was April! The April of twenty-six. The very month that cow first put her case before him! (*Triumphantly*) In other words, the moment he knew it was a bribe, he got rid of it.

CROMWELL (*Nodding judicially*) The facts will bear that interpretation, I suppose.

NORFOLK Oh, this is a horse that won't run, Master Secretary.

CROMWELL Just a trial canter, Your Grace. We'll find something better.

NORFOLK (*Between bullying and pleading*) Look here, Cromwell, I want no part of this.

CROMWELL You have no choice.

NORFOLK What's that you say?

CROMWELL The King particularly wishes you to be active in the matter.

NORFOLK (*Winded*) He has not told me that.

CROMWELL (*Politely*) Indeed? He told me.

NORFOLK But *why*?

CROMWELL We felt that, since you are known to have been a friend of More's, your participation will show that there is nothing in the nature of a "persecution," but only the strict processes of law. As indeed you've just demonstrated. I'll tell the King of your loyalty to your friend. If you like, I'll tell him that you "want no part of it," too.

NORFOLK (*Furious*) Are you threatening me, Cromwell?

CROMWELL My *dear* Norfolk . . . This isn't Spain.

(NORFOLK *stares, turns abruptly and exits.* CROMWELL *turns a look of glacial coldness upon* RICH)

RICH I'm sorry, Secretary, I'd forgotten he was there that night.

CROMWELL (*Scrutinizes him dispassionately; then*) You must try to remember these things.

RICH Secretary, I'm sincerely—

CROMWELL (*Dismisses the topic with a wave and turns to look after* NORFOLK) Not such a fool as he looks, the Duke.

RICH (*Civil Service simper*) That would hardly be possible, Secretary.

CROMWELL (*Straightening his papers, briskly*) Sir Thomas is going to be a slippery fish, Richard; we need a net with a finer mesh.

RICH Yes, Secretary?

CROMWELL We'll weave one for him, shall we, you and I?

RICH (*Uncertainly*) I'm only anxious to do what is correct, Secretary.

CROMWELL (*Smiling at him*) Yes, Richard, I know. (*Straight-faced*) You're absolutely right, it must be done by law. It's just a matter of finding the right law. Or making one. Bring my papers, will you?

(*Exit* CROMWELL. *Enter* STEWARD)

STEWARD Could we have a word now, sir?

RICH We don't require you after all, Matthew.

STEWARD No, sir, but about . . .

RICH Oh yes. . . . Well, I begin to need a steward, certainly; my household is expanding . . . (*Sharply*) But as I remember, Matthew, your attitude to me was sometimes—disrespectful!

(*The last word is shrill*)

STEWARD (*With humble dignity*) Oh. Oh, I must contradict you there, sir; that's your imagination. In those days, sir, you still had your way to make. And a gentleman in that position often imagines these things. Then when he's reached his proper level, sir, he stops thinking about them. (*As if offering tangible proof*) Well —I don't think you find people "disrespectful" nowadays, do you, sir?

RICH There may be something in that. Bring my papers. (*Going, he turns at the exit and anxiously scans* STEWARD's *face for signs of impudence*) I'll permit no breath of insolence!

STEWARD (*The very idea is shocking*) I should hope not, sir. (*Exit* RICH) Oh, I can manage this one! He's just my size! (*Lighting changes so that the set looks drab and chilly*) Sir Thomas More's again. Gone down a bit.

(*Exit* COMMON MAN. *Enter* CHAPUYS *and* ATTENDANT, *cloaked.* ALICE *enters above wearing a big coarse apron over her dress*)

ALICE My husband is coming down, Your Excellency.

CHAPUYS Thank you, madam.

ALICE And I beg you to be gone before he does!

CHAPUYS (*Patiently*) Madam, I have a Royal Commission to perform.

ALICE Aye. You said so.

(ALICE *exits*)

CHAPUYS For sheer barbarity, commend me to a good-hearted Englishwoman of a certain class. . . .

(*Wraps cloak about him*)

ATTENDANT It's very cold, Excellency.

CHAPUYS I remember when these rooms were warm enough.

ATTENDANT (*Looking about*) "Thus it is to incur the enmity of a King."

CHAPUYS A heretic King. (*Looking about*) Yes, Sir Thomas is a good man.

ATTENDANT Yes, Excellency, I like Sir Thomas very much.

CHAPUYS Carefully, carefully.

ATTENDANT It *is* uncomfortable dealing with him, isn't it?

CHAPUYS (*Smilingly patronizing*) Goodness can be a difficulty.

ATTENDANT (*Somewhat shocked*) Excellency?

CHAPUYS (*Recovers instantly his official gravity*) In the long run, of course, *all* good men everywhere are allies of Spain. No good man cannot be, and no man who is not can be good . . .

ATTENDANT Then he is really for us.

CHAPUYS (*Still graciously instructing*) He is opposed to Cromwell, is he not?

ATTENDANT (*Smiling back*) Oh, yes, Excellency.

CHAPUYS (*As a genteel card player, primly triumphant, produces the ace of trumps*) If he's opposed to Cromwell, he's for us. (*No answer; a little more sharply*) There's no third alternative?

ATTENDANT I suppose not, Excellency.

CHAPUYS (*Rides him down, tried beyond all bearing*) Oh—I wish your mother had chosen some other career for you. You've no political sense whatever! (*Enter* MORE) Sir Thomas! (*Goes to him, solemnly and affectionately places hands on his shoulders, gazing into his eyes*) Ah, Sir Thomas, in a better state this threadbare stuff will metamorphose into shining garments, these dank walls to walls of pearl, this cold light to perpetual sunshine.

(*He bends upon* MORE *a melancholy look of admiration*)

MORE (*As yet quite friendly, smiles quizzically*) It sounds not unlike Madrid . . . ?

CHAPUYS (*Throws up his hands delightedly*) Even in times like this, even now, a pleasure to converse with you.

MORE (*Chuckles a little, takes* CHAPUYS *by the wrist, waggles it a little and then releases it as though to indicate that pleasantries must now end*) Is this another "personal" visit, Chapuys, or is it official?

CHAPUYS It falls between the two, Sir Thomas.

MORE (*Reaching the bottom of stairs*) Official then.

CHAPUYS No, I have a personal letter for you.

MORE From whom?

CHAPUYS My master, the King of Spain. (MORE *puts his hands behind his back*) You will take it?

MORE I will not lay a finger on it.

CHAPUYS It is in no way an affair of State. It expresses my master's admiration for the stand which you and Bishop Fisher of Rochester have taken over the so-called divorce of Queen Catherine.

MORE I have taken no stand!

CHAPUYS But your views, Sir Thomas, are well known—

MORE My views are much guessed at. (*Irritably*) Oh come, sir, could you undertake to convince (*Grimly*) King Harry that this letter is "in no way an affair of State?"

CHAPUYS My dear Sir Thomas, I have taken extreme precautions. I came here very much incognito. (*A self-indulgent chuckle*) Very nearly in disguise.

MORE You misunderstand me. It is not a matter of your precautions but my duty, which would be to take this letter immediately to the King.

CHAPUYS (*Flabbergasted*) But, Sir Thomas, your views—

MORE (*With the heat of fear behind it*) Are well known you say. It seems my loyalty to my King is less so!

CHAPUYS (*Glibly*) "Render unto Caesar the things which *are* Caesar's—(*He raises a reproving finger*) But unto God—"

MORE Stop! (*He walks about, suppressing his agitation, and then as one who excuses a display of bad manners*) Holy writ is holy, Excellency.

(*Enter* MARGARET *bearing before her a huge bundle of bracken. The entry of the bracken affords him a further opportunity to collect himself*)

MARGARET Look, Father! (*She dumps it*) Will's getting more.

MORE Oh, well done! (*This is not whimsy; they're cold and their interest in fuel is serious*) Is it dry? (*He feels it expertly*) Oh it *is.* (*Sees* CHAPUYS *staring; laughs*) It's bracken, Your Excellency. We burn it. (*Enter* ALICE) Alice, look at this.

ALICE (*Eying* CHAPUYS) Aye.

MORE (*Crossing to* CHAPUYS) May I? (*Takes the letter to* ALICE *and* MARGARET) This is a letter from the King of Spain; I want you to see it's not been opened. I have declined it. You see the seal has not been broken? (*Returning it to* CHAPUYS) I wish I could ask you to stay, Your Excellency—the bracken fire is a luxury.

CHAPUYS (*With a cold smile*) One I must forgo. (*Aside to* ATTEND-ANT) Come. (*Crosses to exit, pauses*) May I say I am sure my master's admiration will not be diminished. (*Bows, noncommit-tally*) Ladies.

MORE I'm gratified.

CHAPUYS (*Bows to them, the ladies curtsy*) The man's utterly un-reliable.

(*Exit* CHAPUYS *and* ATTENDANT)

ALICE (*After a little silence kicks the bracken*) "Luxury"!
(*She sits wearily on the bundle*)

MORE Well, it's a luxury while it lasts . . . There's not much sport in it for you, is there? (*She neither answers nor looks at him from the depths of her fatigue. After a moment's hesitation he braces himself*) Alice, the money from the bishops. I can't take it. I wish —oh, heaven, how I wish I could! But I can't.

ALICE (*As one who has ceased to expect anything*) I didn't think you would.

MORE (*Reproachfully*) Alice, there *are* reasons.

ALICE We couldn't come so deep into your confidence as to *know* these reasons why a man in poverty can't take four thousand pounds?

MORE (*Gently but very firmly*) Alice, this isn't poverty.

ALICE D'you know what we shall eat tonight?

MORE (*Trying for a smile*) Yes, parsnips.

ALICE Yes, parsnips and stinking mutton! (*Straight at him*) For a knight's lady!

MORE (*Pleading*) But at the worst, we could be beggars, and still keep company, and be merry together!

ALICE (*Bitterly*) Merry!

MORE (*Sternly*) Aye, merry!

MARGARET (*Her arm about her mother's waist*) I think you should take that money.

MORE Oh, don't you see? (*He sits by them*) If I'm paid by the Church for my writings—

ALICE This had nothing to do with your writings! This was charity pure and simple! Collected from the clergy high and low!

MORE It would *appear* as payment.

ALICE You're not a man who deals in appearances!

MORE (*Fervently*) Oh, am I not though. . . . (*Calmly*) If the King takes this matter any further, with me or with the Church, it will be very bad, if I even appear to have been in the pay of the Church.

ALICE (*Sharply*) Bad?

MORE If you will have it, dangerous.

MARGARET But you don't write against the King.

MORE (*Rises*) I write! And that's enough in times like these!

ALICE You said there *was* no danger!

MORE I don't think there is! And I don't want there to be!

(*Enter* ROPER *carrying a sickle*)

ROPER (*Steadily*) There's a gentleman here from Hampton Court. You are to go before Secretary Cromwell. To answer certain charges.

(ALICE *rises and* MARGARET, *appalled, turns to* MORE)

MORE (*After a silence, rubs his nose*) Well, that's all right. We expected that. (*He is not very convincing*) When?

ROPER Now.

ALICE (*Exhibits distress*) Ah—

MORE Alice, that means nothing; that's just technique . . . Well, I suppose "now" means now.

(*Lighting changes, darkness gathering on the others, leaving* MORE *isolated in the light*)

MARGARET Can I come with you?

MORE Why? No. I'll be back for dinner. I'll bring Cromwell to dinner, shall I? It'd serve him right.

MARGARET Oh, Father, don't be witty!

MORE Why not? Wit's what's in question.

ROPER (*Quietly*) While we are witty, the Devil may enter us unawares.

MORE He's not the Devil, son Roper, he's a lawyer! And my case is watertight!

ALICE They say he's a very penetrating lawyer.

MORE What, Cromwell? Pooh, he's a pragmatist—and that's the only resemblance he has to the Devil, son Roper; a pragmatist, the nearest plumber.

(*Exit* ALICE, MARGARET, ROPER, *in darkness. Lights come up. Enter* CROMWELL, *bustling, carrying a file of papers*)

CROMWELL   I'm sorry to invite you here at such short notice, Sir Thomas; good of you to come. (*Draws back curtain from alcove, revealing* RICH *seated at a table, with writing materials*) Will you take a seat? I think you know Master Rich?

MORE   Indeed yes, we're old friends. That's a nice gown you have, Richard.

CROMWELL   Master Rich will make a record of our conversation.

MORE   Good of you to tell me, Master Secretary.

CROMWELL   (*Laughs appreciatively; then*)   Believe me, Sir Thomas —no, that's asking too much—but let me tell you all the same, you have no more sincere admirer than myself. (RICH *begins to scribble*) Not yet, Rich, not yet.

(*Invites* MORE *to join him in laughing at* RICH)

MORE   If I might hear the charges?

CROMWELL   Charges?

MORE   I understand there are certain charges.

CROMWELL   Some ambiguities of behavior I should like to clarify— hardly "charges."

MORE   Make a note of that will you, Master Rich? There are no charges.

CROMWELL   (*Laughing and shaking head*)   Sir Thomas, Sir Thomas . . . You know it amazes me that you, who were once so effective *in* the world and are now so *much* retired from it, should be opposing yourself to the whole movement of the times?

(*He ends on a note of interrogation*)

MORE   (*Nods*)   It amazes me too.

CROMWELL   (*Picks up and drops a paper; sadly*)   The King is not pleased with you.

MORE   I am grieved.

CROMWELL   Yet do you know that even now, if you could bring yourself to agree with the Universities, the Bishops, and the Parliament of this realm, there is no honor which the King would be likely to deny you?

MORE   (*Stonily*)   I am well acquainted with His Grace's generosity.

CROMWELL   (*Coldly*)   Very well. (*Consults the paper*) You have heard of the so-called Holy Maid of Kent—who was executed for prophesying against the King?

MORE   Yes, I knew the poor woman.

CROMWELL (*Quickly*)   You sympathize with her?

MORE   She was ignorant and misguided; she was a bit mad, I think. And she has paid for her folly. Naturally I sympathize with her.

CROMWELL (*Grunts*)   You admit meeting her. You met her—and yet you did not warn His Majesty of her treason. How was that?

MORE   She spoke no treason. Our conversation was not political.

CROMWELL   My dear More, the woman was notorious! Do you expect me to believe that?

MORE   Happily there are witnesses.

CROMWELL   You wrote a letter to her?

MORE   Yes, I wrote advising her to abstain from meddling with the affairs of Princes and the State. I have a copy of this letter—also witnessed.

CROMWELL   You have been cautious.

MORE   I like to keep my affairs regular.

CROMWELL   Sir Thomas, there is a more serious charge—

MORE   Charge?

CROMWELL   For want of a better word. In the May of 1526 the King published a book. (*He permits himself a little smile*) A theological work. It was called *A Defence of the Seven Sacraments.*

MORE   Yes. (*Bitterly*) For which he was named "Defender of the Faith," by His Holiness the Pope.

CROMWELL   By the Bishop of Rome. Or do you insist on "Pope"?

MORE   No, "Bishop of Rome" if you like. It doesn't alter his authority.

CROMWELL   Thank you, you come to the point very readily; what *is* that authority? As regards the Church in Europe; (*Approaching*) for example, the Church in England. What exactly *is* the Bishop of Rome's authority?

MORE   You will find it very ably set out and defended, Master Secretary, in the King's book.

CROMWELL   The book published under the King's name would be more accurate. You wrote that book.

MORE   I wrote no part of it.

CROMWELL   I do not mean you actually held the pen.

MORE   I merely answered to the best of my ability certain questions on canon law which His Majesty put to me. As I was bound to do.

CROMWELL   Do you deny that you *instigated* it?

MORE   It was from first to last the King's own project. This is trivial, Master Cromwell.

CROMWELL   I should not think so if I were in your place.

MORE   Only two people know the truth of the matter. Myself and the King. And, whatever he may have said to you, he will not give evidence to support this accusation.

CROMWELL   Why not?

MORE   Because evidence is given on oath, and he will not perjure himself. If you don't know that, you don't yet know him.

(CROMWELL *looks at him viciously*)

CROMWELL   (*Goes apart; formally*)   Sir Thomas More, is there anything you wish to say to me concerning the King's marriage with Queen Anne?

MORE   (*Very still*)   I understood I was not to be asked that again.

CROMWELL   Evidently you understood wrongly. These charges—

MORE   (*With a sudden, contemptuous sweep of his arm*)   They are terrors for children, Master Secretary—an empty cupboard! To frighten children in the dark, not me.

CROMWELL   (*It is some time now since anybody treated him like this, and it costs him some effort to control his anger, but he does and even manages a little smile as one who sportingly admits defeat*)   True . . . true, Sir Thomas, very apt. (*Then coldly*) To frighten a man, there must be something *in* the cupboard, must there not?

MORE   (*Made wary again by the tone*)   Yes, and there is nothing in it.

CROMWELL   For the moment there is this: (*Picks up a paper and reads*) "I charge you with great ingratitude. I remind you of many benefits graciously given and ill received. I tell you that no King of England ever had nor could have so villainous a servant nor so traitorous a subject as yourself." (*During this,* MORE's *face goes ashen and his hand creeps up to his throat in an unconscious gesture of fear and protection.* CROMWELL *puts down the paper and says*) The words are not mine, Sir Thomas, but the King's. Believe that.

MORE   I do. (*He lowers his hands, looks up again, and with just a spark of his old impudence*) I recognize the style. So I am brought here at last.

CROMWELL   Brought? You brought yourself to where you stand now.

MORE   Yes—Still, in another sense—I was brought.

CROMWELL   Oh, yes. You may go home now. (*After a fractional hesitation,* MORE *goes, his face fearful and his step thoughtful, and he pauses uncertainly as* CROMWELL *calls after him*) For the present. (MORE *carries on, and exits*) I don't like him so well as I did. There's a man who raises the gale and won't come out of the harbor.

RICH (*A covert jeer*) Do you still think you can frighten him?

CROMWELL Oh, yes.

RICH (*Given pause*) What will you do?

CROMWELL We'll put something in the cupboard.

RICH (*Now definitely uneasy*) What?

CROMWELL (*As to an importunate child*) Whatever's necessary. The King's a man of conscience and he wants either Sir Thomas More to bless his marriage or Sir Thomas More destroyed.

RICH (*Shakily*) They seem odd alternatives, Secretary.

CROMWELL Do they? That's because you're not a man of conscience. If the King destroys a man, that's proof to the King that it must have been a bad man, the kind of man a man of conscience *ought* to destroy—and of course a bad man's blessing's not worth having. So either will do.

RICH (*Subdued*) I see.

CROMWELL Oh, there's *no* going back, Rich. I find we've made ourselves the keepers of this conscience. And it's ravenous.

(*Exit* CROMWELL *and* RICH. *Enter* MORE. COMMON MAN *enters, removes a cloth, hears* MORE, *shakes head, exits*)

MORE (*Calling*) Boat! . . . Boat! . . . (*To himself*) Oh, come along, it's not as bad as that. . . . (*Calls*) Boat! (*Enter* NORFOLK. *He stops. Turning, pleased*) Howard! . . . I can't get home. They won't bring me a boat.

NORFOLK Do you blame them?

MORE Is it as bad as that?

NORFOLK It's every bit as bad at that!

MORE (*Gravely*) Then it's good of you to be seen with me.

NORFOLK (*Looking back, off*) I followed you.

MORE (*Surprised*) Were *you* followed?

NORFOLK Probably. (*Facing him*) So listen to what I have to say: You're behaving like a fool. You're behaving like a crank. You're not behaving like a gentleman—All right, that means nothing to you; but what about your friends?

MORE What about them?

NORFOLK Goddammit, you're dangerous to know!

MORE Then don't know me.

NORFOLK There's something further . . . You must have realized

by now there's a . . . policy, with regards to you. (MORE *nods*)
The King is using me in it.

MORE   That's clever. That's Cromwell . . . You're between the upper and the nether millstones then.

NORFOLK   I am!

MORE   Howard, you must cease to know me.

NORFOLK   I do know you! I wish I didn't but I do!

MORE   I mean as a friend.

NORFOLK   You *are* my friend!

MORE   I can't relieve you of your obedience to the King, Howard. You must relieve yourself of our friendship. No one's safe now, and you have a son.

NORFOLK   You might as well advise a man to change the color of his hair! I'm fond of you, and there it is! You're fond of me, and there it is!

MORE   What's to be done then?

NORFOLK   (*With deep appeal*)   Give in.

MORE   (*Gently*)   I can't give in, Howard—(*A smile*) You might as well advise a man to change the color of his eyes. I can't. Our friendship's more mutable than *that*.

NORFOLK   Oh, that's immutable, is it? The one fixed point in a world of changing friendships is that Thomas More will not give in!

MORE   (*Urgent to explain*)   To me it *has* to be, for that's myself! Affection goes as deep in me as you think, but only God is love right through, Howard; and *that's* my *self*.

NORFOLK   And who are you? Goddammit, man, it's disproportionate! *We're* supposed to be the arrogant ones, the proud, splenetic ones—and we've all given in! Why must you stand out? (*Quietly and quickly*) You'll break my heart.

MORE   (*Moved*)   We'll do it now, Howard: part, as friends, and meet as strangers.

(*He attempts to take* NORFOLK's *hand*)

NORFOLK   (*Throwing it off*)   Daft, Thomas! Why d'you want to take your friendship from me? For friendship's sake! You say we'll meet as strangers and every word you've said confirms our friendship!

MORE   (*Takes a last affectionate look at him*)   Oh, that can be remedied. (*Walks away, turns; in a tone of deliberate insult*) Norfolk, you're a fool.

NORFOLK   (*Starts; then smiles and folds his arms*)   *You* can't place a quarrel; you haven't the style.

MORE Hear me out. You and your class have "given in"—as you
rightly call it—because the religion of this country means nothing
to you one way or the other.

NORFOLK Well, that's a foolish saying for a start; the nobility of
England has always been—

MORE The nobility of England, my lord, would have snored
through the Sermon on the Mount. But you'll labor like Thomas
Aquinas over a rat-dog's pedigree. Now what's the name of those
distorted creatures you're all breeding at the moment?

NORFOLK (*Steadily, but roused towards anger by* MORE's *tone*) An
artificial quarrel's not a quarrel.

MORE Don't deceive yourself, my lord, we've had a quarrel since
the day we met, our friendship was but sloth.

NORFOLK You can be cruel when you've a mind to be; but I've
always known that.

MORE What's the name of those dogs? Marsh mastiffs? Bog
beagles?

NORFOLK Water spaniels!

MORE And what would you do with a water spaniel that was afraid
of water? You'd hang it! Well, as a spaniel is to water, so is a man
to his own self. I will not give in because I oppose it—I do—not
my pride, not my spleen, nor any other of my appetites but *I* do
—*I!* (MORE *goes up to him and feels him up and down like an
animal.* MARGARET's *voice is heard, well off, calling her father.*
MORE's *attention is irresistibly caught by this; but he turns back
determinedly to* NORFOLK) Is there no single sinew in the midst
of this that serves no appetite of Norfolk's but is just Norfolk?
There is! Give *that* some exercise, my lord!

MARGARET (*Off, nearer*) Father?

NORFOLK (*Breathing hard*) Thomas . . .

MORE Because as you stand, you'll go before your Maker in a very
ill condition!

(*Enter* MARGARET, *below; she stops; amazed at them*)

NORFOLK Now steady, Thomas. . . .

MORE And he'll have to think that somewhere back along your
pedigree—a bitch got over the wall!

(NORFOLK *lashes out at him; he ducks and winces. Exit* NORFOLK)

MARGARET Father! (*As he straightens up*) Father, what was that?

MORE That was Norfolk.

(*He looks after him wistfully.* ROPER *enters*)

ROPER (*Excited, almost gleeful*) Do you know, sir? Have you heard? (MORE *is still looking off, not answering. To* MARGARET) Have you told him?

MARGARET (*Gently*) We've been looking for you, Father.

(MORE *is still looking off*)

ROPER There's to be a new Act through Parliament, sir!

MORE (*Half-turning, half-attending*) Act?

ROPER Yes, sir—about the marriage!

MORE (*Indifferently*) Oh.

(*Turning back again.* ROPER *and* MARGARET *look at one another*)

MARGARET (*Puts a hand on his arm*) Father, by this Act, they're going to administer an oath.

MORE (*With instantaneous attention*) An oath! (*He looks from one to the other*) On what compulsion?

ROPER It's expected to be treason!

MORE (*Very still*) What is the oath?

ROPER (*Puzzled*) It's about the marriage, sir.

MORE But what is the wording?

ROPER We don't need to know the (*Contemptuously*) wording— we know what it will mean!

MORE It will mean what the words say! An oath is *made* of words! It may be possible to take it. Or avoid it. (*To* MARGARET) Have we a copy of the Bill?

MARGARET There's one coming out from the City.

MORE Then let's get home and look at it. Oh, I've no boat.

(*He looks off again after* NORFOLK)

MARGARET (*Gently*) Father, he tried to hit you.

MORE Yes—I spoke, slightingly, of water spaniels. Let's get home.

(*He turns and sees* ROPER *excited and truculent*)

ROPER But sir—

MORE Now listen, Will. And, Meg, you listen, too, you know I know you well. God made the *angels* to show him splendor—as he made animals for innocence and plants for their simplicity. But Man he made to serve him wittily, in the tangle of his mind! If he suffers us to fall to such a case that there is no escaping, then we may stand to our tackle as best we can, and yes, Will, then we may clamor like champions . . . if we have the spittle for it. And no doubt it delights God to see splendor where He only looked for complexity. But it's God's part, not our own, to bring ourselves to that extremity! Our natural business lies in escaping —so let's get home and study this Bill.

(*Exit* MORE, ROPER *and* MARGARET. *Enter* COMMON MAN, *dragging a cage. The rear of the stage remains in moonlight. Now descends a rack, which remains suspended)*

COMMON MAN *(Aggrieved. Brings the basket on)* Now look! . . . I don't suppose anyone enjoyed it any more than he did. Well, not much more. *(Takes from the basket and dons a coat and hat)* Jailer! *(Shrugs. Pushes basket off and arranges three chairs behind the table)* The pay scale being what it is they have to take a rather common type of man into the prison service. But it's a job. *(Admits* MORE *to jail, turns keys)* Bit nearer the knuckle than most perhaps, but it's a job like any other job—*(Sits on steps. Enter* CROMWELL, NORFOLK, CRANMER, *who sit, and* RICH, *who stands behind them.* MORE *enters the cage and lies down)* They'd let him out if they could, but for various reasons they can't. *(Twirling keys)* I'd let him out if I could but I can't. Not without taking up residence in there myself. And he's in there already, so what'd be the point? You know the old adage? "Better a live rat than a dead lion," and that's about it. *(An envelope descends swiftly before him. He opens it and reads)* "With reference to the old adage: Thomas Cromwell was found guilty of High Treason and executed on 28 July, 1540. Norfolk was found guilty of High Treason and should have been executed on 27 January, 1547, but on the night of 26 January, the King died of syphilis and wasn't able to sign the warrant. Thomas Cranmer"—Archbishop of Canterbury *(Jerking thumb)*, that's the other one—"was burned alive on 21 March, 1556." *(He is about to conclude but sees a postscript)* Oh. "Richard Rich became a Knight and Solicitor-General, a Baron and Lord Chancellor, and died in his bed." So did I. And so, I hope, will all of you. *(He goes to* MORE *and rouses him)* Wake up, Sir Thomas.

MORE *(Rousing)* What, again?

JAILER Sorry, sir.

MORE *(Flops back)* What time is it?

JAILER One o'clock, sir.

MORE Oh, this is iniquitous!

JAILER *(Anxiously)* Sir.

MORE *(Sitting up)* All right. *(Putting on slippers)* Who's there?

JAILER The Secretary, the Duke, and the Archbishop.

MORE I'm flattered. *(He stands, claps hand to hip)* Ooh!

(Preceded by JAILER *he limps across the stage; he has aged and is pale, but his manner, though wary, is relaxed; while that of the Commission is bored, tense, and jumpy)*

NORFOLK (*Looks at him*) A seat for the prisoner. (*While* JAILER *brings a stool from under the stairs and* MORE *sits on it,* NORFOLK *rattles off*) This is the Seventh Commission to inquire into the case of Sir Thomas More, appointed by His Majesty's Council. Have you anything to say?

MORE *No.* (*To* JAILER) Thank you.

NORFOLK (*Sitting back*) Master Secretary.

CROMWELL Sir Thomas—(*He breaks off*) Do the witnesses attend?

RICH Secretary.

JAILER Sir.

CROMWELL (*To* JAILER) Nearer! (*He advances a bit*) Come where you can hear! (JAILER *takes up stance by* RICH. *To* MORE) Sir Thomas, you have seen this document before?

MORE Many times.

CROMWELL It is the Act of Succession. These are the names of those who have sworn to it.

MORE I have, as you say, seen it before.

CROMWELL Will you swear to it?

MORE No.

NORFOLK Thomas, we must know plainly—

CROMWELL (*Throws down document*) Your Grace, *please!*

NORFOLK Master Cromwell!

(*They regard one another in hatred*)

CROMWELL I beg Your Grace's pardon.

(*Sighing, rests his head in his hands*)

NORFOLK Thomas, we must know plainly whether you recognize the offspring of Queen Anne as heirs to His Majesty.

MORE The King in Parliament tells me that they are. Of course I recognize them.

NORFOLK Will you swear that you do?

MORE Yes.

NORFOLK Then why won't you swear to the Act?

CROMWELL (*Impatiently*) Because there is more than that *in* the Act.

NORFOLK Is that it?

MORE (*After a pause*) Yes.

NORFOLK Then we must find out what it is in the Act that he objects to!

CROMWELL Brilliant. (NORFOLK *rounds on him*) God's wounds!

CRANMER (*Hastily*) Your Grace—May I try?

NORFOLK   Certainly. I've no pretension to be an expert in police work.

(*During the next speech* CROMWELL *straightens up and folds arms resignedly*)

CRANMER   (*Clears his throat fussily*)   Sir Thomas, it states in the preamble that the King's former marriage, to the Lady Catherine, was unlawful, she being previously his brother's wife and the—er—"Pope" having no authority to sanction it. (*Gently*) Is that what you deny? (*No reply*) Is that what you dispute? (*No reply*) Is that what you are not sure of? (*No reply*)

NORFOLK   Thomas, you insult the King and His Council in the person of the Lord Archbishop!

MORE   I insult no one. I will not take the oath. I will not tell you why I will not.

NORFOLK   Then your reasons must be treasonable!

MORE   Not "must be"; may be.

NORFOLK   It's a fair assumption!

MORE   The law requires more than an assumption; the law requires a fact.

(CROMWELL *looks at him and away again*)

CRANMER   I cannot judge your legal standing in the case; but until I know the *ground* of your objections, I can only guess your spiritual standing too.

MORE   (*For a second furiously affronted; then humor overtakes him*) If you're willing to guess at that, Your Grace, it should be a small matter to guess my objections.

CROMWELL   (*Quickly*)   You do have objections to the Act?

NORFOLK   (*Happily*)   Well, we know *that*, Cromwell!

MORE   You don't, my lord. You may *suppose* I have objections. All you *know* is that I will not swear to it. From sheer delight to give you trouble it might be.

NORFOLK   Is it material why you won't?

MORE   It's most material. For refusing to swear, my goods are forfeit and I am condemned to life imprisonment. You cannot lawfully harm me further. But if you were right in supposing I had reasons for refusing and right again in supposing my reasons to be treasonable, the law would let you cut my head off.

NORFOLK   (*He has followed with some difficulty*)   Oh yes.

CROMWELL   (*An admiring murmur*)   Oh, well done, Sir Thomas. I've been trying to make that clear to His Grace for some time.

NORFOLK   (*Hardly responds to the insult; his face is gloomy and dis-*

gusted) Oh, confound all this . . . (*With real dignity*) I'm not a scholar, as Master Cromwell never tires of pointing out, and frankly I don't know whether the marriage was lawful or not. But damn it, Thomas, look at those names . . . You know those men! Can't you do what I did, and come with us, for fellowship?

MORE (*Moved*) And when we stand before God, and you are sent to Paradise for doing according to your conscience, and I am damned for not doing according to mine, will you come with me, for fellowship?

CRANMER So those of us whose names are there are damned, Sir Thomas?

MORE I don't know, Your Grace. I have no window to look into another man's conscience. I condemn no one.

CRANMER Then the matter is capable of question?

MORE Certainly.

CRANMER But that you owe obedience to your King is not capable of question. So weigh a doubt against a certainty—and sign.

MORE Some men think the Earth is round, others think it flat; it is a matter capable of question. But if it is flat, will the King's command make it round? And if it is round, will the King's command flatten it? No, I will not sign.

CROMWELL (*Leaping up, with ceremonial indignation*) Then you have more regard to your own doubt than you have to his command!

MORE For myself, I have no doubt.

CROMWELL No doubt of what?

MORE No doubt of my grounds for refusing this oath. Grounds I will tell to the King alone, and which you, Master Secretary, will not trick out of me.

NORFOLK Thomas—

MORE Oh, gentlemen, can't I go to bed?

CROMWELL You don't seem to appreciate the seriousness of your position.

MORE I defy anyone to live in that cell for a year and not appreciate the seriousness of his position.

CROMWELL Yet the State has harsher punishments.

MORE You threaten like a dockside bully.

CROMWELL How should I threaten?

MORE Like a Minister of State, with justice!

CROMWELL Oh, justice is what you're threatened with.

MORE Then I'm not threatened.

704 Robert Bolt

NORFOLK Master Secretary, I think the prisoner may retire as he requests. Unless you, my lord—

CRANMER (*Pettishly*) No, I see no purpose in prolonging the interview.

NORFOLK Then good night, Thomas.

MORE (*Hesitates*) Might I have one or two more books?

CROMWELL You have books?

MORE Yes.

CROMWELL I didn't know; you shouldn't have.

MORE (*Turns to go, pauses. Desperately*) May I see my family?

CROMWELL No! (MORE *returns to cell*) Jailer!

JAILER Sir!

CROMWELL Have you ever heard the prisoner speak of the King's divorce, or the King's Supremacy of the Church, or the King's marriage?

JAILER No, sir, not a word.

CROMWELL If he does, you will of course report it to the Lieutenant.

JAILER Of course, sir.

CROMWELL You will swear an oath to that effect.

JAILER (*Cheerfully*) Certainly, sir!

CROMWELL Archbishop?

CRANMER (*Laying the cross of his vestment on the table*) Place your left hand on this and raise your right hand—take your hat off—Now say after me: I swear by my immortal soul— (JAILER, *overlapping, repeats the oath with him*)—that I will report truly anything said by Sir Thomas More against the King, the Council or the State of the Realm. So help me God. Amen.

JAILER (*Overlapping*) So help me God. Amen.

CROMWELL And there's fifty guineas in it if you do.

JAILER (*Looks at him gravely*) Yes, sir.

(*He goes*)

CRANMER (*Hastily*) That's not to tempt you into perjury, my man!

JAILER No, sir! (*At exit he pauses; to audience*) Fifty guineas isn't tempting; fifty guineas is alarming. If he'd left it at swearing . . . But fifty—That's serious money. If it's worth that much now it's worth my neck presently. (*With decision*) I want no part of it. They can sort it out between them. I feel my deafness coming on.

(*Exit* JAILER. *The Commission rises*)

CROMWELL Rich!

RICH Secretary?

CROMWELL Tomorrow morning, remove the prisoner's books.

NORFOLK Is that necessary?

CROMWELL (*Suppressed exasperation*) Norfolk. With regards this case, the King is becoming impatient.

NORFOLK Aye, with you.

CROMWELL With all of us. (*He walks over to the rack*) You know the King's impatience, how commodious it is!

(NORFOLK *and* CRANMER *exit.* CROMWELL *is brooding over the instrument of torture*)

RICH Secretary!

CROMWELL (*Abstracted*) Yes . . .

RICH Sir Redvers Llewellyn has retired.

CROMWELL (*Not listening*) Mm . . .

RICH (*Goes to the other end of the rack and faces him. With some indignation*) The Attorney-General for Wales. His post is vacant. You said I might approach you.

CROMWELL (*Contemptuous impatience*) Oh, not *now* . . . (*Broods*) He must submit, the alternatives are bad. While More's alive the King's conscience breaks into fresh stinking flowers every time he gets from bed. And if I bring about More's death—I plant my own, I think. There's no other good solution! He must submit! (*He whirls the windlass of the rack, producing a startling clatter from the ratchet. They look at each other. He turns it again slowly, shakes his head and lets go*) No; the King will not permit it. (*He walks away*) We have to find some gentler way.

(*The scene change commences as he says this, and exit* RICH *and* CROMWELL. *From night it becomes morning, cold gray light from off the gray water. Enter* JAILER *and* MARGARET)

JAILER Wake up, Sir Thomas! Your family's here!

MORE (*Starting up. A great cry*) Margaret! What's this? You can visit me? (*Thrusts his arms through the cage*) Meg. Meg. (*She goes to him. Then horrified*) For God's sake, Meg, they've not put *you* in here?

JAILER (*Reassuringly*) No-o-o, sir. Just a visit; a short one.

MORE (*Excited*) Jailer, jailer, let me out of this.

JAILER Yes, sir. I'm allowed to let you out.

MORE Thank you. (*Goes to the door of the cage, gabbling while* JAILER *unlocks it*) Thank you, thank you.

(*He comes out. He and she regard each other; then she drops into a curtsy*)

MARGARET Good morning, Father.

MORE (*Ecstatic, wraps her to him*) Oh, good morning—Good morning. (*Enter* ALICE, *supported by* ROPER. *She, like* MORE, *has aged and is poorly dressed*) Good morning, Alice. Good morning, Will.

(ROPER *is staring at the rack in horror.* ALICE *approaches* MORE *and peers at him technically*)

ALICE (*Almost accusatory*) Husband, how do you do?

MORE (*Smiling over* MARGARET) As well as need be, Alice. Very happy now. Will?

ROPER This is an awful place!

MORE Except it's keeping me from you, my dears, it's not so bad. Remarkably like any other place.

ALICE (*Looks up critically*) It drips!

MORE Yes. Too near the river.

(ALICE *goes apart and sits, her face bitter*)

MARGARET (*Disengages from him, takes basket from her mother*) We've brought you some things. (*Shows him. There is constraint between them*) Some cheese . . .

MORE Cheese.

MARGARET And a custard . . .

MORE A custard!

MARGARET And, these other things . . .

(*She doesn't look at him*)

ROPER And a bottle of wine.

(*Offering it*)

MORE Oh. (*Mischievously*) Is it good, son Roper?

ROPER I don't know, sir.

MORE (*Looks at them, puzzled*) Well.

ROPER Sir, come out! Swear to the Act! Take the oath and come out!

MORE Is this why they let you come?

ROPER Yes . . . Meg's under oath to persuade you.

MORE (*Coldly*) That was silly, Meg. How did you come to do that?

MARGARET I wanted to!

MORE You want me to swear to the Act of Succession?

MARGARET "God more regards the thoughts of the heart than the words of the mouth." Or so you've always told me.

MORE Yes.

MARGARET Then say the words of the oath and in your heart think otherwise.

MORE What is an oath then but words we say to God?

MARGARET That's very neat.

MORE Do you mean it isn't true?

MARGARET No, it's true.

MORE Then it's a poor argument to call it "neat," Meg. When a man takes an oath, Meg, he's holding his own self in his own hands. Like water. (*He cups his hands*) And if he opens his fingers *then*—he needn't hope to find himself again. Some men aren't capable of this, but I'd be loathe to think your father one of them.

MARGARET In any State that was half good, you would be raised up high, not here, for what you've done already. It's not your fault the State's three-quarters bad. Then if you elect to suffer for it, you elect yourself a hero.

MORE That's very neat. But look now . . . If we lived in a State where virtue was profitable, common sense would make us good, and greed would make us saintly. And we'd live like animals or angels in the happy land that *needs* no heroes. But since in fact we see that avarice, anger, envy, pride, sloth, lust and stupidity commonly profit far beyond humility, chastity, fortitude, justice and thought, and have to choose, to be human at all . . . why then perhaps we *must* stand fast a little—even at the risk of being heroes.

MARGARET (*Emotionally*) But in reason! Haven't you done as much as God can reasonably *want*?

MORE Well . . . finally . . . it isn't a matter of reason; finally it's a matter of love.

ALICE (*Hostile*) You're content, then, to be shut up here with mice and rats when you might be home with us!

MORE (*Flinching*) Content? If they'd open a crack that wide (*Between finger and thumb*) I'd be through it. (*To* MARGARET) Well, has Eve run out of apples?

MARGARET I've not yet told you what the house is like, without you.

MORE Don't, Meg.

MARGARET What we do in the evenings, now that you're not there.

MORE Meg, have done!

MARGARET We sit in the dark because we've no candles. And we've no talk because we're wondering what they're doing to you here.

MORE The King's more merciful than you. He doesn't use the rack.

(*Enter* JAILER)

JAILER   Two minutes to go, sir. I thought you'd like to know.

MORE   Two minutes!

JAILER   Till seven o'clock, sir. Sorry. Two minutes.

 (*Exit* JAILER)

MORE   Jailer! (*Seizes* ROPER *by the arm*) Will—go to him, talk to
him, keep him occupied—

 (*Propelling him after* JAILER)

ROPER   How, sir?

MORE   Anyhow! Have you got any money?

ROPER (*Eagerly*)   Yes!

MORE   No, don't try and bribe him! Let him play for it; he's got a
pair of dice. And talk to him, you understand! And take this—
(*He hands him the wine*) and mind you share it—do it properly,
Will! (ROPER *nods vigorously and exits*) Now listen, you must
leave the country. All of you must leave the country.

MARGARET   And leave you here?

MORE   It makes no difference, Meg; they won't let you see me
again. (*Breathlessly, a prepared speech under pressure*) You
must all go on the same day, but not on the same boat; different
boats from different ports—

MARGARET   After the trial, then.

MORE   There'll be no trial, they have no case. Do this for me, I
beseech you?

MARGARET   Yes.

MORE   Alice? (*She turns her back*) Alice, I command you!

ALICE (*Harshly*)   Right!

MORE (*Looks into the basket*)   Oh, this is splendid; I know who
packed this.

ALICE (*Harshly*)   I packed it.

MORE   Yes. (*He eats a morsel*) You still make superlative custard,
Alice.

ALICE   Do I?

MORE   That's a nice dress you have on.

ALICE   It's my cooking dress.

MORE   It's very nice anyway. Nice color.

ALICE (*Turns. Quietly*)   By God, you think very little of me.
(*Mounting bitterness*) I know I'm a fool. But I'm no such fool
as at this time to be lamenting for my dresses! Or to relish com-
plimenting on my custard!

MORE (*Regarding her with frozen attention. He nods once or twice*)
I am well rebuked. (*He holds out his hands*) Al—

ALICE   No!

(*She remains where she is, glaring at him*)

MORE   (*He is in great fear of her*)   I am faint when I think of the worst that they may do to me. But worse than that would be to go with you not understanding why I go.

ALICE   I don't!

MORE   (*Just hanging on to his self-possession*)   Alice, if you can tell me that you understand, I think I can make a good death, if I have to.

ALICE   Your death's no "good" to me!

MORE   Alice, you must tell me that you understand!

ALICE   I don't! (*She throws it straight at his head*) I don't believe this had to happen.

MORE   (*His face is drawn*)   If you say that, Alice, I don't see how I'm to face it.

ALICE   It's the truth!

MORE   (*Gasping*)   You're an honest woman.

ALICE   Much good may it do me! I'll tell you what I'm afraid of: that when you've gone, I shall hate you for it.

MORE   (*Turns from her, his face working*)   Well, you mustn't, Alice, that's all. (*Swiftly she crosses the stage to him; he turns and they clasp each other fiercely*) You mustn't, you—

ALICE   (*Covers his mouth with her hand*)   S-s-sh . . . As for understanding, I understand you're the best man that I ever met or am likely to; and if you go—well, God knows why I suppose—though as God's my witness God's kept deadly quiet about it! And if anyone wants my opinion of the King and his Council they've only to ask for it!

MORE   Why, it's a lion I married! A lion! A lion! (*He breaks away from her, his face shining*) Say what you may—this custard's very good. It's very, very good.

(*He puts his face in his hands;* ALICE *and* MARGARET *comfort him;* ROPER *and* JAILER *erupt onto the stage above, wrangling fiercely*)

JAILER   It's no good, sir! I know what you're up to! And it can't be done!

ROPER   Another minute, man!

JAILER   (*Descending; to* MORE)   Sorry, sir, time's up!

ROPER   (*Gripping his shoulder from behind*)   For pity's sake!

JAILER   (*Shaking him off*)   Now don't do that, sir! Sir Thomas, the ladies will have to go now!

MORE   You said seven o'clock!

JAILER   It's seven now. You must understand my position, sir.

MORE   But one more minute!

MARGARET   Only a little while—give us a little while!

JAILER (*Reprovingly*)   Now, miss, you don't want to get me into trouble.

ALICE   Do as you're told. Be off at once!

(*The first stroke of seven is heard on a heavy, deliberate bell, which continues, reducing what follows to a babble*)

JAILER (*Taking* MARGARET *firmly by the upper arm*)   Now come along, miss; you'll get your father into trouble as well as me. (ROPER *descends and grabs him*) Are you obstructing me, sir? (MARGARET *embraces* MORE *and dashes up the stairs and exits, followed by* ROPER. *Taking* ALICE *gingerly by the arm*) Now, my lady, no trouble!

ALICE (*Throwing him off as she rises*)   Don't put your muddy hand on me!

JAILER   Am I to call the guard then? Then come on!

(ALICE, *facing him, puts foot on bottom stair and so retreats before him, backwards*)

MORE   For God's sake, man, we're saying goodbye!

JAILER   You don't know what you're asking, sir. You don't know how you're watched.

ALICE   Filthy, stinking, gutter-bred turnkey!

JAILER   Call me what you like, ma'am; you've got to go.

ALICE   I'll see you suffer for this!

JAILER   You're doing your husband no good!

MORE   Alice, goodbye, my love!

(*On this, the last stroke of the seven sounds.* ALICE *raises her hand, turns, and with considerable dignity, exits.* JAILER *stops at the head of the stairs and addresses* MORE, *who, still crouching, turns from him, facing audience*)

JAILER (*Reasonably*)   You understand my position, sir, there's nothing I can do; I'm a plain, simple man and just want to keep out of trouble.

MORE (*Cries out passionately*)   Oh, Sweet Jesus! These plain, simple men!

(*Immediately music, portentous and heraldic, is heard. Bars, rack and cage are flown swiftly upwards. The lighting changes from cold gray to warm yellow, re-creating a warm interior. Small coat of arms comes down and hangs, followed by large coat of arms above stairs, then two medium coats of arms. Then the largest*

coat of arms appears. During this the JAILER *takes off jailer's coat,
throws it off, takes off the small chair and moves armchair to the
center. Moves the table under the stairs. He brings on the jury
bench, takes hats from the basket and puts them on poles with a
juryman's hat, takes jailer's hat off head and puts it on a pole.
Seven are plain gray hats, four are those worn by the* STEWARD,
BOATMAN, INNKEEPER *and* JAILER. *And the last is another of the
plain gray ones. He takes a portfolio from the basket and puts
it on the table, and pushes basket into a corner. He then brings
on two throne chairs. While he is still doing this, and just before coats of arms have finished their descent, enter* CROMWELL.
He ringingly addresses the audience as soon as the music ends)

CROMWELL (*Indicating descending props*)

What Englishman can behold without Awe
The Canvas and the Rigging of the Law!

(*Brief fanfare*)

Forbidden here the galley-master's whip—
Hearts of Oak, in the Law's Great Ship!

(*Brief fanfare. To* COMMON MAN *who is tiptoeing discreetly off
stage*) Where are you going?

COMMON MAN   I've finished here, sir.

CROMWELL   You're the Foreman of the Jury.

COMMON MAN   Oh no, sir.

CROMWELL   You are John Dauncey. A general dealer?

COMMON MAN (*Gloomily*)   Yes, sir?

CROMWELL (*Resuming his rhetorical stance*)   Foreman of the Jury.
Does the cap fit?

COMMON MAN (*Puts on the gray hat. It fits*)   Yes, sir.

CROMWELL

So, now we'll apply the good, plain sailor's art,
And fix these quicksands on the Law's plain chart!

(*Several narrow panels, orange and bearing the monogram "HR
VIII" in gold letters, are lowered. Renewed, more prolonged fanfare; during which enter* CRANMER *and* NORFOLK, *who sit on throne
chairs. On their entry* MORE *and* FOREMAN *rise. As soon as the fanfare is finished* NORFOLK *speaks*)

NORFOLK (*Takes refuge behind a rigorously official manner*)   Sir
Thomas More, you are called before us here at the Hall of West-

minster to answer charge of High Treason. Nevertheless, and though you have heinously offended the King's Majesty, we hope if you will even now forthink and repent of your obstinate opinions, you may still taste his gracious pardon.

MORE   My lords, I thank you. Howbeit I make my petition to Almighty God that He will keep me in this, my honest mind, to the last hour that I shall live . . . As for the matters you may charge me with, I fear, from my present weakness, that neither my wit nor my memory will serve to make sufficient answers . . . I should be glad to sit down.

NORFOLK   Be seated. Master Secretary Cromwell, have you the charge?

CROMWELL   I have, my lord.

NORFOLK   Then read the charge.

CROMWELL   (*Formally*)   That you did conspire traitorously and maliciously to deny and deprive our liege lord Henry of his undoubted certain title, Supreme Head of the Church in England.

MORE   (*With surprise, shock, and indignation*)   But I have never denied this title!

CROMWELL   You refused the oath tendered to you at the Tower and elsewhere—

MORE   (*Again shocked and indignant*)   Silence is not denial. And for my silence I am punished, with imprisonment. Why have I been called again?

(*At this point he is sensing that the trial has been in some way rigged*)

NORFOLK   On a charge of High Treason, Sir Thomas.

CROMWELL   For which the punishment is *not* imprisonment.

MORE   Death . . . comes for us all, my lords. Yes, even for Kings he comes, to whom amidst all their Royalty and brute strength he will neither kneel nor make them any reverence nor pleasantly desire them to come forth, but roughly grasp them by the very breast and rattle them until they be stark dead! So causing their bodies to be buried in a pit and sending *them* to a judgment . . . whereof at their death their success is uncertain.

CROMWELL   Treason enough here!

NORFOLK   The death of Kings is not in question, Sir Thomas.

MORE   Nor mine, I trust, until I'm proven guilty.

NORFOLK   (*Leaning forward urgently*)   Your life lies in your own hand, Thomas, as it always has.

MORE   (*Absorbs this*)   For our own deaths, my lord, yours and mine, dare we for shame enter the Kingdom with ease, when Our Lord Himself entered with so much pain? (*And now he faces* CROMWELL, *his eyes sparkling with suspicion*)

CROMWELL   Now, Sir Thomas, you stand upon your silence.

MORE   I do.

CROMWELL   But, Gentlemen of the Jury, there are many kinds of silence. Consider first the silence of a man when he is dead. Let us say we go into the room where he is lying; and let us say it is in the dead of night—there's nothing like darkness for sharpening the ear; and we listen. What do we hear? Silence. What does it betoken, this silence? Nothing. This is silence, pure and simple. But consider another case. Suppose I were to draw a dagger from my sleeve and make to kill the prisoner with it, and suppose their lordships there, instead of crying out for me to stop or crying out for help to stop me, maintained their silence. That *would* betoken! It would betoken a willingness that I should do it, and under the law they would be guilty with me. So silence can, according to circumstances, speak. Consider, now, the circumstances of the prisoner's silence. The oath was put to good and faithful subjects up and down the country and they had declared His Grace's title to be just and good. And when it came to the prisoner he refused. He calls this silence. Yet is there a man in this court, is there a man in this country, who does not *know* Sir Thomas More's opinion of the King's title? Of course not! But how can that be? Because this silence betokened—nay, this silence *was* not silence at all but most eloquent denial.

MORE   (*With some of the academic's impatience for a shoddy line of reasoning*)   Not so, Master Secretary, the maxim is "qui tacet consentire." (*Turns to* COMMON MAN) The maxim of the law is (*Very carefully*) "Silence gives consent." If, therefore, you wish to construe what my silence "betokened," you must construe that I consented, not that I denied.

CROMWELL   Is that what the world in fact construes from it? Do you pretend that is what you *wish* the world to construe from it?

MORE   The world must construe according to its wits. This Court must construe according to the law.

CROMWELL   I put it to the Court that the prisoner is perverting the law—making smoky what should be a clear light to discover to the Court his own wrongdoing!

(CROMWELL's *official indignation is slipping into genuine anger and* MORE *responds*)

MORE   The law is not a "light" for you or any man to see by; the
law is not an instrument of any kind. (*To the* FOREMAN) The law
is a causeway upon which, so long as he keeps to it, a citizen may
walk safely. (*Earnestly addressing him*) In matters of conscience—

CROMWELL (*Smiling bitterly*)   The conscience, the conscience . . .

MORE (*Turning*)   The word is not familiar to you?

CROMWELL   By God, too familiar! I am very used to hear it in the
mouths of criminals!

MORE   I am used to hear bad men misuse the name of God, yet
God exists. (*Turning back*) In matters of conscience, the loyal
subject is more bounden to be loyal *to* his conscience than to any
other thing.

CROMWELL (*Breathing hard; straight at* MORE)   And so provide a
noble motive for his frivolous self-conceit!

MORE (*Earnestly*)   It is not so, Master Cromwell—very and pure
necessity for respect of my own soul.

CROMWELL   Your own self, you mean!

MORE   Yes, a man's soul is his self!

CROMWELL (*Thrusts his face into* MORE'S. *They hate each other
and each other's standpoint*)   A miserable thing, whatever you
call it, that lives like a bat in a Sunday School! A shrill incessant
pedagogue about its own salvation—but nothing to say of your
place in the State! Under the King! In a great native country!

MORE (*Not untouched*)   Is it my place to say "good" to the State's
sickness? Can I help my King by giving him lies when he asks
for truth? Will you help England by populating her with liars?

CROMWELL (*Backs away. His face stiff with malevolence*)   My
lords, I wish to call (*He raises his voice*) Sir Richard Rich! (*Enter*
RICH. *He is now splendidly official, in dress and bearing; even*
NORFOLK *is a bit impressed*) Sir Richard.
(*Indicating* CRANMER)

CRANMER (*Proffering Bible*)   I do solemnly swear . . .

RICH   I do solemnly swear that the evidence I shall give before the
Court shall be the truth, the whole truth, and nothing but the
truth.

CRANMER (*Discreetly*)   So help me God, Sir Richard.

RICH   So help me God.

NORFOLK   Take your stand there, Sir Richard.

CROMWELL   Now, Rich, on 12 March, you were at the Tower?

RICH   I was.

CROMWELL   With what purpose?

RICH   I was sent to carry away the prisoner's books.

CROMWELL   Did you talk with the prisoner?

RICH   Yes.

CROMWELL   Did you talk about the King's Supremacy of the Church?

RICH   Yes.

CROMWELL   What did you say?

RICH   I said to him: "Supposing there was an Act of Parliament to say that I, Richard Rich, were to be King, would not you, Master More, take me for King?" "That I would," he said, "for then you would be King."

CROMWELL   Yes?

RICHARD   Then he said—

NORFOLK   (*Sharply*)   The prisoner?

RICH   Yes, my lord. "But I will put you a higher case," he said. "How if there were an Act of Parliament to say that God should not be God?"

MORE   This is true; and then you said—

NORFOLK   Silence! Continue.

RICH   I said, "Ah, but I will put you a middle case. Parliament has made our King Head of the Church. Why will you not accept him?"

NORFOLK   (*Strung up*)   Well?

RICH   Then he said Parliament had no power to do it.

NORFOLK   Repeat the prisoner's words!

RICH   He said, "Parliament has not the competence." Or words to that effect.

CROMWELL   He denied the title?

RICH   He did.

(*All look to* MORE, *but he looks to* RICH)

MORE   In good faith, Rich, I am sorrier for your perjury than my peril.

NORFOLK   Do you deny this?

MORE   Yes! My lords, if I were a man who heeded not the taking of an oath, you know well I need not to be here. Now I will take an oath! If what Master Rich has said is true, then I pray I may never see God in the face! Which I would not say were it otherwise for anything on earth.

CROMWELL   (*To* FOREMAN, *calmly, technically*)   That is not evidence.

MORE   Is it probable—is it probable—that after so long a silence on this, the very point so urgently sought of me, I should open my mind to such a man as that?

CROMWELL   (*To* RICH)   Do you wish to modify your testimony?

RICH   No, Secretary.

MORE   There were two other men! Southwell and Palmer!

CROMWELL   Unhappily, Sir Richard Southwell and Master Palmer are both in Ireland on the King's business. (MORE *gestures helplessly*) It has no bearing. I have their deposition here in which the Court will see they state that being busy with the prisoner's books they did not hear what was said.

(*Hands deposition to* FOREMAN, *who examines it with much seriousness*)

MORE   If I had really said this is it not obvious he would instantly have called these men to witness?

CROMWELL   Sir Richard, have you anything to add?

RICH   Nothing, Mr. Secretary.

NORFOLK   Sir Thomas?

MORE   (*Looking at* FOREMAN)   To what purpose? I am a dead man. (*To* CROMWELL) You have your desire of me. What you have hunted me for is not my actions, but the thoughts of my heart. It is a long road you have opened. For first men will disclaim their hearts and presently they will have no hearts. God help the people whose Statesmen walk your road.

NORFOLK   Then the witness may withdraw.

(RICH *crosses the stage, watched by* MORE)

MORE   I *have* one question to ask the witness. (RICH *stops*) That's a chain of office you are wearing. (*Reluctantly* RICH *faces him*) May I see it? (NORFOLK *motions him to approach.* MORE *examines the medallion*) The red dragon. (*To* CROMWELL) What's this?

CROMWELL   Sir Richard is appointed Attorney-General for Wales.

MORE   (*Looking into* RICH's *face, with pain and amusement*)   For Wales? Why, Richard, it profits a man nothing to give his soul for the whole world . . . But for Wales!

(*Exit* RICH, *stiff-faced, but infrangibly dignified*)

CROMWELL   Now I must ask the Court's indulgence! I have a message for the prisoner from the King. (*Urgently*) Sir Thomas, I am empowered to tell you that even now—

MORE   No no, it cannot be.

CROMWELL   The case rests! (NORFOLK *is staring at* MORE) My lord!

NORFOLK   The jury will retire and consider the evidence.

CROMWELL Considering the evidence it shouldn't be necessary for them to retire. (*Standing over* FOREMAN) Is it necessary?

FOREMAN (*Shakes his head*) No, sir!

NORFOLK Then is the prisoner guilty or not guilty?

FOREMAN Guilty, my lord!

NORFOLK (*Leaping to his feet; all rise save* MORE) Prisoner at the bar, you have been found guilty of High Treason. The sentence of the Court—

MORE My lord! (NORFOLK *breaks off.* MORE *has a sly smile. From this point to end of play his manner is of one who has fulfilled all his obligations and will now consult no interests but his own*) My lord, when I was practicing the law, the manner was to ask the prisoner *before* pronouncing sentence, if he had anything to say.

NORFOLK (*Flummoxed*) Have you anything to say?

MORE Yes. (*He rises; all others sit*) To avoid this I have taken every path my winding wits would find. Now that the Court has determined to condemn me, God knoweth how, I will discharge my mind . . . concerning my indictment and the King's title. The indictment is grounded in an Act of Parliament which is directly repugnant to the Law of God. The King in Parliament cannot bestow the Supremacy of the Church because it is a Spiritual Supremacy! And more to this the immunity of the Church is promised both in Magna Carta and the King's own Coronation Oath!

CROMWELL Now we plainly see that you *are* malicious!

MORE Not so, Master Secretary! (*He pauses, and launches, very quietly, ruminatively, into his final stock-taking*) I am the King's true subject, and pray for him and all the realm . . . I do none harm, I say none harm, I think none harm. And if this be not enough to keep a man alive, in good faith I long not to live . . . I have, since I came into prison, been several times in such a case that I thought to die within the hour, and I thank Our Lord I was never sorry for it, but rather sorry when it passed. And therefore, my poor body is at the King's pleasure. Would God my death might do him some good . . . (*With a great flash of scorn and anger*) Nevertheless, it is not for the Supremacy that you have sought my blood—but because I would not bend to the marriage! (*Immediately the scene change commences, while* NORFOLK *reads the sentence*)

NORFOLK Prisoner at the bar, you have been found guilty on the charge of High Treason. The sentence of the Court is that you shall be taken from this Court to the Tower, thence to the place of execution, and there your head shall be stricken from your body, and may God have mercy on your soul! (*The trappings of justice are flown upwards.* NORFOLK *and* CRANMER *exit with chairs. The lights are dimmed save for three areas: spots, left, center, and right front, and a black arch cutout is lowered. Through this arch —where the ax and the block are silhouetted against a light of steadily increasing brilliance—comes the murmur of a large crowd, formalized almost into a chant. The* FOREMAN *doffs cap, and as* COMMON MAN *he removes the prisoner's chair and the two benches.* CROMWELL *pushes the table off, takes a small black mask from basket and puts it on* COMMON MAN. *The* COMMON MAN *thus becomes the traditional Headsman. He ascends the stairs, sets up the block from its trap, gets the ax and then straddles his legs. At once the crowd falls silent. Exit* CROMWELL, *dragging basket.* NORFOLK *joins* MORE *in the center spot.* CRANMER *takes his position on the rostrum. The* WOMAN *goes under the stairs*) I can come no further, Thomas. (*Proffering a goblet*) Here, drink this.

MORE   My Master had easel and gall, not wine, given him to drink. Let me be going.

MARGARET   Father! (*She runs to him in the center spot and flings herself upon him*) Father! Father, Father, Father, Father!

MORE   Have patience, Margaret, and trouble not thyself. Death comes for us all; even at our birth—(*He holds her head and looks down at it for a moment in recollection*)—even at our birth, death does but stand aside a little. And every day he looks towards us and muses somewhat to himself whether that day or the next he will draw nigh. It is the law of nature, and the will of God. (*He disengages from her. Dispassionately*) You have long known the secrets of my heart.

(MARGARET *exits with* NORFOLK)

WOMAN   Sir Thomas! (*He stops*) Remember me, Sir Thomas? When you were Chancellor, you gave a false judgment against me. Remember that now.

MORE   Woman, you see how I am occupied. (*With sudden decision goes to her in the left spot. Crisply*) I remember your matter well, and if I had to give sentence now I assure you I should not alter it. You have no injury; so go your way; and content yourself; and trouble me not! (*She exits. He walks swiftly to the stairs, then stops, realizing that* CRANMER, *carrying his Bible, has followed him. Quite kindly*) I beseech Your Grace, go back. (*Of-*

fended, CRANMER *does so. The lighting is now complete, i.e., darkness save for three areas of light, the one at cutout arch now dazzlingly brilliant. When* MORE *gets to head of stairs by the Headsman, he turns to Headsman*) Friend, be not afraid of your office. You send me to God.

CRANMER (*Envious rather than waspish*) You're very sure of that, Sir Thomas.

(*He exits*)

MORE (*Takes off his hat, revealing the gray disordered hair*) He will not refuse one who is so blithe to go to him.

(*Kneeling. Immediately is heard a harsh roar of kettledrums. There is total blackout at head of the stairs, while the drums roar. Then the drums cease*)

HEADSMAN (*Bangs the trap down, in the darkness*) Behold—the head—of a traitor!

(*The lights come up*)

COMMON MAN (*Comes to the center of the stage, having taken off his mask*) I'm breathing . . . Are you breathing too? . . . It's nice, isn't it? It isn't difficult to keep alive, friends—just don't *make* trouble—or if you must make trouble, make the sort of trouble that's expected. Well, I don't need to tell you that. Good night. If we should bump into one another, recognize me.

(*He exits*)

Curtain

Luv

BY

Murray Schisgal

Luv *was first presented by Claire Nichtern at the Booth Theatre,
New York City, on November 12, 1964 with the following cast:*

(*In order of appearance*)

HARRY BERLIN	*Alan Arkin*
MILT MANVILLE	*Eli Wallach*
ELLEN MANVILLE	*Anne Jackson*

Directed by Mike Nichols
Designed by Oliver Smith
Lighting by Jean Rosenthal
Costumes by Theoni V. Aldredge
Music for song by Irving Joseph

ACT ONE

THE TIME: *The Present: evening.*

THE SCENE: *A bridge. The railing of the bridge crosses, rear, at an angle: it is interrupted on the left by a small boxlike alcove, then continues; swooping above and disappearing out of sight on the right is a thick red coil from which cables descend at regular intervals and connect to the railing. Two wooden slab-boarded benches, placed back to back, one facing downstage, the other upstage, are at the right, also at an angle. Farther on the right is an old iron-cast lamppost, which is lit. On the left, forward, is a nondescript unmarked sandbox, no larger in size than three orange crates lying side by side. Farther left, forward, is a public wire-mesh trash basket. A curbstone cuts across the front at an angle and the entire stage is raked.*

The faint sounds of a foghorn, a motor churning in the water, a buoy bell, etc.

HARRY BERLIN (*tall, flabby, with a bristly mustache, in ill-fitting rumpled clothes: a threadbare dark-green corduroy jacket, an open-necked faded blue work shirt, no tie, very large khaki pants tied to his waist by a string, dirty white tennis sneakers*) *leans on the railing in the alcove, rear, facing upstage, and stares at the river below.* MILT MANVILLE (*thin, erect, of less than average height, in a sharply tailored "continental" brown suit, pink shirt with rolled collar, bright yellow tie and pocket handkerchief, large cuff links, and brown suede shoes*) *enters, left, paces up and down, looks at his watch anxiously; his eye soon falls on the trash basket; he is drawn irresistibly toward it; he bends over and examines a worn discarded velvet-collared gray herringbone overcoat.*

HARRY *turns.* MILT *notices him, stares forward, trying to recall where he has seen him before.* HARRY *takes pad, pencil from pocket, writes a note, slaps it on railing; he drops his jacket to ground and climbs up on railing.*

MILT (*With a sense of recognition, moving up to him*)   Is it . . .
(HARRY *turns, stares down at him*) No, Harry Berlin! I thought
so! I just caught a glimpse of you and I said to myself, "I bet that's
Harry Berlin. I just bet that's Harry Berlin." And sure enough, it's
old Harry Berlin himself. (*Taking* HARRY's *hand; shaking it*) How
have you been doing, Harry? What's been happening? (HARRY
squats and slowly comes down from railing) It must be . . . why,
at least fifteen years since I saw you last. We had that party after
graduation, I said, "Keep in touch," you said, "I'll call you in a
few days," and that's the last I heard of you. Fifteen years.

HARRY (*Feigning recognition*)   Is it fifteen years?

MILT   Fifteen years.

HARRY   Hard to believe.

MILT   Fifteen years next month as a matter of fact.

HARRY   Time sure flies.

MILT   It sure does.

HARRY   Fifteen years next month.

MILT   Fifteen years.

HARRY (*Slight pause*)   Who are you?

MILT   Milt! Milt Manville! Your old classmate at Polyarts U.

HARRY (*Grabbing his hand*)   That's right! Milt! Milt Manville!
(*They embrace; laugh joyfully.* HARRY *puts on jacket, then crumples note, throws it over railing as* MILT *speaks*)

MILT   Say, Harry, I've been doing wonderful for myself; terrific. Got
into the brokerage business during the day: stocks, bonds, securities, you know. The money's just pouring in; doing fabulous. Got
into secondhand bric-a-brac and personal accessories at night: on
my own, great racket, easy buck. And, say, I got myself married.
Oh yeah, I went and did it, finally did it. Ellen. A wonderful,
wonderful girl. Do anything for her. A home in the suburbs, no
kidding, thirty-five thousand, and that's not counting the trees,
big tremendous trees; you should see them. Hey. Look at this
watch. Solid gold. Twenty-two carats. (*Opening his jacket to
reveal garish yellow lining*) Notice the label? (*Unbuttons shirt*)
Silk underwear. Imported. Isn't that something? (*Lifts arm*) Hey,
smell this, go ahead, smell it. (HARRY *is reluctant to come too
close;* MILT *presses his head to his armpit; laughing*) Not bad,
huh? (*Solemnly*) Well, how's it been going, Harry? Let's hear.

HARRY (*Mournfully*)   Awful, Milt; awful. It couldn't be worse. I'm
at the end of the line. Everything's falling apart.

MILT (*Perplexed*)   I don't get it.

HARRY   The world, Milt. People. Life. Death. The old questions.
I'm choked with them.

MILT (*Still perplexed*)   Oh.

HARRY (*Arm around him, leads him forward right*)   I must have
been out of school for only a couple of weeks when . . . it happened. Out of the blue. Disillusionment. Despair. Debilitation.
The works. It hit me all at once.

MILT   Oh. Ohhhh.

(HARRY *sits on curbstone.* MILT *puts down white handkerchief,
sits beside him*)

HARRY   I remember . . . I was sitting in the park. It was Sunday,
a hot lazy Sunday. The sun was burning on the back of my neck.
An open book was on my lap and I was kind of daydreaming,
thinking of the future, my plans, my prospects . . . Then . . .
Suddenly . . . Suddenly I looked up and I saw, standing there in
front of me . . . How can I put it in words? It was a dog, Milt. A
fox terrier. I'd swear it was a fox terrier. But who knows, I . . .

MILT (*Interrupting*)   Let's just say it was a dog, Harry.

HARRY   It was a dog. Right.

MILT   A dog. Go ahead.

HARRY   And . . . And he was there, right in front of me, standing
on his hind legs and . . . He looked almost like a little old man
with a little white beard and a little wrinkled face. The thing is
. . . Milt, he was laughing. He was laughing as loudly and as
clearly as I'm talking to you now. I sat there. I couldn't move. I
couldn't believe what was happening. And then, he came up to
me, now he was walking on all fours and . . . When he got up to
me . . . When he got up to me, he raised his leg and . . .

MILT   No.

HARRY (*Nodding, with twisted expression*)   All over my gabardine
pants. And they were wet, through and through. I could swear
to that! Then he turned right around and walked off. The whole
thing was . . . It was all so unreal, all so damn senseless. My mind
. . . I thought . . . (*Emotionally*) Why me? Out of everyone in
that park, out of hundreds, thousands of people, why me? (MILT
looks about bewilderedly) What did it mean? How do you explain
it? (*In control of himself*) That started it; right there was the
beginning. From that minute on, it changed, everything changed
for me. It was as if I was dragged to the edge of the cliff and
forced to look down. How can I make you understand? What
words do I use? I was nauseous, Milt. Sick to my soul. I became

aware . . . aware of the whole rotten senseless stinking deal. Nothing mattered to me after that. Nothing.

MILT   Your plans to go to medical school?

HARRY   I couldn't.

MILT   The book you were writing?

HARRY   (*Throwing up his hands*)   No use.

MILT   Your Greek studies?

HARRY   I couldn't. I couldn't go on. (*Rises; moves to sandbox, paces around it;* MILT *also rises*) No roots. No *modus vivendi*. I had to find some answers first. A reason. I traveled, went everywhere, looked everyplace. I studied with a Brahmin in Calcutta, with a Buddhist in Nagoya, with a Rabbi in Los Angeles. Nothing. I could find nothing. I didn't know where to turn, what to do with myself. I began drinking, gambling, living in whorehouses, smoking marijuana, taking guitar lessons . . . Nothing. Still nothing. Tonight . . . Milt, tonight I was going to end it all, make one last stupid gesture of disgust and . . . that would be it!

MILT   (*Glances at railing*)   You don't mean . . .

HARRY   That's right.

MILT   (*Going to him*)   How terrible. How terrible, Harry. I'm ashamed of you at this minute. I'm ashamed to have been your classmate at Polyarts U.

HARRY   Ask me what I believe in, Milt.

MILT   What do you believe in, Harry?

HARRY   I believe in nothing, Milt.

MILT   Nothing? That's terrible. How can someone go on living without believing in anything?

HARRY   That's the problem I'm faced with. And there's no answer to it, none, except down there!

(*He points to railing, moving to bench*)

MILT   (*Turns* HARRY *toward him*)   Now let's not lose our heads. Let's control ourselves. Keep calm. Keep calm. Now listen to me. I can understand. I can understand everything you said, but, Harry . . . Don't you think it's more than unusual, just a little more than unusual, that I happened to be passing at the very minute, the precise exact minute, that you were contemplating this . . . this horrible thing?

HARRY   (*Pointing upward*)   You don't mean . . . ?

MILT   (*Throwing both hands up defensively*)   I'm not saying it! I didn't say it! (*Wagging finger*) But just remember, science doesn't have all the answers!

HARRY   Talking about it only makes it worse, Milt. You don't know what agony I've been through. It's gotten so bad that sometimes, sometimes, in the middle of the day or night, without a warning of any kind, my whole body becomes paralyzed, I can't move a muscle and . . .

(*In mid-speech his body stiffens like a board and he topples forward.* MILT *catches him at the last moment, shouts and shakes him frantically*)

MILT   Harry! What is it? Harry, for God's sake . . . (*He runs around in a complete circle, holding* HARRY *whose stiff body revolves like the hand of a clock*) Help! Help! Help, here! Help! Help! (*To* HARRY) Look at me! Speak to me, Harry!

HARRY   (*Calmly*)   That's the way it happens.

MILT   (*Sitting on sandbox*)   You scared the life out of me. That's terrible. Why don't you see a doctor, a specialist, someone . . .

HARRY   I don't have to see anyone. I know what it is, Milt. The will to live drops out of me, plops right out of me. Why move? I say to myself. Why do anything? But that's not all of it. Sometimes, sometimes, I can't see, I lose the power of sight completely and I grope about . . . (*Throws up his hands, feigns blindness and moves dangerously close to the edge of the stage*) Milt . . . Milt . . . Where are you? Are you still here, Milt?

MILT   (*Jumps up, grabs him in the nick of time*)   Right here, Harry. I'm right here.

HARRY   (*Clawing behind him at* MILT's *face*)   Help me, Milt. Help me get to the bench.

MILT   (*Pushing him forward*)   Of course. This way, Harry. That's it. Watch your step. Here, here it is.

(*They're seated on bench*)

HARRY   (*Calmly*)   Thank you, Milt.

MILT   Is there . . . anything else I can do?

HARRY   No. I'm all right now. That's the way it happens.

MILT   I would never have believed it.

HARRY   Why see? I say to myself. Why be a witness to it? (*Grabbing* MILT's *lapels*) Why, Milt? Why?

MILT   I don't know, Harry. I don't know.

(*Pulling himself free; straightens tie, etc.*)

HARRY   So I go blind and I don't see. The whole thing becomes completely automatic. I have no control over it.

MILT   But there must be something you can do.

HARRY (*Cupping hand to ear, feigns deafness; loudly*) What did you say, Milt?

MILT I said, "There must be something you can do to correct . . ."

HARRY I can't hear you, Milt. Speak slowly and I'll try to read your lips.

MILT (*Speaking slowly, loudly, drawing out words*) I said, "There must be something you can do to . . ."

HARRY (*Abruptly; calmly*) I hear you now, Milt. That's another one of my . . . my fits. Sound becomes so damn painful to me . . . Why listen? I say to myself. Why listen?

MILT Incredible. I wouldn't have believed it was possible.

HARRY Well, it is. Look at me. I'm a living example of it. Now you can . . .

(*He feigns muteness, his mouth opening wide and closing without uttering a sound; gesturing*)

MILT (*Becoming increasingly distraught*) Harry? Are you speaking to me, Harry? Harry, I can't hear you. Can you speak . . . (HARRY *removes pad and pencil from jacket pocket, jots something on pad*) Oh, God, not that, too. (*Glances at* HARRY's *note*) I understand, Harry. I . . . Give me that. (*Takes pencil and pad from* HARRY; *he starts writing*) "Dear Harry, What we have to keep in mind, no matter what . . ."

(HARRY *pulls pencil out of* MILT's *hand.* MILT *pulls it away from* HARRY)

MILT (*Angrily*) The least you can do is let me finish! (*He starts writing again*)

HARRY I can hear you, Milt.

MILT You can?

HARRY I can't speak when that happens, but I hear all right. Why speak? I say to myself. Words have no meaning; not anymore. They're like pebbles bouncing in an empty tin can.

MILT (*Pockets pad, pencil*) I don't know what to say, Harry.

HARRY What can you say? It's no good, Milt; no good. For cryin' out loud, let me get it over with!

(*Removes rope with noose from jacket pocket as he speaks, puts noose over his head and after throwing rope over crossbar on lamppost, tries to hang himself by pulling on end of rope*)

MILT (*Rises*) No, no! Harry! Harry, will you listen to me? (*Slapping at his hands*) Let go! Let go of it! (HARRY *slumps to foot of lamppost where he sits dejectedly*) There's plenty of time for that! (*He takes rope from lamppost and at the same time re-*

leases pin from crossbar so that it can swing) Did it ever occur to you that you're in the state you're in because you've never known the feeling that comes with money, with power, with influence?

HARRY (*Removes noose from his neck; disparagingly*) Ahhh, Milt . . .

MILT (*Rolling rope together*) Now don't brush it aside. Look at me, Harry, and ask yourself, "Why did he go up so high and I go down so low?" Ask yourself that. (*Moves to the trash basket*) We both started out on the same foot; as a matter of fact you started out ahead of me, you had the money your folks left you. I had nothing but my two hands and a quick eye. When other people slept, I worked. When other people said it couldn't be done, I went out and did it. (*He lifts worn velvet-collared herring-bone overcoat out of basket—it is buttoned; he ties collar with rope, making a bag of it*) And through diligence, self-confidence, perseverance, I've made something of myself!

HARRY (*Rises*) My folks left me a few stinking thousands, that's true, but don't you forget I never lived with them, I was brought up by my grandparents, and it was hell, believe me, it was hell.

MILT (*Drops overcoat to ground*) Ha! You should have lived with my folks for a couple of weeks, then you would have known what hell is really like. Those two were like a pair of cats at each other's throat. And the poverty, the lousy humiliating poverty. I didn't start school until I was eight years old because I didn't have a pair of shoes to wear. Oh, yeah. Lucky for me the kid downstairs was hit by an ice-cream truck and I got his shoes. Even then they were so tight on me I couldn't walk. I was put in a special class for disabled children.

HARRY You think that was bad? My grandparents used to lock me out of the house. They couldn't stand the sight of me because I reminded them of my father. I remember one day I came home from school during a blinding snowstorm and the door was locked. I knocked and yelled and beat my poor little frozen fists on the door . . . They laughed at me. They laughed! Picture that for yourself. A tall skinny kid standing out there in the snowstorm, wearing nothing but a thin torn jacket and a paper bag for a hat, knocking and yelling, "Let me in. Please, let me in!"

MILT Paradise. (*Slight pause*) It was paradise compared to my childhood. Picture this. It's late at night. The wind's blowing outside. A small undernourished boy sits by the cold kerosene stove, feeding his toy wooden horse a bit of bread that he stole during

dinner. The parents are quarreling. "If you don't like it here, get
the hell out," the father shouts. "You're telling me to get out,"
the mother shouts back, and with savage hysterical fury she picks
up the boy's toy wooden horse and throws it at the father. He
ducks and it smashes against the wall. The boy drops down beside
his broken toy horse, the only thing he ever loved, and he cries
quietly.

HARRY (*Moves right, then whirls back to* MILT; *pugnaciously*) Did
you ever get beaten?

MILT (*Emphatically*) I did.

HARRY With what?

MILT A strap, a stick, a radiator cover.

HARRY A chain?

MILT How thick?

HARRY As thick as my wrist.

MILT (*Foiled; moves away, turns*) What did you get for breakfast?

HARRY At home?

MILT At home.

HARRY A glass filled with two-thirds water and one-third milk.

MILT Coffee grounds, that's what I got.

HARRY With sugar?

MILT Not on your life. I ate it straight, like oatmeal.

HARRY (*Foiled; moves away, suddenly turns*) Did your mother
ever kiss you?

MILT Once. When I stuck my head between her lips and a picture of Clark Gable.

HARRY Well, that's better than I did.

MILT (*Foiled; moves about*) What presents did you get for
Christmas?

HARRY Presents? When I was five my grandparents bought a box
of doughnuts and every Christmas until I was seventeen I got a
doughnut.

MILT You were a lucky kid and you didn't know it.

HARRY (*Bawling*) They were cinnamon doughnuts!

MILT Harry, you're missing the whole point. Even if we started
out on the same foot, I went ahead and became a success, I pulled
myself up to a position of responsibility, of respect, of importance.
And don't think it was easy. It was dog-eat-dog all the way.
(*Picks up overcoat, puts wine bottle, magazine into it*) But I
stuck with it, gave it all I had, worked at two jobs, stocks, bonds,

securities during the day, secondhand bric-a-brac and personal accessories at night. (*Takes naked doll from trash basket, waves it in air before inserting it into overcoat*) Rain or shine, sick or well, seven days a week, fifty-two weeks a year. I never let up, not even after I had achieved what I had set out to do. Right to the top. On my own. Every inch of the way. (*Removes baby's chamber pot from trash basket, turns it in his hand before dropping it into overcoat*) And let me tell you, Harry, nothing, nothing succeeds like success.

(*He ties the bottom of the overcoat with a rope*)

HARRY   You know I'm not interested in any of that, Milt. I need something else to go on. A *Weltanschauung*. A reason for living. That isn't easy to come by, either. (*He moves to curbstone, right*) Everything I taste turns sour in my mouth. Everything I touch becomes dust in my hands. It's as if I was standing at the bottom of the world and all I'd have to do is sit down to be dead.

(*He sits down on curbstone*)

MILT   (*Leaving overcoat on ground, moves to him*) Stop talking like that. How could you have changed so much? I still can't believe it. At school you were one of the boys, full of life, ready for a laugh and a good time at the drop of a hat. (*Squatting behind him, holding his shoulder and pointing out into the distance*) Remember, Harry, remember our marching down the football field in our red and gold uniforms, you leading the Polyarts All-Girl Band on the right, with me leading them on the left, our batons twirling in the air . . . (*He rises, struts up and down the bridge, singing, twirling an imaginary baton—he throws it up, catches it, kicks it with the heel of his shoe, catches it, performs tricks of this sort*)

Alma mater, alma mater,
Forward to the fray;
We will win our victory,
And move right on our wa-a-a-a-ay.

(HARRY *nods, mumbles,* "Yes, yes, I remember, yes, yes . . .")

Alma mater, alma mater,
Lift your light up high;
We will win our victory,
And come back by and by.

Da, da, da, da, da, da, da . . .

HARRY (*Rises, breaking spell of past with an anguished shout*) It's no use, Milt. Cut it out. It only makes it worse! (MILT *slumps on bench, panting heavily. Pacing*) You're right, though. At school everything was different. I was different. I expected so much . . . From myself. From the world. From the stars, the sun . . . Do you remember what they used to call me at school?

MILT (*Humbly*) Dostoyevski.

HARRY That's right. Dostoyevski. What ambition I had. What energy. My medical career, my writings, my Greek studies . . . Always had my nose in a book, always scribbling things down, projects, plans, new ideas, new fields to investigate, to explore . . . (*His voice dwindles to a wail; he suddenly pulls off jacket, throws it to ground*) Let me do it now and be done with it! (*He climbs onto railing*)

MILT (*Runs after him*) Harry! Harry! (HARRY *covers his face with his hands, screams and jumps off the railing, landing to his stunned surprise on the bridge; he turns and rushes back to railing.* MILT *grabs him, throws him down to ground*) Listen to me a minute. This is terrible, terrible. That you should treat life so cheaply . . . It's a sin! There. (*He boots him in the backside*) I said it and I'm glad! (*Contemptuously*) Look at you. At your age, worn out, defeated, wrecked in body and soul. It takes guts to go on living, Harry. It takes guts to make something of your life. (*From behind he holds* HARRY *under his arms and lifts him to a sitting position; softer tone*) Harry, listen to me. Love . . .

HARRY Love?

MILT (*Taking chin in his hand*) Yes, Harry. Love, human love, the love of a small boy for his toy wooden horse, the love of an old classmate, the love of a man for a woman. Doesn't that mean anything to you?

HARRY What do you think's been keeping me going this long? (*He rises, moves left, forward*)

MILT (*Rises*) Well?

HARRY I don't know if I can love, Milt.

MILT That's what everyone says until they meet the right woman. And then . . .

HARRY What?

MILT You don't know?

HARRY How could I?

MILT   You don't mean . . . ?

HARRY   (*Shaking his head; mournfully*)   Not once.

MILT   Oh, Harry. Harry, to have lived and not have loved . . . Do you call that living? (*Stepping on sandbox*) You don't know what life is, how can you destroy it?

HARRY   (*Moving right to lamppost. Picks up jacket on way*)   Love. We read about it, all right; we hear a lot about it. But where is it, Milt? Where? I haven't seen it and I've been through the mill and around the world twice.

(*Puts jacket on bench*)

MILT   (*Moving to him*)   It's because your eyes are closed, Harry; your eyes are closed. Do you think I could go on, working day after day, giving my youth, my health, my life itself, for a handful of shekels, for a few clammy coins, if there wasn't some compensation for it, something that made it all worthwhile?

HARRY   You do understand.

MILT   Of course I understand. Ask me what I believe in, Harry.

HARRY   What do you believe in, Milt?

MILT   I believe in love, Harry.

HARRY   Love?

MILT   Love!

HARRY   If I thought there was a chance . . .

MILT   Of course there's a chance. Being alive gives you that chance. And now that we've met . . . I'll help you, Harry; introduce you to people, show you around. You'll meet some woman and, boy, let me tell you, one day you'll get down on your knees and thank me. What do you say?

HARRY   I don't know how I'm going . . . You have to understand . . . (*Turns away from him*) It's not easy . . . Life . . . The stars . . . The sun . . . I . . .

(*He suddenly stiffens and falls backward like a pole;* MILT *catches him, prevents him from falling to ground*)

MILT   Harry! Harry! Don't start that again! (MILT *sits on bench, holding* HARRY's *stiff body*) For God's sake. Harry . . . Love. (*Shouts in his ear*) Love!

HARRY   (*His body relaxing, he slides between* MILT's *legs*)   It . . . It did it, Milt. It worked. I swear. (*Rises*) As soon as you said the word love, I felt my whole body begin to melt and I . . . I suddenly felt . . .

MILT   (*Rises*)   You see? What did I tell you? Give it a chance.

HARRY   (*Enthusiastically*)   Give love a chance.

MILT Why not?

HARRY I have nothing to lose.

MILT What can you lose?

HARRY (*Pointing to rail*) I can . . . always end things if I want.

MILT (*Repeating his gesture*) Of course you can.

HARRY All right, Milt.

MILT (*Retrieves jacket, puts it on* HARRY, *buttons it*) That's my old schoolbuddy. Now you promise . . .

HARRY You have my word on it.

MILT No more of this foolishness.

HARRY (*Sits on bench*) No more.

MILT Wonderful. Wonderful. (*Sits beside him*) There's nothing in the world like it, Harry. It's like getting a new lease on life; it changes everything; one minute you're down in the gutter, the next you're up in the clouds. Do you know I'm more in love today than on the day I married.

HARRY You don't mean . . . ?

MILT That's right. But my wife won't give me a divorce. (*Rises*) She's a wonderful woman, Harry; don't get me wrong. I'd do anything for her. But once love goes, what's left? There's no thrill to it, no excitement, no surprises . . . Look, here's her picture. (*Takes out wallet-photograph*)

HARRY Your wife?

MILT No, no, the girl I want to marry. Linda. Isn't she beautiful? Everything she does has grace and charm, a fascinating Oriental quality. Look at her eyes, Harry, her mouth, her young virgin voluptuousness. Oh, God, you don't know how much I love this woman, Harry. I can't bear being away from her. Not even for a minute. It's sheer torture.

HARRY Why don't you get a divorce?

MILT All I have to do is ask Ellen and . . . You don't know women, Harry. Say no, they'll say yes. Say yes, they'll say no. It can't be done that way. Never. Look at me, Harry. I look happy, don't I? I look as if I have everything in the world to live for. Well, I don't. I'm miserable; positively miserable. (*Moves left, talking to photograph*) Linda, my sweetheart, what's going to happen to us?

HARRY (*Crosses to* MILT, *puts arm about his shoulder*) Come on, Milt; get a hold of yourself.

MILT (*Moves right, with* HARRY's *arm still about his shoulder*) That's easy for you to say, Harry. You don't know what torture it is. We work in the same office; we can't speak to one another, we can't look at one another. (*Both move left, with* HARRY *now stroking* MILT's *neck*) We have to meet in back alleys and bus terminals and crowded, noisy saloons. Do you know what that's like? Any other woman would have given up on me long ago. But she . . . That woman . . . I tell you, I'll go out of my mind! (*Buries his head on* HARRY's *shoulder*)

HARRY (*Consoling him*) It couldn't be that hopeless, Milt. Why don't you . . .

MILT (*Pulls back*) I've tried everything, everything! She won't give me a divorce. I know she won't. I wouldn't even bother asking her. I've been over this a thousand times, Harry. Linda and I do nothing else but talk about it. (*Turns away from* HARRY *in his misery*) There's only one answer and that's if she wants a divorce herself, if she meets someone and . . . meets someone and . . . (*Turns to* HARRY. HARRY *puts his hand up in a gesture of refusal and moves to the bench and sits.* MILT *follows him to bench, puts arm around his shoulder and grabs his hand*) Harry, Harry, buddy, buddy, old classmate of mine. (*Pulling* HARRY's *hand back and forth*) Alma mater, alma mater, forward to the fray; we will . . .

HARRY (*Freeing his hand and stopping* MILT) Oh, no. Definitely not. Don't ask.

MILT Is this what I get for saving your life? Talk about gratitude! Harry, all I want you to do is meet her, just meet her.

HARRY I said no.

MILT (*Humbly*) Dostoyevski.

HARRY That's not going to help. So let's drop it.

MILT Okay. Okay. That's your privilege.
(*Removes jacket, folds it and places it on the bench. Runs to railing left of alcove and jumps up on it*)

HARRY (*Running after him; holds on to his knees*) Milt! Cut it out! Milt!

MILT Let go of me!

HARRY Don't be a fool!

MILT How long do you think I can go on like this, living with one woman, loving another? I can't sleep, I can't eat, I can't work . . . What do you think I'm made of?

HARRY You couldn't be serious.

MILT Couldn't I? Look. Look at this. (*He removes a large wicked-looking knife from a leather sheath on his belt.* HARRY *dances away fearfully*) Did you ask yourself why I came here tonight, Harry?

Did you ask yourself what I'm doing in this godforsaken place?

HARRY   You don't mean . . .

MILT (*Jumps down from railing*) Ellen should be here any minute. Draw your own conclusions.

(*He returns knife to sheath*)

HARRY   No. I don't believe it. That's the ugliest, the most cowardly and revolting . . . You were actually going to . . .

MILT   Yes! Yes! It's her or me. One or the other. I can't go on like this anymore, Harry. Now will you let me . . .

(*He dashes to railing.* HARRY *grabs him. They struggle*)

HARRY   No, Milt! Milt! What are you doing? (*He throws* MILT *to ground; surprised tone*) This isn't like you. (*Sits on* MILT's *backside*) You were always so levelheaded, always so damn anxious to make something of yourself and get ahead in the world. You're not going to throw it all away now, are you?

MILT (*In despair*) I've had as much as I can take of this misery.

HARRY   Always working, from the first day of school, thinking about business, finance, investments, Wall Street . . .

MILT (*Looking up at* HARRY) What's the good of bringing all that up? Don't you see, Harry? I've had it. (*Clutching throat*) Up to here, I've had it!

HARRY   But love, Milt; what about love?

MILT   Love?

HARRY   Love. The thing you were talking about only a minute ago.

(*They rise to their feet*)

MILT   Linda . . .

HARRY   Linda. Exactly.

MILT   Harry, meet her; just meet her.

HARRY   Linda?

MILT   No, no, Ellen. Meet Ellen.

HARRY   Will you promise to stop this nonsense?

MILT   I promise. Yes.

HARRY   And the . . .

(*Points to knife*)

MILT   No more. I promise.

HARRY   Let me have it.

(HARRY *takes the knife from him. Suddenly, unexpectedly, he turns, throws knife at sandbox; it sticks, vibrates rapidly. A mechanical device can be used so that it appears as if he has thrown the knife but in fact the knife is concealed and a second knife is sprung from sandbox.* HARRY *falls back into* MILT, *amazed by his own expertness*)

MILT (*Staring at knife in sandbox, with admiration*) Just meet her, Harry. I know you two will hit it off. She reads, Harry, book after book after book. And she paints, and she plays guitar . . .

HARRY (*Puts jacket on* MILT, *buttons it*) Classical or flamenco?

MILT What's that?

HARRY The guitar. Does she play classical or flamenco?

MILT I don't really . . .

HARRY I play flamenco.

MILT She's good at it; very good at it, whatever it is. And she reads, Harry. That woman reads continuously, books I never heard of . . . with hard covers, too!

HARRY All right. I'll meet her. But that's all I'll do.

MILT That's all I want you to do.

HARRY Don't forget your promise.

MILT I won't. You have my word on it. (ELLEN's *footsteps are heard off right*) Did you hear . . . That's her. She's coming. (*Leads* HARRY *to alcove, left*) Wait here, Harry. I'll bring her over. Wait right here. Don't move.

(MILT *hurries to right where he meets* ELLEN *as she enters. She wears a mink coat, skirt, blouse of same color, alligator bag and shoes, a black kerchief on her head, a pair of dark sunglasses; she carries a rolled graph, about three feet long—a window shade in a wooden casing.* HARRY *tactfully leans over the railing and stares at the river below*)

MILT Ellen, where were you? I was getting worried. (*He removes her kerchief and sunglasses, puts them on bench*) You'll never guess what happened. I ran into an old friend of mine. Harry Berlin. Remember me telling you about Harry Berlin? (*He unbuttons her coat, straightens blouse; on his knees he puts his hand under her dress and pulls her slip down*) We roomed together at Polyarts U. I want you to meet him, El. He's a wonderful guy. You two are going to love one another. (*He takes comb from his breast pocket, starts combing and "teasing" her hair, extravagantly with the finicky adroitness of a couturier. He goes on for a while before he speaks*) I want Harry to see what a lucky guy I am. There that does it. (*He hums contentedly; when he is done he takes compact from her pocketbook: moves her to lamppost for better light, tilts her head back; puts lipstick on her mouth; blots her lips with Kleenex and rouges her cheeks with a long rouge*

brush he takes from his breast pocket) It was the funniest thing.
I came up here to meet you and there he was, like he is now,
leaning over the rail. I recognized him at once. But he's changed,
El. You're going to have to be nice to him. He's been through hell,
the poor guy. Don't you remember me telling you about him? Top
man at Polyarts U. The fellows used to call him Dostoyevski.
What a guy. Plays a terrific guitar. He's sick now. Needs encour-
agement. Love. A reason for living. Don't get frightened if he has
a fit. He comes right out of them. Poor guy. (*He holds compact
under her mouth; she spits uninhibitedly on cake mascara;* MILT
*stands behind her, energetically rubbing brush on mascara; tilting
her head forward, he applies it to her eyes*) We have to darken
these. Does wonders for your eyes. Gives them a deep almost
Oriental look. There, there, that's better. (*Returns compact to her
pocketbook, takes out atomizer, sprays her*) Let me see. You look
positively ravishing, El; beautiful. (*Returns atomizer; takes her
hand*) Now come. I want . . .

ELLEN (*Pulling free; restrained anger*)   No, Milt.

MILT   Why not? He's waiting . . .

ELLEN   He can wait. I want to talk to you.

    (*Returns kerchief and sunglasses to her pocketbook; places
pocketbook beside bench, right*)

MILT (*Annoyed*) El . . .

ELLEN   What I have to say will only take a few minutes. There
may not be many more of them. You didn't come home until
after one last night.

MILT   I told you what happened, hon. I was stuck in the office.
These clients came and the boss was there and I couldn't . . .

ELLEN (*Sharply*) Milt.

MILT   It's the truth, El!

ELLEN   It wouldn't give me any satisfaction to prove you're lying,
so we'll let it stay like that. I have something to show you. I
made this while you were out last night. (*She hooks graph to
lamppost*) Let me explain it to you. (*She pulls graph down to its
full length; points with finger*) These black vertical lines divide
our five years of marriage into months; these blue vertical lines
divide the months into weeks. Now. Each time this red horizontal
line running across the top of the graph hits the blue vertical
line, that indicates the number of sexual experiences over a seven-
day period.

MILT (*Covers graph with his body*) Ellen, for God's sake . . .

(*Looks about in embarrassment*) We can talk about this later.

ELLEN You're always saying later. That's a favorite play of yours. No, Milt. Not tonight. These things must be said while they still can be said. (*Mumbling under his breath* MILT *crosses to bench, sits*) I'd like to continue if you don't mind. Now. You'll notice on this graph how at the beginning of our marriage the red horizontal line touches the blue vertical line at a point of . . . fourteen, fifteen times a week, and how, gradually, the number of contacts become less and less until eighteen months ago, when we have an abrupt break-off, the last time being July twenty-third, the night of your sister's wedding, and after that date the red horizontal line doesn't touch the blue vertical line once, not once! I have nothing further to say, Milt. (*She tugs down on graph so that it snaps up cleanly and disappears in the wooden casing; pause*) When something like this is allowed to happen to a marriage, you can't go on pretending. (*Removes graph from lamppost*) You want to pretend. Oh, the temptation is great to overlook, to find excuses, to rationalize. (*Waving graph*) But here, Milt, here are the facts. Our relationship has deteriorated to such an extent that I don't feel responsible anymore for my own behavior.

MILT (*Rises, arms held out, smiling*) Hon, you're mad at me.

ELLEN (*Still angry*) It isn't a question of being mad at you. We've gone a long ways from that.

MILT I see. (*Takes graph from her*) Just the same I'd like to ask you something, El.

ELLEN Speak. I can't stop you.

MILT Do you think our marriage is a failure?

ELLEN I do.

MILT (*Triumphantly*) I thought so. I thought that was behind it. Well, before I give you a divorce . . .

ELLEN There isn't going to be a divorce.

MILT There isn't?

ELLEN We've made a mistake, but we've got to make the best of it.

MILT We'll act like civilized human beings.

ELLEN I have no intention of doing otherwise.

MILT Good. (*Formally*) Ellen, I'd like you to meet a friend of mine whom I accidentally bumped into a little while before you came and who is now waiting over there for us.

ELLEN (*Stiffly*) I know what my duties are.

MILT Then let me remind you that since he is a friend of mine that you treat him with every courtesy and that any kindness extended to him is considered a kindness by extension to me.

ELLEN   I understand fully.

MILT   Good. Do you have anything more to say?

ELLEN   Nothing.

MILT   Very good. So long as we understand one another. (*Puts graph down on seat of upstage bench and goes to* HARRY) Harry. Harry. Sorry to keep you waiting. (*Arm about* HARRY, *brings him down to where* ELLEN *waits*) Well, here she is. Harry Berlin. Ellen Manville. (*They stare blankly at one another*) Ellen Manville. Harry Berlin. (*Still no reaction from them; he stands between them, arms around their shoulders*) My two best friends. (*Turns head quickly from one to the other; hugs them*) My best classmate . . . My best wife . . . I've looked forward to this for years. I . . . (*Turns head. They don't budge*) I'll tell you what. I'm going to leave you two alone to . . . to get to know one another. (*Slides out from between them, and begins to move left*) I'll be back. Don't go 'way. (*Stops, takes* HARRY *by his arm and pulls him off, left*) Huh . . . Harry. I did a silly thing. Left the house without taking any money. Could you loan me five bucks until later?

HARRY   (*Takes out some crumpled bills and gives him one*) Is it enough?

MILT   Sure, sure, just till later . . . (*Puts money in pocket*) Harry, she's a wonderful girl. But she's had a terribly rough time of it. Try to understand her. (*Moves left; loudly*) See you both soon. You'll love one another, I know you will.

(*Picks up coat and exits. In a second he pops back in, grabs the basket in one jerk and exits. There is a long uncomfortable pause.* ELLEN *takes out a cigarette from a package in her coat pocket, lights it, and leans against the lamppost, front.* HARRY *buttons his shirt, takes a ready-made tie from his jacket pocket, and hooks it onto his collar. He carefully buttons his jacket and brushes his pants. After preparing himself, he crosses to* ELLEN's *right and grabs the lamppost with one hand*)

HARRY   Classical or flamenco?

ELLEN   Flamenco.

HARRY   Me, too. (*Sings a few bars of a flamenco melody. There is no response. A slight pause.* HARRY *points out over audience*) That's the Empire State Building over there.

ELLEN   (*Without looking; wrapped in her own suffering*) I know.

HARRY   I'd like to go there sometime.

ELLEN   I wouldn't.

HARRY   You wouldn't?

ELLEN   I wouldn't.

HARRY   You're probably right. (*Takes off tie and puts it back into his pocket, unbuttons collar and jacket, moves back to the bench and sits left. A pause.* HARRY *looks up*) A star . . . First one. You can hardly see it, it's so weak. "Starlight, starbright, first star I see tonight, wish I may, wish I might . . ." (*To* ELLEN) Make a wish.

ELLEN   I wish . . . I wish I was a lesbian.

HARRY   (*Slowly turns and looks at her*)   You don't mean that.

ELLEN   (*Throws down cigarette and grinds it under her shoe*)   I do. I certainly do. Then I wouldn't have all these demeaning problems.

(*Again he leans against lamppost*)

HARRY   You'd have other problems.

ELLEN   Like what?

HARRY   Like picking up girls, for one.

ELLEN   (*Bitterly*)   That would be simple. All I'd have to do is learn how to be a liar and a hypocrite.

HARRY   There's a lot more to it than that. Do you know what you have to pay for a haircut these days?

ELLEN   I'd pay for it. Gladly. Anything but this heartache; anything.

(*Puts her hand up and grabs lamppost*)

HARRY   Look, you don't have to stay if you don't want to. I can tell Milt . . .

ELLEN   I have nothing else to do.

HARRY   The same here.

(*Pause.* ELLEN *leans against the lamppost, stares up at the sky, one hand clutching the post and one foot pressed to it. She starts to sing in a deep lugubrious voice, softly at first, almost to herself, but with obvious feeling. She is indifferent to* HARRY *who shifts about on the bench nervously*)

ELLEN   (*Sings*)

Love cast its shadow over my heart.
Love changed my life right from the start.

HARRY   (*Uncomfortably*)   I know, Milt told me everything.

ELLEN (*Sings*)

I cried it couldn't be,
Then Love laughed back at me.

HARRY   It'll work out all right.
ELLEN (*Sings*)

Why did you come?
Why did you stay?

HARRY   You have to be patient with him.
ELLEN (*Sings, opening her coat*)

Why did you take me,
Only to play?
Oh, Love. Love. Love. Love.
Look what you've done to me.

HARRY (*Shrugging, with a sigh*)   Well . . . Sometimes it happens that way.

ELLEN (*Wipes a tear from her eye*)   I am sorry. I'm afraid I'm not myself tonight.

HARRY   Don't apologize.

ELLEN (*Leaves post and looks about*)   It is nice out.

HARRY   Probably rain soon.

ELLEN (*Moves downstage and looks out over audience*)   How far down do you think it is?

HARRY   Far enough.

ELLEN   You know, I'm afraid of water. I can't swim a stroke. But tonight . . . with the moon shining on it, it looks quite beautiful and . . . and almost inviting.

HARRY   You shouldn't talk like that.

ELLEN   Shouldn't I? Harry, what do you think I did with my life? What do you think made me the way I am? You don't have to answer that. When I look back . . . (*Looks out once more*) It couldn't have worked out very differently. My childhood was impossible, absolutely impossible. My parents separated when I was three. I spent six months with one, six months with the other; they passed me back and forth like an old sack.

HARRY   That was a lot better than I did. (*Rises; moves left*) My folks left me with my grandparents. I saw them maybe once every four or five years. It was hell, Ellen; believe me, it was hell.

ELLEN   Not as bad as what I went through, Harry. Oh, no.

HARRY   Worse than what you went through, Ellen; lots worse.

ELLEN   You ever live with an alcoholic?

HARRY   My grandfather drank . . .

ELLEN   Enough to have delirium tremens?

HARRY   (*Wagging his hand*) He used to shake a little . . .

ELLEN   Well, it's not the same thing, oh, no, Harry, it's not the same thing.

HARRY   (*Foiled*) Anyone ever call you a bastard?

ELLEN   A relative or a stranger?

HARRY   A relative. (*No answer*) Well, they called me one.

ELLEN   I never had a birthday party.

HARRY   I didn't know when my birthday was until I got a notice from my draft board.

ELLEN   Did anyone ever try to rape you?

HARRY   (*Thoughtfully*) Ahh . . .

ELLEN   I said, "Did anyone ever try to rape you?" When I was fifteen, Harry, only fifteen. Two boys . . . If I hadn't kicked and screamed . . .

HARRY   Where was it?

ELLEN   Where was what?

HARRY   That the two boys grabbed you.

ELLEN   (*Holding head in hands; traumatically*) In Queens. On Parsons Boulevard. When I was walking home from the bus stop.

HARRY   (*Vehemently*) I've never been to Parsons Boulevard. Never. I don't even know where the hell Parsons Boulevard is!

(ELLEN *crosses to* HARRY)

ELLEN   I was lonely, Harry; I was always lonely. (HARRY *moves upstage and begins to walk along rail to the right.* ELLEN *follows him, pulling at his sleeve*) There was no one for me to talk with, or share things with. I couldn't make friends because I never stayed in one place long enough. I went deeper and deeper inside of myself. I read and fantasized and was far too bright for my age. And before I knew it I had grown up, life was for real. (*They continue offstage and with* ELLEN *talking incessantly, turn and come back on, moving to the left of the alcove*) On the one hand, I possessed a cold calculating mind; it was sharp as a razor, incisive, penetrating. Men were afraid of me. They were afraid of my mind, my power of analysis, my photographic memory. They wouldn't discuss things with me. They became resentful and standoffish and avoided me because I was a threat to their feelings of masculine superiority. (ELLEN *stops* HARRY *and both turn downstage*) Ask me a question, Harry.

HARRY   How many states did Al Smith win in the election of 1928?

ELLEN   In the election of 1928 the presidential candidate Alfred E. Smith won eight states: they were the states of Arkansas, Alabama, Georgia, Louisiana, Massachusetts, Mississippi, Rhode Island and South Carolina.

HARRY   (*Nodding, shakes* ELLEN's *hand*)   It's been very nice speaking to you, Ellen. But I really have to go. Tell Milt . . .

ELLEN   Please, Harry. Stay. Don't go yet. (*Stops him, and again begins to move right along the railing with him*) You see, on the other hand, on the other hand, Harry. I was a woman, a woman who wanted to be loved, who wanted to have children, who wanted all the common dreary horrible middle-class things . . . (HARRY *turns back and wearily moves left, leaning on the railing.* ELLEN *not noticing, continues off right*) things that every other woman takes for granted. I willingly . . . (ELLEN *realizes he is no longer with her, and turns and runs left after him. Catching up with him, she continues*) I willingly succumbed to biological and sociological necessity. I willingly confessed my womanhood. But how do I bridge the gap? I didn't ask for universal education. Why was I educated, Harry, if I'm compelled to live this fractured existence?

HARRY   (*Angrily; moves to sandbox and sits*)   Nobody thinks of these things until it's too damn late!

ELLEN   (*Moves right to bench, sits*)   Now there's so little to believe in, so little to keep me going.

HARRY   Love?

ELLEN   Love?

HARRY   Love. What about love?

ELLEN   Oh, I don't know. Once. Yes. Once.

HARRY   Once is enough. It's more than most people had.

ELLEN   You know nothing about women, Harry. For a woman to have never known love isn't tragic. The dream is still there. The dream . . . She needs that more than she does the reality. But to have love become a shabby cynical emotion . . . To watch it change into pettiness and hate . . . That's what destroys her. She loses her dream and . . . (*Through clenched teeth*) It makes an animal of her, a vicious little creature who only thinks of scratching and biting and getting revenge. Look, Harry, look! (*She pulls a large unsheathed bread knife from inside her coat; rises.* HARRY

*looks from the knife in her hand to the one beside him sticking
into the sandbox*) Do you know what I was going to do with this?

HARRY   You don't mean . . . ?

ELLEN (*Moves to left, stabbing air viciously*)   Yes. Milt Manville!
Milt Manville! I was going to use it on him. (HARRY *gets up and
moves upstage to* ELLEN's *right. She turns to him*) I can't go on
like this anymore, Harry. I know he's lying to me. I know he's
seeing another woman. (ELLEN *again turns left and slashes the
air*) I won't have it! I won't let him!

HARRY   Ellen, don't, he's not worth . . .
(*Moves toward her*)

ELLEN (*Suddenly turning with knife so that* HARRY *has to jump back
to avoid being slashed*)   What's left for me? I don't make friends
easily. I can't start again. Don't you see, there's only one thing . . .
Only . . . (*Grabs knife in both hands and raises it over her head*)
Yes! Yes!
(HARRY *grabs her wrists with both hands and struggles with her
to prevent her from plunging the knife into her chest*)

HARRY   Give it to me. Give it . . .

ELLEN   Leave me, Harry. Please . . .

HARRY   A smart girl like you . . .

ELLEN   I want it this way. Please . . . Please . . .
(*The knife turns in her hand and is now pointed at* HARRY's
*Adam's apple. He leans over backward to prevent being stabbed
until he is lying supine on the ground, with* ELLEN, *in a state of
hysteria, bent over him and trying, without knowing it, to plunge
the knife into him*)

HARRY   No, no, Ellen . . .

ELLEN   I won't have it. I won't!

HARRY   What are you . . .

ELLEN   Good-bye, Harry!

HARRY   For cryin' out loud . . .

ELLEN   Good-bye, everyone!

HARRY   You crazy bitch, will you cut it out!
(HARRY *finally manages to turn the knife aside. The knife drops
to the ground. She stands erect, steps over* HARRY, *and moves to
the bench; she weeps quietly into her hands.* HARRY, *after several
attempts, manages to get up. He crosses up to the rail and leans
over it; retches hollowly. He then picks up the knife and moves
to* ELLEN, *offering her his handkerchief*)

ELLEN (*Taking handkerchief*)   Thank you.

HARRY (*Now offers knife*) Do you want this? (*She shakes her head*) Are you sure? (*She nods and he puts knife into his jacket pocket*) You're not going to be this dumb again, are you?

ELLEN No, Harry. I am sorry.

HARRY (*Buttons her coat*) You promise?

ELLEN I promise.

HARRY All right. Let's forget it.

(*And suddenly, unexpectedly,* HARRY *takes the knife from his pocket, whirls to the left and hurls the knife at the sandbox; a second knife appears downstage of the first, vibrating rapidly.* HARRY *moves away with a slight swagger and sits down at the right of the bench*)

ELLEN (*Sits next to him and returns handkerchief to him, placing her head on his shoulder*) I've been a great deal of trouble to you.

HARRY Forget it.

(*Gets up and moves downstage, sitting on the curb*)

ELLEN (*Moves downstage and sits to the right of* HARRY) I don't often meet people who take kindness for granted.

HARRY (*Moves away*) Forget it.

ELLEN (*She moves to him*) I have to tell you . . .

HARRY (*Turning, shouting*) I said forget it! Forget it! (*Rises and moves left away from her*) What's wrong with you? You're giving me a headache! (*Wailing*) Have a little pity for the next guy. (*Sits down on sandbox*)

ELLEN (*Pause*) I am sorry, Harry.

HARRY (*Without turning*) That's all right.

ELLEN Milt has spoken about you. Frequently.

HARRY It's fifteen years since I saw him.

ELLEN He has nothing but good things to say.

HARRY I changed. I changed a lot.

ELLEN You were something of a father figure to him.

HARRY (*Turning to her*) He never told me that.

ELLEN You know how he is.

(*Gets up and moves left*)

HARRY He should have told me. I could have helped him with his homework.

ELLEN Harry, isn't there anything . . .

HARRY Nothing. For me . . . there's nothing.

ELLEN You can't mean that.

HARRY I can't. Ha, ha!

ELLEN You've never been in love, have you?

HARRY Love?

ELLEN Love. It's there. In all of us.

HARRY But I thought . . .

ELLEN It's hard to kill a dream, Harry. (*Sings romantically, directing the song to* HARRY)

Love cast its shadow over my heart,
Love changed my life right at the start,
I cried it couldn't be,

(*Moves to* HARRY *and unbuttons coat*)

Then Love laughed back at me.
Oh, why did you come?
Why did you stay?

(*Touches his face with her hand*)

Why did you take me,

(*Lifts his hand and brings it slowly, steadily upward*)

Only to play?
Oh, Love. Love. Love. Love.
Look what you've done to me.

(*Places his hand on her breast and closes the coat over it*)

HARRY (*As she sings, shifts about agitatedly*) Ellen, stop it; that's enough . . . Why don't you sit down? I want to speak to you, tell you something about myself. I . . . You don't know me, Ellen. I'm a dead man. Dead inside. Dead to everyone and . . . everything. Ellen, will you stop that damn singing! I'm trying to explain. I'm not the kind of man you think. I can't change. (*In despair*) What's the good? The jig's up. The chips are down. No way out. (*Softly*) Ellen . . . Ellen . . . (*As she places his hand on her breast,* HARRY *bolts upright, his eyes widen, and he begins to sing with a great fervor*)

Love cast its shadow over my heart,
Love changed my life right from the start.
Da, da, da, dum, de, dum . . .

(HARRY *gets up and taking* ELLEN *in his arms, with great style and grace and with a formal dip, begins to waltz her about the stage*)

ELLEN (*Exultantly*)   Dance with me, Harry; dance.

HARRY   It's been years . . .

ELLEN   Turn me! Turn me!

HARRY   It's fun. I'm having fun!

ELLEN   Let yourself go, Harry!

HARRY   I feel like singing at the top of my lungs!

ELLEN   Then sing, Harry, sing!

(*Holding hands and carried by the momentum of their emotions, they both sing the following lines superbly as though an aria*)

HARRY (*Singing*)   Oh, Ellen, I think I'm in love with you.

ELLEN (*Singing*)   Oh, Harry, can it possibly be?

HARRY (*Singing*)   I never felt this way before.

ELLEN (*Singing*)   My heart is beating like a banging door.

HARRY (*Singing*)   Oh, how good it feels to be in love with someone like you.

(*They kiss, sink slowly to their knees,* ELLEN *ending cradled in* HARRY'S *arms*)

ELLEN (*Looking up at him*)   Dostoyevski.

HARRY   Ellen Manville.

ELLEN (*Rises to her knees*)   I didn't really think it could happen to me again.

HARRY   I feel like a kid, all weak and sticky inside. Is that . . .

ELLEN   That's part of it. Say it, Harry.

HARRY   Say what?

ELLEN   Just say it!

HARRY   You don't mean . . . ?

ELLEN   Yes, yes, say it!

HARRY   I . . . Ellen, it isn't easy. I never . . .

ELLEN   Say it! Say it!

HARRY (*With great difficulty; voice distorted unnaturally and only after several attempts*)   I la . . . I la . . . I . . . I . . . I l-o-o-o-o-ve . . . ye . . . ye . . . you.

ELLEN   Oh, Harry. (*They kiss and then rise*) Harry, do you still feel that there's nothing . . .

HARRY   Don't say it. No. Life . . . Life is a mystery.

ELLEN (*Turns downstage*)   Do you hear the birds singing?

HARRY (*Behind her, with his arms around her*)   Yes, yes. (*Gesturing*) Here, birdies; here, birdies . . .

ELLEN   Do you see the sun?

HARRY   It's a beautiful sun.

ELLEN   It's our sun, Harry.

HARRY   Sun, I love you!

ELLEN   It's all happening so quickly. I'm dizzy.

HARRY   Me, too. Ellen . . . You say it.

ELLEN   You want me to say it?

HARRY   Yes. Say it. Please.

ELLEN   Harry . . . (*Inhaling deeply*) Harry . . . I like you very much.

HARRY   Like me?

ELLEN   (*Turns to* HARRY)   I think you're one of the nicest and most thoughtful people I ever met.

HARRY   What're you talking about?

ELLEN   Isn't that what you wanted me to say?

HARRY   (*Angrily*)   No. No. Not on your life! You say what I say. I said it. Now you say it. Fair is fair!

ELLEN   (*Sits down on the bench*)   But, Harry, I don't know. Really. I've been hurt once and . . . it's just that I have to be sure. I'm confused. I wasn't prepared for anything like this . . . I . . . (*Turns left to* HARRY) Harry, *how much* do you love me?

HARRY   (*Moves to the bench; outburst*)   A lot! An awful lot!

ELLEN   But *how much?*

HARRY   (*Slight pause; begins to answer; gives it up*)   I see what you mean.

ELLEN   It's a problem. Love isn't a commodity that you can measure. And yet there are different degrees of it. We have to know what we can expect from one another. Am I the first woman you ever loved, Harry? The truth, now.

HARRY   I swear, Ellen. That's the truth. Before I came on this bridge tonight, I never looked twice at any woman.

ELLEN   But you did sleep with other women, didn't you, Harry?

HARRY   And you? What about you?

ELLEN   (*Rises, gets graph from upstage bench, and hands it to him*) Here. Read this. It contains the whole story. But remember, he was my husband, it had nothing to do with personal likes or dislikes. How many, Harry? I'd like to know.

HARRY   Ellen, I don't remember, I couldn't . . .

ELLEN   An approximate figure will do. I just . . .

HARRY   Twenty-eight!

ELLEN   (*Slight pause*)   Twenty-eight different women or one woman twenty-eight times.

HARRY   Six women once and one woman twenty-two times.

ELLEN   Who was she, Harry?

HARRY   I . . . Ellen, I . . .

ELLEN   (*Firmly*)   I want to know who she was, Harry.

HARRY   (*In exasperation*)   Gussie Gooler! Gussie Gooler! But it wasn't love, Ellen. We were kids. Dumb foolish stupid kids. Her brother was my best friend!

ELLEN   Thank you for being honest.

HARRY   Is Milt the only one?

ELLEN   The only one.

HARRY   (*Waves graph before setting it down to the right of the sand-box*)   I'll read this tonight.

ELLEN   (*Softly*)   Harry.

(*They embrace*)

HARRY   You do love me, don't you?

ELLEN   You know I do.

HARRY   How much, Ellen? Tell me.

ELLEN   That's the very problem we're faced with.

HARRY   You're right. That's the problem.

(HARRY *suddenly stamps on* ELLEN's *upstage foot; she howls, hops on the other to the right of the bench*)

ELLEN   Owwwww! What did you do that for?

HARRY   (*Grinning sheepishly*)   Do you still love me?

ELLEN   (*Slight pause*)   Yes . . . (*Limps to him*) Yes, I do.

HARRY   There, there, that proves it! If you could love me after I did something like that to you, there isn't any . . .

(ELLEN *pulls back her arm and punches* HARRY *savagely in the stomach.* HARRY *doubles over in pain, gasps for breath*)

ELLEN   (*Bending over him*)   Has your love for me changed, Harry?

(HARRY *is unable to answer*) Has it, Harry?

HARRY   No. No. It's . . . It's all right.

(*Forces himself erect*)

ELLEN   Now I know I didn't make a mistake! (HARRY *embraces her, with his arms around her, from behind*) And I will be a good wife to you. I have no qualms about getting a job, working, anything, until you get back on your feet. I've learned a good deal being married to Milt and this time, I know, I . . .

(HARRY, *as she talks, grabs the top of her blouse and rips the front of it down*)

HARRY   Well?

ELLEN (*Gulping down her anger, staring at torn blouse*) I love you, Harry.

HARRY The same as before?

ELLEN The same.

HARRY (*Takes her in his arms*) Harry Berlin is happy! For the first time in fifteen years Harry Berlin is actually happy! (*In his exuberance leaves her and steps up on sandbox*) I'm not going to disappoint you, Ellen. I'll come out of it. (ELLEN *reaches into her coat pocket and takes out a pair of scissors. She quietly crosses to* HARRY, *as he talks, and cuts the piece of rope holding up his pants. They fall about his ankles and she puts the scissors back in her pocket*) I'll make good. I know I will. I don't need anything but what I got. I . . .

(HARRY *stops, looks down at his pants. He closes his jacket about himself, modestly*)

ELLEN Have your feelings for me decreased in any way, Harry? (*Slight pause*) Have they, Harry?

HARRY (*Arms crossed*) It's cold.

ELLEN I asked you a question, Harry.

HARRY I love you, Ellen.

ELLEN Despite everything.

HARRY Despite everything.

ELLEN Oh, Harry . . .

(*She gets up on sandbox and embraces him. During the embrace he reaches down, pulls up his pants and fastens them*)

HARRY (*In curt, businesslike tone*) Ellen . . .

ELLEN Yes, Harry.

HARRY Do you love me, Ellen?

ELLEN I love you.

HARRY Please turn around.

ELLEN Harry . . .

HARRY Do what I told you.

ELLEN (*Gets down from sandbox*) I love you, Harry.

HARRY I love you. Now do what I told you.

(ELLEN *turns around.* HARRY *quickly rips the mink coat off her and in a single gesture hurls it over the railing*)

ELLEN (*Running to railing*) My coat! My coat!

(*After looking over railing she turns and doubles over in a fit of soundless hysteria.* HARRY *takes her in his arms and leads her, writhing and floundering about, to the bench. He finally gets her to sit down*)

HARRY   Do you still love me?

ELLEN (*Shouting*)   I bought it with my own money!

HARRY   Yes or no? Do you love me or don't you?

ELLEN (*Sobbing*)   I love you.

HARRY (*Embraces her*)   I love you, too, Ellen. I can't believe it. (*Rises*) Everything's clearing up for me. I have the feeling I can start writing poetry again. I wrote tons of it at school. (*Reciting*) "Under the starlit window, two lovers lie in bed; naked up to their shoulders, for neither has a head. One lover touches the other, the other . . ."

ELLEN (*Coolly; rising*)   Harry.

HARRY (*Going to her*)   Yes, Ellen . . . Darling.

ELLEN   May I have your jacket?

HARRY   My jacket?

ELLEN   Please give it to me.

HARRY   Ellen . . .

ELLEN   I said, please give it to me. (*He gives her his jacket*) Harry, I love you.

HARRY   I love you, Ellen.

ELLEN   I know you do. (*Slight pause*) Harry . . . (ELLEN *gestures upstage.* HARRY *follows her glance to river*) Good-bye.

HARRY   You don't mean . . . ?

ELLEN (*Turning downstage; emotionally, burying her face in his coat*)   I can't watch! I can't!

HARRY (*Nodding; resignedly*)   Good-bye, Ellen.
   (*Moves to railing*)

ELLEN (*Sobbing into hands*)   Good-bye, my dearest; good-bye.

HARRY (*Moves downstage*)   I . . . I love you.

ELLEN   I love you! I love you!
   (HARRY *climbs up on the railing right of the alcove; he is about to throw himself into the river when* MILT *comes in down left.* MILT, *seeing* HARRY, *drops the overcoat he is carrying which is now of enormous size, and running to rail grabs* HARRY *about the legs. He attempts to pull him down but* HARRY *holds on tightly to the cable*)

MILT   Harry! Harry! For God's sake!

HARRY   Get away . . .

MILT   Listen to me.
   (*Trying to pull him down*)

HARRY   Let go!

(*Kicking at* MILT)

MILT   Love, Harry, love!

HARRY   That's what it is, you damn ass! Now will you let . . .

ELLEN   (*After putting on* HARRY's *jacket runs to him*)   No, Harry. Don't. You don't have to. It's true. It's really, really true!

HARRY   Ellen!

(HARRY *slides down the cable to the ground, and embraces* ELLEN. *They kiss.* MILT *stands nearby, viewing them critically*)

MILT   (*Slight pause*)   What's going on here?

ELLEN   (*Breaking the embrace*)   You tell him.

HARRY   No, you better tell him.

ELLEN   I think it wiser if you told him.

HARRY   Do you think so?

ELLEN   I do, Harry.

HARRY   Okay. (*Kisses her hand, crosses to* MILT)   Milt, it worked out all right. We're in love and we'd like . . . (*Turns to* ELLEN) We'd like to get married.

(ELLEN *comes to* HARRY *and they embrace.* MILT *quietly watches*)

MILT   I see. Leave my best friend with my wife alone and this is what happens. You ought to be ashamed of yourself. The both of you!

(MILT *moves down left.* ELLEN *follows down after him and* HARRY *comes to her right and puts his arms about her*)

ELLEN   Milt, I want a divorce. And the sooner you give it to me the easier it'll be for all of us.

MILT   A divorce. I see. Five years of marriage and you come up to me and say, "Milt, I want a divorce," and I'm supposed to take it all, say nothing and go right along with this preposterous and morally contemptible idea!

HARRY   Come on, Milt. Cut it out. You know . . .

MILT   (*Sharply*)   Never mind what I know, Harry. This is between my wife and myself. It has nothing to do with you. Not yet, at any rate.

ELLEN   Milt, we haven't been happy together. It's obvious that our marriage has failed.

MILT   Not completely, El. We've had some good times. Hon, remember when we first moved into our place and the painter locked himself in the bathroom and couldn't get out?

(*He breaks into uncontrollable laughter, which she joins*)

ELLEN   He was banging and screaming . . .

MILT   And the people next door . . .

>   (*Takes* ELLEN *in his arms and moves her away from* HARRY, *to
>   his left*)

ELLEN   The people next . . .

MILT   They thought . . .

ELLEN   They thought . . .

MILT   He was your father . . .

>   (HARRY *attempts to separate* MILT *and* ELLEN)

ELLEN   That he came to take me back and you two were . . .

MILT   We two . . .

ELLEN   Were fighting . . .

>   (HARRY, *having failed to separate or get between them, grabs
>   the bottom of* ELLEN's *jacket and tries to pull her back*)

MILT   (*Rubbing tears from his eyes*)   What a time.

HARRY   Ellen.

ELLEN   (*Ignoring him*)   That was really something.

HARRY   (*Louder*)   Ellen!

MILT   (*Suddenly grim; holding* ELLEN *from* HARRY)   She's still my
    wife, Harry, and so long as she's my wife I have the right to talk
    to her without your interrupting!

ELLEN   (*Conciliatory, takes* MILT *right to bench*)   Milt, we have to
    reach a decision.

MILT   I only want what's best for you, hon.

>   (ELLEN *sits on bench*)

HARRY   Does she get a divorce or doesn't she?

MILT   (*Turns back to* HARRY)   Do you think you know this woman
    well enough so that you can talk of marriage? What do you know
    about her? You met her twenty minutes ago, Harry; only twenty
    minutes ago. Do you know that her mother was an alcoholic? That
    she can't see without glasses? that she shaves her legs and never
    cleans the razor?

ELLEN   (*Protestingly*)   Milt . . .

HARRY   I love her, Milt.

MILT   Love. That's a fancy word. Well, before I give my consent
    to this marriage, Harry, I'm going to make sure that you kids
    know what you're doing. I'm not having this woman go through
    the same lousy deal she had with me, twice! Oh, no. I'm not going
    to let it happen. (*Turning to* ELLEN; *quietly*) Hon, do you know
    that he's a sick man, that he has fits?

ELLEN   I know, Milt . . .

MILT Are you sure . . .

ELLEN I love him.

MILT He doesn't have a job.

HARRY I'm getting a job.

MILT (*To* HARRY, *snapping*) What kind of job?

ELLEN (*Pleadingly*) Milt.

MILT (*To* ELLEN) All right. All right. If that's what you want . . .
(*Moves down left with his back to bench*) I'll give you a divorce,
hon. (HARRY *crosses to bench, sits and embraces* ELLEN) But don't
depend on me for anything. You're both old enough to know your
own minds. (*Moves up right and kneels on upstage bench between them*) Don't come to me asking for help, money, alimony,
legal fees, or anything like that because you won't get it. You
make it on your own or you don't make it. (*Behind them, hands
on their shoulders; as a blessing*) Love one another, live moder-
ately, work together toward a common goal, show patience and
consideration for each other's needs and desires, respect each
other as individuals during the good times and the bad, and you'll
make a go of it. El . . . (*He kisses her on cheek*) Every happiness.
Harry . . . (*Shaking his hand*) You're getting a wonderful girl.
Nobody knows that better than I do. Take care of her.
(MILT *moves left,* HARRY *follows him*)

HARRY Thanks. Ahhh . . . (*Holding* MILT's *arm; whispering*) Say,
Milt, that five bucks . . .
(ELLEN *takes comb out of bag and fixes hair*)

MILT She's a wonderful girl, Harry. You're a lucky guy.

HARRY I know. But that five . . .

MILT You speaking to me, Harry?

HARRY Who do you think I'm speaking to?

MILT That's funny. I can't hear a word you're saying. (*Cheerfully*)
Something's wrong. Speak slowly, Harry, I'll try to read your lips.
(ELLEN *comes up to them*)

HARRY (*Drawing out words*) That five bucks you took from me,
I . . .
(*He glances down to see* ELLEN *staring up at him*)

ELLEN What is it, Harry?

HARRY (*Not wanting her to know*) I . . . I just . . .

ELLEN You can tell me. I want to help you. That's why I'm here.
Only to help you and be with you.

HARRY (*Softly*) Ellen . . .

ELLEN   My Harry . . .
HARRY   Empire State Building?
ELLEN   Yes. Yes. The Empire State Building.
   (*Hand in hand, they run off right, laughing happily*)
MILT (*Watches them go, then cries out in ecstasy*)   Linda! Oh, my
   Linda! (*He runs right, jumps on the bench and springs to the
   crossbar of the lamppost, around which he revolves, singing joy-
   fully, his knees curled under him*) Love cast its shadow over my
   heart, etc.

Curtain

ACT TWO

THE TIME: *Several months later: early evening.*

THE SCENE: *The same as Act One.*

ELLEN *is seated on the right of the downstage bench, in a black leather coat, black high-neck sweater and skirt. She is wearing black tights and low-cut black boots, with a large copper necklace and large hanging copper earrings. Her hair is now in a ponytail, and she is reading a paperback copy of* The Second Sex.

Riding a small Valmobile motor scooter, staring straight ahead, MILT *crosses the bridge, right to left above the bench, and exits. He immediately re-enters and crosses to above the bench, where he stops. He is now wearing a bright brown and yellow flecked sports jacket with a yellow shirt and olive tie, brown slacks, and brown shoes. A brown visored cap completes his outfit. Both he and* ELLEN *speak with exaggerated cheerfulness.*

MILT (*As he stops the scooter*)   El? Ellen? Is that you?

ELLEN (*As if trying to recall who he is*)   Milt. Milt Manville.

MILT   This is incredible.

ELLEN   Isn't it? You're the last . . .

MILT   How are you, El?

   (*Gets off scooter*)

ELLEN   Fine. Fine. You?

MILT (*Parks scooter and shuts off motor*)   Fine. Fine.

ELLEN   Linda?

MILT   Couldn't be better. (*Puts cap aside*) Harry?

ELLEN (*With inarticulate admiration*)   Ahhh, he's . . .

MILT   Happy, huh?

ELLEN   Very very happy, Milt. At times it's frightening. Do I merely thank you or . . . or what?

MILT (*Sits down left* ELLEN)   I knew you were right for each other. Didn't I tell you?

ELLEN It's more than that. Much more. It's . . . (*Glances at wrist-watch*) In an hour or so we're going to the museum.

MILT Is it open at night?

ELLEN Open . . . ? (*Breaks out in deprecating laughter*) Oh, Milt, Milt. Milt Manville. I am sorry. So many memories come back. Yes, Milt. The Modern Museum is open every Thursday evening. (MILT *"ahhh's," "ohhh's" and "ahummmm's, ahummmm's" all through* ELLEN'S *lines, to mitigate if not destroy the sting of her remarks. When* MILT *speaks,* ELLEN *does likewise, laughing artificially, murmuring and by her approval making his remarks innocuous*) Harry and I go to museums together and we borrow books from the public library and we play flamenco duets and it's an entirely different life than what we had. Different, richer, more rewarding . . . I . . . I don't want to hurt your feelings, Milt. Let's . . .

MILT No, no. No, you're not. I'm glad, El. It's worked out perfectly. For both of us. Linda . . . (*Smiles*) My Linda . . . (*He laughs aloud at thought her name evokes*) That woman . . . She . . . She has this dance she does before we go to bed. It's . . . (*Laughs.* ELLEN *murmurs and nods agreeably*) Some sort of Arabian belly dance. She puts a lampshade on her head, you know, and . . . She's fantastic. I don't know where she learned it but . . .

ELLEN That's why I have the greatest and deepest respect for Harry Berlin. I learn from him. Constantly.

MILT The same with Linda. Every day it's something else.

ELLEN The experiences he's had, just being with him is a lesson in itself.

MILT If I told you the things I learned from Linda . . .

ELLEN Do you find you laugh more, Milt?

MILT You hit it, El. That's it. That's the big difference. (*Laughing*) We get up in the morning and we start in laughing . . .

ELLEN (*Laughing*) With Harry, too . . .

MILT (*Laughing*) She carries on . . .

ELLEN (*Laughing*) The tricks and jokes, he's . . .

MILT (*Laughing*) I say, "Linda, Linda, I can't laugh more, no, I'll bust, I'll . . ." (*Suddenly overcome by misery*) Oh, God, oh, God!

ELLEN What is it, Milt?

MILT I can't lie to you. Not to you, El.

ELLEN Lie to me? About what?

MILT She left me. Walked out.

ELLEN When was that?

MILT Two, three days ago. I heard from her lawyer this morning. El, I don't want to be a two-time loser. What's wrong with me? What do people have against me? Tell me. It's driving me out of my mind.

ELLEN Perhaps you ought to go see her, speak to her, see if you can't get her to reconsider.

MILT See who?

ELLEN See Linda.

MILT (*Rises and paces left*) That lazy bitch! Who wants her? She can rot in hell for all I care!

ELLEN That's not nice, Milt.

MILT (*Pacing*) I know it's not nice. I had to live with her!

ELLEN You're exaggerating. She couldn't be that bad.

MILT That's what you say.

ELLEN You always complained that there were no surprises in our marriage. Didn't she have any surprises for you?

MILT She had surprises. Boy, did she have surprises! As soon as we were married . . . It wasn't the same person. She was different. Physically. All over. (*Shudders*) She even started growing a mustache. No kidding. I mean it. I couldn't recognize her. I used to come home and think I was in the wrong apartment.

ELLEN It's not an uncommon affliction among certain women. You should have given her sympathy, not criticism.

MILT I should have given her shaving cream, that's what I should have given her.

ELLEN I won't listen to you, Milt. You're being cruel and unkind. She must have had some assets for you to marry her.

MILT (*Moves to bench, sits left of* ELLEN) El, I don't make accusations lightly, you know that, you know it's not like me; but I'm willing to bet you anything that that woman had me under the influence of drugs or . . . (*Leaning toward her; ominously*) narcotics.

ELLEN How could she have done that?

MILT By intravenous injections. While I was sleeping. (*Rolls up sleeve, shows his forearm; solemnly*) Look at this.

ELLEN (*Examines arm*) Milt, you've had those freckles ever since I've known you.

MILT (*Shrilly*) Purple ones? Did I ever have purple freckles? (*Gets up, paces left*) I know I'm right, El. A human being couldn't change as much as she did. Overnight. Even her voice, it started coming out through her nose. (*Holds fingers to nose, mimicking*)

"Hey, whatta you mean by comin' in here an' leavin' the door open." That's how she sounded. It was incredible.

ELLEN   Did she at least keep the apartment clean?

MILT   Keep it clean? (*Crosses down right, to the front of the bench. Turns back to* ELLEN) El, hit me there. (*Points to back*) Go ahead. Hit me. (*She hits him on back. A thick cloud of dust rises from his jacket.* ELLEN *coughs, waves dust away.* MILT *points out the floating dust*) Now am I exaggerating? Now am I making it all up?

ELLEN   (*Contemptuously*)   That's despicable. That is despicable.

MILT   She quit her job, didn't do a damn thing but lay in bed and eat bonbons all day.

ELLEN   That is ab-so-lutely despicable. (*Heatedly*) I'm sorry. There's just no excuse for it. None. What an obnoxious horrible foul-mouthed rat-faced lascivious woman she must have been.

MILT   She was, she . . .

ELLEN   How could you have lived with her four months? Didn't you have any pride, any sense of self-respect?

MILT   I wanted . . .

ELLEN   *Would I let you leave the house in a jacket like that?*

MILT   (*Shaking head*)   No. No.

ELLEN   Did I lie in bed and eat bonbons all day?

MILT   (*Shaking head*)   No. No.

ELLEN   Why didn't I?

MILT   Because you were good. Because you were unselfish.

ELLEN   Because I was a jerk, that's why. (*Wipes hand on Kleenex from coat pocket*) Because I didn't use sex instead of washing the dishes.

MILT   She did, El, she . . .

ELLEN   You don't have to draw pictures for me. Rat-faced paranoic women. All of them. I'll become ill if I continue to talk about it. You should be happy to be rid of her.

MILT   (*Pained expression*)   Happy? How can I be happy?

ELLEN   Milt, there isn't someone . . . ? (MILT *nods, lips in a pout, with the forlornness of an old man*) You are irresponsible. There's no other word for it. (*Impatiently; puts book in pocketbook*) I have to go. I have my own problems, Milt. I can't spend all night . . .

MILT   I couldn't help it, El. Honest. I couldn't. Do you think I want to throw away my life like a lovesick schoolboy? But she . . . This woman here . . . (*Takes out wallet-photograph and looks at picture so as to arouse* ELLEN's *curiosity*) Beautiful. Too, too beautiful. (*Moves left to center; to photograph*) Sweetheart, if only I had the courage to speak to you . . .

ELLEN (*Crossing to him, peering over his shoulder*) Perhaps you can arrange to . . . Let me see that. (*Surprised*) Milt, this is my photograph!

MILT Of course it's your photograph.

ELLEN You took it at your sister's wedding, the same night . . .

MILT July twenty-third. Don't you think I know it?

ELLEN You don't mean . . . ?

MILT Yes! Yes! (MILT *crosses right to bench, sits.* ELLEN *moves left*) Oh, El . . . How stupid, how inexcusably stupid I was. I didn't realize . . . I didn't think . . . You were all I wanted. Ever, ever wanted. That first night with Linda it came to me, you, you, you, and since then I've been in such misery.

ELLEN (*Her back to* MILT) I don't want to hear any more, Milt.

MILT You have to, El. I've been living with this inside of me for months. It's been tearing me apart. I'm not here by accident. Harry phoned. He asked me to meet him, to collect some money I owe him. But that's not why I'm here. I came because I had to find out how you were doing, what you were doing, what chance I had . . .

ELLEN Whatever you thought, Milt, is totally irrelevant. I'm Mrs. Harry Berlin now, and if you've made a mistake you have no one to blame but yourself.

MILT That doesn't make it easier, El. It was my fault. Okay. I admit it. I was a stupid, selfish, hypocritical, egotistical, narrow-minded nitwit. Just like you always said. But, oh, El, hon . . .

ELLEN (*Moves left*) No. Let's stop it now. There's nothing I can do, Milt. It's too late. Besides other considerations, Harry needs me. He depends on me. (*Paces right to center*) In fact if I don't get home to feed him soon he won't have any dinner.

MILT You feed him?

ELLEN Two-thirds water and one-third milk. That's all he'll take. He . . . He's gotten worse, Milt. He's had a great many fits and . . . It hasn't been easy for me, either. But I know what my duties are. Marriage is more than the two people involved in it. That's something you would never acknowledge. Above everything else, despite my educational background, despite my academic achievements, I want to be a good wife and a good mother. But where is the man to whom I can be a good wife? Where are the children who cry for my arms and the milk in my breasts?

MILT (*Rises, arms outspread*) Here! Here I am!

ELLEN You?

MILT Yes, me. (*Moves to* ELLEN) Don't you see, El? I love you. I always loved you. (ELLEN *moves away left*) For God's sake, have pity. Don't close the door on me.

ELLEN No, Milt. I may have the intelligence of a man . . .

MILT Hey, listen, what was Sugar Ray Robinson's record from 1940 to 1944?

ELLEN From 1940 to 1944 Sugar Ray Robinson had a record of fifty professional bouts. He won forty-nine, thirty-four by knockouts, fifteen by decision, and he lost only one in 1943 to a certain Jake LaMotta.

MILT (*To himself*) I knew that schmuck last night was wrong. (*Moves to* ELLEN) Oh, sweetheart, I missed you so much . . .

ELLEN (*Moving away from him*) The intelligence of a man, Milt, yes, but the emotions of a woman, the innate insecurity of a woman. I refuse to be passed back and forth like an old sack.

MILT I'd never do that.

ELLEN You did it once.

MILT If you gave me another chance . . .

ELLEN You keep forgetting I'm a married woman, Milt.

MILT (*Quacking words like a duck*) Ellie?

ELLEN That's not going to help.

MILT (*Still quacking*) Won't you please reconsider?

ELLEN (*Moves down left to sandbox*) I'm in no mood for any of your games, Milt.

MILT Okay. Okay. Listen. Just tell me you love Harry Berlin, that you're happy with him, and I'll walk away from here and, I promise, you'll never see me again.

ELLEN Love Harry Berlin?

MILT Just say those words and it's good-bye to Milt Manville and his silly stupid but sometimes lovable ways.

ELLEN I . . . I can't. It's impossible. You talk about misery! Ha! (MILT *crosses down to* ELLEN) That makes me laugh. Misery! (MILT *holds his hands out to her*) You can't imagine how it's been. (*She takes his hands and both sit down on the sandbox*) He . . . (*Puzzled expression*) Who is he? What is he? Why didn't you shake me by the shoulders and slap my face and . . . do anything to stop me? He . . . He isn't human, Milt. That man

. . . He lays in the corner of the living room, rocking on his back, wearing a paper bag on his head, yes, a paper bag, mumbling and groaning hour after hour . . . I have to feed him, wash him . . . I can't tell you everything. I'm too ashamed.

MILT The filthy beast!

ELLEN That's what my marriage to Harry Berlin has been like.

MILT Then why? Tell me why?

ELLEN Ask me what I believe in, Milt.

MILT What do you believe in, Ellen?

ELLEN I believe in marriage, Milt. (*Rises, moves left*) I believe in a man coming home at five o'clock with a newspaper rolled under his arm and a silly grin on his face and shouting, "What's for dinner, hon?" I believe in the smell of talcum powder and dirty diapers and getting up in the middle of the night to warm the baby's bottle. I can't help it. I'm made that way. (*Paces up and down stage*) But why did they teach me trigonometry and bio-chemistry and paleontology? Why did they so sharpen my intellect that I find it impossible to live with a man? (*To MILT*) I'll never forgive the Board of Education for that. Never. (*Crosses up right to center*)

MILT (*Moves up to ELLEN's left*) If you'd listen to me . . .

ELLEN I wouldn't have divorced you, Milt. You know that. But you brought it about, coldly and deliberately. You forced me to marry Harry. And now I don't trust you. And where there's no trust there can't be love.

MILT Then . . .

ELLEN It's over.

MILT Nothing I do or say . . .

ELLEN (*Moves to left of bench*) The door is closed, Milt.
(MILT *nods sadly. He sings in a heartbroken voice*)

MILT (*Sings*)

Love cast its shadow over my heart.

ELLEN (*Sits down on bench*) Don't, Milt; please, don't.

MILT (*Sings as he crosses to ELLEN, left of bench and touches her hair*)

Love changed my life right from the start.
I cried it couldn't be.

ELLEN (*Shuddering from his touch*) We can't start all over again.

MILT (*Turns away in anguish*)

Then love laughed back at me.
Oh, why did you come?

ELLEN   It's too late, Milt. No.
(*Flings herself on seat of bench and puts legs up over back of bench*)

MILT (*Sings*)

Why did you stay?
Why did you take me . . .

(*Turns, sees* ELLEN, *stops in surprise. Rushing to bench, he sits and takes her in his arms*) El . . .

ELLEN   Milt . . .
(*As she throws her arms about him, another cloud of dust rises from his jacket*)

MILT   Oh, my sweetheart.
(*They kiss*)

ELLEN (*Staring up at him*)   Dostoyevski.

MILT   No, honey. Milt. Milt Manville.

ELLEN (*Sits up in* MILT's *arms, with legs along bench*)   Milt. Yes. Milt. Oh, I always loved you, Milt. (*Kisses him*) I come here almost every night, hoping you'll show up. I didn't want to marry Harry.

MILT (*Kisses her*)   You didn't want to marry Harry, did you?

ELLEN (*Returning kisses*)   You know I didn't want to marry Harry.

MILT   I know. I know.

ELLEN   I was praying you wouldn't believe what I said before.

MILT   I didn't. Honest.

ELLEN   Harry wasn't taking me to the museum tonight; he doesn't take me anyplace, not even to the movies.

MILT   I know. Now don't worry. It's all going to work out; you'll see. First thing I'm going to do, hon . . . I'm giving up my secondhand bric-a-brac and personal accessories job. I'm through working nights. I'm through scrounging in garbage pails.

ELLEN   But it means so much to you.

MILT   You mean more, much more. Our happiness means more. We're going to have to make some sacrifices, learn to do with less, budget ourselves . . . It won't be easy. (*Rises and crosses left to trash basket*) But every day at five I'm opening that front door

and . . . (*Picks newspaper out of trash basket*) With this newspaper under my arm and a silly grin on my face . . . (*Pantomimes
kicking door open*) "What's for dinner, hon?"

ELLEN Steak, French fries, catsup and mashed baby lima beans,
everything you like!
(*Runs to him and throws herself into his arms*)

MILT (*Twirls her about and then puts her down*) Just the way
I like it.

ELLEN And I'm not contradicting you anymore, Milt. Never. Never.

MILT One job's enough. I'm going to spend every single evening
home with you.
(*About to throw newspaper into basket, looks at it, has second
thoughts and slips it into his side pocket*)

ELLEN I'm not keeping any records and . . . (*Steps up on sandbox*) Ask me a question.

MILT What countries formed the League of Nations in 1919?

ELLEN I don't know.

MILT You don't know?

ELLEN (*Steps down from sandbox*) I don't know and I don't care
to know. I'm submerging my intelligence so that we can be happy
together. (*Embraces* MILT) That's all I want, Milt.

MILT And all I want is you, sweetheart, and the opportunity to be
incredibly rich someday.

ELLEN You will be; you will. But . . . Harry Berlin. What about
Harry Berlin?

MILT You'll get a divorce.

ELLEN He'll never give it to me, Milt.

MILT We'll have him sent away.

ELLEN It would take years, money . . .

MILT I thought of that. El, listen. Harry should be here any minute. (*Looking about*) El, he's a man who's contemplated suicide.
(*Looking about*) If he should happen to lose his balance . . .

ELLEN What are you saying, Milt?

MILT If he fell off the bridge and . . .

ELLEN No, no, don't say any more.

MILT But it's the only way.

ELLEN I won't have it. No.

MILT (*Petulantly, moves up right to right of alcove at the rail*)
Then you really don't love me.

ELLEN (*Crosses up to the left of* MILT) I do, Milt.

MILT   No, you don't.

ELLEN   I do. I swear I do.

MILT   If you really loved me nothing would stand in our way. Nothing in the world!

ELLEN   Don't you understand, Milt? That's murder.

MILT   Murder? Who said anything about murder? Are you out of your mind? All I said . . .

ELLEN   We'll get into trouble. I know we will. What if we get caught?

MILT   (*Moves down right to front of bench*)   You don't love me. I don't think you ever sincerely and truly loved me.

ELLEN   (*Moves down to* MILT's *left*)   That isn't so.
(*Puts out her hand to him*)

MILT   (*Pulls away from her*)   Don't touch me.

ELLEN   Milt.
(*Moves toward him*)

MILT   I said don't touch me.

ELLEN   You're being childish.

MILT   Why? Because I'm asking you to show me your love, to do this one lousy thing for me!

ELLEN   What do you want me to do?

MILT   You know.

ELLEN   Harry Berlin?
(*The sound of halting footsteps are heard off right*)

MILT   Harry Berlin.

ELLEN   It's just that I don't think that's the answer. Can't you . . .
(*Hears the footsteps*) Is that him coming?

MILT   (*Looks right*)   It's him. That's him. (ELLEN *begins to move left*) Come here! (*Excitedly as she comes to him*) Look, El, leave this to me. I'll take care of it. (*Begins to lead her off left*) You walk down here a little. I want to speak to Harry privately. Don't listen and don't watch.

ELLEN   (*Stops and begins to protest*)   You're not . . . Milt, you wouldn't . . .

MILT   (*Pushes her off left*)   Just stand over . . . look. Come here.
(*They exit left.* HARRY *enters, right. He is wearing the worn velvet-collared herringbone coat which had been in the basket in the first act: unshaven, disheveled. He uses a cane, his right leg is stiff, paralyzed. He moves along, dragging his right leg, leaning on cane. He crosses between lamppost and bench and moves up left above the bench*)

HARRY Milt . . . (*Notices the scooter*) Milt? Are you here, Milt? You cheap bastard, where's my five bucks? (*Moves left to center*) Ohhh . . . Ohhh . . . that dog. That crazy dog. On my leg. He did it on my leg. I can still feel it, wet and smelly . . . It's still there . . . Away, get away from me. Away . . . (*Reversing the cane in his hand, he swings it at imaginary dog by his right leg, finally turns, and with cane reversed moves up into alcove. As he does, MILT slowly sneaks out from down left and moves toward him, sinisterly*) Ohhh, Ellen, my sweet, sweet, sweet Ellen. Where are you? (HARRY *turns downstage, barely missing seeing MILT who scurries back off. HARRY turns back to the alcove railing right*) Ohhh, my Ellen, my sweet, sweet Ellen.

(*As he leans on the wrong end of the cane, it slips from beneath him and he falls to the ground. As he puts the cane down, MILT rushes toward him to push him over the railing. When HARRY falls, MILT is unable to stop himself and dives over the right railing of the alcove.*

There is the sound of a large splash, followed by a heavy spray of water which rises above the railing and lands on HARRY. HARRY holds out his hand to check if it's raining, looks up at the sky. Hooking one of the cables with his cane, he pulls himself erect.

ELLEN *enters left*)

ELLEN Milt?

HARRY (*Turning*) Ellen!

ELLEN It's you. Where's Milt?

HARRY Milt?

ELLEN I thought I heard . . . *Moves right, leans over railing; softly.* Milt? Milt? I can't see a thing down there.

HARRY (*Looking over railing in alcove*) Is he down there?

ELLEN I don't know where he is. He was with me a minute ago. He asked . . . (*Looks at* HARRY) Are you sure he wasn't here?

HARRY I was supposed to meet him. What are you . . .

ELLEN Never mind me. Where did he go now?
(*Moves to right of bench*)

HARRY He owes me five bucks. You can't trust anybody.

ELLEN You are interested in money, aren't you, Harry?

HARRY (*Moves downstage*) Not for myself. I wanted to buy you something for your birthday.

ELLEN That's very thoughtful of you. But my birthday isn't until next August.
(*Sits down right of bench*)

HARRY   I was saving for it. Don't start, Ellen. For cryin' out loud. I'm a sick man. Sick! My leg. (*Paces left, his limp very pronounced*) It's paralyzed. I can't move it.

ELLEN   (*Irritably*)   There isn't anything wrong with your leg.

HARRY   (*Limps right*)   There isn't? Then why doesn't it . . . (*Stops, trys to bend his right leg; to his surprise it bends easily and he can raise it*) You're right! (*Joyfully he flexes leg up and down; begins to run in circles about the stage, tossing his cane over the railing*) It's . . . moving! It moved! I can walk again! Look, look, I'm walking. I'm walking!

ELLEN   Harry . . . Harry, I have to speak to you. Please sit down. (*Gestures to bench*)

HARRY   (*Crosses to bench, lies supine on it, his head in ELLEN's lap*) What would I do without you? How would I live? My own sweet precious . . . Oh, Ellen, hold me, hold me, I need you so much . . .

ELLEN   (*Resisting*)   No, Harry. Not tonight. Sit up now. (HARRY *gets up and sits in her lap, facing left*) Sit up properly.

HARRY   (*Tries to embrace her*)   What is it my dear one, my darling, my . . .

ELLEN   Harry, stop it and pay attention. This is important. I've tried . . . I've tried to be a good wife to you. But despite all my efforts our marriage is a failure.

HARRY   (*Dumbfounded, stops his attempts to embrace her*)   Our marriage . . . a failure?

ELLEN   Yes, Harry; a failure.

HARRY   (*Crosses his right leg over his left; there is a pause*)   I . . . I don't know what to say, Ellen. This is a complete shock to me. Up until this minute I thought we were a happily married couple!

ELLEN   You thought . . .

HARRY   I had no idea.

ELLEN   How could you have thought that? Didn't you hear me walking the floors nights; didn't you hear me crying in the bathroom?

HARRY   (*Shaking head*)   No. No.

ELLEN   What did you think I was doing in the bathroom all night?

HARRY   (*Slight pause; desperately*)   Ellen, I love you!

ELLEN   I asked you a question, Harry. (*Bodily picks up HARRY, and sets him on the bench to her left*) What do you think I was doing in the bathroom all night?

HARRY   (*Shaking his head dumbly*)   I didn't want to think about it. I used to get up in the middle of the night and look at the ceiling and wonder to myself: "What could she be doing in the bathroom so long?" But I didn't want to change you, Ellen. I wanted you to be just the way you are. Is that a crime?

ELLEN You should have made it your business to know what I was doing.

HARRY I will. From now on . . .

ELLEN Our marriage has been a failure from the first day. I don't have one memory worth keeping.

HARRY Oh, no. No, Ellen. We had lots of good times. Remember . . .

ELLEN Remember what?

HARRY (*Slight pause; angrily*) Where's my paper hat?

ELLEN I don't have your paper hat and you know it. Our marriage was a mistake, Harry, and anything we can do to terminate it would be a step in the right direction.

HARRY (*Legs over* ELLEN's *lap*) I couldn't, Ellen. I'm responsible for you.

ELLEN (*Pushes them off*) Responsible for me? You must be joking. You haven't worked a day or given me a penny since we were married.

HARRY I was hoping to surprise you.

ELLEN You succeeded in that.

HARRY (*Rises; stands left of bench*) I haven't been wasting my time. I've been doing a lot of thinking, planning . . . I'm going to go back and do what I always wanted. What I should have stuck to. Go back and start right at the beginning. Ellen, in the fall I'm applying for medical school.

ELLEN Harry, it won't do.

HARRY All right. All right. I understand. Night calls, operations, blood all over my clothes . . . It's not all easy going. All right. Law school. In the fall I'm registering for the Bar.

ELLEN No, Harry.

HARRY (*Shouting in frustration*) Why not?

ELLEN Harry, I don't love you anymore. That's all there is to it.
  (*Rises and moves downstage*)

HARRY You don't . . .

ELLEN I doubt if I ever loved you.

HARRY (*Moves to her, arms outstretched, fingers reaching*) Ellen, you don't know what you're saying. Love! Love!

ELLEN What about love, Harry?

HARRY   It's . . .

(*Stops in confusion*)

ELLEN   What is it? I'd like very much to hear your definition.

HARRY   (*Raises his arms to the sky, fingers reaching*)   The birds, the sun, our sun . . .

ELLEN   I don't see any sun, do you?

HARRY   Where's my paper hat?

ELLEN   I don't have your paper hat.

HARRY   (*Angrily*)   Well, somebody's got my paper hat. It's not on my head, is it?

ELLEN   (*Crosses left in front of him, moves left*)   You pretend love means so much to you but it doesn't, Harry. You use it to justify your own indecisiveness. (*Turns back to him*)   What makes me so angry is that you've been using me as well. I do your work, fulfill your obligations . . . How can you say that's love? If anything, love is a giving and taking, an interchange of emotions, a gradual development based on physical attraction, complementary careers and simple social similarities.

HARRY   (*Clasps the back of the bench with one hand, presses the other to his cheek; indignantly*)   So that's what you think!

ELLEN   That's precisely what I think!

HARRY   No romance, no tenderness, no subconscious . . . Love is *ooonly* a gradual development based on physical attraction, complementary careers and simple social similarities. That's *aaaall* it is.

ELLEN   Yes. That's *aaaall* it is.

HARRY   And you're not ashamed to say that to me?

ELLEN   Why should I be ashamed?

HARRY   Love is a gradual development based on physical attraction, complementary careers and simple social similarities!

ELLEN   That's right.

HARRY   (*Moves right to lamppost, turns back to* ELLEN)   I can't get over it. My wife. My own wife. The woman who took the holy vows with me. You can stand there and look at me and say . . .

ELLEN   (*Curtly*)   Love is a gradual development based on physical attraction, complementary careers and simple social similarities!

HARRY   Ellen, do what you want with me, curse me, step on me, tear me to pieces, but I beg you, out of consideration for all the days and nights we lived as man and wife, *do not say* . . .

ELLEN   (*Parrotlike*)   Love is a gradual development based on physical attraction, complementary careers . . .

HARRY (*Moves back to lamppost and cries out*) Ahhhhhh! (ELLEN *stops.* HARRY *moves left to front of bench*) I do not believe that this is happening to us. Not to us. Not to Harry and Ellen Berlin.

ELLEN It is happening to us. And you have to see it for what it is. It's not pleasant but there's no use pretending. There's something else you ought to know, then I'm done. (*Turns away from him*) Harry . . . I'm in love with Milt Manville; and he loves me. (HARRY *freezes in absurd posture;* ELLEN *moves left, not noticing him*) We both realize now that we acted too hastily. It's unfortunate that you came along when you did. I have no doubt that Milt and I would have mended our differences . . . (MILT *enters, right, wearing faded denim trousers which are too short and tight for him, a very large blue and white striped jersey that hangs over his trousers and a small black officer's jacket, without buttons or gold braid; his hair, which is still wet, lies flat on his scalp, and he has on a very small, white, sailor's cap. He is wearing sneakers without socks; he carries his clothes, still dripping, in a package tied by rope under his arm. Enraged, he storms by* HARRY *and paces back and forth center stage*) Milt! What happened to you? Where were you?

MILT Don't ask. Just don't ask. It was terrible.

ELLEN But I . . .

MILT I said don't ask!

ELLEN (*Moves to* MILT) Why are you angry with me?

MILT (*Glaring at* HARRY, *puts his bundle down on upstage bench*) He's at it again, huh? He tried to kill me, did you know that?

ELLEN Harry?

MILT Harry. Your husband. The one you were so worried about.

ELLEN Oh, no.

MILT Oh, yeah. He threw me off the bridge. Right over his shoulder. Lucky for me a barge was passing. They picked me up, gave me these clothes, a cup of coffee and a doughnut. (*Shouting*) It was a cinnamon doughnut.

ELLEN My poor Milt. You don't know how glad I am you're safe.

MILT No thanks to you.

ELLEN Milt! How can you say that?

MILT Well, whose fault is it? I told you there was only one way out of this. It's him or us. One or the other. Ellen, sweetheart, it's not what you think. (*Crosses down right to right of* HARRY) Look at him. He's no good to anyone, not even to himself. (ELLEN *follows and stands left of* HARRY; *both lean their elbows on his shoulders and examine him*) We'd be doing him a favor. When you get down to it . . . What is it? Euthanasia. That's what it is. And remember what you said about euthanasia, hon?

ELLEN   They should be destroyed. Painlessly. By an impartial board of prominent citizens.

MILT   That's what you said. Well, isn't it the same as if we were on that board of prominent citizens? I mean, logically speaking.

ELLEN   There isn't much difference.

MILT   Of course not.

ELLEN   It's one of degree, not of kind.

MILT   Exactly. (*Slight pause*) I love you, El.

(*As* ELLEN *moves to* MILT, HARRY *slowly begins to fall left. They both catch him and hold him up*)

ELLEN   I love you, Milt.

MILT   For all eternity.

ELLEN   For ever and ever.

MILT   El.

ELLEN   I'm so nervous.

MILT   (*Takes her hand*)   Don't be. Just look at my eyes, at me, sweetheart. Don't look at him and don't think about what you're doing. Just look at my eyes and say I love you, Milt Manville.

ELLEN   I love you, Milt Manville.

MILT   (*Facing* HARRY, *puts his arms around him, about his chest, and begins to pull him left*)   I love you.

ELLEN   (*As* HARRY *gets past her, she bends down and picks up one leg in each hand and standing between them, helps* MILT *carry him up left to the alcove*)   My Milton.

MILT   Ellen sweetheart.

(*They stare into each other's eyes*)

ELLEN   How I do love you . . .

MILT   Soon we'll be together. Always together.

ELLEN   My darling husband-to-be.

(*They carry* HARRY *to the right railing of the alcove,* ELLEN *having circled left, so that* MILT *is closest to the railing.* MILT *lays* HARRY's *still-rigid body on his stomach on the railing, while* ELLEN *puts his feet down on the ground*)

MILT   (*At railing*)   Ellen, get him around . . .

ELLEN   (*Butts against* HARRY's *backside with her head in an attempt to push him over*)   I love you, Milt Manville.

(*Repeats line again as she butts* HARRY)

MILT   (*In an effort to pull* HARRY *over,* MILT *puts one leg over railing straddling it, as he pulls at* HARRY. *However,* ELLEN *inadvertently pushes* HARRY *against* MILT, *throwing him off balance*) You're pushing me here . . .

ELLEN I love you, Milt Manville. I love you, Milt Manville. Et cetera.

MILT (*In attempt to regain balance, pulls other leg over railing. But* ELLEN *continues to push* HARRY *against him*) Ellen . . . For God's sake . . . You're pushing me, Ellen . . . Ellen . . .

(MILT *slips off the railing, screaming, with hands clutching empty air. Again a splash, and then a spray of water, which hits* HARRY *as it breaks over the railing.* ELLEN *runs frantically to the railing right and peers over.* HARRY *suddenly comes to with a shudder of his head*)

ELLEN Milt? Milt? Where are you? Are you there, Milt? Answer me! Oh, no, no, no . . .

(*Turning back from rail, begins to sob, wildly*)

HARRY (*Now fully conscious, sees her, and goes to her*) Ellen, don't . . . I'm all right now. It was nothing. (*Embraces her*) You do love me. I knew you loved me. The birds, the sun, our sun . . .

ELLEN Oh, stop it. (*Pulls away from him*) Milt. He fell over. He's down there!

HARRY Milt?

ELLEN He's drowning. Why don't you do something?

HARRY (*Runs to left*) Help. Somebody. Help us!

ELLEN (*Runs to right*) Help! Help!

(*Runs to left*)

HARRY (*Running right*) Help us! Somebody! (*Runs left to alcove and climbs up on railing right of alcove. Shouts*) Milt, hold on, hold on!

ELLEN (*Runs up right to railing left of* HARRY *and looks down*) Do you see him?

HARRY There. That's him. He's getting into a rowboat. Where that light is.

ELLEN (*Waving*) Milt! Milt!

HARRY (*Shouting*) Hey, Milt! What the hell's wrong with you?

ELLEN He can't hear us.

HARRY (*Still shouting*) You dumb bastard!

ELLEN Thank God he's safe. (*Moves right, looks over railing*) How do I get down . . . No. I'll wait here for him. He knows I'll be here.

(*Sits on bench*)

HARRY (*Gets down from railing*) I never thought he'd do anything as stupid as that.

ELLEN He didn't . . . Oh, forget it.

HARRY (*Goes to bench and lies down with head left and feet right in* ELLEN's *lap*) What a world. People trying to kill themselves, jumping off bridges, turning on gas, taking poison . . . They know; they feel it. The sky, look for yourself: it's been trying to rain all night but it can't do it, it can't, it's empty, like everything else, empty and dead. And soon . . .

ELLEN (*Sharply; pushing him off bench.* HARRY *lands on hands and knees*) That's enough of that, Harry. Don't pretend you didn't hear me before. I told you Milt and I . . .

HARRY (*Gets up, moves left*) You told me all right. You told me. But why? What did I do wrong? Explain it to me. Give me a reason.

ELLEN I've given you a dozen reasons. But if they won't do . . . (*Takes a small, rolled paper graph from her bag which is on the ground, right of the bench*) Look. Look at this. (HARRY *sits left of her on bench, and she unrolls graph*) These black vertical lines divide our four months of marriage into days. Now each time the red horizontal line hits the black vertical line that indicates one sexual experience over a twenty-four-hour period.

HARRY Where's the red horizontal line?

ELLEN There is none. (*Rolls up graph*) Now do you understand?

HARRY Why didn't you tell me? I'm trying to be a good husband, but if you don't tell me . . . I was never married before, you were, don't forget that!

ELLEN You're supposed to know some things yourself.

HARRY I was giving you time. I wanted us to become friends first . . . get to know one another, and then . . . (*Gestures*) You should have told me. You definitely should have!

ELLEN A lot of good that would have done.

HARRY Why do you say that?

ELLEN No normal man could have behaved the way you have these past four months. I'd rather not say any more.

HARRY No, no, say it.

(*Crosses legs and leans back on bench*)

ELLEN It'll be painful.

HARRY Say it. Go ahead.

ELLEN Very well. I'll say it. You think you know yourself, Harry, but you don't know yourself at all. You never loved me. You're incapable of that kind of love. You loved . . . All this time . . . You loved . . . Milt.

HARRY   I . . . What?

ELLEN   Yes. Milt. Milt Manville. You always loved him, I imagine. Even back at school. You married me as a substitute-figure because you couldn't confront him and your own latent homosexuality.

HARRY   What are you saying?

ELLEN   I'm saying you're queer, Harry.

HARRY   No, no, it can't be, I . . .

ELLEN   It can be and it is. All this explains your attitude toward life, your fits and (*holding up graph*) everything else. I am sorry but you asked for it.

HARRY   (*Incredulously*)   I love Milt Manville.

ELLEN   I'm afraid you do, Harry.

HARRY   It's ridiculous. I don't even like the guy!

ELLEN   Don't you, Harry? The way he has of laughing, the way his lips curl up when he smiles . . .

HARRY   (*Open-faced*)   His lips . . .

ELLEN   The way he carries himself, like a soldier, and when he's excited, his eyes, how they shine and sparkle . . .

HARRY   His eyes . . .

ELLEN   We both love him, Harry.

HARRY   (*Half convinced*)   Milt.

ELLEN   (*Nodding*)   Milt.

HARRY   (*Regretfully*)   I never sent him flowers.

ELLEN   It's not an easy thing for someone to acknowledge.
    (*Puts graph back into bag*)

HARRY   His lips, his eyes . . . his legs . . . (*Grimaces, expels a sound of repulsion*) No, no, you're crazy, Ellen. It's you I love, you! (ELLEN *rises, moves away right*) I'll show you. I'll prove it to you.
    (*He throws her over his shoulder, runs about madly, indecisively, back and forth across bridge*)

ELLEN   (*Kicking, screaming*)   Harry! Harry!

HARRY   I'll take you away. Someplace. Anyplace. You'll be happy! happy! I'll make you happy!

ELLEN   Put me down!

HARRY   We'll be happy! happy! We're going to be happy! happy!

ELLEN   Harry, will you put me . . .

HARRY   (*Lays her out on bench, smothers her with inept hugs*)

Happy! Happy! Happy! Happy! You little honey-bunny, you . . .
You mousy-wousy hot little flousy . . .

ELLEN Don't! Stop it!

HARRY (*Growling as he kisses and bites the nape of her neck*) Grrrr
. . . Arrrr . . . Grrrrr . . .

ELLEN (*Stamping her feet on bench*) Harry, no more, stop it now!

HARRY (*Suddenly stops, gets up from her, and moves left. Confused*)
What's wrong? I'm trying to do what you told me. (*Shouting*) For
cryin' out loud! Is there no satisfying a woman!

ELLEN (*Sitting up*) Don't talk to me anymore . . . Just leave me
alone and don't talk to me.

(MILT *enters down right, crosses to left, where he paces back
and forth, even more enraged. He is wearing a very large pair of
white bell-bottom trousers, a T-shirt, and a very small, ripped
black wool sweater, sneakers, and a yellow southwester oilskin
cap*)

ELLEN (*Rises and crosses to him*) Milt!

MILT (*Turning on her*) Don't talk to me.

ELLEN What is . . .

MILT I said don't talk to me!

HARRY (*Moves to* ELLEN's *right; to* MILT) It's about time you got
here. I've been waiting . . .

MILT Oh, shut up!

HARRY Where's the five bucks . . .

MILT (*Crosses right, in front of* HARRY; *sits center of bench*) Did
you hear me say shut up!

HARRY Ellen, will you . . .

ELLEN The same goes for me. Shut up!

(*Crosses right to bench; sits right of* MILT. HARRY *defiantly moves
to bench, sits down left of* MILT. *The three of them are now
seated on the bench, grimly, stiffly,* MILT *between the others,
arms folded. A moment passes.* HARRY *takes out a pad and pencil,
begins to write a note.* MILT *glances at him, and* HARRY *turns so
that he cannot read the note; then hands pencil and pad to* ELLEN,
carefully sneaking it over so that MILT *cannot read what he has
written. She, without reading it, tears off note, crumples it and
throws it over her shoulder, writes a brief note to* MILT, *passes
pad and pencil to him. Without reading it, he throws entire pad
over his shoulder. He is about to throw the pencil away as well,
has second thoughts, and begins to put it under his cap.* HARRY
slaps his hand and pulls pencil away from him)

ELLEN (*Quacking; not spoken*)   Miltie? Miltie?

MILT   Don't bother me.

(HARRY *takes a small banana from his coat pocket and begins to peel it*)

ELLEN (*Quacking each word*)   Don't be angry with me.

MILT   Will you stop that stupid quacking.

ELLEN   Why is it my fault?

MILT   I asked you to do a simple lousy thing . . .

(HARRY *begins to eat the banana*)

ELLEN   I tried.

MILT   Not very hard, did you?

ELLEN   I did. Have pity. You're absolutely all I have.

MILT (*Cynically*)   I bet.

ELLEN   Would I be here otherwise, pleading with you like this?

MILT   You still could be lying.

(HARRY *peels it down farther, and continues eating*)

ELLEN (*Sticking her chin out*)   Is this the face of a liar, Milt? Is it?

MILT (*He closely examines her face*)   Why do I keep torturing myself! I'm not made of stone, El. You know me; you know how I am.

ELLEN   Oh, Milt.

(*They kiss in a passionate embrace.* HARRY *watches; then takes final bite of banana, throws peel over his shoulder off the bridge, and pulls* MILT *away from* ELLEN)

HARRY   Hey, cut it out! That's my wife you're kissing there, buster!

MILT   Harry . . . for God's sake. Give us a break, will you?

(*Puts hand on* HARRY's *knee*)

HARRY (*Draws back, glances from corner of eye at* MILT's *hand; meaningfully*)   Don't try anything funny.

MILT   What's that?

(*Puts his arm on top of bench around* HARRY)

HARRY (*Draws back even farther*)   Just don't try anything funny. I love her. Her! Not you! Get that into your thick head! (*Slight pause*) I can't help it.

MILT (*Removes his arm*)   I love her, too, Harry. And I can't help it. Why don't we . . . let her choose between us.

ELLEN   That's fair, Harry.

MILT   It's democratic.

HARRY (*Hesitates, finally deciding, gets up.* MILT *gets up with him*)   Ellen, my life, my . . .

ELLEN (*Rises; abruptly*)   I choose Milt Manville.

(*Taking her bag and* MILT's *hand, she begins to move up left around the bench*)

MILT (*Going with her*) Sorry, Harry.

HARRY (*Moves up left above bench, grabs* ELLEN *and pulls her from* MILT) It's no good. I can't do it. I can't let you go. Don't ask.

(ELLEN *ends up to the left of* HARRY)

ELLEN (*Emphatically*) But, Harry, I don't love you.

HARRY I don't give a damn whether you love me or not! I love you! I love you! (*Placatingly*) Ellen, you loved me once. You can love me again.

ELLEN I'll never love you again, Harry. Now that I've lived with you I find you an utterly obnoxious person.

HARRY All right, that's a beginning; that's a start.

ELLEN (*Crosses right to upstage bench. Puts her bag down on bench*) What are we going to do, Milt?

MILT (*Moves left to* HARRY) Harry, listen to me. Listen. I'm married to a woman at this very minute who has more things in common with you . . .

HARRY Forget it. I'm not interested.

MILT She reads, Harry, and she . . .

HARRY I don't care if she belches Beethoven! I'm satisfied with Ellen.

MILT Are you going to be able to keep an eye on her twenty-four hours a day? Because you're going to have to, Harry. The first chance we get we're checking into a hotel and it's not going to be to watch television, you can take my word on that!

HARRY (*Moves right to* ELLEN) Ha! Ellen isn't the type to . . .

ELLEN Don't count on that, Harry.

HARRY You'd go with a man who's not your husband to some cheap sleazy hotel room that doesn't even have a television set!

ELLEN (*Crosses left to* MILT) It would have a television set, wouldn't it, Milt? (*No response*) Milt?

MILT (*Finally getting word out*) Of . . . of . . . of course! (*Forcefully*) It would be a first-class highly recommended A-1 hotel, with private bath, cocktail lounge, room service, breakfast in bed, everything!

ELLEN (*Turns to* HARRY; *decisively*) I certainly would go to a first-class hotel with a man who's not my husband. And under the circumstances I would not consider it immoral.

HARRY It's all a nightmare. A nightmare. None of it is real. You don't understand. If I lose Ellen, if I stop believing in love, I have nothing, nothing! (*Runs to railing to the right of alcove and jumps up on it*) I might as well jump off the bridge right now!

MILT (*Runs to him, grabs his legs*) Harry . . . you wouldn't . . . ?

ELLEN (*Going to* MILT; *pulls him away*) He has no choice, Milt.

MILT That's true.

(*They both move downstage*)

ELLEN If only I could have loved him more.

HARRY I said, I might as well jump off this bridge right now. Doesn't anybody listen to me?

MILT You tried, hon. Don't blame yourself. You were wonderful to him. I'm to blame for this. He was my best friend and I let him down.

ELLEN You didn't, Milt. Don't even think it.

HARRY What's happening?

(*Stares down at water below*)

MILT I did my best. God knows I did my best.

ELLEN You did. No friend would have done as much. I don't believe it.

HARRY Hey!

MILT There's no helping each other, is there?

ELLEN We're all locked up in ourselves, in little separate compartments.

HARRY Alone. All alone. No love. No hope. Nothing. Nothing. Aww, the hell with it. (*Takes white, woman's bathing cap out of pocket, puts it on*) Let death come early. Yes. Yes. Let death come early. (*Holds nose; falls backward off bridge. There is a splash. As* MILT *runs up to the railing to look over, a spray of water breaks over the railing and hits him. Soaking wet, he turns to* ELLEN, *and squirts out a mouthful of water*)

MILT (*Moving to her*) El!

ELLEN (*Embracing him*) Milt!

MILT We're together.

ELLEN At last. At long last.

MILT My sweetheart.

(*They kiss*)

ELLEN We will have a baby, won't we?

MILT Of course we will.

ELLEN And we'll name him after Harry Berlin?

MILT Harry Manville?

ELLEN Harry Manville. I'm so happy, Milt.

MILT Harry must be happy, too.

ELLEN   He is. I know he is.

MILT   I love you, sweetheart.

(*Kisses her and sweeps her up in his arms. Carries her to scooter as he hums the "Wedding March." She laughs, joins in. He puts her down, and goes to the scooter*)

ELLEN   I love you, my darling first-and-only husband.

MILT (*Taking scooter off stand*)   Not as much as I love you. Never. Never.

ELLEN   More than you love me.

MILT (*Turns to* ELLEN)   You couldn't love me more than I love you.

ELLEN   Much, much, much more.

MILT (*Slight pause*)   How much more?

(*Starts the scooter, gets on*)

ELLEN (*Apprehensively*)   Milt . . .

MILT   That's a reasonable question.

ELLEN (*Gets on scooter behind* MILT)   Don't start.

MILT   Just how much more?

ELLEN   Please, Milt.

MILT (*Beginning to drive off right*)   No, no . . . Never mind "please Milt." What about Harry?

ELLEN   What about Linda?

MILT   I never loved Linda.

(*They are disappearing offstage*)

ELLEN   But, you slept with Linda, didn't you? Didn't you? Didn't you . . . ?

(*As they exit,* HARRY *appears and begins to climb over the railing. He has lost his overcoat, is soaking wet, and is draped in seaweed. As he gets over the railing, he yells after* MILT)

HARRY   Milt! Milt! Where the hell are you going? Ellen, bring him back . . . Where's my five bucks, you cheap bastard!

(*Suddenly a dog dashes onstage from off right.* HARRY *sees it, howls with terror, begins to run left. The dog catches him and begins to pull at his pants leg.* HARRY *runs about in a circle trying to dislodge him, and finally in desperation runs to the lamppost, leaps, and hangs on to the crossbar. He hangs there, with the dog clinging to his pants leg*)

Curtain